The Query Design Screen

You use the query design screen to create queries that isolate selected records. The query shown here searches the CUSTLIST database for customers named Smith.

(CHAPTER 6)

If you want to:	Here's how:	See page:
① Move highlight left and right	Press Tab and Shift-Tab	26
② Extend box downward for OR query	Press ↓	131
③ Add or remove field from a view	Press Field (F5)	149
④ Narrow or widen field in file skeleton	Press Size (Shift-F7)	153
⑤ See results of query	Press Data (F2)	114
⑥ Switch between file/view skeletons	Press Previous (F3) or Next (F4)	152
⑦ Access pull-down menus	Press Menus (F10)	23

Understanding

dBASE IV 1.1

Understanding
dBASE IV™ 1.1

Second Edition

Alan Simpson

 San Francisco • Paris • Düsseldorf • Soest

Acquisitions Editor: Dianne King
Editor: Ami Knox
Technical Editor: Bob Student
Word Processor: Lisa Mitchell
Book Designer: Suzanne Albertson
Chapter Art: Suzanne Albertson
Layout Artist: Lucie Živny
Screen Graphics: Cuong Le
Typesetter: Winnie Kelly
Proofreaders: M. D. Barrera and Bill Cassel
Indexer: Ted Laux
Cover Designer: Thomas Ingalls + Associates
Cover Photographer: Michael Lamotte
Screen reproductions produced by XenoFont.

Library of Congress Card Number: 90-71218
ISBN: 0-89588-633-2
Manufactured in the United States of America
10 9 8 7 6 5 4 3 2

To Susan and Ashley

ACKNOWLEDGMENTS

Many thanks to everyone who helped nurse this book from the idea stage to the finished product in your hands. Though only my name appears on the cover, credit for this book belongs to many people, including

Lyn Cordell, developmental editor at SYBEX, who provided endless support, encouragement, feedback, and ideas through thick and thin.

All of the people at SYBEX involved in producing the first edition of this book, including Judy Ziajka, copy editor; Joel Kroman and Jeff Green, technical editors; Suzanne Albertson, designer and production artist; Rick van Genderen, illustrator; Jocelyn Reynolds and Bob Myren, word processors; Olivia Shinomoto, typesetter; Kristen Iverson, proofreader; Ted Laux, indexer; and Sonja Schenk, who produced the screens.

All of those at SYBEX who worked on the second edition of the book, including Ami Knox, editor; Bob Student, technical editor; Lisa Mitchell, word processor; M. D. Barrera and Bill Cassel, proofreaders; Winnie Kelly, typesetter; Lucie Živny, artist; and Cuong Le, screen graphics artist.

Martha Mellor, who served as the beta tester of the latest version of dBASE IV for the second edition of this book.

Bill and Cynthia Gladstone, my literary agents, for managing the business aspects of this writer's career.

All of you who have read my earlier dBASE books and have taken the time to drop me a line. Your suggestions help make each new book better than the last.

And of course, much credit and special thanks to Susan and Ashley, who were very patient and supportive while Daddy was typing away in the office.

Alan Simpson

CONTENTS AT A GLANCE

TABLE OF CONTENTS

CHAPTER 3

Creating a Database File

CHAPTER 4

Adding and Changing Information

CHAPTER 5

Sorting the Database

CHAPTER 6

Searching the Database

CHAPTER 7

Printing Formatted Reports

CHAPTER 8

Creating Custom Forms

CHAPTER 9

Performing Calculations

CHAPTER 10

Using Memo Fields to Store Documents

CHAPTER 11

Managing Groups of Records

CHAPTER 12

Using Functions to Control Your Data

CHAPTER 13

Managing Related Database Files

CHAPTER 14

Techniques for Managing Your Workspace

CHAPTER 15

Introducing Applications

CHAPTER 16

A Membership Management Application

CHAPTER 17

Adding Power with dBASE IV Commands

CHAPTER 18

Programming Techniques

CHAPTER 19

Business Data Processing

CHAPTER 20

Intelligent Custom Forms for Business Applications

CHAPTER 21

The Business Management Application

APPENDIX A

A DOS Primer

APPENDIX B

Installing dBASE IV

APPENDIX C

Summary of Changes in dBASE

APPENDIX D

Interfacing with Other Programs

APPENDIX E

dBASE IV Functions

APPENDIX F

dBASE IV Commands

APPENDIX G

ASCII Chart

INDEX

INTRODUCTION

dBASE IV is the fourth major revision of the now classic dBASE database management system. Though it initially got off to a rocky start with version 1.0, the dBASE IV approach to managing data is now becoming a standard, and "dBASE IV Compatibility" is quickly outdating earlier versions. Ashton-Tate, the people who brought us the original dBASE, have renewed their commitment to the dBASE IV standard by releasing the much improved dBASE IV version 1.1.

If by any chance you've already seen the documentation that accompanies dBASE IV, you know one thing—dBASE IV is a large (and extremely powerful, I might add) product. I know that just sifting through the myriad of tools and options that dBASE IV offers can be frustrating and confusing, especially for beginners. Therefore, the main purpose of this book is to do some of that sifting for you, to simplify, to explain, and to help you start putting dBASE IV to work productively now.

WHO CAN USE THIS BOOK

This book is written as a tutorial for beginners, but because it focuses on the most practical and efficient techniques for "getting the job done" with dBASE IV version 1.1, experienced dBASE users will also benefit from reading it. The purpose of this book is two-fold. First, it helps you to develop specific skills in using dBASE IV by providing hands-on, step-by-step instructions for managing your data. Second, it attempts to provide a broad understanding of the vast potential and capabilities of dBASE IV through general examples and suggested applications.

Experienced dBASE users who take the time to learn the new features in dBASE IV version 1.1 will find that they can manage their data more easily and effectively and build custom applications with a fraction of the effort required by earlier versions of dBASE.

THE STRUCTURE OF THIS BOOK

This book is designed as a tutorial, not as a technical reference guide. Therefore, you are encouraged to read the chapters in the order that they are presented. Exactly how far into this book you read depends on the complexity of the work you want dBASE to handle. The book is organized as follows:

Chapters 1 through 7: Virtually all readers will want to be familiar with the material presented in Chapters 1 through 7, as these present the most fundamental techniques for storing, retrieving, sorting, searching, and printing information.

Chapters 8 through 14: These chapters describe more advanced techniques for managing information in a database, such as designing custom screens, performing calculations, and managing multiple related database files. Readers whose work requires more than the basics presented in earlier chapters will want to read these chapters.

Chapters 15 through 21: Here you'll find more advanced information for creating custom dBASE IV applications. Experienced dBASE users will especially want to read these chapters, because they demonstrate the new dBASE IV features for building powerful applications with minimal effort.

Appendix A: This optional appendix is provided for readers who have no prior computer experience whatsoever. If you have never used a computer before, you are encouraged to read Appendix A, "A DOS Primer," to become familiar with basic computer terminology and operations that apply to your use of dBASE IV.

Appendix B: This appendix provides instructions for installing dBASE IV on your microcomputer.

Appendix C: This appendix summarizes new features in dBASE IV for experienced dBASE users.

Appendix D: This appendix presents techniques for sharing data with other programs, such as word processors and spreadsheets.

Appendices E through G: These appendices present a categorized summary of all dBASE IV commands and functions and a list of the ASCII character codes.

SPECIAL FEATURES

This book offers several unique features to make your learning easier and more enjoyable.

The Fast Track at the beginning of each chapter summarizes specific skills and techniques discussed within the chapter. Experienced dBASE users can use the Fast Track to locate specific information in the chapter. Beginners may want to refer to the Fast Track after reading the chapter for reminders about how to perform specific tasks.

Three special visual icons are used in the book to identify margin notes:

Identifies a practical tip or hint.

Identifies a special note that augments information in the text or presents reminders about previous techniques.

Identifies a warning about a potential problem.

On the end papers inside the front and back covers of this book, you'll find visual reminders of keys and techniques used in a variety of dBASE IV design screens. You can use these as quick reminders of specific techniques when working with dBASE IV on your own.

A SAMPLE DISK

This book presents many examples of databases, reports, custom screens, and applications. If you would like to use some of these examples without taking the time to type them yourself, you can purchase a disk with all the files (excluding dBASE IV itself, of course) described in this book. The disk includes the membership and business management applications presented in the later chapters. See the coupon near the last page for an order form.

CHAPTER

1

Understanding Database Management

dBASE IV IS A *DATABASE MANAGEMENT SYSTEM*. Although that may sound like something quite complicated, it is not.

A *database* is simply an organized collection of information, such as a list of names and addresses, sales transactions, stock prices, or baseball scores. Even if you've never touched a computer in your life, chances are you've already used quite a few databases. For example, think of a shoe box filled with index cards. On each card, you've written somebody's name and address, as shown in Figure 1.1. The shoebox full of index cards is a *database*, because it contains information. Rolodexes, file cabinets, and library card catalogs are other examples of common databases that you may have used.

A database *management system* is a set of tools to help you manage a database. For example, when you add new cards to your shoebox, arrange the cards into alphabetical order, look up an address, or throw away a card, you are *managing* the shoebox database.

A database management system such as dBASE IV lets you perform these same managerial tasks: adding, changing, deleting, sorting, printing, and looking up information in a database.

Figure 1.1: A ''shoebox'' database with names and addresses

UNDERSTANDING DATABASE FILES

Of course, dBASE doesn't store information on index cards in shoeboxes. Instead, it stores information in *database files* on a computer disk. Each database file consists of *records* (or *rows*) of information. Each record is divided into separate *fields* (or *columns*) of information. For example, Figure 1.2 shows a database file that contains names and addresses.

Notice that John Smith's name and address (from Figure 1.1) is the first record in the file. In all, the file consists of six records (rows) of information, equivalent to six index cards in the shoe box.

Notice also that the information in the database file shown in Figure 1.2 is divided into seven fields, or columns of information: Last Name, First Name, Address, City, State, Zip, and Phone. You need to break information into separate fields like this, because, unlike humans, computers don't understand the meaning of information based on its context.

For example, you and I can look at the index card in Figure 1.1 and figure out that (619)555-1212 is probably a phone number. We can figure this out based upon the context of the information (it "looks" like a phone number).

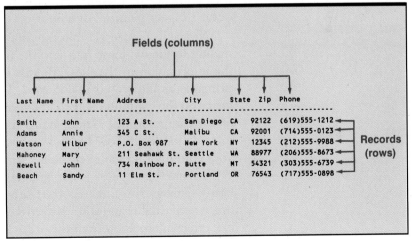

Figure 1.2: A dBASE IV database file of names and addresses

Computers, on the other hand, can't tell a phone number from an address from a potato pancake. (Computers may be fast, but they are definitely not too bright.) Therefore, it is up to you to divide the information on your index cards (or parts list, customer list, or whatever database you are storing) into meaningful fields of information. We'll discuss this topic in more detail in Chapter 2, when you create your first database file.

THE BIGGER PICTURE

Needless to say, most businesses do not store their information in a shoebox. Instead, they store information in such databases as Rolodex files, file cabinets, written lists, and tickler files. In most cases, the information in these databases can easily be stored in a few dBASE IV database files.

But business information is more than just data stored in files. Businesses usually have *forms*, such as credit applications, order forms, and other paper items that are used to gather information. Businesses also use *reports*: printed copies of information in a variety of formats, including invoices, form letters, mailing labels, organized lists, and packing lists, to name a few. Figure 1.3 shows an example of the "bigger picture" of a business database.

Notice in Figure 1.3 that the *forms* are used to provide the information to the database *files*, and the printed *reports* are derived from the information in the files. dBASE IV works on exactly the same principle as illustrated in Figure 1.3. Information is entered into forms on the computer screen and that information is stored in a file on the computer disk. Then, at any time in the future, you can print information from those files on the disk, in any format you wish, on your computer screen or printer.

In some cases, there is not a direct one-to-one relationship among forms, database files, and reports. For example, to print an invoice, you might need a name and address from the customer names and addresses file, order information from the order list, and part names and prices from the parts inventory. But this is no problem; dBASE IV can easily pull together information from separate database files into a single printed report.

Forms

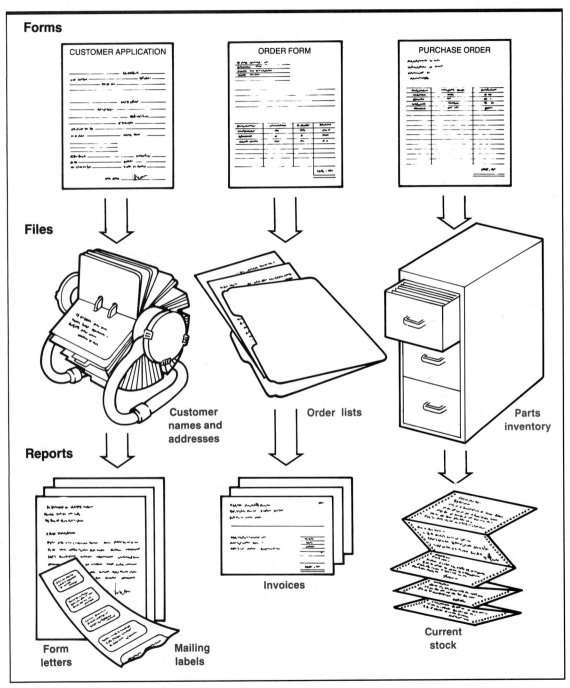

Figure 1.3: The larger view of a business database

LEARNING dBASE IV

Now, especially if you are new to computers, you may be wondering just how you are going to get from here to being able to tell dBASE to perform tasks like those shown in Figure 1.3. After all, *that* looks much more complicated than a shoebox full of index cards.

Using dBASE is not nearly as complicated as it might seem at first glance. Just think of the files in the center of Figure 1.3 as three shoeboxes full of information. All you need to do is learn to manage one database file (shoebox) effectively. In managing a database file, you execute a few basic tasks:

- ADD new information
- CHANGE information as necessary
- DELETE old information as necessary
- SORT information into some useful order (such as alphabetical or zip code order)
- SEARCH for particular types of information (such as an address or all past-due accounts)
- CALCULATE totals, subtotals, counts, averages, and so on, as needed

Once you know how to do these basic tasks, you can learn techniques for creating custom forms and reports, such as mailing labels and form letters. These techniques are easy to learn, because dBASE IV makes them easy.

After you've learned how to do all of these things for one database file, you can use the exact same techniques for creating and managing as many database files as you wish, such as the order list and parts inventory database files in Figure 1.3. So you see, all you really need to learn is to manage one shoebox database file, and in no time, you'll easily be able to manage many.

Of course, if you've never used one before, it may be a little scary to think of using a computer to do tasks that you've always done manually. But, rest assured, this is not nearly as difficult as you might think. There is no math or computer programming involved. You simply select options from *menus*, as you would in a restaurant. Believe me, you'll be a dBASE IV whiz before you know it.

WHAT YOU CAN DO WITH dBASE IV

Virtually any information that you manage without a computer can probably be managed much more quickly, accurately, and efficiently with dBASE IV. The kinds of information management that dBASE IV is especially good for include

- Mailing list management
- Inventory management
- Accounting and bookkeeping, including management of accounts receivable, accounts payable, the general ledger, and billing
- Project management
- Research management, including management of bibliographies, abstracts, and other reference material
- Scientific and statistical data recording and calculation

The main reasons for using dBASE rather than paper and pencil to manage information are speed and efficiency. For example, suppose you have a customer list of 10,000 names and addresses, and you want to send a form letter to all customers living in New York. Doing this by hand could take many hours; you would have to manually retrieve all New York names and addresses, enter them into perhaps a thousand or more letters, and sort them into zip code order for bulk mailing.

Having dBASE IV pull out the appropriate names and addresses and sort them into zip code order would probably take only a few seconds. Then you could tell dBASE to print all the form letters (and mailing labels) while you go out to lunch. The job may be complete before you get back.

How about a database with 15,000 records containing numbers for which you need totals, subtotals, or other calculations? Again, doing this math with a calculator or adding machine would take you a long time, but dBASE IV could do it in a few seconds or minutes.

So now do you think learning dBASE IV might be worth your time? If so, let's move on to the next chapter, where you'll get your first hands-on experience in using dBASE IV.

CHAPTER

2

A Guided
Tour of
dBASE IV

NOW THAT YOU HAVE A BASIC IDEA OF WHAT DATA-base management is all about, it's time to get dBASE IV up and running on your computer and get a feel for the way it works. That's what this chapter is all about.

INSTALLING dBASE IV

Before you can use dBASE IV, it needs to be *installed* on your computer. The installation procedure need be performed only once, not each time you use dBASE. If you are sharing a computer with someone else, find out whether dBASE has already been installed. And while you're at it, ask that person how to start dBASE IV, because they may not have used the usual installation techniques.

If you are using a personal computer and are sure that dBASE IV is *not* already installed on it, then you will need to install the program. Both Appendix B in this book and the *Getting Started with dBASE IV* manual that came with your dBASE IV package provide instructions on how to install dBASE IV. If you do need to install dBASE, follow the instructions for your particular computer and then read the next section.

A QUICK TOUR OF THE KEYBOARD

If this is your first time using a computer, take a moment to locate some special keys on your keyboard that you will use regularly in your work with dBASE IV. Figure 2.1 (pages 15 and 16) shows these special keys on some common keyboards. Locate the keyboard that most closely matches your own and refer to this figure if you have trouble finding a particular key as you work the exercises later in the chapter.

ON ONES AND OH'S

An important point to keep in mind when using a computer is that you cannot use the letter "l" to stand for the number 1, as you can on a typewriter. Nor can you use the letter "o" to stand for zero.

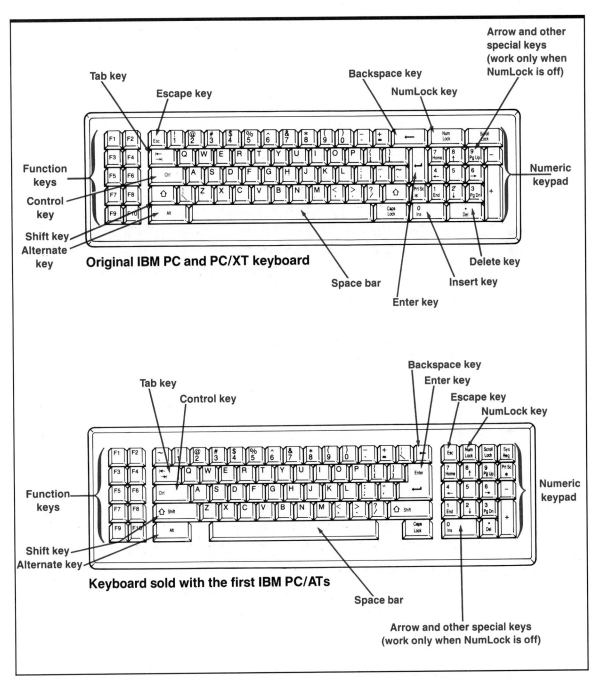

Figure 2.1: Some special keys on different types of keyboards

Figure 2.1: Some special keys on different types of keyboards (continued)

Both the 1 and the 0 must always be typed using the 1 and 0 keys, respectively, at the top of the keyboard, or the numeric keypad on the right side of the keyboard.

COMBINATION KEYSTROKES

During your work with dBASE, you'll often use combination keystrokes, such as Ctrl-N or Alt-F or Shift-F9. Such a combination keystroke means "hold down the first key and tap the second key." Here are some examples:

Ctrl-Y   Hold down the Ctrl key and tap the letter Y.
Alt-F1   Hold down the Alt key and tap the key labeled F1.
Shift-F2   Hold down the Shift key and tap the key labeled F2.

Incidentally, Ctrl stands for control and Alt stands for alternate. The keystroke combination Ctrl-N is pronounced Control N.

STARTING dBASE IV

When you turn on your computer, DOS (the computer's *Disk Operating System*) is in control. To use dBASE IV, you must tell DOS to locate and run the dBASE IV program. We'll lead you through this procedure in a moment.

Although you need not be familiar with DOS to learn dBASE IV, knowing a little about DOS can help you get along with your computer more easily. If you are an absolute beginner and are not familiar with DOS terms such as *drive* and *directory,* you might want to take some time to read Appendix A, "A DOS Primer."

For now, let's forge ahead and get dBASE IV up and running on your computer. Follow these steps (if you make a mistake, use the Backspace key to correct it):

1. Turn on your computer so that the DOS prompt (usually C>) appears on the screen.

TIP

If the name of the directory that you are logged onto does not appear on the screen, you can type the command **PROMPT PG** next to the DOS prompt (and then press ◄┘) to display the current disk drive and directory.

2. Switch to the dBASE directory (the area on the computer hard disk where dBASE IV is stored) by typing the command **CD\DBASE**. Be sure to use a backslash (\) rather than a forward slash (/). Press the Enter key (◄┘) after typing the command.

3. Type the command **DBASE** and press the ◄┘ key.

Depending on how you've installed dBASE IV, you may see a brief message about "cache testing" (described in Appendix C, but not of importance at the moment), followed by the dBASE IV logo, copyright notice, and the message "Press ◄┘ to assent to license agreement and begin dBASE IV." You can press ◄┘ to proceed to the dBASE IV Control Center immediately, or wait a few moments, and you'll arrive there automatically.

If, instead, you see the message "Bad command or file name," then either dBASE is not installed on the computer at all, or dBASE is stored on another disk drive or directory. If someone else installed dBASE, you may need to ask to find out how to start dBASE. The person who installed dBASE may not have used the usual disk drive and directory.

EXPLORING
THE dBASE IV CONTROL CENTER

After the logo and copyright notice disappear, the dBASE IV *Control Center* will appear on your screen, as in Figure 2.2. On your computer, the names of various files may appear in the rectangular panels in the Control Center—particularly if you share a computer with others. Don't worry about that; it won't affect your work.

Let's take a moment to discuss the various parts of the Control Center. Use Figure 2.2 as a guide as you read.

THE MENU BAR

At the upper-left corner of the Control Center is the *menu bar*. On this screen, your menu bar options are Catalog, Tools, and Exit.

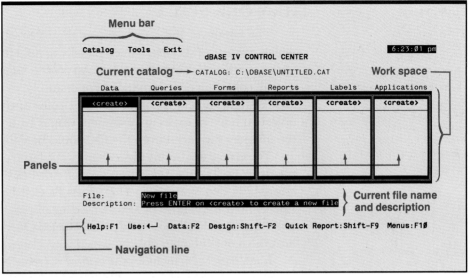

Figure 2.2: The dBASE IV Control Center

Each option has a *pull-down* menu associated with it (which you cannot see at the moment). We'll discuss how to use the pull-down menus a little later in this chapter.

THE CURRENT CATALOG

Centered beneath the title of the Control Center screen is the name of the current catalog. A *catalog* is simply a tool for organizing related information in a database; it is like a department in a corporation. For example, you might store accounts receivable information in one catalog and inventory information in another.

The catalog name actually consists of several parts. In this example, "C:" is the name of the disk drive that contains the catalog, "\DBASE\" is the name of the directory on the hard disk where the catalog is stored, and "UNTITLED.CAT" is the name of the catalog. (Don't worry if your screen is showing something other than C:\DBASE\UNTITLED.CAT.) You'll learn more about catalogs in the next chapter.

THE WORK SPACE

The center of the screen shows the Control Center *work space*, which consists of six *panels*. Each panel will hold the names of various objects within the current catalog. An *object* is simply one piece of the overall collection of information. For example, in an accounts receivable system, the credit application for collecting data would be one object, the file of existing customers would be a second object, and the invoices produced from the file would be a third object.

There may not be any object names displayed on your screen at the moment. But usually, the leftmost panel, titled *Data*, holds the names of *database files* that store data. The panels labeled Forms, Reports, and Labels hold the names of *formats* used to display forms and to print reports and mailing labels. The panels labeled Queries and Applications hold the names of other objects, which you'll learn about in due time.

Each panel also includes the option <create>, which allows you to create your own database file, form, report, or whatever. You'll learn how to create these items later in this book.

THE CURRENT FILE NAME AND DESCRIPTION

The current file name and description section of the screen, beneath the work space, displays the name and description of the file that is currently highlighted in the panel. If <create> is highlighted instead of a file name, this area displays ''New file'' and ''Press ENTER on <create> to create a new file.'' You'll learn how to create files and assign names and descriptions to them in the next chapter.

THE NAVIGATION LINE

The navigation line at the bottom of the screen lists some of the special keys that are currently available to you. For example, the notation Help:F1 tells you that you can get help by pressing the function key labeled F1.

The help screen for creating database files probably won't help you too much right now. You'll learn how to create a database file in the next chapter.

If the arrow keys on your keyboard are combined with the numbers on the numeric keypad, the arrow keys will only work when the NumLock key is in the Off position. If you attempt to use an arrow key and nothing happens or a number appears on the screen, press the NumLock key once to set NumLock Off.

GETTING HELP

You can use the Help key at any time to get help with dBASE IV. The help screens are *context sensitive,* which means they provide help that is relevant to the operation you are currently performing.

Notice, for example, that the <create> option in the Data panel of the Control Center is highlighted at the moment. Go ahead and press the Help key, F1, now. You'll see a help screen (also called a help *window*) titled Create Database Files on your screen, as in Figure 2.3.

Notice that the navigation line at the bottom of the screen says that you can press F4 to see the next screen or F3 to see the previous screen. If you press F4, you'll see the second "page" of help for creating database files. Press F3 to scroll back to the previous page.

There are also a few options—CONTENTS, RELATED TOPICS, and PRINT—displayed at the bottom of the help window. Currently, the CONTENTS option is highlighted. If you press the ← or → key while watching the screen, you'll see the highlight move from one option to the next.

USING THE TABLE OF CONTENTS

Suppose you do not want help with creating database files. Instead, you want more general help with the Control Center. To

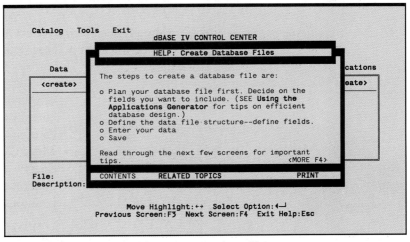

Figure 2.3: Help screen for creating database files

locate the appropriate help area, you need to check the help system's table of contents. Here's how to do so:

1. Press ← or → as necessary to move the highlight to the CONTENTS option.

2. When CONTENTS is highlighted, press ↩ to select it.

You'll see a list of topics concerning database files, but perhaps none that is broad enough for your needs. Notice in the navigation line the two options More General (F3) and More Specific (F4). To see a more general table of contents, press F3. The first entry of this table of contents offers information about the Control Center. To see the help screen for the Control Center, follow these steps:

1. Press the ↑ arrow key several times (or the PgUp key once) to move the highlight to the About the Control Center option.

2. Press ↩ to select that option.

The help screen for the Control Center appears on the screen, as in Figure 2.4. Remember, as the navigation line reminds you, you can use the Previous Screen (F3) and Next Screen (F4) keys to scroll through additional pages of help.

HELP WINDOW OPTIONS

You've already seen how to select an option from those displayed at the bottom of the help window. Each of these options is briefly described here:

CONTENTS	Displays a table of contents for the current topic. When a table of contents is displayed, you can use the More General (F3) and More Specific (F4) keys to change to more general or more specific tables of contents.
RELATED TOPICS	Displays a list of topics that are related to the current topic. (Press Esc if you change your mind.)

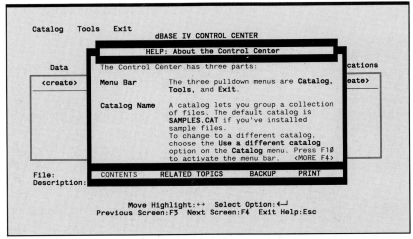

Figure 2.4: Help screen for the Control Center

On a laser printer, you need to eject the page after printing a help screen. See your printer manual for instructions.

BACKUP	Scrolls back to the previous screen. (This option appears only if there is a previous screen.)
PRINT	Prints a copy of the current help window.

LEAVING THE HELP SYSTEM

When you are finished with the help system, you can return to the Control Center by pressing the Esc key. Go ahead and do so now.

Undoubtedly you've noticed that help screens provide only limited information. Such brief instructions may not be very useful while you are learning dBASE IV. But later, when you are more familiar with basic dBASE operations, the help screens will serve as a quick reference to details that you may have forgotten.

USING THE PULL-DOWN MENUS

The pull-down menus attached to the menu bar at the top of the screen are an important tool in dBASE IV. There are two ways that you can access the pull-down menus:

- Press the Menu key (F10).
- Hold down the Alt key and type the first letter of the option you want.

To leave the pull-down menus at any time, just press the Esc key until the menus disappear.

To try the F10 key, follow these simple steps:

1. Press the Menu key (F10) once. A pull-down menu will appear (when no menu has been used previously, F10 pulls down the Catalog menu, as shown in Figure 2.5).

2. Press the Esc key once to leave the pull-down menu and return to the Control Center.

Now try the Alt-key combination, this time to view the Tools pull-down menu:

1. Press Alt-T (hold down the Alt key and type the letter T).

2. Press Esc to leave the Tools pull-down menu.

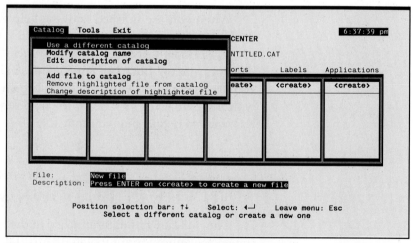

Figure 2.5: Pull-down menu for the Catalog option

Whether you use the F10 key or the Alt-key combination is entirely up to you. Both methods work at any time.

SHADED OPTIONS

Whenever you press F10 or use an Alt-key combination to access a pull-down menu, you may notice that some options on the menu are *shaded* (they appear darker than other items). The shaded options are not available at the moment, usually because they make no sense in the current situation. Even though you cannot use shaded options at a particular moment, they may be available later, in a different situation.

BULLETED OPTIONS

On some pull-down menus, you'll see an arrow (actually a right-pointing triangle) to the left of some options. This arrow means that a *submenu*, another menu containing more options, is available after you select the option.

For example, if you type Alt-T to pull down the Tools menu, you'll see that the options Macros, Import, and Export each have an arrow to the left of them. If you press ↵ while Macros is highlighted, for instance, a *submenu* of macro options will appear, as in Figure 2.6.

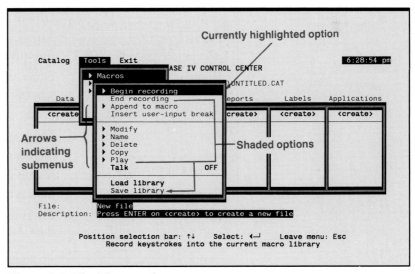

Figure 2.6: The Macros submenu

(If these menu options don't mean much to you at the moment, don't worry.) After you have viewed the submenu, press the Esc key twice to return to the Control Center.

SELECTING MENU OPTIONS

Regardless of whether you use the F10 key or an Alt-key combination to access the pull-down menus, you can use the keys listed in Table 2.1 to navigate the menus and make selections.

Table 2.1: Keys Used to Navigate the Pull-Down Menus

Key	Effect
→	Moves to the menu-bar option on the right, or exits submenu
←	Moves to the menu-bar option on the left, or exits submenu
↓	Moves down to the next available (unshaded) menu option on the current pull-down menu
↑	Moves up to the next available (unshaded) menu option on the current pull-down menu
PgDn	Moves to the last available option on the current pull-down menu
Home	Same as PgUp
PgUp	Moves to the first available option on the current pull-down menu
End	Same as PgDn
↵	Selects the currently highlighted option
First letter of any option	Selects that option
Esc	Backs up to the previous menu or to the Control Center

TIP

As you move the high-light, notice that a brief description of the currently highlighted menu option appears at the bottom of the screen.

Try some of the menu navigating keys now:

1. Press F10 to display the pull-down menus.

2. Press the → or ← keys until the Tools pull-down menu appears on the screen.

3. Press the ↑ or ↓ key until the Export option is highlighted.

4. Press ⏎ to select the Export option. A submenu will display a list of other software products to which you can export dBASE IV data. You really don't want this option at the moment, so let's back up.

5. Press Esc to move back to the previous pull-down menu.

6. Press ← to move to the Catalog option.

7. Press PgDn to move to the last available item on the Catalog menu.

8. Press ↑ to move up one item on the Catalog menu.

9. Press ← and → several times each and watch how the pull-down menu moves from item to item on the menu bar.

10. Press Esc to leave the menus.

Soon you'll start actually using menu options to build a database. For now, this little exercise in *navigating* the pull-down menus is sufficient.

USING TYPEMATIC KEYSTROKES

Most computers offer a *typematic* feature, which allows you to hold down a key to repeat a keystroke. To try this feature, press F10 to pull down a menu. Then hold down the → key for a few seconds. You should see the pull-down menu move quickly from option to option. If the computer starts beeping, release the key that you are holding down. No harm done, but the highlight may take a few seconds to stop moving.

Remember that all the keys on the keyboard are typematic, so you can use this feature whenever you want.

ACCESSING THE DOT PROMPT

dBASE IV offers an optional *command-driven* technique for managing databases, where you type commands rather than select options from pull-down menus. For beginners, the dot prompt is virtually useless.

NOTE

As an alternative to entering the ASSIST command to leave the dot prompt and return to the Control Center, you can just press the F2 function key.

If you start experimenting on your own with menu options and find yourself inadvertently at the dot prompt, with no menus or work space on the screen, you need to return to the Control Center by entering the ASSIST command. Practice this now, so you know what to do if you reach the dot prompt accidentally. Here are the steps:

1. Press F10 to access the pull-down menus.

2. Press → or ← until the Exit pull-down menu appears. (You'll see the options Exit to Dot Prompt and Quit to DOS.)

3. Type E to select Exit to Dot Prompt. The Control Center will disappear, and you'll see only a highlighted bar, a period (dot), and the blinking cursor (see Figure 2.7).

4. To return to the Control Center, type the command **ASSIST** (you can use upper- or lowercase letters).

5. Press the ⬅ key and wait a few seconds.

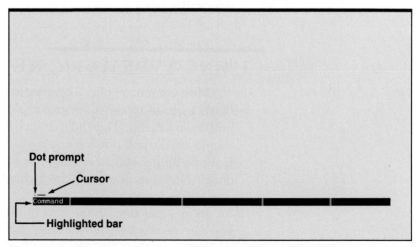

Figure 2.7: The dot prompt

The now-familiar Control Center will reappear on the screen. Keep this technique in mind, in case you should ever find yourself suddenly at the dot prompt, by accident, without the usual assistance you get from the Control Center.

SETTING INSTRUCTIONS ON

dBASE IV offers several modes of operation, which you control through the Settings menu. One setting, Instruct, tells dBASE to display prompt boxes and other aids which you'll see later, to help you learn dBASE. Many of the examples in this book assume that the Instruct setting is On. To make sure that this is indeed the case on your computer, follow these steps:

1. Press Menu (F10) to access the pull-down menus.

2. Press → or ← until the Tools option in the menu bar is highlighted.

3. Either type the letter S, or highlight Settings and press ← to select that option.

4. Type the letter I or use the ↓ key to highlight the Instruct option.

Instruct is a multiple-choice menu item that offers two choices: Off and On. Each time you press ←, the alternate choice appears. Set Instruct to On, as in Figure 2.8. Then, press → twice to move to the Exit option and press ← to return to the Control Center.

EXITING dBASE IV

Whenever you finish a dBASE IV session, you should exit (or quit) dBASE IV before you turn off your computer. If you don't remember to do so, you may find that dBASE IV is not saving your work, and you'll have to reenter all your data.

To exit dBASE IV, follow these simple steps:

1. Press F10 to access the pull-down menus.

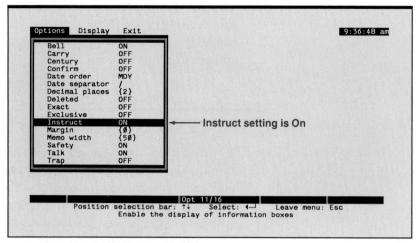

Figure 2.8: The Instruct setting

2. Press ← or → until the Exit pull-down menu appears.

3. Press ↓, if necessary, to highlight the Quit to DOS option.

4. Press ←. (As a shortcut, you can press Alt-E to open the Exit menu, then type Q to select Quit to DOS.)

You'll see the message "∗∗∗ END RUN dBASE IV" on your screen. Depending on how you installed dBASE IV, you might instead see the message "Uninstalled!" Don't be alarmed—the message simply means that the caching program has been removed from memory. dBASE IV is still safely installed on your computer for future use. Again, you need not be concerned about disk caching right now; it only affects the *speed* at which dBASE runs, not the *way* it runs. However, if and when you do want to look into disk caching, you can refer to Appendix C.

The last prompt to appear on your screen will be the DOS command prompt (usually C> or C:\DBASE>). When you see this prompt, dBASE has safely stored all of your information for future use (though in this case, you have not actually entered any specific information). You can now safely turn off your computer or use another program.

WARNING

In the future, *always* quit dBASE IV to return to DOS before turning off your computer. Otherwise, you'll probably lose your work.

USING THE ON-DISK TUTORIAL

As an adjunct to the hands-on exercises that this book offers, you can use the dBASE IV on-disk tutorial, which came with your dBASE IV package. The tutorial program is currently stored on your hard disk if you opted to install the complete dBASE IV package. Here are the steps for using the dBASE IV on-disk tutorial:

1. Make sure you are at the DOS command prompt. If you are using dBASE IV, you must exit and return to DOS.

2. Switch to the directory that the tutorial is stored on (typically \DBASE\DBTUTOR, which you can access by typing the command **CD \DBASE\DBTUTOR** and pressing ↵).

3. Type **INTRO** and press ↵.

4. Follow the instructions as they appear on the screen.

From this point on, the tutorial is pretty self-explanatory. You can try all of the sessions that the tutorial offers, or only a few. As the instructions on the screen will indicate, you can leave the on-screen tutorial at any time by pressing the F5 key, then typing Q to quit at the Introduction to DBASE IV Main Menu.

If you want to pace yourself with the on-screen tutorial, I suggest that you just try the first two sessions—"1 What is a database" and "2 dBASE IV basics"—at this time. These will provide different examples of the concepts you've learned up to this point.

RETURNING TO DBASE IV AFTER THE TUTORIAL

To return to dBASE IV after taking a lesson and exiting back to the command prompt, follow these steps to return to the \DBASE directory and run dBASE IV:

1. Type **CD..** then press ↵.

2. Type **DBASE** then press ↵.

In the next chapter, you'll begin to put your new knowledge and skills to work by creating your first dBASE IV database file.

CHAPTER

3

Creating a Database File

Fast Track

To create a database catalog for organizing information,   36
> forms, and reports, select Use a Different Catalog from the Catalog pull-down menu and <create> from the submenu that appears. Then type the name of the new catalog (using up to eight characters, with no spaces or punctuation) and press ←┘.

To use a previously created catalog,   39
> select Use a Different Catalog from the Catalog submenu and the appropriate catalog name from the submenu that appears.

Every field in a database file must have   42
> a unique name, a data type (Character, Numeric, Float, Date, Logical, or Memo), an assigned width, an assigned number of decimal places (for Numeric and Float data types), and an Index setting.

To create a database file,   45
> select the <create> option from the Data panel in the Control Center. Then enter valid field names, data types, widths, decimal places, and index options for each field in the database design work area.

To enter a plain-English description of a database,   50
> select Layout from the menu bar and Edit Database Description from the pull-down menu. Then type the description and press ←┘.

To save a database file structure,   51
> access the pull-down menu for the Exit option on the menu bar and select Save Changes and Exit.

IN THIS CHAPTER, YOU'LL START BUILDING YOUR first database. Of course, you'll need to have dBASE IV up and running on your computer. If you've forgotten the necessary steps, refer to the instructions in Chapter 2. When the dBASE IV Control Center appears on the screen, you're ready to forge ahead.

CREATING A DATABASE CATALOG

 TIP

Additional information about managing catalogs, which may come in handy when you start managing many files, is presented in Chapter 14.

As mentioned in the previous chapter, a catalog is a tool for grouping together the various components of a database, such as the database files, forms, and report formats. To help you organize your first database, you'll create a catalog named LEARN. The general steps for creating a catalog are simple: You call up the Catalog menu, select Use a Different Catalog, select <create>, and enter a new name for the catalog. Let's create the catalog named LEARN now, following these steps:

1. Press F10 to pull down a menu.

2. If necessary, press → or ← until the Catalog option on the menu bar is highlighted.

3. Use the ↑ or PgUp key, if necessary, to highlight the Use a Different Catalog option.

4. Press ⏎ to select the Use a Different Catalog option. The screen displays a submenu of existing catalog names, as well as the option to create a new catalog, as shown in Figure 3.1. (Don't worry if the submenu on your screen lists other catalog names.)

5. Press ↓ or ↑ until the <create> option is highlighted.

6. Press ⏎. The screen displays the prompt

   Enter name for new catalog: _

The name you enter for a catalog must follow these rules, which also apply to most of the names of the objects you'll create with dBASE IV:

• The name can be no more than eight characters long.

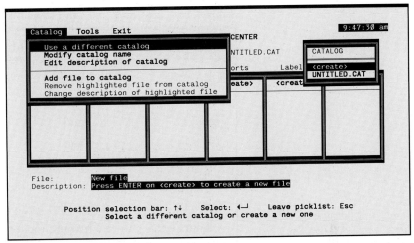

Figure 3.1: Submenu of catalog names

- The name can contain numbers (0 to 9), but *cannot* contain any blank spaces or punctuation marks, such as ? * . $: or ;. The underline character (_) is the only special character allowed.

- You can use upper- or lowercase letters, but lowercase letters are automatically converted to uppercase.

Table 3.1 shows examples of valid and invalid file names.

7. Type the new catalog name **LEARN** (if you make a mistake while typing the catalog name, press the Backspace key to back up and make corrections).

8. Press ⏎.

At this point, your screen should look like Figure 3.2, with only the label < create > at the top of each panel. Note that the current catalog is named LEARN.CAT (dBASE IV automatically adds the *extension* .CAT to the catalog name you provide).

As you build the database and add forms, reports, and mailing labels, you'll see the catalog grow to remind you of the various objects you've created.

NOTE

If somebody else has already created a catalog called LEARN on your computer, or if you've purchased and copied the sample disk described at the end of this book, then the panels will contain several file names. You can either continue to use the existing LEARN catalog or repeat steps 1 through 7 and use a name other than LEARN for your new catalog.

Table 3.1: Examples of Valid and Invalid File Names

File Name	Valid/Invalid
LEARN	Valid
MyData	Valid
June91	Valid
1991Qtr1	Valid
My_Data	Valid
My Data	Invalid; contains a space
Qtr1:91	Invalid; contains a colon
January1991	Invalid; too long
LEARN DBASE	Invalid; too long and contains a space

Figure 3.2: The LEARN catalog

Now let's take a slight detour and discuss how you can quit dBASE at any time and get back to the LEARN catalog to resume your work. This will allow you to take a break at any time as you read along in this book.

TAKING BREAKS

Whenever you want to take a break from the exercises in this book and perhaps turn off the computer, you can exit dBASE using the same techniques discussed in Chapter 2: that is, press F10, highlight the Exit option on the menu bar, highlight the Quit to DOS option, and press ←┘. All of your work will be safely stored on disk for future use.

RETURNING TO THE LEARN CATALOG

To get back to dBASE to resume your work, run dBASE in the usual manner for your computer (as discussed in Chapter 2). When the Control Center appears, follow these steps to return to the LEARN catalog (if it is not already on the screen):

1. Press F10 to access the pull-down menu.

2. Highlight the Catalog option.

3. Highlight Use a Different Catalog and press ←┘.

4. Use the ↓ key to highlight the name LEARN.CAT in the submenu.

5. Press ←┘.

The screen displays LEARN.CAT above the work space as the current catalog name. At this point, you can pick up where you left off in the book.

DESIGNING A DATABASE FILE

Chapter 1 discussed the structure of database files, where information is stored in tabular records (rows) and fields (columns). Before you can store information in a database file, you need to *structure* an empty file that specifies the name and type of data that is stored in each field. There are a few basic rules of thumb to keep in mind when designing a database file, discussed in the following sections.

DEFINING FIELDS

The most important point to keep in mind in structuring a database is that each unique item of information should be stored in its own field. Try not to be influenced by how you want the information to look when it's printed later. The manner in which you *store* information in a database file in no way limits the manner in which you can print it later.

For example, in a file containing names and addresses, you might be tempted to store peoples' names in a single field called Name, like this:

Name

John Smith

Annie Adams

Wilbur Watson

Mary Mahoney

John Newell

Sandy Beach

However, storing the names in this manner creates several problems. For example, you could not tell dBASE to sort the names into alphabetical order by last name because the last name and first name are within the same field. Similarly, you could not tell dBASE to search for the last name Mahoney, because dBASE has no way of isolating the last name as something to search for.

The simple solution to this problem is to store peoples' names in two fields, called LastName and FirstName, as shown here:

LastName	FirstName
Smith	John
Adams	Annie
Watson	Wilbur
Mahoney	Mary
Newell	John
Beach	Sandy

Because the last name and first name are separated, you can isolate the last name for both sorting and searching. If you want to include titles, such as Mr. and Ms., and middle initials, you should break the name into four different fields:

Title	LastName	FirstName	MI
Mr.	Smith	John	J.
Ms.	Adams	Annie	T.
Dr.	Watson	Wilbur	H.
Mrs.	Mahoney	Mary	
Mr.	Newell	John	J.
Miss	Beach	Sandy	B.

The preceding structure gives you the most flexibility in using the names. For example, if you were printing form letters, you could join the four fields together to create an entire name, such as Mr. John J. Smith, and you could just as easily isolate the first name for the greeting in the letter: Dear John:. And of course you could still isolate the last name for sorting and searching.

A common mistake that people make when structuring database files that contain names and addresses is grouping the city, state, and zip code into a single field, as follows:

CityStZip

San Diego, CA 92122

Malibu, CA 92001

New York, NY 12345

Seattle, WA 88977

Butte, MT 54321

Portland, OR 76543

Once again, grouping the data into a single field causes problems. For example, you could not sort the information into zip code order for bulk mailing, because dBASE cannot isolate the zip code. You could not isolate all of the records for a particular state, such as California (CA), or sort the data into state order.

To ensure maximum flexibility in managing your data, be sure to place the city, state, and zip codes in separate fields, as shown here. (Don't worry about the comma you may need between the city and state. You can add that to your printed reports without storing it in the database file.)

City	State	Zip
San Diego	CA	92122
Malibu	CA	92001
New York	NY	12345
Seattle	WA	88977
Butte	MT	54321
Portland	OR	76543

WHAT GOES IN A DATABASE FILE?

Basically, you can put anything that you want into a database file. But remember, dBASE can handle many database files simultaneously, so there is no need to put every bit of information that your business uses into a single file. Instead, use the same common sense that you do when storing information in Rolodex files or file drawers.

For example, you wouldn't mix your customer names and addresses with your parts inventory and accounts receivable in a single Rolodex file. Likewise, you wouldn't want to combine all of this information into a single database file either.

Occasionally, deciding how to divide information into separate database files is a little tricky, but we can save a discussion of these finer points for a later chapter.

ASSIGNING FIELD NAMES

Each field in the database file must have a unique name (that is, no two fields within a single file can have the same name). The name assigned to a field must conform to the following rules:

- The name can include no more than 10 characters.
- The first character must be a letter, but numbers can be used after the first letter.
- Blank spaces and punctuation marks are *not* allowed.
- The underscore character (_) is the only special symbol allowed.

You need not memorize all these rules; when you enter a field name, dBASE will make sure the name adheres to them.

SELECTING DATA TYPES

Each field in a database file must be categorized as a *data type* (or *field type*). dBASE offers six data types, listed in Table 3.2.

The correct data type for a particular field is usually obvious, though not always. For example, when storing phone numbers and zip codes, you might be tempted to use the Numeric data type. After all, we do say phone *number*, and the zip code 92122 certainly looks like a number. However, neither phone numbers nor zip codes are true numbers. Let's discuss why.

To dBASE, a true number is a quantity, such as the number of items purchased or a price or a test score. These numbers can contain only numeric digits (0 through 9) and, optionally, a decimal point (.) and a leading minus sign (–). Other characters, such as letters, parentheses, hyphens, and blank spaces, are not allowed in Numeric fields. A phone number, such as (619) 555-1212, contains parentheses and a hyphen. Some zip codes contain hyphens (such as 92038-2802), and some foreign postal codes contain letters (such as H3X 3T4).

If you give a zip code or phone number field the Numeric data type, you severely limit what you can enter into the field. Thus, before you assign the Numeric (or Float) data type to a field, ask yourself this question: "Is this an item for which I might want to calculate totals?" Certainly, you wouldn't need to total all the zip codes in a database or a group of phone numbers. In general, you should

Table 3.2: The dBASE IV Data Types

Data Type	Description	Examples
Character	Any textual information that has no true numeric value and has maximum length of 254 characters	Jones Spark plug 123 Oak St.
Numeric	Any true numeric value on which you may want to perform arithmetic operations; usually used for quantities and prices	10 – 123.45 100 1234.567
Float	Basically the same as Numeric, with some minor technical differences, as discussed in Chapter 9	10.0 – 123.45 100.00 1234.567
Date	Any date stored in the format mm/dd/yy (for example, 12/31/91); always use this option to store dates	1/1/91 12/31/91 6/12/91
Logical	Contains either a true (.T.) or false (.F.) value and no other information; for example, you could create a field named *Paid* as the Logical data type, with .T. meaning the charge has been paid and .F. meaning it has not been paid	.T. .F.
Memo	Very large volumes of text, perhaps including several paragraphs, up to 64K (about 65,500 characters)	abstracts, comments, lengthy descriptions

use the Numeric and Float data types only for fields on which you need to perform mathematical calculations.

One question that might occur to you is "How can I sort my mailing list into zip code order, if I don't make the zip codes numeric?" Don't worry about this; dBASE knows that the zip code

12345 comes before the zip code 12346 in a sort, regardless of whether the zip code is stored as a Character data type or a Numeric (or Float) data type.

Incidentally, the Numeric and Float (short for floating point) data types are basically the same, with a few minor technical differences. Chapter 9, which presents many aspects of managing numbers, including performing calculations, discusses these technical differences in detail.

You'll see the other data types—Character, Logical, Date, and Memo—in action as you read on.

CREATING A DATABASE FILE

Now let's get back to work and actually create some database files. We'll create a file called CUSTLIST (short for CUSTomer LIST) that stores customers' names and addresses and other useful information. To get started, follow these steps:

1. Use the arrow keys (or Tab key) to move the highlight to the <create> option in the Data panel, as shown in Figure 3.3.

2. Press ↩ while the <create> option is highlighted.

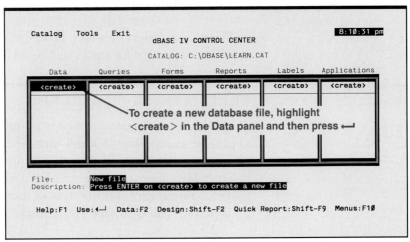

Figure 3.3: Creating a new database file

dBASE will take you to the *database design screen,* as shown in Figure 3.4. Note that the screen includes a table with seven columns labeled Num, Field Name, Field Type, Width, Dec (for decimal places), and Index. You'll define each field in your database structure within this table. Like the Control Center, the database design screen includes pull-down menu options at the top of the screen. The bottom two lines on the screen provide brief help and instructions. Pressing Help (F1) provides additional help.

ENTERING FIELD NAMES

The first database file we'll create will contain the field names LASTNAME, FIRSTNAME, COMPANY, ADDRESS, CITY, STATE, ZIP, PHONE, STARTDATE, and PAID. You can think of CUSTLIST as a database of customers who subscribe to a newsletter. STARTDATE is the date that the subscription started and PAID is a field indicating whether the customer has paid for the subscription.

To enter a field name, first make sure that the blinking cursor is in the Field Name column on the screen. Type the field name and press ←┘. In this example, follow these simple steps:

1. Type the field name **LASTNAME** (if you make a mistake as you type, you can use the Backspace key to make corrections).

2. Press ←┘.

The cursor will jump to the Field Type column, where you need to select a data type for the LASTNAME field.

SELECTING A DATA TYPE

While the blinking cursor is in the Field Type column, you can press the space bar to scroll through the various data types before making a selection. Each time you press the space bar, the name of a data type appears within the highlight, and a brief description of the data type appears at the bottom of the screen. To select the currently displayed data type, just press Enter.

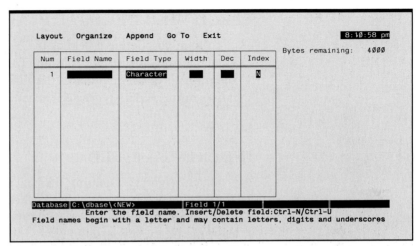

Figure 3.4: The database design screen

A shortcut for entering a data type is simply to type the first letter of its name; for example, type C for Character or D for Date. If you make a mistake, press ← or Shift-Tab to move back to the Field Type column. Then try again.

Follow these two steps to assign the Character data type to the LASTNAME field:

1. If necessary, press the space bar repeatedly until the Character option appears.

2. Press ←.

As soon as you press ←, the cursor jumps to the Width column.

SPECIFYING A FIELD WIDTH

The next step in creating a database structure is to specify a maximum width for the field. The rule of thumb here is to select a reasonable maximum width, with just a touch of frugality. (The wider a field is, the more disk space it consumes.) For the LASTNAME field, a width of 15 should be sufficient. Follow these simple steps:

1. Type **15**.

2. Press ←.

The cursor jumps to the Index column.

SPECIFYING DECIMAL PLACES

When you define a field as the Numeric or Float data type, the cursor jumps to the Dec column. In the Dec column, you specify the number of decimal places that the field requires. Chapter 9 discusses numeric data types and the various special features they offer.

INDEXING A FIELD

In the rightmost column, labeled Index, you can enter either Y (for yes), or N (for no) to indicate whether the field should be *indexed*. You'll learn more about indexing later. For now, just press ⏎ to leave the Index option set to N.

At this point, the highlight jumps down to the next blank row, and you can enter the information for the next field. You can also move around the work area and make corrections or changes.

MAKING CHANGES AND CORRECTIONS

If you notice an error in your file structure or wish to make a change, you can use several keys to move the highlight and cursor around the database design work area. These are listed in Table 3.3.

Note that the keys won't always work if you attempt to leave a field that has incomplete or invalid data. You may have to experiment with several of the keys from Table 3.3 or type Ctrl-U to completely delete an incomplete or invalid field to get the cursor moving in the direction you want.

FINISHING THE CUSTLIST DATABASE

You can now enter the rest of the database file structure shown in Figure 3.5. Notice that ZIP and PHONE are both Character data types (as discussed earlier). When you enter the STARTDATE and

Table 3.3: Keys Used to Change a Database File Structure

Key	Effect
↑	Moves highlight up one row
↓	Moves highlight down one row
←	Moves cursor one character to the left
→	Moves cursor one character to the right
Tab	Moves cursor one column to the right (only if valid information is already in the present column)
Shift-Tab	Moves cursor one column to the left (only if valid information is already in the present column)
Backspace	Moves cursor one space back, erasing along the way
Enter	Completes an entry and moves to the next column or row
Ctrl-N	Inserts a blank field between two existing fields
Ctrl-U	Deletes the current field definition
F3	Moves cursor left one column
F4	Moves cursor right one column
PgUp	Moves cursor to the first row on the screen
PgDn	Moves cursor to the last row on the screen
Home	Moves to Field Name column
End	Moves to Index column

NOTE

A single database file can contain a maximum of 255 fields, or 4,000 characters (bytes) of information, whichever comes first. However, Memo fields can contain over 64,000 characters, as discussed in Chapter 10.

PAID fields as the Date and Logical data types respectively, dBASE will automatically fill in the width as 8 and 1. You cannot (and need not) change the width of these fields.

You have not used the Numeric, Float, or Memo data type in this sample database file. These data types have some unique properties, which are discussed in Chapters 9 and 10.

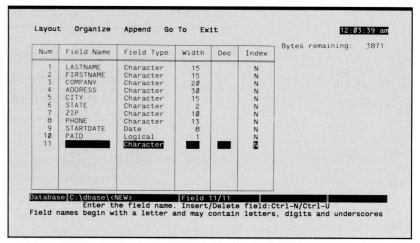

Figure 3.5: The completed CUSTLIST database file structure

ENTERING A DATABASE DESCRIPTION

As the finishing touch for the CUSTLIST database, we'll add a *description*, which is simply a sentence that describes, in plain English, what is stored in the database. To do so, follow these steps:

1. Press F10 to access the pull-down menus.

2. If necessary, use the → or ← key to highlight the *Layout* option on the top menu.

3. Use the ↓ key to highlight the option Edit Database Description in the pull-down menu.

4. Press ◄─┘ to select the menu option.

The screen will display the message "Edit the description of this .dbf file" and present a highlighted bar for you to type in. (Remember that dBASE always adds the *extension* .DBF to a database file name, so the .dbf file that the message refers to is the CUSTLIST database file you just created.) Type the following description:

Customer names and addresses

Press ◄─┘ after typing the description.

SAVING A DATABASE FILE STRUCTURE

TIP

To quickly move from one end of the menu bar to the other, press the arrow key pointing opposite to the direction that you want to go. The highlight will wrap around to the menu option at the opposite end.

Once you've finished entering the structure and description of a database file, you need to save your work. When your screen looks like Figure 3.5, follow these steps to save the new CUSTLIST database file structure:

1. Press F10 to access the pull-down menus.

2. Use the ← or → key to highlight the Exit option on the top menu.

3. If necessary, use the ↑ key to highlight the Save Changes and Exit option.

4. Press ←⎯.

5. When you see the prompt "Save as:" type in the name **CUSTLIST** and press ←⎯.

WARNING

Selecting Overwrite in response to the "File already exists" prompt completely erases all data in the existing database file, replacing it with the empty database structure currently on the screen. Make sure you want to do this before you select the Overwrite option. Chapter 14 discusses file management in detail.

If you attempt to save a database file using a name that already exists, dBASE will beep and display the message "File already exists." You are also given two options: Overwrite, to replace the existing database with the new structure, and Cancel, to stop and use a different file name.

RETURNING TO THE CONTROL CENTER

After you've saved the database structure, you'll be returned to the Control Center. Here you can see the name of the new database file in the Data panel, as shown in Figure 3.6.

Let's take a moment to see what the Control Center now tells us:

NOTE

Appendix A, "A DOS Primer," discusses basic DOS concepts such as *drive* and *directory*.

- Centered near the top of the screen, **CATALOG C:\ DBASE\LEARN.CAT** tells us that the current catalog is named LEARN.CAT, and that catalog is stored on the directory named DBASE on disk drive C.

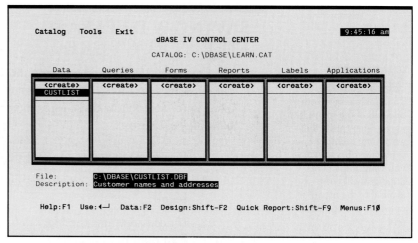

Figure 3.6: The CUSTLIST database file name in the Data panel

- The current catalog contains one database file named CUSTLIST (you can see its name in the data panel).

- The **File:** and **Description:** prompts near the bottom of the screen tell you the complete location and name of the current file—C:\DBASE\CUSTLIST.DBF (dBASE automatically chose the current drive and directory as the place to store the file, and automatically added the .DBF extension). The description, "Customer names and addresses," you added yourself while designing the structure of the database.

- As usual, the keys available to you at this moment are listed at the bottom of the screen.

TIME TO RELAX

So far, so good. You've created a database file (at least, the *structure* of the file), and now you are ready to start storing information in it. However, you may want to take a break now to digest all of the information you've learned so far. To do so, quit dBASE IV now (*before* you turn off your computer, as discussed earlier). Remember, to quit dBASE, you access the Exit pull-down menu and select the option Quit to DOS, as described in Chapter 2.

CHAPTER

4

Adding and
Changing
Information

To add records to a database that already contains information,   70
go to the edit or browse screen and select Add New Records
from the Records pull-down menu.

NOW THAT YOU'VE *STRUCTURED* A dBASE IV DATA-base file, the next step is to put some information into it. But before you can do *anything* to the CUSTLIST database, you need to open it (this is true of any and *all* databases you create with dBASE IV). If you are currently at the DOS command prompt, you have to do several things:

- Get to the proper directory and run dBASE.

- Get to the catalog (which you named LEARN.CAT) that the database is stored in.

- Open the database that you want to work with.

Though we've been through the steps for this procedure in preceding chapters, we'll take it step-by-step in the sections that follow to help reinforce what you've learned so far.

STARTING dBASE IV

Remember that whenever you exit dBASE IV, you need to switch back to its directory and run it again in order to gain access to your database. Assuming that you are currently at the DOS command prompt, and are using C:\DBASE as your dBASE IV drive and directory, follow these steps:

1. Type **CD \DBASE** and press ◄─┘ to switch to your dBASE directory.

2. Type **DBASE**.

Wait a few moments, or press ◄─┘ to leave the copyright notice, and you'll get to the Control Center.

ACCESSING THE LEARN CATALOG

Remember that we put the CUSTLIST database in a catalog named LEARN. Now you need to make sure that LEARN.CAT is the current catalog. You can tell simply by looking at the name next to the CATALOG: prompt centered near the top of the screen. If the LEARN catalog is not the current catalog, here once again are the steps to open that catalog:

1. When the Control Center appears, press F10 to access the pull-down menus.

2. Use the ← or → key, as necessary, to move to the Catalog option on the menu bar.

3. Move the highlight to the Use a Different Catalog option and press ←.

4. When the submenu of catalogs appears, use the ↓ or ↑ key to move the highlight to the LEARN.CAT option. Press ← to select LEARN.CAT.

At this point, LEARN.CAT should appear as the current catalog name in the Control Center, with the CUSTLIST database name in the Data panel, as in Figure 4.1.

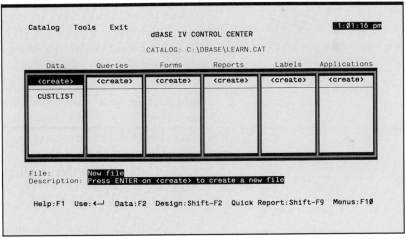

Figure 4.1: The LEARN catalog on the screen, ready for action

SELECTING A DATABASE FILE

NOTE

To view the contents of a database, highlight the database file name in the Data panel, and then press Data (F2). Do not use the pull-down menus.

Any single catalog may contain several database files. Therefore, before you start entering information into a database file, you need to tell dBASE IV which database file you want to use.

To select a database file and access its data (to add, view, or change information), use the arrow keys to highlight the database file name in the Data panel and then press the Data key (F2). Suppose you want to add new information to the CUSTLIST database file. To do so, follow these steps:

1. Press the ←, →, Tab, or Shift-Tab key, as necessary, until the highlight is in the Data panel.

2. When the highlight is in the Data panel, press ↓ or ↑ until the highlight is on the CUSTLIST database file name.

3. Press F2 to view data in the CUSTLIST database file.

ADDING NEW DATA

At this point, you should see the *edit screen* for the CUSTLIST database, as shown in Figure 4.2. (If a different screen appears, press the F2 key.) As you can see, the edit screen looks like a blank form for a single record that you can fill out on the screen. (Later you'll learn how to create much fancier custom forms on the screen.)

Now suppose you want to enter information from the Rolodex card shown in Figure 4.3. To do so, follow the steps presented here. If you make a mistake while typing, just press Backspace to make corrections, or you can wait until we discuss more sophisticated editing techniques a little later in this chapter.

1. Type the last name **Smith** and press ←┘.

2. Type the first name **John** and press ←┘.

3. Type the company name **ABC Co.** and press ←┘.

4. Type the address **123 A St.** and press ←┘.

NOTE

Notice that when your entry completely fills the field, you need not press ⟵; dBASE will beep when you've filled the space provided and automatically move the cursor to the next field.

5. Type the city **San Diego** and press ⟵.

6. Type the state **CA**.

7. Type the zip code **92067** and press ⟵.

8. Type the phone number **(619)555-1234**.

9. Note that in the STARTDATE field, the slashes are already entered for you. To enter the date November 15, 1990, type **11**, then **15**, then **90**. At this point, your screen should look like Figure 4.4.

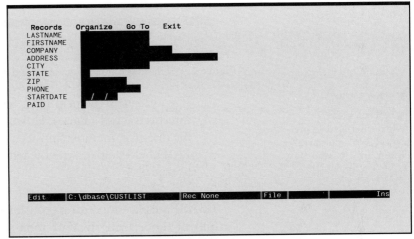

Figure 4.2: Edit screen for a record in the CUSTLIST database

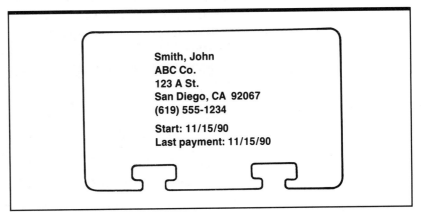

Figure 4.3: A Rolodex card to be entered as a database record

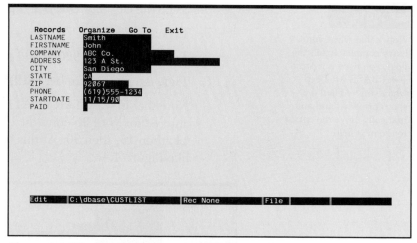

Figure 4.4: The first database record filled in on the screen

When entering data in a
logical field, you can type
T, t, Y, or y for true, or F,
f, N, or n for false.

10. If you leave a Logical field, such as PAID, blank, dBASE
    interprets it as F (False). However, since John Smith has paid
    his dues (or membership fee, subscription, or whatever the
    PAID field holds), type the letter T now to change the entry
    to true.

dBASE displays an edit screen for the next new record. At the
bottom of the screen, EOF/1 means that you are at the end of
the database file, and there is one record above this one.

BROWSING
THROUGH THE DATABASE FILE

In the previous example, you entered new data on an edit screen.
When using the edit screen, you can see only one database record at a
time. You can also add and change data using the *browse screen*. On the
browse screen, you can see several records, though usually not
all the fields from each record.

To switch between the edit screen and the browse screen, you
simply press the Data (F2) key. Do so now, and then press the ↑ key.

You'll see part of the record that you just entered at the top of the database file, as shown in Figure 4.5.

You can scroll to the right to see the fields that are currently hidden by pressing the Tab or ◄─┘ key. Each time you press Tab, the highlight moves one field to the right. To scroll all the way to the right (to the PAID field, which is not currently visible), you can either press the Tab key nine times or just press the End key. Figure 4.6

Figure 4.5: The first database record, displayed on the browse screen

Figure 4.6: Browse screen scrolled to the right

shows the browse screen with the highlight and cursor scrolled all the way to the right.

To scroll back to the left one column at a time, press the Shift-Tab key combination (hold down the Shift key while pressing the Tab key). To quickly scroll all the way back to the leftmost field, press the Home key.

ADDING NEW DATA IN BROWSE MODE

Suppose you want to add a new record while the current record is still displayed on the browse screen. This is simple enough: Just press the ↓ key to move down to the next row. Because there is currently no record there, dBASE will display the prompt " = = = > Add new records? (Y/N)." In this case, you do want to add records, so press Y.

Here is a sample name and address for another database record (but don't begin typing yet):

Annie Adams
345 C St.
Malibu, CA 92001
Tel: (714)555-0123
Start Date = 1/1/91
Paid Yet = No

Now, follow these steps to type the sample record, and you'll learn some new tricks along the way:

1. Make sure the highlight is in the LASTNAME field; then type the last name **Adams** and press ←⏎.

2. Type the first name **Annie** and press ←⏎.

3. Annie has no company affiliation, so press ←⏎ to leave the Company field blank.

4. Type the address **345 C St.** and press ←⏎.

5. Type the city **Malibu** and press ←⏎.

6. You can use the Ditto key (Shift-F8) to copy the State (CA) from the previous record to the current one. Press Shift-F8 now. You'll see CA entered as the state in the current record. Press ←⏎.

7. Type the zip code **92001** and press ←⏎.

8. Type the phone number **(714)555-0123**.

9. To enter the date January 1, 1991, you can type either **1/1/91** or **010191**; dBASE will automatically convert either entry to 01/01/91.

10. When the cursor gets to the PAID field, type **F** to indicate "not paid."

At this point you've filled in the entire second record. Press ↑ twice and End to see the six rightmost fields, shown in Figure 4.7.

```
 Records   Organize   Fields   Go To   Exit

 CITY          STATE  ZIP    PHONE          STARTDATE  PAID
 San Diego     CA     92067  (619)555-1234  11/15/90   T
 Malibu        CA     92001  (714)555-0123  01/01/91   F




 Browse  C:\dbase\CUSTLIST       Rec 1/2         File
```

Figure 4.7: Part of the new record as seen on the browse screen

SAVING NEW RECORDS

You can add as many records as you want, using either the edit screen or the browse screen or by switching back and forth between them with the Data (F2) key. But for now, let's save the two new records and return to the Control Center. Here are the simple steps (which you can perform from either the edit or the browse screen):

1. Press F10 to pull down a menu.

2. Press ← or →, as necessary, to highlight the Exit option on the menu bar.

3. Select Exit by pressing the letter E or by pressing ← while the Exit option is highlighted.

The two new records are saved in the database file, and you are back at the Control Center.

VIEWING DATA

Let's return to the new records now and practice some editing techniques. To view the new data, use the Data (F2) key exactly as before. That is, move the highlight to the name of the appropriate database file in the Data panel (CUSTLIST) and press the F2 key. You'll be returned to the edit or browse screen, depending on which screen you were in when you saved the new data. Of course, you can press the Data key (F2) to switch from one screen to the other.

MAKING CHANGES

Suppose you want to change Annie Adams's address from 345 C St., Malibu, to 3456 Ocean St., Santa Monica. You can make changes whether you are at the edit screen or the browse screen. For this example, let's use the edit screen. Here are the steps to follow:

If you highlight a record in the browse screen and then press F2, that record will appear in the edit screen.

1. If the browse screen is showing, press F2 to display the edit screen.

2. If Annie Adams's record is not on the screen, press PgDn or PgUp until her data appears as in Figure 4.8.

NOTE

Don't forget that if your arrow, PgUp, PgDn, Ins, Del, and other keys share the numbers on the numeric keypad, these keys work only when NumLock is off.

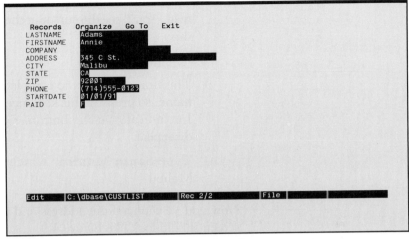

Figure 4.8: Annie Adams's record on the edit screen

3. To change the address, press ↓ three times to move the blinking cursor into the ADDRESS field, like this:

   <u>3</u>45 C St.

4. Press → three times to move the cursor to the right of 345, like this:

   345_C St.

5. Look at the lower-right corner of your screen to see if the indicator "Ins" appears (as it does in Figure 4.8). If it does not, press the Ins (Insert) key until the "Ins" indicator appears. Now you are in Insert mode.

6. Type **6 Ocean**, so the entry looks like this:

   3456 Ocean_C St.

   Notice that the new text you typed was *inserted* into the existing text. That's because the Insert mode (controlled by the Ins key) is currently on.

NOTE

The Ins (Insert) key acts as a *toggle* for the Insert and Overwrite modes. Each time you press the key, dBASE switches from the current mode to the other mode.

7. Now press the Del (Delete) key twice to get rid of the unnecessary characters, so the address looks like this:

   3456 Ocean St.

8. To change the city, press ↵ to move down to the CITY field. You'll see the cursor at the start of the name *Malibu,* like this:

    Malibu

9. This time, you want to completely type over the existing city name, so press the Ins key once to turn off Insert mode. The Ins indicator at the bottom-right corner of the screen will disappear.

10. Type **Santa Monica**, which will completely overwrite Malibu.

Now you've changed the address and city for Annie's record. Your screen should look like Figure 4.9.

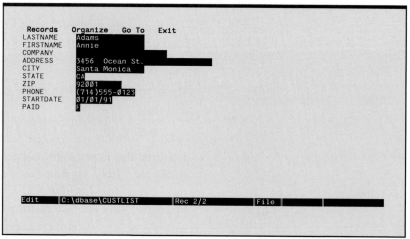

Figure 4.9: Annie Adams's record with the address and city changed

The changes you've made will not be saved until you either scroll to a new record using the PgUp or PgDn key or exit from the edit or browse screen. For now, save these changes in Annie's record by pressing PgUp to move up a record. When you do, the record for John Smith should appear on the edit screen.

You can use the same basic editing techniques you just learned, such as pressing the arrow keys to move the cursor, pressing Del

(Delete) to delete a character, and pressing the Ins (Insert) key to switch between Insert and Overwrite modes, at almost anytime while you are using dBASE IV. They work the same whether you are designing a database structure, creating forms, or creating report formats—and in many other situations as well. Table 4.1 lists these editing keys.

Table 4.1: Navigation and Editing Keys for the Browse and Edit Screens

Key	Effect
↓	Moves cursor down
↑	Moves cursor up
→	Moves cursor right one character
←	Moves cursor left one character
↵	Completes entry and moves to next field
PgDn	Moves down one record on edit screen or one screenful on browse screen
PgUp	Moves up one record on edit screen or one screenful on browse screen
Del	Deletes character over cursor
Backspace	Moves left one character, erasing along the way
Shift-F8	(Ditto) Carries data from same field in previous record to current record
Ctrl-Y	Deletes all characters to right of cursor
Ins	Switches between Insert and Overwrite modes
Home	Moves to first field on browse screen or first character in current field on edit screen
End	Moves to last field on browse screen or end of current field on edit screen
Tab	Moves to next field
Shift-Tab	Moves to previous field
Escape	Leaves current record without saving changes
F1	Displays help

Table 4.1: Navigation and Editing Keys for the Browse and Edit Screens (continued)

Key	Effect
F2	Toggles between browse and edit screens
F3	Same as Shift-Tab
F4	Same as Tab
F10	Accesses pull-down menus (the Exit option saves your work and returns you to Control Center)

UNDOING AN EDIT

Once in a while, you'll probably make the common mistake of changing or erasing a field's contents without paying enough attention to what you are doing. Suddenly, you realize that you've changed the wrong information and do not remember what the old information was. Fortunately, you can easily "undo" accidental changes to a record. To demonstrate, we'll change one field and delete the contents of another, and then reverse those changes:

1. Press ↓ twice (or as many times as necessary) to move the cursor to the COMPANY field.

2. Type **HA HA HO HO** (or any other nonsense that suits your fancy).

3. Press ←┘.

4. Press Ctrl-Y (hold down the Ctrl key and press Y) to erase everything to the right of the cursor (thereby emptying the ADDRESS field).

Suppose now you realize that you are making a mess of things. *Don't* move to another record. (Remember, your changes are not saved until you scroll to a new record or leave the edit or browse screen.) Instead, follow these steps to undo your changes.

1. Press Menu (F10) to pull down a menu.

2. Use ← or →, as necessary, to highlight the Records option on the menu bar.

> **NOTE**
>
> Selecting Undo Change to Record undoes *all* of the changes you've made in the current record, not just the last field you've changed. If you have not made any changes in the record currently on the screen, the Undo Change to Record option is shaded when you call up the Records menu, indicating that there are no changes to undo.

3. Press ↑, if necessary, to highlight Undo Change to Record.

4. Press ↵ to select Undo Change to Record.

You'll see John Smith's record back on the screen, exactly as it was before you made your erroneous changes.

USING THE STATUS BAR

Whether you are at the browse or edit screen, dBASE displays a highlighted *status bar* at the bottom of the screen to help you with your work. Figure 4.10 shows the location of the following information in the status bar:

- Type of screen in use (such as edit screen or browse screen).

- Location and name of the database file currently in use (C:\dbase\CUSTLIST in this example).

- Current record in the database and total number of records. For example, the message "Rec 1/2" means that you are currently viewing record number 1 in a database containing two records.

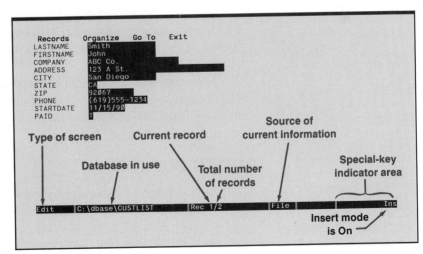

Figure 4.10: The status bar

- Source of the data currently on the screen (a database file in this example).

- Settings of various toggle keys. For example, if "Num" appears, the NumLock key is on. If "Caps" appears, the CapsLock key is on. If "Ins" appears, you are in Insert mode, rather than Overwrite mode. Pressing the NumLock, CapsLock, or Ins key turns these settings (and the appropriate indicators) on and off.

ADDING MORE RECORDS

Now that you are armed with some basic editing techniques, go ahead and enter a few more sample records now (you'll use these in future exercises). To begin entering new records, follow these steps:

1. Press F10 to access the Records pull-down menu.

2. Select the Add New Records option.

Note that originally you did not select Add New Records to add new records to the database. You did not need to do so because the database was empty; dBASE assumed you'd be adding new data. Once you have added data to a database, however, you can add new records either by selecting Add New Records from the Records pull-down menu or by pressing PgDn (from the edit screen) or ↓ (from the browse screen) until you see the prompt " = = > Add new records? (Y/N)." Then type **Y**.

Now type the sample data shown in Figure 4.11. You can use either browse or edit mode to enter these new records. Use the editing keys listed in Table 4.1 as necessary to help you position the cursor and make changes.

SAVING YOUR WORK

After you have finished entering the records shown in Figure 4.11, save your work and return to the Control Center. Here are the steps:

1. Press F10 to pull down a menu.

2. Use ← or → to move to the Exit option.

LastName	FirstName	Company	Address	City	State	Zip	Phone	StartDate	Paid
Watson	Wilbur	HiTech Co.	P.O. Box 987	New York	NY	12345	(212)555-9988	11/15/90	T
Mahoney	Mary		211 Seahawk St.	Seattle	WA	88977	(206)555-8673	12/01/90	T
Newell	John	LoTech Co.	734 Rainbow Dr.	Butte	MT	54321	(303)555-6739	12/15/90	T
Beach	Sandy	American Widget	11 Elm St.	Portland	OR	76543	(717)555-0898	12/15/90	T
Kenney	Ralph		1101 Rainbow Ct.	Los Angeles	CA	96607	(213)555-9988	12/30/90	F
Schumack	Susita	SMS Software	47 Broad St.	Philadelphia	PA	45543	(202)555-9720	12/30/90	T
Smith	Anita	Zeerocks, Inc.	2001 Engine Dr.	Hideaway	CA	92220	(415)555-9854	01/01/91	T

Figure 4.11: New records to add to the CUSTLIST database

3. Select Exit (by pressing E or by pressing ⏎ while Exit is highlighted on the pull-down menu).

You'll be returned to the Control Center, where once again you'll see the CUSTLIST database name in the Data panel.

GETTING SOME PRACTICE

TIP

You might also want to try Session 3 from the on-screen tutorial (described at the end of Chapter 2) to review techniques from Chapters 3 and 4.

If you would like to make some more changes in the CUSTLIST database, use the same techniques discussed previously to return to the data. That is, make sure that the name CUSTLIST is highlighted in the Data panel; then press F2.

You may want to practice with some of the editing keys described in Table 4.1 while the data is on the screen. (Remember that you can undo the changes made to a record by selecting Undo Change to Record from the Records pull-down menu.)

When you have finished experimenting, select Exit from the Exit pull-down menu once again to return to the Control Center. Remember to exit dBASE before turning off your computer.

In Chapter 11 you'll learn more advanced editing techniques, including techniques for deleting records. Already, though, you've accomplished quite a bit. You know how to create a database, add records to it, view those records through the browse and edit screens, and make changes as needed.

HOW MANY RECORDS CAN dBASE IV HOLD?

So far, you've put nine records into the sample database. However, dBASE IV can handle many more. In fact, dBASE can handle approximately a billion (that's 1,000,000,000) records, or 2,000,000,000 characters, whichever comes first.

The CUSTLIST database contains 129 characters per record (the sum of the field widths). Hence, you could have about 15.5 million records in your CUSTLIST database, which should be adequate: After all, if it took you one minute to type each record, you would need about 29 years of nonstop typing to enter 15.5 million records!

CHAPTER

5

Sorting
the Database

TYPICALLY, YOU ENTER INFORMATION INTO A DATA-base as it becomes available to you. Very often, you need to organize, or *sort*, that information into a more useful order, such as alphabetical order by name, or zip code order for bulk mailing. This chapter discusses techniques that you can use to sort your databases into any order you wish.

dBASE IV offers two ways to sort database files. Generally the fastest and most efficient method is *indexing*. A second, slower, and less efficient way to sort is by making a sorted copy of a database file. This chapter discusses both methods, focusing primarily on the preferred index method.

Once again, if you exited dBASE in the previous chapter, be sure to get it up and running on your computer again. If the LEARN catalog does not appear in the Control Center automatically, use the techniques discussed previously to access the LEARN catalog.

SORTING A DATABASE THROUGH AN INDEX

Sorting a database by index is an easy process, and can be accomplished using the Organize pull-down menu at the browse or edit screens (which you learned about in the previous chapter), or the database design screen which you used to initially create the CUST-LIST database in Chapter 3.

Let's take a moment to look at the general steps for creating a sort order (via an index), and then we'll try it out a little later. Here are the general steps:

- Go to the edit or browse screen (F2) or the database design screen (Shift-F2).

- Press Menu (F10) and pull down the Organize menu.

- Select Create New Index.

- Select Name of Index, type in an index name (up to eight characters, no spaces or punctuation), and press ↵.

- Select Index Expression and type in an index expression, or build one using the Expression Builder (Shift-F1), as described in a moment.

- Select Order of Index, and choose between Ascending order (smallest-to-largest) or Descending order (largest-to-smallest) by pressing the space bar.

- Press Ctrl-End when done.

You may have noticed that a couple of other options—"FOR clause" and "Order of index"—are listed on the menu for creating an index. You need not be concerned with those just yet; we'll stick with the basics for now. In the sections that follow, we'll create a couple of indexes to sort the CUSTLIST database you created in the preceding chapters.

SORTING BY LAST NAME

Suppose you want to put the customer names and addresses from the CUSTLIST database into ascending alphabetical order (A-Z) by last name. To do so, follow these steps:

1. In the Control Center's Data panel, move the highlight to CUSTLIST.

2. Press Data (F2) to view its contents.

3. If the edit screen appears (a single record only), press Data (F2) to switch to the browse screen.

4. Press Menu (F10) to access the menus.

5. Press → or ← until the Organize menu is displayed, as in Figure 5.1.

6. Select Create New Index.

7. Select Name of Index.

8. You can assign any file name to the index you wish; for this example, type in LASTNAME and press ←.

9. Select Index Expression.

TIP

Remember that even when an option is highlighted on a menu, you must still press ← to select it.

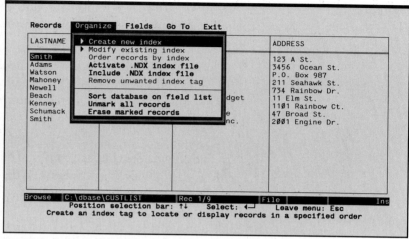

Figure 5.1: The Organize menu on the browse screen

The Index Expression is the name of the field (or fields, as described later) that you want to sort by. You can either type in the field name or select it using the Expression Builder. For this exercise, we'll use the Expression Builder.

10. Press Shift-F1 to open the Expression Builder.

11. Move the highlight to the field named LASTNAME and press ←┘ to select it.

12. Press ←┘ a second time to complete your entry.

13. Press ↓ to move to the Order of Index option.

14. Press the space bar (or ←┘) until ASCENDING appears.

15. Press ↓, and then press the space bar (or ←┘) until NO appears as your selection.

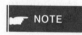

You'll learn about the Operator and Function columns in the Expression Builder a little later; for now we'll just use the Fieldname column.

At this point, your screen should look like Figure 5.2. You can press Ctrl-End to complete your index definition and return to the browse screen. (If you hear a beep and see the message "Index TAG already exists: LASTNAME," don't worry about it; just type the letter O to select Overwrite.)

If you look at your browse screen now, you'll see that your customers are now listed in alphabetical order by last name, as shown in Figure 5.3.

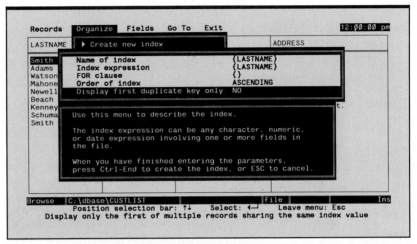

Figure 5.2: Index defined for the LASTNAME field

```
Records   Organize   Fields   Go To   Exit

 LASTNAME        FIRSTNAME        COMPANY          ADDRESS

 Adams           Annie                             3456 Ocean St.
 Beach           Sandy            American Widget  11 Elm St.
 Kenney          Ralph                             1101 Rainbow Ct.
 Mahoney         Mary                              211 Seahawk St.
 Newell          John             LoTech Co.       734 Rainbow Dr.
 Schumack        Susita           SMS Software     47 Broad St.
 Smith           John             ABC Co.          123 A St.
 Smith           Anita            Zeerocks, Inc.   2001 Engine Dr.
 Watson          Wilbur           HiTech Co.       P.O. Box 987

 Browse    C:\dbase\CUSTLIST       Rec 2/9        File
```

Figure 5.3: Records sorted into alphabetical order by last name

SORTING RECORDS BY ZIP CODE

Now let's suppose that you want to put your customer list into zip code order, perhaps for bulk mailing. To do so, you just need to create a second index by following the steps below:

1. Press F10 and pull open the Organize menu.

2. Select Create New Index.

3. Select Name of Index.

4. We'll name this index ZIP, so type ZIP and press ◄──┘.

5. Select Index Expression.

6. Press Shift-F1 to access the Expression Builder.

7. Move the highlight to the ZIP field name.

8. Press ◄──┘ to select ZIP.

9. Press ◄──┘ again to complete your entry.

10. The Order of Index and Display First... options should still be set at ASCENDING and NO respectively, so your index definition is now complete. Press Ctrl-End.

Again, if you hear a beep and see the ''Index Tag already exists...'' message, just type the letter O to proceed. Your records will now be displayed in ascending zip code order (smallest to largest), as you can see by pressing the End key and looking at the ZIP field. Figure 5.4 also shows the records displayed in zip code order.

```
 Records    Organize    Fields    Go To    Exit
┌────────────────┬───────┬───────┬──────────────┬───────────┬────────────┐
│CITY            │STATE  │ZIP    │PHONE         │STARTDATE  │PAID        │
├────────────────┼───────┼───────┼──────────────┼───────────┼────────────┤
│New York        │NY     │12345  │(212)555-9988 │11/15/90   │▐T▌         │
│Philadelphia    │PA     │45543  │(202)555-9720 │12/30/90   │T           │
│Butte           │MT     │54321  │(303)555-6739 │12/15/90   │T           │
│Portland        │OR     │76543  │(717)555-0898 │12/15/90   │T           │
│Seattle         │WA     │88977  │(206)555-8673 │12/01/90   │T           │
│Santa Monica    │CA     │92001  │(714)555-0123 │01/01/91   │F           │
│San Diego       │CA     │92067  │(619)555-1234 │11/15/90   │T           │
│Hideaway        │CA     │92220  │(415)555-9854 │01/01/91   │T           │
│Los Angeles     │CA     │96607  │(213)555-9988 │12/30/90   │F           │
│                │       │       │              │           │            │
│                │       │       │              │           │            │
│                │       │       │              │           │            │
│                │       │       │              │           │            │
│                │       │       │              │           │            │
│                │       │       │              │           │            │
└────────────────┴───────┴───────┴──────────────┴───────────┴────────────┘
 Browse   C:\dbase\CUSTLIST          Rec 3/9        File              Ins
```

Figure 5.4: Records sorted into zip code order

ACTIVATING AN INDEX

Now you have created two indexes, one for displaying names in alphabetical order, the other for displaying them in zip code order. It only took dBASE IV a few seconds to create each one, mainly because this sample database is very small. Believe me, if there were hundreds, or thousands, of records in the CUSTLIST database, the time required to create each index would have been much longer.

However, one of the beauties of indexes is that once you create them, you need never re-create them in the future. Instead, you just select whichever index you want to use to instantly view your database records in a new sort order. The general steps for activating an existing index are quite simple, and they work whether you are at the browse screen, edit screen, or database design screen. Here are the general steps:

- Press Menu (F10) to access the menus.
- Open the Organize pull-down menu.
- Select Order Records by Index.
- Select the name of the index you want to use or Natural Order if you want to view your records in their original (unsorted) order.

To try out these general steps now, let's first view the records in the CUSTLIST database in their original, unsorted order. Assuming that the database still appears on your browse screen, follow these steps:

1. Press Home to move the cursor back to the leftmost field.
2. Press Menu (F10) or Alt-O to open the Organize menu.
3. Select Order Records by Index.
4. Select Natural Order.

The records are now back to their original unsorted order. Now let's activate the LASTNAME index to quickly put them back into alphabetical order by last name. Follow the same basic steps, as listed below:

1. Press Menu (F10) or Alt-O to open the Organize menu.
2. Select Order Records by Index.
3. Select LASTNAME.

Instantly, the records are redisplayed in alphabetical order by name. (Admittedly, this may not be terribly impressive with this small database, but then again, your "real" databases will probably contain hundreds or thousands of records, and dBASE will reorganize those nearly as quickly as it reorganized the records in this small database.)

The real beauty of it all is that dBASE even takes care of the indexes for you at all times. That is, even if you add, change, or delete database records, dBASE will automatically keep all indexes up to date.

PERFORMING SORTS WITHIN SORTS

Sometimes sorting a database on a single field is not sufficient. For example, if you look back at Figure 5.3, you'll notice that John Smith is listed before Anita Smith. In the small CUSTLIST database, this does not create a problem, but if the database contained several hundred Smiths, you'd be hard pressed to find John Smith's records if all the Smiths were in random first-name order.

The ideal way to sort peoples' names is not simply by last name, but by first name within last name, as the telephone book does:

Smith   Anita
Smith   Barbara
Smith   Carla
Smith   Charles
Smith   John
Smith   Karen

To arrange a group of index cards in such an order, you might first sort all the cards into last-name order and then sort them into first-name order within identical last names—a sort within a sort. To sort database records into this kind of an order, you use an *index expression* that lists the fields to sort on, with the fields listed in priority order, with a plus sign between each field name.

For example, to sort records into alphabetical order by LASTNAME, with names alphabetized by FIRSTNAME within identical last names, you would use the index expression LAST-NAME + FIRSTNAME. If this database included a field for middle initial, named MI, you could use the index expression LAST-NAME + FIRSTNAME + MI to sort the database into last-name order, with names alphabetized by first-name and then middle initial within identical last names (for example, Smith, John A. would come before Smith, John B.).

In the next section, you'll learn how to modify an existing index, and in the process will see how to sort the CUSTLIST database into LASTNAME and FIRSTNAME order.

MODIFYING AN INDEX

The Organize menu, which you've already used to create and activate indexes, also lets you modify an existing index. Let's go ahead and modify the LASTNAME index now so that it displays customer names sorted by LASTNAME and by FIRSTNAME within common last names. Here are the steps:

1. Assuming you are still at the browse screen, press Menu (F10) or Alt-O to access the Organize pull-down menu.

2. Select Modify Existing Index from the Organize pull-down menu.

3. Select LASTNAME as the index to modify.

4. Press ↓ to highlight Index Expression and then press ⏎ to select it.

5. At this point, you *could* type + **FIRSTNAME** to change the index expression to LASTNAME + FIRSTNAME. However, we'll use the optional *Expression Builder* once again. Press Shift-F1 to call up the Expression Builder menu.

6. Use the → and ↓ keys to highlight the + operator.

7. When + is highlighted, press ↵.

8. Press Shift-F1 again to bring back the Expression Builder.

9. Use ← and ↓ to highlight FIRSTNAME; then press ↵. The index expression now reads LASTNAME-+FIRSTNAME as shown in Figure 5.5. Press ↵ again to complete the change.

10. Press Ctrl-End to indicate that you've finished modifying the index.

The database appears in the new sort order, as in Figure 5.6. (Press PgUp and Home to scroll to the top of the browse screen, if necessary.) As you can see, Anita Smith is now properly listed before John Smith.

Figure 5.5: Modified index expression for the LASTNAME index

```
   Records   Organize   Fields   Go To   Exit

  ┌──────────────┬──────────────┬──────────────────┬───────────────────┐
  │ LASTNAME     │ FIRSTNAME    │ COMPANY          │ ADDRESS           │
  ├──────────────┼──────────────┼──────────────────┼───────────────────┤
  │ Adams        │ Annie        │                  │ 3456 Ocean St.    │
  │ Beach        │ Sandy        │ American Widget  │ 11 Elm St.        │
  │ Kenney       │ Ralph        │                  │ 1101 Rainbow Ct.  │
  │ Mahoney      │ Mary         │                  │ 211 Seahawk St.   │
  │ Newell       │ John         │ LoTech Co.       │ 734 Rainbow Dr.   │
  │ Schumack     │ Susita       │ SMS Software     │ 47 Broad St.      │
  │ Smith        │ Anita        │ Zeerocks, Inc.   │ 2001 Engine Dr.   │
  │ Smith        │ John         │ ABC Co.          │ 123 A St.         │
  │ Watson       │ Wilbur       │ HiTech Co.       │ P.O. Box 987      │
  │              │              │                  │                   │
  │              │              │                  │                   │
  │              │              │                  │                   │
  │              │              │                  │                   │
  │              │              │                  │                   │
  ├──────────────┴──────────────┴──────────────────┴───────────────────┤
  │ Browse ║C:\dbase\CUSTLIST         ║Rec 2/9        ║File              │
  └─────────────────────────────────────────────────────────────────────┘
```

Figure 5.6: CUSTLIST database sorted by last and first names

EDITING WHEN AN INDEX IS ACTIVE

You may be wondering what would happen if dBASE were displaying records in sorted order on the browse screen and you changed somebody's last name. If you changed the name Adams to Zastrow, for example, when would dBASE re-sort the database to put Zastrow in its proper alphabetical position?

As you may recall from the previous chapter, whenever you change the contents of a database record, the change is not made permanent until you move to another record. (As you've seen, you can undo changes to a record as long as the cursor is still on that record.)

Re-sorting is based on a similar principle. dBASE does not re-sort until you move to a new record. To observe this for yourself, follow these steps:

1. Move the highlight to the last name Adams.

2. Type **Zastrow** in place of Adams and press ←. The records are not in alphabetical order anymore, because Zastrow is still at the top. But remember: An edit is not complete until you move the highlight to a new record.

3. Press PgDn to move down.

4. Press PgUp to scroll back to the top of the database.

As you can see on your screen and in Figure 5.7, dBASE immediately resorted the display and Sandy Beach is now the top record.

Now scroll to the bottom of the browse screen and change Zastrow back to Adams. When you complete the edit (by pressing ↑), Annie Adams returns to her previous place in alphabetical order.

Suppose now that you change a zip code. How will this affect the index for the ZIP field? At the moment, the LASTNAME index controls the sort order of the records, so if you change a zip code, the browse screen will not be re-sorted. However, dBASE hasn't forgotten the ZIP index. dBASE will automatically update the ZIP index behind the scenes. When you later switch to the ZIP index to display records in zip code order, the records will be displayed in correct zip code order.

Note that we've been using the browse screen in these examples because it allows you to see the effects of the re-sorting immediately. If you switch to the edit screen (by pressing F2), you'll only see one record at a time. But as you scroll up and down through records with the PgUp and PgDn keys, records will appear in the sort order determined by the current index.

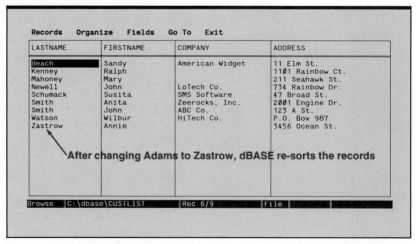

Figure 5.7: dBASE re-sorted the browse screen after changing Adams to Zastrow

WHAT IS AN INDEX?

Now that you've had some experience creating, activating, and modifying indexes, you might be wondering just what's happening "behind the scenes." Well, first of all, a dBASE index is much like the index at the back of this (or any other) book. In a book, the index lists topics in alphabetical order, followed by page numbers. So when you want to look up a topic, you flip through the index, find the appropriate page number, then turn to that page. This, obviously, is much faster than simply reading the book cover-to-cover until you happen upon the topic you are looking for.

A dBASE index works in a similar fashion. When you create an index, dBASE creates a sort of "mini database" that contains only the field (or fields) that you specified in the index expression, followed by the record number of the record. For example, you might envision the contents of the LASTNAME index as follows:

LASTNAME + FIRSTNAME		Record Number
Adams	Annie	2
Beach	Sandy	6
Kenney	Ralph	7
Mahoney	Mary	4
Newell	John	5
Schumack	Susita	8
Smith	Anita	9
Smith	John	1
Watson	Wilbur	3

> **NOTE**
>
> Actually, the "book index" analogy is a simplification—for those of you who are programmers, the index actually has a B + tree structure.

As you can see, the first record you entered into the database, John Smith, is in its proper alphabetical position in the index. The number 1 refers to the fact that John Smith is the first record in the database file.

When you activate an index, dBASE displays records in the order specified in the index. (As you'll learn in the next chapter, you can also use an index to locate information in the database very quickly.)

Even though you may create and activate indexes often, you will never actually see the contents of an index file directly. There is no need to, because once you create or activate an index, dBASE takes care of it for you automatically.

All the indexes that you create for a database file are stored in a file called the *production index file,* which has the same name as your database, but with the extension .MDX. (The .MDX is an abbreviation for "multiple index".) For example, the indexes that you created for your CUSTLIST database are stored in the production index file named CUSTLIST.MDX.

When you open your CUSTLIST database, dBASE automatically opens the CUSTLIST.MDX index file as well. All the indexes within the CUSTLIST.MDX index file are automatically updated as you add, change, or delete data. Whenever you activate one of the indexes in the CUSTLIST.MDX index file, that index then determines the sort order for displaying records.

The name you assign to an index, such as LASTNAME or ZIP in the previous examples, is called the index's *tag.* That is, the indexes that you created for the CUSTLIST.DBF database are stored in a file named CUSTLIST.MDX. CUSTLIST.MDX, in turn, contains two indexes, one tagged (named) LASTNAME, which is based on the expression LASTNAME + FIRSTNAME, and a second index tagged (named) ZIP, which is based on the ZIP field.

DELETING AN INDEX TAG

If for whatever reason you decide to get rid of an index, you can easily remove it from the multiple index file. Once again, you use the familiar Organize pull-down menu, which is available at the browse and edit screens as well as the database design screen. Here are the general steps for future reference (you need not delete an index just now):

- If you are at the Control Center, move the highlight to the database file and press Data (F2) to access the edit or browse screen.

- Open the Organize pull-down menu.

- Select Remove Unwanted Index Tag.

- Move the highlighter to the name of the index you want to remove.

- Press ◄─┘.

That's all there is to it. To leave the Organize menu, simply press the Escape key.

LIMITATIONS ON INDEXES

There are a few limitations that you need to keep in mind when creating or using indexes, as summarized below:

- The maximum number of index tags that you can assign to a single database file is 47.

- You cannot use a Memo field in an index expression, nor can you use a Logical field unless you convert its data type (as described in Chapter 12).

- When combining fields in an index expression, such as LASTNAME + FIRSTNAME, all fields must be the Character data type; otherwise you'll simply receive the error message "Data type mismatch." If you do need to combine multiple data types in a single index expression, you must convert their data types (you'll learn how to do so in Chapter 12).

MANAGING INDEXES FROM THE DATABASE DESIGN SCREEN

As mentioned, you can also access the Organize pull-down menu in the database design screen. The Organize pull-down menu is available at that screen simply for convenience—it does not matter whether you use the Organize pull-down menus from the edit, browse, or database design screen.

The database design screen, however, does offer one alternative technique for creating an index. You can create an index of any single field simply by changing the N in the Index column of that screen to a Y. Using the Index column on the database design screen, however, only lets you define an index for a single field; you cannot use this

technique to index on multiple fields as in the LASTNAME-
+FIRSTNAME example.

When you've finished defining or modifying indexes in the database design screen, press Ctrl-End, or select Save Changes and Exit
from the Exit pull-down menu until you've returned to the Control
Center. Don't forget that in order to see records in the sort order
defined by the index, you must also activate the index on one of the
data screens (for example, either the browse or edit screen).

PREVENTING DUPLICATES

You may have noticed the option Display First Duplicate Key
Only on the Organize pull-down menu. Here, again, is more technical jargon that serves to confuse an otherwise simple feature.

An index *key* is the field (or fields) that defines the sort order. In
the indexes we've created thus far, the ZIP field is the key for the ZIP
index, and the combined LASTNAME + FIRSTNAME field is the
key for the LASTNAME index.

Normally dBASE displays all the records in the database in
sorted order, whether or not you've activated an index. However, if
you set the Display First Duplicate Key Only option to Yes for an
index, dBASE will display records with duplicate keys.

For example, suppose you had a database with 1,000 names and
addresses in it, and created an index based on the STATE field. Furthermore, let's say you also set the Display First Duplicate Key Only
option to Yes while creating this index.

Later, when you activate the index, you would not see 1,000
records. Instead, you'd only see one record for each state in your
database. That is, once dBASE displayed one record with CA in the
STATE field, it would not display any others.

What is the practical significance of this? Well, suppose you purchased mailing lists from several companies, and combined them
into one database. You are not sure if some people's names and
addresses appear on more than one list, nor do you want to take the
time to find out by searching each and every list. However, you do
not want to send more than one item to each address when you
do your own mailing from these combined lists either.

What's the solution? Well, you could create an index using the expression ZIP + CITY + ADDRESS that displays only the first duplicate key, then use that index to print mailing labels. This would help to ensure that only one label was printed for each unique address, city, and zip code combination.

DBASE III PLUS COMPATIBILITY

You may have noticed two other options on the Organize pull-down menu—Activate .NDX index file and Include .NDX index file. These are included simply to provide some compatibility between dBASE IV and its predecessor, dBASE III PLUS.

While dBASE IV combines all indexes in a single file with the .MDX expression, earlier versions of dBASE stored each index in its own file, each with the extension .NDX. With this earlier method, it was very difficult to keep track of which index files belonged to which database, and also hard to make sure all of the indexes were updated properly.

The new method used in dBASE IV, where all indexes are stored in a single .MDX file, is much more convenient and reliable. Therefore, if you are upgrading from dBASE III PLUS to dBASE IV, you might want to re-create all your index files so that they will all be stored in a single .MDX file. (You can save a little time by copying your old dBASE III PLUS .NDX index files using the COPY INDEXES command described in Appendix D.)

One other alternative to re-creating or copying your old .NDX index files to the new dBASE IV format is to keep them in their original format, and use dBASE IV to manage them. The only advantage to this, of course, would be the "downward compatibility" it offers between dBASE IV and dBASE III PLUS. If that compatibility is important in your work, the two options on the Organize pull-down menu (summarized below) will let you keep your old .NDX index files up to date:

- **Activate .NDX index file**: Causes dBASE to search the current directory for a dBASE III PLUS index file with the name you select, then makes that the active (master) index file.

- **Include .NDX index file**: Opens a specified dBASE III PLUS .NDX file for automatic updating (as records are added, changed, or deleted), but does not make it the controlling (master) index.

Again, if you are not concerned about maintaining ''old'' dBASE III (and III PLUS) indexes, you need not be concerned about these two options.

SORTING A DATABASE FILE

As mentioned earlier in this chapter, dBASE IV offers *sorting* as an alternative to indexing a database file to display data in sorted order. However, sorting is generally slower and less efficient than indexing. Nonetheless, some people prefer sorting simply because it seems like a less abstract, more familiar means of putting information into an organized order.

When sorting, dBASE makes a copy of the original database with the records in sorted order. The records remain in their original order in the original database. To access the sorted records, you need to open the sorted copy of the database.

The menu option for sorting a database is on the Organize pull-down menu, like the options for indexing. To try out the sorting feature, follow the steps below to sort the CUSTLIST database record into descending order by the STARTDATE field:

1. If you are currently at the Control Center, move the highlighter to CUSTLIST and press Data (F2) until you get to the browse screen.

2. Press Menu (F10) and pull down the Organize menu.

3. Select Sort Database on Field List.

4. To sort the database into STARTDATE order, first press Shift-F1 to see a list of valid field names.

ASCII, pronounced *askey*, is an acronym for the American Standard Code for Information Interchange.

5. Type **S** or use the ↓ key to highlight STARTDATE.

6. Press ◄┘ to select STARTDATE and then press ◄┘ a second time to complete the entry.

7. The cursor jumps to the Type of Sort column, where you can select from four different sorting techniques, listed in Table 5.1. Note that the basic difference between the Dictionary technique and the ASCII technique is that ASCII considers uppercase letters "smaller than" lowercase letters and hence will place Zeppo before aardvark in an ascending sort.

Table 5.1: Options for Sorting a Database

Order	Example Sort
Ascending ASCII (0..9, A..Z, a...)	123 999 Albert Zeppo van der Pool
Descending ASCII (z..a, Z..A, 9..0)	van der Pool Zeppo Albert 999 123
Ascending Dictionary (0..9, Aa..Zz)	123 999 Albert van der Pool Zeppo
Descending Dictionary (Zz..Aa, 9..0)	Zeppo van der Pool Albert 999 123

Indexes use the ASCII technique to display sort orders. Hence, an index of names places names that begin with lowercase letters (for example, van der Pool) at the bottom of the list (for example, beneath Zeppo). You can alter this order, however, as discussed in Chapter 12.

Both ASCII and dictionary sorts consider numeric characters to be "smaller than" alphabetic characters. Hence, if you sort a list of addresses in ascending order, all addresses beginning with numbers (for example, 123 A St. to 999 Z St.) will be listed before addresses beginning with letters (for example, P.O. Box 2802). If you are sorting a Character field that does not use consistent capitalization, you'll want to use the dictionary technique. If you are sorting any other data type, you can use the ASCII technique instead.

8. For this example, press the space bar until Descending ASCII appears; then press ←. The highlight moves down to let you put more fields into the sort order. These are sort-within-a-sort fields, as discussed under indexing. For example, selecting LASTNAME as the first sort field and FIRSTNAME as the second sort field sorts the records in the same way that the expression LASTNAME + FIRSTNAME sorted the index.

9. Rather than adding more fields to the sort list, press Ctrl-End to finish your work.

10. When dBASE presents the prompt "Enter name of sorted file:" you can enter any valid file name (eight characters maximum length, with no spaces or punctuation). In this example, type the file name **DATEORD** and press ←.

11. When the screen asks for a description of the file, just press ← to leave it blank. (We'll be deleting this file before long, so there's no need to add a description.)

If you press the End and PgUp keys to scroll to the STARTDATE field, you'll see that the records are *not* sorted into date order. Why not? Because the sorted records are in the database file named DATEORD; CUSTLIST has not been sorted.

Let's look at the DATEORD database file. Press F10 to call up the menu, highlight Exit in the menu bar, and select Exit. When you return to the Control Center, you'll see a new database file in the Data panel, as shown in Figure 5.8.

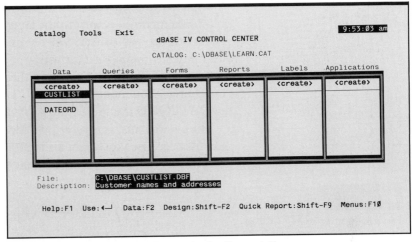

Figure 5.8: DATEORD database in the Control Center

To view the data in the DATEORD database, use ↓ to highlight
DATEORD and then press Data (F2). When the browse screen
appears, press End to scroll to the right. As you can see in Figure 5.9,
the records are in descending date order (from January 1, 1991, to
November 15, 1990).

CITY	STATE	ZIP	PHONE	STARTDATE	PAID
Santa Monica	CA	92001	(714)555-0123	01/01/91	F
Hideaway	CA	92220	(415)555-9854	01/01/91	T
Los Angeles	CA	96607	(213)555-9988	12/30/90	F
Philadelphia	PA	45543	(202)555-9720	12/30/90	T
Butte	MT	54321	(303)555-6739	12/15/90	T
Portland	OR	76543	(717)555-0898	12/15/90	T
Seattle	WA	88977	(206)555-8673	12/01/90	T
San Diego	CA	92067	(619)555-1234	11/15/90	T
New York	NY	12345	(212)555-9988	11/15/90	T

Browse   C:\dbase\DATEORD   Rec 1/9   File

Figure 5.9: Records sorted into descending order by date

When you are done viewing the data, select Exit from the Exit pull-down menu to return to the Control Center.

As mentioned earlier, whenever you create an index, dBASE automatically manages it for you, updating it when you add, change, or delete information. This is *not* the case for sorted copies of files. Any changes you make to the CUSTLIST database have no effect on the DATEORD database (and vice versa).

Because of this, it is *not* a good idea to keep sorted copies of database files because you might accidentally use the wrong database file, and your work could quickly become confused. So let's get rid of the DATEORD database right now, using these steps:

NOTE

Providing Instruct is On (see Chapter 2), when you highlight a database file name and press ◄┘, a *prompt box* for making your next selection appears.

1. Make sure DATEORD is highlighted in the Control Center (if it isn't, use the arrow keys to move the highlight to it).

2. Press Enter and select Close File.

3. Move the highlight to the DATEORD file name in the Data panel.

4. Pull down the Catalog menu (F10).

5. Select Remove Highlighted File from Catalog.

6. The message "Are you sure you want to remove this file from the catalog?" appears. Select Yes.

7. The message "Do you also want to delete this file from the disk?" appears. Select Yes.

DATEORD does not exist anymore, so you need not worry about confusing it with CUSTLIST. (You'll learn more techniques for managing catalogs and files in Chapter 14.)

In the next chapter you'll learn how to *search* for particular records, such as those for all the customers who live in a particular state or all the customers who have not paid. But before we get to that, let's take a moment to recap some of the techniques you've learned so far, focusing particularly on those techniques that you will use consistently in the upcoming chapters.

A QUICK RECAP

One of the most confusing things for beginners is trying to learn new concepts (such as indexing), while at the same time simply trying to remember "what button to push when." Therefore, let's backtrack for a moment and take a look at some of the keys you've used consistently up to this point:

- **Data (F2)**: Always displays the *data* stored within a database. When data is already displayed, switches between the edit (one-record-at-a-time) screen and the browse screen.

- **Design (Shift-F2)**: Displays the underlying design, or structure of a file, for example, the name, type, width, and decimal of each field in the database. (The one exception—when you are at the browse or edit screen, where pressing Shift-F2 takes you to the Query Design screen.)

- **Menu (F10)**: Displays the pull-down menus regardless of whether you are at the Control Center, edit screen, browse screen, database design screen, or any of the other screens you'll encounter in upcoming chapters. The Exit option on the pull-down menus exits the current screen and goes back to the previous screen (unless you are already at the Control Center, in which case you can exit only to the dot prompt or back to DOS).

As Figure 5.10 points out, the bottom of the Control Center screen reminds you that these keys are available. Unfortunately, not *all* screens offer this reminder, but then again you only need to remember that pressing Menu (F10) always displays your options.

In addition to the keys mentioned above, we've used a couple of "shortcut keystrokes," which you'll also find to behave consistently throughout future chapters:

- **Ctrl-End**: Saves any changes on the current screen and returns you to the previous screen (acts as a shortcut to selecting Save Changes and Exit from the Exit pull-down menu).

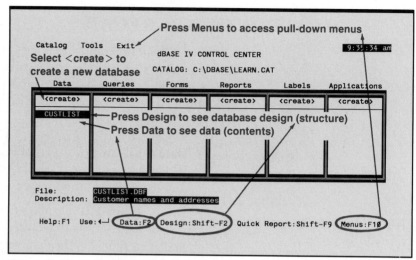

Figure 5.10: Summary of Control Center keystrokes

- **Escape**: Pressing Escape lets you leave a screen without saving any work. That is, it lets you "escape" from any place that you do not want to be (except for the dot prompt, as mentioned earlier).

If you can remember that these five keys are the ones you generally use to move from screen to screen, and if you first try to read the screen or pull down the menus for additional clues when you're feeling lost, you should find it pretty easy to move in and out of the various screens and capabilities that dBASE IV offers.

C H A P T E R

6

Searching
the Database

REGARDLESS OF THE CONTENTS OR SIZE OF YOUR database, dBASE can always help you get to the information you need. In some cases, you may simply want to look up a piece of information, such as a person's address and phone number. In other cases, your searches might be more complex, such as for "all customers who live on the West Coast, subscribed before January 1, and still have not paid."

In this chapter, you'll learn techniques for searching your database. As you'll see, this is an area where dBASE IV shines. Before you begin, get dBASE IV up and running on your computer again and make sure the LEARN catalog appears in the Control Center.

THE BASIC SEARCHES

Both the browse screen and the edit screen include an option titled Go To in the menu bar, which provides options for simple, basic searches. To try some of these, move the highlight to the CUSTLIST database name in the Data panel on the Control Center and press Data (F2) to view its records. If you press Menu (F10) and highlight Go To, you'll see the pull-down menu in Figure 6.1.

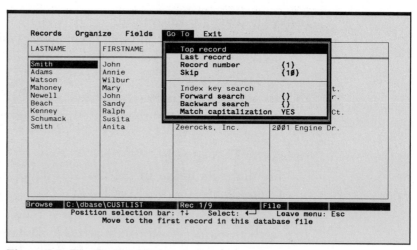

Figure 6.1: The Go To pull-down menu

POSITIONING THE HIGHLIGHT OR SCREEN

The first four Go To options let you position the browse highlight (or edit screen) on a particular record based on its position in the database file. Your options are as follows:

Top record	Moves the edit screen or browse highlight to the top record
Last record	Moves the edit screen or browse highlight to the bottom record
Record number	Moves the edit screen or browse highlight to a particular record based on its position in the database
Skip	Moves the edit screen or browse highlight a certain number of records from its current position

These options are simple to use and experiment with (though they are easier to understand if you first experiment while at the browse screen). For example, if you select Last Record, the highlight jumps to the last database record on the screen. If you press Menu (F10) again and select Top Record, the highlight jumps to the topmost record.

If you select Record Number, dBASE asks you to enter a record number. Type a number between 1 and the total number of records in your database and then press ◄┘. The highlight jumps to the appropriate record. (Note that the record number indicates the record's position in the database and not the index order if an index is in use.)

The Skip option moves the highlight a certain number of records up or down in the database. For example, if you select Skip, type the number 2, and press ◄┘, the highlight (or edit screen) skips forward two records (if possible). If you enter a negative number, such as -3, the highlight or screen jumps backward three records.

These simple searches are of limited value, because they assume you know the location of the record that you want to access. Furthermore, they do little more than mimic the action of the arrow, PgUp, PgDn, and other navigation keys. You'll probably use the lookup options, discussed next, more often.

SEARCHING FOR INFORMATION

 TIP

Remember to move the highlight to the field you want to search before using the Search Forward or Search Backward options from the Go To menu. If the pull-down menu is already displayed, press Esc to close it.

In most cases, you do not simply want to go to a particular position in a database. Instead, you want to find information, such as a person's address or phone number. The bottom half of the Go To menu displays options for locating information. To use the Forward Search and Backward Search options, you first move the highlight into the field that you want to search in the database. You then call up the Go To menu and select either Forward Search, to search forward from the current record, or Backward Search, to search backward from the current record.

After dBASE finds the first record that matches the search requirement, you can use the Find Next key (Shift-F4) or Find Previous (Shift-F3) key to search forward or backward for other matching records. If no match is found, dBASE displays the message "** Not Found **" and waits for you to press any key to resume your work. Let's look at an example.

1. Use the Tab key to move the highlight to the STATE field in the browse screen.

2. Press Menu (F10) to access the Go To pull-down menu.

3. To start from the beginning of the database file, select Top Record.

4. To search for records with CA as the state, first press F10 to bring back the Go To menu.

5. Select Forward Search.

NOTE

The word *string* is a computer term that simply means "a string of characters," which might be a single letter, a word, or several words, such as "X" or "ABC" or "Hello there" or "A-123" or "123 Oak St."

6. When dBASE displays the prompt "Enter search string:" type **CA** (uppercase letters) and press ←. The highlight moves to the first record that has CA in the STATE field. Suppose that this is not the specific record you were looking for, and you want to find the next record with CA in the STATE field.

7. Press Find Next (Shift-F4). The highlight moves to the next record with CA in the state field (record 7).

Each time you press Find Next (Shift-F4), dBASE will scroll forward to the next record in the database that has CA in the STATE field. Each time you press Find Previous (Shift-F3), the highlight will scroll back to the previous record with CA in the STATE field. You may want to experiment with these keys now.

The Backward Search option can be handy for making changes after entering a group of new records. For example, suppose you entered 100 new records and wanted to double-check the new record for Kenney. Rather than scrolling through the database, you could follow these steps:

1. Move the highlight to the LASTNAME field.

2. Press Menu (F10) to access the Go To pull-down menu.

3. Select Last Record to move to the last record in the database (new records are always appended to the end of a database file, so in this case you want to begin your search from the bottom).

4. Press Menu (F10) again to bring back the Go To menu.

5. Select Backward Search.

6. If the previous search value is still displayed next to the "Enter search string:" prompt, press Backspace a few times to erase it.

7. Enter the name to search for—in this example, **Kenney**—and press ↵.

As with forward searches, during backward searches you can use the Find Next and Find Previous keys to find other matching values.

EXPANDING SEARCH CAPABILITIES

When you search a database, dBASE looks for information that exactly matches your request. This can be inconvenient at times. For example, if you are looking for someone who lives on Rainbow St., a search for Rainbow in the ADDRESS field would not help, because the addresses contain the street number as well as the street name. If you were searching for a name but were not sure whether it was spelled Smith, Smyth, or Smythe, a search for Smith would not locate the other spellings.

Luckily, dBASE offers several techniques that you can use to add flexibility to your database search. These are discussed in the following sections.

MATCHING CAPITALIZATION   At the bottom of the Go To pull-down menu, you'll see the option Match Capitalization. When you move the highlight to this option and press the space bar, the option setting changes from Yes to No. When the setting is Yes, a forward or backward search is case sensitive; the upper- and lowercase letters in the search string must match those in the database. When the setting is No, upper- and lowercase designations do not matter.

For example, if Match Capitalization is set to No, then a search for SMITH locates Smith, SMITH, or smith. However, if Match Capitalization is set to Yes, then a search for SMITH finds only SMITH, not Smith, smith, or SmItH, because the upper- and lowercase letters do not match.

WILDCARD SEARCHES   You can use wildcard characters to locate items that match a pattern rather than an exact value. Use the wildcard character **?** to match a single character, and the wildcard character ***** to match any group of characters. For example, a search of the LASTNAME field for Sm* would find Smith, Smyth, Smythe, Smartalec, and any other name beginning with the letters *Sm*. A search for Sm?t* would locate Smith, Smyth, Smythe, and any other name that follows the pattern *Sm*, any other single letter, *t*, any other letters.

In the STARTDATE field, a search for 12/??/90 would locate any record with a date in December 1990. In the ZIP field, a search for either 92??? or 92* would locate a zip code beginning with the numbers 92 (that is, any zip code in the range 92000 to 92999). In the ADDRESS field, a search for *Rainbow* would locate any record with the word *Rainbow* in the address (such as 734 Rainbow Dr. and 1101 Rainbow Ct.). In the PHONE field, a search for (213)* would locate records with 213 as the area code.

The wildcard characters, ? and *, can be fun to experiment with. Also, because they can be used in several other contexts within dBASE (and outside of dBASE as well), you should at least be familiar with them.

INDEX SEARCHES

When you start working with larger databases, you may find the Forward Search and Backward Search options to be quite slow. As an alternative, you can use the Index Key Search option on the Go To pull-down menu. This option uses an index to search for data and can usually find information in any size database in less than a second.

To use the Index Key Search option, you need to activate the index that contains the field you want to search. For example, to search the LASTNAME field using an index, you need to activate an index that uses only LASTNAME as the key, or uses LASTNAME as the first field in the index expression (such as the LASTNAME- + FIRSTNAME index).

ACTIVATING THE SEARCH INDEX

To use Index Key Search, you first need to activate the appropriate index. (If an appropriate index does not exist yet, you can create one using the technique discussed in the previous chapter.) Assume you want to use an index to search for records by people's last names. You activate the LASTNAME index in the CUSTLIST database by following these steps:

1. If you are at the Control Center, highlight CUSTLIST in the data panel, then press Data (F2) to get to the edit or browse screen.

2. Open the Organize pull-down menu (using the F10 key or Alt-O).

3. Select Order Records by Index.

4. From the submenu, select the LASTNAME index.

Now that the index is activated, you can conduct your search.

You can use either the browse or edit screen for this search. For a change of pace, use the edit screen. If the browse screen is displayed, press F2 again to display the edit screen.

PERFORMING THE SEARCH

To search for a last name, follow these steps:

1. Press Menu (F10) and move to the Go To menu option.

2. Select Index Key Search; dBASE presents the prompt

   Enter search string for
   LASTNAME + FIRSTNAME:

   LASTNAME + FIRSTNAME is the expression for the current index; dBASE displays this to tell you what field you currently can search.

3. To find the record for Smith, type **Smith** (using the correct upper- and lowercase letters) and then press ◄┘.

dBASE will immediately locate and display the first record for Smith in the database, as shown in Figure 6.2. You cannot use the Find Next or Find Previous key with an index search to scroll through records for other Smiths. However, because the index groups all the Smiths together (because the records are presented in alphabetical order), you can use the PgDn and PgUp keys to scroll through nearby Smith records.

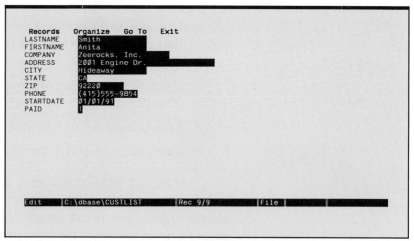

Figure 6.2: Index search locating the first Smith record in the database

INDEX SEARCH LIMITATIONS

Although index key searches are very fast, they are not as flexible as the forward and backward searches discussed previously. An index search works only when upper- and lowercase letters match exactly, even when the Match Capitalization option is off. A search for SMITH would not find Smith, for example.

Also, you cannot use wildcard characters with index searches. A search for Sm?th or Smi* will not find any matching database record. However, dBASE offers some flexibility in index searches. When dBASE searches an index, it looks for a match between the value you are searching for and the leftmost characters in the database field. For example, an index search for Sm would take you to the first record in the database that has *Sm* as the first two letters in the last name. You could then use PgDn (on the edit screen) or ↓ (on the browse screen) to scroll through other nearby records.

The fact that dBASE searches the leftmost characters of the index has a disadvantage as well. For example, even though the index expression for the current index is LASTNAME + FIRSTNAME, you could not use the index to search for the first name John or Anita.

If you do want to search for multiple fields, the following tidbit of information may help you avoid confusion in the future. An index field always has the same width as the field in the database structure. For example, when you created the CUSTLIST database, you assigned a width of 15 characters to the field. Therefore, the LASTNAME in the index has a fixed width of 15 characters. Hence, a search for

Smith Anita

would find no matching record in the database because Smith has only one blank space after it. However, a search for

Smith   Anita

would find Anita Smith's record, assuming that there are 10 spaces between Smith and Anita.

Ten blank spaces are required between Smith and Anita because Smith is five letters long, and the 10 blank spaces pad the last name to the width of the database field: 15 characters in this example. You may have little need of this approach, as there are many other ways to search multiple fields. However, knowing how dBASE works may help you avoid problems when trying to search an index such as LASTNAME + FIRSTNAME for a complete name such as Smith Anita.

To leave the edit screen and return to the Control Center, press Esc or select Exit from the Exit pull-down menu.

USING QUERIES

The searches discussed so far are all alike in one way: They help you *locate* a particular item of information in a database. In some situations, you may instead want to *isolate* or *filter* some type of information. For example, if you want to send a form letter to all California residents in your customer database, you will want to isolate records that have CA in the state field, filtering out all other records.

These kinds of searches are called *queries,* because you query (ask) dBASE for some information, and dBASE answers by displaying only records that meet your requirements. Queries are not handled through the Go To pull-down menu. Instead, they are handled via the *query design screen*.

The technique that you use to construct queries is called *query by example,* often abbreviated QBE. The name comes from the technique you use: dBASE presents a skeleton of the database file in use, and you give examples of the kinds of information that you want dBASE IV to display.

GENERAL STEPS FOR QUERIES

You'll have many hands-on opportunities to actually try some queries in this chapter. But first, let's take a moment to summarize the basic steps involved:

- Make sure the database that you want to query is open (above the line in the Data panel).

- Move the highlighter to the Queries panel.

- Select <create> (by highlighting it and pressing ⏎).

- Move the highlighter to the field you want to search.

- Type the value you want to search for, using proper *delimiters* (described under "Delimiters Used with Queries" later in this chapter).

- Press Data (F2) to perform the query and see the results, and press Data (F2) additionally, if you wish, to switch between the browse and edit screens as usual.

- Press Design (Shift-F2) to return to the Query Design screen when you've finished viewing your data.

- At this point you have several choices:

  - To change the current query, just make your changes, then press F2 to see the results.

  - To get back to the Control Center without saving your query, press Esc or select Abandon Changes and Exit from the Exit pull-down menu, and select Yes when asked about abandoning the current query.

  - To save your query and return to the Control Center, press Ctrl-End, or select "Save Changes and Exit" from the Exit pull-down menu, and enter a valid file name for the query (described in "Saving Queries for Future Use" near the end of this chapter).

Remember that if you start feeling lost or confused while switching among the various screens, there are these quick sources of help available to you:

- Look at the navigation line at the bottom of the screen to see what keys are available at the moment.

- If you are *not* at the Control Center, selecting an option from the Exit pull-down menu will usually get you back to the Control Center (as will pressing Esc).

- Figures inside the front cover of this book will also help you navigate the Control Center and Query Design screens.

Let's go ahead and actually perform a query now, discussing each step in more detail.

SELECTING A DATABASE TO QUERY

Before you can query a database, you must make sure that the database is *open* (in use) at the moment. You can easily see if a database file is open by looking at its position in the Data panel of the Control Center. If the name of the database file appears *above* the line the database is open and ready for action. If the database name is below the line the file is not open and cannot be queried. Figure 6.3 indicates that the CUSTLIST database is in use at the moment.

Once you highlight a database file name and press either Design or Data, dBASE opens that database file and keeps it open. You can also open (or close) a database file at any time by highlighting its name in the Data panel and pressing ◄─┘. A prompt box will present your options. If the database file is not open, you'll be given the option "Use File" to open the database. If the database is open, you'll be given the option "Close File" to close it. You'll also have the option to "Modify Structure/Order" (which takes you to the database design screen), or to "Display Data" (which transfers you to the browse/edit screen). Note that these two options can be used as alternatives to pressing the Design (Shift-F2) and Data (F2) keys.

If you want to try this procedure now, make sure the highlight is on the CUSTLIST database name in the Data panel, and then press ◄─┘. You'll see the three options that we just described. Use the usual

NOTE

Remember, prompt boxes are only available if the Instruct setting, discussed in Chapter 2, is On.

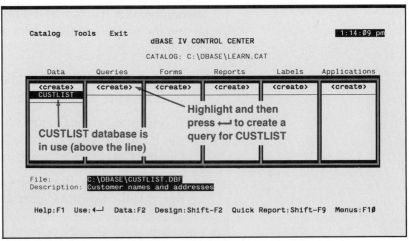

Figure 6.3: The CUSTLIST database is open and ready for use

technique to select an option. When you return to the Control Center, make sure that the CUSTLIST database is still open before you proceed to the next section.

THE QUERY DESIGN SCREEN

To design a query for the currently open database file you need to get to the query design screen. To do so, follow these steps:

1. Use the arrow keys to highlight <create> in the Queries panel.

2. Press ⏎ to select <create>.

You'll find yourself at the query design screen (or *surface*, as it is sometimes called), shown in Figure 6.4. Like other dBASE work areas, the query design screen includes a menu bar at the top of the screen and a status bar and navigation line at the bottom of the screen. The query screen also includes a *file skeleton* and a *view skeleton*.

THE FILE SKELETON The file skeleton is near the top of the screen. In the leftmost column is the name of the database file that

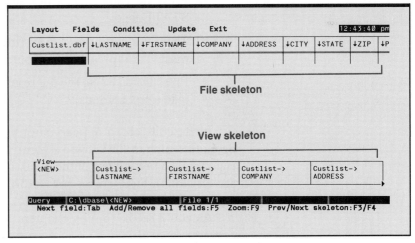

Figure 6.4: The query design screen

the skeleton represents: CUSTLIST.DBF, in this example. Each field name in the database is listed in boxes to the right of the database name. You can use the Home, End, Tab, and Shift-Tab keys to scroll left and right through these field names and to view those that are off the right edge of the screen. You'll use the file skeleton in a moment, to specify search criteria.

THE VIEW SKELETON   The view skeleton, near the bottom of the screen, shows the names of the fields that will be displayed by the query. Initially, the query feature assumes that you want to display all fields, so all fields are included. You'll learn more about how to use the view skeleton later.

DEFINING RECORDS TO DISPLAY

To specify which records you want a query to display, you enter *filter conditions* in the file skeleton near the top of the screen. You put the filter condition under the appropriate box and then press Data (F2) to see the results. Let's create a filter condition to display only records from the CUSTLIST database that have CA in the STATE field. Here are the steps:

1. Press the Tab key six times, so that the highlight moves to the STATE field.

2. Type the condition **"CA"** (including the double quotation marks) and press ◄┘, so your screen looks like Figure 6.5.

3. Press Data (F2) to see the results of the query (dBASE might take a few seconds).

If the edit screen appears after you press F2, press Data (F2) again to switch to the browse screen. Then press End to scroll to the right to get a better view of the query results. As you can see on your screen (and in Figure 6.6), only records that have CA in the STATE field appear.

As you'll see in coming chapters, you can use filtered databases to print mailing labels and form letters, perform calculations, make copies of database files, simplify editing, and facilitate other tasks. In fact, you'll probably find that you use queries more than any other feature of dBASE IV.

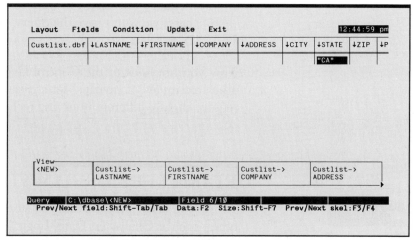

Figure 6.5: A query for records with CA in the STATE field

Figure 6.6: Results of the query for records with CA in the STATE field

To leave the "queried" version of your database and return to the Control Center, follow these steps now:

1. Press Esc, or press Menu (F10) and select Exit from the Exit pull-down menu.

2. A query will ask if you want to save the current query. In this case, we won't save the query, so press ⏎ or type the letter N to select No.

Now you are back to the Control Center. Before we proceed with other examples of queries, let's discuss how different data types require slightly different querying techniques.

DELIMITERS USED WITH QUERIES

NOTE

If you want to take a break during this chapter, select Abandon Changes and Exit from the query design screen Exit menu. When dBASE asks if you are sure you want to abandon, select Yes. You'll be returned to the Control Center, where you can exit dBASE IV gracefully before turning off your computer.

As you know, dBASE lets you store information as various data types, such as Character, Date, Logical, and so forth. Depending on the data type of the field you want to search at the moment, you'll need to use specific *delimiters* (punctuation marks around the information you are searching for). In summary, these delimiters are:

Data Type	Delimiter	Example
Character data	" "	"CA"
Date data	{ }	{12/31/91}
Logical data	. .	.T. or .F.
Numeric or Float	None	123.45

Let's take a look at some examples and get some hands-on practice with queries now.

QUERYING CHARACTER FIELDS

In your first sample query you isolated names and addresses of California residents by searching for "CA" in the STATE field of the CUSTLIST database. You used the quotation marks because

WARNING

If you forget to put quotation marks around the filter condition in a Character field search, dBASE will still accept the value and execute the query. However, the results of the query will probably not be what you had in mind.

WARNING

If you forget to remove the previous filter condition from the query design screen before entering a new one, the old filter condition will affect the new query.

STATE is a Character (data type) field. Let's try another example now, this time searching the LASTNAME field, which is also the Character data type. Follow these steps:

1. Make sure the CUSTLIST database is open.
2. Highlight <create> in the Queries panel.
3. Press ↵ to select <create>.
4. Press Tab to move the highlighter to the LASTNAME field.
5. Type **"Smith"** and press ↵.
6. Press Data (F2) to perform the query.

As you can see in Figure 6.7, only records that have Smith in the LASTNAME field are displayed.

```
  Records   Organize   Fields   Go To   Exit
 ┌─────────────────┬─────────────────┬─────────────────┬─────────────────────┐
 │ LASTNAME        │ FIRSTNAME       │ COMPANY         │ ADDRESS             │
 ├─────────────────┼─────────────────┼─────────────────┼─────────────────────┤
 │ Smith           │ John            │ ABC Co.         │ 123 A St.           │
 │ Smith           │ Anita           │ Zeerocks, Inc.  │ 2001 Engine Dr.     │
 │                 │                 │                 │                     │
 │                 │                 │                 │                     │
 └─────────────────┴─────────────────┴─────────────────┴─────────────────────┘
  Browse   C:\dbase\<NEW>              Rec 1/9          View
```

Figure 6.7: Results of query for records with Smith in the LASTNAME field

Note that the query is carried over to the edit screen if you press Data (F2) now. When the edit screen appears, the record for the first Smith is on the screen. When you press PgDn to move to the next record, the next Smith record appears. If you press PgDn again, dBASE displays the prompt " = = = > Add new records? (Y/N)," as though there were no other records in the database file. For now, answer no by typing N. Then press F2 to return to the browse screen.

QUERYING DATE FIELDS

To isolate "blank" dates, use {} as the search value. To isolate non-blank dates, use {} = .F. as the search value.

When querying a field of the Date data type, such as START-DATE, you must enclose the date you are searching for in curly braces ({}). Let's construct a query to isolate records with START-DATE values of 12/15/90.

1. Press Design (Shift-F2), to return to the query design screen.

2. With the highlight still in the LASTNAME field, press Ctrl-Y to remove "Smith."

3. Press End and then Shift-Tab to move to the STARTDATE field.

4. Type **{12/15/90}** and press ←.

5. To view the results of the query, press Data (F2).

If you scroll to the STARTDATE field in the browse screen, you'll see that only records with 12/15/90 in the STARTDATE field are displayed, as in Figure 6.8.

After viewing the results of the query, press Design (Shift-F2) to get back to the query design screen.

```
  Records   Organize   Fields   Go To   Exit

  CITY        STATE ZIP    PHONE           STARTDATE PAID
  Butte        MT   54321  (303)555-6739   12/15/90  T
  Portland     OR   76543  (717)555-0898   12/15/90  T












  Browse   C:\dbase\<NEW>          Rec 5/9         View
```

Figure 6.8: Results of query for records with STARTDATE {12/15/90}

QUERYING LOGICAL FIELDS

✓ TIP

In Logical fields you can use .T., .t., .Y., or .y. for true; and .F., .f., .N., or .n. for false—where Y and N stand for yes and no. The periods are required by dBASE to distinguish these entries from regular characters.

When you query a field that is the Logical data type, such as PAID in the CUSTLIST database, you can enter either .T. or .F. as the value to search for.

To try this, you'll isolate records in the PAID field that are marked true (that is, they contain T). Follow these steps:

1. At the query design screen, move to the STARTDATE field and press Ctrl-Y to remove {12/15/90}.

2. Press Tab to move to the PAID field.

3. Type **.T.** and press ◄───.

4. Press Data (F2) to execute the query.

When the browse screen appears, press the End key to scroll to the PAID field. Notice that only records marked true (T) are displayed.

After viewing the records, press Design (Shift-F2) to return to the query design screen.

USING OPERATORS IN QUERIES

 NOTE

If you don't use an operator in a query, then equals (=) is assumed. That is, putting "CA" in the STATE field tells dBASE that you want to see records where STATE equals "CA".

dBASE IV includes many *relational operators* that you can use to refine your queries. Table 6.1 lists these operators and their meanings.

These operators can be interesting to play with, and after you learn the basics in this section, you may want to try a few queries on your own.

To use an operator in a query, precede the value that you are searching for with the appropriate operator. To see how this works, create a query that displays records for people whose last names begin with the letters A through M. Here are the steps:

1. At the query design screen, remove the .T. in the PAID field by highlighting that field and pressing Ctrl-Y.

2. Press Home and then Tab to move the highlight to the LASTNAME field.

While building a query, you can select operators from the Expression Builder by pressing Shift-F1. Move the highlight to the Operator panel in the Expression Builder and use PgDn and PgUp to scroll through the operators. To select an operator, highlight it using the arrow keys and then press ◄─┘.

You can edit information on the query design screen using the same techniques that you use to edit information in a database. Use the arrow keys to position the cursor, the Ins key to switch between Insert and Overwrite modes, the Backspace or Del key to delete characters, and so forth.

3. Type the filter condition <"N", including the quotation marks. Press ◄─┘.

4. To see the results of the query, press Data (F2).

The browse screen, as Figure 6.9 shows, displays only records with the appropriate last names. The filter condition <"N" told dBASE to display only records with last names that are less than N, so only records that have last names beginning with the letters A through M are displayed.

If you press Design (Shift-F2) to return to the query design screen, change the filter condition in the LASTNAME field to >="N" (greater than or equal to N), and then press Data (F2), dBASE will display records that have last names beginning with the letters N through Z.

SEARCHING FOR CLOSE SPELLINGS

Suppose you want to look up Ralph Kenney's address, but you misspell the last name as Kinny. When you perform the lookup operation, dBASE informs you that there is no Kinny. This is a good opportunity to use the *sounds-like* operator, which uses a technique

Table 6.1: The dBASE IV Relational Operators

Operator	Meaning
=	Equals
>	Greater than
<	Less than
>=	Greater than or equal to
<=	Less than or equal to
<> or #	Not equal to
$	Contains
Like	Pattern match using wildcard characters
Sounds like	Soundex search for words that sound alike

called *soundex* to locate words that sound alike, regardless of their spelling. Follow these steps:

1. If the browse or edit screen is displayed, press Shift-F2 to return to the query design screen.

2. Move the highlight to the LASTNAME field and press Ctrl-Y to empty that field.

3. Enter the filter condition **Sounds like "Kinny"** (you must use the quotation marks, as in Figure 6.10) and then press ⬅.

4. Press Data (F2) to execute the query.

As Figure 6.11 shows, the query located the record for Kenney.

NOTE

When entering lengthy conditions on the query design screen, the column widens automatically to make room.

PATTERN-MATCHING SEARCHES

Remember the pattern-matching searches discussed previously, where you used the wildcard characters ? to stand for any single character and * to stand for any group of characters? You can use these same wildcards with queries, provided you use the *Like* operator first.

```
  Records    Organize    Fields    Go To    Exit

  LASTNAME         FIRSTNAME        COMPANY            ADDRESS

  Adams            Annie                               3456 Ocean St.
  Mahoney          Mary                                211 Seahawk St.
  Beach            Sandy            American Widget    11 Elm St.
  Kenney           Ralph                               11Ø1 Rainbow Ct.



  Browse   C:\dbase\<NEW>          Rec 2/9          View
```

Figure 6.9: Results of query for records with last names < "N"

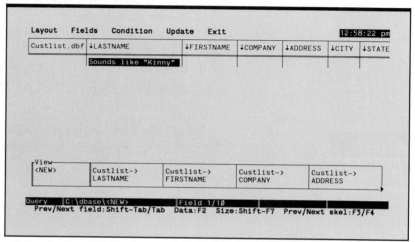

Figure 6.10: Search for records with names that sound like Kinny

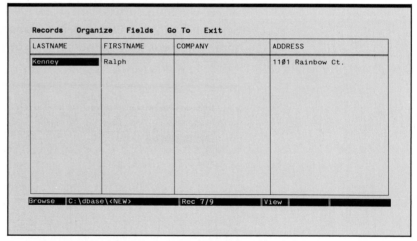

Figure 6.11: Results of query for Sounds like "Kinny"

Suppose you want to search for zip codes that begin with 92. Here are the basic steps:

1. If necessary, press Design (Shift-F2) to return to the query design screen.

2. Erase the current filter condition from the LASTNAME field in the query design screen (using Ctrl-Y).

3. Place the filter condition **Like "92∗"** in the ZIP field, as shown in Figure 6.12.

When you press Data (F2) to see the results of the query, you'll find that only records with zip codes that start with 92 appear on the browse screen. (Press the End key to scroll to the right edge of the browse screen to see the zip codes.) Press Design (Shift-F2) as usual after viewing the data to return to the query design screen. Use Ctrl-Y to erase the filter condition.

EMBEDDED SEARCHES

You can use the *contains* operator, $, to search for text embedded within a Character field. For example, suppose, again, that you want to view records with Rainbow in the street address. Here are the steps:

1. First delete any previous filter conditions from the query design screen.

2. Move the highlight to the ADDRESS field.

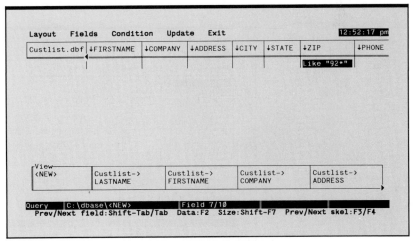

Figure 6.12: Query for records with zip codes beginning with 92

3. Enter the filter condition **$ "Rainbow"** (again, the quotation marks are mandatory).

Figure 6.13 shows how the query design screen should look.

When you press Data (F2) to view the results, you'll see that only records with Rainbow in the ADDRESS field are displayed, as in Figure 6.14.

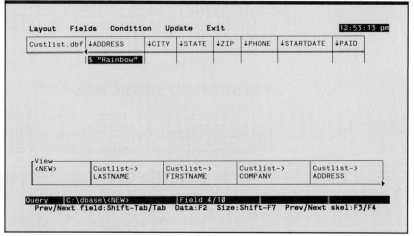

Figure 6.13: Query for records with addresses with Rainbow embedded

Figure 6.14: Results of $ "Rainbow" query of ADDRESS field

EXCEPT SEARCHES

You can use the not-equal-to operator, # or < >, to execute a query that shows all records *except* those that meet some condition. For example, suppose you want to view all the records in CUSTLIST except those with CA in the STATE field. To do so, return to the query design screen and remove the filter condition currently in the ADDRESS field.

Then move the highlight to the STATE field and enter the filter condition # "**CA**", as in Figure 6.15. When you press F2 to execute the query and then scroll to the STATE field in the browse screen, you'll see that none of the records displayed has CA in the STATE field (see Figure 6.16).

By now, you should be feeling that dBASE IV can help you isolate just about any information in your database that you want. You might want to experiment with some queries of your own for a while.

Remember when experimenting on your own: If your query does not produce the results you expected when you press Data (F2), press Design (Shift-F2) to return to the query design screen. Then use the Tab key to scroll through the fields to see if you forgot to erase

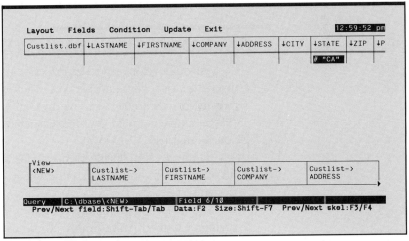

Figure 6.15: Query for records that do not have CA in the STATE field

```
┌─────────────────────────────────────────────────────────────────┐
│                                                                   │
│  Records   Organize   Fields   Go To   Exit                       │
│  ┌──────────────────────────────────────────────────────────────┐│
│  │CITY        STATE ZIP     PHONE          STARTDATE PAID         ││
│  │New York    NY    12345   (212)555-9988  11/15/90  ▪           ││
│  │Seattle     WA    88977   (206)555-8673  12/01/90  T           ││
│  │Butte       MT    54321   (303)555-6739  12/15/90  T           ││
│  │Portland    OR    76543   (717)555-0898  12/15/90  T           ││
│  │Philadelphia PA   45543   (202)555-9720  12/30/90  T           ││
│  │                                                                ││
│  │                                                                ││
│  │                                                                ││
│  │                                                                ││
│  │                                                                ││
│  │                                                                ││
│  └──────────────────────────────────────────────────────────────┘│
│  Browse   C:\dbase\<NEW>          Rec 3/9        View       .  ·  │
│                                                                   │
└─────────────────────────────────────────────────────────────────┘
```

Figure 6.16: Results of query for STATE # "CA"

any filter conditions from the previous query. If you find an old filter condition, remove it (using Ctrl-Y or Del) and try the query operation again.

DESIGNING QUERIES WITH AND

As you develop larger databases, you may want to use more sophisticated queries. For example, you might want to ask dBASE to display records for customers who live in California *and* began subscribing in 1990 *and* have not paid yet. To ask such questions of dBASE, you create queries that use AND logic.

There is a simple rule of thumb for creating AND queries: You put all of the filter conditions for the query on the same row in the query design screen.

Suppose you specifically want to isolate a record (or records) for a customer named Anita Smith. To do so, you need to put **"Smith"** in the LASTNAME field and **"Anita"** in the FIRSTNAME field on the same row in the query design screen, as shown in Figure 6.17. (To speed along the rest of this chapter, instructions assume that you know how to use the Design (Shift-F2) and Data (F2) keys to switch back and forth between the query design and browse screens. We'll also assume that you know how to erase old filter conditions from the query design screen and enter new ones.)

When you press Data (F2) to execute the query, only Anita Smith's record will appear on the browse screen. (Press Shift-F2 to return to the query design screen.)

Suppose you want to list all customers who live on Broad St. in Philadelphia. That is, you want to display all records with Broad St. *embedded* in the ADDRESS field *and* Philadelphia in the CITY field. You need to set up your query as in Figure 6.18.

Once again, notice that the two filter conditions are on the same row within the query. Pressing Data (F2) will display Susita Schumack's record in the CUSTLIST database, the only customer in this database who lives on Broad St. in Philadelphia.

So now, how would you list all customers who have not paid yet, and who began subscribing prior to January 1, 1991—that is, customers with .F. in the PAID field and dates less than 1/1/91 in the

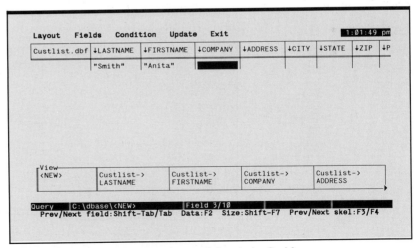

Figure 6.17: A query for records containing Anita Smith

STARTDATE field? Figure 6.19 shows how to set up the query.

Press Data (F2) to execute the query. Press End to scroll to the right edge of the browse screen to view the STARTDATE and PAID fields.

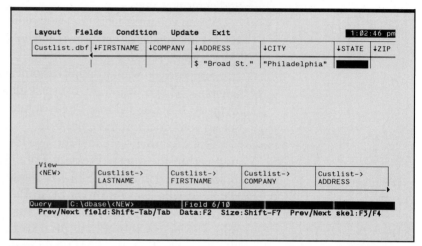

Figure 6.18: A query for records of customers living on Broad St. in Philadelphia

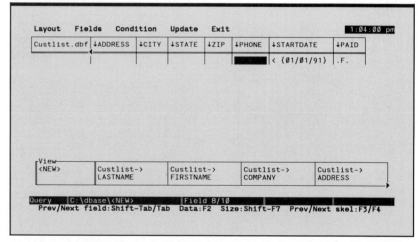

Figure 6.19: Query for records of customers who began subscribing before 1/1/91 and have not paid

If you want to limit the preceding query to California residents who have not paid yet and who began subscribing prior to January 1, 1990, you would just need to add **"CA"** (with quotation marks) to the STATE field in the query design screen. Make sure that "CA" is in the top row of the query screen (the same row as the other filter conditions). Then press F2 to execute the query.

SEARCHING FOR RANGES

Often you need to search for data that falls within some range of values, such as zip codes in the range 92000 to 92555 or names in the alphabetical range A through J. You might want to search for records that fall within a particular range of dates, such as November 15, 1990, to December 15, 1990. Range searches can be particularly useful in Numeric fields: for example, "Display all employees with salaries in the range of $20,000 to $30,000." (Chapter 9 discusses Numeric fields.)

To perform a range search, use an AND query within a single field. Use the $>$ = operator before the low end of the range, and the $<$ or $<$ = operator before the high end of the range; separate the two with a comma.

Suppose, for example, that you wanted to pull out records of people whose last names begin with the letters A through J. The filter condition $>$ = "A", $<$ "K" would do the trick, because it isolates names that begin with any letter that's greater than or equal to "A", but less than "K".

Suppose you want to view customers in the zip code range 80000 to 97000: that is, records with zip codes that are greater than or equal to 80000 *and* are also less than or equal to 97000. To do so, you place the filter condition $>$ = "80000", $<$ = "97000" in the ZIP field, as shown in Figure 6.20. Figure 6.21 shows the results of this query.

Suppose you want to view customers who began subscribing on dates between 11/15/90 and 12/15/90. You use exactly the same kind of filter condition as in the previous examples, including the curly braces for the Date data type. Figure 6.22 shows the appropriate filter condition $>$ = {11/15/90}, $<$ = {12/15/90}, in the STARTDATE field of the query form.

NOTE

To dBASE, "Ja" is *not* less than or equal to "J" alone; "Ja" is greater than "J" alone. Therefore, to search for names beginning with the letters A through J, you could use either $>$ = "A", $<$ = "Jz", or simply $>$ = "A", $<$ "K".

DESIGNING QUERIES WITH OR

Now that you've seen how to construct an AND query, you may be wondering how to create a query that says "Show me all the customers that live in Washington *or* Oregon *or* California." The answer to this question is that you design an OR query.

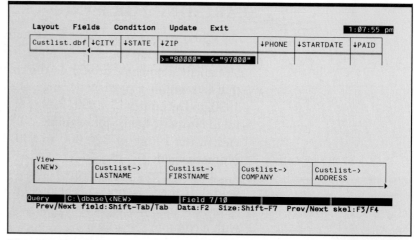

Figure 6.20: Query for records of customers in the 80000 to 97000 zip code range

Figure 6.21: Results of the zip code range query

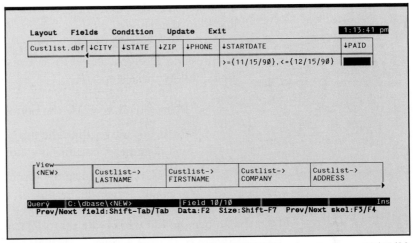

Figure 6.22: A query for records with STARTDATE values between 11/15/90 and 12/15/90

To design an OR query, you need to stagger the values that you are searching for on separate rows within the query design screen. Initially, dBASE IV displays only a single row for entering information into a query form. But you can easily create more rows by pressing ↓. To see how this works, create a query that displays customers who live in either California or Washington:

1. Start with an empty query design screen (use the Tab and Shift-Tab keys to scroll from field to field and use Ctrl-Y to delete any existing filter conditions).

2. Move the highlight to the STATE field in the query design screen.

3. Type **"CA"** to specify California as a state to search for.

4. Press ↓ to add a new row.

5. Type **"WA"** to specify Washington as a state to search for.

6. Press ←. Your query screen should look like Figure 6.23.

Staggering the filter conditions onto two separate rows tells dBASE that you want records that have *either* CA or WA in the STATE field. Press Data (F2) to verify this. After you press the End key to scroll to the right of the browse screen, your screen should look like Figure 6.24.

After viewing the results of the query, return to the query screen by pressing Design (Shift-F2) as usual. To erase both filter conditions, follow these steps:

1. Press Ctrl-Y to erase the bottom filter condition.

2. Press ↑ to move up to the top filter condition (the second row will disappear, because it is now empty).

3. Press Ctrl-Y to erase the top filter condition.

Incidentally, you are not limited to two rows in OR queries. You can use the ↓ key to create up to 12 rows. For example, the query in Figure 6.25 uses 4 rows to display records for residents of PA, NY, MT, or WA (that is, for people who live in PA *or* NY *or* MT *or* WA).

USING OR QUERIES WITH MULTIPLE FIELDS

Suppose you want to view records that have a value in one field *or* some other value in another field? For example, suppose you are a

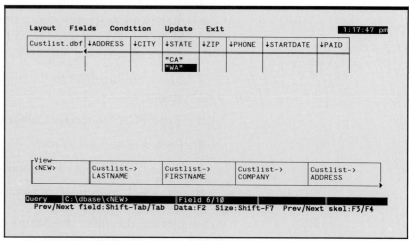

Figure 6.23: A query for records of customers who live in California or Washington

salesperson who works primarily on the phone, and you have been assigned a territory that includes the entire state of California, plus the entire 717 telephone area code (which, for this example, includes, but extends outside of, the state of California).

Figure 6.24: Results of the OR query

Figure 6.25: Query to view records of Pennsylvania, New York, Montana, or Washington residents

You cannot find the appropriate records for your customers by executing a query that asks for records that have CA in the STATE field *and* (717) in the PHONE field, because that query would limit the display to records with the 717 area code within the state of California. Instead, you want to display records that have CA in the STATE field (regardless of area code) *or* 717 in the PHONE field (regardless of the state).

To execute such a query, you need to stagger the STATE and PHONE filter conditions onto two separate rows, to tell dBASE that you want records meeting one condition *or* the other. Figure 6.26 shows how to design such a query. (Remember to use the ↓ key to create a second row in the query design screen before entering $ **"(717)"** into the PHONE field.)

Even though you are searching two different fields in the query shown in Figure 6.26, because the two fields are on two different rows in the query design screen dBASE will understand that you are requesting OR logic in the query. When you press Data (F2), the browse screen will display records that have either CA in the STATE field or (717) embedded ($) in the PHONE field, as shown in Figure 6.27.

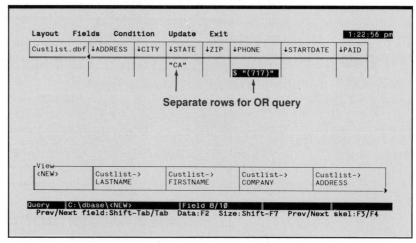

Figure 6.26: A query for records with either CA in the STATE field or (717) in the PHONE field

```
   Records   Organize   Fields   Go To   Exit

   CITY             STATE ZIP      PHONE            STARTDATE PAID

   San Diego        CA    92067    (619)555-1234    11/15/90  T
   Santa Monica     CA    92001    (714)555-0123    01/01/91  F
   Portland         OR    76543    (717)555-0898    12/15/90  T
   Los Angeles      CA    96607    (213)555-9988    12/30/90  F
   Hideaway         CA    92220    (415)555-9854    01/01/91  T




   Browse   C:\dbase\<NEW>              Rec 1/9          View
```

Figure 6.27: Results of the query for either CA in the STATE field or (717) in the PHONE field

COMBINING AND AND OR QUERIES

There is still another type of query that you may need to pose to dBASE IV—a query that combines AND and OR logic. For example, suppose you want to see records for all the people in the states of California, New York, and Washington who have paid. At first you might think that the logic for this requires the query "Locate customers who have paid AND live in Washington or California or New York." If so, you might set up the query incorrectly, as in Figure 6.28.

When you execute the query shown in Figure 6.28, the results will look like Figure 6.29. The query in Figure 6.28 intended to display only CA, NY, and WA records with .T. in the PAID field, but as you can see in Figure 6.29, some records with .F. in the PAID field are displayed. Why?

Actually, dBASE did exactly what you asked. As it considered each record, it asked, "Does this record have WA in the STATE field *and* .T. in the PAID field, *or* does this record have CA in the STATE field, *or* does this record have NY in the STATE field?" The plain-English translation of the query in Figure 6.28 is "Display records that have WA in the STATE field and .T. in the PAID field, or CA in the STATE field (regardless of what's in the PAID field), or NY in the STATE field (regardless of what's in the PAID field)."

However, this is not what you *meant* when you created the query. To see records for all WA, CA, and NY residents who have paid, you need to set up the query as shown in Figure 6.30.

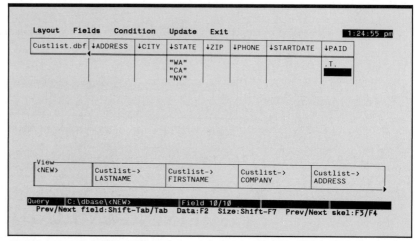

Figure 6.28: *Not* the way to set up the query to display records for all people in California, New York, and Washinton who have paid

```
Records    Organize    Fields    Go To    Exit
CITY           STATE  ZIP      PHONE           STARTDATE  PAID
San Diego      CA     92067    (619)555-1234   11/15/90   T
Santa Monica   CA     92001    (714)555-0123   01/01/91   F
New York       NY     12345    (212)555-9988   11/15/90   T
Seattle        WA     88977    (206)555-8673   12/01/90   T
Los Angeles    CA     96607    (213)555-9988   12/30/90   F
Hideaway       CA     92220    (415)555-9854   01/01/91   T




Browse   C:\dbase\<NEW>            Rec 1/9          View
```

Figure 6.29: Results of incorrect query

The query in Figure 6.30 meets your needs exactly, because when dBASE uses the query, it asks, "Does this record have WA in STATE and .T. in PAID, or CA in STATE and .T. in PAID, or NY in STATE and .T. in PAID?" It then displays only records that meet all these criteria, as Figure 6.31 shows.

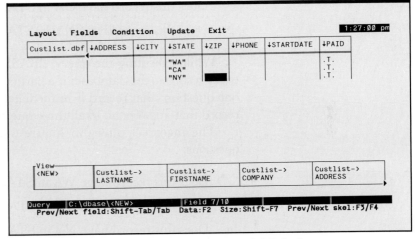

Figure 6.30: A query that combines AND and OR logic

Figure 6.31: Results of query combining AND and OR logic

If you find AND and OR combinations confusing, think of them this way. dBASE considers each row in the query to be a single question. For example, the query in Figure 6.30 can be viewed as three separate questions:

Does this record have WA in STATE and .T. in PAID?

Does this record have CA in STATE and .T. in PAID?

Does this record have NY in STATE and .T. in PAID?

While executing the query, dBASE poses all three questions to every record in the database. If a particular record answers yes to any one question, that record is immediately displayed on the screen. A record that answers no to all three questions is not displayed.

The incorrect query in Figure 6.28 asked each record these questions:

Does this record have WA in STATE, and .T. in PAID?

Does this record have CA in STATE?

Does this record have NY in STATE?

Although they weren't what we wanted, the results displayed by the query were accurate for these questions.

HOW COMPLEX CAN A QUERY BE?

You may be wondering how complex a query you can create. For example, can you design a single query with 12 rows of AND and OR logic, with many sounds-like operators, range searches, and Like pattern matches? The answer is yes—dBASE imposes no limitations on your queries, as long as the query makes sense.

The most common error people make is entering filter conditions into a query that do not make sense. For example, entering "CA","WA" in the STATE field of the CUSTLIST query screen would not display any records because the query asks for records that have both CA *and* WA in the STATE field. But a single person can (presumably) live in only one state. That is, no single record could possibly have both CA and WA in the STATE field at the same time. (Perhaps the creator of the query meant to display records with *either* CA *or* WA in the STATE field, in which case the two filter conditions would have to be staggered onto two separate rows.)

USING QUERIES
TO LOCATE A RECORD

All of the examples presented so far have demonstrated a technique for using queries to *isolate* records that meet some query condition. You can also use queries simply to *find* a particular record in the database. This is a handy technique for locating a specific record in a database, without filtering out any other records. It's also a valuable alternative to the Forward Search option on the Go To menu, because it allows you to search multiple fields, using all of the capabilities of the query design screen.

To use a query to locate a particular record, you enter the filter conditions in the query as usual. Then you enter the word **Find** beneath the database file name in the file skeleton. Figure 6.32 shows an example in which the query will locate the first record with Mahoney in the LASTNAME field and Mary in the FIRSTNAME field.

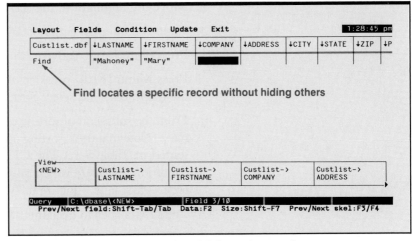

Figure 6.32: Query to locate Mary Mahoney's record

When you press Data (F2) to execute the query, the highlight will be positioned on Mary Mahoney's record. All other database records are still accessible, with the usual arrow, PgUp and PgDn keys.

SORTING QUERY DISPLAYS

So far, the results of all your queries have displayed records in the order that you originally entered them. But there may be times when you want the results of your queries to be sorted. For example, you might want to send form letters to California residents and to print them in zip code order for bulk mailing. Hence, you need a *query* to isolate records with CA in the STATE field and a *sort order* to arrange the records into zip code order.

To sort the results of a query, use the Sort This Field option from the Fields pull-down menu on the query design screen (perhaps after you've already entered your filter conditions). Then execute your query as usual with the Data (F2) key. To see how this works, isolate records that have CA in the STATE field and sort those records into alphabetical order by city. Here are the steps:

1. As usual, work your way to the query design screen and erase any old filter conditions.

2. Move the highlight to the STATE field.

3. Enter the filter condition **"CA"** and press ←┘.

4. Press Shift-Tab to move to the CITY field.

5. Press Menu (F10), press → to move to the Fields option on the menu bar, and select Sort on This Field.

6. From the submenu of sorting options, select Ascending Dictionary. (Note that these sorting options are the same as those presented in Table 5.1.) The CITY field now contains the sort condition *AscDict1,* which stands for "ascending dictionary order—first field." Figure 6.33 shows the completed query.

7. Press Data (F2) to execute the query.

If you scroll to the CITY and STATE fields in the browse screen, you'll see that only records with CA in the STATE field are displayed, and the cities are in alphabetical order, as Figure 6.34 shows.

SORTING MULTIPLE FIELDS You can perform sorts within sorts in a query form, simply by selecting fields to sort on in most-important to least-important order. For example, if you want to sort the results of a query alphabetically by last name and then alphabetically by first name within last names, you move the highlight to the LASTNAME field, select Sort This Field, move the highlight to the FIRSTNAME field, and select Sort This Field again.

dBASE includes a number in the sort condition so that you can see the field's position in the sort order. For example, in Figure 6.35 *AscDict1* indicates that LASTNAME is the first (primary) sort field, and *AscDict2* indicates that FIRSTNAME is the secondary sort field. (The sorted result is the same as when you use LASTNAME + FIRSTNAME in an index.)

Note that dBASE continues to add 1 to the AscDict symbol each time you select Sort on This Field from the Fields menu, as long as you are still in the same querying session. (A query session ends when you exit the query design screen and return to the Control Center.) Therefore, your queries might show symbols like *AscDist3*,

AscDict stands for Ascending Dictionary order. Other abbreviations for sort order options are *DscDict* for Descending Dictionary, *Asc* for Ascending ASCII, and *Dsc* for Descending ASCII order.

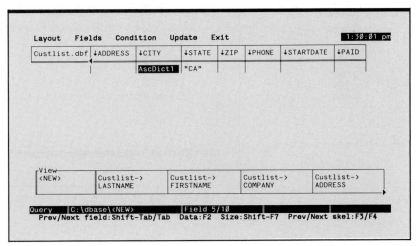

Figure 6.33: Query for records of California residents, sorted alphabetically by city

AscDict4, and so on. Don't worry about this—the sorting precedence remains the same.

For instance, if LASTNAME contains *AscDict1,* and if FIRST-NAME contains *AscDict2,* the data are sorted by first name within common last names. If LASTNAME contains *AscDict3* and FIRSTNAME contains *AscDict4,* you get the same results; first names are still sorted within common last names.

Note that dBASE continues to add 1 to the AscDict symbol each time you select Sort on This Field from the Fields menu, as long as you are still in the same querying session. (A query session ends when you exit the query design screen and return to the Control Center.) Therefore, your queries might show symbols like *AscDist3, Asc-Dict4,* and so on. Don't worry about this—the sorting precedence remains the same.

For instance, if LASTNAME contains *AscDict1,* and if FIRSTNAME contains *AscDict2,* the data are sorted by first name within common last names. If LASTNAME contains *AscDict3* and FIRSTNAME contains *AscDict4,* you get the same results; first names are still sorted within common last names.

> **NOTE**
>
> *AscDict* stands for Ascending Dictionary order. Other abbreviations for sort order options are *DscDict* for Descending Dictionary, *Asc* for Ascending ASCII, and *Dsc* for Descending ASCII order.

```
  Records    Organize    Fields    Go To    Exit
 ┌─────────────┬───────┬───────┬──────────────┬───────────┬─────┐
 │CITY         │STATE  │ZIP    │PHONE         │STARTDATE  │PAID │
 ├─────────────┼───────┼───────┼──────────────┼───────────┼─────┤
 │Hideaway     │CA     │92220  │(415)555-9854 │01/01/91   │T    │
 │Los Angeles  │CA     │96607  │(213)555-9988 │12/30/90   │F    │
 │San Diego    │CA     │92067  │(619)555-1234 │11/15/90   │T    │
 │Santa Monica │CA     │92001  │(714)555-0123 │01/01/91   │F    │
 │      ▲          ▲          California residents                │
 │                                                                 │
 │       Sorted by city                                            │
 └─────────────────────────────────────────────────────────────┘
  Browse    C:\dbase\<NEW>          Rec 1/4         View  ReadOnly
```

Figure 6.34: Results of query for records of California residents, sorted alphabetically by city

COMBINING FILTER AND SORT CONDITIONS   Any field on the query design screen can contain both a filter condition and a sort condition. First put in all of your filter conditions, and then select fields to sort on. dBASE will automatically place the sort condition, preceded by a comma, after the filter condition.

Figure 6.36 shows an example where the query will display only records that begin with the letters "A" through "N." The resulting records will be displayed in alphabetical order by STATE (that is, CA will precede MT, which will precede NY). Within each state, cities will be in alphabetical order (that is, within California, Hideaway will precede Los Angeles, which will precede Malibu, which will precede San Diego).

HOW QUERIES SORT RECORDS

In Chapter 5, we discussed the difference between using an index to display data in sorted order and using the Sort option on the database design screen to create a separate, sorted database file. All of the sorts that we've performed so far in this chapter have actually used the latter technique, sorting to a separate database file. The resulting browse screen displayed the data from the separate, sorted file (not from the original CUSTLIST file).

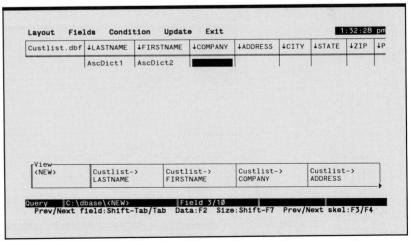

Figure 6.35: Query results sorted alphabetically by name

Whenever dBASE uses a separate file to display the results of a sorted query, the message ReadOnly appears in the status bar of the resulting browse or edit screen (Figure 6.34 shows an example). This message reminds you that the data on this screen can only be read; you cannot enter new data or make changes.

If you attempt to make changes to data on the ReadOnly browse or edit screen, dBASE will beep and reject your keystrokes. This protects you from inadvertently making changes on the sorted copy of the database, rather than on the original database.

As you begin to work with larger databases, you will notice that dBASE takes quite a while to display the results of a sorted query. That's because the query uses the inefficient "sort" method, rather than the quicker and more efficient index method, to organize the records. Again, the delay may not seem significant when you are working with the small CustList database. But when you begin managing databases with hundreds or thousands of records, such sorts can be very time consuming.

You may be wondering if there is some way around these slow, uneditable query results. The answer is yes, there is. And perhaps you will not be too surprised to learn that the answer involves indexes. If you use an index to sort the results of the query, you'll get your results more quickly and you'll be able to make changes in the resulting browse screen.

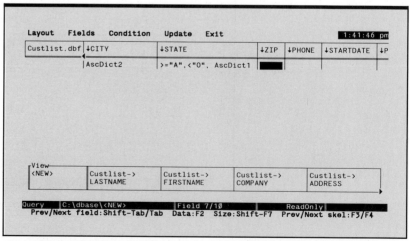

Figure 6.36: A filter and sort condition combined in the LASTNAME field

USING INDEXES TO SORT QUERY RESULTS

Let's start this section with an entirely new query session. (It's not absolutely necessary to do so, but it will be easier to follow step-by-step instructions if you start with a clean slate.) Follow these steps:

1. If the browse screen is showing, press Design (Shift-F2) to return to the query design screen.

2. Select Abandon Changes and Exit from the Exit pull-down menu.

3. If asked about Abandoning, select Yes. You'll be returned to the Control Center.

The CUSTLIST database name should still be above the line in the Data panel, indicating that it is still open and ready for use. To get back to the query design screen, follow these simple steps:

1. Make sure the highlight is on <create> in the Queries panel.

2. Press ←┘.

Now you are back in the query design screen, and can be certain that there are no old filter conditions or sort operators lying around. Let's use the ZIP index that you created in Chapter 5 to sort the results of a query. We'll ask dBASE to display only California residents, and to display them in zip code order. Here are the steps:

1. To include indexes in your query, press Menu (F10), access the Fields pull-down menu, and select the Include Indexes option.

2. To isolate records for California residents, press the Tab key until you get to the STATE field, enter the filter condition "**CA**" (including the quotation marks), and press ←┘.

3. Press the Tab key to move to the ZIP field. Notice that a pound sign (#) appears next to the ZIP field name. This # sign tells you that ZIP is an index field.

4. Press F10 and select Sort on This Field from the Fields pull-down menu.

5. From the submenu, select Ascending ASCII. Notice in Figure 6.37 that the ZIP field now contains the sort operator Asc1, the same sort operator you would use if no index file were involved. However, dBASE automatically uses the ZIP index to speed the sort because it now "knows" that ZIP is an index field.

6. To execute the query, press Data (F2). As you can see in Figure 6.38, the browse screen displays CA residents only, sorted into zip code order. Notice that the ReadOnly message does not appear in the status bar. You can, therefore, change any data in the current browse screen, but there is no need to do so now.

7. Press Design (Shift-F2) to return to the query design screen.

USING COMPLEX INDEXES   In the preceding example, the ZIP field was marked with a pound sign to indicate that it was an index field. What about the LASTNAME + FIRSTNAME index you created in Chapter 5? That's a *complex index* because it uses more than one field. Complex indexes are always displayed to the right of database fields on the query design screen.

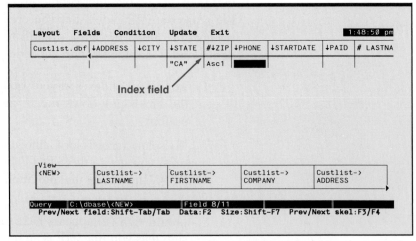

Figure 6.37: Query to display records for California residents, sorted by zip code

To verify this, you can press the End key to move to the rightmost column. In that position you will find the additional field # LASTNAME + FIRSTNAME, with the # symbol again indicating that this is an index field. You can use this field just as you would use any other field in the query design screen, both for sorting and for querying.

Suppose you again want to display records for California residents only, but this time in alphabetical order by last and first name. Here are the steps to do so:

1. Remove the Asc1 operator from the ZIP field.

2. Press the End key to move to the # LASTNAME + FIRST-NAME query field.

3. Select Sort on This Field from the Fields pull-down menu.

4. Select Ascending ASCII. Now you've specified that you want both to search for California residents and to use the index to control the sort order of the display. Figure 6.39 shows how the query form looks.

Figure 6.38: Results of query to display records for California residents, sorted by zip code

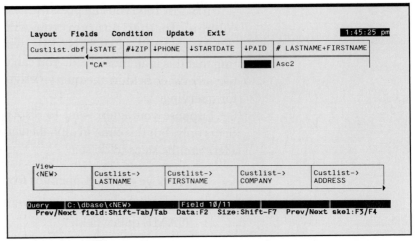

Figure 6.39: Search for CA records, with LASTNAME + FIRSTNAME sort specified

5. Press Data (F2) to execute the query. The browse screen displays only CA records, listed in alphabetical order by last and first name.

6. After viewing the results of the query, press Design (Shift-F2) to return to the query design screen.

By now you've come a long way in gaining access to the data in a database. You've learned how to sort your database records and how to search for records that contain a particular value. In addition, you've seen how to combine sorting and searching. Because you've used indexes to handle your sorting, you've learned the fastest, most efficient techniques for performing these tasks.

Perhaps this would be a good time to take a break. Follow these steps to leave the query design screen and return to the Control Center:

1. Press Menu (F10) and select Abandon Changes and Exit from the **Exit** pull-down menu.

2. When prompted, select Yes to abandon the query design screen.

You'll be returned to the Control Center. From there, you can quit dBASE IV if you wish. To resume with the next section later, get dBASE IV up and running again and open the LEARN catalog using the steps discussed earlier in this chapter.

SELECTING FIELDS TO DISPLAY IN A QUERY

Previously in this chapter, you've used the query design screen to tell dBASE which *records* you want to display in the results of a query. For example, you've designed queries to display records that have "CA" in the STATE field. You can also use the query design screen to display only certain *fields* in the results of a query. To create a personal phone list, for example, you might want dBASE to display only the LASTNAME, FIRSTNAME, and PHONE fields. To determine which fields are displayed in the results of a query, use the view skeleton at the bottom of the query design screen.

We'll go through the steps involved in deciding which fields to display in a moment. But you'll want to start with a new query design screen. If you did not follow steps 1 and 2 to take a break at the end of the preceding section, do so now. We'll start the next steps from the Control Center. First, we need to get to the query design screen:

1. If the CUSTLIST database name is not above the line in the Data panel of the Control Center, move the highlight to it, press ←, and select Use File.

2. Move the highlight to <create> in the Queries panel and press ← to create a new query.

Now you are in the query design screen, where we can start to experiment with the view skeleton. There are several techniques you can use to move field names into and out of the view skeleton. All involve the Field (F5) key. By default, dBASE includes all field names in the view skeleton. You can remove all the field names and put them back in by positioning the highlight beneath the file name in the File Skeleton and pressing F5 (see Figure 6.40).

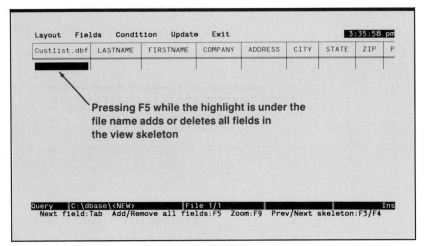

Figure 6.40: All fields are removed from the view skeleton

To try this, first press Home to ensure that the highlight is beneath the file name Custlist.dbf. Then press F5 a few times, and notice that each time you do so, the field names in the view skeleton disappear or reappear.

Now let's try a practical example by creating a personal phone list from the CustList database. Follow these steps:

1. Make sure the highlight is beneath Custlist.dbf in the file skeleton.

2. Press F5 until the view skeleton is empty (no field names appear at the bottom of the screen).

3. Press the End key and then press the Shift-Tab key twice to move the highlight to the PHONE field.

4. Press Field (F5) to copy this field into the view skeleton. You'll notice two things: the Custlist->PHONE field now appears in the view skeleton and the ↓ symbol appears to the left of the field name PHONE in the file skeleton. Both changes serve as reminders that the field will be displayed in the results of the query.

5. Press Home and then the Tab key twice to move the highlight to the FIRSTNAME field.

6. Press Field (F5) to copy the field to the view skeleton.

7. Press Shift-Tab to move the highlight to the LASTNAME field.

8. Press Field (F5) to copy the LASTNAME field to the view skeleton.

As Figure 6.41 shows, the view skeleton now displays the three fields that will be displayed as a result of the query: PHONE, FIRSTNAME, and LASTNAME.

Now you can press Data (F2) to see the results. You'll see that the browse screen displays the PHONE, FIRSTNAME, and LASTNAME fields of all the records in the database, as shown in Figure 6.42.

If you press F2 to switch to the edit screen, it too will display only these three fields. Press Design (Shift-F2) to return to the query design screen after viewing the results of the query.

The file skeleton and view skeleton in the query design screen work somewhat independently of one another in that you can place a filter condition in any field in the file skeleton, regardless of whether the view skeleton includes that field. For example, even though the view skeleton you created tells dBASE to *display* only the PHONE,

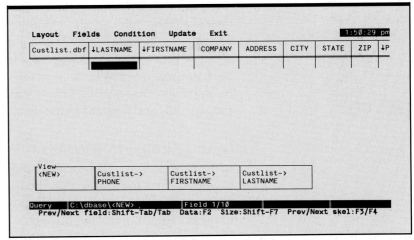

Figure 6.41: PHONE, FIRSTNAME, and LASTNAME fields displayed

```
 Records   Organize   Fields   Go To   Exit
┌────────────────┬─────────────────┬──────────────────────────────┐
│ PHONE          │ FIRSTNAME       │ LASTNAME                     │
├────────────────┼─────────────────┼──────────────────────────────┤
│(619)555-1234│John            │Smith                         │
│(714)555-0123   │Annie           │Adams                         │
│(212)555-9988   │Wilbur          │Watson                        │
│(206)555-8673   │Mary            │Mahoney                       │
│(303)555-6739   │John            │Newell                        │
│(717)555-0898   │Sandy           │Beach                         │
│(213)555-9988   │Ralph           │Kenney                        │
│(202)555-9720   │Susita          │Schumack                      │
│(415)555-9854   │Anita           │Smith                         │
│                │                │                              │
│                │                │                              │
│                │                │                              │
│                │                │                              │
│                │                │                              │
│                │                │                              │
└────────────────┴─────────────────┴──────────────────────────────┘
 Browse  │C:\dbase\<NEW>           │Rec 1/9       │View │
```

Figure 6.42: Results of view skeleton displaying the fields PHONE, FIRST-
NAME, and LASTNAME

FIRSTNAME, and LASTNAME fields, you could still enter **"CA"**
into the STATE field of the file skeleton to limit the phone number list
to California residents.

MANAGING THE VIEW SKELETON

You've seen that you can use the F5 key to move fields into the
view skeleton. You can also work directly with the view skeleton by
pressing the Next key (F4). When you do so, the highlight moves to
the view skeleton and a new set of navigation key options appears at
the bottom of the screen. (One of the options, Prev/Next Skel:F3/F4
reminds you that you can move back to the previous skeleton by
pressing F3, and forward to the next skeleton by pressing F4.)

MOVING FIELDS IN THE VIEW SKELETON   To move a field
in the view skeleton, thereby rearranging the order in which fields are
displayed, first make sure that the highlight is in the view skeleton.
Then use the Tab or Shift-Tab key to highlight the field that you want
to move. Finally, press the Move key (F7). dBASE will highlight the
frame around the field and present the instructions "TAB or BACK-
TAB to move fields. <Return> to end." This means that dBASE

wants you to use the Tab or Shift-Tab key to move the highlighted box to the new location for the field. When the field is in its new location, press ↵. Go ahead and experiment on your own if you like.

SELECTING GROUPS OF FIELDS   While at the view skeleton, you can use the Select key (F6) to highlight a group of adjacent fields to work with. To use Select, move the highlight to the leftmost or rightmost field in the group you want to select. Press Select (F6) and press the Tab or Shift-Tab key to extend the highlight to the left or right, as instructed on the screen (but don't highlight *all* the fields, or you won't be able to move them). Press ↵ after highlighting a group of fields.

Once you have highlighted a group of fields, pressing F5 removes all those fields from the view. Pressing F7 allows you to move that entire group of fields to a new location. After you complete your job, the highlighting disappears. You may want to try some of these features of the view skeleton on your own.

CONTROLLING THE FILE SKELETON COLUMN WIDTHS

As you've undoubtedly noticed by now, whenever you type a query condition into the file skeleton (at the top of the query design screen), the column automatically widens to accommodate your entry. If you enter many wide conditions, you may find it difficult to read your query design screen.

If, for whatever reason, you want to narrow or widen fields in the file skeleton, follow these simple general steps:

- Move the highlighter to the field you want to widen or narrow.
- Press Size (Shift-F7).
- Press ← and/or → to narrow or widen the column to your liking.
- Press ↵

Even if the filter condition within the column is wider than the width you've allotted for it, the query will still work. And, you can still edit the filter condition by scrolling through it with the ← and → keys.

Once you set the column width using this technique, it remains fixed and will not change, even if you change the query within it. If you want to return the column to the normal "elastic" mode, where it adjusts to accommodate its contents, move the highlighter back to the column and press Move (Shift-F7) twice.

Note that changing the width of a column in the file skeleton of the query design screen does not affect the actual width of the field in the database, nor the width of the field as displayed on the browse and edit screens.

SAVING QUERIES FOR FUTURE USE

You can save any query that you create as a file using a valid DOS file name (eight letters maximum, no spaces or punctuation; dBASE will automatically add the extension .QBE to the file name you provide). Then you can reuse that query at any time in the future, without reentering all the keystrokes for filter conditions and so forth.

Figure 6.43 shows a sample query that displays California residents' phone numbers, sorted in alphabetical order by name. The query combines many of the techniques we've discussed in this chapter. You should be able to create it on your own without step-by-step instructions, but I'll give you some hints to help out:

- First, limit the view skeleton to the LASTNAME, FIRST-NAME, and PHONE fields (in that order) using the Field (F5) key, the Previous/Next skeleton keys (F3 and F4), and the other keys described in the navigation line.

- Enter the "CA" filter condition under the STATE field of the file skeleton.

- Include indexes in the file skeleton query to speed up the search. (Use the Include Indexes option from the Fields pull-down menu.)

- Specify LASTNAME + FIRSTNAME index as the index for controlling the sort order (by positioning the highlight and selecting Sort on This Field from the Fields pull-down menu).

When you are done, your query should look like Figure 6.43. To verify that you got it right, execute the query by pressing the usual Data (F2) key. The browse screen should show the four California residents and their phone numbers:

LASTNAME	FIRSTNAME	PHONE
Adams	Annie	(714)555-0123
Kenney	Ralph	(213)555-9988
Smith	Anita	(415)555-9854
Smith	John	(619)555-1234

Suppose you want to save this query for future use so that you can always print current phone numbers for California residents without rebuilding the query. First assign a description to the query by following these steps:

1. Press Design (Shift-F2) to return to the query design screen.

2. Press Menu (F10), highlight the Layout option in the menu bar, and select Edit Description of Query.

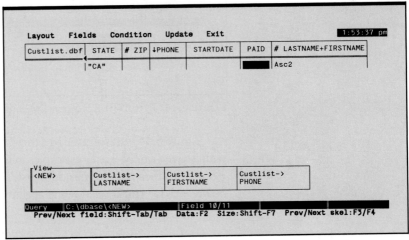

Figure 6.43: Query to display California customers' phone numbers

3. Type a description, such as **California phone numbers**, in this example. Press ←⟩.

To save the query and its description, follow these steps:

1. Press F10 to call up the menu, highlight the Exit option on the menu bar, and select Save Changes and Exit.

2. When dBASE displays the prompt "Save as:" enter a valid DOS file name. In this example, type **PHONELST** and press ←⟩.

You'll be returned to the Control Center where the new PHONELST query will be listed in the Queries panel. When you highlight the PHONELST query, you'll also see its description, as in Figure 6.44.

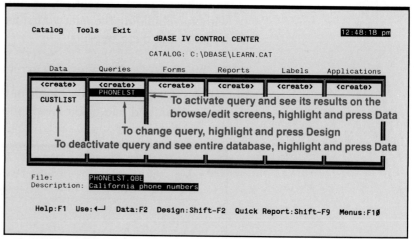

Figure 6.44: PHONELST query listed in the Queries panel

Figure 6.44 also summarizes three basic techniques that you can use with a saved query. Later examples in this book will give you more experience with these techniques. Here we'll discuss them in some detail, but before we do, you'll need some additional background.

In dBASE IV a saved query is also referred to as a *view*. This is because a query provides a particular way of viewing the data in a database. For example, the PHONELST query you just created shows you a particular slice of the CUSTLIST database, the LASTNAME, FIRSTNAME, and PHONE fields with only California residents displayed in alphabetical order by name.

Unlike a database file, a query (view) does not actually contain data. Instead, it contains instructions that dBASE IV reads to see how you want to view the data in a database. Therefore, any changes you make to the original database (CUSTLIST in this example) will indeed be reflected in the view the next time you use it. For example, if you were to change a California resident's phone number in the CUSTLIST database, the next time you used the PHONELST query, the new phone number would be displayed.

Views are a two-way street; because PHONELST shows data that is actually from the CUSTLIST database, if you change any data displayed by the PHONELST view, that change occurs in the CUSTLIST database.

As you'll discover in the following sections, the techniques that you use to manage a view from the Control Center are no different from those you use to manage a database file.

ACTIVATING A SAVED QUERY

To view database data through a saved query, highlight the name of the query in the Queries panel and press Data (F2). (This is similar to viewing the contents of the entire database, where you highlight the name of the database in the Data panel and press F2). If you highlight the PHONELST view and press F2, you'll be taken to the edit or browse screen where you'll see entries from the LASTNAME, FIRSTNAME, and PHONE fields of the CUSTLIST database. From there, you can use the usual F2 key to switch between the edit and browse screens at your convenience.

When you've finished looking at (or editing) the data through the view, select Exit from the Exit pull-down menu or press Esc or Ctrl-End, to return to the Control Center. At the Control Center, you'll notice that the PHONELST name is above the line in the Queries panel, indicating that it is still in use. If you want to view the entire

CUSTLIST database again, open it by highlighting its name in the Data panel and pressing F2.

CHANGING A QUERY

If you want to change the query, highlight its name in the Queries panel and press Design (Shift-F2). You'll be taken to the query design screen where you can make any changes you wish to the query.

While you are in the query design screen, you can modify the query in any way you wish using the same techniques that you used to create queries in this chapter. You can also see the results of the query by pressing Data (F2), as you did in previous examples. To return to the query design screen, press Design (Shift-F2), just as you did before.

When you have finished making changes to the query, select Save Changes and Exit from the Exit pull-down menu, or press Ctrl-End, to return to the Control Center. The name of the query will still be accessible in the Control Center, and any changes you've made will be included the next time you activate the query.

DEACTIVATING A QUERY

When you want to stop using a query and regain access to all the records and fields in your database file, simply opening the database file deactivates the query. For example, to deactivate the PHONELST query and regain access to all the records and fields in the CUSTLIST database, highlight CUSTLIST in the Data panel and press Data (F2). You'll be sent to the browse (or edit) screen, where you will see the entire CUSTLIST database.

To leave the edit or browse screen and return to the Control Center, select Exit from the Exit pull-down menu. When you get back to the Control Center, the CUSTLIST database name will be above the line in the Data panel, indicating that the CUSTLIST database is open and ready for use. The PHONELST query name will be below the line, indicating that it is no longer active (that is, no longer affecting your view of the CUSTLIST database).

ALTERNATIVE TECHNIQUES

Just as the Data panel offers alternatives to the Data and Design keys, so does the Queries panel. If you highlight the name of a saved query in the Queries panel, and press ◄──┘, you'll see three options in a prompt box (available only if the Instruct setting, discussed in Chapter 2, is on). If the query is not already active, the three options will be

Use View   Modify Query   Display Data

If the highlighted query is active when you press ◄──┘, the three options will be

Close View   Modify Query   Display Data

Selecting Use View puts the view name above the line in the queries panel. Selecting Close View deactivates the query, putting its name below the line. Selecting Modify Query takes you to the queries design screen (exactly as though you had pressed the Design key) and lets you make changes to the query. Selecting Display Data activates the view and takes you to the edit or browse screen (as though you had pressed the Data key).

Starting in the next chapter, you'll see how to use saved queries (views) to isolate records for printing information such as mailing labels and form letters. This is where the saved query really comes in handy. It allows you to isolate targeted records (those of New York residents, for example), and then print letters and labels in zip code order to take advantage of cheaper bulk mailing rates.

Printing
Formatted
Reports

Fast Track

To print a report   200
> using a completed format, select the name of the format from the Reports panel in the Control Center and select Print Report and Begin Printing from the menus that follow.

To print labels or reports in sorted order,   210
> activate (or create) the appropriate index on the database design screen. Then print the report or labels as you would normally.

To print labels or reports from the results of a query,   211
> first activate the query by selecting it from the Queries panel in the Control Center and selecting Use View from the submenu that appears. Then print the labels or report as you would normally.

To modify an existing label or report format,   212
> open the associated database or query, highlight the name of the format in the Control Center, and then press Design (Shift-F2).

To control printer operations,   219
> use options from the Print pull-down menu that appears whenever you print labels or a report.

THIS CHAPTER PRESENTS TECHNIQUES FOR USING your printer and formatting your dBASE IV information into a variety of useful reports, such as customer lists, mailing labels, and form letters. As usual, if you exited dBASE IV at the end of the previous chapter, be sure to get it up and running again and bring the LEARN catalog into the Control Center.

USING QUICK REPORT

The quickest and easiest way to get a printed copy of your information is to use the Quick Report option (Shift-F9) from the Control Center. This technique simply dumps data from your database onto the printer, without much regard for formatting. To use Quick Report, you highlight the name of the database file or query that you want to print from, press Shift-F9, and select Begin Printing from the menu that appears. Let's work through an example, printing the results of the PHONELST query that you created at the end of the previous chapter. Here are the steps:

1. Move the highlight to the PHONELST query in the Queries panel.

2. Press Quick Report (Shift-F9).

3. If dBASE asks whether you want to use the current view or PHONELST.qbe, select PHONELST.qbe (you'll learn more about this in a moment).

4. From the submenu that appears, press ◄─┘ to select Begin Printing.

5. Before printing starts, dBASE IV generates a *program* that it uses to print the report. This task may take a few seconds.

6. As dBASE prints the report, you'll see another submenu that allows you to cancel or pause printing. Don't do anything; the submenu will disappear when printing is complete.

Figure 7.1 shows the printed report. As you may recall, the PHONELST query included only the LASTNAME,

```
Page No.    1
01/15/91

LASTNAME        FIRSTNAME       PHONE

Adams           Annie           (714)555-0123
Kenney          Ralph           (213)555-9988
Smith           Anita           (415)555-9854
Smith           John            (619)555-1234
```

Figure 7.1: Printed output from the PHONELST query

FIRSTNAME, and PHONE fields for California residents, so the Quick Report displays only this information. (If you repeat the preceding steps, highlighting CUSTLIST rather than PHONELST in step 1, the report will display all the information in the CUSTLIST database file, probably spread across a few pages.)

SELECTING DATA TO PRINT

Before we go on, let's backtrack for a moment and discuss the choice between the current view and CUSTLIST.DBF that you may have made to print the data in the CUSTLIST file. Understanding that choice will tell you a lot about how to select data for printing in dBASE IV.

In some situations, dBASE IV may not be sure if you want to print data directly from a database file or from a query (for example, if a database file is in use, but a query is highlighted in the Control Center). If dBASE IV is not sure where you want to print from, it displays options that let you clarify the source of the report, as in Figure 7.2.

In Figure 7.2, dBASE asks whether you want to use the current view (or query) or the original CUSTLIST.DBF database file. You can select either option using the usual technique of highlighting and pressing Enter. Keep in mind that database files always have the extension .DBF, and queries (views) always have the extension

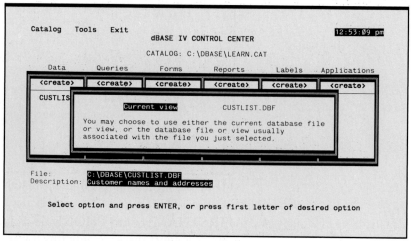

Figure 7.2: dBASE IV prompt for the source of data for the report

QBE. Selecting a .DBF file always prints the entire contents of the database file. Selecting a .QBE query, or view, prints only the fields and records that are specified in the query.

After you've made your selection, you'll see the submenu of printing options, which we'll discuss in more detail later. (As usual, you can press Esc to back out of the submenu and return to the Control Center.)

GENERAL TECHNIQUES FOR DESIGNING AND PRINTING REPORTS

The Quick Report option provides a quick and easy method for printing data in a somewhat formatted matter. When you want more control over the format of your output, such as when printing business reports, mailing labels, form letters, or whatever, you'll want to use the *labels design screen* and *reports design screen* discussed in this chapter.

You'll have an opportunity to create several reports in this chapter. But before proceeding, let's take a moment to summarize the general steps for creating custom report formats, be they mailing labels, form letters, or business reports:

- Make sure the database that you want to print the data from is already open (above the line in the Data panel).

- If you want to print labels, highlight <create> in the labels panel; for any other type of formatted report, highlight <create> in the Reports panel.

- Press ◄┘.

- If you are designing a report rather than labels:
  - Select a Quick Layout from the Fields pull-down menu.
  - Specify margins using the Modify Ruler option from the Words pull-down menu.

- If you are designing labels rather than a report:
  - Define a label size by selecting an option (or options) from the Dimensions pull-down menu.

- Use the techniques described in this chapter (and summarized in Table 7.1 and the inside of the back cover of this book) to design the report format to your liking.

- Press Ctrl-End, or select Save Changes and Exit from the Exit pull-down menu to save the format.

- When prompted, type a valid DOS file name (no extension) and press ◄┘.

NOTE

All techniques for changing and refining formats can be used at any time, regardless of whether you are creating a new format or changing an existing one.

Table 7.1: Keys for Editing Label and Report Formats

Key	Effect
↓	Moves down one row
↑	Moves up one row
→	Moves right one character or to end of field template
←	Moves left one character or to beginning of field template
Ctrl-→	Moves one word to the right

Table 7.1: Keys for Editing Label and Report Formats (continued)

Key	Effect
Ctrl-←	Moves one word to the left
PgUp	Moves to top of screen
PgDn	Moves to bottom of screen
End	Moves to end of line
Home	Moves to beginning of line
Ins	Toggles Insert mode on/off
←	If Insert mode is off, moves down one row; if Insert mode is on, inserts a new line; on reports design, opens and closes bands when cursor is on a border
F1	Provides help
F5	Adds a new field template or changes the currently highlighted one
F6	Selects field template or block
F7	Moves field or block selected with F6
F8	Copies field or block selected with F6
Shift-F7	Changes size of currently selected field template
Ctrl-N	Inserts a new line
Backspace	Erases character to the left
Del	Deletes character, field template, or block selected with F6
Ctrl-T	Removes word or field to right
Ctrl-Y	Removes entire line
Tab	Moves to next tab setting (reformats paragraph in word-wrap editor)
Shift-Tab	Moves to previous tab setting (reformats paragraph in word-wrap editor)
Esc	Abandons current format without saving changes, or unselects currently selected block or template

It may take a few minutes for dBASE to prepare your complete report format, but eventually you'll be returned to the Control Center. At any time in the future, you can print the data in your database using the format you designed by following these general steps:

- Highlight the name of the format in the Reports or Labels column.

- Press ←⊣.

- Select Print label or Print report (depending on which you are printing at the moment).

- Press ←⊣ to select Begin Printing.

You'll be returned to the Control Center when printing is done.

As you will see, there are many features available to you, all designed to give you as much control over the appearance of your printed report as possible. To get some hands-on exercise with these features, we'll start by designing the easiest type of format, mailing labels.

DESIGNING A LABEL FORMAT

To print labels, you first design the appearance, or *format,* of the label using the labels design screen (or *labels design work surface*). Note that dBASE IV uses the term *labels* rather loosely. Not only can you use the labels design screen to print any type of mailing label, but you can also use it to print envelopes, Rolodex-like cards, and general-purpose labels such as identification stickers.

SELECTING A DATABASE

Before you begin to design a label format, you need to make sure the appropriate database file (or query) is open. In this example, you'll design labels for the CUSTLIST database. Recall that if a database or query is currently in use (open), its name appears above the line in the Data panel. If you need to open the CUSTLIST database now, follow these steps:

1. Highlight the name CUSTLIST in the Data panel.

2. Press ←.

3. If the Use File option appears, select it. (Otherwise, press Esc to cancel the selection, because CUSTLIST is already open.)

USING THE LABELS DESIGN SCREEN

After you've specified the database file that you want to print labels from, you need to move to the labels design screen. To do so, move the highlight to the <create> option in the Labels panel and press ← (as shown in Figure 7.3). You'll see the labels design screen.

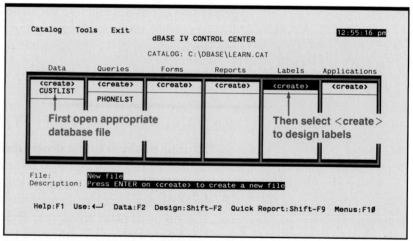

Figure 7.3: Steps for designing labels

As you can see in Figure 7.4, the labels design screen has the same familiar components as most other dBASE screens: a menu bar at the top and a status bar and navigation line at the bottom. The box in the center of the screen represents a blank label, and this is where you design your label format. The ruler above the box shows you the width of the label (in inches). In this example, the printed label will be 3½ inches wide.

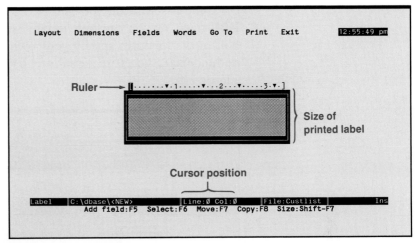

Figure 7.4: The labels design screen

SELECTING A GENERAL LABEL FORMAT

The window at the center of the screen is sized to show the space available on the printed label. Before you actually design the label format, you select your label size. To do so, press Menu (F10) and move to the Dimensions pull-down menu. You'll see the submenu shown in Figure 7.5.

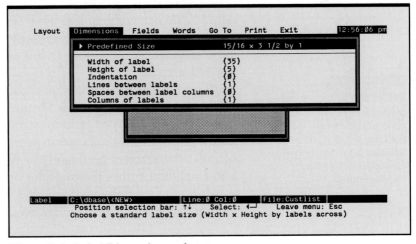

Figure 7.5: Label Dimensions submenu

On this submenu, you can select one of dBASE IV's predefined label sizes, or you can individually select options from the bottom half of the menu to specify your own label size. If you select Predefined Size, you'll see a submenu of common label sizes, as in Figure 7.6.

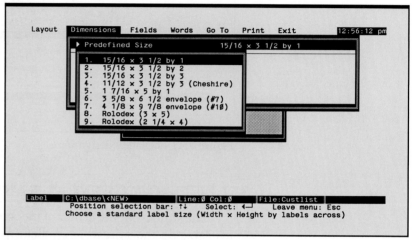

Figure 7.6: Predefined label sizes

The label sizes are described using the height and width in inches and the number of labels printed across each page. For example, the option $^{15}/_{16} \times 3^{1}/_{2}$ by 3 prints labels that are $^{15}/_{16}$ (or about 1) inch tall, $3^{1}/_{2}$ inches wide, and printed three across a page (like many photocopy-machine labels). Select any option you wish by highlighting it and then pressing ←. (In this example, we'll use option 2, for two labels across.)

NOTE

If you do need to create a custom label format, use the Help key (F1) while selecting label dimensions for explanations of the various settings.

If the label size that you want is not available from the predefined sizes, select individual options for the label format from the bottom half of the Dimensions pull-down menu. Note that the Width of Label option assumes that your printer is using the standard print size of 10 characters per inch (*pica* type). Similarly, the Height of Label option assumes the common print size of 6 lines per inch. If your printer uses different print sizes, you may have to adjust these settings accordingly, which might require a little experimentation.

PLACING FIELDS ON A LABEL

After you've selected a label size, you need to tell dBASE how to print each label. You do this by placing *field templates* that show where information from the database is to be printed on the empty label on the screen. To place a field template, you first move the cursor to where you want the data to be printed on the label. Then either press the Field key (F5) or select Add Field from the Fields pull-down menu.

To see how this works, let's create a mailing label format to print labels that look like this:

John Smith
ABC Co.
123 A St.
San Diego, CA 92067

First, notice that the message "Line:0 Col:0" appears centered in the status line near the bottom of the screen. This line tells you the line and column position of the cursor at any given moment. Use this message to help you follow these steps:

1. With the cursor at line 0, column 0, press Field (F5) to add a new field. You'll see a submenu of items that you can place on the label, as in Figure 7.7.

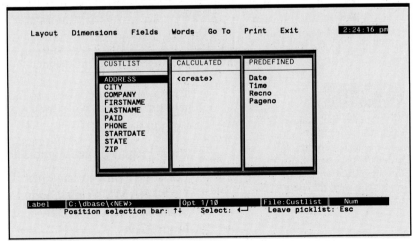

Figure 7.7: Submenu of items that can be placed on the label

2. Use ↓ to highlight FIRSTNAME; then press ←. You'll see information about the field you've selected, with options to change the Template and Picture Functions. These options are irrelevant at the moment, but we'll discuss them later.

3. As instructed in the lower window on the screen, press Ctrl-End to proceed. You'll notice that a series of X's fills in a portion of the screen, as in Figure 7.8. These X's are the field template. They show the maximum amount of space that the information in the FIRSTNAME field from the database will occupy on the printed label. Now you can add the LASTNAME field to the label format.

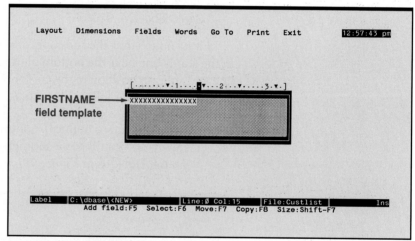

Figure 7.8: FIRSTNAME field added to the sample label

To guarantee that a space separates two fields on a printed label or report, press the space bar when the cursor is at the place where you want the space to appear.

4. Press the space bar to insert a space between the FIRSTNAME and LASTNAME fields (it will appear as a solid box).

5. Press Field (F5) again and select LASTNAME.

6. Press Ctrl-End to leave the Display Attributes menu. The LASTNAME field is added to the sample label. Note the blank space between the first and last names, as shown in Figure 7.9.

Figure 7.9: FIRSTNAME and LASTNAME fields separated by a space

7. Press ◄─┘ to move the cursor down to the next row (line 1, column 0).

8. To place the COMPANY field, press F5 and select COMPANY.

9. Press Ctrl-End to leave the Display Attributes menu.

10. Press ◄─┘ to move the cursor to line 2, column 0.

11. Press F5 and select ADDRESS.

12. Press Ctrl-End.

13. Press ◄─┘ to move the cursor to line 3, column 0.

14. To place the CITY field, press F5 and select CITY.

15. Press Ctrl-End.

16. To place a comma and a space after the city name, type a comma and then press the space bar.

17. To place the STATE field, press F5 and select STATE.

18. Press Ctrl-End.

19. To put two spaces between the STATE and ZIP code fields, press the space bar twice.

NOTE

The comma and space in the format are *text* that will appear on each label. You can actually add *any* text to a label format simply by typing it at the place where you want it to appear on each label.

20. To place the ZIP field, press F5 and select ZIP.

21. Press Ctrl-End.

Your label format should now look like Figure 7.10.

If you made some mistakes along the way, you can use several techniques to correct them. You can use the usual arrow, Ins, Del, and other editing keys to make changes, or you can use some of the techniques discussed in the section "Changing Report and Label Formats" later in this chapter. If you prefer to just start over, you can select Abandon Changes and Exit from the Exit pull-down menu, then Yes from the next window to appear.

SAVING A LABEL FORMAT

To add a description to the label format and save it for future use, follow these steps:

1. Press Menu (F10) and highlight the Layout option on the menu bar.

2. Select Edit Description of Label Design and type **2-across mailing labels** (or any other description you like). Then press ◄—.

Figure 7.10: Completed mailing label

3. Press Menu (F10) again and select Save Changes and Exit from the Exit pull-down menu.

4. When dBASE presents the prompt "Save as:" type a valid file name (maximum eight characters, with no spaces or punctuation). In this example, type **Mailing** and press ←.

There will be a delay while dBASE IV writes a program to print labels in the format you wish. When this is done, you'll be returned to the Control Center. When you return to the Control Center, you'll see the MAILING label format file name in the Labels panel, as in Figure 7.11.

PRINTING LABELS

Now that you have designed the format of the labels, you can use that format to print the names and addresses from the CUSTLIST database. Follow these steps:

NOTE

You can also preview or print labels while designing them, by selecting either Begin Printing or View Labels on Screen from the Print pull-down menu on the labels design screen.

1. Make sure the label format name MAILING is highlighted in the Labels panel.

2. Press ←.

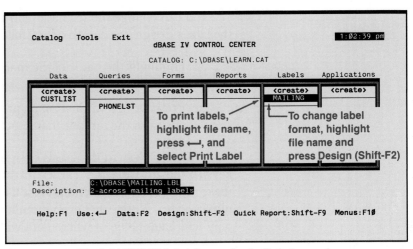

Figure 7.11: The MAILING label format in the Labels panel

3. From the options that appear, select Print Label.

4. From the Print Menu that appears next, select either Begin Printing (to actually print the labels) or View Labels on Screen (to see the labels on the screen only).

If you selected View Labels on Screen, you'll see the labels go by on your screen. dBASE will pause after each screenful and display a prompt at the bottom of the screen indicating that you should press the space bar to scroll to the next screenful. Do so at your leisure until you get back to the Control Center.

If you selected Begin Printing, your printer is probably printing the mailing labels right now. If you have a laser printer, you may need to eject the page to see the printed labels. To do so, repeat steps 1 through 3. Then select Eject Page Now from the Print menu and press Esc to leave the Print menu. Figure 7.12 shows the printed labels.

This exercise assumes that you are printing these sample labels on plain paper. When you print on real mailing labels, you may need to experiment a bit to get the data properly aligned on the labels. See the section "Controlling the Printer" near the end of this chapter for help with label alignment.

MODIFYING THE LABEL FORMAT

You can change the format of labels at any time by returning to the labels design screen. To do so, follow these basic steps:

1. Highlight the name of the mailing label format in the Labels panel (MAILING, in this case).

2. Press Design (Shift-F2), or press ↵ and select Modify layout from the options that appear.

When you get to the labels design screen, you can use editing keys (listed in Table 7.1 earlier in this chapter) and techniques to make changes and corrections (you'll learn more about editing techniques soon). Notice that even though the labels design screen shows only templates (X's) of where data will be printed on the label, you

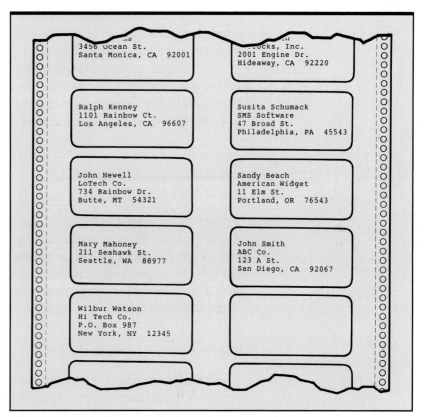

Figure 7.12: Mailing Labels printed from the CUSTLIST database

can easily determine which database field is associated with each template. Just use the usual arrow keys to move the cursor into the template of interest and look at the bottom of the screen.

For example, when the cursor is in the FIRSTNAME field template, the bottom of the screen displays

CUSTLIST->FIRSTNAME Type:Character Width:15 Decimal: 0

This line informs you that the current template will display the contents of the FIRSTNAME field from the CUSTLIST database. The line also indicates the data type, width, and number of decimal places, as defined in the database structure.

When you have finished viewing or editing your label format, select Save Changes and Exit from the Exit pull-down menu. You'll be returned to the Control Center.

Rather than go into any more detail on creating mailing label formats right now, let's discuss how you can use similar techniques to design and create *reports*. As you'll see later, many of the techniques that you use to design reports and labels are identical.

DESIGNING PRINTED REPORTS

Just as the labels design screen lets you specify how data from the database should be displayed on a label, the reports design screen lets you specify how data should be printed on a full page. Unlike labels, full printed pages might consist of many different sections of text, such as page headings, page numbers, totals sections, subtotals sections, and other types of information.

DESIGNING REPORT SECTIONS

Part of designing a report involves deciding what goes into each section of the printed report. Figure 7.13 shows two pages of a somewhat typical report and the various sections displayed in the report. These sections are as follows:

Page header	The page header is printed once at the top of each page.
Report intro	The report introduction is printed once at the beginning of the report.
Detail	The detail section is the body of the report. Typically, this section displays records from a database file.
Report summary	The report summary is printed once at the end of the report and can be used to display totals or closing information about the report.

Figure 7.13: Sections of a typical report

Page footer   The page footer is printed once at the
                       bottom of each page and can be used to
                       display page numbers or other useful
                       information.

When you begin developing a sample report a little later in this
chapter, you'll see how to control exactly what is printed in each section of the report.

GENERAL REPORT FORMATS

To help you design your reports, dBASE offers three general
report layouts: the column layout, the form layout, and the
mailmerge layout. You can use any of the general layouts as the starting point for designing your report. These general formats are summarized here.

Column layout   Data is printed in even-sized columns. A
                       report that presents data as a list or that
                       includes totals or subtotals would likely
                       use a column layout. The sample report
                       in Figure 7.13 uses a column layout to
                       print sales information.

Form layout   Data is not presented in even columns,
                       but is instead stacked or arranged in
                       some other free-form format. (The
                       customer list report shown in Figure 7.14
                       later in this chapter uses the form layout.
                       Note that there are no evenly spaced
                       columns of information on the screen.)

Mailmerge layout   This layout is usually used to combine a
                       large body of text with information from
                       a database. This is the layout you use to
                       create form letters. (*Mailmerge* is a
                       computer term derived from the fact that
                       you *merge* the text of a typewritten letter
                       with names and addresses from a
                       database to create form letters, or *mail*.)

In this book, you'll have opportunities to work with all of these different layouts. However, this chapter focuses on only the Form and Mailmerge layouts.

GENERAL TECHNIQUES FOR THE REPORTS AND LABELS DESIGN SCREENS

Before you actually begin designing fancy reports, let's take a moment to cover some of the most important techniques that you'll be using. Remember, these techniques work with *any* report, including labels, the Column layout, the Form layout, and the Mailmerge layout.

Remember too that throughout these sections *text* refers to normal typed text on the screen, like field names, blank spaces, and punctuation. *Field templates* refer to the templates (like XXXX and MM/DD/YY) that represent fields from the database.

ADDING AND DELETING TEXT

You can place text, such as words, punctuation marks, and blank spaces, anywhere in a report or label format. You've seen examples of this already, when you placed a comma and a space between the CITY and STATE fields on the label format so the contents of those fields would be printed in the format *San Diego, CA*. Here are the general techniques to follow:

INSERTING NEW TEXT   To insert new text into a report or label format

- Move the cursor to where you want the start of the new text to appear.

- Make sure you are in Insert Mode (press the Ins or Insert key until the Ins indicator appears in the status bar, near the lower-right corner of the screen).

- Type your new text (you can also press the space bar to insert blank spaces).

CHANGING EXISTING TEXT If you simply want to change existing text (not insert new text), use the same basic steps above, but without the insert mode on (pressing the Ins or Insert key turns the insert mode on and off). The new text that you type will overwrite existing text. However, any field templates to the immediate right of the cursor will still scroll to the right to make room for new text.

DELETING A SMALL AMOUNT OF TEXT If you want to delete a small amount of text on a single line (such as a few words or characters), just follow these simple steps:

- Move to the leftmost character that you want to delete.
- Press the Del (or Delete) key until all the text is deleted.

Be careful not to delete any field templates, or you'll have to figure out which ones you've deleted, then put them back onto the screen using the techniques for adding fields described later in this section.

ADDING AND DELETING LINES

Any blank lines on a report (or mailing label) format also show up as blank lines on the final printed report and labels. Therefore, you may occasionally want to insert or delete blank lines to gain more control over the spacing between lines in your printed report. You might also need to insert new blank lines into a report or mailing label format in order to insert more fields or text. To insert or delete a line on a report format, the sections that follow will give you the techniques you need:

INSERTING NEW BLANK LINES To insert a new blank line in a label format or a report band, follow these basic steps:

- Move the cursor to the appropriate position:
  - If you want to place a new blank line above all other lines in the band (or on the label), move the cursor to the beginning of the first line (Line: 0 Column: 0) of the report band.

When designing a label format, you can only insert a new row if there is enough room on the label format to fit in another row.

- If you want to insert a new blank row between two existing rows, move the cursor to the left edge (Column 0) of the bottom of those two rows.
- If you want to insert a blank row at the bottom of the report band (below all current rows), move the cursor to the end of the last line in the report band.
- Make sure the Insert mode is on (press the Ins or Insert key until the Ins indicator appears at the right side of the status bar near the bottom of the screen).
- Press ◄─┘.

The blank row is inserted immediately.

DELETING A LINE   To delete an entire line (including the space it occupies), you can usually follow this simple procedure:

- Move the cursor to the start of the line you want to delete.
- Press Ctrl-Y or select Remove Line from the Words pull-down menu.

Note that this does not always let you remove the last line near the bottom of a report band, mainly because dBASE often keeps a blank line between bands so that they will appear on the final report, producing a more neatly formatted report. However, you can delete the last line from a report band by moving text into it, and then perhaps deleting any blank lines above the moved text. See "Moving, Copying, and Deleting Blocks" later in this chapter.

ADDING AND DELETING FIELD TEMPLATES

As you know, a field template indicates the place where the contents of a field will be displayed in the final printed report. You can easily add and delete field templates from any report or label format using the procedures described in the sections that follow.

ADDING FIELD TEMPLATES FROM THE DATABASE   If you want to display a field from the database on your printed label or report, follow these general steps:

- Move the cursor to where you want the start of the field to appear on your printed labels or report.
- Press Add Field (F5).
- Select the name of the field that you want displayed from the leftmost column of the window that appears (move the highlighter to the field name and then press ⏎ to select it).
- Press Ctrl-End to leave the next window that appears.

You'll see the new field template on the screen immediately.

DELETING A FIELD TEMPLATE   To delete a field from the format, follow this simple procedure:

- Move the cursor into the field template that you want to delete.
- Press the Del (or Delete) key.

That's all there is to it.

MOVING, COPYING, AND DELETING BLOCKS

You can easily move, copy, and/or delete *blocks* of text on the reports or labels design screen. A block is simply any section within a report band—be it text, a field template, or any combination of text and field templates.

The basic procedure is fairly simple, but there is always the slight chance that you might inadvertently overwrite or delete some existing text or field templates, and therefore lose some of your work. To avoid this, it's a good idea to first do a "quick save" of your work so far without leaving the reports or labels design screen. The next section describes how.

QUICK SAVE OF A FORMAT   To perform a quick save of a format without leaving the design screen, follow these steps:

- Press Menu (F10) and pull down the Layout menu.
- Select Save This Report or Save This Label Design.
- If you've previously saved the file, just press ◄─┘ to accept the previous name. Otherwise, type in a valid DOS file name (eight letters, no spaces or punctuation), then press ◄─┘.

When dBASE finishes saving the file (and the pull-down menu disappears) you can proceed with your move, copy, or delete operation.

HIGHLIGHTING A BLOCK   To highlight a block on the labels or reports design screen, follow these steps:

- If you are moving a field template, move the cursor into that template. If you are moving a larger block, move the cursor to a corner of that block.
- Press Select (F6).
- If you are moving only a single field template, skip to the next step now. Otherwise, use the →, ←, ↓, and ↑ arrow keys to extend the highlighter over the entire block you wish to move, copy, or delete.
- Press ◄─┘ to complete the selection.
- If you want to delete the highlighted field template or block, press the Del (or Delete) key, then skip the remaining steps.
- To move the highlighted block, press Move (F7); to copy the block, press Copy (F8).
- Use the ↑, ↓, →, and ← arrow keys to move the ''ghost image'' of the block to where you want the highlighted area moved or copied.
- Press ◄─┘ to complete the move/copy.

If you have moved the ''ghost image'' so that it is overlapping existing text and field templates, you'll see the message ''Delete covered text and fields? (Y/N).'' You will need to determine on your own

NOTE

When highlighting a large block, any partially highlighted field templates will be ignored when you copy, move, or delete the block. So if you want to include a template in an operation, be sure the entire template is highlighted.

TIP

It's a good idea to press Esc once after pressing ◄─┘ to complete the move/copy, as this immediately ''unselects'' the current block or template and prevents you from inadvertently deleting the whole thing when you press the Del or Delete key.

whether it's okay to delete the text and field templates that are currently covered by the ghost image.

If you are moving the entire format (that is, all the text and field templates), then you can simply answer Yes (by typing Y) because everything that is being deleted will immediately be replaced as soon as the move/copy is complete.

However, if you are moving or copying a small area, you might want to double check before answering Yes. Select No (by typing N) to see what, exactly, is being covered by the ghost image.

If it's okay to delete the text and field templates that are covered by that image, press ⏎ and answer Yes when asked again about deleting that covered area. If it is not okay to delete the covered text and field templates, use the arrow keys to reposition the ghost image to a new location, then press ⏎ to complete the move/copy. If you cannot find a satisfactory location for the ghost image, press Esc three times in response to the "Delete covered text and fields?" prompt to cancel the operation and "unselect" the currently selected area.

RECALLING THE QUICK SAVE   If during the course of your move/copy/delete operations you manage to make more of a mess than an improvement, but remembered to do your "quick save" before you got started, you can simply abandon the current version of the format and retrieve the copy you previously saved. Here's how:

- Press Esc and answer "Yes" to the prompts about abandoning the current format until you get back to the Control Center.

- At the Control Center, highlight the name of the format you were just working on (chances are, it is already highlighted).

- Press Design (Shift-F2).

A copy of the format as it was when you last saved it is now on the design screen, ready for editing. Any mistakes you made since the last time you saved the format, of course, are not included because they were never saved.

THE CUSTOMER LIST REPORT

To give you some experience with the reports design screen, we'll develop a sample customer list report that displays some CUSTLIST data in the format shown in Figure 7.14. This format is relatively simple. The page header contains only the current date—6/30/91 in the example. The report intro is Customer List. The detail lists the name, address, and other information about each person. The page footer displays the word *Page* and the page number.

To start developing the report, you need to get to the reports design screen. Let's get started.

USING THE REPORTS DESIGN SCREEN

To access the reports design screen, open the database file that contains the data that you want to print and then select <create> from the Reports panel. Here are the steps to begin creating the sample customer list report for this chapter:

1. If CUSTLIST is not currently in use, highlight CUSTLIST in the Data panel, press ←⎯, and select Use File.

2. Highlight <create> in the Reports panel and press ←⎯. You'll see the reports design screen, partially obscured by the Layout menu. For now, press Esc to remove the Layout menu. Your screen should look like Figure 7.15.

As you can see, the reports design screen has many of the same characteristics as other design screens. The menu bar at the top of the screen has pull-down menus associated with it, which you open, as usual, by pressing F10. The ruler just beneath the menu bar shows margins and tab stops. At the bottom of the screen, the navigation line displays special keys that you can use to format your report.

The center of the screen, where you design the format of the report, is currently divided into five *bands*. Each band corresponds to a section of the printed report. Anything that you place within a band is printed only in the corresponding section of the report. For example, any text that you place in the Page Header band is printed at the top of each printed page.

```
06/15/91


                                   Customer List

          Adams, Annie
               3456 Ocean St.
               Santa Monica, CA   92001
               Phone: (714)555-0123
               Starting date: 01/01/91   Paid: N

          Beach, Sandy   American Widget
               11 Elm St.
               Portland, OR   76543
               Phone: (717)555-0898
               Starting date: 12/15/90   Paid: Y

          Kenney, Ralph
               1101 Rainbow Ct.
               Los Angeles, CA   96607
               Phone: (213)555-9988
               Starting date: 12/30/90   Paid: N

          Mahoney, Mary
               211 Seahawk St.
               Seattle, WA   88977
               Phone: (206)555-8673
               Starting date: 12/01/90   Paid: Y

          Newell, John   LoTech Co.
               734 Rainbow Dr.
               Butte, MT   54321
               Phone: (303)555-6739
               Starting date: 12/15/90   Paid: Y

          Schumack, Susita   SMS Software
               47 Broad St.
               Philadelphia, PA   45543
               Phone: (202)555-9720
               Starting date: 12/30/90   Paid: Y

          Smith, Anita   Zeerocks, Inc.
               2001 Engine Dr.
               Hideaway, CA   92220
               Phone: (415)555-9854
               Starting date: 01/01/91   Paid: Y

          Smith, John   ABC Co.
               123 A St.
               San Diego, CA   92067
               Phone: (619)555-1234
               Starting date: 11/15/90   Paid: Y

          Watson, Wilbur   HiTech Co.
               P.O. Box 987
               New York, NY   12345
               Phone: (212)555-9988
               Starting date: 11/15/90   Paid: Y




                                   Page:   1
```

Figure 7.14: The Customer List report

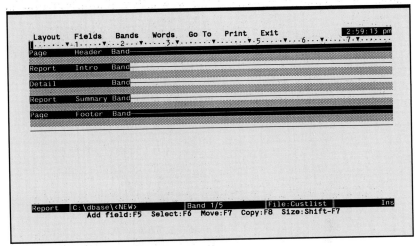

Figure 7.15: The reports design screen

SELECTING A GENERAL FORMAT

As mentioned earlier, dBASE IV lets you select from three general layouts for printing your report: column layout, form layout, and mailmerge layout. You can use a general layout as the starting point for designing your own report. For this particular example, we'll use the form layout as the starting point. Follow these steps:

1. Press Menu (F10) to pull down a menu.

2. Highlight Layout on the menu bar.

3. Select Quick Layouts.

4. Select Form Layout.

dBASE creates a general report format with the page number and date in the Page Header band. The Detail band contains the name of each field in the CUSTLIST database and a template for each field. Figure 7.16 shows this initial report format.

SETTING THE RIGHT MARGIN

After you have selected a general format for your report, it's a good idea to then select margins. Selecting margins now will let you

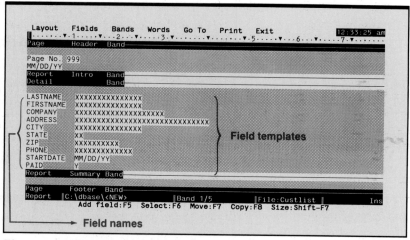

Figure 7.16: Initial form layout suggested by dBASE IV

more easily center titles or other information in your report. When printing on 8 ½ by 11-inch paper, a right margin setting of about 64 will provide adequate left and right margins on the printed page. To set the margins for the customer list report now, follow these steps:

1. Press F10 to access the pull-down menus.

2. Use ← or → to scroll to the Words option on the menu bar.

3. Select Modify Ruler (the cursor will move to the ruler).

4. Press Tab eight times to move to column 64.

5. Type] to mark the right margin (the] key is near the ← key on most keyboards).

6. Press Ctrl-End to finish modifying the ruler.

Notice that you adjusted only the position of the right margin in the preceding steps. There is usually no need to adjust the left margin, because dBASE automatically prints a left margin on the printed page. That is, even if you leave the left margin at column zero (where it is now, as you can see by the [symbol in the ruler), your printed

NOTE

Most tractor-feed printers allow you to slide the paper to the left or right to set the left margin.

report will still have about a 1-inch margin on the left. (See "Controlling Page Length and Margins" under "Controlling the Printer" later in this chapter if you need to adjust the left margin.)

REARRANGING THE INITIAL FORMAT

Now you can rearrange the field templates and text on the initial format into any format that you wish. We'll do so in the sections that follow and make use of many of the reports design screen editing keys (listed in Table 7.1 earlier in this chapter). Figure 7.17 at the end of this section shows the report format that we want for the customer list report as it appears on the reports design screen when completed. You can use that figure as a guide as you rearrange the format in the sections that follow.

Notice that, as with labels, the current position of the cursor is indicated in the status line. Use this indicator to help you position the cursor as you follow the steps below. But be sure that the cursor is in the correct band, because lines are numbered starting at zero within each band.

The cursor's line and column positions do not appear on your screen until the cursor is inside a band.

CHANGING THE PAGE HEADER BAND

First let's delete the page number from the Page Header band. Later, we'll put the page number at the bottom of each page. Here are the steps:

1. Press ↓ to move the cursor to line 0, column 0 in the Page Header band.

2. Press Ctrl-Y twice to delete the next two lines.

3. Press End to move the cursor to the end of the date template (MM/DD/YY).

4. Press Ctrl-N twice to insert two blank lines.

The page header now consists of the current date and two blank lines. dBASE will print this page header at the top of every page.

ADDING A REPORT INTRODUCTION

Now let's add a report introduction, which will appear on the first printed page. Here are the steps:

1. Press ↓ three times to move the cursor to the Report Intro band border. (The line position at the bottom of the screen shows Band 2/5.)

2. Press ↵ to open the band.

3. Press ↓ to move the cursor into the band (the cursor position states that you are at line 0, column 8).

4. Make sure insert mode is on. (If the Ins indicator does not appear in the lower-right corner in the status bar, press the Ins key until it does.)

5. Press ↵. Notice that this adds a new blank line in the Report Intro header, which will in turn print a blank line on the printed report.

6. Type the report heading **Customer List**.

7. To center the heading, press F10 and select Position from the Words pull-down menu. Then select Center from the submenu.

8. Press End and ↵ to add another blank line.

This takes care of the page header and report introduction. Let's get to work on the Detail band now.

> **NOTE**
>
> Pressing ↵ adds new blank lines *only* when Insert mode is on. Pressing Ctrl-N adds a new blank line regardless of whether Insert mode is on.

MODIFYING THE DETAIL BAND

Before we start modifying the Detail band, let's look at what it contains. The field names at the left (such as LASTNAME and FIRSTNAME) are text that will appear on the report exactly as they do on the screen (unless you remove them). The field templates (such as X's, MM/DD/YY, and Y) show where the data from the database will appear (just as in the labels design screen). For example, the name Smith will appear in place of the X's to the right of LASTNAME, and the start date will appear in place of MM/DD/YY to the right of STARTDATE.

Our printed report will not use any of the field names, but will use all of the field templates. Reformatting the field templates into the format we want will require many steps, but these steps will give you some good hands-on experience in using the reports design screen, which you will use to develop your own formatted reports in the future. Also, remember that you have to design a report format only once. You can then use this format over and over again to print data. Therefore, time spent designing a report is time well spent.

1. Press ↓ three times to move the cursor to the *L* in the LASTNAME field name.

2. Press End to move the cursor to line 1, column 26.

3. Type a comma and then press the space bar. This will ensure that a comma and blank space appear after the last name on the printed report.

4. Use the ↓ and ← keys to move the cursor to the FIRSTNAME template (line 2, column 11).

5. Press Select (F6) and then ↵ to select that template (it will be highlighted on your screen).

6. Press Move (F7) to begin to move the template.

7. Use the ↑ and → keys to move the ghost image of the template to line 1, column 28.

8. Press ↵ to complete the move.

9. Press End to move to the end of the template.

10. Press the space bar three times to insert three blank spaces.

11. Use the ↓ and ← keys to move the cursor to the COMPANY field template (line 3, column 11).

12. Press Select (F6) and ↵ to select the template.

13. Press Move (F7) and use the arrow keys to move the ghost image to line 1, column 46.

14. Press ↵ to complete the move.

15. Use the arrow keys to move the cursor to the ADDRESS field template (line 4, column 11).

Remember that whenever the cursor is in a field template, the name of the field appears at the bottom of the screen.

When you press Select (F6) or Move (F7), the navigation line provides instructions regarding what to do next.

NOTE

Ignore the field names to the left of the templates during these steps—you'll be removing them soon anyway.

16. Press Select (F6), End, ↓, and then ← to select the ADDRESS and CITY field templates.

17. Press Move (F7) and use the arrow keys to move the ghost image to line 2, column 16.

18. Press ← to complete the move.

19. Use the arrow keys to move to the end of the CITY field template (line 3, column 31).

20. Type a comma and then press the space bar (so that the printed report will show a comma and blank space).

21. Use the arrow keys to move the cursor to the STATE field template (line 6, column 11).

22. Press Select (F6) and then ← to select the template.

23. Press Move (F7) and use the arrow keys to move the ghost image to the right of the comma and space (line 3, column 33).

24. Press ← to complete the move.

25. Press End to move to the end of the STATE template (line 3, column 35).

26. Press the space bar three times to insert three blank spaces.

27. Use the arrow keys to move the cursor to the ZIP template (line 7, column 11).

28. Press Select (F6) and then ← to select the template.

29. Press Move (F7), move the ghost image to line 3, column 38, and then press ← to complete the move.

30. Move the cursor to line 4, column 16.

31. Type the word **Phone:** and then press the space bar.

32. Move the cursor into the PHONE field template (line 8, column 11).

33. Press Select (F6) and then ← to select the template.

34. Press Move (F7), use the arrow keys to move the ghost image to line 4, column 23, and then press ← to complete the move.

NOTE

Selected (highlighted) text or fields remain selected after moving. You can press Esc once to "unselect" text or fields.

35. Move the cursor to line 5, column 16.

36. Type the words **Starting date:** and press the space bar.

37. Move the cursor to the STARTDATE field template (MM/DD/YY in line 9, column 11).

38. Press Select (F6) and then ◄──┘ to select the template.

39. Press Move (F7), move the ghost image to line 5, column 31, and press ◄──┘.

40. Press End and then press the space bar twice to move the cursor to line 5, column 41.

41. Type the word **Paid:** and then press the space bar.

42. Move the cursor into the PAID field template (the Y in line 10, column 11).

43. Press Select (F6) and then press ◄──┘.

44. Press Move (F7), move the ghost image to line 5, column 47, and then press ◄──┘.

45. Press Home, and ↑ several times until the cursor gets to the *L* in the LASTNAME field name (line 1, column 0).

46. Press Select (F6), press the → key eight times, and press the ↓ key nine times to highlight all the field names (but *not* any of the field templates).

47. Press ◄──┘ to finish highlighting the field names.

48. Press the Del key to delete all the field names.

49. To move all the field templates up and to the left, first move the cursor to line 1, column 11 (to the first X in the LASTNAME field template).

50. Press Select (F6), press End, and press ↓ four times to highlight all the field templates and text. Then press ◄──┘.

51. Press Move (F7), press Home, and press PgUp to move the upper-left corner of the ghost image to line 0, column 0.

52. Press ◄──┘ to complete the move.

53. dBASE displays the message "Delete all covered text and fields? (Y/N)" because the ghost image is overlapping other text and fields. Type **Y** to answer Yes.

54. Press ↓ until the cursor gets to line 5, column 0.

55. Press Ctrl-Y five times to delete blank lines beneath the cursor position, leaving a single blank line at the bottom of the Detail band.

If you are new to computers (and a terrible typist to boot), it may have taken you a while to complete all those steps. But after you get a little practice with the reports design screen, you'll be able to perform these many steps in just a few minutes.

REARRANGING THE PAGE FOOTER BAND

The Customer List report just needs to print page numbers centered at the bottom of each page now, and you'll be done. Here are the steps to follow:

1. Press ↓ to move to the Report Summary band border (the center of the status bar shows "Band 4/5" when you get there).

2. Press ⏎ to close the band (as we will not include a report summary in the customer list).

3. Press ↓ twice to move to the Page Footer band (the status bar now shows that you are at line 0, column 0).

4. Press Ctrl-N to insert a blank line.

5. Press ↓ once to move to line 1, column 0 in the Page Footer band.

6. Type the word **Page:** and then press the space bar.

7. Press the Field key (F5) to add a field template.

8. A menu appears showing all of the fields that can be placed in the current report format. Select Pageno from the column labeled PREDEFINED.

9. Press Ctrl-End to leave the display attributes window.

10. To center the page number, press Menu (F10) and select Position from the Words pull-down menu.

11. Select Center from the submenu.

Note that the page number template appears as 999 on the report format, which indicates that dBASE is saving space for three digits in the page number. We'll discuss the other options that appeared on the screen when you pressed F5 a little later.

You are now finished designing the report. Your screen should look like Figure 7.17.

Figure 7.17: The completed format for the Customer List report

SAVING A REPORT FORMAT

Now let's save all this hard work and then use this format to print a customer list. First, as we've done before, we'll add a description to the format.

1. Press Menu (F10) and highlight Layout on the menu bar.

2. Select Edit Description of Report.

3. Type the description **List of customer names and addresses** and then press ◄┘.

4. To actually save the report format and description, press Menu (F10) again and highlight Exit on the menu bar.

5. Select Save Changes and Exit.

6. When dBASE presents the prompt "Save as:" type a valid file name—**LIST**, in this example—and press Enter.

dBASE will take some time to write a program for itself to print the report later. When that's all done, it will return you to the Control Center. You'll see the LIST report name in the Reports panel.

PRINTING THE CUSTOMER LIST

When you get back to the Control Center, you can use the same basic technique that you used with labels to print the Customer List report; that is, highlight the report name in the Reports panel and press ◄┘. Select Print Report from the options that appear. When the print submenu appears, select either Begin Printing to actually print the report or View Report on Screen to preview the printed report on your screen.

If you'd like to print the customer list report right now, follow these basic steps:

1. Highlight LIST in the Reports panel of the Control Center.

2. Press ◄┘.

3. Select Print Report.

4. To print the report, select Begin Printing. Optionally, to see the report on the screen only, select View Report on Screen.

In the section titled "Controlling the Printer" later in this chapter, we'll solve any formatting problems you may have encountered while printing.

The results should look like the original example of the report shown in Figure 7.14. If you are using a laser printer, you may need to eject the page from the printer. Follow steps 1 through 3 and select Eject Page Now from the Print menu. Then press Esc to return to the Control Center. If you opted to view the report on the screen only, follow the instructions at the bottom of the screen until you are returned to the Control Center.

In the next section, you will create yet another printed report: a form letter. If you are ready to take a break now, go ahead and exit dBASE IV in the usual manner (select Quit to DOS from the Exit pull-down menu). When you are ready to proceed with the next section in this chapter, get dBASE up and running again on your computer and make sure the LEARN catalog is in the Control Center.

CREATING FORM LETTERS

To create form letters with dBASE IV, you can take advantage of a special feature called the *word-wrap editor*, so called because it automatically wraps paragraphs inside of any margins, always breaking lines between words rather than within words. This capability gives you much of the power and flexibility of a word processor—you can easily create, change, delete, and add text to perfect your letter, and the word-wrap editor takes care of the formatting automatically.

Even though the word-wrap editor offers special features, keep in mind that a form letter is like any other report in dBASE. You create the form letter through the reports design screen. After you have saved it, its name appears in the Reports panel of the Control Center, and you can print it at any time using the same techniques you use to print mailing labels and other reports.

Let's create a sample form letter now, so you can gain some experience with the word-wrap editor. Figure 7.18 shows a copy of the letter you will eventually create. Note that the name and address on the letter come directly from the database. dBASE will print a letter for every record in the database or for records you specify in a query (for example, for New York residents only or for people who are late in paying). Follow these steps to get started:

1. If the CUSTLIST database name is not above the line in the Data panel, highlight CUSTLIST, press ↵, and select Use File to open that database.

2. Highlight <create> in the Reports panel and press ↵.

3. When you get to the reports design screen, select Quick Layouts from the Layout pull-down menu.

4. Select Mailmerge Layout to start creating your form letter.

```
01/15/91

Anita Smith
2001 Engine Dr.
Hideaway, CA  92220

Dear Anita:

Believe it or not, this is a form letter!  My new dBASE IV
program lets me add text, delete it, and make changes and
corrections.

Not only can I type up a storm, but I can also use dBASE IV's
many other capabilities with my form letters, including:

         Sorting form letters and matching mailing labels
         into zip code order for bulk mailing.

         Selecting particular people to print letters and
         mailing labels for, such as yourself, Anita.

Sincerely,


Alfred Winstein
```

Figure 7.18: Sample form letter

dBASE automatically closes all report bands except for the Detail band. The Detail band lengthens to accommodate a large body of text. But you are not limited to the space initially displayed in the Detail band; the Detail band will lengthen to accommodate as much text as you enter.

SETTING MARGINS

It's especially important to set your right margin immediately *after* selecting the Mailmerge Layout option from the Quick Layouts menu, but *before* you start typing your text. Otherwise, you will have to reset the right margin for each paragraph you type. So let's go ahead and set the right margin for this form letter now, before typing any text. Follow these steps:

1. Press Menu (F10) and move to the Words pull-down menu.

2. Select Modify Ruler.

3. Press Tab eight times to move the cursor to column 64 on the ruler.

4. Type] to mark the right margin.

5. Press Ctrl-End to finish the operation.

Now that the margins are set, you can start typing the text of your letter.

WRITING THE TEXT OF THE LETTER

Because you selected mailmerge layout as the general format for the report, the Detail band is already in word-wrap mode, which means that you can take advantage of the word-wrap editor right now.

When using the word-wrap editor, there is just one important point to keep in mind: *Do not press the* ◄─┘ *key until you get to the end of a paragraph.* If you are accustomed to typing on a conventional typewriter, you'll be tempted to press ◄─┘ as soon as you get to the end of a line. Or you might be tempted to press ◄─┘ as soon as you get to the end of a sentence. But you'll need to break these habits right now and let dBASE take care of formatting lines and sentences within paragraphs.

Type the first paragraph of the letter now, as shown here. Don't worry about matching the spacing or margins on your screen to those here—just type the paragraph without ever pressing ◄─┘. (You can still use the Backspace and other editing keys to make corrections as necessary.)

> **Believe it or not, this is a form letter! My new dBASE IV program lets me type up a storm. I can add text, delete it, and make changes and corrections.**

After you type the paragraph, you'll no doubt notice that dBASE has automatically word-wrapped the entire paragraph to the margins you've specified. The paragraph is a single *block* of text now. As you'll see, you can do quite a few things with a block of text. But for now, let's proceed with the letter.

Press ◄─┘ twice to start a new paragraph (block). Then type the next block of text (again, without pressing ◄─┘).

> **Not only can I type up a storm, but I can also use dBASE IV's many other capabilities with my form letters, including:**

Now press ← twice and type the following sentence, again without pressing the ← key:

> Sorting form letters and matching mailing labels into zip code order for bulk mailing.

After typing the entire preceding sentence, press ← twice. Then type the following sentence (without pressing ←):

> Selecting particular people to print letters and mailing labels for, such as yourself,

Now press ← twice and type the word **Sincerely,** (including the comma). Then press ← twice again and type the name **Alfred Winstein**.

At this point, the Detail band on your reports design screen should look something like Figure 7.19. Of course, this is only the body of the letter, and we still need to add the name and address. But before we do so, let's take a look at some of the interesting formatting features of the word-wrap editor.

WORKING WITH BLOCKS OF TEXT

You can use all the usual editing keys to make changes and corrections to your form letter, including the arrow keys to position the

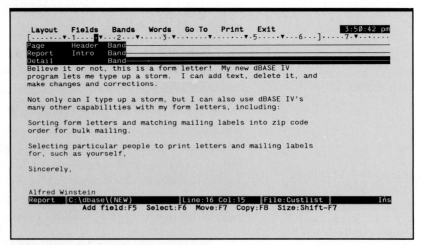

Figure 7.19: The text of the form letter

cursor, the Del key to delete characters, the Backspace key, and the Ins key to switch between insert and overwrite modes. You can also use any special key listed in the navigation line.

As in the customer list report you developed earlier in this chapter, you can mark blocks of text to copy, move, or delete. For example, suppose you want to remove the words "type up a storm. I can" from the first paragraph of the letter. Follow these steps to do so:

1. Press the ↑ and other arrow keys, as necessary, to move the cursor to the blank space in front of the letter *t* in *type* (at line 1, close to column 15).

2. Press Select (F6).

3. Press → until the highlight covers the words *type up a storm. I can* (if you go too far, press ← to back up).

4. Press ⏎ to complete the selection (or highlighting).

5. Press the Del key to delete the highlighted text.

6. The prompt "Press y to perform the block deletion" will appear at the bottom of the screen to double-check your intentions.

7. Press Y, for yes.

Instantly, dBASE removes the highlighted text and automatically reformats the entire paragraph so that it still fits perfectly within the margins. Keep in mind that once you highlight a block of text with the Select (F6) key, you can also move or copy that text using the Move (F7) or Copy (F8) key. (The navigation line at the bottom of the screen reminds you that these features are available.) You may want to experiment with those features on your own later.

REFORMATTING PARAGRAPHS

NOTE

You can control the amount of indentation by changing the tab stops, as discussed later in this chapter.

Now suppose you want to indent the last two sentences (or blocks) in the letter. Indenting is a breeze in the word-wrap editor, as you'll see when you follow these steps:

1. Use the arrow and Home keys to move the cursor to the letter *S* in the word *Sorting* (about line 7, column 0).

2. Press the Tab key.

3. Use the ↓ key to move the cursor to the letter *S* in the word *Selecting* (about line 10, column 0).

4. Press the Tab key again.

Both blocks of text are now indented, and dBASE has reformatted each one accordingly, as shown in Figure 7.20. (If you feel like experimenting a bit, try pressing the Tab key three times to indent further and then press the Shift-Tab key three of times to delete the indent. Watch what happens on the screen each time you press Tab and Shift-Tab.)

ADDING DATABASE FIELDS

Our form letter is not quite ready for printing yet because it is not addressed to anyone. Let's place some field templates from the CUSTLIST database on the form letter to show dBASE where it needs to place names and addresses when it prints the letter.

To place field templates on the letter, use the same techniques that you used when placing field templates on the mailing labels and customer list report. That is, position the cursor where you want the

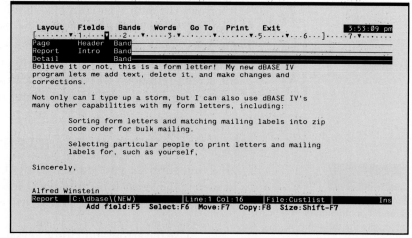

Figure 7.20: Two blocks of text indented using the Tab key

field to begin and press the Field key (F5). Then select the name of the field you want to display and press Ctrl-End. Let's go through this procedure step by step.

1. Press the Home and ↑ keys until the cursor gets to the letter *B* in the word *Believe* (line 0, column 0 in the Detail band).

2. Press Ctrl-N eight times to make room.

3. To place the current date at the top of the form letter, press Field (F5) and select Date from the Predefined column of the submenu that appears.

4. Press Ctrl-End to leave the Display Attributes menu that appears.

5. Press ↓ twice to move to line 2, column 0.

6. Press Field (F5) and select FIRSTNAME from the CUSTLIST panel of the submenu that appears.

7. Press Ctrl-End to leave the Display Attributes menu.

8. Press the End key and then press the space bar to insert a blank space.

9. Press Field (F5), select LASTNAME, and press Ctrl-End.

10. Press ↓, press Field (F5), and select ADDRESS.

11. Press Ctrl-End to leave the Display Attributes submenu.

12. Press ↓, press Field (F5), and select CITY.

13. Press Ctrl-End to leave the Display Attributes menu.

14. Press the End key to move to the end of the CITY field template.

15. Type a comma (,) and then press the space bar.

16. Press Field (F5) and select STATE from the CUSTLIST panel of the submenu that appears.

17. Press Ctrl-End to leave the Display Attributes submenu.

18. Press the End key to move to the end of the STATE field template (line 4, column 19).

19. Press the space bar twice to insert two blank spaces.

20. Press Field (F5), select ZIP, and press Ctrl-End to leave the Display Attributes submenu.

21. Press the ↓ key twice to move to line 6, column 0.

22. Type the word **Dear** and press the space bar to insert a space.

23. Press Field (F5), select FIRSTNAME, and then press Ctrl-End to leave the Display Attributes submenu.

24. Press the End key to move to the end of the FIRSTNAME field template and then type a colon (:).

Steps 22 through 24 set up your form letter to present a greeting at the top of your letter, such as **Dear John:**. At this point, your letter should look like Figure 7.21. (Some of the text is scrolled off the bottom of the screen, but don't worry; it's still there.)

You're not quite finished yet, because the form letter prints the recipient's first name again near the bottom of the letter. Follow these steps to place the FIRSTNAME template accordingly:

1. Press the ↓ key about 13 times and then press the End key to move the cursor to the right of the words "such as yourself,".

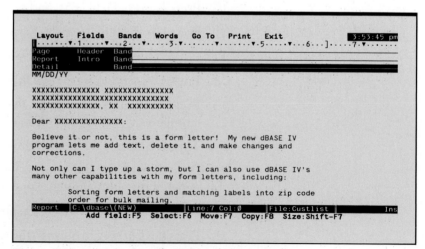

Figure 7.21: Form letter with field templates added

2. Press the space bar to insert a blank space.

3. Press Field (F5) and select FIRSTNAME as the field to place.

4. Press Ctrl-End to leave the Display Attributes submenu.

5. Press the End key to move past the end of the FIRSTNAME field template (about line 19, column 53).

6. Type a period (.).

SAVING THE FORM LETTER

Now you have finished the sample form letter. Go ahead and add a description to the form letter and save it using the file name FORMLET, following these steps:

1. Press Menu (F10) and select Edit Description of Report from the Layout pull-down menu.

2. When prompted, type the description **Example form letter** and then press ←⟋.

3. Press F10 and select Save Changes and Exit from the Exit pull-down menu.

4. When prompted, type a file name such as **FORMLET** and then press ←⟋.

You'll need to wait a few seconds while dBASE prepares a program for printing the form letter. When dBASE is done with this task, it returns you to the Control Center. The name of the form letter, FORMLET, will appear in the Reports panel of the Control Center.

PRINTING THE FORM LETTER

To print the form letter, follow the same basic steps you used to print mailing labels and the customer list report. That is, highlight FORMLET in the Reports panel and then press ←⟋. Select Print

Report from the options that appear and then either Begin Printing or View Report on Screen from the Print menu. Then follow the instructions that appear on the screen.

Figure 7.18 earlier in this chapter presented an example of how the printed letter will appear on your screen or printer. Of course, dBASE will print many letters: one for each record in the CUST-LIST database. The general format of each letter will be the same, but each will be addressed to a single individual in the CUSTLIST database.

SORTING REPORTS AND LABELS FOR PRINTING

To print reports or mailing labels in sorted order, activate the appropriate index and then print the report or labels. The following example prints the Customer List in alphabetical order. Here are the steps:

1. From the Control Center, highlight CUSTLIST in the Data panel and press Data (F2) to get to the edit/browse screen.

2. Press Alt-O, then select Order Records by Index from the Organize menu.

3. Select the LASTNAME index.

4. Press Ctrl-End or select Exit from the Exit pull-down menu.

5. In the Reports panel, highlight LIST and press ←.

6. Select Print Report.

7. Select either Begin Printing or View Report on Screen, whichever you prefer.

The report will be sorted in the order you wanted. To print mailing labels and form letters in zip code order, you follow the same basic steps, but select ZIP as the index for organizing records in step 3.

USING QUERIES
TO PRINT REPORTS AND LABELS

You can use any existing query to filter records that are printed in a report or as labels. The only requirement is that the view skeleton in the query must include all the fields that the form or report displays.

The PHONELST query created in Chapter 6 did not include all the fields from the CUSTLIST database, so let's create a new query now. Here are the steps to create a query called CALCUST to list all California customers in zip code order:

1. If necessary, open the CUSTLIST database by highlighting its name in the Data panel, pressing ←, and selecting Use File.

2. Highlight <create> in the Queries panel and press ←.

3. Tab to the STATE field and enter the filter condition **"CA"** (including the quotation marks). Press ←.

4. Press Menu (F10) and select Include Indexes from the Fields pull-down menu.

5. Tab to the ZIP field, press F10, and select Sort on This Field from the Fields pull-down menu.

6. Select Ascending ASCII. "Asc1" should appear in the ZIP field.

7. Press F10 and select Edit Description of Query from the Layout pull-down menu.

8. Type the description **California customer names and addresses** and press ←.

9. Select Save Changes and Exit from the Exit pull-down menu.

10. Type the file name **CALCUST** and press ← when prompted for a file name.

When you return to the Control Center, you can use the query to print reports (including form letters) or mailing labels by activating the query and then printing the appropriate reports. Here are the exact steps:

1. If CALCUST is not already in use (if it does not appear above the thin line in the Queries panel), highlight CALCUST in the Queries panel, press ◄─┘, and select Use View.

2. Highlight the name of a report or label format in the Reports or Labels panel (either LIST or MAILING in this example) and then press ◄─┘.

3. Select Print Label or Print Report.

4. If dBASE double-checks your intentions, select Current View.

5. Select Begin Printing or View Labels/Report on Screen, whichever you prefer.

The printed report will list only California residents, sorted into zip code order.

The query will stay in effect for any other reports that you print, until you deactivate it either by opening another query or database file, or by selecting the current query name from the Queries panel and choosing Close View.

� NOTE

The remainder of this chapter discusses general options and techniques for printing reports and labels. You may just want to skim through all of this for now and refer to this chapter later if you need help with a particular problem.

MODIFYING AN EXISTING FORMAT

After you've printed your reports or labels, you may decide you want to make some changes to the format. Some changes, such as margins, page length, and page alignment, may be printer issues, in which case you may want to adjust your printer settings rather than the report format. See the section "Controlling the Printer" later in this chapter for more information.

In other cases you might want to change the size and or placement of text and fields in the report or labels. In that case, you want to return to the reports design (or labels design) screen, and make your changes. Here's how:

- Highlight the name of the report or label format that you want to change in the Reports or Labels panel of the Control Center.
- Press Design (Shift-F2).

Here you can use all the techniques we described earlier to add, delete, move, or copy text and field templates. Some additional techniques that you can use to refine the appearance of reports and labels are discussed in the sections that follow.

As usual, whenever you've finished modifying your format, just select Save Changes and Exit from the Exit pull-down menu (or just press Ctrl-End) to save your work and return to the Control Center.

CONTROLLING BLANK LINES

You may find that your report has too few or too many blank lines when printed. Blank lines are caused by two sources: blank lines in the report (or label) format, and the printer's line spacing setting.

Figure 7.22 shows blank lines in the CUSTLIST report format. Compare that figure to the printed report shown back in Figure 7.14

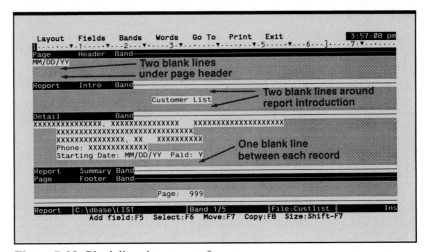

Figure 7.22: Blank lines in a report format

to see exactly how the blank lines on the format become blank lines on the printed report.

If the line spacing on your printed report or labels is too wide or narrow (for example, everything is double-spaced rather than single-spaced), and there are no blank lines in the report format to account for these blank lines, then most likely the printer line spacing is set incorrectly. See the section on line spacing in ''Controlling the Printer'' later in this chapter.

FORMATTING FIELDS

dBASE IV automatically assigns certain Display Attributes to field templates used in label and report formats. Sometimes these automatic attributes may not quite fit your needs, and you may want to change them. You can change the display attribute of a field template in a label or report format by following these steps:

- Move the cursor into the field template that you want to change.

- Press the Field key (F5), or select Modify Field from the Fields pull-down menu.

Either technique displays a submenu that describes the field and presents the Template and Picture Functions options.

CHANGING A FIELD'S PICTURE FUNCTIONS   A *picture function* is a code that tells dBASE how to display a piece of information. dBASE offers many different picture functions, which are listed on a submenu when you select Picture Functions while adding or changing a field template, as shown in Figure 7.23. You can turn any available function on or off by highlighting that option and pressing the space bar. The options relevant to label and report formats are summarized in Table 7.2.

Many of the picture functions affect how data are displayed within the width provided by the field template, as the next section explains.

CHANGING A FIELD'S WIDTH You can control the width of a field on the printed report by changing the size of the field template. By default, dBASE assigns a width that matches the field's width in the database. For example, the LASTNAME field is 15 characters wide, so

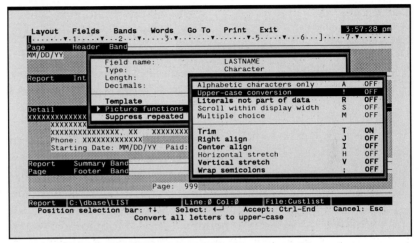

Figure 7.23: Picture Function options for Character fields

Table 7.2: Common Picture Functions for Reports and Labels

Picture function	Symbol	Effect
Uppercase conversion	!	Displays all letters (a–z) in uppercase (A–Z)
Trim	T	Removes leading and trailing blanks
Right Align	J	Right-aligns text within the space allotted for the field
Center Align	I	Centers text within the space provided
Horizontal Stretch	H	Adjusts template width to width of data
Vertical Stretch	V	Wraps text onto several lines within the allotted width

dBASE automatically places the template XXXXXXXXXXXX-XXX in the report or label format to display data from that field.

To widen or narrow a field, you can use either of two techniques:

- Move the cursor to the field template, press Size (Shift-F7), and use the → and ← keys to widen or narrow the field. Then press ◄—.

- Move the cursor to the field template, press F5, and select Template. Press Backspace or Del to narrow the template, or type X's (or other characters from Table 7.2) to widen the template. Press ◄—, then Ctrl-End when done.

Note that if you use the latter technique, dBASE will display a submenu of *character input symbols*. These are more relevant to custom forms than they are to reports, so we'll discuss them in Chapter 8.

How dBASE fits data from the database into the space allotted by the field template on the report depends upon three picture functions: Trim, Horizontal Stretch, and Vertical Stretch. For example, suppose your database contains a field named address that is 30 characters wide, but on your report, you narrow the template to 15 characters (that is, XXXXXXXXXXXXXXX). How would dBASE display the address 3456 Rancho Santa Fe Dr.?

If you assign the Trim picture function to the ADDRESS field, dBASE will *truncate* the data to fit within the template. That is, only the first 15 characters will be displayed, as follows:

3456 Rancho San

If you assign the Vertical Stretch picture function to the ADDRESS field, dBASE will word-wrap the address within the width allotted. Hence, if you print the example address using a template that is 15 characters wide and the Vertical Stretch picture function, the sample address will appear on the report as

3456 Rancho
Santa Fe Dr.

If you assign the Horizontal Stretch picture function, dBASE will automatically adjust the size of the template to fit the data being displayed. Thus, it will not matter what size you make the template. (In fact, you cannot alter the size of a field template that has the Horizontal Stretch function assigned to it.) Hence, regardless of the size of the template, the Horizontal Stretch picture function always displays the full address, in this case

    3456 Rancho Santa Fe Dr.

The Horizontal Stretch function also trims off any leading or trailing blanks when it prints data.

Note that when you assign the Vertical Stretch picture function to a field, the template appears as V's rather than X's. When either V's or X's appear, you can use the Size (Shift-F7) key to size the template. When you assign the Horizontal Stretch picture function to a field, the template appears as H's, and you cannot resize the field template.

The Center and Right Align picture functions also let you determine how data is displayed within the width provided by the field template. If you assign the Center picture function, text will be centered within the width, as in these examples:

    123 Appleton Court
      34 Reposo Alto
        123 A St.
      P.O. Box 3384

If you assign the Right Align attribute to the field, text will be right-aligned within the width allotted by the field template, as follows:

    123 Appleton Court
      34 Reposo Alto
        123 A St.
      P.O. Box 3384

After you've selected options from the Picture Functions pull-down menu, press Ctrl-End to accept those changes and return to the Display Attributes submenu. You can then press Ctrl-End a second time to return to the design screen.

DRAWING LINES AND BOXES

You can draw lines and boxes on a report format using the Box and Line options from the Layout pull-down menu. However, not all printers can print the lines and boxes. Chapter 8 discusses specific techniques for drawing lines and boxes.

SAVING YOUR CHANGES

After you've modified your label or report format, don't forget to save your work by selecting Save Changes and Exit from the Exit pull-down menu. If you do *not* want to save your changes, select Abandon Changes and Exit from the menu instead.

If you want to save your modified format as a new file (leaving the original, unmodified format intact, select Save This Report from the layout pull-down menu and provide a new file name. Then select Abandon Changes and Exit from the Exit pull-down menu.

FINDING TEXT ON THE DESIGN SCREENS

The Go To pull-down menu provides search and replace options for specific text on the reports and labels design screens. (This menu is very similar to the Go To menu discussed in Chapter 6.) These options can be handy for making corrections in a report format. For example, suppose you inadvertently use the word *peace* in place of *piece* in a form letter and want to correct all the mistakes.

Before you use the Replace option with a form letter, make sure that the cursor is in the Detail band.

You could use the Replace option on the Go To pull-down menu to automatically search for and replace the mistakes. To do so, you press F10 and select Replace from the Go To pull-down menu. When prompted, enter **peace** as the search string. Then, when prompted, enter **piece** as the replacement text. dBASE will search for the first occurrence of the word *peace* in the letter, highlight that word, and display these options:

Replace/Skip/All/Quit (R/S/A/Esc)

You can select any single option. Selecting Replace (by typing **R**) replaces the current word and moves on to the next occurrence of the word *peace*. Selecting Skip (by typing **S**) skips the current word without replacing it and moves on to the next occurrence of the word *peace.* Selecting All (by typing **A**) replaces all remaining occurrences of the word *peace* with *piece* without asking for permission. Pressing Esc cancels the search and replace operation.

CONTROLLING THE PRINTER

As you've seen in several of the preceding hands-on examples, all dBASE printing is handled by the Print pull-down menu, shown in Figure 7.24. This menu is available at the Control Center, and at the Reports and Labels Design screens as well.

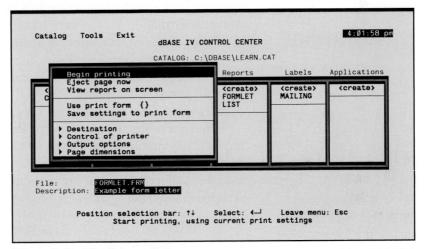

Figure 7.24: The Print pull-down menu

While trying some of the hands-on examples of reports and label formats, you used the Begin Printing option on the Print menu to actually start printing.

You may have also discovered that your printer seems "out of whack." Perhaps text is too far to the left or right, or there's too many or too few lines per page, or perhaps nothing at all printed! Most of these options can be fixed with the other options on the Print pull-down menu. We'll discuss those other options in the sections that follow.

ABOUT PRINT FORMS

Before you start changing individual options on the Print menu, it's useful to get an understanding of *print forms*. A print form is simply a collection of printer settings, or *printer defaults,* that tell dBASE some general things about how to print your report or labels.

Print forms are stored on disk in files with the extension .PRF. One print form, named REPORT.PRF, contains the "global" defaults, that is, the defaults used by all report and label formats that you design.

Each time you create a new report or label format, dBASE automatically creates a print form for that particular format as well. For example, when you created the FORMLET report, dBASE also automatically created a file named FORMLET.PRF that contained printer information for the form letter. Settings in the FORMLET-.PRF file affect only the printing of the FORMLET report.

Notice the option Use Print Form on the Print menu. This option tells you which print form is currently in use. However, if the "global" print form, REPORT.PRF, is in use, this option shows nothing other than two curly braces ({}).

Notice also the Save Settings to Print Form option on the Print menu. That option lets you save any printer settings that you choose from the Print menu for future use. Now, keep in mind the following facts as you read about the various options on the Print menu in the sections that follow:

- If you do not use the Save Settings to Print Form option on the Print menu to save your print settings, those settings affect only the next printing that you perform with the Begin Printing option. The settings are "forgotten" immediately after that printing is finished.

- If you use the Save Settings to Print Form option after making selections from the Print menu to save those settings to a particular print form file, such as FORMLET.PRF for the FORMLET report, then those settings will be used whenever you print the FORMLET report in the future. However, no other report formats will be affected by the settings stored in FORMLET.PRF.

- If you use the Save Settings to Print Form option to save your current settings in a file named REPORT.PRF, then all future reports and labels that you design will use those settings, unless you change them while designing that particular report or label format.

The last option, saving your settings to the REPORT.PRF file, is a very useful one because it lets you determine general settings for your particular printer. Even when the Use Print Form option on the Print menu shows only { } rather than a print form file name, you can rest assured that it is using settings you've previously saved in the REPORT.PRF file.

Keep in mind, however, that saving settings to the REPORT.PRF file affects *only* report and label formats you design in the future. To alter print settings on existing report or label formats, you'll need to change the print settings for those formats individually.

The actual steps for saving printer settings to a print form are listed below:

- Select Save Settings to Print Form from the Print menu.

- If a suggested print form file name is shown, and that selection is acceptable, just press ←⏎. Otherwise, type in a valid file name for the print form (for example, REPORT if you want to make the new settings "global defaults"), then press ←⏎.

- If dBASE asks if it's alright to overwrite the existing file, just press ←⏎ to select Overwrite.

Your printer settings are now saved for future use. To verify this, you can scroll through the other options on the Print menu to make sure the settings are as you want them.

USING MULTIPLE PRINTERS

If you have multiple printers attached to your computer, the first thing you should do before printing is make sure the proper printer is selected. Here's how:

- Get to the Print pull-down menu from either the Control Center or Design screen.

- Select Destination.

- Highlight Write To and press ↵ until PRINTER appears.

- Move the highlighter to the Printer Model option.

- Press ↵ until the printer model you are using appears.

- Press Ctrl-End.

- If you want to save that selection, use the Save Settings to Print Form option as described in the section "About Print Forms" earlier in this chapter.

CONTROLLING VERTICAL ALIGNMENT

When printing reports or labels, you want to make sure that dBASE always starts printing at the top of the page, rather than near the middle or bottom. On tray-fed printers (like most laser printers) this is usually an easy thing to accomplish—basically you don't have to do anything to the paper and/or printer.

But on printers that use tractor-feed paper, you have to make sure that the paper is properly aligned before you start to print. If there is any doubt in your mind about whether the report will be vertically aligned correctly, follow these simple steps:

- Turn off the printer.

- Manually crank the paper in the printer so that there is a page perforation just above the print head (the thing that does the actual printing on your printer).

- Turn the printer back on.

- Begin printing.

Once you complete the steps above, you should never "manually" crank the paper through the printer, as doing so will throw the vertical alignment out of whack (and possibly even damage the printer). Instead, use the Eject Page Now option from the Print menu, or the Form Feed button on your printer, to eject any partially printed pages from your printer.

CONTROLLING EXTRA PAGES

You may find that dBASE prints a blank page before printing your report, and/or does not print the last page of your report (or prints nothing at all when printing a one-page report!). These situations can be handled using the New Page option on the Control of Printer option. Your options there are as follows:

BEFORE	Ejects the current page before printing the report or labels
BOTH	Ejects the current page before and after printing the report or labels
NONE	Does not eject any pages from the printer
AFTER	Ejects the current page after printing the report

The best all-around setting for this option is AFTER, since it wastes the least amount of paper and also helps keep pages aligned properly in the printer. It also prevents the problem of missing pages, which are generally caused by incomplete pages stored within the printer's buffer (memory), waiting to be ejected from the printer.

To change the page eject technique default (for future reports), follow these general steps:

- At the Control Center, move the highlighter to any name in the Data panel (so that an individual report or label will not be selected).
- Press Quick Report (Shift-F9) to get to the Print menu.
- Select Control of Printer.
- Highlight New Page.
- Press the space bar or ⏎ until the option you want is selected (most likely, AFTER).

- Press Ctrl-End.
- Select Save Settings to Print Form.
- Type **REPORT** and press ◀━┛.
- Type **O** to select Overwrite when prompted.

Now the page eject technique you selected will be used in future reports that you design. Remember, existing report formats will continue to use whatever setting is currently in their print form (.PRF) files until you change those settings.

PAGE ADVANCE TECHNIQUE Another way to control how and when pages are broken while printing reports or labels is through the Advance Page Using option on the Control of Printer submenu. Two options are provided:

FORM FEED	Printer settings are used to determine where the top of the next page is
LINE FEEDS	dBASE counts how many lines are necessary to get to the top of the next page

Typically, you use the FORM FEED option when using a standard size paper, such as $8^1/_2 \times 11$ inches, or a size that your printer allows you to use through buttons or options on the printer itself (as described in your printer manual).

If your printer cannot handle an odd page length that you need to use, switch to the LINE FEEDS option (but only for reports or labels that require that odd page size). You will also need to be certain to set the Length of Page option on the Page Dimensions menu to the correct number of lines on each page so that dBASE can accurately count how many lines are needed to get to the top of the next page.

To change this setting, follow these general steps:

- Highlight the name of the report (in the Control Center) that you want to change the page advance method for.
- Press ◀━┛.
- Select Print Report.

NOTE

The Length of Page option is discussed under "Controlling Margins and Page Length" later in this chapter.

- Select Control of Printer.
- Highlight Advance Page Using.
- Press the space bar or ← until the option you want is shown.
- Press Ctrl-End.
- Use the Save Settings to Print Form option to save the selection to the print form file for the current report.

FORCING PAGE BREAKS   Another way to control page breaks is by inserting a page break character right into the report format. You do this using the Insert Page Break option on the Words pull-down menu in the Reports Design screen. See the section on "Creating a Cover Page" near the end of this chapter for an example.

CONTROLLING MARGINS AND PAGE LENGTH

Perhaps the trickiest things to control when printing with dBASE are the margins and page length. Let's take it one step at a time starting with the left margin.

CONTROLLING THE LEFT MARGIN   We usually think of the white space between the left edge of a page and the start of text as the left margin. However, in dBASE terminology, that white space is actually called the *page offset*. The left margin that you set with the [symbol on the design screen tab ruler is actually added to the distance defined by the page offset.

Now, on dot-matrix printers, the offset is largely determined by how the paper is positioned in the printer. On laser printers (and other tray-fed printers), the offset is typically .25 to .30 inches, the width of the roller that feeds the paper through the printer.

Determining an accurate page offset is a matter of adjusting the offset accordingly. For example, suppose your printer's "normal" print size is 10 characters to the inch (which you can easily determine simply by measuring with a ruler any printout you've produced so far with dBASE). Furthermore, let's say dBASE normally prints a ½-inch left margin on your report.

Now, suppose you would prefer a 1-inch margin. Well, you need to add ½-inch to the existing margin. Given that your printer is printing 10 characters to the inch, ½-inch would be five characters. So to get your 1-inch margin, you would need to change the page offset to 5.

The general steps for changing the page offset are listed below (using the "global default" technique, since it is likely that you'll want to use the same margin in most printouts):

- Highlight the name of any database file in the Data panel of the Control Center (so that a particular report or label format is not selected).

- Press Quick Report (Shift-F9).

- Select Page Dimensions.

- Select Offset from Left.

- Type in the number of spaces required to achieve the offset you want (for instance, 5 from the example preceding these steps).

- Press ◄┘.

- Press Ctrl-End.

- Use the Save Settings to Print Form option to save the selection to the REPORT.PRF print form as a general setting for future reports.

Remember, saving the settings to the REPORT.PRF file affects future reports that you design. To change the page offset for an existing report format, you need to save the new offset to the print file for that report.

Controlling the print size is covered a little later in this chapter.

SETTING THE RIGHT MARGIN   Setting the right margin is basically a matter of determining how many lines will fit across the page within the margins you specify. This, of course, is partly determined by how many lines to the inch your printer will print.

For example, suppose you want to print a particular report that uses condensed print on 8½- by 11-inch paper, and you want 1-inch margins on both the left and right side of the page. Furthermore, "condensed print" on your particular printer is about 15 cpi (characters per inch). In this case, you want to print lines that are 6.5 inches wide (the 8.5 inch page width minus the two inches for the margins). At 15 cpi, you can print about 98 characters across a 6.5 inch line (15 times 6.5 is about 98).

Now let's deal with the 1-inch margins. Let's say that when you leave the page offset at 0, your printer usually leaves about a ¼-inch left margin. But in this example you want a 1-inch margin. So, you need to change the page offset to 11 characters using the Offset from Left option on the Page Dimensions submenu from the Print menu. Why 11 characters? Because your printer is already printing a ¼-inch margin, so you need another ¾-inch. At 15 cpi, ¾-inch is about 11 characters (0.75 times 15 is about 11).

Finally, you need to set the right margin to 98. You've already had some experience with setting the right margins (see "Creating Form Letters" earlier in this chapter). As you may recall, you do this in the Reports Design screen using the Modify Ruler option on the Words pull-down menu. In this particular example, you would leave the left margin ([) at zero (since 0 on the ruler is the spot at the right of the page offset), and then set the right margin (]) at 98.

Save the report format as a print form, and when you print the report, you'll have perfect 1-inch margins on both sides of the paper, with 98 characters of text between the margins. The same basic logic used to create this example can be used to control the page layout with any combination of print size, margin size, and paper width.

CONTROLLING THE PAGE LENGTH   The length of the page you are printing on is determined by the number of *printable* lines on the page. Normally, dBASE assumes this to be 66 lines, because most printers print 6 lines to the inch and print on 8½- by 11-inch paper (6 lines per inch times 11 inches is 66 lines).

Many laser printers come factory preset to print only 60 lines per page. If you attempt to print 66 lines on such a printer, some lines from the bottom of page 1 will spill over onto the top of page 2, then page 2 will begin on the next page after that, and so forth.

There is a fairly simple solution to determining the exact number of lines that you can print per page; print one or more pages and

NOTE

You need to count blank lines as well, which can be a little tricky. You may have to experiment to get exactly the right setting.

count how many lines from page 1 spilled over onto page 2. Then subtract that amount from the number of lines printed per page. For example, if 6 lines spill over onto page 2 when the page length is set at 66, simply change the page length to 60. Here are the general steps for changing the page length:

- Get to the Print menu (either from the Control Center or the Reports/Labels design screen.

- Select Length of Page.

- Type in the correct page length (that is, 60 from the example described above).

- Press ←.

- Press Ctrl-End.

- Save the change, either to the current format only, or to the general print form settings in REPORT.PRF (as described earlier).

When using nonstandard-sized paper, such as a preprinted form that is 7½ inches long, you may need to adjust both the page length and the page advance technique, and perhaps use a little trial-and-error experimentation as well. See the earlier section titled "Page Advance Technique" for information on this topic.

CONTROLLING THE TOP AND BOTTOM MARGINS   There are no settings per se for the top and bottom margins of the page in a report printed via the report generator. The amount of white space at the top and bottom of each page is determined by the number of blank lines at the top and bottom of the Page Header and Page Footer bands (respectively), or at the top and bottom of the Report Intro and Report Summary bands (respectively) if the Page Header and Footer bands are closed.

If you change the amount of white space in any of the aforementioned bands, you need not change the page length to accommodate those changes. The blank lines at the top and bottom of each page are just counted as printed lines.

SETTING THE
INDENTATION LEVEL AND TAB STOPS

For the most part, you really need only be concerned with indentation level and tab stops when you are working in a word-wrap band, that is, when you are creating form letters. The indentation level lets you determine how far in the first line of each paragraph will be indented. Changing the tab stops lets you determine how far in an entire paragraph will be indented. In addition, you can create "outdents" (such as numbered lists) by reversing the order of the tab stop and indentation level symbols.

To set the indentation level and tab stops, follow these general steps (after selecting MailMerge Layout from the Quick Layout menu on the Reports Design screen):

- Press Alt-W or access the Words pull-down menu using the Menu (F10) key.
- Select Modify Ruler.
- Use the following keys to change the ruler:

→ ←	Moves cursor to the left and right without making changes
Tab, Shift-Tab	Moves the cursor to the left and right one tab stop
[	Marks the left margin
]	Marks the right margin
#	Sets the indentation level for the first line of a paragraph
!	Marks a tab stop (appears as a triangle)
=	Sets tab stops at even intervals
0	Resets margins and indentation back to zero
Del	Deletes current tab stop (Backspace also does this)

| Esc | Abandons current changes and uses previous settings |
| Ctrl-End | Saves current settings |

- Press Ctrl-End when you've finished modifying the ruler.

Remember that when you are in word-wrap mode, dBASE lets you reset the tab ruler for each paragraph. But to simplify matters, it's a good idea to set your margins, type in the entire body of the letter, then make changes and refinements. That way, you won't have to modify the tab ruler for each paragraph you type in.

CONTROLLING LINE SPACING

Normally dBASE prints everything single spaced. You can, however, switch to double or triple spacing if your printer can do so. To change spacing of the entire report (or all the labels), follow these general steps:

- Access the Print pull-down menu.
- Select Page Dimensions.
- Highlight Spacing of Lines.
- Press ◄─┘ until the spacing you want is shown.
- Press Ctrl-End (or ◄─).

As described earlier, you can save those settings to a print form if you wish.

You can also adjust the spacing in individual bands of a report. For example, you might want to single-space page headers and footers but double-space the body of the report. Here's how to change the spacing of an individual report band:

- Bring the report format to the Reports Design screen.
- Move the cursor to the band that you want to change the spacing of.

- Press Alt-B or use the Menu (F10) key to access the Bands pull-down menu.
- Highlight Spacing of Lines for Band.
- Press ⏎ until the option you want is shown.
- Press Ctrl-End.

Note that if you select DEFAULT as the spacing option, the report will use whatever setting is determined on the Print pull-down menu when you print the report.

PRINTING PART OF A REPORT

You can print any page or group of pages from a report. This is handy for making last minute corrections. For example, suppose you print a 20-page list of names and addresses, and notice an error on page 11. You could correct the error, then print only page 11 rather than the entire report.

To print a specific page or set of pages, follow these steps:

- Highlight the name of the report (or labels) that you want to print in the Reports panel of the Control Center.
- Press ⏎ and select Print Report.
- Select Output options.
- Select Begin on Page.
- Type in the number of the first page you want to print, and press ⏎.
- Select End after Page.
- Erase the old setting with the Delete (Del) key, then type the number of the last page you want printed (if this is the same as the Begin on Page selection, then only that page will be printed).
- Press Ctrl-End.
- Select Begin Printing when you are ready to start printing.

CONTROLLING PAGE NUMBERS

Normally dBASE starts numbering pages from page 1. However, if you are compiling a large report that is made of several smaller reports, you may want to number all the pages sequentially. Therefore, the first page of a report would not necessarily be 1. For example, if the first report constitutes pages 1–50 of a large document, and the second report constitutes pages 51–100, then the first printed page of the second report should be numbered page 51.

To have dBASE start numbering pages from some number other than 1, follow these steps:

- Highlight the name of the report (or labels) that you want to print in the Reports panel of the Control Center.
- Press ⏎ and select Print Report.
- Select Output options.
- Select First Page Number.
- Type in the page number that you want printed on the first page, then press ⏎.
- Press Ctrl-End.
- Select Begin Printing when you are ready to start printing.

PRINTING MULTIPLE COPIES

To print multiple copies of a report (or labels) follow these simple steps:

- Highlight the name of the report (or labels) that you want to print in the Reports panel of the Control Center.
- Press ⏎ and select Print Report.
- Select Output options.
- Select Number of Copies.
- Type in the number of copies you want printed, then press ⏎.
- Press Ctrl-End.
- Select Begin Printing when you are ready to start printing.

PRINTING INDIVIDUAL SHEETS

In some situations you might need to manually feed one page at a time into your printer, for example, if you normally use tractor-feed paper but want to print on letterhead which is not tractor-fed. In these situations, you need to have dBASE pause between each printed page so that you have time to remove the printed page and put in the next page to be printed.

To have dBASE pause between pages, follow these steps:

- Highlight the name of the report (or labels) that you want to print in the Reports panel of the Control Center.

- Press ⏎ and select Print Report.

- Select Control of Printer.

- Highlight Wait between Pages.

- Press ⏎ to change the setting to Yes.

- Press Ctrl-End.

- Select Begin Printing when you are ready to start printing.

SENDING CUSTOM CODES

See Appendix B for special codes for Post-Script printers.

If you want to activate a special printing feature that is not available from the dBASE menus, you can send a code directly to the printer to activate, and deactivate, that feature. The special codes that you need to send to your printer are generally listed in the manual that came with your printer.

For example, in the manual for the Hewlett Packard IID printer, I find that in order to print on manually loaded standard size envelopes, I need to send the code

Esc&l81a2h1O

to the printer. To reset the printer to print on normal paper when the envelopes are done, I need to send the code

EscE

Figure 7.25 shows a suggested label format designed to print on this type of envelope. The text in the upper-left corner is the return address; the *X*s represent fields from the CUSTLIST database in the same format used to print mailing labels in the earlier example in this chapter.

Rather than use the predefined envelope size on the Dimensions pull-down menu (in the labels design screen), I created the following (more accurate) size:

Width of label	95
Height of label	18
Indentation	0
Lines between labels	0
Spaces between label columns	0
Columns of labels	1

On the Print pull-down menu printer, we made the following adjustments:

Destination		
Write to		PRINTER
Printer model		HP LJIID1 6
Control of Printer		
New Page		NONE
Starting Control Code		{ESC}&l81a2h1O
Ending Control Code		{ESC}E

WARNING

Printer control codes are usually fussy about upper- and lowercase letters. The code {ESC}&L81A2H1o is not the same as {ESC}&l81a2h1O.

The printer destination in this example, HP LJIID1 6, is the printer driver for "normal" Laserjet printing (single sided, 6 lines to the inch). However, the Starting Control Code immediately sends a message to the printer to prepare to print envelopes instead.

When you print this label format, the Laserjet blinks and asks you to feed an envelope. You can either feed one envelope at a time or, if you have an envelope feeder, press the printer's Continue button to feed envelopes from a tray.

Figure 7.25: Label format for printing directly on envelopes

As another example of codes, suppose you want to print in landscape mode (sideways on the page), using a very small print size. On the Laserjet IID you can send

{ESC}&l1o5.45C{ESC}(s16.66 H

as the starting control code, and

{ESC}E

as the ending control code. If you set the offset from left of page to 8, and set the right margin to about 155, you'll get a neatly formatted report with about 1/2-inch margins on both sides of the text.

Again, finding the correct code to send to your printer is a matter of locating the codes in your printer manual. Wherever your printer manual tells you to send an Escape, Esc, or ASCII 27 character to your printer, you want to express that as {Esc} when typing in the code at the Print pull-down menu.

Ctrl-key codes are numbers in the range of 1 to 26. For example, Ctrl-A would be expressed as {1}, Ctrl-B would be {2}, Ctrl-C as {3}, and so forth up to Ctrl-Z, expressed as {26}.

ALIGNING LABELS

Getting text to align properly on labels is one of those computer jobs that sometimes takes a lot of patience. There are several tricks to dealing with labels, and exactly which ones you use depends on whether you are using continuous (tractor-fed) labels, or sheet labels—individual sheets often used with all laser printers and other tray-fed papers. The sections below will discuss the differences between these types of labels, and provide some tips for dealing with alignment problems.

TRACTOR-FEED LABELS   With tractor-feed labels you need to be able to align the labels in the printer properly before printing the first label. Therefore, when you put the finishing touches on your label format, you want to be sure the labels are in a position in the printer that will be easy to replicate in the future. Here's a tip on getting started:

- Design a label format, as described in the section titled "Designing a Label Format" earlier in this chapter.

- Turn off the printer (never change paper, or hand-crank paper through the printer, while the printer is turned on).

- If there is paper in the printer instead of labels, remove the paper and insert the labels without changing the position of the paper guide at the left so that you do not alter the left margin position (move the right-margin tractor into the left to align with the holes in the labels).

- Move the label to a position that will be easy to remember and repeat in the future—for example, near the upper-left corner at the print head.

- Turn on the printer (*after* aligning the labels).

- Print at least two labels.

Now, rather than messing with the labels' position in the printer, modify the label format to accommodate the printer, using the suggestions described in "Troubleshooting Label Alignment" later in this chapter.

SHEET LABELS If you want to print labels with a laser printer, first be sure to buy laser printer sheet labels. (Don't use labels designed for copy machines—they may melt inside your printer!) You can usually buy laser printer labels at any office supply or stationery store. (Avery Labels Corporation makes several sizes of laser printer labels.)

Laser printer labels require unique formatting because of the "dead zone" (an area that is never printed on) at the top and bottom of each label page. dBASE IV Version 1.1 offers a small add-in program that can handle the dead zone on laser printers, but you need to tweak things around a bit to use it. Specifically, you need to put the command DTL_LBLOPT = ON in the DOS environment. It's probably best to put the appropriate commands in your AUTOEXEC.BAT file so that they will be there whenever you start your computer. In case you are not a DOS whiz and programmer, here are the exact steps to do so:

- Starting from the Control Center, press Esc and answer Yes to get to the dBASE dot prompt.
- Type **MODIFY COMMAND C:\AUTOEXEC.BAT** (Be sure to use a backslash, \, rather than a slash, /.)
- Press ⏎.
- Press Page Down (PgDn) until the cursor is at the bottom of the file (if the cursor ends up at the end of the past line, press ⏎ to move down to the next blank line).
- Carefully type **SET DTL_LBLOPT = ON** (notice that that's an underscore (_) not a hyphen (-) and the only blank space is after the word SET).
- Press ⏎.
- Press Ctrl-End to save your changes.

Those steps will automatically place the proper command in the DOS environment each time you start your computer in the future.

If the last command in your AUTOEXEC.BAT file starts a program or DOS shell, place the SETDTL_LBLOPT = ON command above that last command.

If you make any mistakes while changing your AUTOEXEC.BAT file, don't save those changes! Instead, press Esc and answer Yes when asked about abandoning.

You can learn more about the AUTOEXEC.BAT file from your DOS manual or book. The dBASE MODIFY COMMAND editor is covered in Chapter 17 of this book.

To make sure, follow the steps below to test your changes now:

- At the dot prompt, type **QUIT** and press ↵ to leave dBASE.

- Prepare your computer for a normal startup. (If your computer starts from the hard disk, drive A should be empty; otherwise, put your DOS startup disk in drive A.)

- Reboot your computer—hold down the Ctrl and Alt keys, then press the Delete (Del) key. Release all three keys.

- When your computer is restarted and you see the DOS prompt, type **SET** and press ↵.

Among the items already in the environment, you should see DTL_LBLOPT = ON. You need never repeat any of the steps above in the future, because the commands are automatically loaded when you start your computer. Now you can run dBASE IV in the usual manner on your computer.

In the future, whenever you change and save a label format, you will see an additional menu before dBASE creates the label format:

Top Margin	(0 to 99)
Bottom Margin	(0 to 99)
Advance By	Default/Line Feeds/Form Feed
Widow Checking	Yes/No

These options are described in the following list:

Top Margin	Specifies the number of blank lines from the top of the page to the top of the first label
Bottom Margin	Specifies the number of blank lines from the bottom of the last label to the bottom of the page
Advance By	The usual setting, DEFAULT, uses whatever is defined on the Print menu when labels are printed. Can be set to FORM FEED for normal 8½- x 11-inch label sheets, or LINE FEEDS for unusual sheet sizes.

| Widow Checking | Prevents labels from being split across two sheets. Change to ON if the last labels on a page are split across two sheets; change to OFF if the last row of labels is not printed at all. |

To change a margin setting on this menu, move the cursor to the option, press ←┘, type in the number, and press ←┘ again. To change the Advance By or Widow Checking option, move the cursor to the option and press ←┘ until the option you want is selected. When you've finished making your selections, press Ctrl-End.

Most laser printer labels already allot space for the dead zone at the top and bottom of each sheet, so you will want to make sure to set the Length of Page option to 60 lines in the label design's print form file, as described earlier in this chapter. Also, the top and bottom margins on most laser printer sheets are usually the same, so the settings on the menu should be equal. For example, if you set the Top Margin to 3, you should also set the Bottom Margin to 3. It might take a little trial-and-error to get the exact margins you want.

TROUBLESHOOTING LABEL ALIGNMENT Here are some tips to help you troubleshoot label alignment problems.

PROBLEM: Text prints too far to the left on the label.

SOLUTION: Increase the offset from the left side of the page using the Page Dimensions option on the Print pull-down menu. Save your change to the print form for the labels.

PROBLEM: Text prints too high on the label.

SOLUTION: If you are using continuous labels, go back to the label design screen by highlighting the name of the label format in the Labels panel and pressing Design (Shift-F2). With the cursor in the upper-left corner of the label design, press Ctrl-N to insert blank lines at the top of the form (as shown in Figure 7.26). This will cause

Figure 7.26: Padding the tops of labels with blank spaces

blanks to be printed at the top, rather than at the bottom of each label. Save the format, and reprint the labels.

If you are using laser printer labels, you may need to adjust the top and bottom margins on the last menu to appear when you save the label format.

PROBLEM: Labels start out ok, but get progressively further out of alignment.

SOLUTION: The number of lines being printed per label is incorrect. For example, if the first label prints properly, but the text on the second label is too high, the number of lines being printed per label is incorrect. Return to the labels design screen and change the number of lines between labels (the Dimensions pull-down menu) or Height of Label option to print more or fewer lines per label.

PROBLEM: Labels in the first column line up properly, but columns to the right are misaligned.

SOLUTION: Go back to the labels design screen and adjust the Spaces between Label Columns option on the Dimensions pull-down menu to put either more or less space between labels, or adjust the Width of Label option on that same menu.

PROBLEM: Labels print perfectly sometimes, terribly at other times.

SOLUTION: This usually happens only with continuous labels, and is usually caused by the labels being misaligned when printing begins. Always remember to turn off the printer, properly align the labels, then turn the printer back on before printing the labels.

You can check the alignment before actually printing by selecting Generate Sample Labels from the Print pull-down menu. This option will fill a row of labels with *X*s so that you can see exactly how the labels are aligned in reference to how text will be printed. After printing a sample label, the screen asks "Do you want more samples? (Y/N)." You can keep typing Y (for Yes) and adjusting the labels until they are perfectly aligned in the printer. Then type N (for No), and dBASE will print the labels.

USING SPECIAL PRINTER FEATURES

Both the labels and reports design screens offer options for taking advantage of any special features that your printer offers, such as controlling the size of print, controlling printer features such as bold-face and italic, and controlling the quality of print. In the reports design screen, you can control these features on a band-by-band manner using the Bands pull-down menu.

It's important to understand that dBASE can only *use* the features that are built into your printer; dBASE cannot force your printer to do something that it's not designed to do.

Unfortunately, dBASE doesn't "know" whether or not your printer has a particular feature either, and this can lead to some confusion. For example, if you tell dBASE to print a report heading in boldface italic in the reports design screen, it will accept your request without a problem. However, if your printer does not support bold-face italic, the heading will appear as normal text when you print the report. In other words, dBASE doesn't warn you that you've selected an unavailable printer feature; it simply ignores your request when you print the report.

So, it's a good idea to check your printer manual and find out what features it offers before you try using them in your reports or labels. That way, you won't be confused when a requested feature does not appear in your printout.

CHANGING PRINT SIZE

If your printer has the ability to print in various sizes, you can change the size of print either for the entire report or just for specific bands within the report. For example, you might want to use a small print size so that you can fit more columns of data across a page.

As with some other features described in this chapter, whether or not this feature actually works depends on whether or not your printer has the capability to print in different sizes. dBASE can only *use* the features that your printer has available; it cannot force your printer to do something it's not designed to do.

dBASE offers four print sizes to choose from:

PICA	10 characters to the inch
ELITE	12 characters to the inch
CONDENSED	Varies, but usually about 16.6 characters per inch (cpi)
DEFAULT	The current setting at the printer

To take full advantage of a specific print size, you'll probably want to adjust the right margin to allow the maximum width, as described under "Setting the Margins and Page Length" earlier in this chapter.

CHANGING THE PRINT SIZE FOR THE ENTIRE REPORT

To change the print size for the entire report, follow these general steps (assuming that you are still at the reports design screen):

- Press Alt-P or use the Menu (F10) key to access the Print pull-down menu.

- Select Control of Printer.

- Highlight the Text Pitch option.
- Press the space bar (or ◂━▸) until the size you want is displayed.
- Press Ctrl-End twice to leave the two menus.

CHANGING THE SIZE FOR A SINGLE BAND   To change the print size for a particular band in the report (assuming that you are still in the reports design screen):

When you mix print sizes in a single report design, the text will not line up on the printed report as it does on the screen, because the screen shows all text as the same size. You will need some trial-and-error adjustments to get text to line up the way you want.

- Move the cursor to the band that you want to change the print size of.
- Press Alt-B or press Menu (F10) and pull down the Bands menu.
- Highlight the Text Pitch for Band option.
- Press the space bar (or ◂━▸) until the size you want is displayed.
- Press Ctrl-End.

You will not notice any change on the screen, but as long as your printer supports the size you chose, you will notice the change when you print the report.

CHANGING PRINT ATTRIBUTES

On laser printers, features like boldface and italic are supported only if the current font supports those features.

When you want text to align neatly into columns on a printed report, you should use a monospaced font such as Courier.

Many printers offer the capability to change the style, or *attribute,* of text and offer boldface, underline, italic, superscript, and subscript. dBASE lets you take advantage of these features in your printed reports and labels as well. You can assign these features from the reports or labels design screen either before or after you've entered text and field templates.

You can also select a font for any portion of your report or label, providing that you've set up dBASE IV to use the fonts that are available for your printer (as discussed in Appendix B). A font is basically a typeface, such as Courier, Times-Roman, or Helvetica. If your printer does offer a wide variety of fonts, you can probably see examples of them in your printer manual.

To assign special print features or fonts to existing text and/or field templates, follow these general steps:

 NOTE

If you have several printers attached to your computer, and will be selecting fonts, be sure to select the correct printer before selecting fonts.

- Move the cursor to the start of the place where you want to activate a print feature, or into the field template that you want to assign a print feature to.

- Press Select (F6).

- If you are changing only a field template, skip to the next step. Otherwise, use the arrow keys to highlight the entire area that should use the print feature you want.

- Press ← to complete your selection.

- Press Alt-W or use the Menu (F10) and arrow keys to pull down the Words menu.

- Select Style.

- Move the cursor to the print feature or font you want, then press ← to turn it on.

You can combine features (such as boldface and italic) simply by repeating the last four steps until all of the features you want activated have been turned on. You cannot, however, combine fonts (it would make no sense to do so, since each font is actually a unique typeface). If you select more than one font while working with a single highlighted block, only the most recent selection will take effect.

If you would like to activate a print feature or font before typing new text, follow these general steps:

- Position the cursor to where you are going to start typing the text.

- Turn on the feature(s) and/or font that you want using the options on the Words pull-down menu.

- When you want to return to "normal" print, select Normal from the Words pull-down menu (both the font and the style return to normal).

None of these options affects the way the report appears on the reports design screen. Also, when "printing" the report or labels to the screen, these print attributes may have an unpredictable effect on the screen. (For example, the screen might interpret ''boldface'' as ''blinking''.) The only way to check your work is to actually print a copy of the report or labels.

CONTROLLING PRINT QUALITY

Some dot-matrix printers offer two or more options for print quality: draft quality (for faster printing) and near letter quality (for neater, though slower, printing). If your printer supports these features, you have three options for controlling the print quality of a report or labels:

YES	Uses the slower, neater near letter-quality print
NO	Uses the faster draft-quality print
DEFAULT	Uses whatever the printer is set to at the moment

To change the print quality overall for report or labels, follow these general steps:

- At either the Control Center or design screen, pull down the Print menu.
- Select Control of Printer.
- Highlight Quality Print.
- Press the space bar (or ◂┘) until the quality you want is selected.
- Press Ctrl-End to return to the Print menu.

As with other printer features mentioned above, you can select a print quality for individual bands in a report design. Follow these general steps to do so:

- In the reports design screen, move the cursor into the band that you want to change the print quality of.
- Press Alt-B or use the Menu (F10) and arrow keys to pull down the Bands menu.

- Highlight the Text Pitch for Band option.
- Press the space bar (or ←┘) until the quality you want is displayed.
- Press Ctrl-End to return to the design screen.

When defining a print quality for an individual band, the DEFAULT option uses the Text Pitch setting on the Print menu.

CREATING A COVER PAGE

Normally dBASE IV prints text from the page header and page footer bands in the report intro band, that is, on the first page of the report. In some cases, however, you might want to use the Report Intro band as an independent cover sheet or cover letter. In this situation, you probably do not want a header and footer printed in the report intro band, and you probably want to eject a page between the cover page and the first printed page of the report. Here are the steps to follow to set up the first page of a report as a cover page, assuming that you are at the reports design screen already:

- Press Alt-W or use the Menu (F10) and arrow keys to pull down the Bands menu.
- Highlight the Page Heading in Report Intro option.
- Press ←┘ to change the option to No (the menu will also disappear from the screen).
- Move the cursor to the last line of text in the Report Intro Band.
- Press the End key to move the cursor to the end of that line.
- Press ←┘.
- Press Alt-W or use the Menu (F10) and arrow keys to pull down the Words menu.
- Select Insert Page Break.

You will see a dotted line across the bottom of the Report Intro band, which indicates that when you print a report, dBASE will start printing remaining bands on the next page.

OPENING AND CLOSING REPORT BANDS

When you print a report, only open bands are printed; closed bands are ignored. Hence, if a band has a blank line in it, that blank line is printed on the report. To prevent that blank line from printing, close the band. The technique for opening or closing a band is the same:

- Move the cursor into the band border (both the upper and lower band borders will be highlighted).

- Press ←⏎.

If the band is already open, pressing ←⏎ will close it. If the band is closed, pressing ←⏎ opens it.

As a shortcut, you can open all the bands in the report format by selecting Open All Bands from the Bands pull-down menu.

PAUSING AND CANCELING PRINTING

While dBASE IV is actually printing, it displays the following instructions:

```
Cancel printing: ESC
Pause printing: CTRL-S
Resume printing with any key

Note that printing might not stop or
pause immediately if your printer has
a buffer
```

If your printer has a *buffer* (a storage area for text that is waiting to be printed), pausing or canceling will not take effect until the buffer is empty.

You can cancel printing altogether by pressing the Esc key. To temporarily pause printing, press Ctrl-S and then press any key later to resume printing.

PRINTING A DATABASE STRUCTURE

Before we leave the topic of printing, note that you can also easily print a copy of your database structure. This can be handy to keep available as an instant reference to the fields in a particular database. To print a copy of a database structure, follow these simple steps:

1. Highlight the database name in the Data panel (CUSTLIST in this example) and press Design (Shift-F2).

2. Select Print Database Structure from the Layout pull-down menu.

3. Select Begin Printing.

4. If you need to eject the page from the printer, select Print Database Structure from the Layout menu again and Eject Page Now from the submenu. Then press Esc.

5. Select Abandon Changes and Exit from the Exit menu to return to the Control Center.

Figure 7.27 shows a printed copy of the structure of the CUST-LIST.DBF database file.

```
Page #      1

Structure for database:  C:\DBASE\CUSTLIST.DBF
Number of data records:        9
Date of last update    : 01/15/91
Field   Field Name  Type        Width    Dec    Index
      1   LASTNAME    Character     15              N
      2   FIRSTNAME   Character     15              N
      3   COMPANY     Character     20              N
      4   ADDRESS     Character     30              N
      5   CITY        Character     15              N
      6   STATE       Character      2              N
      7   ZIP         Character     10              Y
      8   PHONE       Character     13              N
      9   STARTDATE   Date           8              N
     10   PAID        Logical        1              N
**  Total  **                      130
```

Figure 7.27: Printed copy of the CUSTLIST database structure

In the next chapter, we'll discuss how to create custom forms for entering and changing data. Many of the techniques that you learned while using the reports design and labels design screens in this chapter also apply to the forms design screen discussed in Chapter 8.

8

Creating
Custom
Forms

THIS CHAPTER DISCUSSES TECHNIQUES FOR CREAT-
ing custom forms for entering and editing data. As you'll see, custom
forms have several advantages over the simple edit screen that you've
used previously for adding and changing records. Besides looking
better, custom forms can actually do some of the work involved in
entering data and can trap and correct errors before they are stored in
the database.

Figure 8.1 shows an example custom form for the CUSTLIST
database that you'll develop in this chapter. As you can see, the custom form is quite a bit more attractive than the standard form presented on the edit screen. For instance, field names (such as
LASTNAME) are replaced with plain-English descriptions (such as
Last Name). The box at the top of the screen provides information
about the purpose of the form (for example, Enter/Edit Customer
Information), and the box at the bottom of the screen lists important
keys. The PAID field accepts the more natural Y and N (for yes and
no), rather than T and F (for true and false).

As you'll see in this chapter, the dBASE IV forms design screen
lets you be as creative as you wish when developing custom forms for
your database files.

If you've exited dBASE IV, be sure to get it up and running and
then bring the LEARN catalog into the Control Center so you can
try the techniques discussed here.

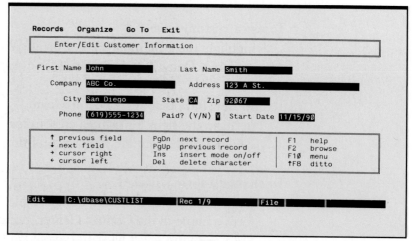

Figure 8.1: A custom form for the CUSTLIST database

USING THE FORMS DESIGN SCREEN

To create a custom form, you first open the database file for which you want to design the form and select <create> from the Forms panel of the Control Center. To do so, follow these steps:

1. If CUSTLIST is not already open, highlight CUSTLIST in the Data panel, press ←┘, and select Use File.

2. Highlight <create> in the Forms panel and press ←┘.

You'll be taken to the forms design screen, with the Layout pull-down menu already displayed. You'll notice that the forms design screen is similar to the reports design screen except that the word "Form" appears in the lower-left corner of the screen, and there are no bands.

CREATING A QUICK LAYOUT

The easiest way to create a form is first to allow dBASE to create a simple form similar to the standard edit screen on the forms design screen. To do so, select Quick Layout from the Layout pull-down menu. Your screen will look like Figure 8.2. You can use this initial form as the starting point for designing your own custom form.

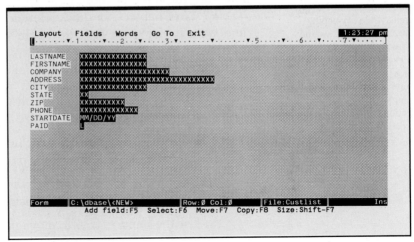

Figure 8.2: Quick layout of a form on the forms design screen

Now let's rearrange the quick layout and add text and boxes to create the custom form shown in Figure 8.1.

PLANNING A FORM

Before you start actually moving items around on the form, keep in mind a few important points. First, note that the current row and column position of the cursor is displayed in the center of the status bar near the bottom of the screen. A custom form can be as wide as the screen (from column 0 to column 79).

Second, when you use the form later to enter or change data, the top row of the screen (row 0 on the form) will display the menu bar and rows 22, 23, and 24 at the bottom of the screen will display the status bar and other messages. Therefore, when designing a form, try to use only rows 1 through 21.

MOVING TEXT AND FIELDS

If you need to take a break while developing this form, see the section "Saving Your Form" later in this chapter to save the work you've done so far. To resume your work later, see the section "Modifying an Existing Form."

The basic editing keys for rearranging and designing a custom form are the same as those used for report and label design. (See Table 7.1 in Chapter 7 for quick reference.) If you are feeling creative and want to use those keys to design your own form, then by all means feel free to do so. However, if you want some help designing the exact form shown in Figure 8.1, follow these steps to get started:

1. Make sure Insert mode is on (press the Ins key until the "Ins" indicator appears in the status bar).

2. With the cursor at row 0, column 0, press ← six times to insert six blank lines at the top of the form.

3. Use the arrow keys to move the cursor to row 2, column 6 and then type **Enter/Edit Customer Information**.

4. Use the ↓ and ← keys to move the cursor to row 5, column 2 and then type **First Name**.

5. Press ↓ three times to move the cursor to the FIRSTNAME template (row 8, column 11).

6. Press Select (F6) and then ←.

7. Press Move (F7), move the ghost image to row 5, column 13, and press ←.

8. Move the cursor to row 5, column 34 and type **Last Name**.

9. Move the cursor to inside the LASTNAME template (row 7, column 11).

10. Press the Select key (F6) and then the ← key.

11. Press Move (F7), move the cursor to row 5, column 44, and then press ←.

12. Move the cursor to row 7, column 0 and press Ctrl-T to remove the LASTNAME field name.

13. Press ↓ to move to row 8, column 0 and then press Ctrl-T again to remove the FIRSTNAME field name.

14. Move the cursor to row 7, column 5 and type **Company**.

15. Move the cursor to the COMPANY template (row 9, column 11), press Select (F6), and press ←.

16. Press Move (F7), move the cursor to row 7, column 13, and press ←.

17. Move the cursor to row 7, column 36 and type **Address**.

18. Move the cursor to inside the ADDRESS template (row 10, column 11).

19. Press Select (F6) and then ←.

20. Press Move (F7), move the ghost image to row 7, column 44, and press ←.

21. Move the cursor to row 9, column 0 and press Ctrl-T.

22. Press ↓ to move the cursor to row 10, column 0 and press Ctrl-T to erase ADDRESS.

23. Use the arrow keys to move the cursor to row 9, column 8 and type **City**.

24. Press ↓ to move to the CITY template, press Select (F6), and press ↵.

25. Press Move (F7), move the ghost image to row 9, column 13, and press ↵.

26. Move the cursor to row 9, column 30 and type **State**.

27. Move the cursor to the STATE template (row 12, column 11), press Select (F6), and press ↵.

28. Press Move (F7), move the ghost image to row 9, column 36, and press ↵.

29. Move the cursor to row 9, column 40 and type **Zip**.

30. Move the cursor to the ZIP template (row 13, column 11), press Select (F6), and press ↵.

31. Press Move (F7), move the ghost image to row 9, column 44, and press Enter.

32. Move the cursor to row 11, column 0 (the "C" in CITY).

33. Press Select (F6), press ↓ five times, press → eight times so that all remaining field names are highlighted, and then press ↵.

34. Press the Del key to delete the highlighted block.

35. Move the cursor to row 11, column 7 and type **Phone**.

36. Move the cursor to the PHONE template (row 14, column 11), press Select (F6), and press ↵.

37. Press Move (F7), move the ghost image to row 11, column 13, and press ↵.

38. Move the cursor to row 11, column 30 and type **Paid? (Y/N)**.

39. Move the cursor to the PAID template (the "L" in row 16, column 11), press Select (F6), and press ↵.

40. Press Move (F7), move the ghost image to row 11, column 42, and press ↵.

41. Move the cursor to row 11, column 45 and type **Start Date**.

42. Move the cursor to the STARTDATE template (MM/DD/YY in row 15, column 11).

43. Press Select (F6) and then ↵.

44. Press Move (F7), move the ghost image to row 11, column 56, and press ↵.

At this point, your screen should look like Figure 8.3. (If you made a mistake, you should be able to rearrange things on your own by now to make your form look like the figure.)

ADDING BOXES AND LINES

NOTE

You can draw boxes and lines on the reports design screen too, using the same techniques discussed here. However, not all printers can display the boxes or special graphics characters.

Now let's add some boxes and lines to our form to make it look a little better. Options for drawing boxes and lines are on the Layout pull-down menu. The technique is quite easy, as the following steps demonstrate:

1. Move the cursor to row 1, column 0, the upper-left corner of the first box you'll draw.

2. Press Menu (F10) and select Box from the Layout menu.

3. Select Double Line.

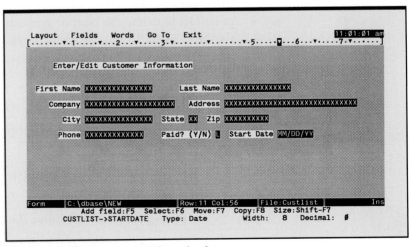

Figure 8.3: Fields rearranged on the form

4. At the bottom of the screen, dBASE displays the instructions "Position upper left of box with cursor keys, complete with ENTER." The cursor is already positioned, so just press ←.

5. The instructions now read "Stretch box with cursor keys, complete with ENTER." Press ↓ twice, hold down the → key until the lower-right corner moves to row 3, column 78, and then press ←. You'll see a double-line box around the form title.

Now draw the box at the bottom of the form.

1. Move the cursor to row 13, column 0.
2. Select Box from the Layout pull-down menu.
3. Select Double Line.
4. Press ← to mark the upper-left corner of the box.
5. Use the ↓ and → keys to extend the box to row 18, column 78.
6. Press ←.

Notice that while the cursor is on the box frame, the frame is highlighted. As long as the frame is highlighted, you can manipulate the box. For example, you can use the Select key to select the box and then press the Move or Copy key to move or copy the box. You can press Del to delete the box, or you can press Size (Shift-F7) to resize the box, using the usual arrow keys. Keep these options in mind whenever you draw boxes.

Now let's add a line to the lower box. Here are the steps:

1. Move the cursor to row 14, column 25.
2. Select Line from the Layout pull-down menu.
3. Select Single Line.
4. Press ← to mark the current cursor position as the start of the line.
5. Press ↓ four times to move the cursor to row 18, column 25.
6. Press ← to complete the line.
7. To copy the line to column 55, move the cursor to row 14, column 25.

8. Press Select (F6).

9. Press ↓ three times to highlight the entire line.

10. Press ←⏎.

11. Press Copy (F8).

12. Move the ghost image to row 14, column 55 and press ←⏎.

As you've seen in the preceding steps, box drawing and line drawing use the same basic techniques. That is, you select either Box or Line from the Layout pull-down menu, and you select a style: either single line or double line. Then you mark the starting point for the box or line by pressing ←⏎, draw the box or line using the arrow keys, and complete the box or line by pressing ←⏎ again. The bottom of the screen provides instructions to help you as you work.

The only difference between drawing boxes and lines is that the Box option always draws an even, rectangular box. The Line option is generally used to draw straight lines, but it can actually be used to draw any shape or even a single special graphics character, as you'll see in the next section.

ADDING GRAPHICS CHARACTERS

While you were drawing boxes and lines, you may have noticed the option Using Specified Character on the submenu. This option allows you to use characters other than the single- and double-line characters to draw boxes. This option can also be used to individually place special graphics characters on the screen. When you select this option, you'll see a submenu of graphics characters and ASCII numbers assigned to those characters. Use the PgDn and PgUp keys to scroll through the menu. When the character you want is highlighted, press ←⏎ to select it.

To demonstrate, let's add some cursor arrows to the current form.

1. Move the cursor to row 14, column 5.

2. Select Line from the Layout pull-down menu.

3. Select Using Specified Character.

4. Press PgDn and then ↓ seven times until you get to the ↑ symbol (number 24 in the leftmost column of the submenu).

5. Press ◄── to select the ↑ symbol.

6. You now need to draw a line that is one character long. To do so, press ◄── to mark the start of the line, → once to draw the short line, and then ◄── again to complete the line. The arrow now appears on the screen.

7. Move the cursor to row 15, column 5.

8. Select Line and Using Specified Character from the Layout submenu.

9. Use ↓ to highlight character 25 on the submenu and ◄── to select it.

10. Press ◄──, then →, and then ◄── again to place the arrow on the screen.

11. Move the cursor to row 16, column 5.

12. Select Line and Using Specified Character from the Layout menu.

13. Use ↓ to highlight character number 26 on the submenu and ◄── to select it.

14. Press ◄──, then →, and then ◄── again to place the character on the screen.

15. Move the cursor to row 17, column 5.

16. Select Line and Using Specified Character from the Layout menu.

17. Use ↓ to highlight character number 27 on the submenu and ◄── to select it.

18. Press ◄──, then →, and then ◄── again to place the character on the screen.

In the form, we will use ↑ to stand for the Shift key next to F8 (because there is not enough room to spell out Shift). You can copy

TIP

To draw the ↵ symbol on a form, you can place the ASCII characters numbered 17, 196, and 217 next to each other on the forms design screen.

the ↑ arrow to the appropriate place by following these steps:

1. Move the cursor to row 14, column 5 (the ↑ symbol).

2. Press Select (F6) and ↵.

3. Press Copy (F8), move the cursor to row 17, column 60, and press ↵.

The form is nearly complete now. You just need to add some helpful text inside the box at the bottom of the screen. You should be able to do this on your own by now, without step-by-step instructions. However, before you begin typing the text, you should be sure to turn insert mode off (press Ins until the Ins indicator disappears from the lower-right corner of the screen).

To type the text, just position the cursor, using the arrow keys, to where you want the text to begin. Then type the text. Use the completed form shown in Figure 8.4 as a guide to help you position the cursor and enter the text. If you make a mistake, remember that all of the standard editing keys are available to you at all times (including Backspace, Del, the arrow keys, and the special keys listed in the navigation line at the bottom of your screen).

After you've added the remaining text to the bottom of the form, the basic appearance of the form is complete. But before you save the

Figure 8.4: The custom form so far

form and test it, let's take a look at some additional features that you can use to enhance your form. Specifically, we'll focus on techniques that make it easier to enter and edit data using the completed form and techniques that allow the form to trap errors before they get into the database. (You'll see these features in action later, after you finish designing and saving the form.)

CONTROLLING INPUT

There are three ways that you can control what is actually entered into a field on the form so you can trap errors as they occur, before they are actually stored in the database. The same techniques can also ensure that data in a field is consistent: for example, that all phone numbers are entered with an area code, in the format (999)999-9999. You can control input using template characters, picture functions, and edit options. The following sections discuss these methods.

MODIFYING FIELD TEMPLATES

As you know from experience in the labels and reports design screens, a field template marks the place where actual database data will appear. Initially, Character fields use templates such as XXXX-XXXXXXXX, Date fields use the template MM/DD/YY, and Logical fields use the template L. You can also use other template characters, as summarized in Table 8.1.

Here are some examples of templates and template characters:

!XXXXXXXXXXXXXX	Accepts any characters, but capitalizes the first character; for example, entering **smith** produces Smith
AAAAAAAAAAAAAA	Accepts only letters, such as Smith or SMITH, but would not accept 123 A St. (because of the numbers) or Tom Jones (because of the space)

Table 8.1: Characters Used in Field Templates

Symbol	Description
A	Accepts only alphabetic characters A-Z and a-z and no numbers, spaces, or punctuation
N	Accepts alphabetic and numeric characters, A-Z, a-z, and 0-9, but no spaces or punctuation
Y	Accepts either Y or N
#	Accepts numeric digits 0-9, spaces, periods (.), and plus (+) and minus (-) signs
L	Accepts T, F, Y, and N
X	Accepts any character
!	Accepts any character and converts letters to uppercase
9	Accepts real numbers only, including plus and minus signs
Other	Any other characters are *literal* characters and are actually stored in the database

(999)999-9999	Accepts any numbers, 0-9, and automatically adds parentheses and hyphens; hence, entering **2139876543** produces (213)987-6543
999-99-9999	Accepts any number and inserts hyphens; for example, entering **123456789** produces 123-45-6789
!-!!!	Accepts any characters, but converts letters to uppercase and inserts a hyphen; for example, entering **a1j3** produces A-1J3

!-999 — Accepts a character followed by any three numbers, converting the character to uppercase; hence, entering **x555** produces X-555 (you could not enter a1j3 into this field, because the "j" appears where a number is required)

WARNING

When changing template characters, make sure that Insert mode is off so you don't change the size of the template.

To try some of these template characters, we'll make some changes to the current form. Remember, you cannot actually see the effects of these changes until after you've completed and saved the form (you're still designing it right now). The general technique that you use to change field templates includes these steps:

- Highlight the field template you want to change.
- Press the Field key.
- Make your changes.
- Press Ctrl-End when you are done.

The exact steps we'll use in this sample form are as follows:

1. Make sure Insert mode is off.
2. Move the cursor to the FIRSTNAME field template (row 5, column 13).
3. Press F5, and you'll see a submenu of options.
4. Select Template. A list of template characters appears, and the cursor is readied to make changes, as shown in Figure 8.5.
5. Press Home to move to the first character in the template.
6. Type ! and then press ←⏎.
7. Press Ctrl-End to save the change.

The template for the FIRSTNAME field now looks like this:

!XXXXXXXXXXXXX

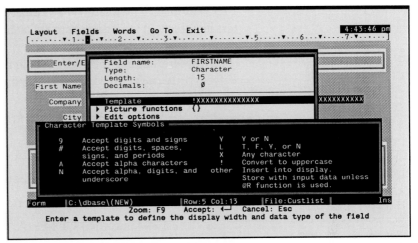

Figure 8.5: Template characters displayed on the screen.

To change the template for the LASTNAME field, move the cursor to the LASTNAME field template (row 5, column 44) and then repeat steps 3 through 7.

Now let's add a template to the PHONE field that will insert parentheses and hyphens. Here are the steps:

1. Move the cursor to the PHONE field template (row 11, column 13).

2. Press F5.

3. Select Template.

4. Press Home.

5. Type the new template **(999)999-9999** and press ←⏎.

6. Press Ctrl-End.

Note that the PHONE field template includes parentheses and a hyphen, which are not special characters listed in Table 8.1. These "other" characters are called *literal characters*, or just *literals*. Literal characters actually become part of the data stored in the field.

As you'll see later when you actually use the form, the (999)999-9999 template will allow you to type any 10 numeric digits into the

PHONE field. The form will automatically display the literal characters like this: ( ) - , and these will actually be stored in the database after you type a phone number.

Now let's change the PAID field template so that it accepts only a Y (yes) or N (no) entry by following these steps:

1. Move the cursor to the PAID field template (row 11, column 42).

2. Press F5.

3. Select Template (note your options on the screen).

4. Press ← and then type the letter **Y**.

5. Press ↵ and then Ctrl-End.

You can now see the new template characters in their fields, as shown in Figure 8.6. Before we test these, let's look at another technique for controlling data entered onto the screen: using picture functions.

USING PICTURE FUNCTIONS

Whereas template characters control the individual characters that are typed into a field, picture functions affect the entire field.

Figure 8.6: New template characters on the form

Table 8.2 summarizes the picture functions. (They are discussed in more detail later in the chapter.)

The basic technique for assigning a picture function to a field is to highlight the field, press F5, select Picture Functions, and then select the functions you want. To see how this works, we'll assign the ! (uppercase) function to the STATE field in the current form. (You'll use some other picture functions later.) Here are the steps:

1. Move the cursor to the STATE template (row 9, column 36).

2. Press F5.

3. Select Picture Functions.

4. Highlight Uppercase Conversion and press the space bar to turn the option on.

5. Press Ctrl-End to leave the submenu. You'll now see the picture function displayed as {!}.

6. Press Ctrl-End to save the change.

You won't notice any change on the design screen, because picture functions do not appear in the field template. (Of course, you can see what picture functions are assigned to a field template at any time by moving the cursor into the template and pressing F5.)

CONTROLLING EDIT OPTIONS

Another way that you can control what is entered into a field is through edit options. These options are summarized in Table 8.3 and discussed in more detail later in this chapter.

Let's use some edit options on the current form. We'll use the Default Value option to display the current date in the START-DATE field and the Message option to display a message when a field is highlighted.

1. Move the cursor to the STARTDATE template (row 11, column 56).

2. Press F5 and select Edit Options.

3. Select Message and type **Press Enter to accept suggested date, or type in a new date**.

Table 8.2: Picture Functions for Custom Forms

Function	Effect
A	Accepts alphabetical characters only (entire field)
!	Accepts any data, but converts all letters to uppercase
R	Removes literal characters from entry before storing them on the database
S	Allows long text to be entered into short field displays
M	Allows multiple-choice options to be displayed in a form and selected by pressing ◄—
T	Removes leading and trailing blank spaces
J	Right-aligns data in field template
I	Centers data in field template

4. Press ◄— after typing the entire message.

5. Select Default Value.

6. Type **DATE()** (a special dBASE function, discussed in Chapter 12, that displays the current date) and press ◄—.

7. Press Ctrl-End to leave the submenu.

8. Press Ctrl-End to save your selections.

Note that you will not see any immediate effects on the form that you are designing. However, you'll see these edit options in action when you use the completed form.

SAVING YOUR FORM

At this point, you can add a description to the form and then save it. Here are the steps:

1. Press Menu (F10) and select Edit Description of Form from the Layout pull-down menu.

Table 8.3: Edit Options for Custom Forms

Edit option	Effect
Editing Allowed	If Yes, field contents can be changed; if No, field contents can be viewed, but not changed
Permit Edit If	Allows you to enter a logical formula to determine when a field can be changed
Message	Lets you enter a message that is displayed at the bottom of the screen when the field is highlighted
Carry Forward	If Yes, data entered into one record is automatically carried over to the next record when you add new records (data for only the current field is carried forward)
Default Value	Lets you automatically place a suggested value into a field, which can be accepted, or changed, when you actually enter data
Smallest Allowed Value	Specifies the smallest allowable value for the field
Largest Allowed Value	Specifies the largest allowable value for the field
Accept Value When	Lets you define a logical formula that determines whether a value can be entered into a field
Unaccepted Message	Lets you define a message that is displayed on the screen if an unacceptable value is entered into a field

2. Type the description **Form for entering/editing customer information** and press ←⤶.

3. Press Menu (F10) and select Save Changes and Exit from the Exit pull-down menu.

4. When prompted, type the file name **CUSTFORM** and press ↵.

After dBASE creates the appropriate form (in its own language), you'll be returned to the Control Center. You'll see the name of the new form, CUSTFORM, in the Forms panel of the Control Center.

USING A FORM

To use any custom form, you simply highlight its name on the Forms panel of the Control Center and press Data (F2). To use the CUSTFORM form that you just created, follow these simple steps:

1. If necessary, use the arrow keys to highlight CUSTFORM in the Forms panel.

2. Press Data (F2).

The form will appear, looking just like Figure 8.1 at the beginning of this chapter. You can use the usual keys, including PgDn and PgUp to scroll through records and to enter and change information. Also, you can still use the Data key (F2) to switch back and forth between the custom form and the browse screen.

USING A FORM TO ADD NEW DATA

Let's use the custom form to add a new record to the CUSTLIST database and test some of the features we put into the form. Here are the basic steps:

1. If the browse screen is displayed, press F2 to get back to the custom form.

2. Press Menu (F10) and select Add New Records from the Records menu.

You'll see the custom form on the screen with most of its fields empty, as in Figure 8.7. Notice that Start Date already displays the current date.

Now, type **fred** as the First Name entry. Notice that your entry is immediately converted to Fred. Press ◄──┘ and type **jones** as the Last Name entry. Your entry is converted to Jones. Both of these instant conversions are caused by the !XXXXXXXXXXXXX templates that you specified for these fields in the form design.

You did not customize the COMPANY, ADDRESS, or CITY field templates, so you need to enter data correctly in these fields. For Company, enter **American Sneaker**. For Address, enter **P.O. Box 3381**. For City, enter **Newark**. When you get to State, type **nj**. You'll see the entry immediately converted to **NJ**, because of the ! picture function you assigned to the STATE field. For Zip, enter **01234**.

When you get to the Phone entry line, first try typing **ABC**. dBASE will beep and reject the letters, because you specified the field template (999)999-9999, and the 9 template character does not accept letters. Now type **2025550987**. dBASE already displays the parentheses and hyphen, so the phone number reads (202)555-0987.

For Paid, try entering a letter such as **J** or **Q**. Once again, dBASE beeps and rejects the entry, because you used the Y template, which accepts only Y or N for the PAID field. Type **Y** now.

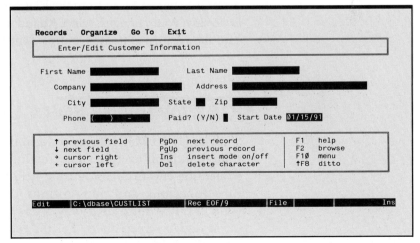

Figure 8.7: Blank custom form, ready to accept a new record

When you get to Start Date, you'll see the message "Press Enter to accept suggested date, or type in a new date" at the bottom of the screen. (This is the custom message that you entered during forms design.) The Start Date line will already display the current (system) date. You can either type a new date or just press ← to accept the current date.

After you press ←, dBASE scrolls down to a new blank record. (To change the previous record, you can press PgUp.) You could add more new records now. But for the time being, return to the Control Center by selecting Exit from the Exit pull-down menu (or by pressing ← while a blank record is displayed).

> **NOTE**
>
> The rest of this chapter discusses general features for designing custom forms. If you wish, you can refer to these sections as you need them, rather than reading them now.

MODIFYING A FORM

To change an existing form design, first make sure the appropriate database file is open (in this example, the CUSTLIST file name must be above the line in the Data panel). Then highlight the name of the form that you want to edit and press ←. Select Modify Layout from the menu that appears.

You can use the same techniques used to create the form to make changes in the form. When you are done making changes, select Save Changes and Exit from the Exit pull-down menu. (If you prefer *not* to save your changes, select Abandon Changes and Exit instead.) You'll be returned to the Control Center.

MORE OPTIONS FOR CUSTOM FORMS

The CUSTFORM custom form that you just created provided some hands-on exercises for creating custom forms and demonstrated the effects of customizing field templates and assigning picture functions and edit options to fields in the form. The CUSTFORM form used only a few of the many options that the forms design screen offers. For the remainder of this chapter, we'll discuss additional options and features of the forms design screen. You may want to use some of these in the future when you begin creating your own custom forms.

PICTURE FUNCTIONS

Picture functions operate on data as it is entered into or changed in a custom form. To assign picture functions to a field template in the forms design screen, you move the cursor to the appropriate field template and press the Field (F5) key. The Picture Function option on the menu that appears will display the currently assigned picture functions (if any) between curly braces. To add or change picture functions, highlight the Picture Functions option and press ←.

You will see a menu of picture function options that are available for the current data type. Each option can be turned on or off by highlighting the option and pressing the space bar. The picture functions available for the Character data type are discussed in the following sections. (Picture functions for the Numeric data type are discussed in Chapter 9.)

ALPHABETIC CHARACTERS ONLY If you assign the Alphabetic Characters Only picture function to a field template, the field will only accept letters (A to Z and a to z) later when you use the completed form. Note that the field will not even accept blank spaces. Thus, a field template that has this picture function turned on could not accept ''123 Appleton Way'' or ''Pulver-Smith'' as an entry.

UPPERCASE CONVERSION The Uppercase Conversion picture function, when turned on, converts all lowercase letters entered in the field to uppercase. For example, suppose you assign this picture function to a database field named PARTCODE. Later when you use the form to add or edit data, dBASE will convert an entry such as Ak7-7jl to AK7-7JL.

LITERALS NOT PART OF DATA The Literals Not Part of Data picture function, when turned on, removes all literals from data typed in a form before storing the data in the database. Normally this option is turned off. For example, suppose you specify the field template (999)999-9999 for entering data into a field named PHONE. When you type a phone number into the field, dBASE will fill in the literals (the parentheses and hyphen) and store your entry in the database with these characters included. But if you turn on the Literals Not Part of Data picture function for the PHONE field, dBASE will remove the literals after you enter a phone number. That is, the form will still *display* the phone number with the parentheses and hyphen inserted, but dBASE will *store* only the numbers in the database. Hence, if you enter (213)555-1212 as the phone number, the actual database record will contain 2135551212.

The only advantage of using the Literals Not Part of Data picture function is that it saves a little bit of disk space by not storing the repetitive parentheses and hyphen. However, when designing report formats, you would always need to be certain to include the (999)999-9999 template to display data from the PHONE field; otherwise, phone numbers would be printed without the parentheses and hyphen.

SCROLL WITHIN DISPLAY WIDTH You can define a width of up to 254 characters for the Character data type when you create a database. However, a standard screen is only 80 characters wide. Now suppose you created a database with a Character field named REMARKS and a width of 100 characters. (Perhaps you use this field to enter general comments about customers or whatever other information is stored in the database.) How would you place such a field in a custom form?

Your best bet is to modify the field template to whatever size best fits on your custom form. You could use the full 80-character width of the screen or any smaller width.

Let's assume that you use a field template that consists of 40 X's to display the REMARKS field on your custom form. To ensure access to the full 100 characters that the REMARKS field offers, you would need to turn on the Scroll within Display Width picture function. Later, when you use the completed custom form, the form will display a highlight that is 40 characters wide for entering data into the REMARKS field. But when the cursor gets to that field in the form, you can still type up to 100 characters into the field. As you type beyond the fortieth character, the text in the field will scroll to the left to make more room.

When viewing existing data through the completed form, the form will initially display only the first 40 characters stored in the REMARKS field. But once the cursor gets to the REMARKS field, you'll be able to use the ← and → keys to scroll to the left and right within the field and thereby view all 100 characters.

MULTIPLE CHOICE The Multiple Choice picture function allows you to create a multiple-choice field on your custom form. A multiple-choice field is one that allows only certain entries. For example, suppose you create a database of members in a club, and that database includes a Character field named STATUS. Any given member can have the status REGULAR, OFFICER, HONORARY, or EXPIRED. Because only these four options are acceptable entries for the field, there is no need to even allow the field to accept other data.

When you use a completed custom form that has a multiple-choice field in it, the form initially displays one of the acceptable values in the field. When the cursor gets to that field on the form, you can press ◄─┘ to use the displayed value or press the space bar to view other possible options. When the option that you want to enter in the field is displayed on the form, you press the ◄─┘ key to accept it.

Actually, the STATE field in the CUSTLIST custom form could be defined as a multiple-choice field, because it allows only two-letter state abbreviations (which implies that all customers in the CUSTLIST database live in the United States). To see a multiple-choice field in action, follow these steps to modify the CUSTLIST form:

1. If the CUSTLIST database is not in use (that is, if its name is not above the line in the Data panel of the Control Center), highlight CUSTLIST, press ◄─┘, and select Use File.

2. To modify the CUSTFORM form, highlight CUSTFORM in the Forms panel and press Design (Shift-F2).

3. Use the arrow keys to move the cursor to the STATE field template (row 9, column 36).

4. Press the Field key (F5).

5. Select Picture Functions.

6. Highlight Multiple Choice and press ◄─┘. The screen displays the prompt ''Enter multiple choices:''

7. Type all the possible entries for the field, separating entries with a comma. (It's best to enter them in alphabetical order.) For this example, type the two-letter state abbreviations shown here. Do not include any blank spaces and do not

WARNING

Never use double quotation marks ('') when listing options for a multiple-choice field.

press ⏎ until you've typed all the two-letter abbreviations. Use the Backspace key to make corrections.

> AK,AL,AR,AZ,CA,CO,CT,DC,DE,FL,GA,GU,HI,IA,ID,IL,
> IN,KS,KY,LA,MA,MD,ME,MI,MN,MO,MS,MT,NC,ND,NE,
> NH,NJ,NM,NV,NY,OH,OK,OR,PA,RI,SC,SD,TN,TX,UT,VA,
> VI,VT,WA,WI,WV,WY

8. Press ⏎ after typing all the abbreviations.

9. Press Ctrl-End twice to leave the menus.

10. Select Save Changes and Exit from the Exit pull-down menu to save the change.

Now you can try the new multiple-choice field. To use the CUSTLIST form, make sure its name is highlighted in the Forms panel and press Data (F2). Then press the ↓ key until the cursor reaches the State highlight on the form. While the cursor is in the State highlight, you can experiment with the following techniques to select a state:

• Type the first letter of a state abbreviation (such as *M*) to see the first option that begins with that letter.

• Type the first letter of a state abbreviation repeatedly to see all state abbreviations that start with that letter.

• Press the space bar to scroll through state abbreviations without regard to the first letter in the abbreviation.

Feel free to experiment with the multiple-choice field for as long as you want. When you are finished, you can just press the Esc key to quickly return to the Control Center. (Any changes you made will not be saved.)

When you are creating a multiple choice field and defining the list of acceptable options, remember to type those options in alphabetical order and separate each with a comma. If you want an empty Character field to be an acceptable entry, start the list of acceptable options with a comma. dBASE will consider the "nothing" in front of the first comma to mean "a blank entry is acceptable." In a Numeric or Float field, use 0 rather than a blank entry.

Normally, the first item in the list of acceptable choices is the one that is displayed on the screen later when you are adding new records. You can, however, have the field display any other value from the list of acceptable entries by using that value as the Default Value on the Edit Options menu.

TRIM, RIGHT ALIGN, AND CENTER ALIGN   The Trim, Right Align, and Center Align picture functions determine how data is displayed within the field template. Normally, character data is left-aligned within the width provided by the field template. If you turn on the Trim option along with the Right Align or Center align picture function, you can align character strings in different ways. Some examples follow (where the | characters mark the width of the field highlight on the form):

```
| Smith                  |  Left-Aligned (default)
|            Smith       |  Centered
|                 Smith  |  Right-aligned
```

EDIT OPTIONS

In the CUSTLIST custom form, you used the Default Value edit option to display the current date in the StartDate field highlight as the default date. You also used the Message edit option to define a custom message at the bottom of the screen whenever the cursor landed in the StartDate field highlight on the custom form. This section discusses all of the edit options available for custom forms.

The general technique you use to assign or change an edit option for a field is similar to the technique you use to change templates and picture functions. You need to get to the forms design screen and move the cursor inside the appropriate field template. Then you press the Field (F5) key and select Edit Options from the menu that appears. The Edit Options submenu will appear on the screen, where you can use the usual technique of highlighting and pressing ← to select any option.

EDITING ALLOWED   The Editing Allowed edit option lets you determine whether a particular field can be edited. By default, all fields on a custom form can be changed when the completed form is used. If you change the Editing Allowed option to no, the form will display the contents of a field, but you will not be able to change those contents.

PERMIT EDIT IF   The Permit Edit If option lets you enter an expression that defines when a field can be edited. The expression you enter can take the form of any filter condition that you would use in a query, except that it must be a *complete expression*. For example, in the query design screen, you can place the *incomplete expression* "CA" in the STATE box to limit the display to California residents. But when creating an expression for the Permit Edit If edit option, you need to use the complete expression, STATE = "CA".

Use the Permit Edit If option when you want your custom form to permit a field to be edited only when some other field's contents meet a particular condition. For example, suppose you have a database with two Character fields named PARTCODE and PARTNAME. To ensure that a part is assigned a part code before the part name is entered onto the custom form, you could use the Permit Edit If expression PARTCODE <> "   " (part code does not equal blank) in the PARTNAME field.

Table 8.4 shows examples of expressions that you could use in the Permit Edit If edit option (though, as mentioned, you can use any valid expression, and dBASE poses virtually no limitations). You'll see further examples of valid expressions as you read through this book. In addition, Chapter 12 discusses dBASE IV functions, such as DATE( ), that can be useful in custom form edit options.

Remember that when you use your custom form in the future, dBASE will always move the cursor from field to field from left to right and from top to bottom. Therefore, when placing a field on your custom form, place any field that depends on the contents of another field below (or to the right of, if the fields are on the same line) the field that it depends on. This placement allows the independent field to be filled before the dependent field decides whether to permit editing.

For example, when you use the PARTCODE and PARTNAME fields discussed previously, make certain that the field template for the PARTNAME field, which depends on the PARTCODE field, is either

Table 8.4: Examples of Valid Expressions

Expression	Meaning
LASTNAME <> " "	True when the first character in a Character field named LASTNAME is not a blank space
STARTDATE < = DATE( ) + 30	True when the Date field named STARTDATE contains a date that is no more than 30 days beyond the current date
"-" $ PARTCODE	True when the Character field named PARTCODE has a hyphen (-) embedded in it
PAID	True when the Logical field named PAID contains .T.
.NOT. PAID	True when the Logical field named PAID contains .F.

to the right (on the same row) or below the PARTCODE field template when you design your form. That way, when you use the form later to enter data, the cursor will first land in the PARTCODE field, letting you fill in a part code before you fill in a part name. Figure 8.8 illustrates this placement.

MESSAGE　As you saw in the sample CUSTFORM form that you developed earlier in this chapter, the Message edit option lets you create a custom message that appears centered at the bottom of the screen when the cursor is in the appropriate field. You can create a separate and unique message for each field in your custom form. The message can be no more than 79 characters wide and cannot contain double quotation marks ('').

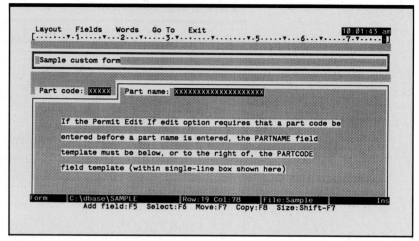

Figure 8.8: Placement of dependent fields on a custom form

CARRY FORWARD Normally when you enter new records into a database, each new record is displayed with empty fields (except those that use a default value, as discussed later). Alternatively, you can tell dBASE to carry the value entered into a particular field in a new record to the next new record. In the next new record, you can accept the value carried forward by pressing ⟵ when the cursor gets to that field, or you can type a new value.

For example, suppose that you set the Carry Forward option to Yes for the STATE field in the CUSTLIST database. Then when you use the form to enter new records, you specify CA as the state for the first new record. When you finish entering all the data for that record and dBASE scrolls to the next new record, you'll see CA in the STATE field, because the previous entry was carried forward.

Each new record that you add will display CA in the STATE field, until you enter a new state for a particular record. From that point on, the new state will be carried forward to additional new records. Each time you change the state in a particular record, that new value is carried forward to the ensuing new records.

DEFAULT VALUE The CUSTFORM custom form that you developed earlier in this chapter used the dBASE DATE( ) function to display the current date in the STARTDATE field highlight on the custom form. As you saw when you used the completed form, the default value is displayed as a suggestion when you add new records to the database. You can either accept the suggested value as is (by pressing ◄◄ when the cursor is in the field) or type a new value.

You can enter any value as a default value, as long as you use the correct data type. For example, if most of the records in the CUSTLIST database will have Los Angeles as the city, then you can assign "Los Angeles" as the default value for that field. (The quotation marks are required, because the CITY field is the Character data type.) To use a specific date as the default value for a Date field, enclose the date in curly braces: {01/01/91}. You can also specify .T. or .F. as the default value for a Logical field.

SMALLEST AND LARGEST ALLOWED VALUE You can use the Smallest Allowed Value and Largest Allowed Value edit options independently or together to define ranges of acceptable values for a specific field in a database. Remember to use the proper delimiters for the data type of the field (for example, quotation marks for Character fields and curly braces for dates).

For example, suppose the current year is 1991 and you want the CUSTLIST custom form to accept only STARTDATE values in the range January 1, 1991, to December 31, 1991. To restrict the data entered in this way, you specify {01/01/91} as the lowest acceptable value for the field and {12/31/91} as the highest acceptable value.

Or suppose you have a database of part codes, part names, and so forth. The field named PARTCODE on this database is the Character data type, and all codes in your business begin with a letter between *M* and *P* (for example, perhaps M-000 to P-999). To ensure that no part numbers outside this range are entered into the database, you could specify "M-000" (including the quotation marks) as the lowest acceptable value for the field and "P-999" as the highest acceptable value.

Later, when you use the custom form to enter data in the database, entering an invalid value will cause dBASE to beep and display the message

Range is 01/01/91 to 12/31/91 (press SPACE)

or the message

Range is M-000 to P-999 (press SPACE)

at the bottom of the screen. You must then press the space bar and enter a new, valid value before proceeding.

ACCEPT VALUE WHEN   The Accept Value When edit option is similar to the Smallest and Largest Allowed Value options just discussed, but provides a little more flexibility. You can use any valid expression (such as the expressions discussed in the section "Permit Edit If") to test the data as soon as it is entered in the field when the form is in use. Later, when you use the completed form to enter and edit data, the field will accept only entries that cause the expression to evaluate to true. Any other entry will be rejected and will need to be reentered.

For example, suppose you created a database for storing accounts receivable that included a field named DATEPAID. The DATE-PAID field would be the Date data type. To ensure that no backdated payments could be entered into the database, you would want the DATEPAID field to accept only dates greater than or equal to the current date.

To make dBASE do so, you enter **DATEPAID > = DATE( )** as the Accept Value When expression for the DATEPAID field. (Remember, DATE( ) is a dBASE IV *function* that always represents the current date.) Later, when you use the form to enter or edit data, any date that you enter into the DATEPAID field will have to be greater than (later than) or equal to the current date. Any earlier date will be rejected.

Note that the example expressions displayed in Table 8.4 work with both the Accept Value When edit option and the Permit Edit If edit option.

UNACCEPTED MESSAGE   The Unaccepted Message edit option lets you define a message that is displayed whenever an invalid value is entered into a field that uses the Accept Value When edit option. For example, if you created the DATEPAID field and Accept Value When edit option discussed in the previous section, you could also add an Unaccepted Message such as "Date must be today's date, or later."

Later, when you used the custom form to enter or edit data, an unacceptable entry into the DATEPAID field would cause dBASE to beep and display the message "Date must be today's date, or later (press SPACE)" at the bottom of the screen. You would need to press the space bar and enter a new date.

Note that you can use any character other than the double quotation mark ('') in your message.

THE GO TO MENU

The Go To pull-down menu on the forms design screen works exactly as it does on the reports and labels design screen. The sample form letter in Chapter 7 provided an example of using the Go To menu to locate and replace all occurrences of a particular word on the design screen. You can use the same technique on the forms design screen.

COLORING CUSTOM FORMS

You've already seen how to select a box frame, field template, or any other area of a custom form on the forms design screen using the Select (F6) key. You can color any selected area by selecting Display from the Words pull-down menu on the forms design screen.

If you are using a monochrome monitor, you'll be given the options Intensity (to display letters in a bright boldface), Underline (to underline words), Reverse Video (to reverse the light and dark shades used for letters and their background), and Blink (to cause letters to blink on and off).

If you are using a color monitor, you will see the dBASE IV *electronic palette* for selecting a foreground and background color combination, as well as an option for blinking. (See the section "Changing the Display Colors" in Chapter 14 for information about selecting foreground and background colors).

Note that after you select a display attribute or color combination and return to the forms design screen, the selected area that you colored will still be highlighted, so your selection might not be readily apparent. To unselect the area and see the effects of your selection, press Select (F6) and then press the Esc key.

MULTIPLE-PAGE CUSTOM FORMS

A single dBASE IV database file can contain up to 255 fields per record. Needless to say, if you were to create a database with that many fields in it, you'd be hard pressed to squeeze all those fields onto a single screen. To solve this problem, dBASE IV lets you divide any custom form into several pages (or screensful) of fields.

Figure 8.9 shows a portion of a sample database, named TAXES.DBF, that contains 112 fields for entering income tax data. An accountant or tax preparer might create such a database to store income tax data. Each record in the database can hold enough data to fill in an income tax form for each client.

```
Structure for database: TAXES.DBF

Field   Field Name   Type       Width    Dec    Index
    1   CLIENT_NO    Character      4             Y
    2   LASTNAME     Character     15             N
    3   FIRSTNAME    Character     15             N
    4   MI           Character      1             N
    5   ADDRESS      Character     25             N
    6   CITY         Character     20             N
    7   STATE        Character      2             N
    8   ZIP          Character     10             N
    9   PHONE        Character     13             N
   10   SSN          Character     12             Y
   11   SPOUSESSN    Character     12             N
   12   OCCUPATION   Character     30             N
   13   SPOUSEOCC    Character     30             N
   14   ELECT_FUND   Logical        1             N
   15   SP_ELECFND   Logical        1             N
   16   FILESTATUS   Character     25             N
   17   SP_DE__
                                                  N
        _____YR      Numeric        2             N
  100   IRADEDUCT    Numeric       10      2      N
  101   IRAPAY       Numeric       10      2      N
  102   KEOGH        Numeric       10      2      N
  103   PENALTY      Numeric       10      2      N
  104   ALIMONYPD    Numeric       10      2      N
  105   COUPLEWRK    Numeric       10      2      N
  106   TAXWITHELD   Numeric       10      2      N
  107   ESTPAYMNTS   Numeric       10      2      N
  108   EARNEDINC    Numeric       10      2      N
  109   EXTEN_PD     Numeric       10      2      N
  110   EXCESS_SSN   Numeric       10      2      N
  111   FUEL_CRDIT   Numeric       10      2      N
  112   RIC_CREDIT   Numeric       10      2      N
```

Figure 8.9: A portion of the sample TAXES database

To enter and edit information in this database would require several pages of custom forms. For example, Figure 8.10 shows how the first page of the form might look on the screen, and Figure 8.11 shows how the second page on the form might appear. For convenience, the fields on each page are roughly organized to resemble the fields on the paper form.

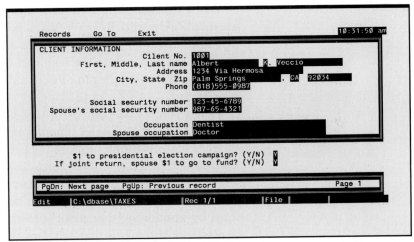

Figure 8.10: First page of form for entering tax data

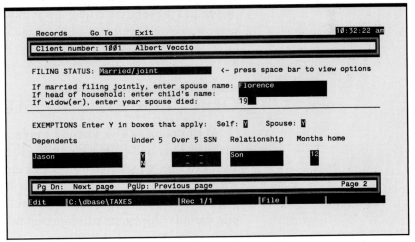

Figure 8.11: Second page of form for entering tax data

To create multiple-page custom forms, you use the standard forms design screen that you used earlier in this chapter. Initially, the forms design screen displays only enough space to create a single page (on which you would use rows 1 through 21). However, you can use the PgDn and PgUp keys to scroll through additional pages on the forms design screen. A single custom form can actually contain over 1600 screen pages.

When using a completed form that contains multiple pages, you use the PgUp and PgDn keys to scroll forward and backward through individual pages. When you are at the last page of the form, pressing PgDn scrolls to the next record in the database. When you are at the first page, pressing PgUp scrolls back to the previous database record.

When you create your own multiple-page custom forms, it is a good idea to display useful identifying information on each page of the form. For example, Figure 8.11 displays the customer number and name from page 1 of the form so that you can see at a glance to which client the information on the screen refers.

You can repeat any field or fields on any page of a multiple-page form by positioning the cursor, pressing F5, and selecting the field name from the menu that appears. Note that because the field is repeated, there is no need to edit it on every page in the form. Therefore, you can set the Editing Allowed edit option to No for repeated fields and prevent the cursor from moving into the field highlight on page 2 and subsequent pages.

YOUR PROGRESS SO FAR

At this point you've learned a great deal about dBASE IV in general and have had quite a bit of hands-on experience in using some of the program's many features and capabilities. If you look at the dBASE IV Control Center now, you'll see that you have used five of the six panels presented in the Control Center to create, modify, and use various objects, as summarized here:

- *Data panel*: The Data panel lets you create, modify, and use a particular database and index (sort order).

- *Queries panel*: The Queries panel lets you create, modify, and use a query, which isolates particular records in the database, such as California residents or records within a particular range of dates.

- *Forms panel*: The Forms panel lets you create, modify, and use a custom form for entering and editing database data.

- *Reports panel*: The Reports panel lets you create, modify, and use a format for printing database data in a format that you specify.

- *Labels panel*: The Labels panel lets you create, modify, and use a format for printing labels.

Each panel uses a consistent set of keys and options for creating, modifying, and using an object, as summarized here:

- Highlighting <create> and pressing ◄── in any panel lets you create a new object.

- Highlighting an existing file name within a panel and pressing Design (Shift-F2) takes you to a design screen, where you can modify an object.

- Highlighting an existing file name and pressing Data (F2) uses (or activates) the completed object.

- As an alternative to using the Design and Data keys, you can highlight any file name in any panel and press ◄── to see a menu of options for modifying or using a particular object (if the Instruct setting is On).

Remember also that the menu bar at the top of any screen is accessible by pressing Menu (F10), and that the navigation line at the bottom of the screen displays special keystrokes and instructions to help you along.

Before we move on to the sixth panel in the Control Center, Applications, let's take some time to round out the skills you've learned so far and increase your database management abilities. We'll begin with a discussion of the Numeric data type, which lets you add the power of calculations to your work with dBASE IV.

CHAPTER 9

Performing Calculations

Fast Track

To change the appearance of numbers or forms and reports, 315
  highlight the field template on the design screen and press F5. Then select either Template or Picture Functions and make your changes. (Table 9.3 lists numeric picture functions.)

To display the results of calculations in custom forms, 318
  create a custom form and then create calculated fields using the same techniques as used in the reports design screen.

To perform calculations quickly, without using forms or reports, 319
  use the queries design screen. Like the reports design screen, the queries design screen offers both calculated fields and summary operators such as Average, Count, Max (highest value), Min (lowest value), and Sum.

To calculate a date that is *x* number of days away, 330
  add or subtract the number of days from a date.

To calculate the number of days between two dates, 331
  subtract the earlier date from the later date.

To compare two fields in queries, 331
  put an *example* (placeholder) into one field and use it in the filter condition in the other field. The placeholder can be any letter or word.

dBASE IV OFFERS GREAT POWER AND FLEXIBILITY for performing calculations in reports, forms, and queries. Whether you need to add 6.5 percent tax to sales transactions, print a subtotaled report of outstanding orders, list accounts receivable over 30 days past due, or count the customers in each state in a customer list, dBASE will help you get the information you need.

USING NUMERIC FIELDS

dBASE IV offers two different data types for numbers: Float (floating point) and Numeric. You can use all of the techniques discussed in this chapter with either type of number. The only difference between the two is the way dBASE handles them behind the scenes, which affects the type of number you use for a particular application.

THE NUMERIC DATA TYPE

The Numeric data type is best for most business applications, where numbers usually have a fixed number of decimal places. For example, sales quantities, such as 10 or 190, usually have no decimal places. Dollar amounts, such as $1.98, always have two decimal places. The Numeric data type is the most accurate for performing calculations with such numbers.

THE FLOAT DATA TYPE

> **NOTE**
>
> dBASE automatically displays extremely large numbers in scientific notation; for example, a 30-digit number might be displayed as .37789318629576E + 30.

The Float data type is best for scientific applications that involve extremely large or extremely small numbers with no fixed number of decimal places. If a single field has a very large number, such as 123,456,789,876.1, in one record and a very small number, such as 0.00000000000012, in another, and you need to perform calculations on these numbers, then you should use the Float data type.

ARITHMETIC OPERATORS

dBASE IV offers the arithmetic operators shown in Table 9.1 for performing calculations. The relational operators that you've seen in

Table 9.1: Arithmetic Operators

Operator	Performs	Example
+	Addition	$2 + 2 = 4$
–	Minus	$5 - 3 = 2$
*	Multiplication	$3*5 = 15$
/	Division	$10/2 = 5$
^ or **	Exponentiation	$3\char`^2 = 9$ $3**2 = 9$
()	Grouping	$(1 + 2)*5 = 15$ $1 + (2*5) = 11$

earlier queries, such as < (less than), > (greater than), < = (less than or equal to), > = (greater than or equal to), = (equal), and # or < > (not equal), can also be used to compare numbers.

ORDER OF PRECEDENCE

dBASE IV follows the standard mathematical order of precedence when performing calculations. That is, exponentiation takes place first, followed by multiplication and division, followed by addition and subtraction. Therefore, the formulas $2*5 + 1$ and $1 + 2*5$ both produce the same result, 11, because the multiplication takes place first.

When in doubt about order of precedence, use parentheses to group operations. For example, the formula $(1 + 2)*5$ results in 15, because the parentheses force the addition to take place before the multiplication. When using parentheses in a mathematical formula, you must make sure that the formula contains an equal number of opening and closing parentheses. Otherwise, dBASE responds with an error message, such as "Syntax error" or "Unbalanced parentheses."

NEGATIVE NUMBERS

To enter a negative number into a field, simply precede the number with a minus sign (hyphen) as you would in everyday arithmetic. For example, – 10 is negative 10 (or minus 10).

SIZING NUMBERS

When you create a database with Numeric or Float data types (as you'll do in a moment), you need to define both a width and a number of decimal places for those fields. If you need only whole numbers, then you can set the number of decimal places to zero. For example, a numeric field with a width of four characters and zero decimal places can handle any number in the range −999 to 9999 (the minus sign requires a place in the width you specify).

When sizing numbers that require decimal places, remember that the decimal point takes up one digit in the width you assign. Therefore if you assign a width of nine characters and two decimal places to a field, then the field can hold any number in the range −99999.99 to 999999.99.

CREATING A SAMPLE DATABASE FOR PERFORMING CALCULATIONS

We'll create a database named ORDERS.DBF in this chapter to view techniques for performing calculations. Be sure that the LEARN catalog is in the Control Center. If necessary, select Use a Different Catalog from the Catalog pull-down menu and LEARN-.CAT from the submenu that appears.

To create this database, select <create> from the Data panel on the Control Center and then type the information for each field, as shown in Figure 9.1. As you can see, the Qty field has a width of three characters and zero decimal places, and UNITPRICE has a width of nine characters and two decimal places. Notice also that the PARTNO field is marked Y for indexing.

You may have noticed that we stored fields for the quantity and unit price of each order in the ORDERS database, but not for the extended price (that is, the quantity times the unit price). That's because the extended price is the result of a calculation. It's best not to store the results of calculations in a database, for two reasons. First, any calculations can easily be performed while you are displaying data, so it's a waste of disk space to store the results of calculations in a database. Second, if you do store the results of calculations in a

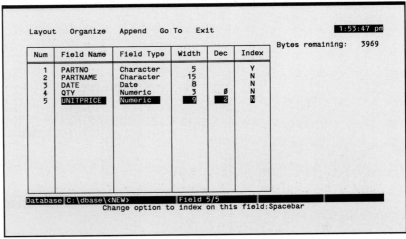

```
  Layout   Organize   Append   Go To   Exit                    1:53:47 pm
                                                    Bytes remaining:   3969
 ┌─────┬──────────────┬────────────┬───────┬──────┬───────┐
 │ Num │  Field Name  │ Field Type │ Width │ Dec  │ Index │
 ├─────┼──────────────┼────────────┼───────┼──────┼───────┤
 │  1  │ PARTNO       │ Character  │   5   │      │   Y   │
 │  2  │ PARTNAME     │ Character  │  15   │      │   N   │
 │  3  │ DATE         │ Date       │   8   │      │   N   │
 │  4  │ QTY          │ Numeric    │   3   │  0   │   N   │
 │  5  │ UNITPRICE    │ Numeric    │   9   │  2   │   N   │
 │     │              │            │       │      │       │
 └─────┴──────────────┴────────────┴───────┴──────┴───────┘
 Database C:\dbase\<NEW>                    Field 5/5
                Change option to index on this field:Spacebar
```

Figure 9.1: Structure of the ORDERS database

field, then any time you change a number in another field that affects the calculation, you'll have to make sure that all other calculated fields were also changed accordingly. This wastes time and increases the likelihood of errors.

After you've created the database structure, select Edit Database Description from the Layout pull-down menu and enter the description **Outstanding orders**. Then select Save Changes and Exit from the Exit pull-down menu and enter the file name **ORDERS** when prompted. You'll be returned to the Control Center, where you'll see the ORDERS database name in the Data panel.

To add some sample data to the database, highlight ORDERS in the Data panel, and press Data (F2). Use either the edit or browse screen to enter the records shown in Figure 9.2. Select Exit from the Exit pull-down menu after entering the 10 records shown.

NOTE

Because you *always* need to press ↵ after entering a value in dBASE IV, from now on this book will use instructions such as "enter **ABC**" instead of "type **ABC** and press ↵."

TIP

Use the Ditto key (Shift-F8) to save some typing when adding new records to the ORDERS database.

PERFORMING CALCULATIONS IN REPORTS

If you highlight ORDERS in the Data panel and press Quick Report (Shift-F9) to print a report of its data, you'll see that the report already contains totals of the numeric fields QTY and UNIT-PRICE, as Figure 9.3 shows.

Figure 9.2: Sample data in the ORDERS database

Figure 9.3: Quick report from the ORDERS database

In most cases, you will probably want reports that offer a better format than Quick Report provides. For the ORDERS database, a column showing extended prices and a total of the extended prices would certainly be helpful. Let's start designing a report that provides this information.

1. Make sure the ORDERS database is open (its name should appear above the line in the Data panel).

2. Move the highlight to the Reports panel and select <create>.

3. Select Quick Layouts from the Layout pull-down menu.

4. Select Column Layout.

Numeric fields in column reports are wider than the width defined in the database structure to accommodate totals at the end of each column. The field widths of other data types may be widened to match the width of the field name.

dBASE creates a report format that is identical to the format used for Quick Reports. Templates for all fields are spread across the Detail band, and templates for the totals of numeric fields appear in the Report Summary band. The names of the database fields, which appear as column headings in the printed report, appear within the Page Header band, as Figure 9.4 shows.

This example intentionally uses a database that has very few fields, so all the data will easily fit across one row on the screen and on one printed page. When you create columnar reports with larger databases, the fields might extend well beyond the right margin of the screen and printed page. You can move field templates (or remove them) using the basic techniques discussed in Chapter 7.

SETTING THE REPORT MARGINS

Before you begin arranging fields in the report, set the right margin for 8½-by-11-inch paper following these steps:

1. Press Menu (F10) and select Modify Ruler from the Words pull-down menu.

Figure 9.4: Initial column layout for a report

2. Press Tab eight times to move the cursor to column 64.

3. Type].

4. Press Ctrl-End.

Now you can proceed with adding calculated fields and arranging the report format.

ADDING A CALCULATED FIELD

Let's add a calculated field to the report format to display the extended price. The basic steps are the same as those used to place any other field: You position the cursor where you want the field to appear and then press Field (F5). Here are the exact steps:

1. Move the cursor to column 55 in the Detail band (to the right of all other field templates within the Detail band).

2. Press Field (F5). You'll see a menu of options, as in Figure 9.5.

3. Select <create> from the CALCULATED column, because you want to create a calculated field.

4. At this point, you are given options to define a name, description, expression, and display attributes for the calculated field.

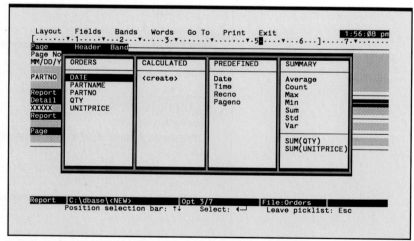

Figure 9.5: Options for placing fields in the report format

5. Select Name and enter a name such as **EXTPRICE**.

6. Select Description and enter a plain-English description, such as **Extended price**. (The description is optional, but is useful for future reference.)

7. Select Expression and enter the expression **Qty * UnitPrice** to multiply the quantity by the unit price in this calculated field.

Your screen should now look like Figure 9.6. You could change the display attributes (that is, the template and picture functions) for the calculated field, but there is no need to do so right now (we'll discuss these options later in this chapter). Just press Ctrl-End to leave the submenu.

Now you'll see the new calculated field template in the report format. You might also want to take a moment to rearrange the Page Header band, improve the column titles, and add a title for the new field, just to tidy things up, as in Figure 9.7.

Notice that when the cursor is in the calculated field template, the bottom line of the screen describes the field, as follows:

EXTPRICE   Expression: Qty * UnitPrice

This information can be helpful in the future, when you need to know what a field template contains.

Figure 9.6: Calculated field defined

CALCULATING TOTALS

To display the total of the extended price in the report, you need to use a *summary field*. A summary field summarizes the information in a group of records. The summary might be a total or subtotal, an average, a count, or some other calculation. Table 9.2 lists the summary options.

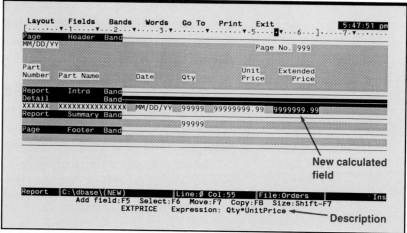

Figure 9.7: Calculated field added to the report format

Table 9.2: Summary Field Options

Option	Operation
Average	Displays the average for a group of numbers
Count	Counts the number of records in a group
Max	Displays the largest value in a group
Min	Displays the smallest value in a group
Sum	Displays the total of values in a group
Std	Displays the standard deviation (a statistical measure) for a group
Var	Displays the variance (a statistical measure) for a group

Right now you need a summary field to total all the extended prices in the ORDERS database. You want this total to appear once at the end of the report, so you need to place it in the Report Summary band. You don't need the total of the UNITPRICE field that is currently in the format, so you can remove that now. Here are the steps to do so:

1. Move the cursor to the summary field template for the UNITPRICE field (the description at the bottom of the screen will show "Operation: SUM Summarize: UNIT-PRICE" when the cursor is in the correct template).

2. Press the Del key to remove the template.

3. Staying within the Report Summary band, move the cursor to column 55.

4. Press Field (F5).

5. You want a summary field that calculates a total (sum), so move the cursor to the SUMMARY column and select Sum.

6. Select Name and enter a name for the field (such as **SUMEXT**).

7. Select Description and enter the description **Sum of extended prices**.

8. Select Field to Summarize On and then select EXTPRICE from the submenu that appears (because you want to total the EXTPRICE field).

9. Press Ctrl-End.

The template for the summary field will appear on the screen. To improve the report format a bit, you can use equal bars to create a double line between the detail band and the totals. Follow these steps:

1. Press Home to move the cursor to column 0 in the Report Summary band.

2. Press Ctrl-N to insert a blank line.

3. Place a string of equal signs above the 99999 and 9999999.99 templates, as in Figure 9.8.

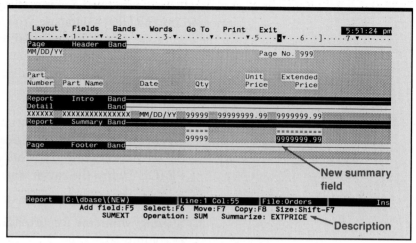

Figure 9.8: Summary field added to the report format

Figure 9.8 shows the report format with the new summary field and the equal bars. Notice that when the cursor is within the template for the summary field, its name, the operation it performs, and the name of field it summarizes are displayed at the bottom of the screen, as follows:

SUMEXT   Operation: SUM Summarize: EXTPRICE

(The name is optional in summary fields. If you don't create one, the Operation and Summarize information still appears at the bottom of the screen. In the Add Field menu that appears when you press F5, unnamed summary fields are displayed in the format SUM(QTY)— that is, sum-of-qty).

Use the usual technique now to save the report format: Select Edit Description of Report from the Layout pull-down menu and enter a description such as **Total sales.** Then select Save Changes and Exit from the Exit pull-down menu. When asked to name the report, enter **TOTALS**. After dBASE creates a program for printing the report, it returns you to the Control Center. From there, use the usual techniques to print the report (select its name from the Reports panel). The printed report will look like Figure 9.9.

```
07/08/91                                          Page No.    1


  Part                                          Unit   Extended
  Number   Part Name      Date      Qty         Price     Price

  B-222    Banana Man     06/01/91     2       100.00    200.00
  B-222    Banana Man     06/01/91     1       100.00    100.00
  A-111    Astro Buddies  06/01/91     2        50.00    100.00
  C-333    Cosmic Critters 06/01/91    1       500.00    500.00
  A-111    Astro Buddies  06/02/91     3        50.00    150.00
  A-111    Astro Buddies  06/05/91     4        50.00    200.00
  B-222    Banana Man     06/15/91     1       100.00    100.00
  C-333    Cosmic Critters 06/15/91    2       500.00   1000.00
  C-333    Cosmic Critters 06/15/91    1       500.00    500.00
  C-333    Cosmic Critters 07/01/91    2       500.00   1000.00
                                     =====            ==========
                                        19               3850.00
```

Figure 9.9: The printed TOTALS report

CALCULATING SUBTOTALS

Suppose you want to print a report that shows not only overall totals, but also subtotals for each part number. To display subtotals, you need to add *group bands* to the report format. A group band tells dBASE to group similar items on the report. You can group records in any manner you wish. For instance, in the ORDERS database you might want to group records by part number or date (or both). In the CUSTLIST database you could group customers by city, state, or zip code.

A group band actually consists of two parts: a Group Intro band, and a Group Summary band. Information in the Group Intro band is displayed once at the top of each group. For example, a report grouped by part number might display the group headings "Part number: A-111" for one group and "Part number: B-222" for the next. The Group Summary band displays its contents once at the bottom of each group. This is where you place summary fields to display subtotals.

Let's add a group band to the TOTALS report format to subtotal records by part number. Our goal will be to make the report format look like Figure 9.10. Here are the steps:

1. Make sure that ORDERS is still the database in use.

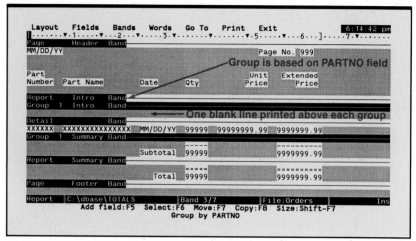

Figure 9.10: Report format for subtotals

2. Move the highlight to TOTALS in the Reports panel and press Design (Shift-F2).

3. To insert a group band, move the cursor to the Report Intro band border (the indicator in the status bar will read ''Band 2/5'').

4. Press Menu (F10) and select Add a Group Band from the Bands pull-down menu.

5. Select Field Value from the submenu.

6. Select PARTNO as the field to group by.

You'll see the new group band appear in the report format. While the cursor is still on the group band, the message ''Group by PARTNO'' appears centered at the bottom of the screen. If you were to print the report now, however, you would not see any subtotals, because the Group Summary band is still empty. We'll rectify that situation right now by adding some summary fields.

1. Press ↓ five times to move the cursor down to the blank line between the Group 1 Summary band and the Report Summary band.

If you need help placing hyphens and subtotal fields, use Figure 9.10 as a guide.

2. Move the cursor to column 35 and place hyphens beneath the Qty (99999) and EXTPRICE (9999999.99) templates, (directly above the equal signs in the Report Summary band).

3. Press Ctrl-N to insert a blank line.

4. Move the cursor to line 1, column 35, directly below the hyphens you just entered.

5. Press Field (F5) and select Sum from the SUMMARY column.

6. Select Name and enter a name for the field (such as **SUBQTY**).

7. Select Description and enter a description (such as **Subtotal of Qty field**).

8. Select Field to Summarize On and then select QTY.

9. Select Reset Every and then select PARTNO.

10. Select Template and press Backspace until the template reads 99999. Then press ⏎.

11. Press Ctrl-End.

Step 9 is required so that dBASE will reset the subtotal to zero each time it encounters a new part number while printing the report. If the Reset Every option is set to REPORT, dBASE will accumulate the subtotals as it prints the report, giving you running totals rather than subtotals. Step 10 ensures that the template for the subtotal matches the template used elsewhere for the Qty field.

Let's add a subtotal field for the Extended Price field now.

1. Press → until the cursor is in column 55 (above the equal bars).

2. Press Field (F5).

3. Select Sum from the SUMMARY column.

4. Select Name and enter **SUBEXT**.

5. Select Description and enter **Subtotal of extended price**.

6. Select Field to Summarize On and EXTPRICE from the submenu.

7. Select Reset Every and then PARTNO.

8. Press Ctrl-End.

Now your report will print subtotals as well as grand totals. You might want to add the words **Subtotal** and **Total** to the report format as well, as shown in Figure 9.10.

Rather than use this format to *replace* the previous TOTALS report, let's save this format as a new, separate file. That way, you'll still be able to use the TOTALS report format. Here are the steps:

1. Press Menu (F10) and select Edit Description of Report from the Layout pull-down menu.

2. Press Home and then Ctrl-Y to erase the previous description. Then enter the description **Subtotals by part number (requires PARTNO index)**. (This description will be explained in a moment.)

3. Press Menu (F10) and select Save This Report from the Layout pull-down menu.

4. Press Backspace 10 times to remove the previous file name.

5. Type the new name **SUBTOTAL** and press ◄─┘.

6. When dBASE finishes creating its program, select Abandon Changes and Exit from the Exit pull-down menu.

In the last step, it was okay to select Abandon Changes and Exit because you had already saved your changes under a new file name. The original TOTALS report remains unchanged, and the new format is saved with the name SUBTOTAL. You can use this technique whenever you design a report that is similar to some existing report, so that you don't have to build each report format from scratch.

PRINTING SUBTOTALED REPORTS

Before you print the new subtotaled report, there is one catch you have to be aware of. The records in the printed report will be grouped properly only if the database is indexed (or sorted) on the field on which the grouping is based. Why? Because the report format tells dBASE only how to *display* the groups, not how to *create* the groups.

Let's assume that you printed the SUBTOTAL report without first using the PARTNO index to organize the records. dBASE would "see" the records in their unsorted order, like this:

B-222

B-222

A-111

C-333

A-111

A-111

B-222

C-333

Each time dBASE encounters a new part number while printing the report, it considers that record to be the start of a new group. Hence, it would print the first two records, with part number B-222, and then print subtotals for those two records before moving on to records containing part number A-111. It would print the record containing part number A-111 and a subtotal for that one record before moving on to the next part number. Then it would print the next record with part number C-333 and a subtotal for that one record, before moving on to the next record with part number A-111.

However, if you use an index to organize the records by part numbers, dBASE will "see" the data in this order before printing the report:

A-111

A-111

A-111

B-222

B-222

B-222

C-333

C-333

The sort order automatically groups similar records together. Hence, when dBASE prints a report from the data organized in this manner, it prints all the records containing A-111, and then a subtotal for those records, before moving on to the records with the next part number, B-222. Then it prints all the records with part number B-222, and a subtotal for those records, before moving on to the records with part number C-333.

So you need to organize the records in the ORDERS database into PARTNO order before printing the SUBTOTAL report. As you may recall, we indexed the PARTNO field when we designed the database structure, so now you just need to put that index into action. Here are the steps:

1. Highlight ORDERS in the Data panel.

2. Press Data (F2).

3. Press Alt-O, then select Order Records by Index from the Organize pull-down menu.

4. Select PARTNO.

5. Press Ctrl-End to return to the Control Center.

Now you can print the SUBTOTAL report by selecting it from the Reports panel in the usual manner. The results should look something like Figure 9.11.

It's often hard to remember to activate an index before printing a report with groups, probably because we expect dBASE to be smart enough to do this for us. No such luck. If you do forget, no harm done; the report will still be printed, but groups and subtotals will be in haphazard order. It helps to put a reminder in the description of the report format, as we did just before we saved the SUBTOTAL report. Then each time you highlight the report's name in the Control Center you'll be reminded that an index is required.

```
07/08/91                                          Page No.    1


Part                                              Unit   Extended
Number  Part Name        Date      Qty            Price     Price

A-111   Astro Buddies    06/01/91    2            50.00    100.00
A-111   Astro Buddies    06/02/91    3            50.00    150.00
A-111   Astro Buddies    06/05/91    4            50.00    200.00
                                   -----                 ----------
                         Subtotal    9                    450.00

B-222   Banana Man       06/01/91    2           100.00    200.00
B-222   Banana Man       06/01/91    1           100.00    100.00
B-222   Banana Man       06/15/91    1           100.00    100.00
                                   -----                 ----------
                         Subtotal    4                    400.00

C-333   Cosmic Critters  06/01/91    1           500.00    500.00
C-333   Cosmic Critters  06/15/91    2           500.00   1000.00
C-333   Cosmic Critters  06/15/91    1           500.00    500.00
C-333   Cosmic Critters  07/01/91    2           500.00   1000.00
                                   -----                 ----------
                         Subtotal    6                   3000.00
                                   =====                 ==========
                         Total      19                   3850.00
```

Figure 9.11: Subtotaled report from the ORDERS database

ORDER OF PRECEDENCE IN CALCULATIONS

When creating your own reports to perform calculations, keep in mind that there are four ways to perform calculations in report bands, and dBASE follows a certain order of precedence when performing calculations as summarized below:

Named   When you create a calculated field and give it a name (such as ExtPrice), the results of that calculation can be used as part of another calculation. These named calculated fields are calculated left-to-right, top-to-bottom within the band. Hence, if a calculated field uses the results of another calculated field, the second calculated fields should be to the right of or below the first calculated field.

Unnamed   When you create a calculated field, you must provide an expression (such as Qty * UnitPrice), but the name is required only if another calculated field needs to use that name as part of its expression. Unnamed calculated fields are calculated last.

Hidden   When creating a calculated field, you have the option to change it to a Hidden field so that it can perform an intermediate calculation but not display the results of that calculation on the report. The hidden calculated fields in a band are always calculated first in a band, in the order in which they were created.

Summary   Summary fields, such as those used for subtotals and totals in this chapter, calculated left to right, top to bottom within each band, along with the named calculated fields, unless the summary field is dependent on a calculated field. In that case, the summary field is calculated after all hidden and named calculated fields.

In practice, what this all boils down to is that how calculations are performed in a report depends both on the type of field performing the calculation, and its position within the band. You should always check the results of calculations in a printed report carefully, and make sure the proper data from the proper record is displayed on each page.

If you find that a value is being calculated incorrectly, try moving the field to the right of or below any other fields that its calculation depends on so that the other fields will be calculated first.

Or, if the calculated field is named, but does not need to be because no other fields depend on it, remove its name to convert it to an unnamed calculated field.

MANAGING REPORT BANDS

As you add new bands to your report format, your screen may become increasingly cluttered and difficult to read. You can close bands that you are not using at the moment by moving the cursor to the band border and pressing ◄┘. Just remember to reopen the band before you print the report, because closed bands do not print. To open a closed band, move the cursor to the band border and press ◄┘ again. You also can select Open All Bands from the Bands pull-down menu to open all closed bands.

To permanently remove a group band from a report format, place the cursor in the band's border and press the Del key or select Remove Group from the Bands pull-down menu. To change the field that a group band is based on, move the cursor to the group band border and select Modify Group from the Bands menu.

FORMATTING REPORT BANDS

You can specify the pitch, quality, and spacing of lines for an individual band by moving the cursor to the band border and selecting the appropriate option from the Bands submenu. These are the same printer features that were discussed in Chapter 7; however, they affect only the current band when specified in this manner.

REMOVING REPETITIOUS FIELDS

In Figure 9.11, the part numbers and part names are repeated within each group. To display repetitious data only once in a group, move the appropriate field templates into the Group Intro band, as in Figure 9.12.

Keep in mind that you cannot move the ghost image of a field from one report band to another. Before you press Move, you must select the field you want to move and move the cursor to the new location for the field template. To try this for yourself, follow these steps:

1. At the Control Center, make sure the ORDERS database is still open (that its name appears above the line in the Data panel).

2. Highlight SUBTOTAL in the Reports panel and press Design (Shift-F2).

3. Press ↓ repeatedly, until the cursor appears in the Group 1 Intro band.

CH. 9

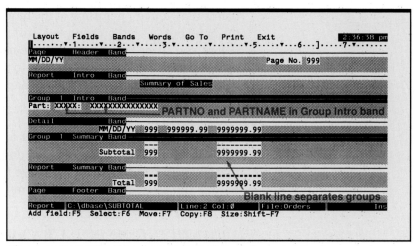

Figure 9.12: PARTNO and PARTNAME fields in the Group Intro band

4. Type **Part:** (including the colon).

5. Press ↓ and ← until the cursor is in the PARTNO field template (the bottom of the screen will show the field name ORDERS->PARTNO when the cursor is properly positioned).

6. Press Select (F6).

7. Press → until both the PARTNO and PARTNAME field templates are highlighted (the highlight should extend to column 22).

8. Press ↩ to complete the selection.

9. Press the ↑ and ← keys to move the cursor to the right of the newly typed word **Part:** (column 6).

10. Press Move (F7) and then ↩.

11. The move is now complete, but you may want to add a colon between the part number and the part name. To do so, press → and type the colon (:).

12. Press the End key to move to the end of the field templates.

13. Press ↩ to insert a blank line in the Group 1 Intro band.

You may also want to remove the field name headings from the Page Header band using the usual Ctrl-Y key. To place the Summary of Sales heading, shown in Figure 9.12, in the Report Intro band, first move the cursor to the Report Intro band border and press ← to open the band. Press ↓, type the heading, and select Position and Center from the Words pull-down menu to center the heading. Add a blank line by pressing Ctrl-N with the cursor positioned at the right of the heading.

You might also wish to shift the contents of the Detail, Group1 Summary, and Report Summary bands to the left. You can use the Select (F6) and Move (F7) keys to do so, but you must change each band independently because you cannot extend the selector highlight outside of the current band. When you are finished formatting the report, follow these steps to save it with a new file name:

1. Press F10 and select Save This Report from the Layout pull-down menu.

2. When prompted, press the Backspace key six times to erase part of the original file name.

3. Type in the number **2** to change the file name to SUBTOT2.

4. Press ←.

5. When dBASE finishes creating the program to print the report, press F10 and select Abandon Changes and Exit from the Exit pull-down menu.

When you return to the Control Center, remember that the database must still be sorted into part number order before you print the report. Use the same techniques that you used to print the SUB-TOTAL report to print the new SUBTOT2 report.

Figure 9.13 shows a printed copy of the new report. Notice that the part number and part name are printed only once at the top of each subtotal group and that a single blank line beneath each subtotal separates the groups.

HANDLING GROUPS AND PAGE BREAKS

Normally, if a particular group on the report continues to the next printed page, the Group Intro is not repeated on the new page.

You can change this so that the Group Intro *is* repeated on the new page by changing the Group Intro on Each Page option on the Bands menu from No to Yes.

```
07/08/91                                              Page No.   1

                             Summary of Sales

    Part: A-111: Astro Buddies

                        06/01/91      2      50.00      100.00
                        06/02/91      3      50.00      150.00
                        06/05/91      4      50.00      200.00
                                    -----              ----------
                        Subtotal      9                  450.00

    Part: B-222: Banana Man

                        06/01/91      2     100.00      200.00
                        06/01/91      1     100.00      100.00
                        06/15/91      1     100.00      100.00
                                    -----              ----------
                        Subtotal      4                  400.00

    Part: C-333: Cosmic Critters

                        06/01/91      1     500.00      500.00
                        06/15/91      2     500.00     1000.00
                        06/15/91      1     500.00      500.00
                        07/01/91      2     500.00     1000.00
                                    -----              ----------
                        Subtotal      6                 3000.00

                                    =====              ==========
                        Total       19                 3850.00
```

Figure 9.13: Report printed by the format in Figure 9.12

You can print groups successively, as in the examples in this chapter, or you can print each new group band on a separate page. Move the cursor to the appropriate band border and then highlight Begin Band on New Page in the Bands menu. Change the setting to Yes to start each printed group on a new page.

NESTING GROUPS WITHIN GROUPS

You can *nest* group bands inside of each other to produce groups within groups. For instance, suppose you place a group band for

PARTNO in the format of a report and then a group based on the DATE field within that group. You could then print a report that subtotals sales for particular products and, for each product, subtotal sales by date.

However, printing reports that have groups within groups requires complex indexes, and creating these can be tricky. Rather than opening up that can of worms right now, let's stay with the basic topic at hand. Chapter 12 will help you master complex indexes and report groupings.

FORMATTING NUMBERS

The templates in reports formats are slightly larger than database field width to provide extra space for totals.

In Chapters 7 and 8, you saw how to use templates and picture functions to format Character and Logical fields in reports and forms. You can also format numbers, using similar techniques, when designing reports and forms.

NUMERIC TEMPLATES

To change the format of an existing numeric template in a form or report design, move the cursor into the field template and press F5.

When you place a numeric field in a report or form design, you'll see a template that reflects the width and decimal places assigned to the number in the database. For example, if a number is assigned a width of six digits and two decimal places, the template for that field will automatically be 99999.99.

Unlike Character data, numeric data is never truncated to fit within the space provided by a template. When a number is too large for the space allotted, dBASE displays only asterisks. For example, the template 999 displays only numbers with three or fewer digits. It displays any larger number, such as 1,000, as asterisks (***). Therefore, if you change a template on a form or report format, be sure to specify enough digits to accommodate the largest possible number for the field or calculation.

To specify how many decimal places to display in printed numbers, insert a decimal point in the appropriate position in the template. dBASE will round the number to fit the template. For example, the template 99999 displays the value 12345.678 as 12346 (no decimal places displayed). The template 99999.99 displays the same value as 12345.68. The template 99999.9999 displays the value as 12345.6780.

To display numbers with embedded commas, such as 12,345 (rather than 12345), insert commas into the template wherever you want them to appear in the printed number. If you use the template 999,999.99 to display extended prices, then the value 3850.00 will be displayed as 3,850.00. The number 123.45 will still be displayed as 123.45, because it is not large enough to require a comma.

NUMERIC PICTURE FUNCTIONS

Numeric picture functions let you further refine the format of printed numbers. Whenever you add or modify a field template and select Picture Functions from the Display Attributes menu, you'll see the options shown in Figure 9.14. You can move the highlight to any option and press the space bar to turn it on or off.

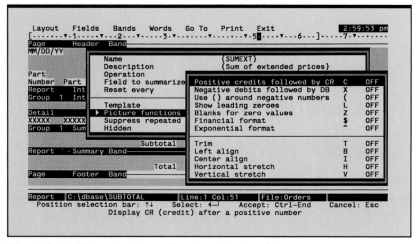

Figure 9.14: Numeric picture functions displayed in a menu

Table 9.3 shows picture functions that you can assign to numeric fields and calculations, and examples of how those functions affect the numbers 0, – 123, and 98765.43. Each example assumes that the current template is 999,999.99.

Table 9.3: Numeric Picture Functions

Picture function	Symbol	Examples
Follow positive credits by CR	C	0.00 CR – 123.00 98,765.43 CR
Follow negative debits by DB	X	0.00 123.00 DB 98,765.43
Use ( ) around negative numbers	(	0.00 (123.00) 98,765.43
Show leading zeroes	L	000000.00 – 000123.00 098,765.43
Use blanks for zero values	Z	– 123.00 98,765.43
Use financial format	$	$0.00 $ – 123.00 $98,765.43
Use exponential format	^	.00000000000E + – .123 .123000000000000E + 3 .987654300000000E + 5

You can combine picture functions if you like. For example, combining C and X places CR after positive numbers and DB after negative numbers. Combining Z and (prints positive numbers normally, negative numbers in parentheses, and zeros as blank spaces (rather than as 0 or 0.00).

ADDING CALCULATED FIELDS TO FORMS

You can create calculated fields in custom forms using techniques similar to those used in reports. The calculated fields will be displayed on the form whenever you scroll through existing records in the database. However, the calculations are *not* updated on the screen automatically as you add or change data, so calculated fields on a custom form are of somewhat limited value.

As discussed in the previous chapter, you create a custom form by first opening the appropriate database and then selecting <create> from the Forms panel in the Control Center. Then you can select Quick Layout from the Layout menu on the forms design screen to bring the field names and field templates into the new form.

To add a calculated field to a custom form, position the cursor where you want the field to appear and then press Add Field (F5). Select <create> from the CALCULATED column of the submenu that appears. You'll be given a menu of options to define the name, description, expression, template, and picture functions for the new field (exactly as when placing a calculated field in a report format).

Figure 9.15 shows a form design for the ORDERS database. Notice that there are three calculated fields, each with its own expression. The expression Qty*UnitPrice displays the extended price. The expression 0.065*(Qty*UnitPrice) displays the sales tax at 6.5 percent. The expression 1.065*(Qty*UnitPrice) displays the total sale (the extended price with 6.5 percent tax added).

Chapter 12 shows how to limit tax calculations to only taxable items in a database.

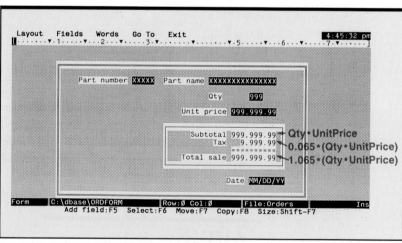

Figure 9.15: A form design with calculated fields

After you save the form design, you can select its name from the Forms panel in the Control Center to activate it. Figure 9.16 shows how the form design in Figure 9.15 appears when you use it to view records in the ORDERS database. As you can see, the form calculates and displays the subtotal, tax, and total sale for each record. As you scroll through records with the PgDn and PgUp keys, the calculations will adjust to new quantity and unit-price values.

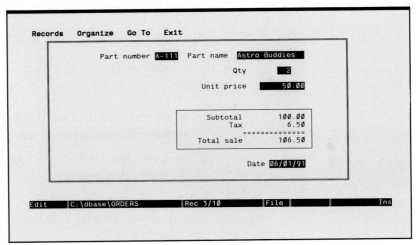

Figure 9.16: Custom form displaying calculations

PERFORMING CALCULATIONS ON THE FLY

You can use the queries design screen to perform some quick calculations without going through all the steps involved in creating a form or report format. This is useful when you just want to experiment with data and calculations and do not need a neatly formatted report.

USING CALCULATED FIELDS IN QUERIES

The general steps for performing calculations through queries are

- Create a query for the appropriate database.
- Select Create Calculated Field from the Fields pull-down menu.

- Enter the expression (formula) required to perform the calculation, using database field names and arithmetic operators.

- Press Field (F5) to include the calculated field in the view skeleton so its results will be displayed.

- When prompted, enter a field name for the calculated field.

- Press Data (F2) as usual to see the results of the query.

To try an example for yourself using the ORDERS database, follow these steps:

1. Make sure that the ORDERS database is open (that its name appears above the line in the Data panel).

2. Select <create> from the Queries panel. This brings you to the query design screen.

3. Press F10 and select Create Calculated Field from the Fields pull-down menu. The screen displays a skeleton titled "Calc'd Flds."

4. Type the formula **Qty * UnitPrice** into the Calc'd Flds box (the cursor is already in position).

5. Press ◄─┘ after typing in the formula.

6. Press F5 to move the calculated field to the view skeleton at the bottom of the screen.

7. When prompted, type in a name such as **ExtPrice** and press ◄─┘.

Figure 9.17 shows the completed query. If the calculated field is scrolled off the right of your screen, you can press Next (F4) and then the End key to view the right side of the view skeleton.

When you press F2 to execute the query, the results will include a copy of the calculated field, as shown in Figure 9.18. The calculated field will appear in both the browse and edit screens. Remember that you can print the results of this or any other query simply by pressing Quick Report (Shift-F9) while the results are on the screen. To return to the query design screen, press Design (Shift-F2).

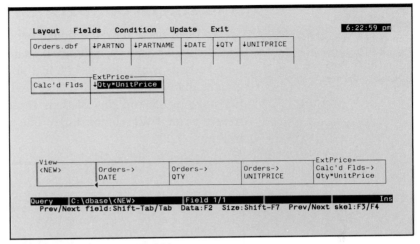

Figure 9.17: Calculated field in a query

```
 Records   Organize    Fields    Go To    Exit

 PARTNO PARTNAME          DATE      QTY UNITPRICE EXTPRICE

 B-222  Banana Man        06/01/91    2   100.00         200.00
 B-222  Banana Man        06/01/91    1   100.00         100.00
 A-111  Astro Buddies     06/01/91    2    50.00         100.00
 C-333  Cosmic Critters   06/01/91    1   500.00         500.00
 A-111  Astro Buddies     06/02/91    3    50.00         150.00
 A-111  Astro Buddies     06/05/91    4    50.00         200.00
 B-222  Banana Man        06/15/91    1   100.00         100.00
 C-333  Cosmic Critters   06/15/91    2   500.00        1000.00
 C-333  Cosmic Critters   06/15/91    1   500.00         500.00
 C-333  Cosmic Critters   07/01/91    2   500.00        1000.00




 Browse   C:\dbase\<NEW>          Rec 1/10       View              Ins
```

Figure 9.18: Results of query shown in Figure 9.17

You can add up to 20 calculated fields to a query, simply by selecting Create Calculated Field from the Fields submenu. Each new calculated field that you create will be added to the right of existing calculated fields.

Remember: You use the F3 and F4 keys to move up and down from one skeleton to the next.

USING FILTER CONDITIONS WITH NUMBERS

You can use filter conditions freely in queries containing calculated fields. The query in Figure 9.19 uses two filter conditions to display records that have A-111 in the PARTNO field *and* a value greater than 100 in the calculated ExtPrice field. (Both filter conditions are in the top row of their respective skeletons, so they are treated as an *AND* relationship.) The results of the query are shown in Figure 9.20.

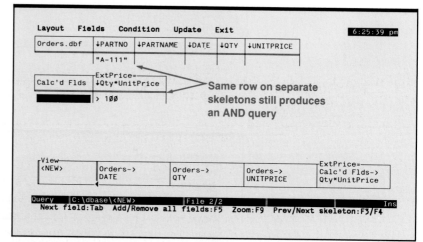

Figure 9.19: Filter conditions added to calculated field query

Figure 9.20: Results of the query shown in Figure 9.19

Figure 9.21 shows a query that isolates records with extended price values in the range $100 to $200.

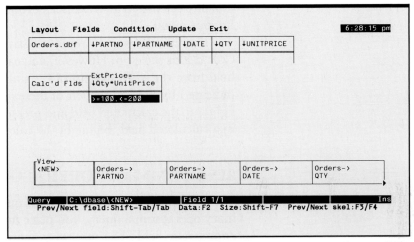

Figure 9.21: Query for records with extended prices in the range $100 to $200

You'll learn more about the use of .AND. and .OR. in Chapter 16.

If you want to set up an OR query that uses fields from both the database file skeleton and a calculated field you need to create a *condition box* by selecting Add Condition Box from the Condition pull-down menu. Use the .AND. and .OR. operators to create AND and OR queries. For example, the query in Figure 9.22 displays records that have quantities greater than 3 or extended prices over $500.

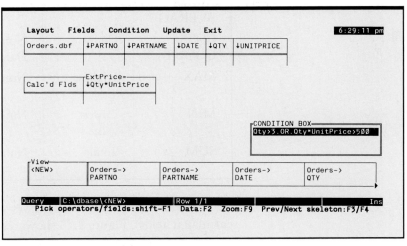

Figure 9.22: A sample OR query

REMOVING CALCULATED FIELDS

To remove all of the calculated fields from a query, put the cursor into any calculated field and select Remove File from Query from the Layout menu.

There is no way to remove a single calculated field from the Calc'd Flds skeleton. However, you can easily remove the calculated field from the View skeleton (if it's already in the View skeleton as indicated by the ↓ to the left of the expression) by moving the highlighter to the calculated field and pressing F5. To erase the expression in a calculated field, highlight the calculated field and press Ctrl-Y.

USING SUMMARY OPERATORS

Like reports, queries offer summary operators. To use a summary operator in a query, you place its name beneath the box in the appropriate field. The summary operator must be spelled correctly, as listed in the left column of Table 9.4. The table also lists the data types with which each summary operator can be used.

Table 9.4: Summary Operators Used in Query Forms

Summary operator	Calculates	Data types
AVG or AVERAGE	Average	Numeric, Float
CNT or COUNT	Count	Numeric, Float, Character, Date, Logical
MAX	Highest value	Numeric, Float, Character, Date
MIN	Lowest value	Numeric, Float, Character, Date
SUM	Total	Numeric, Float

You can use summary operators with database fields only (not calculated fields). Figure 9.23 shows a sample query that displays the sums of the QTY and UNITPRICE fields.

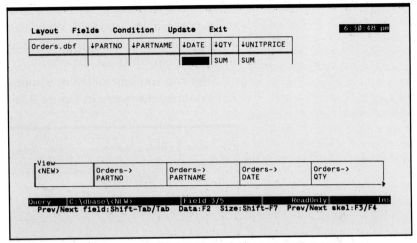

Figure 9.23: Query to sum the QTY and UNITPRICE fields

Figure 9.24 shows the results of the query. As you can see, only the summed fields are displayed. It would not make much sense to display any other fields, because the sums include all records, not just those for a particular part number or part name.

PARTNO	PARTNAME	DATE	QTY	UNITPRICE
		/ /	19	2450.00

(Browse screen: menu line — Records Organize Fields Go To Exit; status line — Browse C:\dbase\<NEW> Rec 1/1 View ReadOnly Ins)

Figure 9.24: Results of the query shown in Figure 9.23

You can combine filter conditions and summary operators in separate fields or in the same field. When combining the two in a single field, separate them with a comma, as in Figure 9.25. (The query counts the number of records in the database with part number A-111.)

You can combine different summary operators in a single query. For example, the query in Figure 9.26 will display the highest (latest)

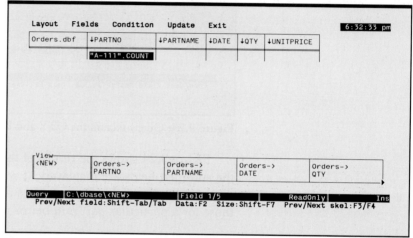

Figure 9.25: A query to count the number of records with A-111 in the PARTNO field

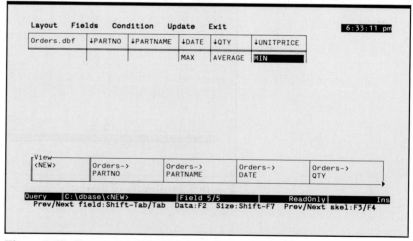

Figure 9.26: Summary operators combined in a query

date, the average quantity, and the lowest unit price. You could still use a filter condition, such as **A-111** in the PARTNO field, to limit the calculation to part number A-111.

GROUPS AND SUBTOTALS IN QUERIES

Unlike reports, queries don't require indexes to print subtotals or groups.

Queries can generate quick calculations that involve groups or subtotals, without the use of report formats or indexes. To group the results of a query, place the Group By operator in the field that you want records grouped by and include at least one summary operator to perform a calculation. Figure 9.27 shows an example query that groups records by the PARTNAME field and sums the QTY field for each group.

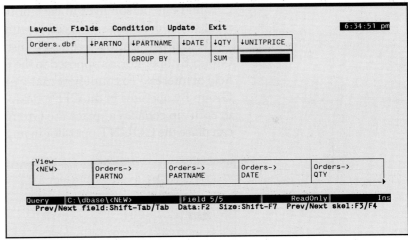

Figure 9.27: Query to subtotal QTY by part name

The results of the query are shown in Figure 9.28. Note that the results of the query show *only* the resulting summaries, and not the individual details within each group.

By default, dBASE will sort the results of queries that use the Group By operator into ascending order, based on the Group By field. You can override this default sort order by using the Sort on This Field option from the Fields pull-down menu in the query design screen. For example, if the query in Figure 9.27 used Group By, Dsc1 in the PARTNO field, the results would have been displayed in descending order.

CALCULATING FREQUENCY DISTRIBUTIONS

You can combine the Group By and Count summary functions in a query to calculate a *frequency distribution* (a count of all records that have a specific value). For example, suppose that in the CUSTLIST database you want to know how many customers lived in each state.

First, you have to select the CUSTLIST database from the Control Center to open it. Then you must create a query like the one shown in Figure 9.29.

Figure 9.30 shows the results of the query. Four people live in CA, and one person lives in each of the other states. (Obviously the results would be more impressive with a larger database.)

When performing frequency distributions, remember that the Group By operator, as opposed to the Count operator, is placed in the field of interest. To count how many people live in each city, place the Group By operator in the CITY field. To count the number of people in each zip code area, place the Group By field in the ZIP field. You can place the COUNT operator in any other field in the query design

Figure 9.28: Results of the query in Figure 9.27

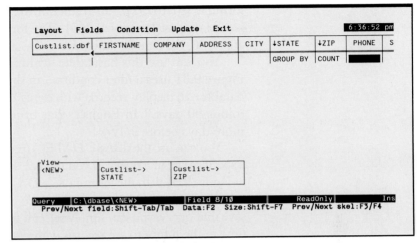

Figure 9.29: Frequency distribution query

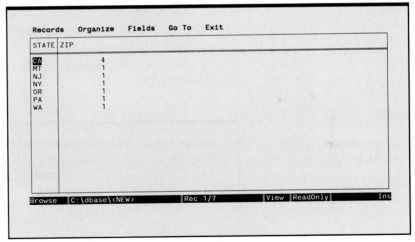

Figure 9.30: Results of the frequency distribution query

screen. To ensure that the results of the query are easy to read, include only the fields that contain the GROUP BY and COUNT operators in the view skeleton.

CALCULATING DATES

You can add a number to a date, or subtract a number from a date, to determine the date a certain number of days away. For example, the formula {01/01/91} + 90 results in the date 04/01/91, the date that is 90 days past January 1, 1991. The formula {12/15/90}-60 results in 10/16/90, the date 60 days prior to December 15, 1990.

You can use this basic date arithmetic in queries. The query in Figure 9.31 uses a filter condition in the Date field of the ORDERS database to display records with dates "less than or equal to 9/12/91 minus 90 days." In English, that translates to dates that are 90 or more days before 9/12/91.

You can use the dBASE DATE( ) (today's date) function in place of a specific date in a query. If you replace the formula < = {9/12/91}-90} in Figure 9.31 with the formula < = DATE( )-90, the query will display records with dates that are 90 or more days before today. If you then save that query, you can simply select it from the Control Center at any time in the future to see records with dates from 90 or more days ago. This feature is very handy for accounts receivable.

You can also subtract one date from another to determine the number of days between two dates. For instance, the formula {12/15/91} – {12/01/91} results in the number 14, because 12/15/91 is 14 days "larger than" (that is, after) 12/01/91. The formula {01/01/91} – {03/01/91} results in – 59, because 1/1/91 is 59 days "smaller than" (that is, before) 3/1/91.

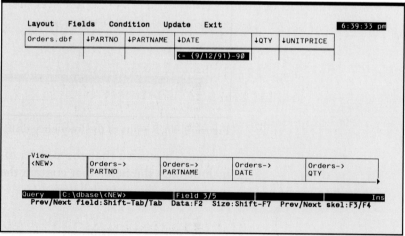

Figure 9.31: Request for records with dates 90 or more days before 09/12/91

This kind of date arithmetic can be very useful in databases that store starting and ending dates for projects. For instance, suppose a database contained two fields named STARTDATE and ENDDATE, and both are the Date data type. You could create a calculated field (either in a report or query) that used the expression ENDDATE – STARTDATE to quickly display the number of days between each starting and ending date.

COMPARING FIELDS

Once in a while, you might want to perform a query that compares values in one field to values in another field. Neither the CUSTLIST nor ORDERS database can provide a good example, but the database of stock prices shown in Figure 9.32 can. Suppose you want to isolate records from this database that have a difference of three or more dollars in the opening and closing stock prices.

To perform such a query, you need to use an *example*, or *placeholder*, in the query. The placeholder can be any letter or word (such as X, Y, or Zookie). Put the placeholder in one of the fields in the comparison and then use the placeholder in the filter condition of the other field in the comparison.

Figure 9.33 shows an example where several placeholders are used for comparisons and calculations. The placeholder for the

Figure 9.32: Database of stock prices

OPEN field was typed in as StartofDay (though again, any letter or word would do). The CLOSE field uses the query expression $> = StartofDay + 3$ to limit the resulting records being displayed to those in which the closing price is at least $3.00 higher than the opening price.

To calculate and display the difference between the opening and closing prices, a calculated field named CHANGE was also created and added to the View skeleton. As you can see, EndofDay was typed into the CLOSE field as an example (placeholder). Then the calculated field displays the result EndofDay-StartofDay, the difference between the closing and opening stock prices. Figure 9.34 shows the results of the query.

Returning to our date arithmetic, suppose you want to isolate records with 90 or more days between their starting and ending dates. You could put a placeholder in the STARTDATE field and a filter condition in the ENDDATE field that looks for ending dates that are 90 or more days "greater than" the starting date. Figure 9.35 shows such a query.

Figure 9.36 shows the results of this query, using a hypothetical database of projects.

NOTE

Examples (placeholders) are required only when comparing fields in filter conditions.

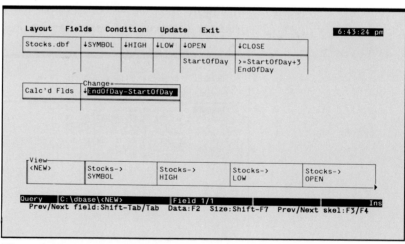

Figure 9.33: A query comparing two fields

You'll be learning still more features and capabilities of reports, forms, and queries in coming chapters. For now, you've seen a good portion of dBASE's math capabilities.

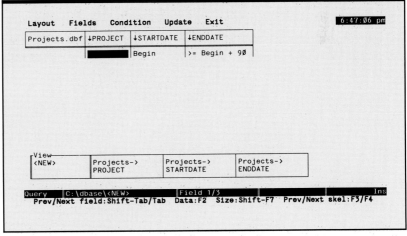

Figure 9.34: Results of the query in Figure 9.33

Figure 9.35: Query for records with ending dates 90 or more days past their starting dates

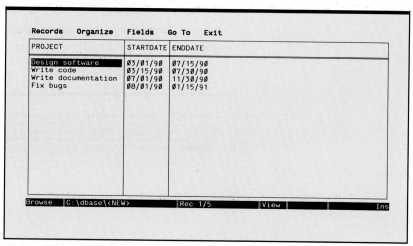

Figure 9.36: Results of the query in Figure 9.35

CHAPTER

10

Using Memo Fields to Store Documents

IN SOME DATABASES, YOU MIGHT WANT TO STORE an entire written document with each database record. For example, you might want to store resumes in a personnel database. In a real estate office, you could store descriptions of each property in your database. You could store abstracts of journal articles in a database of scientific research references or reviews of performances in a music collection.

You can store a large body of text in a *memo field*. A memo field can hold over 64,000 characters, or about 18 single-spaced pages of text. dBASE offers many features for managing memo fields, including the dBASE IV *editor,* which provides tools for creating, changing, and formatting the text in a memo field.

GETTING STARTED

In this chapter we'll create a new catalog and database to demonstrate techniques for managing memo fields. The database will list references to journal articles and include an abstract of each article. Because most of the techniques you use in this chapter will be the same as those you've used in previous chapters, this chapter won't present step-by-step instructions for every object you create. If you need help with specific techniques in this chapter, refer to the appropriate chapter in this book.

To create a new catalog named RESEARCH, go to the Control Center and follow these steps:

1. Select Use a Different Catalog from the Catalog pull-down menu.

2. Select <create> from the submenu.

3. When prompted, type the catalog name **RESEARCH** and press ←┘.

You should see the Control Center, with all the panels empty, and the name of the RESEARCH.CAT catalog centered near the top of the screen.

THE DATABASE STRUCTURE

To create a database structure for storing references, use the usual steps: select <create> from the Data panel of the Control Center and fill in field names and other information in the usual manner. Figure 10.1 shows the database structure that we'll use in this chapter. Note that the field named ABSTRACT is the memo data type. dBASE automatically assigns a width of 10 characters to the field. But don't worry; you can still enter up to 18 pages of text in the memo field, as you'll soon see.

Also, as you can see in the figure, the AUTHORS and DATE fields are marked Y for indexing, so that you can easily display references in alphabetical order by name or in date order.

After you've created the database structure, select Edit Database Description from the Layout pull-down menu and enter the description **References to journal articles**. Then select Save Changes and Exit from the Exit pull-down menu. When prompted, type REFERENC as the file name and then press ◄┘. You'll be returned to the Control Center.

NOTE

You cannot create an index of a memo field.

ENTERING DATA INTO MEMO FIELDS

To add or change memo field data, you first use the usual techniques for entering or changing database records. That is, make sure that REFERENC is highlighted in the Data panel and then press Data (F2). You'll notice that the memo field appears as a highlight with the word *memo* inside it. The word *memo* is used as a *marker* to remind you that this field can actually contain a much larger memo. Go ahead now and type the sample reference shown in Figure 10.2.

You can use any one of three techniques to enter text into the memo field:

• Move the cursor to the memo marker and press Ctrl-Home.

• Move the cursor to the memo marker and press Zoom (F9).

• If the cursor is in the field directly above the memo field, pressing Next (F4) moves the cursor into the memo field, automatically preparing the screen for data to be added or modified. If

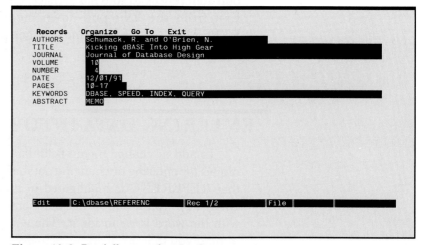

Figure 10.1: Database structure with a memo field

Figure 10.2: Partially completed reference

the cursor is in the field beneath the memo field, pressing Previous (F3) automatically takes you to the memo field editor.

In this example, the cursor is already in the memo field, so press Ctrl-Home. You'll be taken to the memo field editor, where you can enter your text.

USING THE MEMO FIELD EDITOR

The memo field editor is virtually identical to the word-wrap editor that you used in the reports design screen to create a form letter. Like a word processor, the memo field editor automatically *word wraps* long sentences into paragraphs, so that if you change something in a paragraph, the entire paragraph is reformatted automatically.

Most of the editing keys used with the memo field editor are identical to the editing keys you've already used to design reports and custom forms. These keys are listed in Table 10.1. Note that many operations provide alternative keystrokes. For example, to move the cursor right one space, you can press either → or Ctrl-D. The alternative keystrokes are identical to those in some popular word processing programs, such as WordStar. They are provided for dBASE IV users who are already familiar with such programs.

 TIP

Many of the alternative keystrokes shown in Table 10.1 are available in other dBASE editing modes as well. If you prefer the alternative keystrokes, feel free to try them at any time.

Table 10.1: Editing Keys Used in the Memo Field Editor

Keys	Alternative	Action
→	Ctrl-D	Moves cursor right one character
←	Ctrl-S	Moves cursor left one character
↓	Ctrl-X	Moves cursor down one line
↑	Ctrl-E	Moves cursor up one line
Ins	Ctrl-V	Toggles between Insert and Overwrite modes; when Insert mode is on, cursor appears as a blinking square, and when Insert mode is off, cursor appears as a blinking underline
Del	Ctrl-G	Deletes character at cursor
Ctrl-T		Deletes word to the right of the cursor
Ctrl-Y		Deletes entire line
Backspace	Ctrl-H	Moves cursor left one character and erases along the way

Table 10.1: Editing Keys Used in the Memo Field Editor (continued)

Keys	Alternative	Action
↵	Ctrl-M	Marks end of a paragraph; adds a new blank line if Insert mode is on
Ctrl-N		Inserts a blank line, regardless of whether Insert mode is on
Home	Ctrl-Z	Moves cursor to beginning of line
End	Ctrl-B	Moves cursor to end of line
Ctrl-→	Ctrl-F	Moves cursor to beginning of next word
Ctrl-←	Ctrl-A	Moves cursor to beginning of previous word
PgDn	Ctrl-C	Scrolls down one screen or to bottom of existing text on the current page
PgUp	Ctrl-R	Scrolls up one screen or to top of existing text on the current page
Tab	Ctrl-I	Moves cursor to next tab stop
Ctrl-End	Ctrl-W	Saves changes and exits
Ctrl-Q	Escape	Abandons changes and exits

The top of the editor screen displays a menu bar and a ruler (see Figure 10.3). Within the ruler, the left bracket ([) shows the left margin, and the right bracket (]) shows the right margin. By default, the left margin is set at 0 and the right margin is set at 65, about the right width for printing on 8½-by-11 inch paper with proper margins. The triangles show tab stops, which are used for indenting and outdenting memo field paragraphs.

ENTERING PARAGRAPHS

When you type paragraphs of text into a memo field, the main point to keep in mind is that you do not press ↵ until you get to the

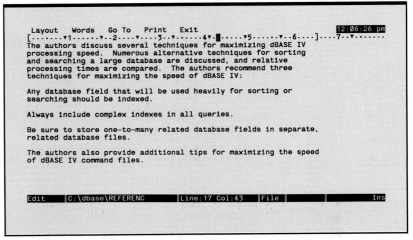

Figure 10.3: Paragraph typed into a memo field

end of a paragraph; unlike a conventional typewriter, dBASE automatically word wraps text within a paragraph when you attempt to type past the right margin. To enter the memo field text, type the first paragraph shown in Figure 10.3 without pressing ← until you get to the colon (:) at the end of the paragraph.

After you've finished typing the first paragraph, press ← twice before typing in the next two lines of text. Type the entire memo as shown in Figure 10.3, pressing ← twice at the end of each paragraph (wherever you see a blank line in the figure).

SAVING A MEMO FIELD

After you've finished entering your memo field, you can use either of the following techniques to save your work and return to the edit screen:

- Select Save Changes and Exit from the Exit pull-down menu.

- Type Ctrl-End.

When you get back to the edit screen, you'll notice that the marker in the ABSTRACT field now reads "MEMO." When a memo field contains information, its marker is shown in uppercase letters, so you can tell when a memo field contains data without going to the editor.

After entering the first record, select Exit from the Exit pull-down menu to return to the Control Center.

USING MEMO FIELDS IN CUSTOM FORMS

The standard edit and browse screens always indicate memo fields with markers. When you create your own custom forms, you can display memo fields as markers (as on the standard edit and browse screens), or you can display parts of memo fields in a *memo window*. The window technique is very handy because it lets you see at least a portion of the memo field while still viewing other fields in the database.

Figure 10.4 shows the first record in the REFERENC database displayed in a custom form, with the memo field displayed in a memo window. The memo window in this example shows the first few lines of the Abstract field. When you create your own custom forms with memo windows, you can make the memo window any size you wish.

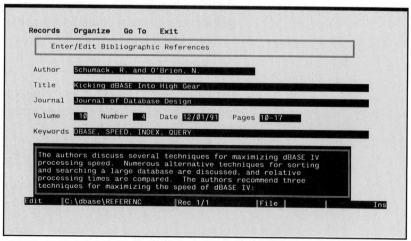

Figure 10.4: A memo field displayed in a memo window

To create a custom form with a memo window, start with the usual steps for creating a custom form. That is, make sure the appropriate database file is in use and then select <create> from the Forms panel. When you get to the forms design screen, select Quick Layout from the Layout pull-down menu. Then you can use the techniques discussed in Chapter 8 to add, change, move, and copy field templates and text on the screen.

Initially, the memo field will be displayed as a marker on the custom form. If left as such, only the marker ''memo'' or ''MEMO'' will be displayed on your custom form (exactly as on the standard browse and edit screens). If you want to change the marker to a memo window, first rearrange all other fields on the form, leaving enough space to accommodate the memo window. For example, Figure 10.5 shows the current form with fields rearranged, a title added, and some blank space near the bottom where the memo field will be placed.

BUILDING A MEMO WINDOW

To create a memo window, you first change the memo field display format from Marker to Window and select a border for the window. Then you use the Size (Shift-F7) and Move (F7) keys to size

Figure 10.5: Custom form with memo field displayed as a marker

and move the window into position. Using the form in Figure 10.5 as a starting point, follow these steps to create a memo window:

1. Move the cursor to inside the memo field template (so that the cursor is on the first M in MEMO).

2. Press the F5 key.

3. Highlight the Display As option in the menu and press the space bar to change the setting to Window.

4. Select Border Lines.

5. Select any border type you wish (this example uses Double Line).

6. Press Ctrl-End to leave the submenu.

When you return to the design screen, a large memo field window filled with X's will appear on the forms design screen.

Now you need to size and position the window. Here are the steps for this example:

1. Move the cursor to any position inside the memo window.

2. Press Move (F7) and move the cursor to row 15, column 2 (as indicated in the center of the status bar near the bottom of the screen).

3. Press ← to complete the move.

4. Press Size (Shift-F7).

5. Use the ↑ and → keys to move the lower-right corner of the memo window to row 21, column 71.

6. Press ← to finish sizing the window.

After moving and sizing the memo window, press ↑ (or PgUp) as necessary to get back to the top of the screen. Figure 10.6 shows the memo window on the forms design screen. The window actually extends down to row 21, but you cannot see the bottom of the window in the figure because it is partially obscured by the status bar and navigation line of the design screen.

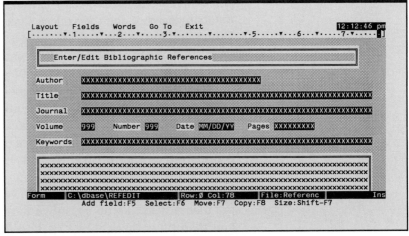

Figure 10.6: Memo window on the forms design screen

After placing the memo window, save the form by selecting Save Changes and Exit from the Exit pull-down menu. When prompted, assign a valid name to the form, such as **RefEdit**.

USING THE MEMO WINDOW

Now that you've created and saved the custom form, you can use it in the usual manner. That is, you can highlight its name in the Forms panel of the Control Center, press ◄━┛, and select Display Data. You can edit existing records, or you can select Add New Records from the Records pull-down menu to add new records.

To add or change the data in the memo window, move the cursor into the window and press Ctrl-Home or Zoom, just as you would when a marker is displayed. To expand the memo window to full screen, press Zoom (F9). After making your changes, press Ctrl-End. You'll be returned to the custom form.

DISPLAYING MEMOS IN REPORTS

You can place memo fields in report formats just as you can any other database field. By default, the memo field will be displayed in a template 50 characters wide, using the Vertical Stretch picture function so that all text is word-wrapped within the allotted width.

To create a sample report, make sure that the REFERENC database is in use and then select <create> from the Reports panel. When you get to the reports design screen, select Quick Layouts from the Layout pull-down menu and Form Layout from the submenu. Then use the usual keys and techniques to format the report.

Figure 10.7 shows a sample report format, which was initially created by selecting Form Layout from the Quick Layouts submenu. The usual editing keys and techniques were used to change text and to arrange the field templates. Notice that the Abstract field template is displayed as a series of 50 V's.

You cannot change the template assigned to a memo field; it must be V (for Vertical Stretch). However, you can widen or narrow the memo field. To do so, move the cursor into the field template and then press Size (Shift-F7). Use the ← or → key to narrow or widen the template and then press ↵ when you are done. Later, when you print the report, all text in the memo field will be word-wrapped within the width of the field template on the report.

Because the Abstract field uses the Vertical Stretch picture function, the text within the margin will extend downward when the report is printed. Remember to place at least one blank line beneath the memo field template in the Detail band if you want to print a blank line at the bottom of the memo field.

Figure 10.7: Sample report format with a memo field

Figure 10.8 shows a single record printed from the sample report format. Note that the text in the memo field is word-wrapped within the default width of 50 characters.

QUERYING MEMO FIELDS

In the queries design screen, you can use the $ (embedded in) operator in a condition box to isolate records that have a particular word or group of words in the memo field. For example, Figure 10.9 shows a query that will search the REFERENC database for records with "dBASE IV" embedded in the Abstract field.

When using a condition box to create filter conditions, you can press Zoom (F9) to zoom into and out of the box. Use .AND. and .OR. operators for AND and OR queries. For example, the filter condition in Figure 10.10 searches for records that have dBASE IV in the Keywords or Abstract field.

NOTE

To create a condition box in the query design screen, select Add Condition Box from the Condition pull-down menu.

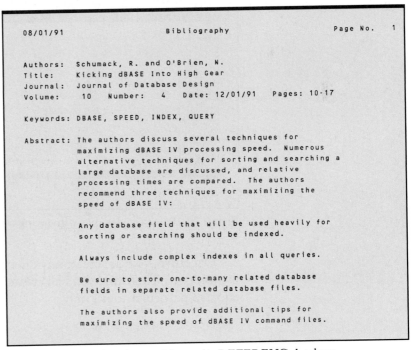

```
08/01/91                    Bibliography                    Page No.    1


Authors:  Schumack, R. and O'Brien, N.
Title:    Kicking dBASE Into High Gear
Journal:  Journal of Database Design
Volume:    10   Number:    4   Date: 12/01/91    Pages: 10-17

Keywords: DBASE, SPEED, INDEX, QUERY

Abstract: The authors discuss several techniques for
          maximizing dBASE IV processing speed.  Numerous
          alternative techniques for sorting and searching a
          large database are discussed, and relative
          processing times are compared.  The authors
          recommend three techniques for maximizing the
          speed of dBASE IV:

          Any database field that will be used heavily for
          sorting or searching should be indexed.

          Always include complex indexes in all queries.

          Be sure to store one-to-many related database
          fields in separate related database files.

          The authors also provide additional tips for
          maximizing the speed of dBASE IV command files.
```

Figure 10.8: A printed record from the REFERENC database

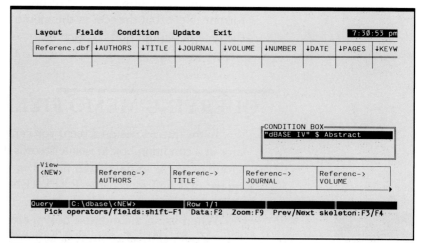

Figure 10.9: Query for records with "dBASE IV" in the Abstract field

```
 Layout   Fields   Condition   Update   Exit                    2:46:47 pm
┌CONDITION BOX─────────────────────────────────────────────────────────────
│"dBASE IV" $ Keywords .OR. "dBASE IV" $ Abstract
│
│
│
│
│
│
│
│
│
│
│
│
└────────────────────────────────────────────────────────────────────────
┌View─────────────────────────────────────────────────────────────────────
│<NEW>        Referenc->    Referenc->    Referenc->    Referenc->
│             AUTHORS       TITLE         JOURNAL       VOLUME
└────────────────────────────────────────────────────────────────────────
Query    C:\dbase\<NEW>            Row 1/1
      Pick operators/fields:shift-F1   Data:F2   Zoom:F9   Prev/Next skeleton:F3/F4
```

Figure 10.10: A complex query involving a memo field

Of course, you can create any query, save it, and use it for printing a report. That way, you can create bibliographies that list references to particular topics only.

MANAGING MEMO FIELD TEXT

You can use many techniques within the word-wrap editor to polish the format of your memo field data. This section discusses these techniques.

MOVING, COPYING, AND DELETING BLOCKS OF TEXT

To move, copy, or delete a block of text, you must first select a block using the Select (F6) key. Position the cursor at the first character of the block you wish to select and press Select. Then use the arrow keys to extend the selection (the selected text will be highlighted). As an alternative to pressing an arrow key, you can press F6 a second time to select a word, or press F6 a third time to select an entire paragraph. Press ← after highlighting the entire block of text.

To move or copy the selected block of text, move the cursor to the new location on the screen. Then press Move (F7) or Copy (F8). To delete the selected block, press the Del key.

FORCING PAGE BREAKS

When you print memo fields, dBASE will automatically start a new page when the current page is filled. If you prefer, you can force a page break to occur at a specific place in a memo field. To do so, position the cursor where you want a new page to begin. Then select Insert Page Break from the Words pull-down menu. You'll see a dashed line across the screen where the new page will begin when the memo field is printed.

If you change your mind about the page break and want to delete it, just move the cursor to the dashed line and press Del.

COPYING TEXT FROM ONE MEMO FIELD TO ANOTHER

Suppose you want to use the text in one memo field in the memo field of another record. To do so, you need to copy the text from the source (original) memo field to a disk file. Then you need to move into the memo field of the target record (the one that is receiving the copy) and read in the file. Here are the basic steps:

1. Display the source record (the one that contains the memo field that you want to copy) on the edit screen.

2. Move the cursor to the memo field and press Ctrl-Home to get to the editor.

3. Use the Select key (F6) to highlight the block of text you want to copy (or all the text in the memo field, if you prefer).

4. Press Menu (F10) and select Write/Read Text File from the Words pull-down menu.

5. Select Write Selection to File from the submenu.

6. When prompted, enter a valid DOS file name (for example, you could enter **MEMCOPY**) but no extension. Then press ←⏎.

7. Press Ctrl-End to return to the edit screen.

8. Display the target record (the one you want to copy the text into) on the edit screen (or select Add New Records from the Records pull-down menu to add a new record).

9. Move the cursor to the memo field of the target record and press Ctrl-Home.

10. Position the cursor where you want the incoming text to appear.

11. Press F10 and select Write/Read Text File from the Words pull-down menu.

12. Select Read Text from File from the submenu.

13. When prompted, enter the name of the file in which you stored the text (MEMCOPY, in this example), or press Shift-F1 to see all file names with the .TXT extension.

14. Press Ctrl-End to save the copied text.

Note that if you write the memo field text to a file that already exists, dBASE will beep and warn you that you are about to overwrite an existing file. If you are going to be copying memo field text often, you might want to reserve a special file name (MEMCOPY, for example) just for copying memo fields (dBASE automatically adds the extension .TXT to the file name you provide). That way, when dBASE warns that you are about to overwrite a file with the same name, you'll know that the existing file is the MEMCOPY file you created during the previous copy operation and can be safely overwritten.

FORMATTING PARAGRAPHS

You can indent a paragraph in a memo field by moving the cursor to the first character of the paragraph and pressing the Tab key. Each time you press the Tab key, the entire paragraph is indented by one tab space. Pressing Shift-Tab has the opposite effect; it outdents the paragraph by one tab stop.

SOME TECHNICAL ASPECTS OF MEMO FIELDS

While you are using a database that contains a memo field, it will appear that you are working with a single database file, and that the memo field is just another field. But the actual events that are taking place behind the scenes are a little different than they look on the screen.

For instance, the contents of memo fields are not actually stored in the database file. Instead, they are stored in a separate file that has the same name as the database file, but the extension .DBT. For example, in this chapter, the file REFERENC.DBF holds all the fields except the memo field; the file REFERENC.DBT holds only the memo field.

The ABSTRACT field in the REFERENC.DBF database file contains a *pointer,* a special code that tells dBASE the location of the appropriate memo field in the separate .DBT file. The reason that memo fields are always assigned a width of 10 characters when you design a database is that this pointer occupies 10 characters in the record.

None of this information is particularly important to know unless you use commands outside of dBASE to copy, rename, or delete files.

For example, if you were to use the DOS command **COPY REFERENC.DBF REFBAK.DBF** to copy the REFERENC.DBF database to a file called REFBAK.DBF, DOS would not automatically copy the REFERENC.DBT file in the process.

If you later tried to use REFBAK.DBF through dBASE, an error message would appear telling you that dBASE could not find the memo file and asking whether you want to create a new, empty memo file. In other words, dBASE is telling you that REFBAK.DBF has a memo field in it, but there is no file named REFBAK.DBT that contains the memos.

To avoid such errors, either use dBASE IV to copy, rename, and delete all files, or use the extension .DB? rather than .DBF when copying dBASE files in DOS. For example, entering the DOS command **COPY REFERENC.DB? REFBAK.DB?** automatically copies REFERENC.DBF and REFERENC.DBT to two files named REFBAK.DBF and REFBAK.DBT. See Chapter 14 for more information about managing files.

11

Managing
Groups of
Records

To mark a record for deletion,   358
> move the cursor to the appropriate record and type Ctrl-U or select Mark Record for Deletion from the Records pull-down menu.

To temporarily delete, or *hide,* records marked for deletion,   359
> select Settings from the Tools menu in the Control Center and set the Deleted option to On.

To unmark records that are marked for deletion,   360
> first set Deleted to Off. Then return to the browse or edit screen, position the cursor in the marked record, and press Ctrl-U or select Clear Deletion Mark from the Records pull-down menu.

To permanently delete marked records from the database,   361
> select Erase Marked Records from the Organize menu on the database design screen.

To make a change to all records that meet a filter condition,   364

1. Create a query with the appropriate filter conditions.
2. Enter the word **REPLACE** beneath the file name in the file skeleton.
3. Enter the word **WITH** and the value or expression defining the replacement in the field that contains the values to be replaced.
4. Select Perform the Update from the Update pull-down menu.

To mark all records that meet some filter condition,
set up the appropriate filter condition in a query and enter the word **MARK** beneath the file name in the file skeleton.

To unmark records that meet some filter condition,
set up the appropriate filter condition in a query and enter the word **UNMARK** beneath the file name in the file skeleton.

To unmark all records in a database,
highlight the name of the database in the Control Center and press Design (Shift-F2). Then select Unmark All Records from the Organize pull-down menu.

IN MANAGING YOUR DATABASE, YOU MAY SOME-
times want to perform an operation on an entire group of records.
For example, you might want to raise the unit price of part B-222 by
10 percent in all records that contain this part number. This chapter
discusses techniques for performing such tasks, as well as general
techniques for hiding and deleting records and customizing the
browse screen.

Once again, we'll use the database files in the LEARN catalog
for demonstrations. If the LEARN catalog is not currently in the
Control Center on your screen, select Use a Different Catalog from
the Catalog pull-down menu, and LEARN.CAT from the submenu
that appears.

DELETING DATABASE RECORDS

There are two techniques for deleting database records. The first
is to *mark* a record for deletion. This does not actually remove the
record from the database, but instead allows you to hide, or temporarily delete, the record. You can bring marked records out of hiding
and unmark them at any time.

The second method for deleting records is often called *packing*.
Packing a database permanently removes from the database
all records currently marked for deletion. Any records beneath
a deleted record move up a notch to fill the void left by the deleted
record (hence the term *packing*). There is no way to recover de-
eted records once you've packed the database.

MARKING RECORDS FOR DELETION

Whether you are using the edit or browse screen or a custom form,
you use the same techniques to mark a record for deletion. First, use the
usual arrow, PgUp, and PgDn keys to move the cursor to the record
you want to mark. Then use one of the following ways to mark the
record:

- Select Mark Record for Deletion from the Records pull-
  down menu.

• Press Ctrl-U.

Suppose Wilbur Watson has not placed an order in many months and you decide to delete him from the CUSTLIST database. Move to his record on the browse screen and type Ctrl-U to mark his record for deletion. The only indication that the record has been marked is the word ''Del'' in the status bar at the bottom of the screen. Figure 11.1 shows Wilbur Watson's record marked for deletion on the browse screen.

HIDING MARKED RECORDS

You can hide marked records without permanently deleting them. First you need to select Exit from the Exit pull-down menu to return to the Control Center. At the Control Center, follow these steps:

1. Press Menu (F10) and highlight Tools on the menu bar.

2. Select Settings.

3. Highlight the Deleted option and press the space bar to change the option from Off to On, as in Figure 11.2.

4. Select Exit to Control Center from the Exit pull-down menu.

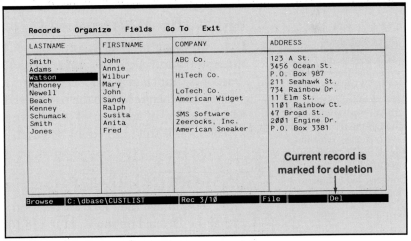

Figure 11.1: Watson's record marked for deletion

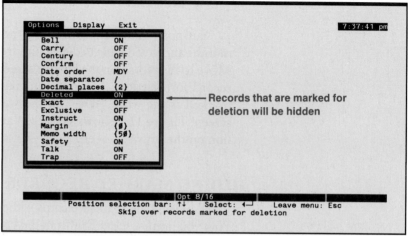

Figure 11.2: Deleted option set to On

If you now highlight CUSTLIST in the data panel and press Data (F2) to view its records, you'll see that Wilbur Watson's record no longer appears, as Figure 11.3 shows. If you use the ↓ key to scroll through records, you might notice that the Rec indicator skips from 2 to 4 when you scroll from Adams to Mahoney. That's because Wilbur's record (number 3) still exists; it's just hidden for the time being.

BRINGING MARKED RECORDS OUT OF HIDING

When the Deleted option is On, marked records are excluded from *all* dBASE operations, as though the records do not exist. Always remember to set the Deleted option to Off when you no longer need to hide marked records.

To bring marked records out of hiding, return to the Control Center and follow the same steps that you followed to hide the records, but change the Deleted setting from On back to Off. If you do so and then return to the browse screen, you'll see Wilbur's record once again. In addition, if you move the cursor to his record, you'll see that it is still marked for deletion.

UNMARKING RECORDS

To remove the mark for deletion from a record, first make sure that the Deleted option is set to Off (otherwise, you won't be able to see the marked record that you are trying to unmark). Then move

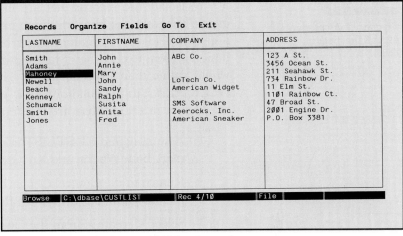

```
    Records   Organize   Fields   Go To   Exit
   ┌──────────────┬───────────────┬──────────────────┬──────────────────┐
   │ LASTNAME     │ FIRSTNAME     │ COMPANY          │ ADDRESS          │
   ├──────────────┼───────────────┼──────────────────┼──────────────────┤
   │ Smith        │ John          │ ABC Co.          │ 123 A St.        │
   │ Adams        │ Annie         │                  │ 3456 Ocean St.   │
   │ Mahoney      │ Mary          │                  │ 211 Seahawk St.  │
   │ Newell       │ John          │ LoTech Co.       │ 734 Rainbow Dr.  │
   │ Beach        │ Sandy         │ American Widget  │ 11 Elm St.       │
   │ Kenney       │ Ralph         │                  │ 1101 Rainbow Ct. │
   │ Schumack     │ Susita        │ SMS Software     │ 47 Broad St.     │
   │ Smith        │ Anita         │ Zeerocks, Inc.   │ 2001 Engine Dr.  │
   │ Jones        │ Fred          │ American Sneaker │ P.O. Box 3381    │
   │              │               │                  │                  │
   │              │               │                  │                  │
   │              │               │                  │                  │
   │              │               │                  │                  │
   │              │               │                  │                  │
   ├──────────────┴───────────────┴──────────────────┴──────────────────┤
   │ Browse │C:\dbase\CUSTLIST    │Rec 4/10          │File               │
   └─────────────────────────────────────────────────────────────────────┘
```

Figure 11.3: Marked record hidden from view

the cursor to the record that you want to unmark and use one of these techniques:

- Select Clear Deletion Mark from the Records pull-down menu.
- Press Ctrl-U.

Notice that Ctrl-U acts as a toggle. That is, each time you press Ctrl-U, the current record's status changes from marked to unmarked. You'll see the Del indicator in the status bar appear or disappear each time you press Ctrl-U. For now, leave Wilbur's record marked for deletion.

> **☞ NOTE**
>
> The Clear Deletion Mark option appears on the Records pull-down menu *only* if the current record is already marked for deletion. Otherwise, the option reads Mark Record for Deletion.

ERASING MARKED RECORDS

Because packing the database permanently removes all marked records from the database, use this option with a good deal of caution. A good approach is to isolate all marked records and look at them on the browse screen before you pack the database. Use Ctrl-U or the Clear Deletion Mark option to unmark any records that you do not want permanently removed; *then* pack the database.

Chapter 12 discusses
dBASE functions in
detail.

To isolate the records that are marked for deletion, you use a query, but place the filter condition in the *condition box* rather than in a specific field. (The condition box is like any other box on the query design screen, except that it takes into consideration the record as a whole, rather than a specific field.) Then place the dBASE function DELETED( ) in the condition box, which isolates records that are marked for deletion. Here are the steps:

1. Assuming that CUSTLIST is currently on the browse screen, mark both Watson and Kenney's records for deletion.

2. Return to the Control Center by selecting Exit from the Exit pull-down menu (or by pressing Ctrl-End).

3. Select <create> from the Queries panel.

4. Press Menu (F10) and select Add Condition Box from the Condition pull-down menu.

5. Enter the function **DELETED( )** into the condition box, as in Figure 11.4.

6. Press Data (F2) to execute the query.

The browse screen appears, showing only those records that are marked for deletion, as in Figure 11.5. You can scroll through the

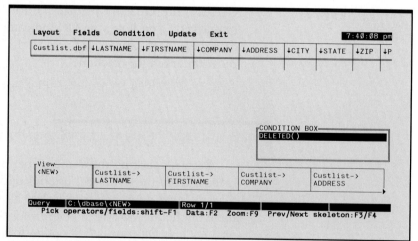

Figure 11.4: Query to isolate records marked for deletion

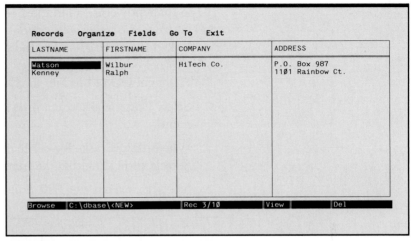

```
 Records   Organize   Fields   Go To   Exit

 LASTNAME          FIRSTNAME       COMPANY        ADDRESS

 Watson            Wilbur          HiTech Co.     P.O. Box 987
 Kenney            Ralph                          1101 Rainbow Ct.




 Browse  C:\dbase\<NEW>          Rec 3/10        View        Del
```

Figure 11.5: Marked records isolated on the browse screen

records and use the Ctrl-U key or Clear Deletion Mark option to unmark any records that you do not want permanently removed.

Note, however, that unmarking a record may not immediately remove it from the browse screen. However, the Del indicator will disappear from the status bar when you unmark a record. To be safe, you can switch back and forth from the query to the browse screen until you are certain only records that you want permanently removed are marked, as described in the following steps:

1. Move the cursor to Kenney's record and press Ctrl-U (so the Del indicator disappears).

2. Select Transfer to Query Design from the Exit pull-down menu, or just press Design (Shift-F2) to return to the query design screen.

3. Execute the same query again, to double-check the marked records, by pressing Data (F2).

Now only Wilbur Watson's record should appear in the browse screen, because step 1 removed the deletion mark from Kenney's record. Assuming you want to leave Wilbur's record marked for deletion, go ahead and select Exit from the Exit pull-down menu. dBASE will ask if you want to save the query that displays marked records. For now, select No to return to the Control Center.

To permanently erase all marked records from the database, you need to return to the browse/edit or database design screen and select Erase Marked Records. Here are the steps:

1. Highlight CUSTLIST in the Data panel and press Data (F2).

2. Select Erase Marked Records from the Organize pull-down menu.

3. When dBASE asks for confirmation, select Yes. A box will appear, indicating that the marked records are being erased.

4. Select Exit from the Exit pull-down menu to return to the Control Center.

If you view the data for the CUSTLIST database now, you'll see that Wilbur Watson's record is gone (press PgUp to view all remaining records). If you move the highlight to Mahoney's record you'll see that the record is now number 3, rather than number 4. All records following Watson's have moved up to fill the void left by the deletion.

CHANGING SEVERAL RECORDS AT ONCE

Up to now, most of your changes to the database have involved a single record. With dBASE IV's *global editing* capability, you can extend that power to change several records simultaneously. For example, with global editing you can perform any of the following tasks in a single operation:

- Increase or decrease the unit price of all orders for part A-111 by 10 percent.

- Add or subtract 30 days from shipping dates for part number C-333.

- Mark or unmark for deletion all California residents' records.

The tool for performing global editing is the *update query*. You use the usual query design screen and filter conditions, but specify an update operator in the file skeleton. You can either type the update operator directly beneath the file name in the skeleton or choose it from a menu by selecting Specify Update Operation from the Update pull-down menu. The following update operators are discussed in this chapter:

REPLACE   Replaces the contents of fields that meet the filter condition with some new value

MARK   Marks for deletion those records that meet the filter condition

UNMARK   Unmarks those records that meet the filter condition

Unlike other queries, where you press Data (F2) to see the results, update queries require you to select Perform the Update from the Update pull-down menu on the query design screen. Let's look at some examples using the ORDERS and CUSTLIST databases from the LEARN catalog.

REPLACING CHARACTER DATA

Suppose that product number B-222, Banana Man, is not doing well in the marketplace, and a corporate decision is made to change the product's name to Mondo Man. Your job is to change all references to Banana Man in the ORDERS database to Mondo Man. To change all the records without retyping them, follow these steps:

1. Open the Orders database by selecting ORDERS from the Data panel in the Control Center and Use File from the submenu.

2. Go to the query design screen by selecting <create> from the Queries panel in the Control Center.

3. To limit the update operation to part number B-222, enter the filter condition **"B-222"** (including the quotation marks) under the PARTNO field name in the file skeleton, as in Figure 11.6.

```
Layout    Fields    Condition    Update    Exit                    7:44:40 pm
Orders.dbf   ↓PARTNO  ↓PARTNAME  ↓DATE  ↓QTY  ↓UNITPRICE
             "B-222"




    ┌View────
    │<NEW>          │Orders->    │Orders->    │Orders->    │Orders->
    │               │PARTNO      │PARTNAME    │DATE        │QTY              ▶
Query    C:\dbase\<NEW>           Field 1/5
    Prev/Next field:Shift-Tab/Tab  Data:F2  Size:Shift-F7  Prev/Next skel:F3/F4
                                Unterminated string
```

Figure 11.6: Filter condition for part number B-222

4. Press Data (F2) just to make sure you've isolated the appropriate records.

The browse screen should show only records with part number B-222 in the PARTNO field in the browse screen. This step may seem superfluous to you, since you already know that putting **"B-222"** under PARTNO in the query design screen will produce this result. However, when performing update queries, it's a good idea always to enter your filter condition first and test it by pressing the Data key.

If you do not perform this step to test your filter condition, you might inadvertently change the wrong records. For example, suppose you created an update query to change part names to Mondo Man and simply forgot to include the filter condition that would limit changes to records with part number B-222. dBASE would not filter out other part numbers from the query. Hence, the update query would change *all* part names in the database to Mondo Man, and there would be no easy way to undo the erroneous (and extensive) change.

In this example the filter condition is not too complex, so it's easy to be sure that the appropriate records are displayed. But when you start using REPLACE operators with very complex filter conditions, it's easy to make a mistake. Therefore, whenever you execute *any* update

NOTE

When executing update queries on your own important data, you can take the extra precaution of backing up your original database before making global changes. Chapter 14 tells you how to make backup copies.

query, *always* enter the filter condition first and test that filter condition by pressing Data (F2). Scroll through the browse screen and make sure that *only* the records that you want to change are displayed.

If the appropriate records are not displayed, be sure to adjust the filter condition accordingly. Switch back to the query design screen by pressing Design (Shift-F2), modify the filter condition, and test the condition again by pressing Data (F2). Keep doing so until only the records that you want to change are displayed in the browse screen.

Assuming that your filter condition is accurate now, and only records for part number B-222 are displayed, follow these steps to change your basic query into an update query.

1. Press Design (Shift-F2) to return to the query design screen.

2. Press Shift-Tab to move the highlight to the space beneath the database name in the file.

3. Type the update operator REPLACE and press ←, or select Replace Values in ORDERS.DBF from the Specify Update Operation submenu of the Update pull-down menu.

4. If dBASE tells you that it will delete the view skeleton, select Proceed. (You don't need the view skeleton because it is used to display data, and update queries do not *display* data, they *change* it.)

5. Move the highlight to the PARTNAME field.

6. Tell dBASE that you want to replace the current part name for product number B-222 *with* Mondo Man by typing **WITH "Mondo Man"** (including the quotation marks) in the highlighted area.

7. Press ←.

Your query should now look like Figure 11.7. Notice that the query is actually quite descriptive. The word "Target" above the file name tells which database file is about to be changed (ORDERS.DBF in this case). The filter condition specifies records with B-222 in the PARTNO field. The update operation is to replace PARTNAME with Mondo Man (for records with B-222 in the PARTNO field). Now you are

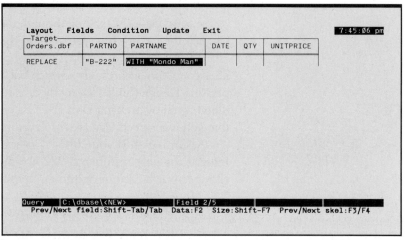

Figure 11.7: Query to replace the part number B-222 part name with Mondo Man

ready to actually execute the update query:

1. Press Menu (F10) to access the pull-down menus.

2. Use ← or → to display the Update pull-down menu.

3. Select Perform the Update from the Update pull-down menu and wait a few seconds while dBASE does its work.

You may hear your computer's disk drive whirring or buzzing as dBASE makes the change. Update queries do not show any immediate results, so you need to return to the browse screen to see what happened. There is no need to save this query, because its job is done, so follow these steps:

1. When prompted, press any key to continue.

2. Select Abandon Changes and Exit from the Exit pull-down menu.

3. When dBASE asks for confirmation before abandoning the query, select Yes.

4. When you get back to the Control Center, highlight ORDERS in the Data panel and press Data (F2).

As you'll see on the browse screen, and as Figure 11.8 shows, all part names for records with part number B-222 have been changed to Mondo Man. The change is complete and permanent. To return to the Control Center, select Exit from the Exit pull-down menu.

CHANGING NUMERIC DATA

Suppose that the price of Astro Buddies (part number A-111) is increased by 10 percent on June 1, 1991. Your job is to add 10 percent to any orders for Astro Buddies that come in after June 1. To perform this task, you need to isolate records that have order dates later than 06/01/91 in the Date field *and* that have part number A-111 in the PARTNO field and then increase the UNITPRICE value by 10 percent for those records.

To begin, you need to set up the basic filter condition for the query, as in Figure 11.9. Note that the query isolates records that have A-111 in the PARTNO field and dates greater than 6/1/91 in the DATE field. Press Data (F2) to make sure that the filter conditions isolate the appropriate records. After testing the query, press Design (Shift-F2) to return to the query design screen.

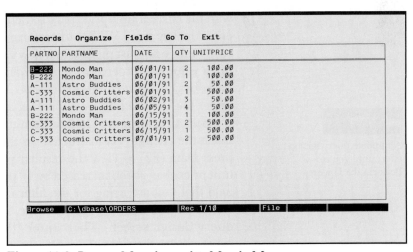

Figure 11.8: Banana Man changed to Mondo Man

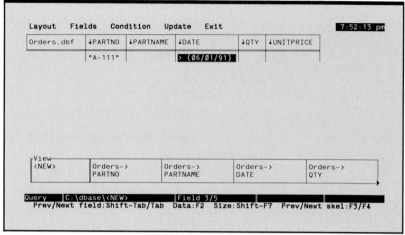

Figure 11.9: Query to isolate orders for A-111 after June 1

Now you need to enter the REPLACE update operator under the file name in the file skeleton of the query design screen. Press Home, type the word **REPLACE**, and then press ←┘. Select Proceed when dBASE reminds you that the view skeleton will be removed.

Now you need to tell dBASE to replace the current unit price with the current unit price plus 10 percent. Once again, you need to enter the key word WITH to perform the replacement. Also, in this case you are not just putting in a new value. Instead, you are increasing a value by 10 percent, so you want to multiply the current unit price by 1.10. Enter the expression WITH 1.10 * UNITPRICE under the UNITPRICE field name, as in Figure 11.10.

Select Perform the Update from the Update pull-down menu to make the change. As instructed on the screen, press any key, then press Data (F2) to view the results; you'll see that the appropriate unit prices have been increased by 10 percent, as Figure 11.11 shows. field that you are using for the filter condition, then enter the filter condition into the field first, test the basic query, and return to the query design screen. Then enter **"WITH"** and a replacement expression to the right of the filter condition, preceded by a comma.

For example, to add 30 days to the date 06/01/91 in the ORDERS database, first enter the filter condition {06/01/91} into

NOTE

An update query has no effect until you select Perform the Update.

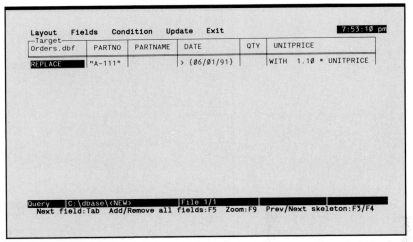

```
 Layout   Fields   Condition   Update   Exit                    7:53:10 pm
 ┌Target─────────────────────────────────────────────────────────────────
 │Orders.dbf │ PARTNO │ PARTNAME │ DATE      │ QTY │ UNITPRICE
 ├───────────┼────────┼──────────┼───────────┼─────┼───────────────────────
 │REPLACE    │ "A-111"│          │ > {06/01/91} │   │ WITH  1.10 * UNITPRICE








 Query   C:\dbase\<NEW>              File 1/1
      Next field:Tab  Add/Remove all fields:F5  Zoom:F9  Prev/Next skeleton:F3/F4
```

Figure 11.10: Query to increase the orders for part number A-111 after 6/1/91 by 10 percent

```
 Records   Organize   Fields   Go To   Exit
 ┌──────┬───────────────┬──────────┬─────┬───────────
 │PARTNO│ PARTNAME      │ DATE     │ QTY │ UNITPRICE
 ├──────┼───────────────┼──────────┼─────┼───────────
 │B-222 │ Mondo Man     │ 06/01/91 │  2  │ 100.00
 │B-222 │ Mondo Man     │ 06/01/91 │  1  │ 100.00
 │A-111 │ Astro Buddies │ 06/01/91 │  2  │  50.00
 │C-333 │ Cosmic Critters│ 06/01/91│  1  │ 500.00   Unit prices in two records
 │A-111 │ Astro Buddies │ 06/02/91 │  3  │  55.00   increased by 10 percent
 │A-111 │ Astro Buddies │ 06/05/91 │  4  │  55.00
 │B-222 │ Mondo Man     │ 06/15/91 │  1  │ 100.00
 │C-333 │ Cosmic Critters│ 06/15/91│  2  │ 500.00
 │C-333 │ Cosmic Critters│ 06/15/91│  1  │ 500.00
 │C-333 │ Cosmic Critters│ 07/01/91│  2  │ 500.00



 Browse   C:\dbase\ORDERS           Rec 1/10        File
```

Figure 11.11: Results of update query in Figure 11.10

> **TIP**
>
> Use the Zoom key (F9) as a toggle in the query design screen to zoom into and out of the current box.

the Date field on the query design screen. Press Data (F2) to test the query and then Design (Shift-F2) to return to the query. Then enter the REPLACE operator under the file name and the expression **,WITH Date + 30** next to the filter condition in the Date box, as in Figure 11.12.

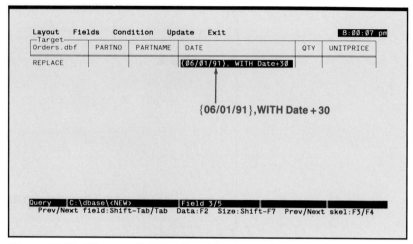

Figure 11.12: Filter condition and replacement value in one box

MARKING GROUPS OF RECORDS

To mark for deletion all records that meet some filter condition, enter the appropriate filter condition on the query design screen and test it. Then return to the query design screen and enter the update operator MARK under the field name in the skeleton. For example, Figure 11.13 shows a query to mark all records in the CUSTLIST database that have CA in the STATE field.

If you select Perform the Update from the Update pull-down menu after setting up the query shown in Figure 11.13 and then press Data (F2), you will still see California residents in the database. However, as you scroll through the records, you'll notice that the records of all California residents are marked for deletion. Of course, if you set Deleted to On (as discussed earlier in this chapter) and then view the data, the records for all California residents will be hidden, as in Figure 11.14.

UNMARKING MULTIPLE RECORDS

To unmark records that meet some filter condition, use the UNMARK update operator in the file skeleton, as in Figure 11.15. And of course, remember to select Perform the Update from the Update pull-down menu.

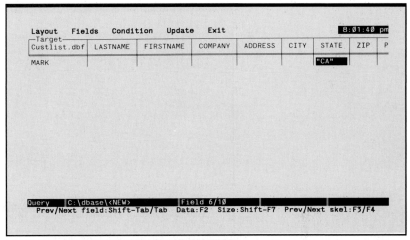

Figure 11.13: Query to mark all records that have CA in the STATE field

```
Records    Organize    Fields    Go To    Exit

COMPANY                    ADDRESS                       CITY          STATE  ZIP
                          211 Seahawk St.               Seattle        WA    8897
LoTech Co.                734 Rainbow Dr.               Butte          MT    5432
American Widget           11 Elm St.                    Portland       OR    7654
SMS Software              47 Broad St.                  Philadelphia   PA    4554
American Sneaker          P.O. Box 3381                 Newark         NJ    0123




Browse    C:\dbase\CUSTLIST           Rec 10/10         File
```

Figure 11.14: Records for California residents are hidden

To unmark all of the records in a database, you can either use the UNMARK update operator in a query with no filter conditions or select Unmark All Records from the Organize menu in the database design screen. If you use the latter method, the Deleted setting must be off.

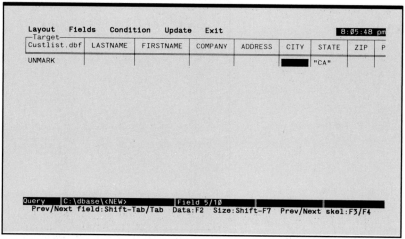

Figure 11.15: Query to unmark records

CUSTOMIZING THE BROWSE SCREEN

The browse screen offers several features to help you edit a database, which are particularly useful when you work with larger databases. All of these features are available from pull-down menus from the browse screen.

LOCKING FIELDS

The Lock Fields on Left option on the Fields pull-down menu lets you lock one or more fields at the left of the database so that they do not disappear when you scroll to the right. When you select this option, dBASE will ask how many fields you want to remain stationary. Enter a number and press ←┘.

Figure 11.16 shows the CUSTLIST database on the browse screen with the two fields, LASTNAME and FIRSTNAME, locked. Notice that the cursor is scrolled all the way to the PAID field, but the two locked fields, LASTNAME and FIRSTNAME, are still on the screen.

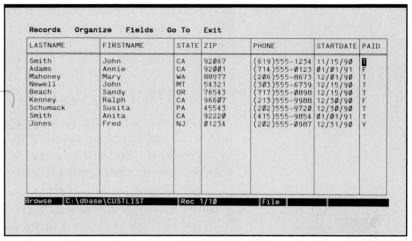

Figure 11.16: LASTNAME and FIRSTNAME fields locked on the browse screen

FREEZING A FIELD

The Freeze Field option on the Fields pull-down menu lets you isolate a particular field on the browse screen. When you select this option, dBASE asks for the name of the field to freeze. Type the field name and press ⏎.

The highlight will move to the field you've named and cannot be moved out of that field. Pressing ← and → moves the highlight up and down, rather than across fields. To unfreeze the field, select the option again and press the Backspace key to remove the field name.

BLANKING A FIELD OR RECORD

The Blank Record option leaves an empty record in a database. It does not mark or delete the record.

To empty the contents of a field, move the cursor to the appropriate field and select Blank Field from the Fields pull-down menu. To empty all the fields in a record, select Blank Record from the Records pull-down menu. If you accidentally blank the wrong field or record, select Undo Change to Record from the Records pull-down menu.

SIZING COLUMNS

You can expand or contract the size of a column on the browse screen by moving the highlight to the appropriate column and selecting

Size Field from the Fields pull-down menu, or by pressing Size (Shift-F7). After selecting the option, use the ← or → key to widen or narrow the field; then press ↵.

PREVENTING AUTOMATIC RE-SORT

When you are using an index to maintain a sort order on the browse screen, changing values in the index field causes the records to be re-sorted. (You saw an example of this in Chapter 5 when you changed Adams's last name to Zastrow.)

If you do not want the cursor to follow records to their new sorted positions while you are editing, select Follow Record to New Position from the Records pull-down menu and change its setting from Yes to No.

LOCKING RECORDS

If you are using dBASE IV on a network, other users working on the same database may change information in the database while you are viewing it. To prevent other users from changing the data in a record while you are viewing it, select Lock Record from the Records pull-down menu. The record will remain locked until you move the highlight to a different record.

At this point, you can create and manage just about any database, because you know all the basic techniques. Occasionally, though, you may need a sort order, report grouping, or calculation more complex than those we've discussed so far. No matter how complex a particular operation is, a dBASE function can probably handle it, as you'll see in the next chapter.

CHAPTER

12

Using Functions to Control Your Data

ExtPrice for records that have .T. in the Taxable field, and 0 for records that have .F. in the Taxable field.

To include Logical fields in an index expression,   409
you can use the IIF( ) function to convert .T. and .F. to letters. For example, the index expression IIF(Paid,''T'',''F'') + LASTNAME + FIRSTNAME displays records sorted into two groups: paid and unpaid. Within each group, records are displayed in alphabetical order by name.

When nesting functions in complex expressions,   411
be sure to use appropriate open and closing parentheses for each function: for example, SQRT(ABS(<*field-name*>)).

dBASE IV OFFERS MANY FUNCTIONS TO HELP YOU refine your queries, forms, and reports. A *function* is a predefined procedure that performs an immediate operation on one data item. All functions use the same basic syntax: a word or abbreviation followed by a pair of parentheses. You've already seen a few functions in action: DATE( ), which returns the current date, and DELETED( ), which can be used in a query to isolate records that are marked for deletion.

Some dBASE IV functions require one or more *arguments:* data to operate on, which is enclosed in parentheses. For example, the PAYMENT( ) function, which calculates the payment on a loan, requires three arguments: *principal, interest,* and *term.* The arguments are always separated by a comma. Hence, if a database contained loan parameters in three fields named Principal, Interest, and Term, than a calculated field containing the expression PAYMENT(Principal,Interest,Term) would display the payment for each record.

All functions *return* a value. The DATE( ) function returns the current date. The DELETED( ) function returns .T. if a record is marked for deletion, and .F. if it is not. In the expression PAYMENT(Principal,Interest,Term), the PAYMENT function returns the payment on the loan.

When speaking, it is common to use the word *of* between a function and its argument. For example, the SQRT( ) function returns the square root *of* a number. For the expression SQRT(81), you could say "the square root of 81."

dBASE offers over 140 functions, though many of these are used only in dBASE IV programming (a topic we'll discuss in Chapter 17). This chapter focuses on functions that are useful for refining your queries, forms, reports, and sort orders.

REFINING SORT ORDERS

As you may recall from Chapter 5 and examples since then, you can use an index to control the order in which records are displayed and printed. In case you've forgotten, the basic procedure for creating an index is summarized below:

- In the Data panel of the Control Center, highlight the name of the database that you want to use.
- Press Data (F2).
- Press Alt-O, or use the Menu (F10) and arrow keys to open the Organize pull-down menu.
- Select Create New Index.
- Select Name of Index and type in a valid name (up to eight letters, no spaces or punctuation). Press ◄──┘.
- Select Index Expression, and type in the index expression or press Shift-F1 to access the Expression Builder. Press ◄──┘ after defining your index expression.
- Press Ctrl-End when done.

You can see the new sort order immediately if you are at the browse screen. (If you are at the edit screen, just press F2 to switch to the browse screen.)

Once you create an index, you need not re-create it in the future. Instead, simply select it from the Organize pull-down menu. Once again, as a quick reminder, the basic steps are as follows:

- If you are at the Control Center, highlight the database name in the Data panel and press Data (F2) to get to the browse or edit screen.
- Press Alt-O, or use the Menu (F10) and arrow keys to open the Organize pull-down menu.
- Select Order Records by Index.
- Move the highlight to the index you want to activate to control the sort order. As you scroll through the index names, the expression for each index is displayed to the left of the menu. (The Natural Order option means "no index"; records are displayed in the order in which they were entered into the database.)

- Press ◄─┘ to make your selection and return to the edit/ browse screen.

Chapter 5 also discussed how you can do a sort within a sort using an index by combining two or more fields in the index expression. For example, the index expression LASTNAME- +FIRSTNAME could be used to display records in alphabetical order by last name and by first name within last names (for example, Ann Smith would come before Bob Smith, as in the phone book).

This technique of combining fields to produce a sort within a sort works fine *only* if the fields involved are the Character data type. If you try to mix data types, dBASE just beeps and displays the error message "Data Type Mismatch" while you are creating the index expression.

For example, in the CUSTLIST database, LASTNAME is a Character field, while STARTDATE is a Date field. If you tried to create an index based on the expression LASTNAME +START- DATE, dBASE would reject your entry because you cannot mix the two data types. (The reason that you cannot combine data types has to do with how the computer and dBASE store information, but we need not get into all of that here.) However, you *can* mix data types in an index expression if you convert all the data types in the expression to Character data, and dBASE offers several *conversion functions* that allow you to do precisely that. Two of the most widely used functions are DTOS (Date to String) and STR (string), discussed in the next two sections.

COMBINING DATE AND CHARACTER DATA

To combine the Date and Character data types, you use the DTOS (Date to String) function. This function converts a date to a character string in the format *yyyymmdd*. For example, the date 12/31/91 would be converted to 19911231, which is the correct format for sorting dates. (Because you are using DTOS in an index expression, the converted date is used only within the index; you never actually see the date in yyyymmdd format.)

As an example, suppose you have a database of medical patients and appointment dates; the patient names are stored in Character fields LASTNAME and FIRSTNAME, and the appointment dates are stored in a Date field named APTDATE. You want to display the records with patients listed in alphabetical order by last and first name, and then in chronological order by appointment date for each patient.

You cannot use the index expression LASTNAME-+FIRSTNAME+APTDATE because you'd be mixing data types. However, if you use the index expression LASTNAME-+FIRSTNAME+DTOS(APTDATE) after selecting Index Expression from the Organize pull-down menu, dBASE will accept your entry and display records in the order you want.

As another example, if you used the index expression DTOS (APTDATE)+LASTNAME+FIRSTNAME, dBASE would display the records in chronological order by date. Within each date, the names would be alphabetized.

COMBINING NUMERIC AND CHARACTER DATA

The STR function lets you convert data stored as the Numeric or Float data type to the Character data type. This function uses the general format

STR(*number,length,decimals*)

The following list describes the arguments in this format:

number	An actual number or the name of the field that contains Numeric or Float data
length	The total length of the converted data (If you leave this argument out, dBASE assigns a length of 10.)
decimals	The number of decimal places that dBASE rounds to when converting the data (If you leave this argument out, dBASE uses 0 decimal places. You must specify a length if you want to specify the number of decimal places.)

When using STR to convert data for sorting purposes, you'll usually want to use the same *length* and *decimals* as specified in the

NOTE

The structure of the
ORDERS database is
shown back in Figure 9.1
near the beginning of
Chapter 9.

database structure. Let's look at some examples.

The ORDERS database you created in Chapter 9 contains two Numeric fields—QTY, with a length of 3 and no decimal places, and UNITPRICE, with a length of 9 and two decimal places. The PARTNO field in that database is the Character data type.

Now, suppose you want to display records from that database in part code (PARTNO) order, and by quantity within each part code. You cannot use the expression PARTNO + QTY because the data types are different. However, if you use the index expression PARTNO + STR(QTY,3), dBASE will accept the index expression and display records in the order you wish.

Suppose you wanted to view records in price (UNITPRICE) order and alphabetically by part code within each identical unit price. The index expression in this case would need to be STR(UNITPRICE,9,2) + PARTNO.

COMBINING DATES AND NUMBERS

If you are combining both dates and numbers in an index expression, convert both to the Character data type. For example, if you want to sort records in the ORDERS database in date order and then by quantity within each date, you use the index expression DTOS-(DATE) + STR(QTY,3). If you want to sort records by date and then by part number within each date and then by quantity within each part number, you use the index expression DTOS(DATE) + PARTNO + STR(QTY,3).

MIXING ASCENDING AND DESCENDING ORDERS

Whenever you create an index, dBASE gives you the opportunity to specify the entire sort in either ascending or descending order. In some situations, you might want to combine ascending and descending sort orders. For example, suppose you want to display records from the ORDERS database in *ascending* part number order (for example, A-111 to C-333), but within each part number, you want records displayed in *descending* quantity order (largest to smallest), like this:

PARTNO	QTY
A-111	4
A-111	3
A-111	2
B-222	2
B-222	1
B-222	1
C-333	3
C-333	2
C-333	1

You need to index on the *inverse* of the quantity by subtracting each quantity from the largest possible quantity. Recall that the QTY field has a width of 3, with no decimal places, so the largest possible number in QTY is 999. Because you are combining this value with PARTNO, the result has to be converted to Character data. Hence, the appropriate index expression is PARTNO + STR(999 – QTY,3). (You would still select ASCENDING as the overall sort direction, to make sure the part numbers are in ascending order.)

Recall that the UNITPRICE field has a width of 9 and two decimal places. Hence, the largest possible number in the UNITPRICE field is 999999.99. Therefore, to display the unit price field in descending order within an ascending index, you would invert the unit prices with the basic formula 999999.99 – UNITPRICE. To convert this to a Character string, you can use the STR function with a width of 9 and two decimal places, like this: STR(999999.99 – UNITPRICE,9,2).

You can reverse the order of dates within an ascending index order by subtracting each date from the latest possible date in the field. For example, suppose you want to list records in ascending part number order, but in descending order by date, as follows:

A-111   07/01/91
A-111   06/15/91
A-111   06/01/91

B-222   07/01/91
B-222   06/15/91
B-222   06/14/91

C-333   06/15/91
C-333   06/10/91
C-333   06/01/91

In this database, we'll assume that the latest possible date is 12/31/1999. Hence, the entire index expression is PARTNO + STR({12/31/99} – DATE)—again using an ascending order for the overall index. Note that, in this case, the STR( ) function is used to convert the numeric result of subtracting two dates to the Character data type.

There is no reliable technique for inverting Character data. For example, you cannot subtract peoples' last names from ZZZZZZ to invert the sort order. To display records in descending order in a Character field, you must select descending as the overall sort order for the index. But you can still invert a Date or Numeric field to present their sort orders in the opposite direction.

Just remember that an inverted Numeric or Date field is always displayed in the opposite order of the overall index. That is, the expression PARTNO + STR(999 – QTY,3) displays part numbers in ascending order and quantities in descending order when the overall index order is ascending. However, this same index expression displays part numbers in descending order and quantities in *ascending* order when the overall sort order is descending.

SORTING BY THE RESULTS OF CALCULATIONS

We stored quantities and unit prices of transactions in the ORDERS database, but we did not store the extended price.

Suppose you want to display records in the ORDERS database in extended price order (that is, from the smallest total sale to the largest, or vice versa). To do so, you index on a calculated field, just as you display the extended price as a calculated field.

To display records in extended-price order from smallest to largest total sale, you use the index expression QTY*UNITPRICE and ascending as the overall sort order. To display records in order from largest to smallest extended price, you use the same index expression, but descending as the overall sort order. (To see the results of the index, you need to use a query or report format, such as TOTALS, that includes a calculated field to display the extended price.)

What if you want to display records sorted by part number and by extended price within each part number? You need to convert the results of the calculation QTY*UNITPRICE to a Character data type. To ensure an adequate width in the Character field, use the sum of the widths within the STR function. QTY has a width of 3, and UNITPRICE has a width of 9, so within the STR function, you specify a width of 12.

For example, to display records in ascending part number and extended price order, you use the index expression PARTNO + STR(QTY*UNITPRICE,12,2). To display records in ascending part number order and descending extended-price order, you use the following index expression instead: PARTNO + STR(999999999.99 − QTY*UNITPRICE,12,2). This index produces the sort order shown here, where part numbers are sorted into ascending order, and extended prices are sorted into descending order within each part number:

A-111	220.00
A-111	165.00
A-111	100.00
B-222	200.00
B-222	200.00
B-222	100.00

C-333	1000.00
C-333	1000.00
C-333	500.00
C-333	500.00

SORTS-WITHIN-SORTS WITH NUMBERS

If you want to combine numbers in an index to obtain a sort within a sort, convert both numeric fields to the Character data type. Otherwise the index will contain the sum of the two numeric fields—that is, the result of a calculation—rather than a combination of the two fields.

For example, suppose you had a database with the following floor numbers and office numbers stored in two fields named FLOOR and ROOM:

FLOOR	ROOM
1	1
1	2
1	3
1	4
2	1
2	2
2	3

If you created an index based on the expression FLOOR + ROOM, the index would contain the *sums* of the room and floor numbers and would therefore display the FLOOR and ROOM column in the order shown here:

ROOM + FLOOR	FLOOR	ROOM
2	1	1
3	1	2
3	2	1

ROOM + FLOOR	FLOOR	ROOM
4	1	3
4	2	2
5	1	4
5	2	3

To obtain a correct sort-within-sort order, you would convert both numeric fields to character strings using the index expression STR(FLOOR,1,0) + STR(ROOM,1,0). The resulting index would contain character strings that combine the numeric digits (shown in quotes) and would yield the sort order, as shown here:

STR(FLOOR,1,0) + STR(ROOM,1,0)	FLOOR	ROOM
"11"	1	1
"12"	1	2
"13"	1	3
"14"	1	4
"21"	2	1
"22"	2	2
"23"	2	3

DICTIONARY SORTS VIA INDEX

Chapter 5 discussed the difference between dictionary sorts and ASCII sorts. Indexes use the ASCII method, in which all lowercase letters are considered to be "larger than" all uppercase letters. Hence, an index of the LASTNAME field puts a name such as van der Pool after Zastrow in a sort order.

To get around this problem, you can convert all values in a Character field to uppercase using the UPPER( ) function in the index expression. For example, the index expression UPPER(LASTNAME) creates the following sort order (even though the names in the actual database are stored with both uppercase and lowercase letters):

ADAMS

BAKER

CARLSON

MILLER

VAN DER POOL

WILSON

ZASTROW

Remember that only the index contains words converted to uppercase; the names in the actual database are still in their original format. If you want to combine first and last names in the sort order, place the usual expression in the UPPER( ) function, like this: UPPER(LASTNAME + FIRSTNAME).

SEARCHING COMPLEX INDEXES

When you are using an index to display records in the browse or edit screen, you can use the Index Key Search option on the Go To menu to quickly look up a value. However, keep in mind that this option searches the *index,* not the actual database file. Therefore, any special techniques that you used in creating the index must be used when searching the index.

For example, suppose you used the index expression UPPER(LASTNAME + FIRSTNAME) to sort the CUSTLIST database and that index is in effect while you are at the browse screen. You want to quickly locate the first Smith record, so you select Index Key Search from the Go To pull-down menu. dBASE displays the index expression and allows you to type a value to search for.

When you see the expression UPPER(LASTNAME + FIRSTNAME), remember that all the values in the index are in uppercase, so whatever you want to search for must be specified in uppercase. Therefore, you would enter **SMITH**, rather than **Smith** in this case (as shown in Figure 12.1) to locate the first Smith record.

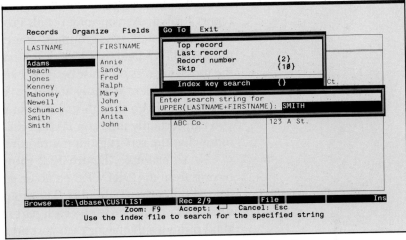

Figure 12.1: An index search for the first Smith record

Suppose you had organized records in the ORDERS database into descending DATE order and ascending PARTNO order within each date, using the index expression STR({12/31/1999} – DATE) + PARTNO. If you want to search this index for a particular date, you need to convert that date in exactly the same manner that you converted the dates in the index. That is, to search for the first record with 06/01/91 in the date field, you would need to enter STR({12/31/1999} – {06/01/91}) as the Index Key Search value.

Unfortunately, the Index Key Search option may not provide enough space for entering such a large, complex expression. To get around this problem, you could create one index with the complex expression STR({12/31/1999} – DATE) + PARTNO to define a sort order only, and another index with the simple field name DATE for searching. Then, when searching for dates, you could use the index with the simpler expression so that you do not need to convert the date for searching.

FUNCTIONS AND REPORT GROUPINGS

Chapter 9 touched on some potential problems of using groups within groups in report formats; for instance, when you need a complex index to presort a database into the groups specified in the report format. As you may recall, groups within groups require an index that matches the grouping. For example, if group 1 is based on the PARTNO field and group 2 is based on the DATE field, then the index expression must be PARTNO + DATE.

This problem is easily solved by using functions in your index expression. Even though you cannot index on PARTNO + DATE, you can certainly index on PARTNO + DTOS(DATE) to create the index that the report grouping requires.

As an example, Figure 12.2 shows a report format that prints records from the ORDERS database grouped by part number and by date within each part number. The group-2 summary band displays the subtotal for each date within each part number. The group-1 summary band prints a subtotal for each part number.

Note that to create such a report, you would need to use the Add a Group Band option from the Bands pull-down menu twice, basing the outermost band on the PARTNO field and the innermost band on the DATE field.

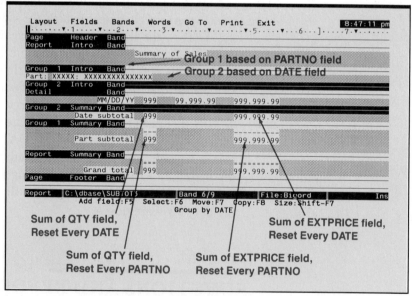

Figure 12.2: Report format to subtotal by date within parts

Before printing the report, you need an index with an expression that matches the group order. That is, the report uses PARTNO as group 1 and DATE as group 2, so you need the index expression PARTNO + DTOS(DATE).

Here are the general steps you would go through to create the index:

- If you are still at the reports design screen, save your report format by pressing Ctrl-End or by selecting Save Changes and Exit from the Exit pull-down menu.

- At the Control Center, highlight the database name (ORDERS in this example) in the Data panel.

- Press Data (F2) to get to the Edit/Browse screens.

- Press Alt-O or use the Menu (F10) key to access the Organize pull-down menu.

- Select Create New Index, and enter a valid file name (such as PARTDATE in this example). Press ←.

- Select Index Expression and type in the appropriate index expression—PARTNO + DTOS(DATE) in this example, as in Figure 12.3. Press ←.

- Press Ctrl-End.

In the future, whenever you print the report, you'll need to first activate the PARTDATE index. In this particular case, that index is active because you just created it, but in future dBASE sessions you'll need to activate the index before printing the report. So the complete steps for printing the report in the future would be as follows:

- Move the highlighter to the name of the database in the Data panel at the Control Center.

- Press Data (F2) to get to the edit/browse screens.

- Press Alt-O or use the Menu (F10) key to access the Organize pull-down menu.

- Select Order Records by Index.

Figure 12.3: Index for report with part number and date subtotals

- Select the appropriate index for the report (PARTDATE in this example).

- Press Ctrl-End to get back to the Control Center.

- In the Reports panel, highlight the name of the report you want to print (SUBTOT2 in this example) and press ⏎.

- Select Print Report and whatever options you wish from the Print menu.

Figure 12.4 shows the printed SUBTOT2 report using some hypothetical data that aren't actually in the ORDERS database right now. But what's important here is the grouping (sort order). As you can see, the records are grouped by part number, and within each part number, records are sorted by date. And it's the combination of the group bands in the report format and the sort order of the PART-CODE index that allows the records to be displayed in that manner.

Now let's suppose that after printing the first copy of the report you decide you would rather display the records in *descending* (latest to earliest) date order rather than in ascending order by date. Would you need to change the report format? No—because the groups will still be based on the same two fields, PARTNO, and within each PARTNO, DATE.

```
                              Summary of Sales

            Part: A-111: Astro Buddies
                            06/01/91      2         50.00           100.00
                            06/01/91      4         50.00           200.00
                            06/01/91      2         50.00           100.00
                            06/01/91      4         50.00           200.00
                            06/01/91     10         50.00           500.00
                   Date subtotal        22                        1,100.00
                            06/15/91      3         50.00           150.00
                            06/15/91      4         50.00           200.00
                            06/15/91      5         50.00           250.00
                            06/15/91      3         50.00           150.00
                   Date subtotal        15                          750.00
                                       ---                     ----------
                   Part subtotal        37                        1,850.00

            Part: B-222: Mondo Man
                            06/01/91      2        100.00           200.00
                            06/01/91      2        100.00           200.00
                            06/01/91      8        100.00           800.00
                            06/01/91     10        100.00         1,000.00
                            06/01/91      1        100.00           100.00
                   Date subtotal        23                        2,300.00
                            06/15/91      1        100.00           100.00
                            06/15/91      5        100.00           500.00
                            06/15/91      1        100.00           100.00
                            06/15/91      1        100.00           100.00
                            06/15/91      6        100.00           600.00
                   Date subtotal        14                        1,400.00
                                       ---                     ----------
                   Part subtotal        37                        3,700.00

            Part: C-333: Cosmic Critters
                            06/01/91      1        500.00           500.00
                            06/01/91      2        500.00         1,000.00
                            06/01/91      1        500.00           500.00
                            06/01/91      1        500.00           500.00
                            06/01/91      2        500.00         1,000.00
                            06/01/91      1        500.00           500.00
                   Date subtotal         8                        4,000.00
                            06/15/91      3        500.00         1,500.00
                            06/15/91      2        500.00         1,000.00
                            06/15/91      6        500.00         3,000.00
                            06/15/91      4        500.00         2,000.00
                            06/15/91      8        500.00         4,000.00
                            06/15/91      2        500.00         1,000.00
                            06/15/91      1        500.00           500.00
                   Date subtotal        26                       13,000.00
                                       ---                     ----------
                   Part subtotal        34                       17,000.00

                                       ===                     ==========

                   Grand total        108                       22,550.00
```

Figure 12.4: Sample report grouped by part number and date

What you need to change is the sort order, which means changing the index. Hence, you'd want to get back to the Organize pull-down menu (at the browse or edit screen), select Modify Existing Index from the Organize pull-down menu, select PARTDATE as the index to modify, and change the index expression to

PARTNO + STR({12/31/1999}-DATE)

so that dates will be displayed in descending order. Press Ctrl-End until you get back to the Control Center to save the change.

In the future, when you activate the PARTCODE index and print the report, the records would be listed in the order shown in Figure 12.5, with later dates preceding earlier dates within each part number group.

The important thing to remember is that the group bands in a report format do not *force* a particular sort order on a database, they just *use* the current sort order to group data. If the database records are in random (or natural) order when you start printing the report, they'll be in random order in the printed report. Remember, it's entirely up to you to remember to activate the appropriate index at the browse or edit screen prior to printing the report.

Actually, there are three alternatives to having to remember to activate an index yourself before printing a grouped report, though two of them involve topics that we have not yet discussed:

- Before you create the report format, create a query that sorts data into the order you need (as discussed in Chapter 6), then use that query to design the report and to print the report in the future (Chapter 7).

- Record the keystrokes required to activate the index and print the report in a keystroke macro so you need not repeat all of those keystrokes in the future (see Chapter 14).

- Create a command file that sets up the sort order and prints the report. (Command files are discussed in Chapters 17 and 18).

Just keep these three alternatives in mind for the time being—there's no need to try any of them out right now. Instead, let's get back to the main topic at hand, using dBASE functions.

NOTE

When you subtract two dates, the result is a number; the STR( ) function here converts that result to character data.

```
                          Summary of Sales

        Part: A-111: Astro Buddies
                          06/15/91      3        50.00         150.00
                          06/15/91      4        50.00         200.00
                          06/15/91      5        50.00         250.00
                          06/15/91      3        50.00         150.00
                  Date subtotal        15                      750.00
                          06/01/91      2        50.00         100.00
                          06/01/91      4        50.00         200.00
                          06/01/91      2        50.00         100.00
                          06/01/91      4        50.00         200.00
                          06/01/91     10        50.00         500.00
                  Date subtotal        22                    1,100.00
                                       ---                  ----------
                  Part subtotal        37                    1,850.00

        Part: B-222: Mondo Man
                          06/15/91      1       100.00         100.00
                          06/15/91      5       100.00         500.00
                          06/15/91      1       100.00         100.00
                          06/15/91      1       100.00         100.00
                          06/15/91      6       100.00         600.00
                  Date subtotal        14                    1,400.00
                          06/01/91      2       100.00         200.00
                          06/01/91      2       100.00         200.00
                          06/01/91      8       100.00         800.00
                          06/01/91     10       100.00       1,000.00
                          06/01/91      1       100.00         100.00
                  Date subtotal        23                    2,300.00
                                       ---                  ----------
                  Part subtotal        37                    3,700.00

        Part: C-333: Cosmic Critters
                          06/15/91      3       500.00       1,500.00
                          06/15/91      2       500.00       1,000.00
                          06/15/91      6       500.00       3,000.00
                          06/15/91      4       500.00       2,000.00
                          06/15/91      8       500.00       4,000.00
                          06/15/91      2       500.00       1,000.00
                          06/15/91      1       500.00         500.00
                  Date subtotal        26                   13,000.00
                          06/01/91      1       500.00         500.00
                          06/01/91      2       500.00       1,000.00
                          06/01/91      1       500.00         500.00
                          06/01/91      1       500.00         500.00
                          06/01/91      2       500.00       1,000.00
                          06/01/91      1       500.00         500.00
                  Date subtotal         8                    4,000.00
                                       ---                  ----------
                  Part subtotal        34                   17,000.00

                                       ===                  ==========

                  Grand total         108                   22,550.00
```

Figure 12.5: Parts in ascending order, dates in descending order

MORE COMPLEX GROUPINGS

There is no limit to the number of group bands that you can place in a report format. Just be certain to use the appropriate index expression to print the report. For example, suppose you have a database that includes fields named SALESREP, PARTNUMBER, DATE, QTY, and UNITPRICE and you want to print a report with subtotals by sales representative, by date within each sales representative, and by partnumber within each date. Furthermore, you want records displayed in descending order by quantity within each date.

In the report format, SALESREP would be the group-1 field, DATE would be the group-2 field, and QTY would be the group-3 field. The basic index expression for the report groups would be SALESREP + DTOS(DATE) + PARTNO. However, to ensure that quantities are displayed in descending order within each part number, the complete index expression would be SALESREP + DTOS(DATE) + PARTNO + STR(QTY,3).

GROUPING BY EXPRESSION

Selecting Add a Group Band from the Bands pull-down menu displays three options: Field Value, Expression Value, and Record Count. As you've seen, selecting Field Value lets you specify a particular field to group by, such as PARTNO in the SUBTOTAL report.

The Expression Value option lets you group by an expression rather than a field. The expression you enter can be a combination of Character fields joined with a plus sign, such as LASTNAME + FIRSTNAME, in which case each group would consist of people with the same last and first names. You can also use expressions with functions in them, just like the index expressions discussed earlier. There are a few functions, however, that are especially useful for report groupings, as summarized in Table 12.1.

GROUPING BY MONTH Suppose you want to group records in a report by month, regardless of the particular day. If you use Date alone as the grouping field, your report will display a separate group for each specific date. However, if you use the expression value

Table 12.1: Functions Used in Grouping

Function	Returns	Used with data type
CMONTH( )	The month of a date	Date
YEAR( )	The year of a date	Date
CDOW( )	The day of the week	Date
LEFT( )	Leftmost characters	Character

CMONTH(DATE) to determine groups, all of the records for January will be grouped together, followed by all of the records for February, and so forth. Figure 12.6 shows a sample report format that uses the CMONTH( ) function for grouping.

Before printing the report, you need to activate an index that puts the records in date order. This could be a simple index of the DATE field or a complex index using DTOS(DATE) combined with another field, just so long as the records are presorted into date, or month, order. Figure 12.7 shows a sample report printed by this format, using DATE as the field for the index.

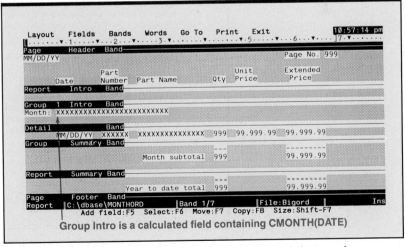

Figure 12.6: Sample report format for grouping records by month

NOTE

When you subtract two dates, the result is a number; the STR( ) function here converts that result to character data.

GROUPING BY FIRST LETTER With Character fields, you can use the LEFT( ) function to group records by the leading characters in each field. To use the LEFT function, you must include both the field name and the number of characters within the parentheses. For example, suppose you want to print a customer list grouped by the first

```
03/15/91                                              Page No.  1


                    Part                      Unit        Extended
           Date     Number  Part Name     Qty Price       Price

Month: January

           01/01/91 B-222   Mondo Man        2  100.00      200.00
           01/05/91 B-222   Mondo Man        2  100.00      200.00
           01/09/91 A-111   Astro Buddies    2   50.00      100.00
           01/11/91 C-333   Cosmic Critters  1  500.00      500.00
           01/12/91 A-111   Astro Buddies    4   50.00      200.00
           01/15/91 A-111   Astro Buddies    2   50.00      100.00
           01/20/91 B-222   Mondo Man        8  100.00      800.00
           01/21/91 C-333   Cosmic Critters  2  500.00    1,000.00
           01/30/91 C-333   Cosmic Critters  1  500.00      500.00
                                            ---            ---------
                            Month subtotal  24            3,600.00

Month: February

           02/02/91 C-333   Cosmic Critters  1  500.00      500.00
           02/11/91 A-111   Astro Buddies    4   50.00      200.00
           02/12/91 A-111   Astro Buddies   10   50.00      500.00
           02/12/91 A-111   Astro Buddies    4   50.00      200.00
           02/15/91 A-111   Astro Buddies    3   50.00      150.00
           02/20/91 B-222   Mondo Man       10  100.00    1,000.00
           02/21/91 B-222   Mondo Man        1  100.00      100.00
                                            ---            ---------
                            Month subtotal  33            2,650.00

Month: March

           03/01/91 A-111   Astro Buddies    5   50.00      250.00
           03/03/91 C-333   Cosmic Critters  2  500.00    1,000.00
           03/05/91 C-333   Cosmic Critters  1  500.00      500.00
           03/05/91 A-111   Astro Buddies    3   50.00      150.00
           03/09/91 B-222   Mondo Man        5  100.00      500.00
                                            ---            ---------
                            Month subtotal  16            2,400.00

                                            ===            =========
                         Year to date total 73            8,650.00
```

Figure 12.7: Orders subtotaled by month

letter in people's last names (that is, all the A's, then all the B's, and so forth). To do so, you need to base the grouping on the expression LEFT(LASTNAME,1), with the 1 indicating that only the first letter is to be used for breaking groups. Figure 12.8 shows a sample report format to group records by the first letter in the LASTNAME field.

Once again, before printing the report, you need to put the records into alphabetical order. You can use any appropriate index expression, such as LASTNAME or LASTNAME + FIRSTNAME. Figure 12.9 shows a sample printed report that used the LASTNAME + FIRSTNAME index expression and the format shown in Figure 12.8.

Suppose you want to group customers by a general zip code area, such as all the 91's followed by the 92's, the 93's, and so forth. If the zip codes are stored as the Character data type in a field named ZIP, then the expression for grouping is LEFT(ZIP,2). In this case, you need to activate an index of the ZIP field before printing the report.

GROUPING BY RECORD COUNT

You can group records by record count, which simply separates printed rows into equal-sized blocks. To do so, select Record Count from the Add a Group Band submenu and enter the number of

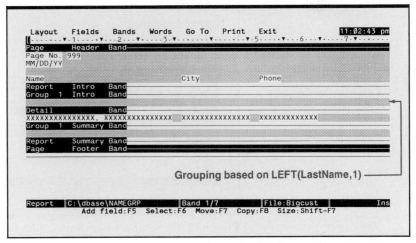

Figure 12.8: Report format to group letters by first letter of last name

```
Page No.   1
08/01/91

Name                              City              Phone

Adams, Annie                      Santa Monica      (714)555-0123
Adroit, Bob                       Palm Springs      (714)555-9987
Agajaninan, Roo                   Oakland           (415)787-5233
Amanda, Rhonda                    Newark            (217)555-0990
Anastasie, Steve                  Hatboro           (215)543-9283
Atritia, Ted                      Buffalo           (208)756-9320


Beach, Sandy                      Portland          (717)555-0898
Boon, Lenny                       New Orleans       (606)551-1212
Byers, Bob                        Torrance          (213)756-9320


Carlyle, Tim                      Glendora          (818)550-3345
Caruthers, Candy                  Ocean Beach       (619)465-3968
Casanova, Juan                    Azusa             (818)776-5464
Coulter, Lou                      San Diego         (619)225-0998
Cuisine, Zeke                     Carmel            (404)649-2453


Davis, Randi                      Newport Beach     (714)564-3648
Delorrio, Maria                   Orange            (818)555-0989
Devine, Deedra                    Santa Ana         (714)800-5434
Dillon, Jack                      Indianapolis      (317)800-5434
Divin, Adam                       Los Angeles       (213)655-8956
```

Figure 12.9: Names grouped by first letter

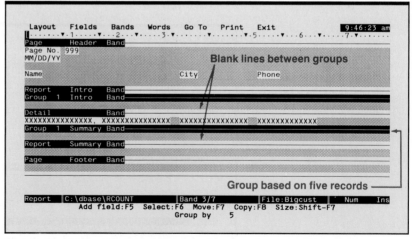

Figure 12.10: Sample report format with records grouped by count

records you want within each group. Figure 12.10 shows a sample report format with grouping based on groups of five records.

Figure 12.11 shows a sample report printed by the previous format. Notice that the records are organized into groups of five, regardless of their contents. As usual, the number of blank spaces that appears between each group is determined by the number of blank lines within the group band in the report design.

```
Page No.    1
01/01/91


Name                            City            Phone


Adams, Annie                    Santa Monica    (714)555-0123
Beach, Sandy                    Portland        (717)555-0898
Adroit, Bob                     Palm Springs    (714)555-9987
Agajaninan, Roo                 Oakland         (415)787-5233
Amanda, Rhonda                  Newark          (217)555-0990


Anastasie, Steve                Hatboro         (215)543-9283
Atritia, Ted                    Buffalo         (208)756-9320
Boon, Lenny                     New Orleans     (606)551-1212
Byers, Bob                      Torrance        (213)756-9320
Caruthers, Candy                Ocean Beach     (619)465-3968


Carlyle, Tim                    Glendora        (818)550-3345
Casanova, Juan                  Azusa           (818)776-5464
Coulter, Lou                    San Diego       (619)225-0998
Cuisine, Zeke                   Carmel          (404)649-2453
Davis, Randi                    Newport Beach   (714)564-3648


Delorrio, Maria                 Orange          (818)555-0989
Devine, Deedra                  Santa Ana       (714)800-5434
Dillon, Jack                    Indianapolis    (317)800-5434
Divin, Adam                     Los Angeles     (213)655-8956
```

Figure 12.11: Report with groups of five records

A DECISION-MAKING FUNCTION

One of dBASE IV's most powerful and versatile functions is IIF( ) (an abbreviation for immediate IF). This function makes a spur-of-the-moment decision about which of two alternative actions to take. The plain English syntax for this function is

IIF(*this-is-true,do-this,otherwise-do-this*)

The first argument must be either the name of a Logical field (which is always either true or false) or an expression with a true or false result. For example, the expression PARTNO = "A-111" is either true or false, because a specific PARTNO either is or is not equal to "A-111." The expression QTY > 10 also results in either a true or a false value, because a specific QTY either is or is not greater than 10.

The other two arguments (both are required) in an IIF function can be any expression; these arguments usually reflect the contents of a calculated field. To see how IIF works, we'll create a query that adds 6.5 percent sales tax only to taxable items in the ORDERS database.

USING IIF IN A QUERY

Suppose that the ORDERS database contains a Logical field named TAXABLE, which contains .T. if a particular transaction is taxable and .F. if the transaction is not taxable. Figure 12.12 shows the structure of the ORDERS database with this field added.

```
  Layout   Organize   Append   Go To   Exit                          2:54:56 pm

                                                        Bytes remaining:    3959
  ┌─────┬────────────┬─────────────┬───────┬─────┬─────────┐
  │ Num │ Field Name │ Field Type  │ Width │ Dec │  Index  │
  ├─────┼────────────┼─────────────┼───────┼─────┼─────────┤
  │   1 │ PARTNO     │ Character   │    5  │     │    Y    │
  │   2 │ PARTNAME   │ Character   │   15  │     │    N    │
  │   3 │ DATE       │ Date        │    8  │     │    N    │
  │   4 │ QTY        │ Numeric     │    3  │  Ø  │    N    │
  │   5 │ UNITPRICE  │ Numeric     │    9  │  2  │    N    │
  │   6 │ TAXABLE    │ Logical     │    1  │     │    N    │
  └─────┴────────────┴─────────────┴───────┴─────┴─────────┘



  Database C:\dbase\ORDERS            Field 6/6
                    Enter the field name. Insert/Delete field:Ctrl-N/Ctrl-U
  Field names begin with a letter and may contain letters, digits and underscores
```

Figure 12.12: TAXABLE field added to the ORDERS database

Within the ORDERS database records, transactions involving part numbers A-111 and C-333 are marked as taxable, and those involving part number B-222 are marked as not taxable. Figure 12.13 shows the ORDERS database with the TAXABLE field filled in.

Now suppose you want to execute a query that calculates tax. Select <create> from the Queries panel and then select the Create Calculated Field option from the Fields pull-down menu for each calculated field that you wish to add. Be sure to name each calculated field and move a copy of each field into the view skeleton (by pressing F5). If you want to use a calculated value in another calculated field's expression, place an example in the box beneath the expression.

Figure 12.14 shows a query with three calculated fields. The first, named ExtPrice, calculates the extended price before taxes using the usual expression Qty*UnitPrice. The second calculated field, named Tax, contains the expression IIF(Taxable,0.065*EPrice,0). In English, this expression says, "If the taxable field is .T. in this record, then display 6.5 percent times the extended price; otherwise display zero." (That is, if the Taxable field is .F. for a particular record, then the tax to be added is 0.)

The third calculated field, TotSale, calculates the total sale by adding the tax to the extended price using the expression TotTax +EPrice. TotTax, in turn, is used as an example in the calculated

Figure 12.13: Transactions marked as taxable or nontaxable

Tax field. Figure 12.15 shows the results of the query (compressed so that you can see all the data) after you press Data (F2). Of course, you can enter any filter conditions you wish into the query to confine this display to only certain records (such as part number A-111).

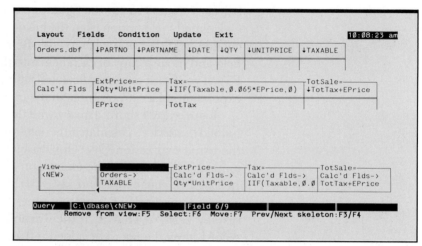

Figure 12.14: Query to calculate taxes for taxable transactions

PARTNO	QTY	UNITPRICE	TAXABLE	TAX	TOTSALE
B-222	2	100.00	F	0.00	200.00
B-222	1	100.00	F	0.00	100.00
A-111	2	50.00	T	6.50	106.50
C-333	1	500.00	T	32.50	532.50
A-111	3	55.00	T	10.73	175.73
A-111	4	55.00	T	14.30	234.30
B-222	1	100.00	F	0.00	100.00
C-333	2	500.00	T	65.00	1065.00
C-333	1	500.00	T	32.50	532.50
C-333	2	500.00	T	65.00	1065.00

Browse   C:\dbase\TAXCALC   Rec 1/10   View   Ins

Figure 12.15: Results of tax-calculation query

USING IIF IN A REPORT FORMAT

Suppose you wish to develop a report format that shows the tax, and the total sale price including the tax, for each transaction. Just as in the preceding sample query, the calculated fields in the report design will need to ''decide'' whether to tax transactions based on the contents of the TAXABLE field.

Figure 12.16 shows a sample report format (assuming the TAXABLE field was added to the ORDERS database, as discussed previously). A calculated field, named EXTPRICE, calculates and displays the extended price using the expression QTY*UNITPRICE.

To the right of the Extended Price column, notice the calculated field named TAX, which uses the expression IIF(TAXABLE,0.065 *EXTPRICE,0) to display the tax. The template for the field was reduced to 999.99, and the Blanks for Zero Values picture function was set to On so the report would display blanks in place of the number 0.

To the right of the TAX column in the detail band is a calculated field named TOTSALE that uses the expression EXTPRICE +TAX to calculate the total sale. (Hence, if tax is zero, no tax is added to the total.) Summary fields using the Sum operator total the

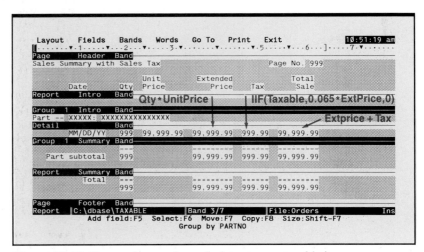

Figure 12.16: Report format that calculates tax on taxable items

EXTPRICE, TAX, and TOTSALE columns within each group (based on the PARTNO field) and at the end of the report.

Figure 12.17 shows an example of the printed report. Note that no tax is added to transactions involving part number B-222. Blanks, rather than zeroes, are displayed in the Tax column for those parts because the {Z} Picture function was assigned to the calculated TAX field in the report format. (Because the report is also grouped by part number, you must activate the PARTNO index before printing the report.)

USING IIF IN CUSTOM FORMS

You can use the IIF function in a custom form in exactly the same way you would in either a query or report format. Simply place a calculated field on the form design screen and use the IIF function as you normally would. For example, Figure 12.18 shows a form on the

```
Sales Summary With Sales Tax                                    Page No.    1

                          Unit        Extended              Total
            Date     Qty  Price         Price     Tax        Sale

Part --  A-111: Astro Buddies
            06/01/91   2    50.00       100.00     6.50     106.50
            06/02/91   3    55.00       165.00    10.73     175.73
            06/05/91   4    55.00       220.00    14.30     234.30
                       ---                         ------    --------   ---------
            Part subtotal  9            485.00    31.53     516.53

Part --  B-222: Mondo Man
            06/01/91   2   100.00       200.00     0.00     200.00
            06/01/91   1   100.00       100.00     0.00     100.00
            06/15/91   1   100.00       100.00     0.00     100.00
                       ---                         ------    --------
            Part subtotal  4            400.00     0.00     400.00

Part --  C-333: Cosmic Critters
            06/01/91   1   500.00       500.00    32.50     532.50
            06/15/91   2   500.00     1,000.00    65.00   1,065.00
            06/15/91   1   500.00       500.00    32.50     532.50
            07/01/91   2   500.00     1,000.00    65.00   1,065.00
                       ---                         ------    --------
            Part subtotal  6          3,000.00   195.00   3,195.00

            Total     ===          =========  ======  =========
                       19          3,885.00   226.53   4,111.53
```

Figure 12.17: Sample report with tax calculations

forms design screen with calculated fields to display the tax (assuming, once again, that the TAXABLE field has already been added to the ORDERS database).

INDEXING LOGICAL FIELDS

Earlier you learned that you cannot include Logical fields in index expressions. However, just as with the Numeric and Date fields, if you convert the Logical field to the Character data type within the index expression, you most certainly can index on Logical fields. Just use the IIF function to convert the .T. or .F. to the letter ''T'' or ''F.''

For example, the CUSTLIST database includes a Logical field named PAID. Suppose you want to sort this database into customers who have paid and customers who have not and then display the names in each group in alphabetical order. You would use the usual techniques to create an index, using the index expression IIF (PAID,''T'',''F'') + LASTNAME + FIRSTNAME. After you select Order Records by Index to activate the new index and press Data (F2) to view your data, you'll see all customers who have not paid listed before all those who have paid (because the letter ''F'' is ''less than'' the letter ''T'').

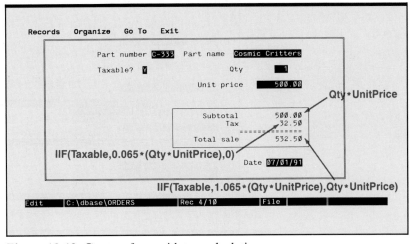

Figure 12.18: Custom form with tax calculations

If you want to place the trues before the falses in the sort order, use a "lower" letter for the trues. For example, the index expression IIF(Paid,"A","Z") + LASTNAME + FIRSTNAME would place all those who have paid before those who have not. (Remember, though, that if you wanted to search the Paid field using an index search, you would need to search for the letter "A" to find a .T. value, and the letter "Z" to search for an .F. value.)

Of course, once you create an index based on the Paid field, you can create a report format that groups the customers into two lists: those who have paid and those who have not. Figure 12.19 shows an example format. Note the use of a calculated field in the Group Intro band to display the group headings. If the group that is about to be printed has paid, the heading "PAID CUSTOMERS" is printed. If the group about to be printed has not paid, the heading "STILL NOT PAID" is printed. (This Intro is just for demonstration; you can use any Group Intro you want.)

Figure 12.20 shows the printed report based on the index expression IIF(Paid,"A","Z") + LASTNAME + FIRSTNAME, which, as discussed earlier, lists customers who have paid before those who have not paid.

Now, you may be wondering how the group heading was able to decide whether the PAID field was .T. or .F., when the index

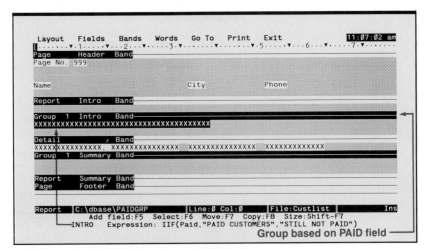

Figure 12.19: Report format that groups on the PAID field

```
Page No.    1


Name                                City              Phone

PAID CUSTOMERS

Beach, Sandy                        Portland          (717)555-9988
Jones, Fred                         Newark            (202)555-0987
Mahoney, Mary                       Seattle           (206)555-8673
Newell, John                        Butte             (303)555-6793
Schumack, Susita                    Philadelphia      (202)555-9720
Smith, Anita                        Hideaway          (415)555-9854
Smith, John                         San Diego         (619)555-1234


STILL NOT PAID

Adams, Annie                        Santa Monica      (714)555-0123
Kenney, Ralph                       Los Angeles       (213)555-9988
```

Figure 12.20: Report grouped by the contents of the PAID field

"cheated" by converting these to the letters "A" and "Z." Remember, the index defines only the order in which records are displayed. As dBASE prints the report, it always looks at the original database data to decide when to end one group and start another. Hence, it does not matter how you convert the values in the index, so long as the index puts the records into the appropriate sort order for the grouping.

NESTING FUNCTIONS

You can nest functions within each other to combine their power. However, when you do so, you must make sure that each function has its appropriate number of opening and closing parentheses and that the parentheses are properly placed.

For example, the SQRT( ) function returns the square root of a positive number; thus, the expression SQRT(81) returns 9. You cannot take the square root of a negative number, so attempting to perform a calculation such as SQRT(– 81) would cause dBASE to display an error message such as "Execution error on SQRT( ) : Negative." To avoid such errors, you could nest the ABS( ) (absolute value) function within the SQRT( ) function to convert any negative number to a positive number.

Hence, the expression SQRT(ABS(–81)) returns 9, because the ABS function converted the –81 to 81 before the SQRT function did its work. (dBASE always works from the innermost to the outermost function when functions are nested.) Note that the expression SQRT (ABS(–81) will generate a syntax error rather than the result you want because it contains two opening parentheses, but only one closing parenthesis. One of the functions is missing a closed parenthesis.

The expression SQRT(ABS)(–81) will also generate an error, even though there are an equal number of parentheses. The error in this case is that the ABS function is not fully nested within the SQRT function. The inner function, ABS(–81), must be fully nested within the outer function, SQRT, like this:

```
SQRT( ABS( – 81) )
```

When nesting functions, it is also important to remember that the inner function must return the correct data type for the outer functions. For example, the LEFT( ) function operates only on the Character data type. Therefore the expression LEFT(DATE( ),2) would produce an error, because the DATE( ) function returns the Date data type. On the other hand, the expression LEFT(DTOS (DATE( )),4) is valid because DTOS( ) converts the results of the DATE( ) function to the Character data type (for instance, "19910810") before the LEFT( ) function returns the four leftmost characters ("1991").

QUERIED INDEXES

Up to this point, you've seen how indexes can be used to control the sort order of records, and how queries can be used to display only certain types of records. You've also seen that queries can be used to control the sort order of records, using the Asc or AscDict operators.

At the risk of confusing things, perhaps now is a good time to mention that indexes can actually be used for simple queries. For example, you can create an index that includes only records that have CA in the STATE field. Whenever you activate that index, records without CA in the STATE field will be "invisible."

Now you may be thinking, "If queries can do sorts, and indexes can do queries, why have both?" There are several answers to this question. But suffice it to say for now that indexes only let you do rudimentary querying, and do not offer all the features of the queries design screen such as file linking, a view skeleton, and so forth.

To create a "query" index, you need to create a *FOR clause* on the Organize pull-down menu for that index. You can do so either after selecting Create New Index or Modify Existing Index from the Organize pull-down menu (at the edit, browse, or database design screen). After selecting the FOR Clause option, you can press Shift-F1 to access the Expression Builder if you want help creating your expression.

The expression you use in a FOR clause should follow the general syntax shown below:

fieldname operator value

The arguments in this syntax are described below:

fieldname	The name of the field to be queried
operator	The comparison method, such as = (equal), < > (not equal), > (greater than), < (less than), $ (embedded in), and so forth, as discussed in Chapter 6
value	The value being searched for such as "CA" or {12/31/91} or 123.45, using the same data type delimiters described in Chapter 6

For example, if you wanted your index to include only CA residents, the FOR clause expression would be

STATE = "CA"

as shown in Figure 12.21.

Whenever you use this index to organize your database records (by selecting Order Records by Index from the Organize pull-down menu), only records with CA in the STATE field will be displayed.

Figure 12.21: Creating an index for CA residents only

(In this example, the records will be in alphabetical order by name.)

If you wanted to create an index that includes only records with today's date in a Date field named STARTDATE, the FOR clause expression would be:

STARTDATE = DATE( )

If you wanted to create an index that displays only records that have a value of $1,000.00 or more in a Numeric field named PRICE, you would use the expression:

PRICE > = 1000

What's the advantage to using a FOR clause with an index to "query" a database? At this point, there really is none other than the fact that you could instantly activate the "query" from the browse or edit screen by activating the index from the Organize pull-down menu—thereby eliminating the need to go to the queries design screen.

However, you will probably find it easier and less confusing to stick with the queries design screen, for now, to perform your queries. Later, if you get into programming with dBASE IV (starting in Chapter 17) you may find some interesting applications of this feature.

MORE ON FUNCTIONS

This chapter has introduced some of dBASE IV's many functions and provided some practical suggestions for using them in your work. For a quick reference to all of dBASE IV's functions, see Appendix E.

13

Managing
Related
Database
Files

UP TO NOW, WE HAVE FOCUSED ON WORKING WITH A single database at a time. Now it's time to add a new dimension to your database management skills by learning to manage multiple *related* files. But before we discuss the specific techniques involved, let's discuss *database design theory*.

DATABASE DESIGN

In most business applications, it is simply not practical to store all information in a single database file. Suppose, for instance, that you want to store accounts receivable information for customer charge account transactions in which a customer can charge any number of items in a month. You can attempt to store the accounts receivable information in a single database file using either one record per transaction or one record per customer. Neither of these approaches is satisfactory, however.

If you base each record on a single charge transaction, as in Figure 13.1, the database will store the correct information, but the database will not be efficient or convenient to use because

- Repeating names and addresses wastes a lot of disk space.

- If the person entering the information has to retype the name and address for every order, much time is wasted.

- If a customer changes address, this change must be made in many different records.

LastName	FirstName	Address	City	State	Zip	Amount	Date
Smith	John	123 A St.	San Diego	CA	92067	$276.69	01/01/91
Smith	John	123 A St.	San Diego	CA	92067	$600.26	01/01/91
Smith	John	123 A St.	San Diego	CA	92067	$962.91	01/01/91
Smith	John	123 A St.	San Diego	CA	92067	$291.88	02/02/91
Smith	John	123 A St.	San Diego	CA	92067	$972.70	02/02/91
Beach	Sandy	11 Elm St.	Portland	OR	76543	$331.77	01/01/91
Beach	Sandy	11 Elm St.	Portland	OR	76543	$100.63	01/01/91
Beach	Sandy	11 Elm St.	Portland	OR	76543	$698.52	01/01/91
Beach	Sandy	11 Elm St.	Portland	OR	76543	$183.15	02/02/91
Beach	Sandy	11 Elm St.	Portland	OR	76543	$217.41	02/02/91

Figure 13.1: A poorly designed accounts receivable database

If you base each record on a customer, rather than a transaction, and use multiple fields for charge transactions, you eliminate the problem of repeated names and addresses. Figure 13.2 shows an example in which charge amounts are stored in fields named Amount1, Amount2, and Amount3, and dates are stored in similarly named fields. This second design, however, has a different set of problems:

- There is a limit to the number of fields that a database record can have, so there is a limit to the number of charges a customer can make.

- If you want to query for all charge transactions that occurred, for example, on 01/01/91, you would need to include each Date field in the query (Date1 = 01/01/91 or Date2 = 01/01/91 or Date3 = 01/01/91 . . . and so on).

- You could not easily distinguish charges that have been invoiced or paid from those that have not.

At the heart of this accounts receivable problem is the fact that there is a natural *one-to-many* relationship between customers and their charges. Any *one* customer may have *many* charges, and in fact may have any *unpredictable* number of charges.

The best way to store information when there is a one-to-many relationship involved is to place the information on two separate databases in such a manner as to minimize repetition of information. Hence, the best way to store information about customers and their charges is to use two separate database files: one for names and addresses and another for charge transactions. That way, you will

LastName	FirstName	Address	City	State	Zip	Amount1	Date1	Amount2	Date2	Amount3	Date3
Smith	John	123 A St.	San Diego	CA	92067	$468.39	01/01/91	$926.61	01/01/91	$54.66	01/01/91
Adams	Annie	345 Ocean St.	Santa Monica	CA	92001	$702.02	01/01/91	$253.07	01/01/91	$684.76	01/01/91
Mahoney	Mary	211 Seahawk	Seattle	WA	88977	$632.50	01/01/91	$351.02	01/01/91	$702.53	01/01/91
Newell	John	734 Rainbow	Butte	MT	54321	$665.33	01/02/91	$892.19	01/02/91	$294.24	01/02/91
Beach	Sandy	11 Elm St.	Portland	OR	76543	$75.96	01/02/91	$970.92	01/02/91	$99.69	01/02/91
Kenney	Ralph	1101 Rainbow	Los Angeles	CA	96607	$582.68	01/02/91	$307.47	01/02/91	$523.95	01/02/91
Schumack	Susita	47 Broad St.	Philadelphia	PA	45543	$990.16	01/03/91	$598.00	01/03/91	$943.32	01/03/91

Figure 13.2: A second poor design for the accounts receivable database

not need to repeat information unnecessarily, and the number of charge transactions that a customer can make will not be limited.

However, separating customers and their transactions into two separate database files does create one new problem. How do you ensure that each charge in the charge transaction database is billed to the correct customer? The solution to this problem is the *common field*.

RELATING DATABASE FILES

If you store customer information in one database and charges in another, you need some way to *relate* each charge to the appropriate customer. To do this, you create a common field: a field that exists in both databases. This field must contain information that is unique to each customer. If the linking information is not unique to each customer, problems will arise.

For example, if you use the customer's last name to link charges to customers, dBASE can look at any single charge and link it to a specific customer, such as Smith. But what if there are two or more Smiths? How does dBASE decide which Smith gets the bill?

You could use two fields, LastName and FirstName in the Charges database to specify which customer a charge belongs to, but you still run into the same problem if there are two customers named John Doe. You could further clarify who a charge belongs to by adding the Address field to the Charges database, but by this point, you're back to repeating too much information from the Customer database in the Charges database.

The best way to solve this problem of relating the two databases is to assign each customer a unique customer number, or code, and to store this code with each record in the Charges database. As long as no two customers have the same customer number, there can be no confusion about who is responsible for each charge transaction.

Figure 13.3 shows an example in which a field named CUSTNO exists in both the CHARGES database and the CUSTOMER database. Notice that each customer has a unique customer number, so there is no doubt about who gets billed for charges to customer number 1002, or any other number.

```
CUSTOMER database

CustNo  LastName  FirstName  Address        City          State  Zip
1001    Smith     John       123 A St.      San Diego     CA     92067
1002    Adams     Annie      345 Ocean St.  Santa Monica  CA     92001
1003    Mahoney   Mary       211 Seahawk    Seattle       WA     88977
1004    Newell    John       734 Rainbow    Butte         MT     54321
1005    Beach     Sandy      11 Elm St.     Portland      OR     76543
1006    Kenney    Ralph      1101 Rainbow   Los Angeles   CA     96607
1007    Schumack  Susita     47 Broad St.   Philadelphia  PA     45543


                  CHARGES database

                  CustNo  Amount    Date
                  1001    $468.39   01/01/91
                  1001    $702.02   01/01/91
                  1001    $632.50   01/01/91
                  1001    $665.33   01/02/91
                  1002    $75.96    01/02/91
                  1002    $582.68   01/02/91
                  1002    $990.16   01/03/91
                  1002    $926.61   01/01/91
                  1003    $253.07   01/01/91
                  1003    $351.02   01/01/91
```

Figure 13.3: The best way to store accounts receivable data

Of course, the design shows only a basic structure for the accounts receivable application. Realistically, you would probably want to store more information about each charge, such as the item purchased, the quantity, and the unit price. You could certainly add such fields to the CHARGES database.

In an accounts receivable system, you also need to keep track of payments. But this is no problem now, because you can just create a third database, perhaps named PAYMENTS, and use the CUSTNO field to identify the customer to which each payment belongs. The following small sample database presents an example:

CustNo	CheckNo	AmtPaid	DatePaid
1001	285	$100.00	01/30/91
1002	998	$300.00	01/29/91
1003	335	$50.00	02/01/91

As you can see, it's quite easy to see which customer made each payment in this database, because the CustNo field clearly links each payment to a specific customer.

There is always the temptation to kill two birds with one stone by putting hidden meaning into common fields that relate two files. For example, you might assign each customer a code such as SD41291, where SD stands for San Diego, 4 stands for an excellent credit rating, and 1291 stands for a starting date. But if you try to use a scheme like this and end up with two or more San Diego residents with credit ratings of 4 and start dates of 12/91, you have a problem on your hands. When you enter a charge transaction for customer number SD41291, dBASE will not know to *which* customer SD41291 the transaction belongs.

Using an arbitrary and meaningless number is the best (albeit most impersonal) way to relate two files. For example, if you have fewer than 9,000 customers, assign those customers numbers in the range 1001 to 9999. Starting at 1001 ensures that each customer has a four-digit number, which adds consistency to the numbering scheme.

CREATING
MULTIPLE RELATED DATABASES

When developing multiple related databases, you create each separate database using the same techniques you've used elsewhere in this book. That is, you select <create> from the Data panel in the Control Center and define each field. But you need to be sure that each of the related databases includes a field that has the same name, data type, width, and decimal places in both files. It also is a good idea to index this field in both databases, as this will speed up later operations.

To see how multiple related databases work, we'll modify the CUSTLIST and ORDERS databases in the LEARN catalog to link orders to customers. Be sure dBASE IV is up and running on your computer right now and that the LEARN catalog is in the Control Center.

1. Highlight CUSTLIST in the Control Center Data panel and press Design (Shift-F2).

2. Press Esc to leave the Organize menu and then press Ctrl-N to insert a new field.

3. Enter a new field named **CUSTNO**, with the **Numeric** data type, a width of **4**, **0** decimal places, and **Y** in the index column, as shown in Figure 13.4.

4. Press Ctrl-End to complete the addition.

5. When dBASE asks for permission to make the change, select Yes.

The next step is to assign a number to each customer. You could go the browse or edit screen and do this record by record—but you also can take a shortcut:

1. Select <create> from the Queries panel of the Control Center.

2. Type the update operator **REPLACE** beneath the file name in the file skeleton and press ⏎.

3. Select Proceed when dBASE warns you about removing the view skeleton.

4. Press Tab and enter the update expression **WITH RECNO( ) + 1000** under the CUSTNO field name, so your screen looks like Figure 13.5.

5. Select Perform the Update from the Update pull-down menu.

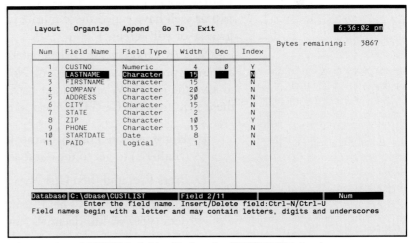

Figure 13.4: CUSTNO field added to the CUSTLIST database

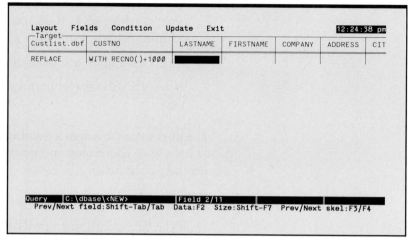

Figure 13.5: Query to add customer numbers

6. When the update is complete, press Data (F2) to see the results.

Your screen should look like Figure 13.6 now, where each customer has a unique number starting at 1001. The update query told dBASE to replace the current (empty) contents of the CUSTNO field with the record number (using the RECNO( ) function) plus 1000, so the customers now have numbers 1001, 1002, 1003, and so forth. (Again, this is just a shortcut for your convenience; you could just as well have typed these numbers into the blank field from the browse or edit screen.)

Now let's modify the Orders database. Leave the current browse screen by pressing Esc and selecting No when dBASE asks if you want to save the query. When you get back to the Control Center, follow these steps to add a CUSTNO field to the ORDERS database:

1. Highlight ORDERS in the Data panel and press Design (Shift-F2) to get to the database design screen.

2. Press Esc, and then Ctrl-N to insert a new field.

3. Add the CUSTNO field, using the exact same field name, data type, width, decimals, and index option as used in the CUSTLIST database, as shown in Figure 13.7.

4. Press Ctrl-End and select Yes when prompted.

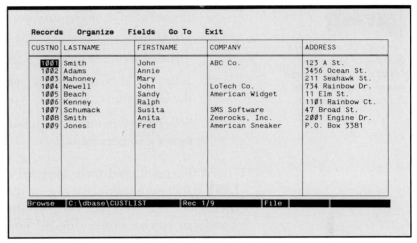

Figure 13.6: A number assigned to each customer

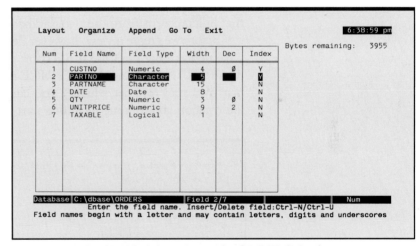

Figure 13.7: CUSTNO field added to the ORDERS database

5. To deactivate the CUSTNO index before adding new records, press ↵ and select Close File.

Now you need to assign each order in the ORDERS database to a customer. Follow these steps:

1. Highlight ORDERS and press Data (F2) to get to the browse screen. (If the edit screen appears instead, press F2 again.)

NOTE

After you've added the indexed CUSTNO field, you must close the file to deactivate the index so that dBASE will not re-sort records as you enter customer numbers later.

Press Alt-O, select Order
Records by Index, then
Natural Order to prevent
record re-sort while add-
ing customer numbers.

2. Press PgUp to make sure you are at the topmost record in ORDERS.

3. Type customer numbers, as in Figure 13.8.

4. If the "Add New Records" prompt appears after you enter the last customer number, type **N** for no.

5. Select Exit from the Exit pull-down menu after entering customer numbers for orders.

At this point, you have assigned each customer in the CUSTLIST database a unique customer number. Also, you've assigned transactions in the ORDERS database to individual customers. That's *all* you've done. dBASE does not yet "know" that the CUSTNO field in ORDERS is in any way related to the CUSTNO field in the CUSTLIST database. However, as you will see in a moment, you can use the common CUSTNO field to create a view that links records from the two databases.

Before we create a view, however, let's clarify one point. You may have noticed that the ORDERS database contains repeated information: PARTNAME and UNITPRICE are repeated for each part number. You may wonder whether you can create a third database with information about parts, including part number, part name, and unit

```
 Records   Organize   Fields   Go To   Exit

CUSTNO  PARTNO  PARTNAME        DATE      QTY  UNITPRICE  TAXABLE
1001    B-222   Mondo Man       07/01/91    2     100.00  F
1002    B-222   Mondo Man       07/01/91    1     100.00  F
1001    A-111   Astro Buddies   07/01/91    2      50.00  T
1001    C-333   Cosmic Critters 07/01/91    1     500.00  T
1002    A-111   Astro Buddies   06/02/91    3      55.00  T
1003    A-111   Astro Buddies   06/05/91    4      55.00  T
1003    B-222   Mondo Man       06/15/91    1     100.00  F
1004    C-333   Cosmic Critters 06/15/91    2     500.00  T
1005    C-333   Cosmic Critters 06/15/91    1     500.00  T
1006    C-333   Cosmic Critters 07/01/91    2     500.00  T




Browse   C:\dbase\ORDERS              Rec 1/10        File
```

Figure 13.8: Customer numbers added to the ORDERS database price, and then include only the part number in the ORDERS database to avoid the repetitions. The answer is yes, you can.

For now, however, we will focus on techniques for managing just two related database files. Once you've learned how to manage two related databases, you'll see that managing three or more is just as easy.

COMBINING INFORMATION FROM RELATED DATABASES

Suppose you want to view all the records in the ORDERS database, with the name of the customer who placed each order. You need some information from ORDERS and some from CUSTLIST to accomplish this. Therefore, you need to create a view that links the two databases by their common field, CUSTNO. A view essentially is a query that includes two or more file skeletons and an *example* (or *placeholder*) to relate the common fields. The example used in the query design screen must show dBASE that records with identical values in the common field on both databases are related. Let's build a view now to link ORDERS and CUSTLIST, following these steps:

1. If the ORDERS database is not currently in use (above the line in the Data panel), highlight its name, press ←┘, and select Use File from the submenu that appears.

NOTE

Basic techniques for using the query design screen were presented in Chapter 6.

2. To start building the view, highlight <create> in the Queries panel, and press ←┘, which brings you to the query design screen.

3. Select Include Indexes from the Fields pull-down menu to change its setting to Yes (a # symbol appears next to the indexed fields).

4. Now, to bring a file skeleton of the CUSTLIST database into the design screen, select Add File to Query from the Layout pull-down menu.

5. From the submenu that appears, select CUSTLIST.DBF.

6. Activate the CUSTLIST index by selecting Include Indexes from the Fields pull-down menu.

7. To tell dBASE that the two databases are related through the CUSTNO field, press Tab to move the highlight to the CUSTNO field in the CUSTLIST file skeleton and select Create Link by Pointing from the Layout pull-down menu. (Note that the placeholder LINK1 appears in the box, and instructions appear at the bottom of the screen.)

8. Press Previous (F3) and Tab to move the highlight to the CUSTNO field in the ORDERS database file skeleton.

9. Press ⏎ to complete the link.

dBASE adds the placeholder LINK1 to the CUSTNO field of each file skeleton. The query presents an example to dBASE, where the CUSTNO field from each database contains the same placeholder. dBASE will follow this example when you execute the query and will display records that have the same value in the CUSTNO field.

Before you execute the query, you need to adjust the view skeleton to include fields from both databases. As you may recall, the view skeleton defines which fields will be displayed in the results of the query. At the moment, the view skeleton includes only fields from the ORDERS database. To view the customer's name with each order you need to include the LASTNAME and FIRSTNAME fields from the CUSTLIST database in the view skeleton. Follow these steps to include those fields and rearrange the view skeleton:

1. Press Next (F4) to move the highlight to the CUSTLIST database file skeleton.

2. Press the Tab (or Shift-Tab) key as necessary to move the highlight to the LASTNAME box.

3. Press F5 to copy the field to the view skeleton (an arrow appears next to the field after you press F5, indicating that the field is now included in the view skeleton).

4. Press Tab to move the highlight to the FIRSTNAME box.

5. Press F5 to copy it to the view skeleton.

6. Now, to display customer names next to the customer numbers, you need to rearrange the view skeleton. First press Next (F4) to move the highlight to the view skeleton.

NOTE

The Create Link by Pointing menu option uses LINK1 as the placeholder, but you can type any letter or word into the common fields, so long as you use the same letter or word in both file skeletons.

NOTE

Remember: You use the F3 and F4 keys to move the highlight from one skeleton to the next and the F5 key to move fields into and out of the view skeleton. Use Select (F6) and Move (F7) to rearrange the order of fields in the view skeleton.

7. Press End to move to the end of the view skeleton.

8. Press Select (F6) and then press Shift-Tab to highlight the LASTNAME and FIRSTNAME boxes.

9. Press ⬅ to finish highlighting.

10. Press Home to move back to the beginning of the view skeleton.

11. Press Move (F7), then ⬅ to move the selected boxes, LASTNAME and FIRSTNAME, to the right of the CUSTNO box.

At this point, your query should look like Figure 13.9. Notice that the view skeleton shows both the database and field name in each box. The box containing Orders – >CUSTNO will display the CUSTNO field from the Orders database. The Custlist – >LASTNAME and Custlist – >FIRSTNAME boxes will display the LASTNAME and FIRSTNAME fields from the Custlist database. (Some additional fields are beyond the right edge of the display.)

When you've completed the query, press Data (F2) to execute it. A browse screen will appear showing all the fields that you specified in the view skeleton. Figure 13.10 shows an example with LASTNAME and FIRSTNAME from the CUSTLIST database and CUSTNO, PARTNO, PARTNAME, QTY, and UNITPRICE from the

Remember, a # in the file skeleton indicates that the field is indexed and Include Indexes on the Fields pull-down menu is set to YES. A ↓ in the file skeleton indicates that the field is included in the view skeleton (by pressing F5).

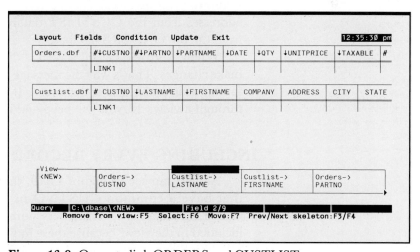

Figure 13.9: Query to link ORDERS and CUSTLIST

Figure 13.10: Data from CUSTLIST and ORDERS combined in a view

ORDERS database. (If your screen shows other fields, use the Tab key to scroll horizontally through the browse screen.)

The browse screen makes it appear as though a single database contains repetitive customer names with each order. However, we know that there is actually no such database; the browse screen is just presenting information from two related database files *as though* the names were stored repeatedly. As you'll see, you can use a view such as this to print invoices. That is, you can print customer names and addresses from the CUSTLIST database, along with transactions from the the ORDERS database.

When a browse or edit screen is displaying a view, you cannot make changes. That's why the message ReadOnly appears in the status bar near the bottom of the screen. If you attempt to make changes through a view, dBASE will beep and ignore your keystrokes.

INCLUDING EVERY RECORD

As you can see in Figure 13.10, the view presents only records that have a common CUSTNO in both the CUSTLIST and ORDERS databases. Customers numbered 1007 to 1009 are not included in the view, because these individuals had no records in the ORDERS database. However, in some situations you *might* want to include all records from a database file, even if the related file contains no information for some of the records.

To include all records from a file in a view, use the *Every* operator in the query, placing it before the linking example in the appropriate file skeleton (the file skeleton for the database that is not having all its records displayed: CUSTLIST in this example). Follow these steps to make this change:

1. Select Transfer to Query Design from the Exit pull-down menu.

2. Press F3, then move the highlight to the CUSTNO field in the CUSTLIST file skeleton.

3. Change the entry to **Every LINK1**, as shown in Figure 13.11 (you can type over the existing entry or insert the word Every if Insert mode is on).

4. Press Data (F2) to execute the query.

Figure 13.12 shows the results of the query. Notice that even though there are no orders for Susita Schumack, Anita Smith, or Fred Jones, their records are included in the view. Fields from the ORDERS database for these customers are empty, because there is no related

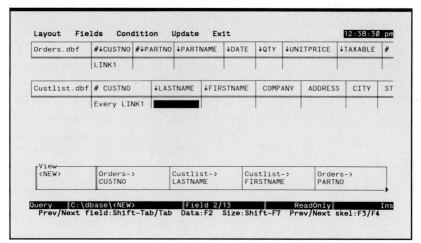

Figure 13.11: Query to include all records from CUSTLIST

```
 Records   Organize   Fields    Go To     Exit

 CUSTNO  LASTNAME          FIRSTNAME        PARTNO  PARTNAME            QTY  UNITPRICE  TA

  1001   Smith             John             B-222   Mondo Man            2    100.00    F
  1001   Smith             John             A-111   Astro Buddies        2     50.00    T
  1001   Smith             John             C-333   Cosmic Critters      1    500.00    T
  1002   Adams             Annie            B-222   Mondo Man            1    100.00    F
  1002   Adams             Annie            A-111   Astro Buddies        3     55.00    T
  1003   Mahoney           Mary             A-111   Astro Buddies        4     55.00    T
  1003   Mahoney           Mary             B-222   Mondo Man            1    100.00    F
  1004   Newell            John             C-333   Cosmic Critters      2    500.00    T
  1005   Beach             Sandy            C-333   Cosmic Critters      1    500.00    T
  1006   Kenney            Ralph            C-333   Cosmic Critters      2    500.00    T
         Schumack          Susita                                             .
         Smith             Anita                                              .
         Jones             Fred                                               .



 Browse   C:\dbase\<NEW>                   Rec 1/9          View  ReadOnly            Ins
```

Figure 13.12: Results of query for Every customer

information. (The CUSTNO field contains blanks because the view skeleton is showing Orders – >CUSTNO. If you changed the view skeleton to show CustList – >CUSTNO, then customer numbers for these three individuals would be displayed.)

ADDING FILTER CONDITIONS

NOTE

If a query includes both a filter condition and an Every operator, the filter condition takes precedence.

You can still place any filter condition in the query to isolate records that meet some search criterion. If the filter condition is based on one of the linking fields, enter the LINK example first, followed by a comma and the filter condition. For example, the query shown in Figure 13.13 limits the display to orders for customer number 1002. Figure 13.14 shows the results of this query.

You can place filter conditions in any other field boxes in the usual manner and use the rows from each skeleton to create *AND* and *OR* relationships. For example, placing **"CA"** (with the quotation marks) in the STATE field of the CUSTLIST database limits output to California residents. Placing **"CA"** in the top row of the CUST-LIST file skeleton and **"A-111"** in the top row of the ORDERS skeleton, under the PARTNO field, limits the display to records that have CA in the STATE field *and* A-111 in the PARTNO field. Placing **"CA"** in the first row of the CUSTLIST skeleton and **"A-111"** in the second row of the ORDERS skeleton displays records that have CA in the STATE field *or* A-111 in the PARTNO field.

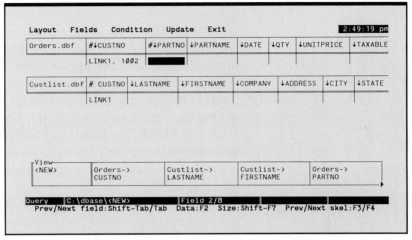

Figure 13.13: Query combining a filter condition and linking examples

```
Records    Organize    Fields    Go To    Exit
CUSTNO  LASTNAME          FIRSTNAME         PARTNO  PARTNAME            QTY  UNITPRICE  TA
 1002   Adams             Annie             B-222   Mondo Man             1    100.00   F
 1002   Adams             Annie             A-111   Astro Buddies         3     55.00   T




Browse    C:\dbase\<NEW>                Rec 2/9            View  ReadOnly              Ins
```

Figure 13.14: Results of query for orders by customer 1002

PRINTING REPORTS
FROM RELATED DATABASES

To print a report from two databases, you first need to create a query that links the databases. Also, make sure that all the fields that

you need in the printed report are included in the view skeleton.
If the report that you want to print involves any groups, be sure to
use the Sort on This Field option from the query Fields menu to
arrange the records into proper order for the grouping.

Figure 13.15 shows an example query, which we'll use to design
a report to print invoices. The LINK1 placeholder is included to set
up the link between CustList and Orders based on the common
CUSTNO field. The Every operator ensures that all customers will
be included in the view (though you could omit this operator if you
wanted to print invoices for only those individuals who have outstanding orders).

Using the Asc1 operator in the Orders – >CustNo field ensures
that the orders are sorted into customer number order. (The sort is
particularly important in this case because, when printing invoices, a
group band based on customer number is needed to print each customer's charges on a single invoice.)

All fields from both database file skeletons, except Orders
– >CUSTNO, are included in the view skeleton. Orders – >
CustNo is not included in the view skeleton because, as you saw in an
earlier example, this field is blank when displaying customers for
which there are no charge transactions. We want to print a customer
number on each invoice, so the query uses the CustNo field from the
CustList database (which contains all customer numbers).

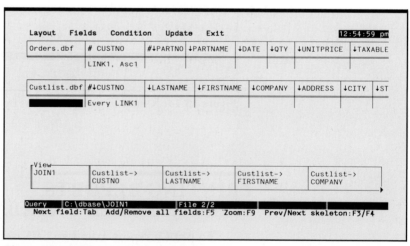

NOTE

To quickly put all fields
from CustList into the
view skeleton, first remove
Orders – >CUSTNO by
highlighting it and pressing
F5. Then put the highlight
beneath CustList.DBF and
press F5.

Figure 13.15: View to print a report

After creating the query and testing it by pressing the Data (F2) key, press Design (Shift-F2) to return to the query design screen. Then select Edit Description of Query from the Layout pull-down menu and enter a description such as **View to link ORDERS and CUSTLIST**. Then select Save Changes and Exit from the Exit pull-down menu. When prompted, enter the file name **JOIN1**.

Next you need to use the view as the basis for building a report format. If JOIN1 is not already above the line in the Queries panel, highlight its name, press ⏎, and select Use View. Then highlight <create> in the Reports panel and press ⏎.

When you get to the reports design screen, select the Column Layout option from the Quick Layout submenu to start with a column layout. The initial layout will include all fields that are in the view (though some may initially be off the right edge of your screen). As far as the reports design screen is concerned, a view is no different from a database file, so you are now free to use the same techniques you've used previously with single database files to design a report format to your liking.

To ensure that charges for a single customer are grouped together on one invoice, move the cursor to the Report Intro band (Band 2/5) and select Add a Group Band from the Bands pull-down menu. Select Field Value and then CUSTNO as the field to base the groups on.

To print each invoice on a separate page, leave the cursor in the Group 1 Intro band border. Then press F10 and change the Begin Band on New Page option on the Bands pull-down menu to Yes.

Figure 13.16 shows a sample report format after adding, rearranging, and deleting some field templates. The field template furthest to the right in the detail band is a calculated field named ExtPrice, based on the expression Qty*UnitPrice. The template beneath that one is a summary field that sums the ExtPrice field. Be sure to set Reset Every to CUSTNO for this summary field so that the total is reset to zero for each customer.

After creating the report format, use the Save Changes and Exit option from the pull-down menu to save it. Enter **INVOICES** as the file name when prompted. When you get back to the Control Center, you can select INVOICES from the Reports panel to print the invoices. Figure 13.17 shows an invoice printed from the report format.

To move the cursor to field templates that are off the right edge of the screen, move the cursor into the detail band and press End to move to the rightmost template or Ctrl-→ to move to the next template.

You could also use the IIF function in a calculated field to display the tax and total sale in this report, using techniques discussed in the previous chapter.

The sample application in Chapter 21 also prints invoices.

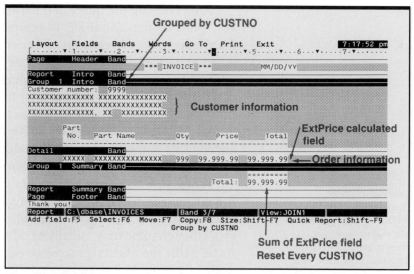

Figure 13.16: Report format for printing invoices

```
                    *** INVOICE ***                    07/30/91

        Customer number: 1003
        Mary Mahoney
        211 Seahawk St.
        Seattle, WA    88977


             Part
             No.    Part Name          Qty      Price       Total
             -----------------------------------------------------
             A-111  Astro Buddies        4      55.00      220.00
             B-222  Mondo Man            1     100.00      100.00
                                                        ==========
                                               Total:      320.00



        Thank you!
```

Figure 13.17: An invoice printed from the JOIN1 view

USING FORMS WITH RELATED FILES

Just as you can use the fields in a view to lay out a report format, you can use a view to lay out a custom form. But remember, when the view is active, you cannot change any data in the database. Hence, your custom form would only be useful for viewing data on the screen.

The sample business management application in Chapter 20 demonstrates some advanced techniques for creating and using custom forms that access multiple related database files.

LINKING MORE THAN TWO FILES

A common field is also known as a linking field or a key field.

Linking three or more files is no more difficult than linking two. Just be sure that you include proper common fields so that you can set up the links. For example, Figure 13.18 shows a modified version of the CUSTLIST and ORDERS databases with a third database, named PARTLIST, added. The PARTLIST database contains information about the product inventory.

PARTNO is the common field that links the PARTLIST database to the ORDERS database. It has the same name, data type, width, decimal places, and index option as the PARTNO field in the ORDERS database, as is required when creating a common field.

To set up a query to link the three files, you need to include file skeletons for all three files (using the usual Add File to Query option from the Layout pull-down menu to add each new skeleton). Select Create Link by Pointing to set up the link between CUSTLIST and ORDERS and then select Create Link by Pointing a second time to set up the link from ORDERS to PARTLIST. (dBASE will automatically use LINK2 as the placeholder for the second link.)

Figure 13.19 shows the completed query. Note that in the figure, Asc1 will display records sorted by the CUSTNO field in the ORDERS database. The view skeleton includes selected fields from all three files (though some fields are beyond the left and right edges of the screen).

Figure 13.20 shows the results of the query. Just as in the example with two databases, the customer's name, the part number, the part name, the unit price, and other information for each order is readily available and appears to be on one database. Of course, you can save this query and use it as the basis for developing report formats.

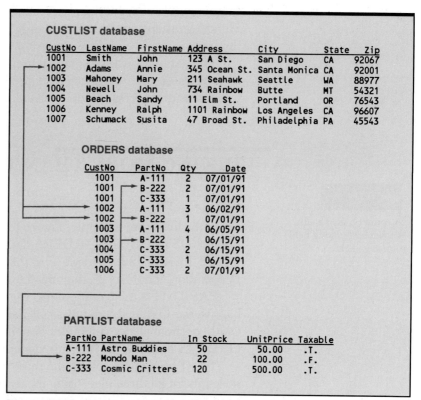

Figure 13.18: Database design with three related files

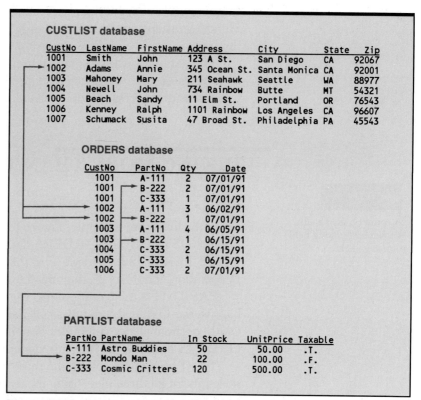

Figure 13.19: View linking three related files

CUSTNO	LASTNAME	FIRSTNAME	PARTNO	PARTNAME	QTY	UNITPRICE	TA
1001	Smith	John	B-222	Mondo Man	2	100.00	T
1001	Smith	John	A-111	Astro Buddies	2	50.00	T
1001	Smith	John	C-333	Cosmic Critters	1	500.00	T
1002	Adams	Annie	B-222	Mondo Man	1	100.00	
1002	Adams	Annie	A-111	Astro Buddies	3	50.00	T
1003	Mahoney	Mary	A-111	Astro Buddies	4	50.00	T
1003	Mahoney	Mary	B-222	Mondo Man	1	100.00	
1004	Newell	John	C-333	Cosmic Critters	2	500.00	T
1005	Beach	Sandy	C-333	Cosmic Critters	1	500.00	T
1006	Kenney	Ralph	C-333	Cosmic Critters	2	500.00	T

Records   Organize   Fields   Go To   Exit

Browse   C:\dbase\tmp\LINK3   Rec 1/10   View ReadOnly

Figure 13.20: Results of view linking three databases

THE MANY-TO-MANY DESIGN

The preceding example has actually brought us into the realm of another common database design based on a *many-to-many* relationship. Whereas there is a one-to-many relationship between customers and orders (every one customer may place many orders) and a one-to-many relationship between Orders and Parts (each part may appear in many different orders), there is a many-to-many relationship between customers and parts—that is, many customers can order many different parts.

This type of relationship occurs quite often in applications that involve scheduling. For example, a school offers many different courses, and each course is attended by many different students. To set up a database design for such an application, you need three database files: one to list students, one to list courses, and one to list student's numbers and the courses in which they are enrolled. The design assumes that each student and each course has a unique number.

Figure 13.21 shows the three databases and the links among them. The common field between STUDENTS and LINKER is StudentID, a Character field that is 11 spaces wide in both databases. The common field linking COURSES to LINKER is CourseID, a Character field that is 5 spaces wide in both databases.

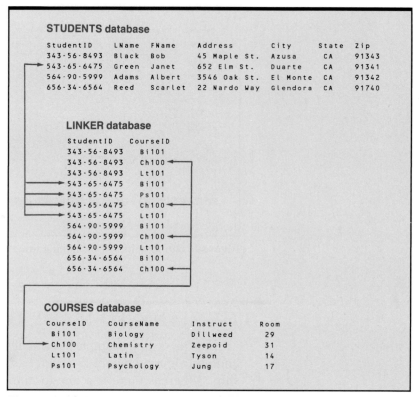

STUDENTS database

StudentID	LName	FName	Address	City	State	Zip
343-56-8493	Black	Bob	45 Maple St.	Azusa	CA	91343
543-65-6475	Green	Janet	652 Elm St.	Duarte	CA	91341
564-90-5999	Adams	Albert	3546 Oak St.	El Monte	CA	91342
656-34-6564	Reed	Scarlet	22 Nardo Way	Glendora	CA	91740

LINKER database

StudentID	CourseID
343-56-8493	Bi101
343-56-8493	Ch100
343-56-8493	Lt101
543-65-6475	Bi101
543-65-6475	Ps101
543-65-6475	Ch100
543-65-6475	Lt101
564-90-5999	Bi101
564-90-5999	Ch100
564-90-5999	Lt101
656-34-6564	Bi101
656-34-6564	Ch100

COURSES database

CourseID	CourseName	Instruct	Room
Bi101	Biology	Dillweed	29
Ch100	Chemistry	Zeepoid	31
Lt101	Latin	Tyson	14
Ps101	Psychology	Jung	17

Figure 13.21: Three related databases used for scheduling

In Figure 13.21, you can see that course identifiers use a department abbreviation combined with a number (for example, Bi101). In a sense, this identification scheme goes against earlier advice about using arbitrary identifiers in common fields. However, in this particular case, so long as the school makes certain that each department has a unique abbreviation, and that each course in each department has a unique number, then each course will be ensured a unique code.

Figure 13.22 shows a query to display information from the three files, with records sorted by the StudentID field in the LINKER database. The view skeleton includes some fields from all three files (several fields are beyond the right edge of the screen). Note that all of the linking fields are indexed (as indicated by the # symbol).

You could press F2 to see the immediate results of the query. Optionally, you could save the query and use it as a basis for creating

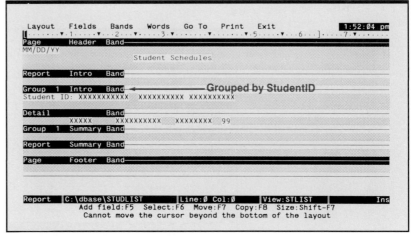

```
 Layout   Fields   Condition   Update   Exit                    1:50:02 pm
┌─────────────┬──────────────┬───────┬───────┬──────────┬──────┬───────┬──────┐
│Students.dbf │ # STUDENTID  │↓LNAME │↓FNAME │↓ADDRESS  │↓CITY │↓STATE │↓ZIP  │
│             ├──────────────┤       │       │          │      │       │      │
│             │ LINK1        │       │       │          │      │       │      │
└─────────────┴──────────────┴───────┴───────┴──────────┴──────┴───────┴──────┘

┌─────────────┬──────────────┬──────────┐
│Linker.dbf   │#↓STUDENTID   │#↓COURSEID│
│             ├──────────────┼──────────┤
│             │ LINK1, Asc1  │ LINK2    │
└─────────────┴──────────────┴──────────┘

┌─────────────┬──────────────┬─────────────┬──────────┬───────┐
│Courses.dbf  │ # COURSEID   │↓COURSENAME  │↓INSTRUCT │↓ROOM  │
│             ├──────────────┤             │          │       │
│             │ LINK2        │             │          │       │
└─────────────┴──────────────┴─────────────┴──────────┴───────┘

┌─View────┬─────────────┬─────────────┬─────────────┬─────────────┐
│ stlist  │ Linker->    │ Students->  │ Students->  │ Linker->    │
│         │ STUDENTID   │ FNAME       │ LNAME       │ COURSEID    │▶
└─────────┴─────────────┴─────────────┴─────────────┴─────────────┘
 Query    C:\dbase\STLIST        Field 1/11                        Ins
        Remove from view:F5  Select:F6  Move:F7  Prev/Next skeleton:F3/F4
```

Figure 13.22: Query to display data from many-to-many related files

the report format shown in Figure 13.23. In this report, the group band is based on the StudentID field.

Figure 13.24 shows the output from the report format. Because the query sorts records into StudentID order, student numbers are printed in ascending order and grouped according to the group band field, StudentID.

```
 Layout   Fields   Bands   Words   Go To   Print   Exit        1:52:04 pm
[......▼..1....▼....2...▼.....3.▼......▼.......▼.5....▼....6...]....7.▼.....
Page       Header   Band────────────────────────────────────────────────
MM/DD/YY
                            Student Schedules
Report     Intro    Band
Group 1    Intro    Band◀───────────Grouped by StudentID──────────
Student ID: XXXXXXXXXX  XXXXXXXXXX XXXXXXXXXX
Detail              Band
           XXXXX      XXXXXXXXXX   XXXXXXX  99
Group 1    Summary  Band
Report     Summary  Band
Page       Footer   Band────────────────────────────────────────────────


Report    C:\dbase\STUDLIST      Line:0 Col:0    View:STLIST          Ins
          Add field:F5  Select:F6  Move:F7  Copy:F8  Size:Shift-F7
          Cannot move the cursor beyond the bottom of the layout
```

Figure 13.23: Report format to display students and courses

```
07/21/91
                            Student Schedules

Student ID: 343-56-8493   Bob Black

                Bi101      Biology        Dillweed      29
                Ch100      Chemistry      Zeepoid       31
                Lt101      Latin          Tyson         14

Student ID: 543-65-6475   Janet Green

                Bi101      Biology        Dillweed      29
                Ps101      Psychology     Jung          17
                Ch100      Chemistry      Zeepoid       31
                Lt101      Latin          Tyson         14

Student ID: 564-90-5999   Albert Adams

                Bi101      Biology        Dillweed      29
                Ch100      Chemistry      Zeepoid       31
                Lt101      Latin          Tyson         14

Student ID: 656-34-6564   Scarlet Reed

                Bi101      Biology        Dillweed      29
                Ch100      Chemistry      Zeepoid       31
```

Figure 13.24: Report grouped by students

If you want a list of courses and the students enrolled in each, you set up the links in the query design screen, as usual, and base the sort order on the CourseID field in the LINKER database. Figure 13.25

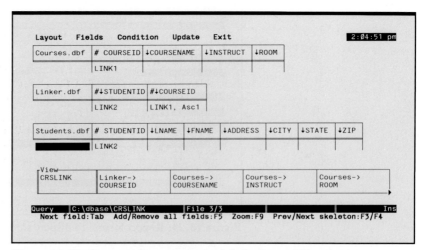

Figure 13.25: Query to list course schedule in CourseID order

shows the appropriate query. (Once again, some of the fields included in the view skeleton are off the right edge of the screen.)

Using this query as the basis for a report design, you could create a format with a group band based on the CourseID field, as shown in Figure 13.26. The actual report printed by the format is shown in Figure 13.27.

The two preceding examples illustrate the importance of selecting an appropriate sort field in the queries design screen if you want to print the results in a grouped report. To print a report with records grouped by students, the results of the query must be sorted by student number. To print a report with records grouped by courses, the results of the query must be sorted by course number.

AUTOMATIC UPDATING

In many business applications, you'll want dBASE to automatically update information in one database file based on information in another database file. For example, suppose you have a database for your master inventory that includes the in-stock quantity of each item. A second database stores orders or sales transactions, including the part number and quantity of each item sold. To calculate the true

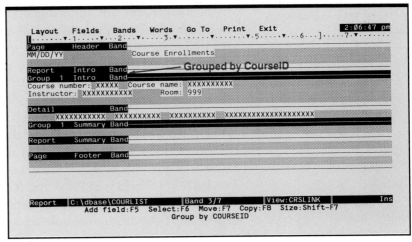

Figure 13.26: Report format to print course list

```
07/21/91                                Course Enrollments

Course number: Bi101   Course name: Biology
Instructor: Dillweed              Room:  29

           564-90-5999   Adams        Albert      3546 Oak St.   El Monte
           343-56-8493   Black        Bob         45 Maple St.   Azusa
           543-65-6475   Green        Janet       652 Elm St.    Duarte
           656-34-6564   Reed         Scarlet     22 Nardo Way   Glendora

Course number: Ch100   Course name: Chemistry
Instructor: Zeepoid               Room:  29

           564-90-5999   Adams        Albert      3546 Oak St.   El Monte
           343-56-8493   Black        Bob         45 Maple St.   Azusa
           543-65-6475   Green        Janet       652 Elm St.    Duarte
           656-34-6564   Reed         Scarlet     22 Nardo Way   Glendora

Course number: Lt101   Course name: Latin
Instructor: Tyson                 Room:  14

           564-90-5999   Adams        Albert      3546 Oak St.   El Monte
           543-65-6475   Green        Janet       652 Elm St.    Duarte
           343-56-8493   Black        Bob         45 Maple St.   Azusa

Course number: Ps101   Course name: Psychology
Instructor: Jung                  Room:  17

           543-65-6475   Green        Janet       652 Elm St.    Duarte
```

Figure 13.27: Report grouped by course list

in-stock quantity for each product in the inventory, you need to subtract the quantities sold from the in-stock quantities.

To understand how automatic updating works, assume that you have three database files, named MASTER, SALES, and PURCHASE. The MASTER database stores information about each item in the inventory, including the part number, part name, in-stock quantity, unit price, and reorder point, as well as other useful information. Figure 13.28 shows the database structure on the database design screen. Note that the PARTNO field is indexed. Figure 13.29 shows some sample records in the database.

Individual sales transactions are stored in the database named SALES. Figure 13.30 shows the structure of the SALES database. The PARTNO field is indexed and is the common field that will be used to link sales transactions to items in the MASTER database. Figure 13.31 shows some sample records in the database.

```
 Layout   Organize   Append   Go To   Exit                    8:38:19 pm

                                                    Bytes remaining:   3958
  ┌─────┬────────────┬────────────┬───────┬─────┬───────┐
  │ Num │ Field Name │ Field Type │ Width │ Dec │ Index │
  ├─────┼────────────┼────────────┼───────┼─────┼───────┤
  │  1  │ PARTNO     │ Character  │   5   │     │   Y   │
  │  2  │ PARTNAME   │ Character  │  15   │     │   N   │
  │  3  │ IN_STOCK   │ Numeric    │   3   │  0  │   N   │
  │  4  │ ON_ORDER   │ Numeric    │   3   │  0  │   N   │
  │  5  │ REORDER    │ Numeric    │   3   │  0  │   N   │
  │  6  │ UNITPRICE  │ Numeric    │  12   │  2  │   N   │
  │  7  │ TAXABLE    │ Logical    │   1   │     │   N   │
  │  8  │            │ Character  │       │     │   N   │
  │     │            │            │       │     │       │
  └─────┴────────────┴────────────┴───────┴─────┴───────┘

 Database  C:\dbase\invent\MASTER    Field 8/8
                Enter the field name.  Insert/Delete field:Ctrl-N/Ctrl-U
 Field names begin with a letter and may contain letters, digits and underscores
```

Figure 13.28: Structure of the MASTER database

```
 Records   Organize   Fields   Go To   Exit

 PARTNO PARTNAME        IN_STOCK ON_ORDER REORDER UNITPRICE    TAXABLE

 A-111  Amplifier           10       5      25      495.00  T
 B-222  CD Player           10       5      25      295.00  T
 C-333  Boise speakers      10       5      25      800.00  T




 Browse   C:\dbase\MASTER          Rec 1/3           File
```

Figure 13.29: Sample data in the MASTER database

The business purchases items to sell. All completed purchase transactions, for this example, are stored in the database named PURCHASE. Figure 13.32 shows the structure of the PURCHASE database. Figure 13.33 shows some sample records in the database.

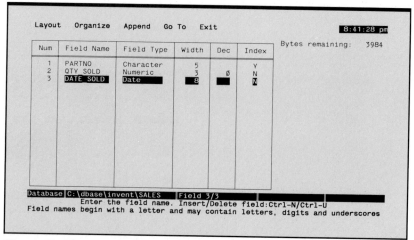

Figure 13.30: Structure of the SALES database

```
     Records   Organize   Fields   Go To   Exit
     PARTNO QTY_SOLD DATE_SOLD
     A-111        1 01/01/91
     A-111        1 01/01/91
     A-111        1 01/01/91
     A-111        5 01/01/91
     B-222        1 01/01/91
     B-222        1 01/01/91
     B-222        1 01/01/91
     C-333        1 01/01/91
     C-333        1 01/01/91
     C-333        1 01/01/91
     C-333        1 01/01/91




     Browse   C:\dbase\SALES            Rec 3/11        File
```

Figure 13.31: Sample sales transactions in the SALES database

To subtract the quantities of items sold in the SALES database from IN_STOCK quantities in the MASTER database, you need to create an UPDATE query that links the two databases. Figure 13.34 shows a sample query that will do the job. Notice that the MASTER file (the one containing the REPLACE operator) is the target of the replacements.

The QTY_SOLD field contains the placeholder, Sold. The IN_STOCK field uses the expression WITH In_Stock – Sold to

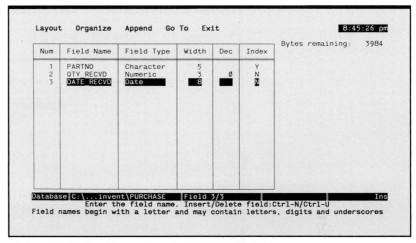

```
  Layout   Organize   Append   Go To   Exit                          8:45:26 pm
                                                        Bytes remaining:   3984
  ┌─────┬────────────┬────────────┬───────┬──────┬───────┐
  │ Num │ Field Name │ Field Type │ Width │ Dec  │ Index │
  ├─────┼────────────┼────────────┼───────┼──────┼───────┤
  │  1  │ PARTNO     │ Character  │   5   │      │   Y   │
  │  2  │ QTY_RECVD  │ Numeric    │   3   │  Ø   │   N   │
  │  3  │ DATE_RECVD │ Date       │   8   │      │   N   │
  │     │            │            │       │      │       │
  └─────┴────────────┴────────────┴───────┴──────┴───────┘


  Database C:\...invent\PURCHASE      Field 3/3                            Ins
            Enter the field name.  Insert/Delete field:Ctrl-N/Ctrl-U
  Field names begin with a letter and may contain letters, digits and underscores
```

Figure 13.32: Structure of the PURCHASE database

```
  Records   Organize   Fields   Go To   Exit
  ┌────────┬───────────┬────────────┐
  │ PARTNO │ QTY_RECVD │ DATE_RECVD │
  ├────────┼───────────┼────────────┤
  │ A-111  │      5    │ Ø1/11/91   │
  │ B-222  │      5    │ Ø1/11/91   │
  │ C-333  │      5    │ Ø1/11/91   │
  │        │           │            │


  Browse  C:\dbase\PURCHASE          Rec 1/3             File
```

Figure 13.33: Sample data in the PURCHASE database

subtract the quantity sold from the quantity in stock. When you select Perform the Update to execute this query, dBASE will step through each record in the nontarget database (SALES), look for a record in the target database (MASTER) that has the same part number (because LINK1 sets up the link), and then perform the WITH calculation in the IN_STOCK field.

After dBASE executes the update, the MASTER database will contain the information shown in Figure 13.35. Notice that there are

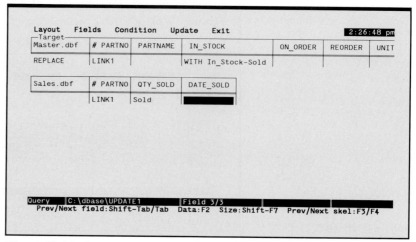

Figure 13.34: Query to subtract sold quantities from in-stock quantities

PARTNO	PARTNAME	IN_STOCK	ON_ORDER	REORDER	UNITPRICE	TAXABLE
A-111	Amplifier	2	5	25	495.00	T
B-222	CD Player	7	5	25	295.00	T
C-333	Boise speakers	6	5	25	800.00	T

Figure 13.35: Sales quantities subtracted from in-stock quantities

now two amplifiers in stock, because eight were sold. The in-stock quantities for CD players and Boise speakers have also been adjusted.

To update the MASTER database using the quantities in the PURCHASE database, you need to add the quantities received to the in-stock quantities and subtract the quantities received from the on-order quantities. (Presumably, the items received were previously on order, but now that they have been received, the on-order quantity needs to be decreased accordingly.)

The query to perform the update appears in Figure 13.36. The REPLACE update operator specifies a replacement update. The word *Recvd* is a placeholder for the value in the QTY_RECVD field. The expression WITH In_Stock + Recvd replaces the in-stock value with its current value plus the quantity received. The expression WITH On_Order – Recvd replaces the on-order value with its current value minus the quantity received. Again, because the PARTNO fields in the two file skeletons contain the same LINK1 placeholder, the replacement takes place only in the MASTER file record that has the same part number as the record in the SALES database.

After you create the query and execute it by selecting Perform the Update from the Update menu, the MASTER database will contain the information shown in Figure 13.37. Seven amplifiers are now in stock, and none are on order, because five were received. The other records have been updated as well.

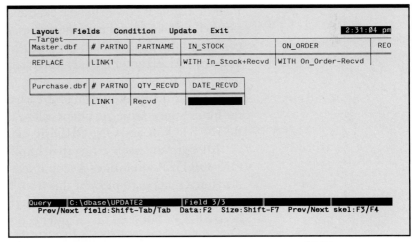

Figure 13.36: Query using PURCHASE to update MASTER

Figure 13.37: MASTER database after updating from the PURCHASE database

HANDLING OLD TRANSACTIONS

One issue that arises when you print invoices and perform automatic updating is how to handle old transactions that have already been printed on invoices and used in updates. For example, after dBASE has completed the updates from the SALES and PURCHASE databases, both the SALES and PURCHASE databases will still contain the same data. dBASE has no way of knowing that their records have already been used in an update. Therefore, each time you perform the update in the future, these same quantities will be added to, and subtracted from, the IN_STOCK and ON_ORDER values in the MASTER database.

Of course, each time this happens, the IN_STOCK and ON_ORDER quantities become less accurate. It's up to you to develop a scheme to prevent this from happening. There are several techniques you can use. You can flag the records as having already been used, or not used, in an update, or you can move updated transactions from the SALES and PURCHASE databases to history files that contain only *posted* transactions (that is, transactions already used in an update).

Either technique, unfortunately, takes several steps to accomplish and is therefore prone to errors if each step is not fully completed. The safest way to ensure that all steps are handled properly is to combine them into a *batch process*, so that pressing a single button performs the entire update operation, including handling posted transactions. You'll see how to do this in Chapters 19 through 21, where we develop a complete inventory management system.

Techniques for Managing Your Workspace

THIS CHAPTER PRESENTS GENERAL TECHNIQUES for managing catalogs, files, and settings, as well as techniques for interfacing with DOS. Many of the tasks discussed in this chapter are referred to as housekeeping chores, because they help you keep your files in order. Housekeeping chores that you'll want to perform on your computer from time to time include

- Finding particular files

- Erasing outdated files

- Copying files to floppy disks as backup copies or for use on another computer

- Changing the names of files

- Deleting unnecessary files to conserve disk space

You may find that you need to use only a few of the techniques presented in this chapter. Therefore, don't worry about trying all of them. Instead, you can just become familiar with the options available to you and then refer to this chapter later as necessary.

MANAGING CATALOGS

As discussed in Chapter 2, a catalog is a tool for helping you keep the names of files that belong together visible in the Control Center. Any time you create a file (be it a database file, report format, custom screen, or whatever), dBASE automatically adds the file name that you assign the file to the current catalog, and that name appears in the Control Center. (You've already seen many examples of this.)

Because a catalog consists of only the names of files, you can include the same file in more than one catalog. As you create and work with multiple catalogs, you may eventually want to add, change, or delete file names in a catalog. The Catalog pull-down menu in the Control Center offers all the techniques you'll need to manage catalogs.

> **TIP**
>
> To avoid confusing *catalogs* and *directories*, remember that a directory (or subdirectory) is a place on the disk where files are stored, and a catalog is simply a list of file names.

CREATING A NEW CATALOG

To create a new catalog, select Use a Different Catalog from the Catalog pull-down menu above the Control Center and then select <create> from the submenu that appears. When the screen asks for a name, type a valid file name (eight letters maximum, no spaces) and press ←┘. That new catalog will become the current catalog, and the panels in the Control Center will be empty. Any new files that you create while using the new catalog will be listed in the catalog automatically.

SELECTING A CATALOG

When working with multiple catalogs, you can switch from one to another by selecting Use a Different Catalog from the Catalog pull-down menu in the Control Center. Select the name of the catalog that you want to use from the submenu of catalog names that appears.

CHANGING A CATALOG DESCRIPTION

To change the description of a catalog, select Edit Description of Catalog from the Catalog pull-down menu. Use the usual editing keys to change the description (or type a new description) and press ←┘. The description of the catalog appears when you scroll through catalog names after selecting Use a Different Catalog.

ADDING FILE NAMES TO A CATALOG

Suppose you create a file while using one catalog and want that file name to appear in a different catalog. To add a file name to a catalog, select the catalog to which you want to add the file name and then move the highlight to the panel that describes the type of file that you want to add. For example, if you are adding a database file name to the current catalog, move the highlight to the Data panel.

Next, select Add File to Catalog from the Catalog pull-down menu. A submenu will list all files in the current directory that match the type of file you are adding (for example, all .DBF files if the highlight is in the Data panel). The submenu will also list options to change to a different disk drive, to the parent directory, or to another subdirectory. If necessary, switch to the appropriate directory to locate the file name. Then select the file name from the submenu.

You can either edit the description of the file or just press ← to use the current description. The name of the file will appear in the appropriate panel of the Control Center.

☞ NOTE

Chapter 17 lists other dBASE file name extensions and the types of files they represent.

If you are adding a query, form, report, or label file name to the current catalog, the submenu will display every file name with every extension (such as CUSTFORM.FRM and CUSTFORM.SCR). You need select only one of these multiple names, using the appropriate extension, as listed here.

File type	Extension to select
Query	.QBE
Update query	.UPD
View query	.QBE
Form	.SCR
Report	.FRM
Labels	.LBL
Application	.APP

Note that if you add the name of a file that is stored on a floppy disk to a particular catalog, that floppy disk must be in its disk drive whenever you use that catalog; adding a file name to a catalog does not copy the file to the current drive or directory. If you do want to copy the file from the floppy disk onto your hard disk, use the copying techniques discussed later in this chapter and then add the file name to the hard disk catalog.

REMOVING FILE NAMES FROM A CATALOG

To remove a file name from the current catalog, first highlight the file name that you wish to remove. Then select Remove

Highlighted File from Catalog from the Catalog pull-down menu. dBASE will double-check your request by asking

**Are you sure you want to remove
this file from the catalog?**

No   Yes

Select Yes if you do want to delete the file. Next, dBASE will ask,

**Do you also want to delete
this file from the disk?**

No   Yes

If you select No, then the file name is removed from the catalog, but the file remains intact on the disk (and its name can be added to some other catalog). If you select Yes, then the file is permanently removed from the disk and cannot be recovered. (So use this option with caution!)

CHANGING A FILE DESCRIPTION

To change the description that you've assigned to a file, first highlight the file name in the Control Center. Then select Change Description of Highlighted File from the Catalog pull-down menu. Use the usual arrow and Backspace keys to position the cursor and erase, as needed, and then save the new description by pressing ←┘. The new description will appear below the Control Center panels whenever the file name is highlighted.

CHANGING THE NAME
OF THE CURRENT CATALOG

If you start dBASE IV from a directory that contains no catalogs, it will automatically create a catalog named UNTITLED.CAT that includes all of the dBASE IV database files on the current directory. To change the name of the current catalog, select Modify Catalog

Name from the Catalog pull-down menu. Press Backspace to erase the current name and then enter the new name. (You need not enter the .CAT extension; dBASE will add it automatically. Do not enter a different extension.)

MANAGING FILES

Appendix A discusses basic DOS concepts and is especially useful for dBASE users new to computers.

The computer's disk operating system (DOS) handles all basic file management tasks, including saving, retrieving, copying, moving, and deleting files, as well as managing directories. dBASE IV lets you interact with DOS to manage files on your own via the DOS utilities screen.

Whereas the Catalog pull-down menu lets you manage the file *names* that appear in a catalog, the DOS utilities screen offers options for actually manipulating files, including techniques for copying, moving, deleting, and renaming files. To get to the DOS utilities screen, select DOS Utilities from the Tools pull-down menu above the Control Center. You will see a box containing a *file list* that includes all subdirectory names (directories beneath the current directory) and files, as in Figure 14.1. (Of course, some of the file and subdirectory names on your screen will be different.)

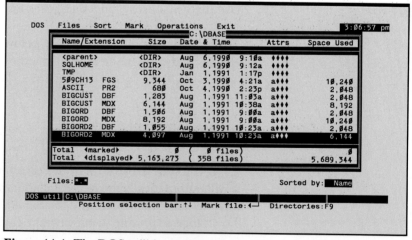

Figure 14.1: The DOS utilities screen

The current drive and directory, C:\DBASE in this example, are displayed at the top of the box. Within the file list, the Name/ Extension column lists subdirectory names enclosed in < > brackets (for instance, <DBDATA>) and file names. The Size column displays the number of characters in the file (or <DIR> for directory names). The Date & Time column shows the date and time that the file was created or last changed.

The Attrs (Attributes) column lists the DOS attributes assigned to each file, in the order Archive, Hidden, Read-Only, and System. (These attributes need not concern you just now.) The Space Used column shows how much real disk space the file occupies. This information differs from that in the Size option because the computer stores files in clusters, which have some minimal size. For example, if your computer uses a cluster size of 2,048 bytes, then even the smallest file occupies at least 2,048 bytes.

The Total Marked information at the bottom of the box lists the total size and number of files that are currently marked (zero in the figure). The Total Displayed information lists the size and number of files displayed. Use the PgUp, PgDn, Home, and End keys to scroll through file names.

The indicator "Files:*.*" means that all files are currently displayed. (The *.* wildcard pattern means "files with any name, followed by any extension.") The "Sorted by: Name" indicator means that file names are currently sorted by name (though subdirectory names are listed above file names).

TEMPORARILY CHANGING DIRECTORIES

You can use the ↑ and ↓ keys to move the highlight through the file list. To switch to a subdirectory, select the subdirectory name using the usual technique of highlighting and press ←. To switch to the parent directory, select <parent>.

To get a better view of the overall directory structure, press Zoom (F9). dBASE then presents the directory structure in a tree format, as in the example in Figure 14.2. Note that subdirectory names are indented beneath the name of their parent directory. The current directory is indicated by a pointer to the left of the directory name.

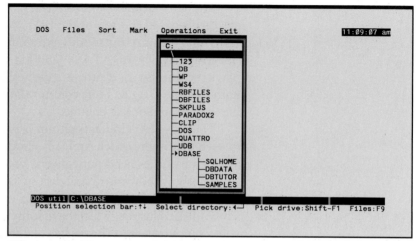

Figure 14.2: Sample directory tree

To switch to any directory or subdirectory while the directory tree is displayed, highlight the appropriate name and press ←┘. The file list will appear, showing the names of files on the new current directory.

You can also switch to a new drive and directory by selecting Change Drive:Directory from the Files pull-down menu. When you select this option, you'll be given the opportunity to enter a new drive and directory or press Pick (Shift-F1) to view the directory tree.

Note that the techniques discussed in this section affect only the DOS utilities screen display. When you return to the Control Center, the directory that was in effect before you went to the DOS utilities will still be in effect.

NOTE

The Set Default Drive: Directory option on the DOS pull-down menu lets you permanently change the default directory (see page 422).

SELECTING FILES TO DISPLAY

You can limit the file names displayed on the DOS utilities screen to only those that match some wildcard pattern. As with searches, you can use ? to stand for any single character and * to stand for any group of characters. To change the wildcard pattern, select Display Only from the Files pull-down menu and type the new wildcard pattern.

For example, to view only database file names (those with the extension .DBF), change the wildcard pattern to ***.DBF**. To view only file names that begin with the letters CUST, change the wildcard pattern to **CUST*.***. Note that subdirectory names and the <parent> option are still displayed, regardless of the wildcard pattern you use.

SORTING FILE NAMES

The Sort pull-down menu lets you select a sort order for viewing file names. When you highlight Sort on the menu bar, you'll be given a menu of choices:

Name	Lists files alphabetically by file name (the default setting)
Extension	Lists files alphabetically by extension
Date & Time	Lists files in ascending order by date and time
Size	Lists files by size, from smallest to largest

MARKING FILES

Sometimes you may want to perform operations on groups of files. dBASE provides several techniques for marking files. The simplest approach is to scroll the highlight to the file that you want to mark and then press ←. You can mark as many files as you wish in this manner. (Note that ← works as a toggle: Each time you press it, it either marks or unmarks the current file name.)

You can also use options from the Mark pull-down menu to mark and unmark records. The Mark All option marks all currently displayed file names. Hence, if the wildcard pattern CUST*.* is in effect and you select Mark All, then all files beginning with the letters CUST will be marked. Changing the wildcard pattern does not affect the marks, so you can mark several groups of files by changing the wildcard pattern and selecting Mark All.

The Unmark All option on the Mark pull-down menu unmarks all currently displayed file names. The Reverse Marks option swaps the file marks, so that unmarked files are marked, and marked files become unmarked. This option is handy when, for example, you want to copy two groups of files to two floppy disks. You could mark one set of files and copy those files to one floppy disk. Then you could reverse the marks and copy the now-marked files to another floppy disk.

COPYING, MOVING, DELETING, AND RENAMING FILES

To copy, delete, move, or rename files, select the appropriate option on the Operations pull-down menu. You'll first see a sub-menu with these options:

Single File	Includes only the currently highlighted file name in the operation
Marked Files	Includes all currently displayed marked files in the list in the operation
Displayed Files	Includes only the currently displayed files in the operation

Note that the phrase ''currently displayed'' as used here refers to all files that match the current wildcard pattern. Hence, any file names that are not visible at the moment simply because they are scrolled off the bottom of the screen are still included in the operation. The Marked Files option includes only marked files that are currently displayed (that is, marked files that match the current wildcard pattern).

If the highlight is on a directory name when you choose a group of files for an operation and you select Single File, then the operation will be performed for all files in that directory.

After you've selected the files to include in the operation, you'll be given further information and options relevant to that operation, as discussed in the following sections.

COPYING FILES   If you selected Copy as the file operation, you will be prompted to specify the destination and file names for the copy operation. Enter the appropriate disk drive and directory for the copy operation and press ←┘. For example, to copy files to a floppy disk in drive A, delete the current destination and type the new destination **A:** (be sure to type the colon). Then press ←┘.

If you are copying a single file, its name will be displayed as the name for the copied file. You can change that name (so that the copied file has a different name than the original file) or press ←┘ to use the same name. If you are copying a group of files, enter ***.*** as the destination file name to ensure that copied files have the same names as the original files.

If you prefer, you can assign new names to the copied files. In the destination file name, use a combination of the new name (for that part of the file name that you want to change) and a wildcard (for the part that you want to remain the same). For example, suppose you mark the files CUSTLIST.DBF and CUSTLIST.MDX as the file group to copy. If you enter **CUSTBAK.*** as the destination file name, the copied files will have the names CUSTBAK.DBF and CUSTBAK.MDX.

If you want to place copied files in the same directory as the original files, you must specify a new name for the copied files (a directory cannot have two files with the same name). For example, suppose you want to copy C:\DBASE\ORDERS.DBF and C:\DBASE\OR-DERS.MDX to two backup files in the same directory. You would keep the destination for the copy as C:\DBASE, but enter a file name with a wildcard character, such as **OLDORDER.***, so that the copies would have the file names OLDORDER.DBF and OLDORDER.MDX.

When you have finished filling in the destination and file name for the copy, press Ctrl-End to begin the copy operation. Note that you can also copy a single file by highlighting its name in the files list and pressing Copy (F8).

Using * rather than a specific file name helps to ensure that all the appropriate files are copied. For example, if a database contains a memo field, the memos are stored in a separate file with the extension .DBT. Therefore, if you named the database REFERENC, and copied REFERENC.*, you'd be sure that all the appropriate files, REFERENC.DBF, REFERENCE.DBT, and REFERENCE.MDX, were copied.

Keep in mind that when you copy files, the copies are stored in the directory you specified, but in no particular catalog. When you've completed your Copy operation, you'll need to either select an existing catalog, or create a new catalog to put the file names in. Then add the file names as discussed in "Managing Catalogs" earlier in this chapter.

DELETING FILES   If you select Delete as the operation, dBASE displays the options Proceed and Cancel. If you are sure you want to delete all the files described, select Proceed. But use this option with

Before deleting all marked or displayed files, use PgDn and PgUp to scroll through the file list to make certain that you know exactly which files will be deleted. Also, make sure that the highlight is not on a subdirectory name when you select Delete; otherwise you might inadvertently delete the entire directory.

caution, because once you delete a file, you cannot retrieve it. If you are unsure about deleting the files, select Cancel.

You can also delete any single file by moving the highlight to the appropriate file name in the file list and pressing Del. You'll still be given the option to proceed or cancel.

MOVING FILES   The Move option lets you move a file from one disk drive directory to another. This option works in the same manner as Copy, except that the original file is deleted from its original drive and directory after being copied to its new destination. The general technique used is identical to that used for copying. After you select the option, you specify a disk drive or directory to move the file to or press Pick (Shift-F1) to select a new directory from the directory tree.

After specifying the disk drive and directory to move the file to, you'll be prompted to enter a new name for the moved file. If you are moving a single file, its name will be displayed, and you can just press ←┘ to retain the name. If you are moving a group of files, enter the wildcard patterns *.* to move all files and retain their current names. Press Ctrl-End after responding to both prompts (or press Esc to abort the operation).

You can also move a single file by highlighting its name in the file list and pressing Move (F7).

RENAMING FILES   The Rename option lets you change the name of a file, group of files, or a subdirectory. When you select this option, you'll be prompted to enter the new name. If you are renaming a group of files, be sure to use a wildcard character in the new file name. For example, if you want to rename all files named CUST-BAK to OLDCUST, enter **OLDCUST.** * as the new file name. Each file previously named CUSTBAK will be renamed OLDCUST, but will still have the original extension. (Hence, CUSTBAK.DBF becomes OLDCUST.DBF, and CUSTBAK.MDX becomes OLD-CUST.MDX.)

If the new name that you assign to a file is the same as an existing file name, an information box will warn you that the existing file will be erased. The screen will display options to overwrite the existing file or to skip the renaming operation. Unless you are absolutely sure that you wish to replace the currently named file with the new one, select Skip.

MAKING BACKUP
COPIES OF IMPORTANT FILES

TIP

Use the general techniques described in this section to make backup copies of all your database files from time to time. That way, if you ever inadvertently lose any files from your hard disk, you can just copy the backup files from the floppy disks back onto your hard disk.

To see how to use the DOS utilities screen as a tool for making backup copies of important files, we'll go through the steps necessary to copy the CUSTLIST and ORDERS databases to a formatted disk in drive A. (This example assumes that you have a formatted disk with at least 51K of blank space on it readily available, and that your floppy disk drive is named A. If you need help creating a formatted floppy disk, see the FORMAT command in your DOS manual. But be careful when using the format command, because it permanently erases any files already on the disk.)

From the Control Center, select DOS Utilities from the Tools pull-down menu. When the file list appears, select Display Only from the Files pull-down menu and change the wildcard pattern to **CUSTLIST.***. Then select Mark All from the Mark pull-down menu to mark the files named CUSTLIST.DBF and CUSTLIST.MDX (the .MDX file contains the indexes for CUSTLIST.DBF). You may have to press PgDn a few times to see the marked file names.

Next, select Display Only from the Files pull-down menu and change the wildcard pattern to **ORDERS.***. Once again, select Mark All from the Mark pull-down menu. Select Display Only from the Files pull-down menu again and change the wildcard pattern to ***.*** (or just press Ctrl-Y to blank the option; dBASE will change it to *.* after you press ◄─┘).

If you use the PgDn and PgUp keys now to scroll through the files list, you'll see that the CUSTLIST and ORDERS files are the only ones marked. Also, beneath the file list you can see that the total amount of space used by the marked files is about 51,200 bytes (about 50K, because a kilobyte contains 1,024 characters).

To begin the copy operation, first place the floppy disk in drive A. Then select Copy from the Operations menu and Marked Files from the submenu. Press Ctrl-Y to erase the current drive and directory names suggested by the prompt and then enter the destination drive, **A:**. Then press ◄─┘ and enter ***.*** as the file name, so that copied files retain their same names and extensions. To perform the copy operation, press Ctrl-End.

dBASE will begin copying all the marked files onto the disk in drive A. Note that if the disk already contains copies of these files, you will be given the option to overwrite (replace) the current file or skip (not copy) the file with the currently displayed name.

To verify the copy operation, select Change Drive:Directory from the Files pull-down menu and change the setting to **A:**. After you press ◄—, you should see the names of the copied files on the disk in drive A. (If there are other files on the floppy disk in drive A, you may need to use PgDn and PgUp to scroll through the file list.)

To return to the C:\DBASE directory, select Change Drive:Directory from the Files pull-down menu once again and replace A: with **C:\DBASE**. Then press ◄—. Files from the C:\DBASE drive and directory will be displayed in the file list once again.

CHANGING THE
DEFAULT DRIVE AND DIRECTORY

To change the default drive and directory for *all* operations in the current dBASE session, select Tools from the Control Center menu bar and DOS Utilities from the pull-down menu. Then select Set Default Drive:Directory from the DOS pull-down menu. You can then either type the name of the new drive and directory to log on to or press Pick (Shift-F1) to select an option from the directory tree.

Note that this change tells dBASE to look for and save all files on the new drive and directory. It does not immediately affect the current files list. (To view files on the new default drive and directory, you need to select Change Drive:Directory from the Files pull-down menu and type or select the name of the new default drive and directory.)

After you leave the DOS utilities screen and return to the Control Center, you'll see that dBASE is logged on to the new drive and directory (the catalog name centered above the Control Center will include the current drive and directory). dBASE will search only this new default directory for any files that you request. Any new files that you create also will be saved on the new drive and directory.

ACCESSING DOS

dBASE IV offers two techniques for accessing DOS commands without quitting dBASE. Both are available by selecting DOS Utilities from the Tools menu at the Control Center and DOS from the DOS Utilities menu.

The Perform DOS Command option lets you enter a single DOS command. When the DOS command completes its job, you'll be prompted to press any key to return to dBASE IV.

The Go to DOS option on the DOS pull-down menu temporarily leaves dBASE IV and displays the DOS prompt. If any marked files are currently in the file list, dBASE will warn you that all marked files will be unmarked and ask whether you want to proceed or to cancel the operation.

If you select Proceed, you'll be taken to the DOS prompt, with dBASE IV suspended in memory. You can enter whatever DOS commands you wish. To return to dBASE IV, type the command **EXIT** at the DOS prompt and press ◄──┘, as instructed on the screen.

Whenever you select Go to DOS, be sure to return to dBASE IV and exit dBASE in the usual manner before turning off your computer.

CHANGING ENVIRONMENTAL SETTINGS

In previous chapters, you saw how to use the Settings submenu to turn the Instruct and Deleted options on and off. This section discusses the other options on the Settings submenu. To get to the Settings menu from the Control Center, select Settings from the Tools pull-down menu.

CHANGING OPTIONS

To permanently change a setting so that it affects all future dBASE IV sessions, use the DBSETUP program discussed in Appendix B.

When you first select Settings, you'll see the Options pull-down menu, which displays a list of the most commonly used settings, as shown in Figure 14.3. The effects of changing the settings are summarized in Table 14.1. Note that changing these settings affects only the current dBASE IV session. When you exit and then return to dBASE IV later, the original settings will be in effect.

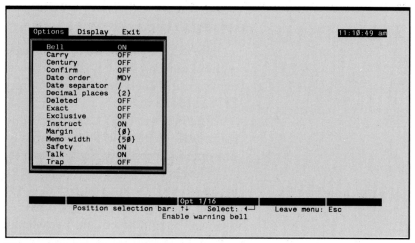

Figure 14.3: The Settings Options submenu

Table 14.1: Settings Options

Option	Effect of settings
Bell	When on, beeps whenever a field on an edit screen or custom form is filled or an error occurs. When off, doesn't beep.
Carry	When on, copies all information from the current record to the next new record while you are entering new data. When off, starts each new record with blank fields.
Century	When off, displays dates with two-digit years (for example, 12/31/91). When on, displays dates with four-digit years (for example, 12/31/1991).
Confirm	When off, automatically moves the cursor to the next field when you fill a field during data entry or editing. When on, keeps the cursor in the current field until the ◄┘ key is pressed.

Table 14.1: Settings Options (continued)

Option	Effect of settings
Date Order	Lets you determine the order of month, day, and year in date displays (press the space bar to scroll through the options). Options are MDY (12/31/91), DMY (31/12/91), and YMD (91/12/31).
Date Separator	Determines the character used in date displays (space bar scrolls through options). Slash (/) displays dates as 12/31/91, hyphen (-) displays dates as 12-31-91, and period (.) displays dates as 12.31.91. Can be used in conjunction with Date Order to create various international date formats (for example, 91.12.31).
Decimal Places	Determines the number of decimal places displayed in the results of calculations, in the range 0 to 18. The default setting is 2.
Deleted	When off, displays records that are marked for deletion. When on, hides from view, and from all operations, records marked for deletion.
Exact	When off, matches strings of different lengths in a search. When on, matches only strings of the same length. Hence, when Exact is off, a search for **"AB"** locates "ABC Co." When on, a search for **"AB "** matches only "AB ".
Exclusive	When off, lets other network users access the file you are currently using. When on, does not let other network users access the file you are currently using.
Instruct	When on, displays information boxes each time you use a feature for the first time. When off, does not display information boxes.

Table 14.1: Settings Options (continued)

Option	Effect of settings
Margin	Adjusts the left margin for all printed output, as measured in characters. Thus, entering **10** adds a one-inch margin to the left side of the page (assuming that 10 characters to the inch are printed).
Memo Width	Adjusts the default width of memo field displays during certain operations. Can accept a value in the range 5 to 250. (Widths defined in custom forms and reports override this setting.)
Safety	When on, displays a warning before dBASE overwrites an existing file and provides an option to cancel the operation. When off, displays no warning and immediately overwrites the existing file.
Talk	When on, displays results of various dBASE operations on the screen. When off, does not display results on the screen (used mainly in custom programming).
Trap	In custom programming, determines whether the dBASE IV debugger is activated when an error occurs in a program.

CHANGING THE DISPLAY COLORS

NOTE

The color options available to you depend on the type of color monitor you have.

If you have a color monitor, you can use the options on the Display pull-down menu to change display colors. The Display pull-down menu provides a list of areas to color. When you select an area, you'll see a list of possible foreground and background colors for that area, as shown in Figure 14.4.

The Standard – All option affects the general color of text and background on normal (that is, unhighlighted) sections of the screen. The Enhanced – All option sets the general color for all highlighted

TIP

When creating a custom form, you can also select colors that affect only that form, as discussed in Chapter 8.

text, such as text in the menu, status bar, and input fields of a custom form. You can color more specific areas by selecting options under Standard – All and Enhanced – All. Some examples of these specific areas are shown in Figure 14.5.

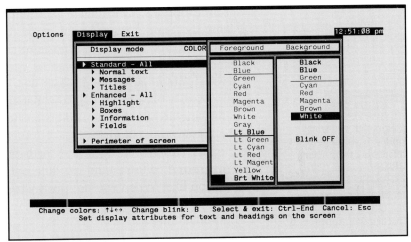

Figure 14.4: Display menu and color options

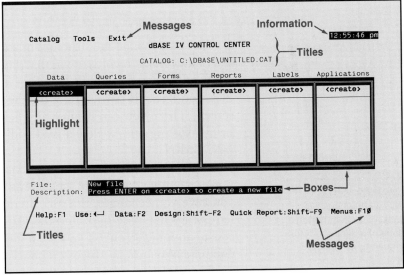

Figure 14.5: Some areas that can be colored

After you select an area to color, the menu of foreground and background options appears. A small square indicates the current foreground color. You can use ↑ and ↓ to scroll up and down and select a different foreground color.

After selecting a foreground color, press → to move the background options. Once again, you can scroll through color options using the ↑ and ↓ keys. As you scroll through foreground and background colors, the screen adjusts to show color combinations. For example, if you select Lt Cyan as your foreground color and then scroll through background colors, you'll see Lt Cyan displayed with all possible backgrounds in the Background column and the currently highlighted background color behind all foreground colors in the Foreground column.

You can switch back and forth between the Background and Foreground columns and try different combinations until you find one you like. When you do, press Ctrl-End. You can color as many areas as you wish and then select Exit to Control Center from the Exit pull-down menu.

NOTE

Colors that you select under the Settings menu affect only the current dBASE session. To change the colors used in all dBASE sessions, use the DBSETUP program discussed in Appendix B.

MODIFYING A DATABASE STRUCTURE

You can change the structure of a database at any time, regardless of how many records are in that database. To do so, highlight the name of the database in the Control Center and press Design (Shift-F2). You'll see the structure of the database on the database design screen. There you can change any field definitions, add new fields below existing ones, delete a field with Ctrl-U, or insert a new field with Ctrl-N.

As soon as you enter the database design screen, dBASE IV makes a temporary copy of the records in the current database. After you save your changes, dBASE attempts to copy records from the temporary database back into the original database. It will be successful at doing so only if you use a little caution while changing the database structure, as discussed here.

If you delete a field from the database structure, keep in mind that you are also deleting all the data in that field. In other words, if you have a database with 10,000 names and addresses in it and you

TIP

As an added precaution, make your own backup copy of a database before changing its structure, using the techniques described earlier in this chapter.

delete the City field from that database structure, you have just lost all the cities that were in that field. To get them back you have to type each one in again by hand—not a pleasant task!

To change the position of a field in the database structure, first note the exact spelling of the field name, the data type, the width, and the number of decimal places. Then delete the field from its current position using the Ctrl-U key. Use Ctrl-N to insert a new blank field, or add the new field beneath the existing field names. Be sure to use the same spelling, data type, width, and number of decimal places. Do not perform any other operations at this time; save your changes and exit immediately.

You can change the name of a field *only* if you do not add, change, move, or delete any fields during the same operation. If you change field names and rearrange fields in the same operation, dBASE will become confused, and there is no telling how things might be arranged after you save your changes.

Again, your best bet is to use the DOS utilities screen to make a copy of the entire database before you even begin to modify its structure.

SAVING TIME
WITH KEYSTROKE MACROS

Some operations require many keystrokes to accomplish. As an alternative to rekeying each time you want to perform one of these operations, you can record all the necessary keystrokes in a *keystroke macro,* and then play them back at any time. To demonstrate, we'll record the keystrokes required to display the names of all database (.DBF) files in the list of DOS utilities.

TIP

While macros are one of the main tools for creating applications in word processors and spreadsheets, they play a minor role in database management. Therefore, it's not essential to invest a lot of time in learning about keystroke macros in dBASE IV.

RECORDING KEYSTROKES

Assuming that the Control Center is currently displayed on your screen, follow these steps to start recording keystrokes:

1. Press F10 and select Macros from the Tools pull-down menu.

2. Select Begin Recording.

3. A submenu will appear, as in Figure 14.6, instructing you to choose the key that will activate the macro once it is recorded.

4. You can pick any letter key or function key to call your macro; for this example, type the letter D as your choice. (After you record a macro, its name is listed in the macro submenu.)

5. The navigation line informs you that keystrokes are now being recorded, so you can type the keystrokes that you want to save.

6. Press Alt-T to access the Tools pull-down menu.

7. Type D to select DOS Utilities.

8. Press Alt-F to access the Files pull-down menu.

9. Type the letter D to select Display Only.

10. Press Ctrl-Y to erase the current entry.

11. Type ***.DBF** and press ⟵ to display the names of database files only. (The screen will continue to display the names of directories as well.)

12. Press PgDn as many times as necessary to view the names of database (.DBF) files.

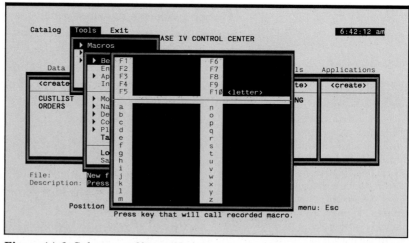

Figure 14.6: Submenu of keystroke macros

13. Assuming that you want your recorded keystrokes to stop at this point, press Shift-F10, and select End Recording.

The navigation line now informs you that macro recording has stopped. To return to the Control Center, select Exit to Control Center from the Exit pull-down menu.

PLAYING BACK RECORDED KEYSTROKES

Macro means *large* (the opposite of *micro*); a *keystroke macro* is a single keystroke that plays back many keystrokes—that is, a "large keystroke."

Now let's suppose that you want to view the names of all .DBF files on the current directory. You need not enter all the usual keystrokes to do so. Instead, just play back your recorded keystrokes by following these steps:

1. Press F10 and select Macros from the Tools pull-down menu.

2. Select Play from the submenu that appears.

3. Type the letter D to play back the macro that you just created.

4. dBASE IV plays back the recorded keystrokes, leaving you at the DOS utilities screen with the names of all .DBF files displayed.

Once the recorded keystrokes are all played back and dBASE IV returns to normal, you can either do more work in the DOS utilities screen, or select Exit to Control Center from the Exit pull-down menu.

SAVING KEYSTROKE MACROS

When you first save recorded keystrokes in a macro, they are only stored in RAM, not on disk. If you want to save a keystroke macro for all future sessions in your work with dBASE IV, you must save the macro in a *macro library* on disk. To do so, follow these steps:

1. Select Macros from the Tools pull-down menu above the Control Center.

2. Select Save Library from the submenu that appears.

3. Enter a valid DOS file name with no extension (such as MYMACROS), and press ◄━┘.

A single macro library can contain up to 34 macros. When you want to use a saved macro or add more macros to an existing macro library, you must first be sure that that macro library is loaded.

LOADING A MACRO LIBRARY

To reload a saved macro library into RAM, follow these steps:

1. From the Control Center, select the Macros option from the Tools pull-down menu.

2. Select Load Library.

3. Select the macro library name from the submenu that appears.

Now you can either play one of the previously recorded macros by selecting Play, or you can create a new macro by selecting Begin Record and a name (key) for the macro. Optionally, press Esc to return to the Control Center. The loaded macro library stays loaded for the duration of the current dBASE session or until you load a different macro library.

AVOIDING COMMON MACRO ERRORS

If your recorded macro accesses pull-down menus, use Alt-<*first letter*>, rather than F10, to access the pull-down menus, when you record macro keystrokes. Alt-<*first-letter*> always pulls down a specific menu, whereas F10 pulls down the last-used menu. This is why you used Alt-T and Alt-F to pull down menus while recording keystrokes in the preceding example. If you use F10 to pull down a menu while recording keystrokes, the recorded F10 keystroke may pull down a different menu when you play back the macro.

Similarly, when selecting options from pull-down menus, type the first letter of the option, rather than highlighting and pressing ◄━┘, to select the option. In this way, you ensure that the macro will not select the wrong option because the highlighter is in a different position during playback than it was when you recorded the macro.

If you want the macro to select an option from a panel in the Control Center, or a submenu of file or field names, type out the name rather than just highlighting it. Submenus of file and field names change as you add and delete objects, so the position of a field or file name in a submenu may vary. If you type out the file or field name while recording keystrokes, you need not be concerned about its position when you later use the macro.

RECORDING KEYSTROKES WITHOUT THE TOOLS MENU

Suppose that you regularly create form letters and at the top of each new letter you always type your own name and address. To save time, you decide to record the keystrokes required to type this information. First, you go to the reports design screen and create a blank Mailmerge report format.

When you are ready to start recording keystrokes, the first thing you notice is that there is no Tools pull-down menu on the reports design screen. So how do you record your keystrokes? Easy—you use the shortcut method of pressing Shift-F10. Doing so displays a sort of "mini-macros" menu with these options:

Begin Recording   Cancel

To start recording your keystrokes, select Begin Recording. The screen displays the message "Press the key that will call this macro." Press any letter key or function key. If you select one that is already assigned to a macro, the screen displays the message "Do you really want to overwrite <letter>? (Y/N)." If you select No, the operation is canceled and you can start over. If you select Yes, dBASE begins recording keystrokes immediately. When you've finished recording your keystrokes, type Shift-F10 and select End Recording.

To save the recorded macro in the current macro library, you will eventually need to return to the Control Center, select Macros from the Tools pull-down menu, and then Save Library from the submenu.

PLAYING BACK MACROS WITHOUT THE TOOLS MENU

To play back a recorded macro without using the Tools menu, press Alt-F10. You will be asked to "press an alphabetic key of the macro to play back." Type the letter name you assigned to the keystroke macro to start playing it back.

NAMING KEYSTROKE MACROS

Initially, all macros have only the single-letter name that you assign to them. If you need a reminder as to what a particular macro does, you can add an additional name. To do so, select Macros from the Tools pull-down menu and Name from the submenu. Type the letter name of the macro to which you want to add a name. You'll be prompted to enter a macro name up to 10 letters long. The additional macro name appears in the list of existing macros for the current library, but you still use the single-letter name to play back the macro.

INSTANT MACROS

When you assign one of the function keys to a macro, you can play back that macro by simply holding down the Alt key and pressing the appropriate function key. For example, if you assign F5 as the macro name when you begin recording a macro, you can play back the macro by simply pressing Alt-F5.

ADDING A MACRO

You can add more recorded keystrokes to a macro by selecting the Append to Macro option from the Macros menu. When you select this option, you'll see a list of existing macros. Press the name of the macro that you want to add more keystrokes to. You'll see a prompt at the bottom of the screen indicating that the keystrokes are being recorded. Type the keystrokes that you want to record, then press Shift-F10 and E.

When you play back the macro, it will perform all of its original keystrokes, then all of the ones that you just added to it.

MAKING A MACRO PAUSE

You might want to create a macro that performs a series of keystrokes, pauses for some unique entry, then continues playing back additional keystrokes. For example, you might want to create a macro that takes you from the control center to the screen for selecting an existing index. Then it pauses while you select an index, and then takes you back to the Control Center.

To create such a macro, you record the keystrokes as you normally would. Then when you get to the place where you want the macro to pause, press Shift-F10 and select Input User-Input Break. Then continue recording the remaining keystrokes for the macro. When you've finished, stop recording keystrokes in the usual manner—by pressing Shift-F10 and selecting End Record.

When you play back the macro, the message "Macro Playback suspended, press Shift-F10 to resume macro playback" appears in a window on the screen when the input break is reached. You can type or press any keys you wish (for example, move the highlighter to a menu option), then press Shift-F10 to resume the macro playback.

EDITING A KEYSTROKE MACRO

Sometimes when you create a macro or append keystrokes to an existing macro, you make mistakes, and when you play back the macro, the mistakes are also played back. One way to fix such mistakes would, of course, be to re-record all the keystrokes. But dBASE also offers an alternative way to fix macro problems; you can edit the recorded keystrokes directly. To edit a keystroke macro, you follow these general steps:

- At the Control Center, press Alt-T or use the Menu (F10) key to access the Tools pull-down menu.

- Select Macros.

- Select Modify.

- Press the "macro name" key (for example, type B to edit macro B).

At this point you'll see the contents of the macro on an edit screen, similar to the edit screen used to edit memo fields. Any text that the macro types directly is displayed simply as text. You can use the usual arrow, Del, Backspace, and other keys to make changes and corrections to the contents of your keystroke macros.

Within a keystroke macro, special keys, like ⟵, →, PgUp, and so forth, are displayed within curly braces, as shown in Table 14.2. If you wish to add a special keystroke (or input break command) to your macro while editing it, you must use the format shown in the

Table 14.2: Names of special keys/commands in keystroke macros.

Keystroke	Macro Symbol
⟵	{Enter}
Esc	{Esc}
←	{leftarrow}
→	{rightarrow}
↑	{uparrow}
↓	{downarrow}
Delete (Del)	{Del}
Insert (Ins)	{Ins}
Backspace	{Backspace}
Tab	{Tab}
Page Up (PgUp)	{PgUp}
Page Down (PgDn)	{PgDn}
Home	{Home}
End	{End}
Ctrl	{Ctrl-
Shift	{Shift-
Alt	{Alt-
F1, F2...	{F1}, {F2}...{{{}
User Input Break	{InpBreak}

second column of that table (upper/lowercase is not important—{LEFTARROW}, {LeftArrow}, and {leftarrow} are all the same).

Because the Alt, Shift, and Ctrl keys are always used in conjunction with another key, the two keys are shown together between one pair of braces. For example, the keystroke combination Alt-F5 is represented as {Alt-F5}.

If you want a macro to actually type a left curly brace, you must use {{} to represent this. Otherwise, dBASE "thinks" that the { is the first character to a special key.

When you've finished modifying your keystroke macro, press Ctrl-End to save your changes (or press Esc to abandon those changes).

DELETING A MACRO

To delete a macro from a macro library, first stop recording keystrokes (if you have not already) by pressing Shift-F10 and typing E. Then, select Macros from the Tools pull-down menu and Delete from the Macros menu. Then press the name of the macro for example A or the F5 key, and type Y (for Yes) and press ◄┘ when dBASE asks for confirmation.

C H A P T E R

15

Introducing
Applications

An application is a group of database objects   490
    linked together by a custom menu system. Unlike a catalog,
    which displays the names of related database objects, an appli-
    cation "hides" the names of objects from the user and lets the
    user interact with the database through a menu of actions (such
    as Add New Records or Print a Report).

To develop a quick application   494
    for a single database, custom screen, report format, and mail-
    ing label format,

1. Select <create> from the Applications panel of the Control
   Center.

2. Select Applications Generator from the submenu and fill in
   the Application Definition form.

3. Select Generate Quick Application from the Application
   pull-down menu.

4. Fill in the names of the objects to be used by the application
   and press Ctrl-End.

To use a completed application,   496
    highlight the application name in the Applications panel of the
    Control Center, press ◄┘, and select Run Application from
    the dialog box that appears.

When developing larger applications of your own,   498
    it's best to break the overall project into a series of steps:

1. Define the goals of the application.

2. Design and create the database objects.

3. Design a menu structure.

4. Build the application.

5. Test and refine the application as necessary.

THIS CHAPTER INTRODUCES YOU TO dBASE IV AP-
plications and to the dBASE IV Applications Generator. In this chapter,
we'll discuss applications in general and generate a sample application
to give you some hands-on experience. Later in the chapter, we'll discuss techniques for designing and developing larger applications.

WHAT IS AN APPLICATION?

An *application* is a customized menu system that simplifies access
to database files, forms, reports, queries, and other related database
objects. Unlike the Control Center, which simply displays the names
of files in a catalog, an application lets you build a menu system that
is based on *actions*, rather than file names.

To clarify the difference between a catalog and an application,
suppose you develop several databases, forms, views, and so forth to
manage an inventory, and you include them in a single catalog. Figure 15.1 shows how the file names might appear in the Control Center. If you, personally, had created all these files, managing the
inventory might be easy because of your knowledge of how to select
items from the Control Center, what each file in the panels stands
for, how to use dBASE menus, and so on.

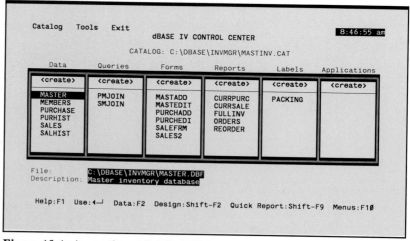

Figure 15.1: A sample catalog for managing an inventory

But suppose that you wanted someone else, perhaps an employee, to use all the files in the catalog to manage the inventory. If this person (who we will refer to as the *user*) had no prior computer experience, you might need to invest quite a bit of time teaching him or her the basics of dBASE IV and the purpose of each file in the Control Center.

An application, on the other hand, would be much easier for the novice to learn. To start with, your application could bypass the Control Center altogether and display a personalized *sign-on banner*, as in Figure 15.2.

After pressing ◄—, the novice user would see a custom menu (that you designed) dedicated to managing the inventory. This custom menu system would replace the dBASE IV menus and provide options specifically geared toward managing the inventory. Figure 15.3 shows a menu for the sample inventory application with a custom pull-down menu for managing the master inventory displayed.

Notice that the application menu clearly defines specific jobs involved in managing the inventory. From the Master Inventory pull-down menu, currently displayed on the screen, the user can add new products, change or delete products, browse through the inventory, or print reports. The pull-down menus under Sales and Purchases offer these same basic options for managing sales transactions and purchases.

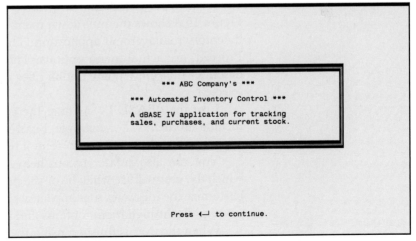

```
              *** ABC Company's ***

          *** Automated Inventory Control ***

          A dBASE IV application for tracking
          sales, purchases, and current stock.




              Press ◄—' to continue.
```

Figure 15.2: Sign-on banner for the inventory application

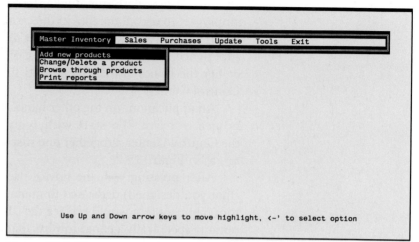

Figure 15.3: Custom menu for managing the inventory

The user does not need to know anything about the underlying files, forms, reports, or views or even that such things exist. All the user really needs to know is how to move through the menus and how to select items. The application menus operate in a manner similar to the dBASE IV menus. That is, the user can move the highlight across the menu bar or up and down a pull-down menu to highlight any option. Pressing ← selects the currently highlighted option.

When you create an application, you can further simplify matters for the user by adding descriptive text to menus. For example, Figure 15.4 shows the pull-down menu for the Update option in the inventory management application. The first two items, Cancel and Proceed, are actual menu options. The underline and text beneath describe what the Update option does and cannot be highlighted or selected.

Like the dBASE IV menus, the application menu system can include submenus. For example, Figure 15.5 shows such a menu that appears when the user opts to print a report.

You can also create custom help screens for your application, which the user will see when he or she presses Help (F1), and you can customize the messages that appear at the bottom of the screen as the user scrolls through menu options and makes selections.

When the user is finished using the inventory application, he or she can select Exit from the menu bar and be returned to the DOS

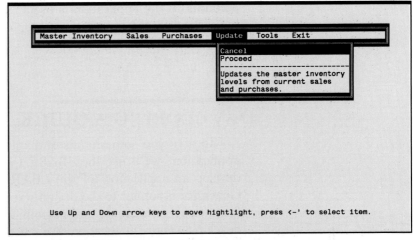

Figure 15.4: Pull-down menu with descriptive text

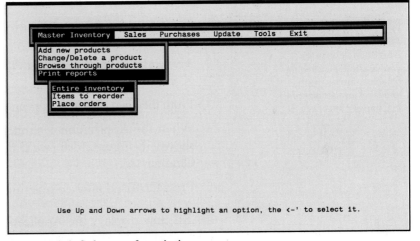

Figure 15.5: Submenu for printing reports

prompt, without ever seeing the Control Center. In fact, the user need not even know that dBASE IV is involved, or that such a thing as dBASE IV exists! From the user's perspective, only the inventory application itself exists.

In addition to meeting your own needs, some of your custom applications may meet the needs of others as well. For example, suppose you own a construction company, and you develop a very powerful and easy-to-use application for managing time, materials, and accounts. If the application is useful for others in the construction business, you could market your application, perhaps sell hundreds of copies, and turn quite a profit.

DEVELOPING A QUICK APPLICATION

To give you some hands-on experience in using a completed application, we'll use the dBASE IV Applications Generator to develop an application for the LEARN catalog. The Applications Generator is similar to the design screens you used to create report formats, label formats, and custom forms, except that it lets you develop an entire application. We'll use the *quick application* technique to create a simple application. Follow these steps to begin generating the sample application:

This example assumes you've already created the database, forms, report, and label formats described in Chapters 3–8.

1. Make sure the LEARN catalog is displayed in the Control Center.

2. Move the highlight to the Applications panel and select <create>.

3. From the dialog box that appears, select Applications Generator.

4. When the Application Definition form appears, fill it in as shown in Figure 15.6 (we'll discuss this form in detail in Chapter 16).

5. Press Ctrl-End after completing the form.

dBASE now displays the Applications Generator work surface. Like other work surfaces, it has a menu bar and pull-down menus. Initially, the Applications Generator work surface looks like Figure 15.7.

USING A QUICK APPLICATION

Your next step is to create a quick application:

1. Press Menu (F10) and select Generate Quick Application from the Application pull-down menu.

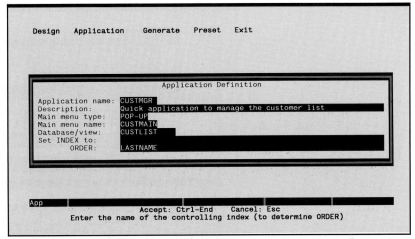

Figure 15.6: Completed Application Definition form

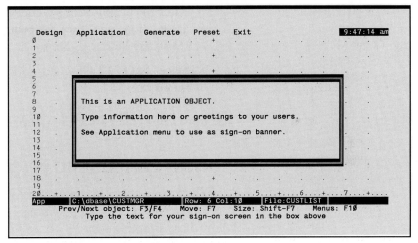

Figure 15.7: The Applications Generator work surface

2. Fill in the quick application form as shown in Figure 15.8. Rather than typing file names, you can press Pick (Shift-F1) to select them from a submenu.

3. Press Ctrl-End after filling in the quick application form.

4. Select Yes from the dialog box that appears.

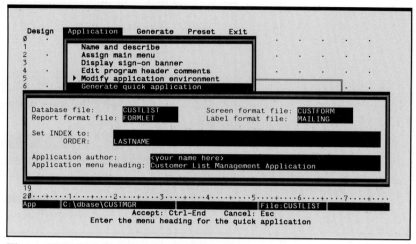

Figure 15.8: Quick application form filled out

5. After the Applications Generator writes the program for the application, you'll see the prompt, "Generation is complete. Press any key . . ." Do so.

6. Select Save All Changes and Exit from the Exit pull-down menu.

You have finished creating the sample application.

RUNNING THE APPLICATION

When you return to the Control Center, you'll see the name of your application in the Applications panel. To run the application, follow these simple steps:

1. Highlight the name of the application in the Applications panel and press ◄─┘.

2. Select Run Application from the submenu that appears.

3. Select Yes when dBASE asks for verification.

After a few seconds the application main menu appears on the screen, as shown in Figure 15.9. The quick application technique does not create a menu bar with pull-down menus. Instead, it presents a smaller sign-on banner at the top of the screen and a single

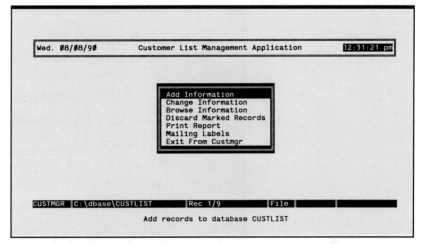

```
┌──────────────────────────────────────────────────────────────┐
│ Wed. Ø8/Ø8/9Ø        Customer List Management Application    12:31:21 pm │
│                                                                │
│                                                                │
│                   ┌──────────────────────────┐                 │
│                   │ Add Information           │                 │
│                   │ Change Information        │                 │
│                   │ Browse Information        │                 │
│                   │ Discard Marked Records    │                 │
│                   │ Print Report              │                 │
│                   │ Mailing Labels            │                 │
│                   │ Exit From Custmgr         │                 │
│                   └──────────────────────────┘                 │
│                                                                │
│                                                                │
│ CUSTMGR  C:\dbase\CUSTLIST        Rec 1/9        File          │
│                  Add records to database CUSTLIST              │
└──────────────────────────────────────────────────────────────┘
```

Figure 15.9: The quick application main menu

pop-up menu centered on the screen. The pop-up menu is identical to a pull-down menu, except that it is not directly attached to a menu-bar option.

Feel free to experiment with the application. The Add and Change options will take you to the CUSTFORM form, where you can add or edit records. The Browse option will take you to the familiar browse screen. Exiting these screens returns you to the application main menu, where you can select another option.

The Discard Marked Records option packs the database (that is, permanently erases records that are marked for deletion). The Print Report option and Mailing Labels option behave a little differently than they usually do in dBASE. The screen shows the names and data types of each field in the database. A pop-up menu in the center of the screen provides options for locating a starting record, as shown in Figure 15.10.

To start printing a report from the first record, select GOTO Record and then Top from the submenu. You may also want to experiment with the SEEK and LOCATE commands, but don't be too concerned with these right now. When you develop your own applications later, you'll probably want to devise other techniques for printing reports.

Because indexes are susceptible to power failures and other disasters that occasionally strike computers, the Reindex Database option

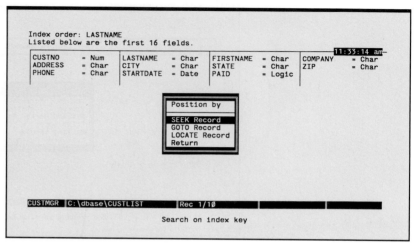

```
Index order: LASTNAME
Listed below are the first 16 fields.
                                                              11:33:14 am
CUSTNO    = Num    LASTNAME   = Char   FIRSTNAME  = Char   COMPANY  = Char
ADDRESS   = Char   CITY       = Char   STATE      = Char   ZIP      = Char
PHONE     = Char   STARTDATE  = Date   PAID       = Logic

                        ┌─────────────────┐
                        │ Position by     │
                        ├─────────────────┤
                        │ SEEK Record     │
                        │ GOTO Record     │
                        │ LOCATE Record   │
                        │ Return          │
                        └─────────────────┘




  CUSTMGR   C:\dbase\CUSTLIST          Rec 1/10
                        Search on index key
```

Figure 15.10: Quick application printing technique

is included on the quick application main menu. When you create
your own applications, it's a good idea to include such an option.
That way, if some catastrophe erases your indexes, you can repair
them immediately using a simple menu selection.

Feel free to experiment with the sample application as much as
you wish, but don't worry about mastering or understanding every
aspect of it. When you've finished experimenting, select Exit From
CustMgr to return to the Control Center.

DEVELOPING LARGER APPLICATIONS

The quick application technique generates only the simplest possible application, but it has allowed us to experiment with a sample
application. In the future, you may want to create some more sophisticated and powerful applications of your own. However, before you
start pounding the keyboard to bring your great application idea to
fruition, you should take some time to design the end product.

You can think of the application development process as several
separate tasks, as follows:

- Define the goals of the application.

- Design and create the objects (that is, databases, forms, and reports) of the application.

- Design a menu structure for the application.

- Build the application using the Applications Generator.

- Test and refine the finished application as necessary.

The following sections discuss each of these tasks in more detail, breaking them into a series of steps. (The next chapter uses these same steps to actually build a very powerful membership management system.) Keep in mind that application development is seldom linear; it is usually a series of refinements. You need not rigidly follow the steps described here; you can backtrack and make changes along the way.

STEP 1: DEFINE THE GOALS OF THE APPLICATION

The first step in building an application is simply to jot down some notes about what you want the application to do. If you are automating an existing manual system, analyze the manual system and get copies of forms and reports that are currently used in the system. Note what information is currently stored in manual files (such as Rolodexes, index cards, forms, and so forth). This information will help you design the databases.

If you are writing the application for a client, find out in as much detail as possible what the client wants. Given your knowledge of dBASE and its capabilities, you can offer suggestions to make the client's work easier.

As you make notes, start with a broad description of your goal, such as this:

Develop an order entry and inventory management application.

Then refine the broad definition into specific goals and features, focusing on the fundamental aspects of database management: database structure, sorting and searching requirements, types of reports needed, and specific types of updating or other processes that are required. For example, you can refine the description of your goal as follows:

Develop an order entry and inventory management application that

- Stores the current product inventory, sales transactions, and purchases for ABC Company

- Allows users to sort any database into part number order and search for any part number

- Allows users to print the entire inventory, a reorder report, orders that need to be placed, a sales summary, and a purchases summary

- Updates current in-stock and on-order quantities by quantities sold and quantities received from the Sales and Purchases database

- Provides utilities for backing up the databases, copying the application, and repairing corrupted indexes

As you refine the written definition, try to break the overall goal of the application into smaller, more manageable tasks. That way, each task becomes a smaller goal in itself. It's much easier to achieve a big goal (for example, to create a large application) if you break it into a series of smaller, more manageable goals.

STEP 2: DESIGN AND TEST THE DATABASES

The next step is to determine which fields are required to store the information needed in the application. To ensure the most efficient database design, you may need to use several related database files. In Chapter 13, you saw how trying to combine customer names and addresses with each charge transaction in an accounts receivable database led to a great deal of repeated information.

To eliminate redundancy, customer information and charge transactions were stored on two separate databases, and the two database files were linked by a common field named CustNo. To ensure that there would be no errors in linking charges to customers, each customer was assigned a unique customer number.

When designing your own database structures, use these same techniques to structure the databases for your application. If you need a reminder about one-to-many and many-to-many database designs, refer to Chapter 13.

After you have decided what information needs to be stored in the database file (or files), create each one in the usual manner (by selecting <create> from the Data panel of the Control Center). Index any common fields that relate two or more database files as well as any fields that will be used regularly for sorting or for quick lookups, to speed these operations. After creating each database file, enter some sample data so you can test the components of the application as you build them.

STEP 3: DESIGN THE VIEWS

If any forms or reports in your query will require data from two or more related database files, create the views to link the files, using the usual techniques (start by selecting <create> from the Queries panel of the Control Center). For maximum speed, always include indexes in each file skeleton by selecting Include Indexes from the Fields pull-down menu in the query design screen.

Remember to use the Create Link by Pointing option from the Layout pull-down menu (or identical placeholders) to link the common fields. Also, if the output of a printed report is to be sorted or grouped, use the appropriate sorting operators in the query design screen. Test the view to ensure that it links the files in the proper manner. When you are certain that the view works, save it and assign it a name.

You need not be concerned about creating simple search queries, such as those that isolate all New York residents or records with a particular range of dates. You can enter appropriate filter conditions while developing the application, without using a query. You'll see how to do this in the next chapter.

STEP 4: DESIGN THE FORMS

The next step is to design and create the custom forms used by the application. If a form needs to use data from two or more database files, be sure to build the form from a view rather than a database.

When designing forms for complex applications, use the techniques listed here to simplify the user's work:

- If information being typed on the screen is coming from an existing paper form, try to make the form on the screen resemble the paper form. Most important, be sure that the order of fields (left to right and top to bottom) on the screen form matches the order of fields on the manual form.

- Always place the most important information near the center of the screen, as this is where the user always looks first.

- Be consistent when placing similar information on different forms. For example, if each form displays the current date and time, always place that information in a particular corner of the screen.

- If a large database requires several screens full of information to add or edit a record, repeat some identifying information on each screen. For example, suppose a database accepts all information necessary to fill in a tax form, and the user needs to use several screens to enter all the information. If the taxpayer's name appears on each screen, the user will not have to scroll back to the first screen to remember the current taxpayer's name.

- Use templates and validation techniques to trap faulty entries before they are stored in the database.

- Use boxes, lines, and graphics characters (such as arrows) to enhance the form, but don't clutter the form. A form with open space is easier to comprehend than an overcrowded form.

After you've created each form, test it by entering and editing some data. When you are satisfied that all forms are working as expected, you can move on to the next step.

STEP 5: DESIGN THE REPORTS

The next step is to create the report and mailing label formats for the application. Use the usual reports and labels design screens to create these. Use each format to print some sample data. When you are satisfied with each report and label format, you can start on the next step.

STEP 6: DESIGN THE MENU STRUCTURE

Before you fire up the Applications Generator, take some time to design the menu structure for your application on paper. Place main menu-bar options across the top row of the design and pull-down menus (or submenus) beneath the menu bar in a hierarchical manner.

Figure 15.11 shows a menu structure for an inventory application like the one presented earlier in this chapter. Note the hierarchical structure, from the general to the specific, for the pull-down menus. That is, under the general option of Master Inventory are several options for managing that information. Beneath the Print Reports menu option is a submenu of specific reports to choose from.

When you actually begin to develop the application, you will need to assign valid DOS file names (eight letters maximum, no spaces) to each menu in your application. You might want to note the menu names on your design to help you keep track of them later. Figure 15.12 shows an example.

You might also want to jot down some notes about the databases, objects, and actions associated with each menu option. Later, when you start developing the application, these notes will help you remember all of the details. Figure 15.13 shows an example with the menu and submenu under the Master Inventory option.

In the example, the Master Inventory option opens the menu named InvMenu. The Add New Products option lets the user add new records using a custom form named MASTADD. The Print Reports option opens a submenu named InvRep. The Items to Reorder option prints a report using a format named REORDER. All options use the MASTER.DBF database in PARTNO order.

STEP 7: DESIGN BATCH PROCESSES

A *batch process* is a series of operations assigned to a single menu selection. For example, suppose you want your application to provide a menu option that copies all database files and their indexes to the floppy disk in drive A. Furthermore, assume that the application

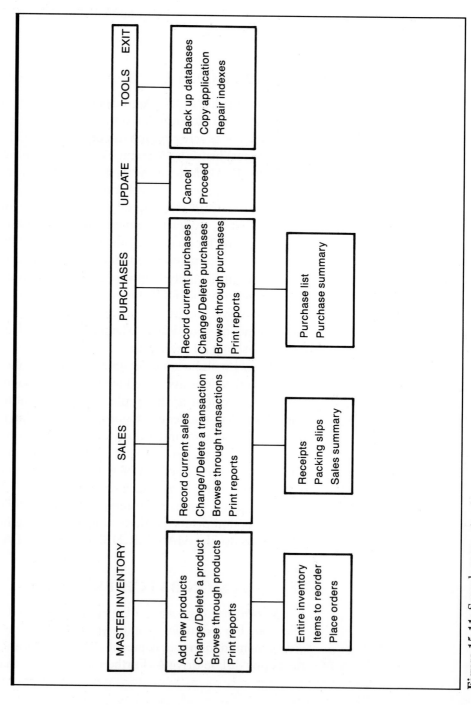

Figure 15.11: Sample menu structure

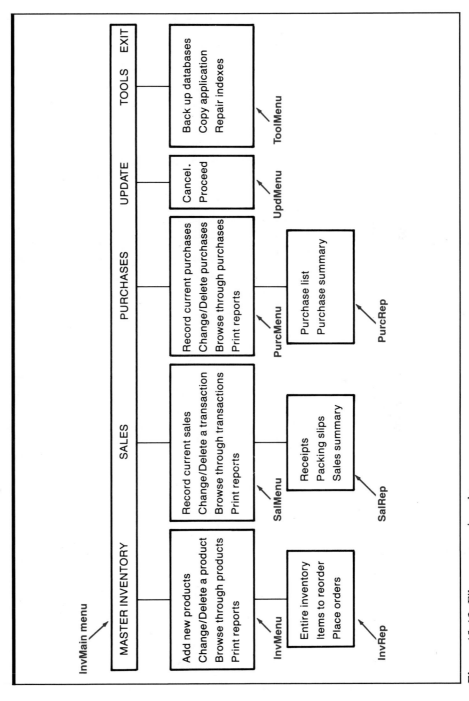

Figure 15.12: File names assigned to menus

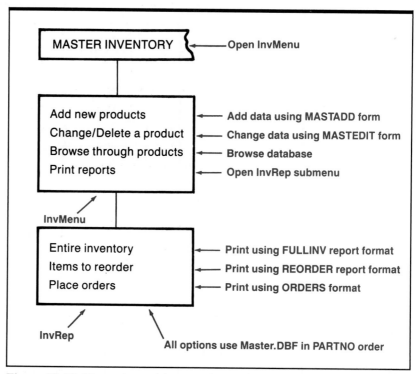

Figure 15.13: Notes about objects used at each menu option

(like the inventory example) uses three databases: MASTER.DBF, SALES.DBF, and PURCHASE.DBF. When the user selects the Backup option, the application must perform three steps:

```
Copy MASTER.* to A:
Copy SALES.* to A:
Copy PURCHASE.* to A:
```

(The * wildcard is used to ensure that the .mdx index files are copied with each .dbf database file.) To design a batch process such as this, assign an eight-letter file name to the process and list the required steps in English. Figure 15.14 shows an example. The Backup Database option is attached to a batch process named BACKUP.

Batch processes can become quite sophisticated and complex. But don't be too worried right now if you are not sure what types of

Figure 15.14: Batch process defined and assigned to a menu option

batch operations are possible. As you gain more experience with the Applications Generator in the chapters that follow, you'll find it much easier to develop batch processes of your own.

STEP 8: DEVELOP, TEST, AND REFINE

After you have a created all the appropriate objects for your application and designed your menu structure, you can begin using the Applications Generator to develop the application. The Applications Generator will allow you to "draw" each menu and attach an action to each menu option.

After you create the application, use it and check to make sure that everything works as expected. Sometimes, developing an application is an iterative process. You start with a design, develop the application, and then use the application for a while. After a time, you might decide to make some improvements and changes. You can do so, again using the Applications Generator to modify the existing application. You can repeat this process of testing and refining several times until you create a satisfactory (if not perfect) application.

When you are completely satisfied with the application, you may want to add some embellishments, such as custom help screens, messages, and colors. It's easiest to add these embellishments after you are finished with the overall application. That way, you won't need to concentrate on these extras while you are refining your application.

The steps presented here offer a somewhat simplified version of *program design*. If you should ever start developing large, complex applications on your own, you might want to look into this topic in more detail, either in a book devoted to program design and development or in an advanced book on dBASE IV programming and application development.

For the time being, however, the basic techniques discussed here should be sufficient to get you started. In the next chapter, we'll develop a sophisticated application, following the steps discussed in this chapter so you can see them in action.

16

A Membership
Management
Application

To assign actions to items in your custom menus,   *539*
> highlight the menu option to which you want to assign an action and then select Change Action from the Item pull-down menu.

To create a batch process,   *557*
> select Batch Process from the Design pull-down menu on the applications design screen and list the steps (in plain English) that the process is to perform. Then assign actions to each step in the process, using the same techniques that you use to assign actions to menu options.

Whenever you create or modify an application,   *564*
> you must generate the application code. To do so, choose Select Template from the Generate pull-down menu and specify MENU.GEN as the template to use. Then select Begin Generating from the same menu.

After generating (or regenerating) an application,   *573*
> select Save All Changes and Exit from the Exit pull-down menu to return to the Control Center.

THIS CHAPTER PRESENTS A COMPLETE EXAMPLE OF application design and development. Starting from scratch and following the basic steps of application design and development discussed in the previous chapter, we will develop an application to manage a membership database. First, we'll define the goals of the application, and then we'll develop the various objects, such as the database, custom forms, and report formats. Next, we will design a menu system, and finally we'll use the Applications Generator to create the finished product.

This chapter assumes that you are now familiar enough with the database, labels, reports, and forms design screens to create these objects with minimal assistance. Of course, when you start using the Applications Generator later in the chapter, step-by-step instructions will be provided. The techniques that you learn here will help you build your own applications, as well as the larger, more complex business management application presented in Chapter 21.

CREATING A SUBDIRECTORY FOR THE APPLICATION

To keep individual applications from becoming entangled, it's a good idea to create each new application on a unique subdirectory. In this chapter, you'll store the membership application on a subdirectory named \DBASE\MEMBERS on the hard disk. Follow these steps to create and switch to this new directory:

1. If you are currently running dBASE IV, select Quit to DOS from the Exit pull-down menu above the Control Center.

2. At the DOS prompt, type the command **MD\DBASE \MEMBERS** and press ↵. (If the error message "Unable to Create Directory" appears, the directory already exists—proceed with step 3.)

3. To log on to the new directory, type the command **CD \DBASE\MEMBERS** and press ↵.

Appendix A discusses DOS commands, directories, and paths in more detail.

If the subdirectory name \DBASE\MEMBERS does not appear next to the C > prompt, type the command **PROMPT PG** and press ←┘. This DOS command will display the directory name.

You should be able to run dBASE IV from the directory by entering the usual command **DBASE** (followed by ←┘, of course). If the error message ''Bad Command or File Name'' appears, your PATH setting does not include the directory on which dBASE IV is stored. You can run dBASE by including the path in the command. For example, if dBASE IV is stored on the \DBASE directory, you can enter the command **\DBASE\DBASE** (or substitute the correct directory name in place of the first DBASE).

Remember that whenever you wish to use the membership system in the future, you must be logged on to the \DBASE\MEMBERS directory. To do so, you can use the command **CD\DBASE\MEMBERS** at the DOS prompt (before you run dBASE). If dBASE is already running, you can log on to the \DBASE\MEMBERS directory by selecting DOS Utilities from the Tools pull-down menu at the Control Center. From the DOS Utilities DOS menu, select Set Default Drive:Directory and type **C:\DBASE\MEMBERS** as the new default directory.

GOALS OF THE MEMBERSHIP APPLICATION

The membership application will be designed to allow the membership committee of a computer user's group to automate tasks that they currently perform manually. The application will allow the group to do the following:

- Store members' names and addresses, membership starting and expiration dates, and other useful information
- At any time during the month—

    Add, change, and delete members' records

    Print a current membership roster, alphabetized by name

Print mailing labels, sorted by zip code, for each active member

Update records when a membership is renewed

- At any time during the month, perform the following basic housekeeping tasks:

    Change the system date

    Make a backup copy of the database

    Copy the entire application to a diskette

    Repair corrupted indexes

- The application will also automate printing of the following monthly form letters:

    Welcome letters and mailing labels for new members

    Renewal reminders and labels for memberships that expire next month

    Overdue notices and labels for memberships that expired in the previous month

NOTE

If you would like to take a look at the completed application, refer to the section "Testing the Application" near the end of this chapter.

At this point, you might want to start refining each feature of the application by sketching on paper a database design and a form design and draft form letters. However, in this chapter we'll design and create simultaneously to save some space and time. If you have not done so already, log on to the \DBASE\MEMBERS directory and get dBASE IV up and running, so the Control Center is displayed on your screen.

DESIGNING THE MEMBERSHIP APPLICATION DATABASE

The membership application database, named MEMBERS.DBF, is structured to manage information about each group member. You can create this database structure now by selecting <create> from the Data panel on the Control Center. Type the field information as shown in Figure 16.1 (of course, you can't type the description of each field). Note that the ZIP field is marked Y for

```
Num Field Name  Type       Width Dec Index  Description
  1  TITLE      Character      4       N     Mr./Mrs. title
  2  FIRSTNAME  Character     12       N     First name
  3  MI         Character      2       N     Middle initial
  4  LASTNAME   Character     12       N     Last name
  5  COMPANY    Character     25       N     Company
  6  DEPARTMENT Character     25       N     Department
  7  ADDRESS    Character     32       N     Address
  8  CITY       Character     20       N     City
  9  STATE      Character      2       N     State
 10  ZIP        Character     10       Y     Zip code
 11  PHONE      Character     13       N     Phone number
 12  EXTENSION  Character      4       N     Phone extension
 13  STATUS     Character      8       N     Membership status
 14  STARTDATE  Date           8       N     Starting date
 15  EXPIRES    Date           8       N     Next expiration date
 16  CURRENT    Logical        1       N     Is memberhip current?
 17  RENEWED    Logical        1       N     Renewed this month?
```

Figure 16.1: Structure of the MEMBERS database

indexing. After completing the structure, select Save Changes and Exit from the Exit pull-down menu and assign the file name MEMBERS to the database.

CREATING AN ALPHABETICAL SORT ORDER

To create a complex index for alphabetizing names, move the highlight to the MEMBERS database name in the Control Center and press Design (Shift-F2). Select the Create New Index option from the Organize pull-down menu to create a complex index with these characteristics:

Name of index	LASTNAME
Index expression	LASTNAME + FIRSTNAME + MI
FOR clause	
Order of index	ASCENDING
Display first duplicate key only	NO

Press Ctrl-End after defining the index. Then select Save Changes and Exit from the Exit pull-down menu to return to the Control Center.

CREATING A CUSTOM FORM
FOR THE MEMBERSHIP SYSTEM

The membership application will use a custom form, named MEMFORM, to allow the user to enter and edit membership data. Use the MEMBERS database and select <create> from the Forms panel to create the form. Use the usual editing techniques to arrange the fields as in Figure 16.2. (Note that a small portion of the custom form is below the bottom of the screen; you'll see the missing portion in the next figure.)

Some of the fields in the form can be improved by specialized templates or picture functions. These fields are listed in Table 16.1 (those not listed use the default template and picture function and do not need to be changed). Remember: To change a template or picture function, move the cursor into the field template and press F5.

The STARTDATE, EXPIRES, and CURRENT fields use Edit Options to display default (suggested) values. To assign a default value, move the cursor to the field template, press F5, select Edit Options, and then select Default Value. Type the default value and press Ctrl-End. The STARTDATE field uses the default value DATE() to display the current date. The EXPIRES field uses the current date plus one year,

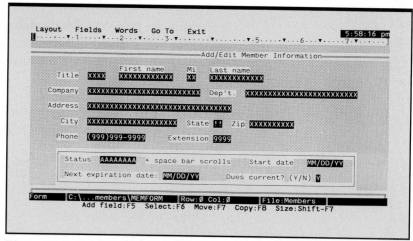

Figure 16.2: MEMFORM form for the membership application

Table 16.1: Templates and Picture Functions in MEMFORM

Field	Template	Picture function
STATE	!!	
PHONE	(999)999-9999	
EXTENSION	9999	
STATUS	AAAAAAA	Multiple choice {M} with options REGULAR, OFFICER
CURRENT	Y	

DATE() + 365, as the default value. Because most members pay immediately when they join, the CURRENT field uses a default value of .T. (for true).

Note that the RENEWED field is not included on the form. This field is used in a browse screen to *flag* (identify) members who have renewed their membership. You'll see the RENEWED field put to use later.

After you create the form, save it and assign the name MEMFORM. When you get back to the Control Center, highlight MEMFORM in the Forms panel and press Data (F2). You should see the form appear on the screen as in Figure 16.3. Note that the default starting date on your screen will match the current date, and the default expiration date will be one year beyond the current date.

To test the form, let's add a sample record. When entering data in the STATUS field, you should be able to switch from REGULAR to OFFICER and back again by pressing the space bar. Now enter the following record (regardless of the suggested start and expiration dates that appear on the screen, enter the start and expiration dates in the example shown here):

```
Mr. Andy A. Adams
ABC Technology
Engineering Dep't
13307 Artesia Ave
Los Angeles    CA    90165
```

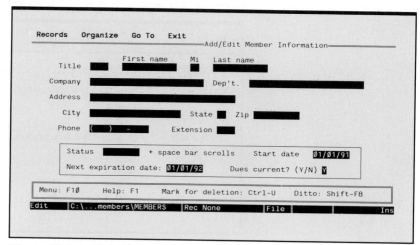

Figure 16.3: MEMFORM form ready to accept data

(818)555-0101 Extension 123
Status: REGULAR   Start date: 01/01/91
Next expiration date:01/01/92   Dues current? Y

After entering the sample record, select Exit from the Exit pull-down menu to return to the Control Center. Now you can begin developing the reports that the application will use.

CREATING
MEMBERSHIP APPLICATION REPORTS

The membership application in this example uses four report formats, three of which are form letters. Create each of the report formats using the usual <create> option from the Reports panel of the Control Center. Use the MEMBERS database as the basis for each report format.

The first report format, named ROSTER, will display a list of all members. Use the usual editing techniques on the reports design screen to format the report to your liking. Figure 16.4 shows an

Figure 16.4: Format of the ROSTER report

example, where the fields are arranged as shown here:

```
LASTNAME, TITLE FIRSTNAME MI
    COMPANY
    DEPARTMENT
    ADDRESS
    CITY, STATE ZIP PHONE EXTENSION
    Status: STATUS  Current?: CURRENT
    Start Date: STARTDATE  Expiration Date: EXPIRES
```

A single blank line is included in the Detail band to separate printed records. Select Save Changes and Exit from the Exit pull-down menu after completing the format.

The other three reports are form letters, each of which uses an identical name and address format near the top of the letter. To speed the development of the form letters, first select <create> from the Reports panel in the Control Center. Then select Quick Layouts and Mailmerge Layout from the Layout pull-down menu. Using the usual techniques, arrange the fields as shown in the next example. (The MM/DD/YY template is for the current date, which you can place by pressing F5 and selecting Date from the PREDEFINED column of the menu that appears.)

```
MM/DD/YY
TITLE FIRSTNAME MI LASTNAME
COMPANY
```

DEPARTMENT
ADDRESS
CITY, STATE ZIP

Dear FIRSTNAME:

After arranging the fields as shown, make three copies of the current format by following these steps:

1. Select Save This Report from the Layout pull-down menu.

2. Enter **WELCOME** as the report name and press ←⏎.

3. Select Save This Report from the Layout pull-down menu.

4. Use the Backspace key to erase WELCOME.FRM; then enter **RENEWAL** as the report name and press ←⏎.

5. Select Save This Report from the Layout pull-down menu.

6. Use the Backspace key to erase RENEWAL.FRM; then enter **OVERDUE** as the report name and press ←⏎.

7. Select Abandon Changes and Exit from the from the Exit pull-down menu.

When you return to the Control Center, you can complete each form letter by highlighting its name in the Control Center and pressing Design (Shift-F2). Figures 16.5, 16.6, and 16.7 show examples of

Figure 16.5: Format for the WELCOME letter

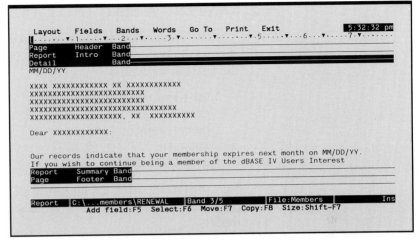

Figure 16.6: Format for the RENEWAL letter

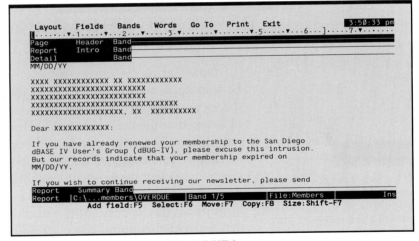

Figure 16.7: Format for the OVERDUE letter

three form letters. (Most of each letter is scrolled off the bottom of the screen, but you'll undoubtedly want to create your own form letters anyway.)

After creating each report format, you can print a test copy by highlighting the report name in the Control Center and pressing ←. Then select Print Report and either Begin Printing or View Report on Screen from the Print submenu.

CREATING A MAILING LABEL FORMAT

The application also needs a format for printing labels. Select <create> from the Labels panel in the Control Center and arrange the fields as follows:

```
TITLE FIRSTNAME MI LASTNAME
COMPANY
DEPARTMENT
ADDRESS
CITY, STATE ZIP
```

Save the format using the file name MEMLABEL and then test it by printing a label, using the same basic technique you use to print reports.

DESIGNING THE MEMBERSHIP APPLICATION MENU STRUCTURE

Now that you've created and tested all the objects for the membership application, you can begin designing the menu structure. (Some people prefer to design the menu structure early in the design phase so that they can refine the written definition before creating any objects. There is certainly no harm in doing so.)

Figure 16.8 shows the menu structure for the membership application, including the names in the horizontal bar menu and the pull-down menus. Figure 16.9 shows the menu structure with the names of objects, sort orders, filter conditions, and the batch process defined. (At this point, filter conditions are in plain English; for example, "new members" is a filter for printing welcome letters.)

> **TIP**
>
> If you have a copy machine nearby, you might want to copy Figures 16.8 and 16.9 and keep them in front of you as you develop the application to help you keep track of each menu and menu option.

DESIGNING THE MEMBERSHIP APPLICATION BATCH PROCESS

The membership application uses a single batch process, named RENEW.BCH, to help the user renew memberships (dBASE automatically adds the .BCH extension). The batch process performs

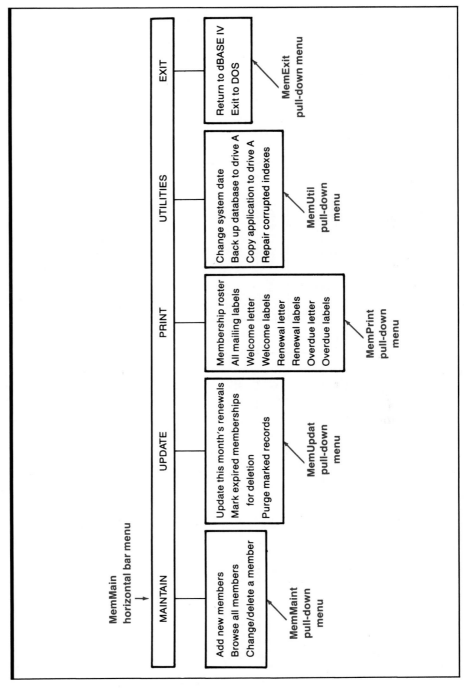

Figure 16.8: Menu structure for the membership application

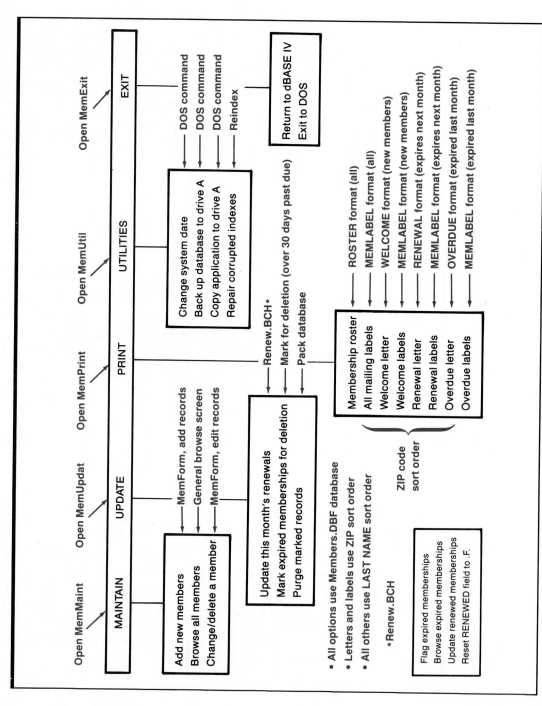

Figure 16.9: Objects, filters, sort orders, and batch processes sketched out

four operations to automate the task of updating memberships each month. To see what each operation in the process does, assume that the current date is February 28, 1992, and the database contains the following four records (only relevant fields are used in this example). Note that Andy Adams' CURRENT field is already marked .F., because his membership expired last month:

LASTNAME	FIRSTNAME	STARTDATE	EXPIRES	CURRENT	RENEWED
Adams	Andy	01/01/91	01/01/92	.F.	.F.
Baker	Bob	02/01/91	02/01/92	.T.	.F.
Carlson	Cara	02/28/91	02/28/92	.T.	.F.
Davis	Deedra	03/31/91	03/31/92	.T.	.F.

The batch process performs four operations.

OPERATION 1: FLAG EXPIRED MEMBERSHIPS

The first operation in the batch process automatically changes the CURRENT field to .F. for all memberships that have expired. Again, given that the current date is 02/28/92, this operation will modify two of the four records, bringing the CURRENT field up to date in all records, as follows:

LASTNAME	FIRSTNAME	STARTDATE	EXPIRES	CURRENT	RENEWED
Adams	Andy	01/01/91	01/01/92	.F.	.F.
Baker	Bob	02/01/91	02/01/92	.F.	.F.
Carlson	Cara	02/28/91	02/28/92	.F.	.F.
Davis	Deedra	03/31/91	03/31/92	.T.	.F.

OPERATION 2: BROWSE EXPIRED MEMBERSHIPS

The next operation in the batch process displays only expired memberships on a browse screen. The user, who presumably has payments from all renewed members, can then change the RENEWED field from .F. to .T. for members who have renewed. For convenience, the cursor is locked into the RENEWED field, and the field is displayed to the left of other fields. Figure 16.10 shows the browse screen with some sample data.

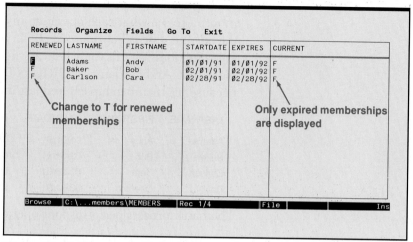

Figure 16.10: Browse screen for indicating renewed memberships

Suppose Adams and Baker have renewed their memberships, so the user changes the .F. to .T. in the RENEWED field for each of their records and then saves these changes. The database now contains the following data:

LASTNAME	FIRSTNAME	STARTDATE	EXPIRES	CURRENT	RENEWED
Adams	Andy	01/01/91	01/01/92	.F.	.T.
Baker	Bob	02/01/91	02/01/92	.F.	.T.
Carlson	Cara	02/28/91	02/28/92	.F.	.F.
Davis	Deedra	03/31/91	03/31/92	.T.	.F.

OPERATION 3:
UPDATE RENEWED MEMBERSHIPS

Now that the database has been saved with renewed memberships marked with a .T., the third operation in the batch process automatically marks the appropriate CURRENT fields as .T. and extends the expiration dates by one year (to 1993) as follows:

LASTNAME	FIRSTNAME	STARTDATE	EXPIRES	CURRENT	RENEWED
Adams	Andy	01/01/91	01/01/93	.T.	.T.
Baker	Bob	02/01/91	02/01/93	.T.	.T.
Carlson	Cara	02/28/91	02/28/92	.F.	.F.
Davis	Deedra	03/31/91	03/31/92	.T.	.F.

OPERATION 4:
RESET RENEWED FIELD TO FALSE

All records with renewed memberships now have .T. in the CURRENT field and have had their expiration dates extended by a year. The user can now deposit the payments and need not be concerned about these memberships for another year. (They won't even appear on the updating browse screen for another year.)

However, the batch process is not quite complete, because even though the third operation in the batch process completed the renewal process, those records still have .T. in the RENEWED field. If the user were to run this batch process again, those records would have their expiration dates extended by *another* year (in this case, to 1994). To prevent this mistake, the fourth operation in the batch process resets all the values in the RENEWED field to .F., as follows:

LASTNAME	FIRSTNAME	STARTDATE	EXPIRES	CURRENT	RENEWED
Adams	Andy	01/01/91	01/01/93	.T.	.F.
Baker	Bob	02/01/91	02/01/93	.T.	.F.
Carlson	Cara	02/28/91	02/28/92	.F.	.F.
Davis	Deedra	03/31/91	03/31/92	.T.	.F.

Now the database is accurate for the current month and ready for next month's updates. Adams and Baker need not be renewed again until next year. When March rolls around and the user repeats the batch operation, Carlson and Davis will appear on the browse screen for possible renewal. The user will identify those members (if any) that have renewed by placing .T. in the RENEWED field, and the the batch process will once again update all appropriate memberships for the month of March.

You'll see how to create and use this batch process later in this chapter. Let's go ahead now and start developing the application.

DEVELOPING THE APPLICATION

Now that you have created the database, forms, label, and report formats for the membership application and planned the batch process, you can use the Applications Generator to develop the application. Developing the application involves a series of steps:

• Define the application name and default settings.

- Create a sign-on banner for the application (this step is optional).

- Create the menu bar and pull-down menus.

- Attach *actions* to each menu option.

- Create batch processes.

- Generate the application.

- Save all changes and exit.

NOTE

If you do exit dBASE now, remember to log on to the \DBASE\MEM-BERS subdirectory before resuming your work on the application later.

Completing all of the necessary steps might take quite a bit of time, particularly in large applications that contain many menu options. In the sections that follow, you'll complete the first three steps and then take a break. Still, it may take half an hour or more for you to complete those steps, so if you are pressed for time at the moment, you may want to start developing the application later.

To get started, follow these steps:

1. Select <create> from the Application panel in the Control Center.

2. Select Applications Generator from the submenu.

DEFINING THE APPLICATION

The first dialog box to appear when you enter the Applications Generator will ask for the application definition. You need to name the application, using a valid DOS file name. For this example, we'll use the name MEMMGR (an abbreviation for Membership Manager). You also need to enter a name for the main menu, which will be MEMMAIN in this example.

At this step, you need to assign a default database, index file, and sort order. These default settings will be used by all menu selections, except those that you specifically change. For example, the membership application will use the default alphabetical sort order for edit screens, browse screens, and the membership roster. But menu options that print form letters and mailing labels will override the default setting and use zip code order.

Figure 16.11 shows the completed application definition for the membership application. Press Ctrl-End after you complete the definition.

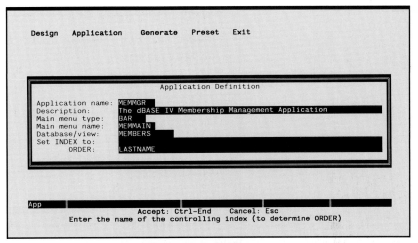

Figure 16.11: Completed application definition

THE APPLICATION DESIGN SCREEN

After you have saved the application definition, you'll be taken to the application design screen. Here is where you will create the *application objects* that make up the application. The application objects include the menus, batch processes, and optional sign-on banner. Currently, the sign-on banner is centered on the design screen, as shown in Figure 16.12.

Like other dBASE IV design screens, the application design screen has a menu bar at the top and pull-down menus. However, unlike other dBASE IV menus, this menu bar changes from time to time to reflect the type of object that you are creating at the moment. At first, this can be a little confusing, but as you develop the membership application in this chapter, you'll see how and when the changes occur.

THE SIGN-ON BANNER

You can use the application object that is currently on the design screen as a sign-on banner, which will appear each time the user runs the completed application. Use Ctrl-Y to delete the text that is currently in the box and type your own sign-on information. You can type the application title, a description, author name, copyright

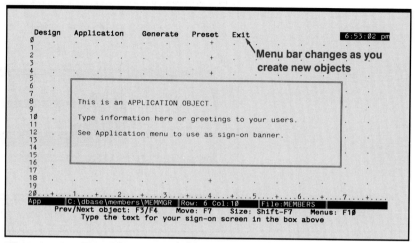

Figure 16.12: The application design screen

notice, or any other text in the sign-on banner. You can use the usual editing keys to make changes if necessary.

You can also resize and move the frame that contains the sign-on banner (as well as most other objects that you create). To change the size of the frame, press Size (Shift-F7). The border will blink. Use the arrow keys to expand or reduce the size of the box; then press ◄─┘ when you are done. To move the box, press Move (F7) and then use the arrow keys to move the box to a new location. Press ◄─┘ to complete the move operation.

Figure 16.13 shows a suggested sign-on banner for the membership application. In this example, the box has been reduced slightly in size and moved up a few rows. Once you've completed the banner, you need to make a few menu selections to ensure that it is displayed when the user boots the application. Here are the steps to do so:

1. Press Menu (F10) and select Display Sign-On Banner from the Application pull-down menu.

2. Select Yes from the options that appear.

CREATING THE HORIZONTAL BAR MENU

Next you can create the horizontal bar menu (the main menu) that appears across the top of the screen when the user runs the

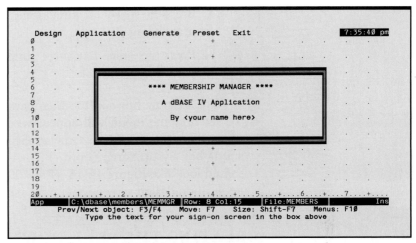

Figure 16.13: Sign-on banner for the membership application

application. (In Figure 16.8, this is the horizontal menu named MEMMAIN.) To create the menu, follow these steps:

1. Select Horizontal Bar Menu from the Design pull-down menu.

2. Select <create> from the submenu that appears.

3. In the dialog box that appears, enter **MEMMAIN** as the menu name.

4. Enter **Membership application main menu** as the description.

5. Leave the message line prompt blank for now.

6. Press Ctrl-End when you are done.

Now you can place menu options inside the menu bar. To enter an option, press the F5 key, type the option text, then press F5 again. Here are the steps to enter the menu options Maintain, Update, Print, Utilities, and Exit:

1. Press F5, type **Maintain**, and press F5 again.

2. Press the space bar three times, press F5, type **Update**, and press F5 again.

3. Press the space bar three times, press F5, type **Print**, and press F5 again.

NOTE

After you have created the horizontal bar menu, it becomes the current object, and the second option in the Application Design menu changes from Application to Menu.

4. Press the space bar three times, press F5, type **Utilities**, and press F5 again.

5. Press the space bar three times, press F5, type **Exit**, and press F5 again.

You've now finished the membership application main menu. To see how the menu will appear when the user actually runs the application, you can remove the application design screen menu and status bar by pressing Zoom (F9). After you do so, your screen should look like Figure 16.14. (Press Zoom again to bring back the application design screen menu and status bar.)

CREATING THE PULL-DOWN MENUS

The Pop-Up Menu option on the Design menu is used to create both pop-up and pull-down menus.

Creating the pull-down menu for each main menu option is the next step. (The options on each pull-down menu were defined in Figure 16.8.) The general procedure to create each pull-down menu is the same: You start with a blank pop-up menu, increase its size as necessary, and then type menu options and optional text. You can then resize the menu to tighten the frame around the options and move the menu to where you want it to appear when the user runs the application.

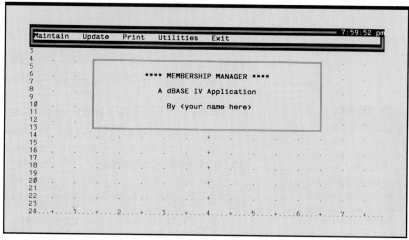

Figure 16.14: Horizontal bar menu for the membership application

THE MAINTAIN PULL-DOWN MENU   Follow these steps to create the pull-down menu for the application's Maintain option:

1. Press F10 and select Pop-up Menu from the Design menu.

2. Select <create> from the submenu.

3. Enter **MEMMAINT** as the menu name.

4. Leave the other options blank for the time being.

5. Press Ctrl-End.

6. Press Size (Shift-F7) and press → five times to widen the box. Then press ◄—┘.

7. Type the option **Add new members** and press ◄—┘.

8. Type **Browse all members** and press ◄—┘.

9. Type **Change/delete a member**.

10. Press Size (Shift-F7) again and press ↑ five times to remove blank lines in the box. Press ◄—┘.

11. Press Move (F7) and select Entire Frame to begin moving the menu.

12. Use the arrow keys to move the menu to beneath the Maintain option, as in Figure 16.15. Press ◄—┘ after completing the move.

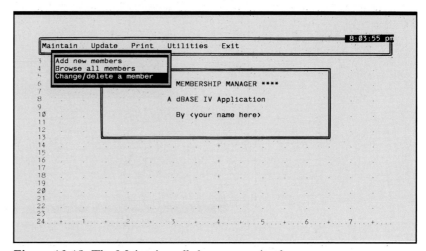

Figure 16.15: The Maintain pull-down menu in place

After completing the MEMMAINT pull-down menu, save it and put it away (hide it temporarily to reduce screen clutter) by selecting Put Away Current Menu from the Menu pull-down menu. When prompted, select Save Changes.

THE UPDATE PULL-DOWN MENU To create the pull-down menu for the application Update option, use the same general techniques as you used for the Maintain option to get started. That is, select Pop-Up Menu from the Design pull-down menu and <create> from the submenu. Enter **MEMUPDAT** as the name of the menu. You can leave the description and message line prompt blank for the time being and just press Ctrl-End.

When the menu frame appears, you'll need to enlarge it (using Shift-F7) to accommodate all the options (you can resize the menu frame at any time, so don't worry about getting the frame right the first time). Then type the following items and text:

> Update this month's renewals
> Mark expired memberships for deletion
> Purge marked records

After typing all three options, you can use Size (Shift-F7) to tighten the frame around the options if necessary. Then press Move (F7), select Entire Frame, and align the completed menu beneath the application Update option, as in Figure 16.16.

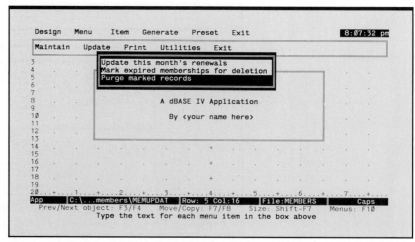

Figure 16.16: The Update pull-down menu in place

Once again, to reduce screen clutter and save the new menu, select Put Away Current Menu from the Menu pull-down menu and select Save Changes when prompted.

THE PRINT PULL-DOWN MENU   Now you can create the pull-down menu for the Print option of the membership application. Start with the usual steps: Select Pop-Up menu from the Design pull-down menu, select <create> from the submenu, and enter **MEMPRINT** as the name of the menu. Press Ctrl-End to leave other options blank.

Use Shift-F7 to enlarge the initial frame to accommodate the menu options and then type the options and text shown here (use hyphens for the dividing line):

```
Membership roster
All mailing labels
Welcome letters
Welcome labels
Renewal letters
Renewal labels
Overdue letters
Overdue labels
- - - - - - - - - - - - - - - - - - - - -
Complete all options
on the Update menu
before printing
monthly letters.
```

After completing the pull-down menu, resize it (using Shift-F7) to tighten the frame around the options. Then move it (using F7) so that it is aligned beneath the Print option on the application horizontal bar menu, as shown in Figure 16.17.

After completing the MEMPRINT pull-down menu, select Put Away Current Menu from the Menu pull-down menu and Save Changes from the submenu.

THE UTILITIES PULL-DOWN MENU   To create the pull-down menu for the application Utilities option, select Pop-Up Menu from the Design pull-down menu and <create> from the submenu. Enter **MEMUTIL** as the menu name and press Ctrl-End to leave

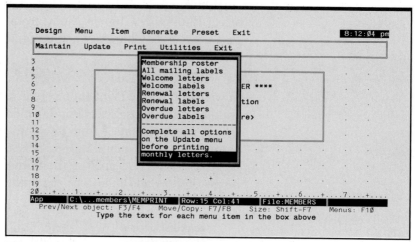

Figure 16.17: The Print pull-down menu in place

the other options blank. Use Shift-F7 to widen the blank frame and then fill in the options as follows:

Change system date
Back up database to drive A
Copy application to drive A
Repair corrupted index

When you are done, use Shift-F7 again, if necessary, to tighten the frame around the menu options and then use Move (F7) to reposition the menu beneath the Utilities option, as shown in Figure 16.18.

Select Put Away Current Menu from the Menu pull-down menu and Save Changes from the submenu to save your work and clear some work space.

THE EXIT PULL-DOWN MENU   Finally, use the usual techniques to create the pull-down menu for the application Exit option. That is, select Pop-Up Menu from the Design pull-down menu and <create> from the submenu. Enter the name **MEMEXIT** and press Ctrl-End to leave all other options blank for the time being. Fill in the box with these two options:

Return to dBASE IV
Exit to DOS

Size the frame for a tight fit and move the frame to the appropriate location beneath the Exit option on the menu bar, as in Figure 16.19.

SELECTING THE CURRENT OBJECT

Before putting away the Exit menu, you might want to experiment with the Previous (F3) and Next (F4) keys for a moment. Whenever there are multiple objects on the applications design

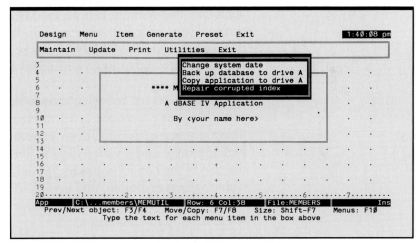

Figure 16.18: The Utilities pull-down menu in place

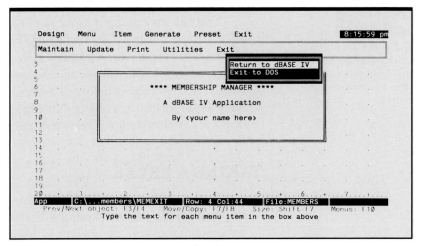

Figure 16.19: The Exit pull-down in place

screen, these keys allow you to scroll from one application object to the next.

If you press either of these keys repeatedly now, you'll notice that the current object switches among the pull-down menu, the horizontal bar menu, and the sign-on banner. The *current* object always has its frame highlighted and overlays any other objects on the screen.

To bring a hidden object (one that you've already put away) back to the design screen, select the type of object you want to bring back from the Design pull-down menu and then select the object name from the submenu. For example, to bring the MEMPRINT pop-up menu to the design screen, press F10 and select Pop-Up Menu from the Design pull-down menu and MEMPRINT from the submenu. The MEMPRINT menu appears on the design screen and automatically becomes the current object.

You can resize, move, or change the current object at any time, using the same keys you used to create the object. If the current object is a pop-up (or pull-down) menu, you can delete an option by highlighting it and pressing Ctrl-Y. To insert a new option, increase the size of the box as necessary, position the highlight to where you want to insert an option, and press Ctrl-N. You may want to experiment a bit with these options now and correct any mistakes you made while developing the menus.

PUTTING AWAY ALL OBJECTS

The Save Changes and Exit option from the Exit pull-down menu also saves all application objects.

You can save and put away all of the objects in an application by selecting the Clear Work Surface option from the Menu pull-down menu (or the Application pull-down menu). Go ahead and select that option now. dBASE will ask whether you want to save changes made to each unsaved object before dBASE puts it away. In this case, select Save Changes for each object. Note that the sign-on banner is always displayed on the design screen and cannot be put away.

TAKING A BREAK

Now you have created the entire menu structure for the membership application. Your next step will be to assign actions to each menu option. But first you might want to take a break. To do so, select Save

All Changes and Exit from the Exit pull-down menu. You'll be returned to the Control Center, where you can exit dBASE in the usual manner before turning off the computer.

To resume your work later, first make sure to log on to the C:\DBASE\MEMBERS directory; then run dBASE IV in the usual manner. Highlight MEMMGR in the Application panel at the right side of the Control Center and then press Design (Shift-F2). You'll be returned to the application design screen, with the sign-on banner displayed in the center of the screen. Other objects will be hidden.

You can use the techniques discussed here to take a break and then resume your work at any time as you complete the application in the following sections.

ASSIGNING ACTIONS TO MENU ITEMS

Your next step is to attach actions to each menu option in the application. The general procedure is to highlight the option to which you want to attach an action, select Change Action from the Item pull-down menu, and then select an appropriate action. In this section, we'll attach actions to all menu options in the membership application.

ATTACHING MENU-BAR ACTIONS

We'll start by attaching actions to the options in the application horizontal bar menu. First, you must reveal the horizontal bar menu and make it the current object by following these steps:

1. Select Horizontal Bar Menu from the Design pull-down menu.

2. Select MEMMAIN from the submenu.

Now you can assign actions to each option on the horizontal menu. Let's start with the Maintain option.

ASSIGNING AN ACTION TO THE MAINTAIN OPTION If the user selects the Maintain option from the horizontal bar menu, you want the application to display the MEMMAINT pull-down menu. Here are the steps to assign the appropriate action:

1. Press F10 and select Change Action from the Item pull-down menu.

2. Select Open a Menu as the action.

3. Press the space bar until the Pop-Up option appears; then press ◄─┘.

4. Type the name of the appropriate pull-down menu (**MEM-MAINT**) or press Pick (Shift-F1) and select MEMMAINT from the submenu that appears.

5. Press Ctrl-End.

NOTE

While the Item pull-down menu is displayed, you can use the PgUp and PgDn keys to scroll through options on an application menu.

At this point, you'll be returned to the Item pull-down menu. Take a moment to look at the status bar near the bottom of the screen. You'll notice that in the center it displays the current menu option, Maintain. Whenever you assign an action to a menu option, take a quick look at the option displayed in the status bar to make sure you are working with the correct menu option.

ASSIGNING AN ACTION TO THE UPDATE OPTION If the user selects the UPDATE option from the horizontal bar menu, you want the application to display the MEMUPDAT pull-down menu. Here are the steps to assign the appropriate action:

1. Press PgDn so that the Update option is current (it appears centered in the status bar near the bottom of the screen).

2. Select Change Action.

3. Select Open a Menu.

4. Press the space bar until the Pop-Up option is displayed; then press ◄─┘.

5. Press Pick (Shift-F1) and select MEMUPDAT as the menu to attach.

6. Press Ctrl-End.

Repeat steps 1 to 6 for the Print, Utilities, and Exit menu options. Substitute the appropriate menu option in step 1 and, in step 5, the pull-down menu name for each bar menu option, as listed here (you can refer to Figure 16.8 for a visual display).

Menu option (step 1)	Pull-down menu name (step 5)
Print	MEMPRINT
Utilities	MEMUTIL
Exit	MEMEXIT

When you are finished, press Ctrl-End to leave the Item menu and return to the application design screen.

CONVERTING POP-UP MENUS TO PULL-DOWN MENUS

Even though pop-up menus and pull-down menus are formatted identically, they behave in slightly different ways. Pop-up menus are not displayed until the user *selects* the higher-level menu item by highlighting and pressing ←. Pull-down menus, on the other hand, are displayed as soon as the higher-level menu option is highlighted (the user need not press ← to see the pull-down menu).

To convert the pop-up menus beneath the membership application bar menu to pull-down menus, follow these simple steps:

1. Select Attach Pull-Down Menus from the Menu pull-down menu.

2. Select Yes from the submenu that appears.

When you attach pull-down menus to a menu bar, the pull-down menus automatically *inherit* many characteristics of the menu bar, including the database in use, index and order in use, and colors. You can, however, override any of these inherited characteristics, as you'll see later.

ASSIGNING ACTIONS TO THE MAINTAIN MENU

Now you need to begin attaching actions to the pull-down menus. (These actions were summarized previously in Figure 16.9.)

Before you can assign actions to the Maintain pull-down menu, you need to take it out of hiding by following these steps:

1. Select Pop-Up Menu from the Design pull-down menu.

2. Select MEMMAINT from the submenu.

You'll see the Maintain pull-down menu appear on the screen with its frame highlighted, indicating that it is the object currently in use. Now you can assign an action to each menu option.

ADD NEW MEMBERS   The Add New Members option allows the user to add (*append*) new records to the MEMBERS database, using the MEMFORM custom screen you created earlier. Follow these steps:

1. Press Menu (F10) and select Change Action from the Item pull-down menu.

2. Select Edit Form (Add, Delete, Edit) from the submenu.

3. Press Pick (Shift-F1) and select MEMFORM as the form to use to add records.

4. When the cursor is in the Mode box, press the space bar, if necessary, to change the option to APPEND.

5. Leave all other options at their default values, as in Figure 16.20.

6. Press Ctrl-End.

BROWSE ALL MEMBERS   The second option on the Maintain pull-down menu, Browse All Members, allows the user to change the MEMBERS database through a browse screen. (This is a general-purpose browse screen, unlike the browse screen displayed during membership renewals, which displayed only expired memberships.) Here are the steps to attach the appropriate action to the menu option:

1. Press PgDn to move to the next menu option (Browse All Members should appear in the center of the status bar).

2. Select Change Action.

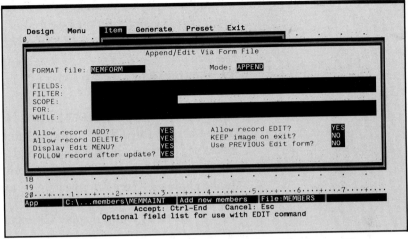

Figure 16.20: Append/Edit Form for the Add New Members option

3. Select Browse (Add, Delete, Edit).

4. Press ◄┘ five times to move to the FORMAT file option.

5. Press Pick (Shift-F1) and select MEMFORM as the related format file.

6. Press Ctrl-End to leave all other settings at their default values.

In the previous steps, you directed the Applications Generator to display the data on a browse screen when the user selects Browse All Members. However, steps 4 and 5 told the Applications Generator to use the MEMFORM custom screen. This creates a contradiction, because the browse screen displays multiple database records in rows and columns, and the MEMFORM screen displays a single record at a time.

dBASE resolves this contradiction by displaying the browse screen as usual, but using any special templates, picture functions, and edit options defined for the MEMFORM custom form. For example, even though the data is displayed on a browse screen, the user will still be able to press the space bar to scroll through the REGULAR and OFFICER options in the STATUS field, because you defined this as a multiple-choice field in the MEMFORM custom form (see Table 16.1).

All other features that you added to the MEMFORM custom form, such as default dates, will also be carried over to the browse screen, because you specified MEMFORM as the FORMAT file for the browse screen. You'll have a chance to test this later when you use the completed application.

CHANGE/DELETE A MEMBER   Now you need to assign an action to the third item on the Maintain menu, Change/Delete a Member. This option displays a single record from the MEMBERS database on the MEMFORM custom screen and allows the user to make changes. Here are the steps to assign the menu action:

1. Press PgDn to display Change/Delete in the status bar.

2. Select Change Action.

3. Select Edit Form (Add, Delete, Edit).

4. Type or select (using Pick, Shift-F1) MEMFORM as the form to use.

5. In the Mode box, specify Edit as the mode (pressing the space bar if necessary).

6. Press Ctrl-End to complete the operation and leave all other settings at their default values.

Now you have assigned actions to all three items on the Maintain pull-down menu. You can save and put away that menu now by following these steps:

1. Select Put Away Current Menu from the Menu pull-down menu.

2. Select Save Changes from the submenu.

ASSIGNING ACTIONS TO THE UPDATE MENU

Now you need to assign actions to the application Update pull-down menu. First, take that menu out of hiding and make it the current object by following these steps:

1. Press F10 and select Pop-Up Menu from the Design pull-down menu.

2. Select MEMUPDAT from the submenu.

The Update pull-down menu appears on the application design screen, and you are ready to assign actions to its options.

UPDATE THIS MONTH'S RENEWALS   As discussed earlier in the chapter, the Update This Month's Renewals option automates the steps involved in updating renewed memberships. When the user selects this option, the application executes a batch process named RENEW.BCH (dBASE adds the file extension .BCH). We'll create the actual batch process later, but you can assign the action to the menu option. Here are the steps:

1. Make sure that the Update This Month's Renewals option is highlighted in the pull-down menu.

2. Press F10 and select Change Action from the Item pull-down menu.

3. Select Run Program.

4. Select Execute Batch Process.

5. Type the batch process name **RENEW** and press ←┘.

Now you can move on and assign the action to the next menu option.

MARK EXPIRED MEMBERSHIPS FOR DELETION   The Mark Expired Memberships for Deletion option marks for deletion all records of members whose membership expired 60 or more days ago (and was never renewed). The option performs this task automatically for the entire database, so that the user need not scroll through and mark these records one at a time. Here are the steps to assign the appropriate action to the menu option:

1. Press PgDn to move to the Mark Expired Memberships for Deletion option.

2. Select Change Action.

3. Select Perform File Operation.

4. Select Mark Records for Deletion.

5. Enter the expression **DATE() – Expires > 60 .AND. .NOT. Current** as the FOR option, as shown in Figure 16.21.

The expression that you entered as the FOR option acts as a filter condition, just like the filter conditions you created in queries in Chapter 6. As with queries, the expression must result in a true or false verdict, as in the expression PartNo = ''A-111'' or Qty < 10. However, when using the Applications Generator, you do not stagger filter conditions onto separate rows to create AND and OR queries. Instead, you use the operator .AND. for an AND condition and the operator .OR. for an OR condition.

You can also use the .NOT. operator, which, when used with the Logical data type, means that the result of the expression should be false, rather than true.

Logical data types always contain either a true or a false value, so you need not use a complete expression to test this particular data type. Just using the logical field name, such as CURRENT, implies the expression CURRENT = .T. Using the .NOT. operator in front of the Logical field's name, as in the expression .NOT. CURRENT, is the same as using the expression CURRENT = .F.

In this particular example, the expression used as the FOR condition, DATE() – Expires > 60 .AND. .NOT. Current, specifies

NOTE

To make complex expressions more readable, it is common practice to type function names, such as DATE(), in all uppercase letters and field names, such as Expires, with only the first letter capitalized. However, you can use whatever upper- and lowercase conventions you wish.

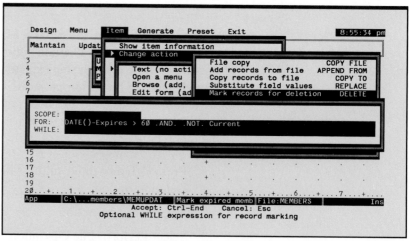

Figure 16.21: FOR condition for marking expired memberships

records with membership expiration dates that are 60 or more days "less than" (earlier than) the current date and in which membership has not been renewed (that is, the CURRENT field contains .F.). When the user selects this menu option, the application will automatically mark such records for deletion.

To permanently delete records that are marked for deletion, the user needs to select the next menu option, Purge Marked Records. Before moving on to the next menu option, however, press Ctrl-End to save the current menu action.

PURGE MARKED RECORDS   The next item on the Update menu is Purge Marked Records. This option packs the database, permanently removing all records that are marked for deletion. This purging includes records that were marked in the previous operation, as well as any that were marked by the user (using Ctrl-U) while editing or browsing. To assign an action to this option, follow these steps:

1. Press PgDn to move to the Purge Marked Records option (check the status bar to be sure you have the correct option).

2. Select Change Action.

3. Select Perform File Operation.

4. Select Discard Marked Records.

5. Select OK when prompted.

That completes the actions for the Update pull-down menu for the time being, until later when we create the RENEW.BCH batch process. For now, select Put Away Current Menu from the Menu pull-down menu and Save Changes from the submenu.

ASSIGNING ACTIONS TO THE PRINT MENU

The Print pull-down menu in the membership application presents options for printing reports and mailing labels. To assign actions to these menu options, first make the Print menu the current object by following these steps:

1. Select Pop-Up Menu from the Design pull-down menu.

2. Select MEMPRINT from the submenu.

MEMBERSHIP ROSTER   The Membership Roster option allows the user to print a list of all members, using the format you created earlier and named ROSTER. To assign the appropriate action to this menu, follow these steps:

1. Press F10 and select Change Action from the Item pull-down menu.

2. Select Display or Print.

3. Select Report.

4. Press Pick (Shift-F1) and select ROSTER.

5. Press ← to leave the HEADING box blank.

6. Complete other print options as follows (all are multiple-choice options that you can scroll thorough by pressing the space bar):

Report format:	FULL DETAIL
Heading Format:	INCLUDE DATE AND PAGE
Before printing:	SKIP TO NEW PAGE
Send output to:	PRINTER

7. Press Ctrl-End when you are done.

ALL MAILING LABELS   The second option on the Print menu lets the user print all mailing labels. It uses the MEMLABEL format that you created earlier. Here are the steps to assign the action:

1. Press PgDn to scroll to the All Mailing Labels menu option.

2. Select Change Action.

3. Select Display Or Print.

4. Select Labels.

5. Press Pick (Shift-F1) and select MEMLABEL.

6. Set the Send Output To option to PRINTER.

7. Set the Print Sample? option to Yes.

8. Press Ctrl-End.

TIP

If you change Send Output to ASK AT RUN-TIME, the user can decide where to send output.

WELCOME LETTERS   The Welcome Letters option on the Print menu prints the WELCOME form letter for new members who joined this month. To assign the action to this menu option,

1. Press PgDn to move to the Welcome Letters option.
2. Select Change Action.
3. Select Display or Print.
4. Select Report.
5. Press Pick (Shift-F1) and select Welcome from the Pick menu.
6. Fill in other options as shown in Figure 16.22.

Note the filter condition used with the FOR box in the dialog box: MONTH(StartDate) = MONTH(DATE()) .AND. YEAR-(StartDate) = YEAR(DATE()). This filter condition limits printing of the welcome letters to members who joined in the current month of the current year (that is, this month's new members). Press Ctrl-End after completing the dialog box.

WELCOME LABELS   The Welcome Labels option prints a mailing label for each letter that the Welcome Letters option printed. It uses the MEMLABEL format and the same filter condition that the Welcome Letters option uses. To assign the action, follow these steps:

1. Press PgDn to move to the Welcome Labels option.
2. Select Change Action.
3. Select Display or Print.
4. Select Labels.
5. Press Pick (Shift-F1) and select the MEMLABEL format.
6. In the FOR box, enter the same filter condition used in Figure 16.22:

    MONTH(StartDate) = MONTH(DATE()) .AND.
    YEAR(StartDate) = YEAR(DATE()).

7. Press Ctrl-End.

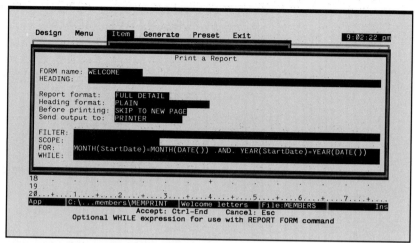

Figure 16.22: Dialog box for printing welcome letters

RENEWAL LETTERS   The Renewal Letters option in the membership application prints the RENEWAL form letter for each person whose membership will expire next month. Unfortunately, defining "next month" in terms that dBASE will understand is not as easy as you might think.

First, for the months January through November, "next month" can be expressed simply as MONTH (DATE()) + 1, because the MONTH() function returns a number between 1 and 12, and adding 1 to this value produces the number for the next month (for example, in January, the expression MONTH (DATE()) + 1 produces 2, the month number for February). However, in December, the expression MONTH(DATE()) + 1 produces 13, obviously not the month number for January.

To solve this problem, you can divide the month number by 12 and then add one to the *modulus* (the remainder after division) to determine the next month. This approach works because dividing any number below 12 by 12 produces a modulus that equals the current month. For example, 1/12 produces zero and a modulus of 1. Dividing February, month 2, by 12 produces zero and a modulus of 2. Dividing the twelfth month, December, by 12 (12/12) produces 1 and a modulus of zero; adding 1 to zero produces 1, the month after December.

The dBASE MOD() function returns the modulus of one argument divided by a second argument. Hence, the expression MOD (MONTH(DATE()),12) + 1 always returns the number of the next month, even in December. But this does not solve all problems for the membership application, because renewal letters should be sent only to people whose memberships expire in the next month of the current year.

Once again, however, you cannot use the simple expression YEAR(DATE( )) to specify the current year, because in December, next month is also next year (that is, the month following December 1991 is January 1992). But if you divide any month number from January to November (month number 1 to 11) by 12, the integer portion of the division is zero (for example, 11/12 = 0 if you exclude the decimal portion of the result). Dividing December (month 12) by 12 (12/12), however, produces 1. If you add the integer portion of the results of the division to the current year, the result will be the appropriate year.

To isolate the integer portion of a number (with the decimal value completely removed), you use the dBASE INT() function. Therefore, the complete expression used for isolating appropriate years in the EXPIRES field is YEAR(Expires) = YEAR(DATE()) + INT (MONTH(Expires)/12).

Actually, there is a third problem to contend with. The space allotted for a FOR filter condition in the Applications Generator does not provide enough room for the complete expression that renewal letters require: MONTH(Expires) = MOD(MONTH(DATE()),12 + 1 .AND.YEAR(Expires) = YEAR(DATE()) + INT(MONTH (Expires)/12). But, as you may have guessed, there is a way around this limitation too, as you'll see in a moment. Let's get back on track now and assign the appropriate action to the Renewal Letters menu option, following these steps:

1. Press PgDn until Renewal Letters appears in the status bar.

2. Select Change Action from the Item menu.

3. Select Display or Print.

4. Select Report.

5. Type the report format name **RENEWAL**, or press Pick (Shift-F1) and select RENEWAL from the Pick submenu.

6. Fill in the rest of the Print a Report Dialog box as shown in Figure 16.23.

As you can see in the dialog box, both the FILTER and FOR options contain filter conditions. The FILTER condition YEAR(Expires) = YEAR(DATE()) + INT(MONTH(Expires)/12) isolates records that have the appropriate expiration year (the current year for the months January through November and the next year for December). The FOR condition MONTH(Expires) = MOD (MONTH(DATE()),12) + 1 isolates records that have expiration dates in the next month. The FOR and FILTER options are additive, so placing filter conditions in both is equivalent to placing the single long filter condition YEAR(Expires) = YEAR(DATE()) + INT(MONTH(Expires)/12).AND.MONTH(Expires) = MOD (MONTH(DATE()),12) + 1 into the FOR (or FILTER) condition box.

After filling in the dialog box (paying close attention to parentheses in the expressions), press Ctrl-End.

RENEWAL LABELS Mailing labels for the renewal letters can be printed using the usual MEMLABEL format and the same filter

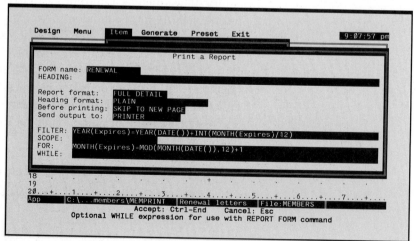

Figure 16.23: Dialog box for printing renewal letters

condition as is used to print renewal letters. Follow these steps to assign an action to the application Renewal Labels menu option:

1. Press PgDn to move to the Renewal Labels menu option.

2. Select Change Action.

3. Select Display or Print.

4. Select Labels.

5. Fill in the Print Labels dialog box as shown in Figure 16.24.

6. Press Ctrl-End after filling in the dialog box.

OVERDUE LETTERS   The Overdue Letters option prints the OVERDUE form letter for people whose memberships expired 30 or more days ago, and who have still not renewed. Here are the steps to assign the action to the menu option:

1. Press PgDn to make Overdue Letters the current menu option.

2. Select Change Action.

3. Select Display or Print.

4. Select Report.

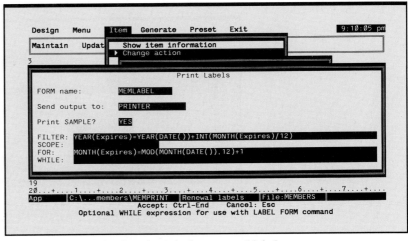

Figure 16.24: Dialog box for printing renewal labels

5. Fill in the screen as shown in Figure 16.25.

6. Press Ctrl-End.

OVERDUE LABELS   The Overdue Labels option prints mailing labels for the overdue letters. It uses the MEMLABEL format and the same filter condition as the overdue letter. Here are the steps to assign the action:

1. Press PgDn to make Overdue Labels the current menu option.

2. Select Change Action.

3. Select Display or Print.

4. Select Labels.

5. Enter **MEMLABEL** as the label format.

6. Enter **DATE() – Expires>30.AND..NOT.Current** as the FOR condition.

7. Press Ctrl-End.

This completes the menu options for the Print menu. To save the menu and put it away, select Put Away Current Menu from the Menu pull-down menu and Save Changes from the submenu.

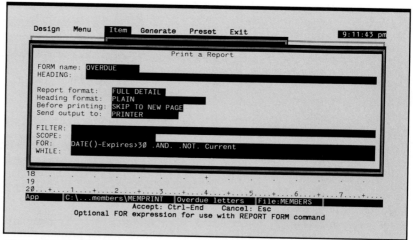

Figure 16.25: Dialog box for printing overdue letters

ASSIGNING ACTIONS TO THE UTILITIES MENU

To assign actions to the Utilities menu, first make it the current menu by following these steps:

1. Press F10 and select Pop-up Menu from the Design menu.
2. Select MEMUTIL from the submenu.

Now you can assign actions to the Utilities menu options.

CHANGE SYSTEM DATE   The Change System Date option allows the user to change the current (system) date without exiting the application. It does so by running the external DOS command, DATE. Here are the steps to assign the action to this option:

1. Press F10 and select Change Action from the Item menu.
2. Select Run Program.
3. Select Run DOS Program.
4. Next to the prompt ''Program:'' enter the command **DATE**.
5. Press Ctrl-End.

BACK UP DATABASE TO DRIVE A   The Back Up Database to Drive A option uses the DOS command COPY MEMBERS.* A: to copy MEMBERS.DBF and MEMBERS.MDX to a diskette in drive A. Here are the steps to assign the action:

1. Press PgDn to move to the Back Up Database menu option.
2. Select Change Action.
3. Select Run Program.
4. Select Run DOS Program.
5. In the dialog box, enter **COPY** as the program name.
6. Enter **MEMBERS.* A:** in the parameters box.
7. Press Ctrl-End.

COPY APPLICATION TO DRIVE A   The Copy Application to Drive A command copies all files on the \DBASE\MEMBERS directory to a floppy disk in drive A. This option can be used both for making backup copies and for making extra copies to give to others to use. Here are the steps for assigning the action:

1. Press PgDn to move to the Copy Application to Drive A option.

2. Select Change Action.

3. Select Run Program.

4. Select Run DOS Program.

5. Enter **COPY** as the name of the program to run.

6. Enter ***.* A:** as the parameters.

7. Press Ctrl-End.

REPAIR CORRUPTED INDEXES   Repair Corrupted Indexes helps the user to recover from power outages and other situations that can corrupt indexes. To assign the action to this menu option, follow these steps:

1. Press PgDn to move to the Repair Corrupted Indexes menu option.

2. Select Change Action.

3. Select Perform File Operation.

4. Select Reindex Database.

5. Select OK.

That completes the actions for the Utilities menu. Select Put Away Current Menu from the Menu pull-down menu and Save Changes from the submenu.

ASSIGNING ACTIONS TO THE EXIT MENU

The Exit menu provides two options: Return to dBASE IV, which leaves the application and returns the user to the Control Center, and Exit to DOS, which returns the user to DOS. Make the Exit menu the current object by following the usual steps:

1. Press F10 and select Pop-Up Menu from the Design pull-down menu.

2. Select MEMEXIT from the submenu.

RETURN TO dBASE IV   To assign the action to the Return to dBASE IV option, follow these steps:

1. Press F10 and select Change Action from the Item menu.

2. Select Quit.

3. Select Return to Calling Program.

4. Select OK.

EXIT TO DOS   To assign the action to the Exit to DOS option, follow these steps:

1. Press PgDn to move to the next menu option.

2. Select Change Action.

3. Select Quit.

4. Select Quit to DOS.

5. Select OK.

Now you can select Put Away Current Menu from the Menu pull-down menu and Save Changes from the submenu.

At this point, you have assigned an action to every menu option in the membership application. However, you still need to perform a few steps to complete the application.

BUILDING THE BATCH PROCESS

As you probably recall, you assigned the action Execute Batch Process to the Update This Month's Renewals menu option earlier and specified RENEW as the name of the batch process. Now you need to create that batch process. Two steps are involved: First you list the operations in the batch process, and then you assign an action to each operation. Let's create RENEW.BCH now.

LISTING THE
OPERATIONS IN THE BATCH PROCESS

The first step is to list each operation (or step) in the batch process, in plain English. This procedure is similar to writing options into a pop-up menu frame. Here are the steps:

1. Press F10 and select Batch Process from the Design pulldown menu.

2. Select <create> from the submenu.

3. Enter **RENEW** as the batch-process name.

4. Enter **Automate monthly renewals** as the description.

5. Press Ctrl-End.

6. Press Size (Shift-F7) and widen the frame by at least two spaces. Then press ←⏎.

7. Type plain-English descriptions of each operation in the batch process, as shown in Figure 16.26.

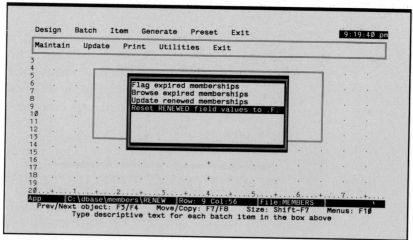

Figure 16.26: Descriptions of batch-process operations

ASSIGNING ACTIONS TO A BATCH PROCESS

Now you need to assign an action to each operation in the batch process, using a technique similar to that used to assign actions to menu options.

FLAG EXPIRED MEMBERSHIPS   The Flag Expired Memberships operation in the batch process places .F. in the CURRENT field for all memberships that have expired. Follow these steps to assign the appropriate action:

1. Press ↑ until the topmost item, Flag Expired Memberships, in the box is highlighted.

2. Press F10 and select Change Action from the Item pull-down menu.

3. Select Perform File Operation.

4. Select Substitute Field Values.

5. Fill in the Substitute Field Values dialog box as shown in Figure 16.27.

6. Press Ctrl-End when you are done.

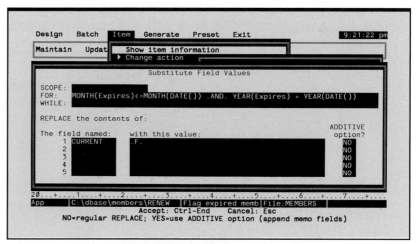

Figure 16.27: Dialog box for the first batch-process operation

BROWSE EXPIRED MEMBERSHIPS The second operation in the batch process displays all expired memberships on a browse screen so the user can quickly and easily identify renewed memberships. To simplify matters further, the cursor is locked into the RENEWED field, which is displayed in the leftmost column of the browse screen. Furthermore, the browse screen displays only selected, relevant fields (Figure 16.10 showed an example).

To assign the appropriate action to this second batch-process operation, follow these steps:

1. Press PgDn to move to the next step, Browse Expired Memberships.

2. Select Change Action.

3. Select Browse and fill in the form as in Figure 16.28.

4. Press Ctrl-End.

In Figure 16.28, the FIELDS box lists the fields that are to be displayed in the browse screen, in the order in which they are to be displayed. The FILTER box indicates that only records with .F. in the CURRENT field are to be displayed. The maximum column width of 15 allows all the fields to fit on the screen (only the first 15 letters of the COMPANY field will be visible on the screen; all other fields are less than 15 characters wide).

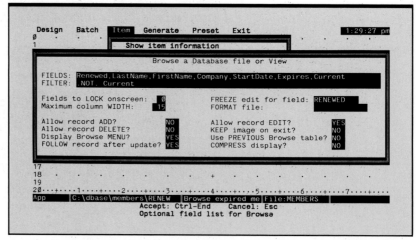

Figure 16.28: Dialog box for renewing memberships through a browse screen

The FREEZE Edit for Field: RENEWED option locks the cursor into the RENEWED field, thereby making it easier to scroll up and down from record to record without scrolling left and right. (You'll see this feature in action later when we test the application.)

UPDATE RENEWED MEMBERSHIPS   The third operation in the batch process changes the CURRENT field for all renewed memberships to .T. and increments their expiration dates by one year. Here are the steps to assign the appropriate action:

1. Press PgDn to move to the next batch operation.

2. Select Change Action.

3. Select Perform File Operation.

4. Select Substitute Field Values.

5. Fill in the dialog box as shown in Figure 16.29.

6. Press Ctrl-End.

In Figure 16.29, the FOR condition limits the operation to records that have .T. in the RENEWED field. For each of these renewed memberships, the date in the EXPIRED field is replaced

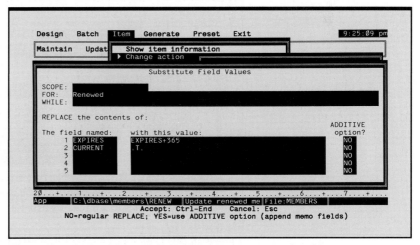

Figure 16.29: Dialog box for updating renewed memberships

with its current value plus 365 (thereby adding one year to the expiration date). The contents of the CURRENT field is replaced with .T.,
indicating that the membership is now current.

RESET RENEWED FIELDS TO FALSE   The fourth operation in
the batch process resets the RENEWED field to false in all database
records, so that no expiration dates are accidentally extended by
another year the next time the user updates memberships. To assign
the action to this operation, follow these steps:

1. Press PgDn to move to the next batch operation.

2. Select Change Action.

3. Select Perform File Operation.

4. Select Substitute Field Values.

5. Fill in the Substitute Field Values form as in Figure 16.30.

6. Press Ctrl-End.

In Figure 16.30, the SCOPE option indicates that all records in
the database should be included in the operation, and that the

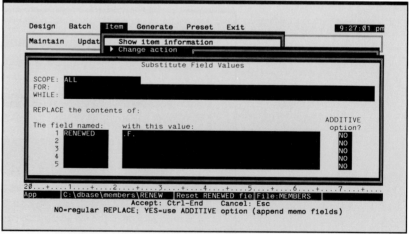

Figure 16.30: Dialog box for resetting all RENEWED fields to false

RENEWED field needs to be set to .F. At this point, you have completed the RENEW.BCH batch process. Follow these steps to save it and put it away:

1. Select Put Away Current Batch Process from the Batch pull-down menu.

2. When prompted, select Save Changes.

Now that the batch process is complete, there is only one more task to perform.

DEFINING SORT ORDERS

As you may recall, when you first started developing the application you defined MEMBERS as the default database and LASTNAME as the default index order. All options that display data (such as edit, browse, and the various reports) will use these default settings. However, we want letters and mailing labels to be printed in zip code order, so we need to override those settings for a few of the menu options.

1. Select Pop-Up Menu from the Design pull-down menu.

2. Select MEMPRINT from the submenu.

3. Press ↓ to highlight All Mailing Labels.

4. Press F10.

5. Select Reassign Index Order from the Item pull-down menu.

6. When the prompt ''Set ORDER to:'' appears, type ZIP and press ←⏎.

7. Press PgDn to move to the next menu option.

Repeat steps 5 through 7 six times to assign the ZIP index order to the remaining report and label options. When you are done, select Put Away Current Menu from the Menu pull-down menu and select Save Changes.

GENERATING THE APPLICATION

The membership application is now complete, but before you can use it, you need to *generate* the application programs (or *code*). Unlike forms and reports, this step is not automatic when you develop an application. So follow these steps to generate the application programs:

1. Press F10, select Select Template from the Generate pull-down menu, and enter **MENU.GEN**.

2. Select Display During Generation and Yes.

3. Select Begin Generating.

You will see the code that the Applications Generator creates pass by in a window on the application design screen. When this operation is complete, you'll see the message ''Generation is complete—press any key to continue.'' Press any key and proceed.

GENERATING DOCUMENTATION

The Applications Generator can also create written documentation that can help you to refine your application later. Follow these steps to create this written documentation:

1. Select Select Template from the Generate pull-down menu.

2. Enter **DOCUMENT.GEN** as the template to use.

3. Select Begin Generating.

4. Enter either **Y** or **N** when asked if you have an IBM graphics or compatible printer (enter **N** if you are not sure).

When the document is completed, you'll again be prompted to press any key. Follow these steps:

1. Press Menu (F10).

2. Select Save All Changes and Exit from the Exit pull-down menu.

You'll be returned to the Control Center, where you can now test, and then use, the membership application.

TESTING THE COMPLETED APPLICATION

Before you give a completed application to the user (or before you use the application for serious work, if you are the user), you need to test it thoroughly. Use the application with some sample data and try every menu option. This section describes how to use the finished application and also provides a few examples for testing the application.

RUNNING THE MEMBERSHIP APPLICATION

To run the membership application, highlight MEMMGR in the Application panel, press ←, and select Run Application. Select Yes from the dialog box that appears. After a few seconds, you'll see the sign-on banner. Press ← to move on to the menus. You'll see the application horizontal menu bar and the Maintain pull-down menu on the screen.

You can use the arrow keys to scroll through menu options in the usual manner. Note, however, that the highlight will not land on text within a menu. Figure 16.31 shows the application menu bar and Print pull-down menu on the screen. Now let's test each option to make sure the application works as expected.

ADDING NEW MEMBERS

To add new members to the database, select Add New Members from the Maintain menu. You'll be taken to a blank form for entering new records. The default starting date should match the current system date, and the default expiration date should be one year beyond the starting date.

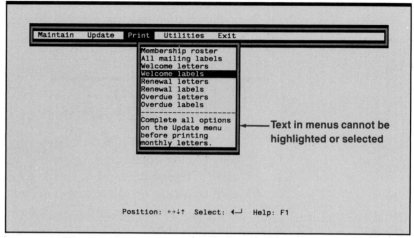

Figure 16.31: Print menu in the membership application

For testing purposes, enter the following three records, using the dates specified in the samples rather than the default dates shown on your screen:

Mr. Bob B. Baker
Boeing International
Ballistics Dep't.
2744 Bering St.
El Monte, CA 91704
(818)555-1232 Ext. 999
Status: REGULAR
Start date: 02/01/91   Expiration date: 02/01/92
Dues Current?: Y

Miss Cara C. Carlson
Cookie Haven
Purchasing Dep't.
3211 Cantamar
Cucamonga, CA 91655
(818)555-9988
Status: OFFICER
Start date: 03/15/91   Expiration date: 03/15/92
Dues Current?: Y

Dr. Deedra D. Davis
Doctor's Hosptal
15th Floor
8843 Donga Dr.
Duarte, CA 91555
(818)555-9910 Extension 8851
Status: REGULAR
Start date: 04/30/91   Expiration date: 04/30/92
Dues current? Y

After entering the sample records, select Exit from the Exit pull-down menu to return to the application menu.

CHANGING MEMBER DATA

The application offers two options for editing membership data: Browse All Members and Change/Delete a Member. Test each method now (but don't change any starting or expiration dates). Note that records should be displayed in alphabetical order by last name.

You should be able to perform an index search from either the custom form or the browse screen. To test this, press Menu (F10) and select Index Key Search from the Go To pull-down menu. Enter a valid last name, such as Carlson (with proper upper- and lowercase letters), and press ◄─┘.

You can mark (and unmark) any record for deletion using the usual Ctrl-U keystroke. (The Del indicator appears in the status bar.) For the current test session, however, do not leave any records marked for deletion yet.

After testing each option, select Exit from the Exit pull-down menu to return to the membership application main menu.

UPDATING THE MEMBERSHIP ROSTER

Suppose now that you are the user of the application, and you want to update the membership database to reflect renewed members and delete records where memberships have expired. The following sections present the steps you would take (they are the same steps you can use to test the application).

CHECK THE SYSTEM DATE   First, make sure the current (system) date is accurate. For testing purposes, we'll assume that the current date is March 30, 1992. Select Change System Date from the Utilities pull-down menu. The following DOS prompt appears on the screen (with the actual system date displayed in place of Mon 1-02-91):

Current date is Mon 1-02-91
Enter new date (mm-dd-yy): _

Type the test date 3-31-92 and press ◄─┘ to return to the menu.

UPDATE THIS MONTH'S RENEWALS   Next, select Update This Month's Renewals from the Update pull-down menu. You'll see a brief message as the application replaces the CURRENT field of expired memberships with .F. Then a browse screen will appear showing the expired memberships, as in Figure 16.32.

Mark the record for Carlson with a **T** (assume that hers is the only renewed membership). Note that the cursor stays locked into the RENEWED field, even if you press ◄─ or ─►.

After updating the one record, select Exit from the Exit pull-down menu. You'll see some brief messages as the application updates the records with renewed memberships. Then you'll be returned to the application main menu.

			Del			
RENEWED	LASTNAME	FIRSTNAME	COMPANY	STARTDATE	EXPIRES	CURRENT
F	Adams	Andy	ABC Technology	01/01/91	01/01/92	F
F	Baker	Bob	Boeing Internat	02/01/91	02/01/92	F
F	Carlson	Cara	Cookie Haven	03/15/91	03/15/92	F

Figure 16.32: Expired memberships ready for renewal

To verify that the update was accurate, select either Browse All Members or Change/Delete a Member from the Maintain pull-down menu. You should see Carlson's membership extended to 1992, and the CURRENT field for the record marked T. Select Exit from the Exit pull-down menu to return to the membership application main menu.

DELETE EXPIRED MEMBERSHIPS Now it's time to delete memberships that expired 60 or more days ago and have not been renewed. Select Mark Expired Memberships for Deletion from the Update pull-down menu. You'll see a brief message as the application marks one record for deletion (Andy Adams). Next, select Purge Marked Records from the Update menu. Again, you'll see a message as the application packs the database.

To verify that the deletion was accurate, select Browse All Members from the Maintain pull-down menu. You'll notice that Andy Adams' record has been permanently deleted.

PRINTING THE MEMBERSHIP ROSTER

At any time during the month, the user can print a list of all members by selecting Membership Roster from the Print pull-down menu. If you do so now, the application will print a list of all members currently in the Members database. These should be in alphabetical order.

PRINTING ALL MAILING LABELS

If you select All Mailing Labels from the Print pull-down menu, the application should print a sample mailing label and display the message "Do you want more samples? (Y/N)." Type **Y** if you want to test the label alignment again or **N** to begin printing labels. The application should print three mailing labels in zip code order and then return you to the application menus.

PRINTING RENEWAL LETTERS AND LABELS

Each month the user can print letters and labels, reminding members whose memberships expire next month that it's time to

NOTE

If you try to print Welcome, Renewal, or Overdue Letters, and none are pending, you'll see an End of File message. Just type I to select Ignore.

renew. Select Renewal Letters from the Print pull-down menu. The application should print a letter for Deedra Davis, whose membership expires next month (April 1992). Select Renewal Labels, and the application will print a label for this member.

PRINTING OVERDUE LETTERS AND LABELS

Each month the user can print Overdue letters and labels, reminding late payers that their memberships expired last month, and that they still have not renewed. Currently, Bob Baker is the only member who meets this description (his membership expired in February 1992, and he has not renewed yet).

Select Overdue Letters from the Print pull-down letter. You should see a single letter printed for Bob Baker. Select Overdue Labels from the Print pull-down menu to print a mailing label for this letter.

PRINTING WELCOME LETTERS AND LABELS

Each month, the user can print a batch of welcome letters and matching mailing labels for all new members (those who joined in the current month and year). Currently, no records in the test database meet this description, so you'll need to alter the current date to test print at least one letter. Select Change System Date from the Utilities pull-down menu and change the current date to **3-31-91**.

NOTE

Changing the system date in this chapter is *only* for testing with a small database. In actual use with real data, you would never need to change the date to print a particular type of letter or mailing label.

Select Welcome Letters from the Print pull-down menu. You should see a welcome letter printed for Cara Carlson. Select Welcome Labels, and after printing samples, you should see a single label, again for Cara Carlson.

You may now want to reset the current date back to 3-31-92 or to the actual current date.

TESTING THE UTILITIES

You've already had a chance to test the Change System Date option on the Utilities menu. Now you can test the other three options on that menu. If you have a blank, formatted disk available, place it in drive A of your computer and select Back Up Database to Drive A from the Utilities pull-down menu. You should hear the disk drive whir and see the file names MEMBERS.DBF and MEMBERS.MDX on the screen as the application makes the backup copy.

Next, select Copy Application to Drive A from the Utilities menu. Once again, you should hear the disk drive and see the names of all files being copied on the screen as the application copies the entire \DBASE\MEMBERS subdirectory to the disk in drive A.

Finally, select Repair Corrupted Indexes from the Utilities menu to test that option. (Even though the indexes are probably not corrupted at the moment, the option will still rebuild them.) You'll see several messages on the screen as the indexes are rebuilt.

EXITING THE APPLICATION

If you select Return to dBASE IV from the Exit pull-down menu, you'll be returned to the Control Center. Selecting Exit to DOS from the Exit pull-down menu returns you all the way to the DOS prompt.

MODIFYING THE MEMBERSHIP APPLICATION

If you discovered an error during your testing phase, or if you wish to refine the application, use the Applications Generator to make changes. In this section, we'll discuss general techniques for modifying an existing application.

PRINTING THE DOCUMENTATION

As you may recall, you use the Applications Generator to generate some documentation earlier in this chapter. You might want to make a printed copy of this document now, as it can be handy when you are making changes. The document is always stored with the same name as the application, but with the extension .DOC (as MEMMGR.DOC in this example). To print this documentation, first exit dBASE IV and return to the DOS prompt. Be sure you are logged on to the \DBASE\MEMBERS directory and then type the command

TYPE MEMMGR.DOC >PRN

Press ⬅ after typing the command. If you have a laser printer that won't eject the last printed page, enter the following command at the DOS prompt (hold down the Ctrl key and press the letter L where you see <Ctrl-L>):

```
ECHO <Ctrl-L> >PRN
```

The command will appear on the screen as ECHO ^L >PRN. Press ⬅ after entering the command.

The documentation will provide pictures of all menus and descriptions of the actions and objects assigned to each menu option. For example, the ninth page of the MEMMGR application documentation displays this for the Welcome Letters option on the Print menu:

```
----------------------------------------------------------------
Bar: 3
    Prompt: Welcome letters
    Action: Run Report Form WELCOME.frm
    Command Options:
    FOR MONTH(StartDate) = MONTH(DATE())
    .AND.YEAR(StartDate) = YEAR(DATE())
    Print mode: Send to default printer
    Set Order to:  ZIP
----------------------------------------------------------------
```

If any options in your application are not working as expected, perhaps the first place you should check is the printed documentation to see what the action is doing. Then you can return to the Applications Generator and make changes if necessary.

RETURNING TO THE APPLICATIONS GENERATOR

When you are ready to modify your application, follow these steps to return to the Applications Generator:

1. Highlight the application name in Application panel of the Control Center.

2. Press ⬅ and select Modify Application from the dialog box.

When you get back to the application design screen, you can select a particular menu to work with by selecting the type of object from the

Design pull-down menu (for example, Horizontal Bar Menu or Pop-Up Menu) and then the name of the object you wish to work with from the submenu that appears (for example, MEMPRINT).

As discussed previously, you can resize or move the menu using the Size and Move keys. You can delete options by pressing Ctrl-Y and insert options pressing Ctrl-N. (If the frame is already tightened around the menu options, you'll need to expand it to make room for the insertion.)

To change all or any part of an action assigned to a menu option, highlight the menu option and select Change Action from the Item pull-down menu. The action that is currently assigned to the menu option will be highlighted in all submenus. You can keep or change the current action at any level (that is, on any submenu).

SAVING YOUR CHANGES

It's important to remember that any changes you make to an application will *not* be reflected in the actual application until you save all those changes and regenerate the entire application. Therefore, any time that you make a change to an application, you should follow these exact steps before leaving the Application Generator design screen:

1. Select Clear Work Surface from the Menu, Batch, or Application pull-down menu.

2. When prompted, select Save Changes.

3. Choose Select Template from the Generate pull-down menu and make sure MENU.GEN is in use.

4. Select Begin Generating from the Generate pull-down menu.

5. Enter **Y** when you are asked whether you want to overwrite the existing application.

6. If you want to regenerate the documentation, choose Select Template and use DOCUMENT.GEN.

7. Select Begin Generating from the Generate menu.

8. Enter **Y** when you are asked whether you want to overwrite the existing documentation.

9. Select Save all Changes and Exit from the Exit pull-down menu.

REFINING THE MEMBERSHIP APPLICATION

When we created the membership application, we did not add help screens or message line prompts. If you wish to add some of these now, highlight MEMMGR in the Application panel of the Control Center, press ◄──┘, and select Modify Application.

ADDING MESSAGE LINE PROMPTS

Currently, the application always displays the message line prompt "Position: ← → ↓ ↑ Select: ◄──┘ Help: F1." You can replace this default prompt with your own prompt. In fact, you can assign a different message line prompt to each menu option in your application to provide further instructions or information about each option to your user. (The message line prompt appears when the menu option is highlighted.)

To add message line prompts, follow these general steps (this example uses the Add New Members option from the Maintain menu):

1. Select Pop-Up Menu from the Design pull-down menu.

2. Select MEMMAINT.

3. Highlight Add New Members.

4. Select Assign Message Line Prompt from the Item pull-down menu.

5. Type the message line prompt **Add new members to the membership database** and press ◄──┘.

You can press PgDn to scroll to the next item and then add a message line to that menu prompt. After assigning message lines to all items, select Put Away Current Menu from the Menu pull-down menu and Save Changes from the dialog box.

You may want to repeat the preceding steps for each menu and menu option in the application, substituting appropriate text. You can make up your own message line prompt for each menu option.

ADDING CUSTOM HELP SCREENS

You can also add a custom help screen to each menu option, which the user will see when he or she presses F1 when the option is highlighted. To add custom help screens to your application, use the same basic steps as for adding message line prompts, but rather than selecting Assign Message Line Prompt from the Item pull-down menu, select Write Help Text. You'll be given an entire screenful of space in which to type your help text. (Press Ctrl-End when you are done.) Again, remember to select Put Away Current Menu and Save Changes after adding help screens.

Don't forget to regenerate the entire application after adding message line prompts and help screens.

TIPS ON USING THE MEMBERSHIP APPLICATION

If you have actual data to store in the membership database, delete the example records by selecting Browse All Members from the application Maintain pull-down menu. Mark each record for deletion using Ctrl-U and exit from the browse screen. Then select Purge Marked Records from the Update pull-down menu.

Next, type at least some portion of your real data. When you start using the membership system with real data, keep in mind a few points:

- When you first run the application, select Change System Date from the Utilities menu and correct the current system date if necessary.

- Make a habit of always printing monthly letters on the same day each month (preferably the last day of the month).

- If for some reason you miss a month and want to print the previous month's letters in the current month, change the system date to the month that you are printing for. For example, if you don't get around to printing February's letters until March 2, change the system date to February 28, so that the application behaves as though it were still February. Be sure to restore the correct system date when you are done.

- Before printing any monthly letters, always perform all the operations on the Update menu in the order they are presented. That is, update the month's memberships, mark the expired memberships, and then purge the marked records. This will ensure that your mailing is based on current, accurate data.

- Make a habit of backing up the database to the disk in drive A at least once a month, using the Back Up Database to Drive A option on the Utilities pull-down menu. The best time to make this backup copy is after you print monthly letters, when the database is thoroughly up to date.

- You can designate renewed memberships by placing T in the RENEWED field when using the Browse All Members option on the Maintain pull-down menu. However, don't change the expiration date if you do so. The next time you select Update This Month's Renewals from the Update menu, the expiration date will be extended by one year (so long as the RENEWED field still contains .T.).

If you were previously using a manual technique to manage your membership records, you may want to use both the manual technique and the membership application for a few months to make sure the application is performing the way you want it to. This is called running the application in parallel with the existing system and is one of the most common techniques used to test all types of applications.

Adding
Power with
dBASE IV
Commands

Fast Track

To store "scratchpad" data in temporary memory variables,   586
use the STORE command, or type a variable name followed by
an equal (=) sign and a value to store in the memory variable.
For example, both the commands STORE 10 TO Age and
Age = 10 store the number 10 in a memory variable named Age.

To see the names, data types, and contents   588
of all current memory variables, enter the command **DIS-
PLAY MEMORY** at the dot prompt.

To get quick help with the syntax and options of a command,   589
type the command **HELP** at the dot prompt, type the com-
mand you want help with, and press the ◄┘ key.

A dBASE IV command file, or program,   592
lets you store a series of commands in a file. Later, when you
execute the command file, each command will be executed, one
after the other, in the order you entered them.

To create a dBASE IV command file,   592
enter the command **MODIFY COMMAND** <file name> at
the dot prompt (replacing <file name> with a valid DOS file
name). When the editor appears, type the commands that you
want the command file to perform.

To run a completed command file,   593
enter the command **DO** <file name>, replacing <file name>
with the name of the command file that you want to run.

AT THIS POINT, YOU HAVE EXPERIENCE WITH ALL six panels in the Control Center and with each associated design screen: the reports design screen, the applications design screen, and so on. For many of you, the material covered in the preceding chapters will be sufficient to handle all of your database management tasks.

However, as you gain experience using the Control Center, design screens, and Applications Generator, you may find that you need more power and flexibility to achieve some goal. This is particularly true if you want to develop large, complex business applications for big jobs like inventory management or accounts payable and receivable. When you need that added power and flexibility, it is available in the dBASE IV *programming language.*

THE dBASE IV
PROGRAMMING LANGUAGE

The dBASE IV programming language is the program's most advanced and powerful feature. The programming language consists of *commands* that tell dBASE specific tasks to perform and functions (some of which you used in Chapter 12). Every action dBASE performs—including actions that you initiate from the Control Center, design screens, and pull-down menus—is actually handled by a dBASE command.

In most cases, the dBASE IV command used to perform an action is invisible to you. dBASE intentionally "hides" the command or commands involved in performing operations because many people don't really want, or need, to know what's going on "behind the scenes." In this respect, dBASE is no different from machines such as televisions and automobiles that we use every day. Almost everyone can use these machines, but very few people can explain exactly how they work, and even fewer can actually build a car or television from scratch.

When you are using dBASE IV, however, sometimes you can see what's going on behind the scenes. For example, in the previous chapter, after you designed the membership application and selected

Begin Generating from the Generate pull-down menu, you saw a lot of code whiz by on the screen. You were watching dBASE IV convert your application design into a series of programming language commands. When you run your completed application, dBASE IV uses that series of commands to actually display the menus and perform the actions that you specified while designing the application.

We'll look at this relationship between the Control Center, the design screens, and the programming language more closely later in this chapter. For now, just keep in mind that the Control Center and design screens are an *alternative* to the programming language and are provided as a convenience. Everything you do at the Control Center or on a design screen is automatically converted into a dBASE IV command, usually without your realizing it.

Now let's get a little hands-on practice using dBASE IV commands directly at the dot prompt, outside of the Control Center. Some of the commands that you will enter will perform operations identical to those you can perform by making selections from the Control Center. Don't let this confuse you. There is no particular rule that says you must use the Control Center in one situation and a command in another. In many situations, the Control Center and programming commands are simply alternative ways to do the same thing. The only reason we use commands rather than the Control Center in this chapter is because commands are the topic at hand.

USING COMMANDS INTERACTIVELY

You can enter most dBASE IV commands directly at the dot prompt and get immediate results. (A few commands work only when used in dBASE IV programs, as discussed later. If you enter one of these commands at the dot prompt, dBASE IV will remind you of this.)

If you'd like to try some commands, log on to the \DBASE directory (the one you used in Chapters 1 through 15 in this book) before you start dBASE. If dBASE IV is already running and you are not logged on to the \DBASE directory, select DOS Utilities from the Tools pull-down menu above the Control Center. Then select Set

Default Drive/Directory from the DOS pull-down menu. If necessary, enter **C:\DBASE** as the drive and directory, press ←, and select Exit to Control Center from the Exit pull-down menu.

When you get to the \DBASE directory, you should see the LEARN catalog in the Control Center. To get to the dot prompt from the dBASE IV Control Center, you can use either of the following techniques:

- Press Menu (F10) and select Exit to Dot Prompt from the Exit pull-down menu.

- Press Esc and select Yes from the dialog box that appears.

When you get to the dot prompt, you'll see only the status bar at the bottom of the screen and a period (dot) with the cursor blinking to the right. You can type any valid dBASE IV command, followed by ←, whenever you see the dot prompt. Try some sample dBASE IV commands to get a feel for the way commands work.

OPENING A DATABASE FILE

The dBASE IV USE command opens a database file. For example, to open the CUSTLIST database, you enter the command

    USE CustList

You can use any combination of upper- and lowercase letters in a command. This book presents commands in uppercase letters and information that the command uses (such as the file name CustList in the preceding example) in lowercase or mixed-case letters.

After you enter the USE CustList command, you'll see the dot prompt again (not much appears to have happened, but the CUSTLIST database is indeed open, as you'll see momentarily). If you made an error while typing the command, something else will happen, as discussed next.

HANDLING ERRORS

If you make a mistake while typing a command, you can use the Backspace key to make changes (before you press ←). If you enter a command that dBASE cannot process, you'll see a dialog box with an error message that briefly describes the problem and the command you entered and presents the options Cancel, Edit, and Help.

For example, if you enter the command **US CustList** (instead of USE CustList), dBASE displays an error dialog box with the error message ''*** Unrecognized command verb:'' (the first word in a dBASE IV command is the *verb,* and the error message is telling you that dBASE IV does not recognize US as a valid command verb). Figure 17.1 shows the error dialog box.

After the error dialog box appears, you can select Cancel to completely cancel the request and return to the dot prompt. If you select Edit, the cursor will return to the end of the faulty command, and you can use the ←, →, and other standard dBASE IV editing keys to make changes. After making changes, press ◄┘ to reenter the command. If you aren't sure what an error message means or don't know how to correct an error, select Help and you'll be taken to the dBASE IV help system.

NOTE

You can also reenter or edit a previous dot-prompt command by pressing ↑ and ↓ at the dot prompt to scroll through the last ten commands entered. You can change any command with the Backspace and arrow keys and reenter the command by pressing ◄┘.

THE LIST COMMAND

To verify that the CustList database is now open, you can use the LIST command to view the records in the file. You can limit the

Figure 17.1: A sample error dialog box

display to specific fields if you wish. For example, if you now enter the command

LIST LastName, FirstName, Company

and then press ←, you'll see data from the CUSTLIST database on your screen, as in Figure 17.2.

RETURNING TO THE CONTROL CENTER

You can leave the dot prompt and return to the Control Center at any time by using the ASSIST command. Enter the command

ASSIST

(remembering to press ←), and you'll be returned to the Control Center. You will notice that CUSTLIST is above the line in the Data panel, indicating that that database is still open (because of the USE CustList command you entered at the dot prompt).

WHY TWO MODES?

Many dBASE IV commands perform exactly the same functions as options in the Control Center. You may be wondering why

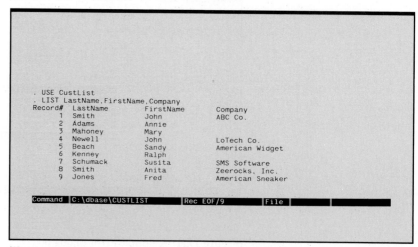

Figure 17.2: Results of entering the LIST command

dBASE offers two modes—Control Center and dot prompt—to perform the same operations.

The answer to this question lies partly in dBASE IV's history. The first version of dBASE, dBASE II, offered only the dot-prompt mode for interacting with dBASE (there was no Control Center). The Control Center was added to dBASE IV simply because it is easier to select options from menus than it is to memorize and type commands. But the Control Center provides access to only the most essential dBASE IV capabilities.

Again, for the most common uses of dBASE, the essential capabilities are enough, and you may never need to use commands or the dot prompt. But if you do begin to develop large, complex business applications, the dot-prompt and programming language commands will let you take advantage of more advanced dBASE IV capabilities.

dBASE IV: THE CALCULATOR

One particularly handy feature of the dot prompt is that it allows you to get immediate answers to questions. You can use the ? command to display information or the results of a calculation. You can think of ? as a kind of PRINT command or WHAT IS? command.

For example, leave the Control Center now to get to the dot prompt. Then type the command

    ? 50*50

and press ←┘. dBASE displays the results of 50 times 50, which is 2500.

Suppose you need to find the cube root of the number 127. You can ask dBASE for the result of raising 127 to the power (1/3) by entering the command

    ? 127^(1/3)

dBASE responds with the answer: 5.03.

You can use any dBASE function with the ? command. For example, to find the square root of 81, you can enter the command

    ? SQRT(81)

and dBASE will respond with the answer: 9.

USING MEMORY VARIABLES

Up to this point, you've stored data in database files on disk. When programming, you will often want to store data temporarily in RAM (the computer's random-access memory). You can use RAM as a scratchpad for temporarily storing data that you want to use for only a short time. (Programming examples presented later demonstrate the power of storing data in RAM.)

You store temporary data in RAM through *memory variables* (also called *MemVars,* or *variables*). There are two ways to store data in memory variables: by using the STORE command or by using the equal (=) sign in an expression, with the variable name on the left and the value to store on the right. For example, if you enter the command

```
STORE 150000 TO Principal
```

a memory variable named Principal will be created containing the number 150,000. To verify that the variable exists, you can enter the command

```
? Principal
```

and dBASE will display 150000.

To try the other method for storing data in variables, enter the command

```
APR = 9.75
```

Again, if you then enter the command

```
? APR
```

you'll see that this variable now exists and contains the number 9.75.

Enter the command

```
Years = 30
```

and press ◄┘. Now suppose you want to know what the monthly payment on a loan with the principal, interest rate, and term (years) you've entered would be. You can use the PAYMENT( ) function with the ? command to find the result. Remember, though, that you must divide the annual interest rate by 1200 to convert it to the

The annual interest rate must be divided by 1200 because the percentage value, 9.75, must be divided by 100 to produce the decimal value, 0.975, before the annual rate is divided by 12 to produce the monthly rate, 0.813.

monthly interest rate and multiply the years by 12 to determine the number of monthly payments. Hence, you enter the command

```
? PAYMENT(Principal,APR/1200,Years*12)
```

The result is 1288.73.

MEMORY VARIABLE DATA TYPES

Just like the data that you store in databases, memory variables store different data types. dBASE determines the data type by the delimiters you use in the command. For example, Principal, APR, and Years in the preceding examples are all Numeric data types because no delimiters were used when storing data.

To store Character data, surround the value being stored with quotation marks. For example, entering the commands

```
String1 = "Hello"
String2 = "there"
```

creates two Character memory variables, named String1 and String2. If you then enter the command

```
? String1,String2
```

dBASE displays the result: Hello there.

To enter variables of the Date data type, use curly braces as delimiters. For example, enter the following two commands:

```
StDate = {01/01/91}
EndDate = {06/15/91}
```

StDate and EndDate are now memory variables that contain dates.

To determine the number of days between StDate and EndDate, subtract the earlier date from the later date by entering the command

```
? EndDate – StDate
```

dBASE displays the result: 165.

The rules for memory variable names are the same as the rules for field names. A memory variable name can be up to 10 characters long, must begin with a letter, and may not contain spaces or punctuation. (But it may contain the underline (_) character.)

DISPLAYING MEMORY VARIABLES

To see a list of all memory variables currently stored in RAM, enter the command

DISPLAY MEMORY

at the dot prompt. You'll see all of the variables that you've created so far listed on the screen, as follows:

			User Memory Variables	
ENDDATE	pub	D	06/15/91	
STDATE	pub	D	01/01/91	
STRING2	pub	C	"there"	
STRING1	pub	C	"Hello"	
YEARS	pub	N	30	(30.000000000000000)
APR	pub	N	9.75	(9.7500000000000000)
PRINCIPAL	pub	N	150000	(150000.00000000000)

7 out of 500 memvars defined (and 0 array elements)

The left column lists memory variable names. The second column lists *pub*, which stands for public. (We'll discuss public and private variables later.) The third column lists the data types (D for Date, C for Character, and N for Numeric). The fourth column lists the value stored in the variable. For the Numeric data type, the fourth column shows how the contents of the variable are displayed on the screen. The fifth column shows how dBASE actually stores the value (with up to 18 decimal places of accuracy).

You can press any key to scroll through other pages of information that DISPLAY MEMORY produces. (This additional information is not relevant to us at the moment.) When you get past the last page, you'll be returned to the dot prompt.

THE LIFE OF A VARIABLE

You learned earlier that variables are used for storing temporary, or scratchpad, data. As soon as you exit dBASE IV, all memory variables are erased. (Some variables, as you'll see later in the chapter, are erased even sooner than that.) Admittedly, the preceding examples with the ? commands did little more than turn your computer and dBASE IV into an overpriced pocket calculator. But as you'll see soon, memory variables are very powerful and important tools when you start developing dBASE IV programs.

GETTING HELP WITH COMMANDS

So far in this chapter, you've used a few dBASE IV commands, including USE (to open a database file), LIST (to display database records), and ? (to display results). dBASE actually offers about 200 commands (see Appendix F).

To use a command properly, you need to use the correct *syntax*. To get some quick help with a command and to see its *syntax chart,* you can enter the command HELP at the dot prompt, followed by the name of the command in question. For example, if you enter the command

HELP LIST

dBASE will display a help screen for the LIST command, as in Figure 17.3. Note that the top portion of the help screen displays the *syntax chart,* the second paragraph describes the command, and the bottom portion of the screen describes the various options that the command supports.

```
Layout   Words   Go To   Print   Exit
||......▼1......▼..2....▼....3..▼.....4▼.......▼5......▼..6....▼...7..▼......
******************************* Loop2.PRG
SET TALK OFF
CLEAR

*------ Open the database and use LastName index.
USE CustList ORDER LastName

*---- Begin loop.
GO TOP
DO WHILE .NOT. EOF()
   ? TRIM(FirstName),LastName
   SKIP
ENDDO

?
? "All done!"



Program  C:\dbase\LOOP2              Line:1 Col:1                        Ins
```

Figure 17.3: Help screen for the LIST command

At first, the command help screen may seem more confusing than helpful. However, after you understand how syntax charts work, you'll find it tells you a lot.

SYNTAX CHARTS

The syntax chart for a command displays the components of a command and the order in which they are to be typed. dBASE uses the following symbols in a syntax chart:

[ ]   Items in square brackets are optional and can be omitted from the command.

/   One item or the other can be used, but not both.

< >   Items in angle brackets are to be replaced with specific information.

?   In some commands, the **?** can be used in place of specific information in angle brackets to see what objects are available in the current catalog (for example, **USE ?** displays a menu of database file names).

Following are some examples of the specific information that you provide in place of angle brackets and how it appears in a syntax chart.

<condition>   You must enter a valid filter condition, such as **State = "CA"** or **StartDate> = {01/01/91} .AND. StartDate< = {02/28/91}**.

<expression list>   You must enter an expression, or several expressions separated by commas. The expression might be a field name, variable name, or calculation (such as **Qty∗UnitPrice**, where Qty and UnitPrice are field names from the currently open database).

<expC>   You must enter the name of a Character field, actual character data (enclosed in quotation marks), or an expression that results in the Character data type.

\<expN>	You must enter the name of a Numeric (or Float) field, actual numeric data, or an expression that results in the Numeric or Float data type.
\<expD>	You must enter the name of a Date field, an actual date enclosed in curly braces ({}), or an expression that results in the Date data type.

For example, any of the following LIST commands is valid (assuming that the CUSTLIST database is open at the moment). Note that even though the commands in the left column are broken into several lines, you must type each command as one long line next to the dot prompt.

LIST	Lists all fields and records from the current database.
LIST LastName,FirstName	Lists the LastName and FirstName fields from the current database (LastName,FirstName substitutes for \<expression list>).
LIST FIELDS LastName,FirstName	Same as the preceding command, but includes the optional component FIELDS.
LIST StartDate, StartDate + 30 OFF	Lists the StartDate field and the start date with 30 days added. Omits record numbers because the OFF option is specified.
LIST RECORD 5	Displays the fifth record in the database (RECORD 5 is used in place of \<scope>).
LIST City,State,Zip FOR State = "CA"	Lists the City, State, and Zip fields for records that have CA in the State field (State = "CA" substitutes for \<condition>).
LIST LastName, FirstName, Company TO PRINTER	Lists the LastName, FirstName, and Company fields, sending output to the printer.

☞ NOTE

If you are using a laser printer, enter the command **EJECT** at the dot prompt to eject the page.

As you can see from these examples, the LIST command offers quite a bit of flexibility, as do most dBASE IV commands. It takes some time and practice to fully master all of the commands in dBASE IV, but using the HELP command and understanding the syntax charts makes this learning experience much easier and more productive.

CREATING COMMAND FILES

A *command file*, or *program*, is a file that contains a list of commands that dBASE will execute in a series. The beauty of command files is that you can enter a few, or even hundreds of, commands into a single file and then have dBASE execute all of the commands in response to a single command by you.

You can create and edit command files using the dBASE IV editor. To get to the editor from the dot prompt, enter the command **MODIFY COMMAND** <**file name**> (where <file name> is a valid DOS file name, with no extension). For example, to create a program named Test, enter the command **MODIFY COMMAND Test** at the dot prompt.

When you get to the editor, you can type each command for your program, following each command with ◄┘ to ensure that each command is on a separate line. You can also use editing keys to make changes and corrections. The keys used to create and edit command files are identical to those you use to manage memo field data (see Table 10.1 in Chapter 10 if you need a reminder). The options on the pull-down menus are also similar to those you use when editing memo fields.

To create a sample command file now, type the commands that follow. Be sure to press ◄┘ after you type each command. Note that the commands you enter will do nothing right now, because you are just storing them in a file. The commands will be executed later when you *run* the command file.

```
CLEAR
? "Here are the names in CustList..."
USE CustList
LIST LastName,FirstName
?
? "All done!"
```

When you are done, your screen should look like Figure 17.4.

To save the command file, press Menu (F10) and select Save Changes and Exit from the Exit pull-down menu. (You can also press Ctrl-End to save a command file and leave the editor.) You'll be returned to the dot prompt. dBASE will add the extension .PRG to the file name you provide, so the command file is actually stored as TEST.PRG.

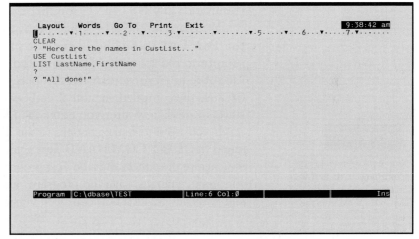

```
   Layout   Words   Go To   Print   Exit                    9:38:42 am
 |........▼.1....▼...2...▼.....3.▼.......▼........▼.5....▼...6...▼....7.▼.....
 CLEAR
 ? "Here are the names in CustList..."
 USE CustList
 LIST LastName,FirstName
 ?
 ? "All done!"




 Program  C:\dbase\TEST            Line:6 Col:0                        Ins
```

Figure 17.4: The Test command file on the dBASE IV editor screen

RUNNING A COMMAND FILE

To run an existing command file, you use the DO command, followed by the name of the command file. For example, to run the Test command file that you just created, enter this command at the dot prompt:

```
DO Test
```

dBASE will take a moment to *compile* the program (more on this in the next section). When compilation is complete, you'll see the results of the command file. First, the CLEAR command clears the screen (except for the status bar). The command ? ''Here are the names in CustList..." displays the message "Here are the names in CustList..." The command LIST LastName,FirstName displays the FirstName and LastName fields from the database. The command ? prints a blank line, and ? "All done!" displays the message "All done!"

Figure 17.5 shows how the screen looks after all the commands in the program have been executed. (The message at the top may scroll off on your screen.) Note that when dBASE finishes executing all the commands in CUSTLIST, it returns you to the dot prompt.

You can run the program as many times as you wish by entering the **DO Test** command at the dot prompt (or press ↑ at the dot prompt to redisplay the command and then press ◄─┘ to reenter it). On subsequent runs, dBASE will not need to recompile the program, because the compiled version already exists. Therefore, the program starts immediately after you enter the DO command.

If you need to make changes to the Test program, enter the command **MODIFY COMMAND Test** again at the dot prompt. You'll be returned to the editor, with the Test program displayed on the screen. If you make changes, save the program, and then rerun it, dBASE will automatically make a new compiled version of the program.

TIP

You can abbreviate any command to its first four letters. For example, MODI COMM is the same as MODIFY COMMAND.

LEVELS OF INTERACTING WITH THE COMPUTER

Now you know how to enter dBASE IV commands at the dot prompt, as well as how to store a group of commands in a command file and then execute the entire group serially using the dBASE DO command. You may be surprised to learn that the command file you created in this chapter is not the first one you've created in this book. In fact, you've created dozens of command files. Actually, dBASE has created them for you, but has done so behind the scenes or "under the hood," so to speak. Every time you design a query, a label format, a report format, or a custom form using one of the design screens, dBASE uses the information from the design screen to create a command file. The command file contains all the dBASE IV commands and functions (the code, or *source code*, that is) required

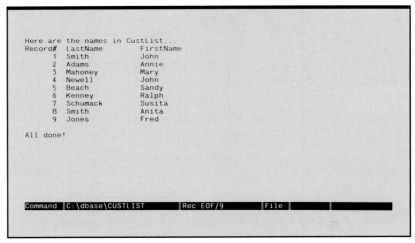

```
Here are the names in CustList...
Record#  LastName       FirstName
      1  Smith          John
      2  Adams          Annie
      3  Mahoney        Mary
      4  Newell         John
      5  Beach          Sandy
      6  Kenney         Ralph
      7  Schumack       Susita
      8  Smith          Anita
      9  Jones          Fred

All done!




Command  C:\dbase\CUSTLIST          Rec EOF/9      File
```

Figure 17.5: Results of the TEST.PRG command file

to turn your design into a series of instructions the computer can interpret and execute.

Not only does dBASE automatically create a command file for each object you create, it also creates a compiled copy of the command file that the computer can read directly. Figure 17.6 shows this series of events from the "highest" level, the Control Center, to the "lowest," the actual computer hardware.

In the first 16 chapters of this book, you worked at the highest level, the Control Center. When you created the sample command file in this chapter, you worked directly at the second level from the top. That is, you personally created a command file rather than having the Control Center do it for you.

The third level down, the *object code*, is simply too technical and abstract for most people to deal with directly. But the computer can use it and execute its instructions very quickly. (You may be wondering where DOS fits into this scheme. Suffice it to say that the object code and DOS interact in a variety of ways. But this topic is very technical and need not concern you right now.)

PEEKING UNDER THE HOOD

By taking a peek at some of the files on your hard disk, you can see for yourself that dBASE creates all these files. Assuming that

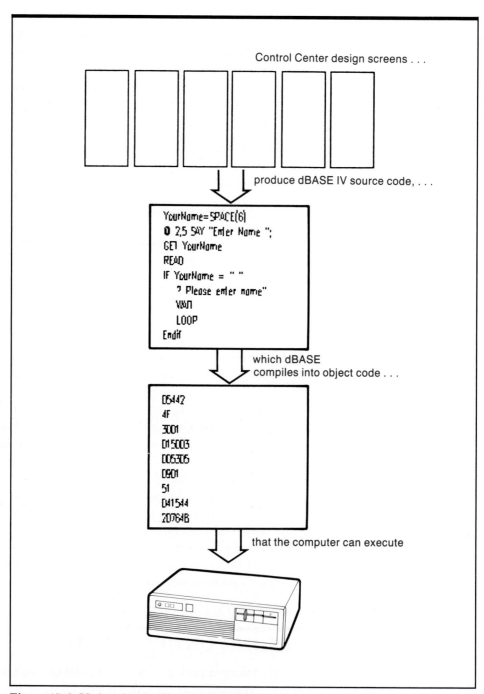

Figure 17.6: Various levels of interacting with the computer

dBASE IV is still running and you are still logged on to the \DBASE directory, you can enter the command **DIR CUSTFORM.** * to see a list of all files with the file name CUSTFORM. (The command tells dBASE to display the names of all files on the current directory that have the first name CUSTFORM and any extension.) Assuming that you created the CUSTFORM custom form in Chapter 8, you should see the following list:

```
CUSTFORM.SCR
CUSTFORM.FMT
CUSTFORM.FMO
```

The file with the .SCR extension contains information pertaining to how you designed the form on the labels design screen. The .FMT file contains the source code for displaying the screen. The .FMO file displays the compiled object code.

You can look directly at the contents of the .FMT file (that is, the source code), but don't be alarmed if its contents do not mean anything to you now. To see the source code, enter this command at the dot prompt:

```
MODIFY COMMAND CustForm.FMT
```

When the source code appears, you can use the PgUp and PgDn keys to scroll through the entire file. When you are done, press F10 and select Abandon Changes and Exit from the Exit pull-down menu to return to the dot prompt. (The .SCR and .FMO files do *not* contain code that you can read directly, so don't try using the MODIFY COMMAND editor to view their contents.)

The file name extensions for the various files created for each object are listed in Table 17.1. If you wish, you can look at the source code file for any type of object. Note that database files (those with a .DBF extension) contain only data, not code, and so there is no compiled copy of those files.

SO WHY PROGRAM?

If the dBASE IV design screens can create source code programs automatically, why should you bother creating your own dBASE IV

Table 17.1: File Name Extensions for Various Objects

	Design screen file	Source code	Object code
Queries	\<None\>	.QBE	.QBO
Labels	.LBL	.LBG	.LBO
Reports	.FRM	.FRG	.FRO
Forms	.SCR	.FMT	.FMO
Applications	.APP	.PRG	.DBO

programs? The only real reason for writing your own programs is to create a program that the design screens cannot create for you. It is really a matter of personal choice and personal need.

Again, as discussed at the beginning of this chapter, you may find the Control Center, design screens, and Applications Generator sufficient for all your data processing needs. On the other hand, if you want to develop larger and more complex applications, you probably will need to learn the programming language. The next chapter discusses some general programming techniques that you can use to build powerful and efficient programs of your own.

C H A P T E R

18

Programming
Techniques

THE PRECEDING CHAPTER INTRODUCED dBASE IV commands and showed you how to create your own command files (or programs) using the MODIFY COMMAND editor. In this chapter, you'll learn about programming *techniques* that give you precise control over what occurs when dBASE executes your command file, and thus over what happens to your data.

The techniques presented in this chapter are general and probably won't provide a quick fix for your accounts receivable, inventory management, and other data processing problems. But beginning in the next chapter, you will see these techniques used in some very practical applications that may well give you the solutions you need.

INTERACTING WITH THE USER

Command files are particularly useful for interacting with the user of a program (or application). They allow the program to ask the user questions and store the answers in memory variables. Later the program can use these answers to perform calculations, make decisions, or display information. The dBASE IV commands that you use to interact with a user are ACCEPT, INPUT, WAIT, and @.

THE ACCEPT COMMAND

NOTE

This chapter describes basic command syntax using a format similar to dBASE IV's HELP screens, as discussed in Chapter 17.

The ACCEPT command displays a prompt on the screen and waits for the user to type an answer and press ←. The user's answer is stored in a memory variable as the Character data type. The basic syntax for the ACCEPT command is

ACCEPT [<prompt>] TO <memvar>

To try out the ACCEPT command at the dot prompt, enter this command:

ACCEPT "What is your name? " TO Name

As soon as you press ← after entering the command, the screen displays the prompt "What is your name?" and waits for a response. Type your name and then press ←. To verify that the command stored your name in a memory variable called Name, enter the command

? Name

or the command:

DISPLAY MEMORY

(Normally you would use user interface commands only in a command file, but here we'll test them at the dot prompt just for demonstration. Sample command files will follow.)

THE INPUT COMMAND

The INPUT command is similar to the ACCEPT command, except that it does not automatically create a Character data type memory variable. Instead it takes a best guess as to the data type based on what the user enters. The syntax is basically the same as the ACCEPT command:

INPUT [<prompt>] TO <memvar>

To try the INPUT command at the dot prompt, enter this command:

INPUT "How old are you? " TO Age

As soon as you press ◄─┘ after entering the command, the screen displays its prompt and waits for an answer. Type your age and press the ◄─┘ key. To verify that the command worked, enter the command

? Age

or the command

DISPLAY MEMORY

THE WAIT COMMAND

The WAIT command presents a prompt and waits for a single keypress. WAIT uses the syntax

WAIT [<prompt>] [TO <memvar>]

If no prompt is provided, WAIT displays the prompt "Press any key to continue...." If the [<TO memvar>] component is omitted, the user's keystroke is not saved in a memory variable (but the command still pauses and waits for a keystroke).

To try this command, enter the following command at the dot prompt:

WAIT "Are you ready to proceed? (Y/N) " TO Ready

As soon as you press ←┘ after entering the command, the screen displays the prompt "Are you ready to proceed? (Y/N) " and waits for a keypress. You can press any key (preferably Y or N). You need not press ←┘, because WAIT expects only a single keystroke.

To verify that the command worked, enter the command **? Ready** or **DISPLAY MEMORY** at the dot prompt. Note that if you press ←┘ or the space bar, the ? Ready command will not display a letter (but the DISPLAY MEMORY command will verify that the variable exists).

THE @...SAY...GET READ COMMANDS

The @ command is the most powerful and sophisticated of the user interface commands. It provides many optional features and can be used for entering and editing memory variable and database data. The basic syntax (excluding many options) for the @ command is

@ <row>,<col> [SAY <exp>] [GET <variable/field>]

NOTE

Beyond its basic syntax, the @ command offers options too numerous to list here.

The <row> and <col> variables must be valid row and column positions on the screen. The <exp> option can be any valid dBASE expression, including a prompt enclosed in quotation marks. The <variable/field> option must be the name of an *existing* memory variable or a field in the currently open database. If the variable or field already contains data, the @ command displays the existing value.

The @...SAY...GET commands only display information on the screen. To allow the contents of the GET field or variable to be entered or changed, you must use a separate READ command beneath the @...SAY...GET commands. Rather than demonstrate this at the dot prompt, let's create a command file that demonstrates all of the user-interface commands. We'll name this command file TestUser. To get started, enter the command

MODIFY COMMAND TestUser

at the dot prompt. When you get to the editor, type the command file exactly as shown in Figure 18.1.

After creating the command file, select Save Changes and Exit from the Exit pull-down menu. To run the command file, enter the command

    DO TestUser

at the dot prompt. The screen will clear, and you'll see the prompt "What is your name?" Type your name and press ◄─┘. Next the prompt "What is your age?" appears. Type your age and press ◄─┘. Now you'll see the prompt "Enter your birthdate [/ /]." Type your birthdate in MM/DD/YY format, but do not press ◄─┘.

After filling in your birthdate, you'll see the following results (with your own name, age, and number of days displayed):

    Hello Alan
    How does it feel to be 35?
    You were born 12999 days ago!
    Press any key to view memory variables...

Press any key, and you'll see a list of all current memory variables, including those shown here:

    BIRTHDATE   priv D   03/31/55 TESTUSER (@ testuser.prg)
    USERAGE   priv N   35 (35.00000000) TESTUSER (@ testuser.prg)
    USERNAME   priv C   "Alan"   TESTUSER (@ testuser.prg)

Figure 18.1: The TestUser command file

Note that the variables created in the TestUser file are defined as *priv*, for *private*. Unlike memory variables that you create at the dot prompt, variables that are created in a command file are *private* to that command file and disappear as soon as the command file is finished running. (TestUser is actually still running at this moment, so the variables have not yet disappeared.) The TESTUSER (@ testuser.prg) columns of the display show that the memory variable was created in a program named TestUser.PRG.

You can press any key several times until DISPLAY MEMORY finishes its display. Then you'll be returned to the dot prompt. At this point, TestUser is finished running. To see that its memory variables have indeed been erased, enter the command **DISPLAY MEMORY** now. Only public memory variables (if any exist) will appear in the list of user memory variables.

Let's take a moment to discuss how this program worked. The SET TALK OFF command at the top of TestUser.PRG prevents dBASE IV extraneous messages (such as the immediate results of creating memory variables) from being displayed on the screen. Many command files use SET TALK OFF, because the extraneous messages can be distracting if they appear while a program is running. The CLEAR command clears the screen.

The ACCEPT and INPUT commands act exactly as they did at the dot prompt in earlier examples (except that these examples use different variable names). The command BirthDate = { / / } creates a Date memory variable that contains a blank date. (It is necessary to create this variable *before* using it in the @...SAY...GET command.) The command @ 10,1 SAY ''Enter your birth date '' GET BirthDate positions the cursor at the tenth row, first column of the screen. The SAY portion displays the prompt ''Enter your birth date.'' The GET BirthDate part displays the current contents of the BirthDate variable in a highlighted box on the screen.

The READ command tells dBASE to put the cursor in the highlighted box on the screen, so that the user can enter or change information in that highlighted box. When the highlighted box is filled (or the user presses ◄─┘), the READ command is done, and processing resumes with the next command.

The two ? commands each print a blank line on the screen. The command ''Hello'',UserName displays the word *Hello* followed by a space and the contents of the UserName variable. The command How does it feel to be " + STR(UserAge,2,0) + "?" displays the message "How does it feel to be" followed by the user's age and a question mark. The STR() function converts the numeric UserAge variable to a character string, so that it can be combined with the characters enclosed in quotation marks. This conversion is required when you use + in ? commands, just as it is when you use + in index expressions (as discussed in Chapter 12).

The next command, ? "You were born +"STR(DATE() – BirthDate,5,0) + " days ago!", calculates the number of days between the current date (DATE()) and the user's birthdate. The STR() function converts the result to a character string, so that it can be combined with the Character data enclosed in quotation marks in the command.

The command WAIT "Press any key to view memory variables" pauses execution, and waits for a keypress. As soon as the user presses a key to proceed, the DISPLAY MEMORY command displays all active (current) memory variables. After you scroll through the various pages of the DISPLAY MEMORY screens, the command file ends and returns control to the dot prompt.

DECISION MAKING IN COMMAND FILES

One of the most powerful capabilities of command files is their ability to make decisions "on the fly," based on user responses, data in database files, or current events. The following sample command files demonstrate this capability.

THE IF...ELSE...ENDIF COMMANDS

One of the most common set of commands for inserting a decision-making capability into a command file is IF...ELSE...ENDIF. The general syntax for this set of commands is

```
IF <condition>
    <do these commands>
```

```
[ELSE
    <do these commands>]
ENDIF
```

IF...ELSE...ENDIF can
only be used in command
files, not at the dot
prompt. You can simu-
late IF...ELSE...ENDIF
within a command by
using the IIF function
discussed in Chapter 12.

Every IF command must have exactly one ENDIF command associated with it. The ELSE portion of the command is optional. The <condition> portion of the command can be any expression that yields a true or false result (exactly like the filter conditions that you enter into Applications Generator dialog boxes to create FOR and FILTER conditions).

The <do these commands> portions within IF...ELSE...ENDIF commands can be any number of dBASE IV commands, each on a separate line. If the <condition> portion of the command is true, then all <commands> between the IF and ELSE commands are executed, and any commands between ELSE and ENDIF are ignored. If the <condition> proves false, all commands between the IF and ELSE commands are ignored, and only the commands between ELSE and ENDIF (if any exist) are executed.

To try a simple program with IF...ELSE...ENDIF commands in it, enter the command **MODIFY COMMAND TestIf1** at the dot prompt. When the editor appears, type the command file shown in Figure 18.2. When you've finished entering the program, select Save Changes and Exit from the Exit pull-down menu to save it.

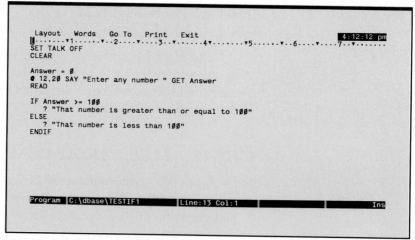

Figure 18.2: Sample TestIf1 program

To test the program, enter the command **DO TestIf1** at the dot prompt. The screen will display a prompt asking you to enter any number. Enter a number and then press ◄┘. If the number that you entered was greater than or equal to 100, the program displays the message "That number is greater than or equal to 100." If the number you entered was not greater than or equal to 100, the program displays the message, "That number is less than 100." The program ends after displaying its results and returns you to the dot prompt.

Let's see how the program works. The first commands, SET TALK OFF and CLEAR, turn off the TALK setting and clear the screen. The command Answer = 0 creates a Numeric memory variable named Answer, which contains the number zero. The command @ 12,20 SAY "Enter any number" GET Answer displays its message and the contents of the Answer variable in a highlighted box on the screen. The READ command moves the cursor into the highlighted box so the user can change the contents of the Answer variable.

After you enter a number, the command IF Answer > = 100 checks to see if the Answer variable contains a number that is greater than or equal to 100. If it does, then the command, ? "That number is greater than or equal to 100", is executed, and dBASE ignores the command between ELSE and ENDIF. If the number in the Answer variable is not greater than or equal to 100, then dBASE ignores the command between IF and ELSE and executes only the command between ELSE and ENDIF (that is, ? "That number is less than 100").

Note that the IF...ELSE...ENDIF commands must each be on a separate line in a command file. Yet, in a sense, they act like a single command because every IF must have an ENDIF command associated with it and you can only use an ELSE command between an IF and an ENDIF command. Commands with this type of structure can be thought of as programming *clauses*. For example, although there are five commands listed here, there is only one *IF clause*:

```
IF City = "San Diego"
    TaxRate = 6.75
ELSE
    TaxRate = 6.25
ENDIF
```

Let's look at a more practical example that includes two IF clauses that do not use the optional ELSE command. Figure 18.3 shows a sample command file named TestIf2.PRG that demonstrates the use of

IF...ENDIF clauses in a program similar to the TestUser command file. To create the command file, enter the command **MODIFY COMMAND TestIf2** at the dot prompt. To save some typing, select Write/ Read Text File from the Words pull-down menu, then select Read Text from File. When dBASE asks for the name of the file to insert, type Test-User.PRG and press ←⏎. You'll see a copy of the TestUser program that you created earlier.

Modify the command file as shown in Figure 18.3. (To insert a blank line, position the cursor where you want the new line to appear and press Ctrl-N. To delete a line, position the cursor to the line and press Ctrl-Y.) Save the command file after modifying it. When you get to the dot prompt, enter the command

    DO TestIf2

to run the command file.

At first, the modified program will run exactly as the TestUser program did, except that it will display the prompt "Send results to

```
SET TALK OFF
CLEAR

ACCEPT "What is your name " TO UserName
INPUT "What is your age " TO UserAge

BirthDate = (  /  /  )
@ 10,1 SAY "Enter your birth date " GET BirthDate
YesNo = "N"

@ 20,10 SAY "Send results to printer? (Y/N) " GET YesNo PICTURE "!"
READ

IF YesNo = "Y"
   SET PRINT ON
ENDIF

?
? "Hello",UserName
? "How does it feel to be "+STR(UserAge,2,0)+"?"
? "You were born "+STR(DATE()-BirthDate,5,0)+" days ago!"

IF UPPER(YesNo) = "Y"
   EJECT
   SET PRINT OFF
ENDIF
```

Figure 18.3: Sample command file with IF...ENDIF clauses printer? (Y/N) [N]" near the bottom of the screen. After filling in all of the preceding prompts, type **Y** to send results to the printer or **N** to display them on the screen only. After printing or displaying the results, dBASE returns to the dot prompt.

Let's discuss the new commands in the TestIf2 program. First, the command YesNo = ''N'' creates a memory variable named YesNo that contains the character *N*. Then the command @ 20,10 SAY Send results to printer? (Y/N) '' GET YesNo PICTURE ''!'' displays the prompt "Send results to printer? (Y/N) '' at row 20, column 10 of the screen. The PICTURE ''!'' component converts the entry in the YesNo variable to uppercase. (The PICTURE component is identical to the Template option in the forms design screen.)

After the user enters Y or N, the IF YesNo = ''Y'' command checks to see whether the user entered Y. If so, the SET PRINT ON command activates the printer. All subsequent display commands will send their results to the printer. If the user did not enter Y, dBASE ignores the SET PRINT ON command and does not send any output to the printer.

The ? commands that follow the first IF clause display their results normally (whether YesNo was entered as Y or N), because the ? commands are outside of the first IF...ENDIF clause and therefore are not affected by it. The second IF command once again checks to see if the YesNo variable contains a Y. If it does, the EJECT command ejects the page from the printer, and then the SET PRINT OFF command deactivates the printer (so that future displays are sent to the screen only).

When you test this program, be sure to try it both ways. That is, run the program once, entering **N** in response to the "Send results to printer" prompt. Then run the program again, entering **Y** in response to that prompt.

If your understanding of this command file is a little shaky, think of it this way: dBASE always executes the commands in a command file from left to right, top to bottom (in exactly the same progression that you read a page in a book). When dBASE encounters an IF command, it tests the condition to see if the result is true. If the result is true, dBASE continues executing commands until it encounters an ELSE command (if any exists). Once it encounters an ELSE command, it skims over all commands (not performing them) until it encounters ENDIF. Once it finds the ENDIF command, it forgets all about the IF condition and executes all remaining commands normally.

On the other hand, if dBASE encounters an IF command and its condition proves false, dBASE skims over all commands until it encounters an ELSE or ENDIF command. If it encounters an ELSE command, it resumes normal processing. When it encounters an ENDIF command, it forgets all about the IF condition and resumes normal processing.

THE DO CASE...ENDCASE COMMANDS

Like other "clause" commands discussed in this chapter, DO CASE...ENDCASE is valid only in command files; it cannot be used at the dot prompt.

The IF...ELSE...ENDIF clause is handy for simple either-or decisions, but some situations require that the program decide what to do based on several possibilities. In those situations, DO CASE...ENDCASE is preferable. The basic syntax for DO CASE is

```
DO CASE
    CASE <condition>
        <do these commands>
    [CASE <condition>
        <do these commands>
    [additional CASE and commands allowed]
    [OTHERWISE
        <do these commands>]
ENDCASE
```

Every DO CASE command must have exactly one ENDCASE command associated with it. You can have any number of CASE <condition> commands between DO CASE and ENDCASE. The OTHERWISE command is optional. The <condition> portion must be an expression that results in a true or false result. The <do these commands> portion can be any number of commands, each on a separate line.

Like the IF...ELSE...ENDIF commands, the DO CASE, CASE, OTHERWISE, and ENDCASE commands must be on separate lines in a command file, and also form clauses, which are called *CASE clauses*. The DO CASE command must be the first command in a CASE clause. It can be followed by any number of CASE commands and an optional OTHERWISE command. The ENDCASE command is required to complete the clause.

To see how a DO CASE...ENDCASE clause works, use the MODIFY COMMAND editor to create a program named Test-Case. Type the command file exactly as shown in Figure 18.4.

Save the command file after typing it and then run it by entering the command **DO TestCase** at the dot prompt. The screen will display the prompt, "Enter a number between 1 and 5 [0]." Type a number, and the program will display the appropriate message. For example, if you enter **1**, the program displays, "You entered a one." If you enter a number that is less than one or greater than five, the program displays the message, "I said from 1 to 5!" (You can run the program several times to try different numbers.)

Let's discuss how the program works. The Answer = 0 command creates a Numeric variable named Answer that contains a zero. The command @ 2,5 SAY "Enter a number between 1 and 5 " GET Answer PICTURE "9" displays the prompt in quotation marks and then displays the current contents of the Answer variable in a highlighted box. The PICTURE "9" component is a template (identical to the templates in the forms design screen) that displays the number as a single digit and accepts only a single numeric digit. The READ command then moves the cursor into the highlighted box and waits for the user to enter a number.

The user's answer is stored in the variable named Answer. Once dBASE receives that number, it resumes processing at the next command after READ (DO CASE in this example). It tests each CASE

```
 Layout  Words  Go To  Print  Exit                        4:16:00 pm
[.......1......▼..2....▼....3..▼....4▼......▼5......▼..6....▼....7..▼.......
SET TALK OFF
CLEAR
Answer = 0
@ 2,5 SAY "Enter a number between 1 and 5 " GET Answer PICTURE "9"
READ

DO CASE
    CASE Answer = 1
         ? "You entered a one"
    CASE Answer = 2
         ? "You entered a two"
    CASE Answer = 3
         ? "You entered a three"
    CASE Answer = 4
         ? "You entered a four"
    CASE Answer = 5
         ? "You entered a five"
    OTHERWISE
         ? "I said from 1 to 5!"
ENDCASE
Program  C:\dbase\TESTCASE          Line:20 Col:9                    Ins
```

Figure 18.4: Sample program to test DO CASE...ENDCASE

condition to see if it is true. If a CASE condition proves false, dBASE moves on to the next CASE condition. If a CASE condition proves true, dBASE executes all commands following that CASE condition, up to the next CASE condition. Then it completely ignores all remaining CASE conditions and the OTHERWISE command and resumes processing after the ENDCASE command. (In this example, there are no commands after ENDCASE, so the program just ends and returns control to the dot prompt.)

If none of the CASE conditions proves true (and *only* if none of the CASE conditions proves true), then the commands between OTHERWISE and ENDCASE are the only commands that dBASE executes. The optional OTHERWISE command must be listed beneath all preceding CASE commands.

You might think that the DO CASE...ENDCASE clause is similar to a series of stacked IF...ENDIF clauses, but it is not. There is a subtle difference, in that the DO CASE...ENDCASE clause executes only the *first* condition that proves true, whereas a series of IF...ELSE clauses executes all true conditions. To see this, note the series of commands in Figure 18.5.

In Figure 18.5, dBASE stores A-111 in the PartNumb variable and 100 in the Qty variable. The first IF command is true, as is the second, so the results of running this program are the following

```
******** Two stacked IF...ENDIF clauses.

*----- Assign values to memory variables.
PartNumb = "A-111"
Qty = 100

*----- Does PartNumb contain A-111?
IF PartNumb = "A-111"
   ? "Part number is A-111"
ENDIF

*----- Is Qty greater than 10?
IF Qty > 10
   ? "Qty is greater than 10"
ENDIF
```

Figure 18.5: Two stacked IF clauses

messages displayed on the screen:

Part number is A-111
Qty is greater than 10

Now observe the next series of commands in Figure 18.6. The result of that command file is

Part number is A-111

What happened to the second CASE statement? After all, it is true that Qty is greater than 10. But here is where the subtle difference in logic comes in. Once a CASE statement in a DO CASE...ENDCASE clause evaluates to true, all other CASE (and optional OTHERWISE) commands are completely ignored. Therefore, even though it is true the Qty is greater than 10 in Figure 18.6, dBASE never sees that CASE command, and hence it does not print any result.

Note that if none of the CASE options in a DO CASE...END-CASE clause proves true and there is no OTHERWISE alternative, the entire clause does absolutely nothing. After all the CASE conditions prove false, processing resumes normally with the first command after the ENDCASE command.

```
******************* A DO CASE...ENDCASE clause.

*----- Assign values to memory variables.
PartNumb = "A-111"
Qty = 100

DO CASE
    *----- Does PartNumb contain A-111?
    CASE PartNumb = "A-111"
        ? "Part number is A-111"

    *----- Is Qty greater than 10?
    CASE Qty > 10
        ? "Qty is greater than 10"

ENDCASE
```

Figure 18.6: A DO CASE command

STRUCTURED PROGRAMMING

Before we begin to develop more complicated command files in this chapter, we should discuss structured programming. *Structured programming* is a technique for creating programs that are more readable from a human standpoint. The techniques do not affect the way a program runs; they only affect the way the program looks to you (and whoever else sees the program source code). The two main guidelines of structured programming are

1. Use programmer comments to identify the meaning of commands.

2. Use indentations to align commands that are embedded in clauses.

PROGRAMMER COMMENTS

Programmer comments are notes to yourself that you embed in command files for future reference. They have no affect whatsoever on how the program runs and are, in fact, excluded from the compiled version of the program. There are two ways to enter comments into a command file:

- If the comment begins as the first character in a line, it must be preceded by at least one asterisk (*), the word NOTE, or two ampersands (&&).

- If the comment appears to the right of a command line, it must be preceded by two ampersands (&&).

Comments are useful for identifying the name and purpose of a program, the purpose of specific routines (or tasks) within the program, and the meaning of complex conditions. For example, Figure 18.7 shows TestIf2.PRG with comments added, as well as some blank lines to separate specific routines.

USING INDENTATIONS

You may have noticed that in all examples involving commands with multiple clauses, the commands within each clause are

```
********************************************** TestIf2.PRG
*-----------------  Sample program with IF...ENDIF clauses.

SET TALK OFF
CLEAR

*----- Get information from the user.
ACCEPT "What is your name " TO UserName
INPUT "What is your age " TO UserAge

*------- Create birth date variable, and let user fill it in.
BirthDate = ( / / )
@ 10,1 SAY "Enter your birth date " GET BirthDate

*------ Create initial YesNo variable as N, then let user change it.
YesNo = "N"
@ 20,10 SAY "Send results to printer? (Y/N) " GET YesNo PICTURE "!"
READ

*------- If user wants results printed, set printer on.
IF YesNo = "Y"
   SET PRINT ON          && Send output to printer.
ENDIF

*------- Print the results.
?
? "Hello",UserName
? "How does it feel to be "+STR(UserAge,2,0)+"?"
? "You were born "+STR(DATE()-BirthDate,5,0)+" days ago!"

*------- If the results were printed, eject the page and
*------- deactivate the printer.
IF UPPER(YesNo) = "Y"
   EJECT                 && Eject printed page.
   SET PRINT OFF         && Deactivate printer.
ENDIF
```

Figure 18.7: TestIf 2.PRG with comments added

You can use the Tab and Shift-Tab keys to indent and un-indent commands in a command file.

Some dBASE programmers believe that adding comments and indentations to a program slows it down, but this is not true.

indented. A program will run fine if you do not indent commands within clauses. However, if you leave the indentations out, it is very difficult to see how the program is structured. For example, look at the version of the TestIf 2.PRG program in Figure 18.8.

Even though the program in Figure 18.8 does *exactly* the same thing as the TestIf 2.PRG program in Figure 18.7, it is much more difficult to read and understand. The logical structure of the program is not apparent. Trying to modify or debug (remove the errors from) such a program would certainly be difficult.

Another technique you can use to add structure to your program is to use uppercase and lowercase letters consistently. For example, in

```
SET TALK OFF
CLEAR
ACCEPT "What is your name " TO UserName
INPUT "What is your age " TO UserAge
BirthDate = {  /  /  }
@ 10,1 SAY "Enter your birth date " GET BirthDate
YesNo = "N"
@ 20,10 SAY "Send results to printer? (Y/N) " GET YesNo PICTURE "!"
READ
IF YesNo = "Y"
SET PRINT ON
ENDIF
?
? "Hello",UserName
? "How does it feel to be "+STR(UserAge,2,0)+"?"
? "You were born "+STR(DATE()-BirthDate,5,0)+" days ago!"
IF UPPER(YesNo) = "Y"
EJECT
SET PRINT OFF
ENDIF
```

Figure 18.8: Unstructured version of TestIf 2.PRG

this book (and the dBASE IV manuals), all commands, functions, and command options are displayed in uppercase letters. Field names, variable names, and comments are displayed in mixed upper- and lowercase letters.

LOOPING

Looping allows a program to repeat a task as many times as necessary to complete a job. dBASE IV offers two looping commands: DO WHILE...ENDDO and SCAN...ENDSCAN.

THE DO WHILE...ENDDO COMMANDS

The DO WHILE...ENDDO clause repeats all commands between the DO WHILE and ENDDO commands, as long as the WHILE condition is true. The general syntax for DO WHILE...ENDDO is

```
DO WHILE <condition>
   <commands>
ENDDO
```

Every DO WHILE command must have exactly one ENDDO command associated with it. The <condition> component is an expression that results in a true or false result. The <commands> component is any number of commands, each on a separate line, that are all performed with each pass through the loop. If the <condition> statement is false when dBASE first encounters the DO WHILE loop, it ignores all commands between DO WHILE and ENDDO.

If <condition> is true to begin with, but never results in a false result, the loop attempts to run forever (such a structure is called an *infinite loop*). To escape from an infinite loop, you need to press the Esc key (perhaps several times) and select Cancel from the dialog box that appears.

Earlier we noted that dBASE always executes a program in the same way we read books, starting at the top and reading left to right from top to bottom. Loop commands are one exception to this top-to-bottom execution, because they can cause a series of commands to be repeated several times (as if you read to the end of this paragraph and then started at the top of the paragraph and read it again).

Figure 18.9 illustrates how a loop works. Note that the commands *between* the DO WHILE and ENDDO commands are executed, top-to-bottom, as long as the condition controlling the loop is true. As soon as the condition controlling the loop becomes false, execution resumes at the first command after the ENDDO command.

Figure 18.10 shows a sample loop that repeats two commands 15 times. To try this program, enter **MODIFY COMMAND Loop1** and type the command file exactly as shown in the figure.

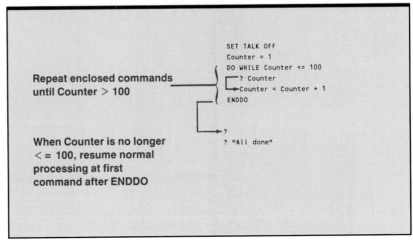

Figure 18.9: A loop causes enclosed commands to be executed several times

After creating and saving the command file, you can run it by entering the command DO Loop1 at the dot prompt. After the program runs its course, your screen will look like Figure 18.11.

Let's discuss each line in the sample program. The first two lines are comments (preceded by lots of asterisks, just to make them stand out). The SET TALK OFF and CLEAR commands turn TALK off and clear the screen.

```
   Layout   Words   Go To   Print   Exit                           4:32:57 pm
[.......▼1......▼..2....▼....3..▼.....4▼..▪..▼5......▼..6....▼....7..▼......
******************************* Loop1.PRG
*---- Test the DO WHILE...ENDDO commands.
SET TALK OFF
CLEAR

*---- Initialize Counter memory variable.
Counter = 1

*---- Begin loop.
DO WHILE Counter <= 15
    ? "Counter = ",Counter           && Display Counter
    Counter = Counter + 1            && Increment Counter by 1
ENDDO                                && Counter <= 15

?
? "All done with loop (and program)."



Program  C:\dbase\LOOP1              Line:18 Col:45                      Ins
```

Figure 18.10: Sample program with a loop

```
    Counter =                   1
    Counter =                   2
    Counter =                   3
    Counter =                   4
    Counter =                   5
    Counter =                   6
    Counter =                   7
    Counter =                   8
    Counter =                   9
    Counter =                  10
    Counter =                  11
    Counter =                  12
    Counter =                  13
    Counter =                  14
    Counter =                  15

    All done with loop (and program).



Command
```

Figure 18.11: Results of running the Loop1 program

The command Counter = 1 creates a numeric memory variable that contains the number 1. The command DO WHILE Counter < = 15 tells dBASE to repeat all commands between here and the ENDDO command as long as the Counter variable contains a number that is less than or equal to 15.

Within the loop, the command ? "Counter = ",Counter displays the message "Counter = " followed by the value that is currently stored in that variable. The command Counter = Counter + 1 increments the value of Counter by 1. For example, when the Counter variable contains the number 5, the command Counter = Counter + 1 adds 1 to that value and stores the result, 6, in the variable named Counter.

The ENDDO command marks the bottom of the loop. As soon as dBASE encounters the ENDDO command, it passes control back to the DO WHILE command, which checks to see whether the condition (Counter < = 15) is still true. If the condition is true, all commands between the DO WHILE and ENDDO are executed again. If the condition is not true, processing resumes at the first command after ENDDO. In this example, there are no commands after ENDDO, so the program ends and returns control to the dot prompt.

The text && Counter < = 15 next to the ENDDO command is a programmer comment and could be excluded. It is only a reminder to the programmer about the condition that is controlling the loop and has no effect whatsoever on the loop or the program. (The other comments preceded by && in the program also have no effect on the program.)

To get some extra practice with the DO WHILE command, you might want to try changing the number in the DO WHILE Counter < = 15 command. (Enter the command **MODIFY COMMAND Loop1** to edit the program.) For example, if you change the command to **DO WHILE Counter < = 100**, then the loop will be repeated 100 times. (If you enter a very large number and get tired of waiting for the loop to finish when you run the program, press the Esc key and select Cancel from the dialog box.)

You can set up a DO WHILE loop that repeats itself as many times as necessary to perform some operation on every record in the database. The general technique to do so is to make sure the appropriate database file is open, the record that you want to begin processing at is the current record, and the condition in the DO WHILE loop is .NOT. EOF(). EOF() is a dBASE function that returns .T. when the record pointer goes past the last record in the database.

Figure 18.12 shows a sample program that uses such as loop. (The example does basically the same thing that a simple command such as LIST TRIM(FirstName),LastName would do, but it demonstrates how the loop works nonetheless.) To create the command file, enter the command **MODIFY COMMAND Loop2** at the dot prompt, typing it exactly as shown in the figure.

After entering and saving the program, enter the command **DO Loop2** to test it. The results of running the program are shown in Figure 18.13 (but may be different on your screen if your CustList database has different records in it).

Let's discuss each command in the program. We've discussed the opening comments and SET TALK and CLEAR commands elsewhere. The command USE CustList ORDER LastName opens the CustList.DBF database (and, automatically, the CustList.MDX index file) and sets the sort order to the LastName index. (This command assumes that CustList.DBF and CustList.MDX exist on the current directory, and that an index named LastName has been created previously through the database design screen.)

The command GO TOP ensures that the record pointer starts at the top of the indexed sort order. (Actually, this command is somewhat redundant, because when you first open a database, the record pointer is automatically at the top of the database. But it's a good

Figure 18.12: Sample program with DO WHILE .NOT. EOF() loop habit to remember to position the record pointer before you start a loop that processes records.)

The command DO WHILE .NOT. EOF() tells dBASE to process all commands between itself and the ENDDO command, until the EOF() function returns .T. The command ? TRIM(FirstName), LastName prints the FirstName from the current record, with trailing blanks removed, followed by a space and the LastName. (The **,** operator automatically places a blank space between two printed Character strings.)

The command SKIP tells dBASE to skip to the next record in the database (or, if an index order is in use, to the next record in the appropriate sort order). The SKIP command is vital to a DO WHILE .NOT. EOF() loop because, without it, the loop would print the same record over and over again. The only way to terminate the loop while the program was running would be to press Esc.

The ENDDO command marks the bottom of the loop. After the record pointer passes beyond the last record in the database, processing begins at the first command beneath the ENDDO command. In this case, ? prints a blank line and ? "All done!" prints the message "All done!" Then the program ends and returns control to the dot prompt.

THE SCAN...ENDSCAN COMMANDS

You can also use the SCAN...ENDSCAN commands to set up a loop that individually processes the records in a database. The

Figure 18.13: Results of the Loop2.PRG command file

SCAN...ENDSCAN loop, however, is generally used to process specific records (those that meet a filter condition) in a database. The general syntax for SCAN...ENDSCAN is

```
SCAN [<scope>] [FOR <condition>] [WHILE <condition>]
     <commands to perform>
ENDSCAN
```

The <condition> component must be a valid expression that results in a true or false result. The <commands to perform> component can be any number of commands, each on a separate line. Exactly one ENDSCAN command is required for every SCAN command.

Figure 18.14 shows a sample SCAN...ENDSCAN loop that acts upon every record in the CustList database that has .F. in the Logical field, Paid. To create the command file, enter the command **MODIFY COMMAND TestScan** at the dot prompt, typing it exactly as shown in the figure.

After creating and saving the command file, you can run it by entering the command **DO TestScan** at the dot prompt. The results will show the first name, last name, and paid status of records that have .F. in the Paid field, as follows:

```
Annie    Adams     .F.
Ralph    Kenney    .F.
All done.
```

```
   Layout   Words   Go To   Print   Exit                           4:37:56 pm
 ▌·······▼1·······▼··2····▼····3··▼·······4▼·······▼5·······▼··6····▼····7··▼·······
 *****************************************TestScan.PRG.
 *-- Process records that have .F. in the Paid field.
 SET TALK OFF
 CLEAR

 *---------- Open database file.
 USE CustList

 *- Scan for records with .F. in the Paid field.
 SCAN FOR .NOT. Paid
        ? FirstName, LastName, Paid
 ENDSCAN

 ?
 ? "All done."




 Program  C:\dbase\TESTSCAN           Line:1 Col:1                          Ins
```

Figure 18.14: Sample program with SCAN...ENDSCAN commands

The command file uses the command USE CustList to open the CustList database (which is presumably in the current directory). SCAN automatically starts processing from the first record in the database, so there is no need to use GO TOP to ensure that the record pointer is properly positioned. The command SCAN FOR .NOT. PAID tells dBASE to look at each record in the database, starting at the top and working downward (either in the natural order or in the order imposed by the current index, if one is in use).

In this example, dBASE automatically ignores every record that has .T. in the Paid field. As soon as dBASE encounters a record with .F. (that is, a record with .NOT. Paid), it processes all commands between the SCAN and ENDSCAN commands. In this case, it simply prints the contents of the FirstName, LastName, and Paid fields.

A SKIP command is not required in a SCAN...ENDSCAN clause, because the ENDSCAN command automatically skips records as it scans the database. When SCAN...ENDSCAN encounters the end of the file, it automatically passes control to the first command beneath the ENDSCAN command. In this example, the commands are ? (to print a blank line) and ? "All done." (to print the message "All done.").

Note that, again, this example is not very practical, because you could get the same results that the SCAN...ENDSCAN loop produces with the much simpler command LIST LastName, FirstName, Paid FOR .NOT. Paid (even by entering the command directly at the dot prompt). However, for now we'll stick with simple programs that demonstrate the basics of these commands. In a real-life application, you might have many commands in a DO WHILE...ENDDO or SCAN...ENDSCAN clause that could not be duplicated with any single command.

PROGRAMS THAT CALL OTHER PROGRAMS

To run a program at the dot prompt, you enter the DO command followed by the name of a command file. Any command file that you create can also contain a DO command to run another program. As soon as dBASE encounters a DO command within a command file, it automatically executes the commands in the program that was *called by* (specified in) the DO command. When dBASE has executed all commands in the called program, processing resumes at the next command line in the calling program.

To see how programs that call other programs work, we'll create three command files: Main.PRG, Sub1.PRG, and Sub2.PRG. Main-.PRG will call Sub1.PRG, which will in turn call Sub2.PRG. Each command file will display some messages and create one memory variable. Sub2.PRG will return control to Sub1.PRG after it finishes its jobs, and Sub1.PRG will return control to Main.PRG after it finishes its jobs.

To try the command files, enter the command **MODIFY COM-MAND Main** at the dot prompt and create the Main.PRG command file as shown in Figure 18.15. Save the command file after creating it, but don't run it yet.

After creating and saving Main.PRG, enter the command **MODIFY COMMAND Sub1** at the dot prompt and create the Sub1.PRG command file as shown in Figure 18.16. Then save the command file, but don't run it yet.

After creating and saving Sub1.PRG, enter the command **MODIFY COMMAND Sub2** at the dot prompt and type the Sub2.PRG command file exactly as shown in Figure 18.17. Save the command file after typing it, but don't run it yet.

```
   Layout   Words   Go To   Print   Exit                    6:15:31 pm
   [.......▼1......▼..2...▼....3...▼....4▼......▼5......▼..6....▼...7..▼......
   *********************************** Main.PRG
   *-- Calls separate Sub1 and Sub2 command files.
   SET TALK OFF
   CLEAR

   ? "Am currently running Main.PRG. Here I will create"
   ? "a memory variable named MainVar."

   MainVar = "Created in Main.PRG"
   ?
   ? "Now I will call Sub1.PRG"

   *--------- Call the Sub1.PRG command file.
   DO Sub1
   ?
   ? "Back to me, Main.PRG, now.  Sub1 and Sub2 have finished their jobs."
   ?
   WAIT "Now press any key to see remaining memory variables."

   DISPLAY MEMORY
   Program  C:\dbase\MAIN              Line:20 Col:17
```

Figure 18.15: The Main.PRG command file

After creating and saving all three command files, run the Main-.PRG command file by entering the command **DO Main** at the dot prompt. Your screen will show the results shown in Figure 18.18.

Note that each command file displayed its results on the screen. That's because each was called by a DO command in the preceding program. Also, Sub2.PRG and Sub1.PRG both used the RETURN command to pass control back to the calling program. Study the results

```
 Layout   Words   Go To   Print   Exit                          6:10:24 pm
[.......▼1.█....▼..2....▼...3..▼......4▼.......▼5......▼..6....▼...7..▼......
***************************************** Sub1.PRG.
* ---------------- Sample command file called by Main.PRG.
?
? "        Hello.  Now I, Sub1.PRG, am running, and will"
? "        create a memory variable named Sub1Var"

Sub1Var = "I was created in Sub1.PRG"

?
? "        Now I will call Sub2.PRG"

*----------- Call Sub2.PRG
DO Sub2

?
? "        Back to me, Sub1.PRG now.  I'll just RETURN control to Main.PRG"

*--------- Return control to calling program.
RETURN
Program  C:\dbase\SUB1              Line:20 Col:12
```

Figure 18.16: The Sub1.PRG command file

```
 Layout   Words   Go To   Print   Exit                          6:11:22 pm
[.......▼1......▼..2....▼...3..▼......4▼.......▼5......▼..6█...▼...7..▼......
***************************** Sub2.PRG.
* Sample command file called by Sub1.PRG.
?
? "            Howdy howdy.  It's me, Sub2.PRG running now."
? "            I'll create a memory variable named Sub2Var"

Sub2Var = "I was created in Sub2.PRG"

?
? "            Now I will RETURN control to Sub1.PRG"

*--- Return control to calling program.
RETURN




Program  C:\dbase\SUB2              Line:16 Col:61
```

Figure 18.17: The Sub2.PRG command file

of running Main.PRG and refer to the original source code in Figures 18.15 through 18.17 to follow the exact steps that dBASE followed.

When you press any key to see all existing memory variables, you may be surprised to see that only one variable of the three created in Main.PRG, Sub1.PRG, and Sub2.PRG still exists, as shown here:

MAINVAR   priv   C   "Created in Main.PRG"   MAIN @ main.prg

What happened to the memory variables that were created in Sub1.PRG and Sub2.PRG?

As mentioned earlier, some variables have a shorter life than others. The rule of thumb is that any variable created in a command file is automatically erased when the program returns control to a calling program or to the dot prompt. Therefore, the Sub1Var and Sub2Var variables have been erased, because they were created in programs that eventually returned control to a calling program.

Press any key to scroll through the DISPLAY MEMORY screens until you get back to the dot prompt. If you then enter the command **DISPLAY MEMORY** at the dot prompt, you'll see that even the MainVar variable has been eliminated. That's because when Main.PRG ended and returned control to the dot prompt, the variable that it created, MainVar, was also erased.

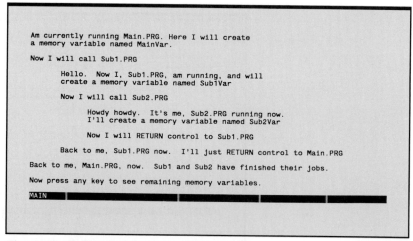

Figure 18.18: Results of running Main.PRG

PRIVATE AND PUBLIC MEMORY VARIABLES

In some situations, you may want to retain variables that were created in a called program after that program returns control to its calling program. To do so, you must declare the variables that you want to keep as public, using the PUBLIC command. A variable must be declared public before it is created.

To see how PUBLIC works, enter the command **MODIFY COMMAND Main** and add the command **PUBLIC MainVar, Sub1Var, Sub2Var** near the top of Main.PRG, as shown in Figure 18.19 (beneath the CLEAR command). This PUBLIC command declares all three memory variables created in the three separate programs as PUBLIC before any of them are created.

After making the change to Main.PRG and saving the modified command file, enter the command **DO Main** at the dot prompt to test the results. On the surface, the program will produce exactly the same results that it produced the first time you ran it. However, after you press any key to see remaining memory variables, you'll see that all three memory variables still exist, as follows:

```
SUB2VAR    pub    C    "I was created in Sub2.PRG"
SUB1VAR    pub    C    "I was created in Sub1.PRG"
MAINVAR    pub    C    "Created in Main.PRG"
```

```
   Layout   Words   Go To   Print   Exit                        6:13:36 pm
   [.......▼1......▼..2....▼....3.█▼.....4▼......▼5......▼..6....▼...7..▼......
   ************************************* Main.PRG
   *-- Calls separate Sub1 and Sub2 command files.
   SET TALK OFF
   CLEAR
   PUBLIC MainVar,Sub1Var,Sub2Var
   ? "Am currently running Main.PRG. Here I will create"
   ? "a memory variable named MainVar."

   MainVar = "Created in Main.PRG"
   ?
   ? "Now I will call Sub1.PRG"

   *--------- Call the Sub1.PRG command file.
   DO Sub1
   ?
   ? "Back to me, Main.PRG, now.  Sub1 and Sub2 have finished their jobs."
   ?
   WAIT "Now press any key to see remaining memory variables."

   DISPLAY MEMORY
   Program │C:\dbase\MAIN              │Line:5 Col:32    │        │
```

Figure 18.19: Main.PRG with PUBLIC command added

In fact, if you press any key a few times to scroll through the remaining pages of the DISPLAY MEMORY display until you get to the dot prompt and then enter the command **DISPLAY MEMORY** again, you'll see that these same three memory variables still exist.

PROCEDURES AND PARAMETERS

As you know, dBASE IV offers many commands for building programs and managing your data. But dBASE IV's commands are very general, and you may need specialized commands for your own particular work that dBASE does not offer. Even though you cannot simply create your own commands, you can create procedures (also called *subroutines*) that are almost like custom commands.

For example, dBASE IV does not offer a command to center text on the screen; that is, you cannot enter the command **CENTER "Sales Summary Report"** to automatically have the title in quotation marks centered on the screen. However, you can create a procedure named CENTER that does indeed center any title on the screen. You could then access this procedure from any command file or application or even from the dot prompt with a command such as DO Center WITH "Sales Summary Report".

Procedures are generally stored in a *procedure file,* which is separate from any command files that you create. After you create a procedure file, you need to open it with the command SET PROCEDURE TO <file name>, where <file name> is the name of the procedure. Once the procedure file is open, you can access any of its procedures at any time.

Within the procedure file, each procedure uses the general syntax

```
PROCEDURE <procedure name>
[PARAMETERS <parameter list>]
        <commands>
RETURN
```

where <procedure name> is a unique name up to eight characters long that must begin with a letter and cannot contain blank spaces or punctuation. The PARAMETERS command assigns variable

Programming Techniques **631**

names to data that is passed to the procedure. In the <parameter list> component, you list these variable names, separating each with a comma. The <commands> component can be any number of dBASE IV commands, each on a separate line. Every procedure must end with a RETURN command.

WARNING

No two procedures in the same procedure file can have the same name.

CREATING A PROCEDURE FILE

To develop a procedure file, you use the usual MODIFY COMMAND editor. Let's create a procedure file that contains a procedure similar to the Center procedure discussed earlier. We'll name the procedure file ProcLib1 (for Procedure Library 1), so at the dot prompt enter the command **MODIFY COMMAND ProcLib1**. When the editor appears, type the CENTER procedure as shown in Figure 18.20.

Note that the procedure is named Center in the PROCEDURE command. We've told dBASE that we will be passing two PARAMETERS to this procedure file, which the procedure can store in memory variables named Title and RMargin.

Within the body of the procedure, the first command Padding = SPACE((RMargin/2) – LEN(TRIM(Title))/2) calculates how many blank spaces are required to center the title and creates the appropriate number of spaces. Let's see how dBASE does

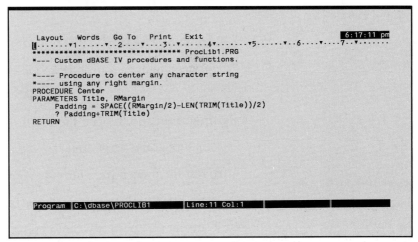

Figure 18.20: The Center procedure in the ProcLib1 file

this. Suppose that the right margin (RMargin) is 80, and the Title to be centered is initially "Sales Summary Report." First, dBASE fills in the data in place of the variable named RMargin and Title, so the expression looks like this:

```
Padding = SPACE((80/2) – LEN(TRIM("Sales Summary Report"))/2)
```

Because dBASE works from the innermost parentheses out, it next trims off any trailing blanks from the title. (In this example, however, there are no trailing blanks.) Next, the LEN() function returns the length of the title, which is 20 characters in this example, so the expression now looks like this:

```
Padding = SPACE((80/2) – 20/2)
```

Next, dBASE does the division, so the expression looks like this:

```
Padding = SPACE(40 – 10)
```

The subtraction takes place, producing 30, so the Padding variable is assigned SPACE(30)—thirty blank spaces.

The command ? Padding + TRIM(Title) prints the leading blank spaces, followed by the title with any trailing blank spaces removed. Hence, the title is printed with exactly enough leading blank spaces to center it on an 80-character-wide screen.

After typing the entire procedure, select Save Changes and Exit from the Exit pull-down menu to save it.

OPENING A PROCEDURE FILE

You need to open a procedure file before you can use any of the procedures stored in it. To open a procedure file, you use the SET PROCEDURE command. In this example, you need to enter the following command to open the ProcLib1.PRG procedure file:

```
SET PROCEDURE TO ProcLib1
```

To test the procedure, enter the command

```
DO Center WITH "Sales Summary Report",80
```

You'll see the title perfectly centered on your screen (assuming that your screen is 80 characters wide).

You can also pass data stored in memory variables to the procedure. For example, if you enter the following commands at the dot prompt (making sure to follow each with a press on the ◄┘ key), you'll see the title "Accounts Receivable Aging Report" centered on the screen:

```
CenTitle = "Accounts Receivable Aging Report"
Right = 80


DO Center WITH CenTitle,Right
```

Note that in the preceding example, the DO Center command uses different variable names than were specified in the PARAMETERS statement of the procedure. This is perfectly okay, because the PARAMETERS statement assigns its own variable names to the data passed to it. You can use the same variable names as the PARAMETERS statement if you wish, but there is no need to do so.

Now suppose you are printing reports on paper that is 130 characters wide. To center a title on the wide paper, you pass 130 as the right margin to the parameter, as follows:

```
DO Center WITH "Customer List",130
```

As you can see, the procedure offers considerable flexibility, because you can pass any character string and any right margin to it.

Another feature that adds flexibility to procedures is dBASE's treatment of memory variables always as private (local) to the current command file or procedure. Therefore, you need never worry about what memory variables are being created or changed within a procedure. After a procedure finishes its job, it erases all its own memory variables and returns control to the calling program. Any memory variables that happened to have the same names as memory variables created and used in the procedure file will retain their original values.

You can access a procedure only when the procedure file is open. Once you open a procedure file using the SET PROCEDURE command, the file stays open until you either exit dBASE IV or enter the command **CLOSE PROCEDURE** or **CLOSE ALL**. If you attempt to access a procedure that is not in a currently open procedure file, dBASE responds with the error message, "File does not exist."

MODIFYING A PROCEDURE FILE

If you need to modify a procedure file, you should first enter the command **CLOSE PROCEDURE** to close the procedure file. Then use the MODIFY COMMAND editor to make your changes. After saving the modified procedure and returning to the dot prompt, enter the SET PROCEDURE TO < file name > command to open the new, modified procedure file.

USER-DEFINED FUNCTIONS

You've seen how to create procedures that act something like custom dBASE IV commands. You can also create your own custom dBASE IV functions, called *user-defined functions* (or UDFs). For example, suppose you often need to present dates in the format *January 15, 1991,* rather than in the MM/DD/YY format that dBASE offers.

dBASE does not offer any particular function to make this conversion for you automatically. But you can create your own function to make this conversion and use it in any command, report column, custom screen, or dBASE IV program, just as you use any other dBASE IV function.

Like procedures, user-defined functions can be stored in a procedure file. The general syntax for creating a user-defined function is similar to that used to create a procedure, as shown here:

```
FUNCTION <name>
PARAMETERS <passed to function>
        <commands>
RETURN <result of function>
```

The name of the function, < name >, can be up to eight characters long, must begin with a letter, and cannot contain blank spaces or punctuation marks. The < passed to function > component assigns a memory variable name to whatever information is passed to the function. The assigned memory variable name is private to the current function and will not affect any previously defined variable that has the same name.

The < commands > component can be any series of valid dBASE IV commands, but each one must be entered on a separate

Actually, the dBASE MDY( ) function displays dates in the format *December 06, 1990,* but our function displays dates in *December 6, 1990* format.

No two functions in a procedure file can have the same name.

line. The <result of function> component specifies what should be returned to the calling command.

To see how user-defined functions work, we'll add such a function, named PropDate(), to the ProcLib1 procedure file. To do so, first enter the command **CLOSE PROCEDURE** (just to make sure that the procedure file is not still open from the previous exercise). Then enter the command **MODIFY COMMAND ProcLib1** at the dot prompt. When the procedure file appears on the screen, press the PgDn key to move the cursor to the bottom of the file. If you need to add some blank lines beneath the Center procedure, press the End key and then press ⏎ a couple of times. Type in the user-defined function as shown in Figure 18.21.

Let's discuss how the function works. The FUNCTION command assigns the name PropDate. The PARAMETERS command assigns the private variable name ThisDate to whatever date is passed to the function. The next command, Month = CMONTH (ThisDate), stores the month name (for example, June) in a variable named Month.

The command Day = LTRIM(STR(DAY(ThisDate),2,0)) converts the day of the month to a Character data type. For example, if the date being converted is 06/05/90, then DAY(ThisDate) returns the number 5, the STR( ) function converts that number to a

```
    Layout   Words   Go To   Print   Exit                        6:17:55 pm
    [.......▼1.......▼█.2...▼....3..▼.....4▼......▼5......▼.6....▼...7..▼......
    ***************************** ProcLib1.PRG
    *--- Custom dBASE IV procedures and functions.

    *---- Procedure to center any character string
    *---- using any right margin.
    PROCEDURE Center
    PARAMETERS Title, RMargin
         Padding = SPACE((RMargin/2)-LEN(TRIM(Title))/2)
         ? Padding+TRIM(Title)
    RETURN

    *--- Function to convert MM/DD/YY dates to proper format.
    FUNCTION PropDate
    PARAMETERS ThisDate
        SET TALK OFF
        Month    = CMONTH(ThisDate)
        Day      = LTRIM(STR(DAY(ThisDate),2,0))
        Year     = STR(YEAR(ThisDate),4,0)
        ThisDate = Month+" "+Day+", "+Year
    RETURN ThisDate
    Program  C:\dbase\PROCLIB1             Line:20 Col:18
```

Figure 18.21: Sample user-defined function

Character string with two spaces and no decimal places (that is, " 5"), and LTRIM trims off any leading blanks (producing "5").

The command Year = STR(YEAR(ThisDate),4,0) converts the year (for example, 1991) to a four-digit Character string with no decimal places. Because all three components have been converted to Character data, they can be combined into a single character string; the ThisDate = Month + " " + Day + ", " + Year command takes care of that step.

Note that to insert a blank space between the month and the day, the command uses + " " +, rather than a comma. This entry is necessary because a comma is allowed only in commands that *display* data (such as ?). When combining character strings to *store* them in a memory variable or field, you must use + " " + to insert a blank space.

The last command, RETURN ThisDate, returns the value stored in the ThisDate variable to the calling command.

After creating the function, select Save Changes and Exit from the Exit pull down menu. When you get back to the dot prompt, enter the command **SET PROCEDURE TO ProcLib1** to open the procedure file.

There are several ways you can use the PropDate( ) function. To see the current date translated to the new format, enter the command **? PropDate(DATE( ))**. You will see the current date expressed in the format December 31, 1991.

If the CUSTLIST database is available on the current directory, you can enter this series of commands to list all dates in their original and converted formats (be sure to press ⏎ after typing each command at the dot prompt):

```
USE CustList
```

```
LIST StartDate,PropDate(StartDate)
```

The resulting display should look something like this:

Record #	StartDate	PropDate(StartDate)
1	11/15/90	November 15, 1990
2	01/01/91	January 1, 1991
3	12/01/90	December 1, 1990
4	12/15/90	December 15, 1990
5	12/15/90	December 15, 1990
6	12/30/90	December 30, 1990

7	12/30/90	December 30, 1990
8	01/01/91	January 1, 1991
9	07/01/90	July 1, 1990
10	07/25/90	July 25, 1990

When the ProcLib1 procedure file is open, you can use the Prop-Date( ) function in any report format, label format, custom screen, or application. For example, you could add a calculated field that contains the expression PropDate(DATE()) to the top of a form letter to print the current date, in proper format, above the recipient's name and address. (The ProcLib1 format file must be open when you print the form letter that uses the PROPDATE() function.)

PROCEDURE FILE LIMITATIONS

A single procedure file can contain a maximum of 1,092 procedures and user-defined functions. However, an open procedure file is always stored in RAM (random-access memory). Therefore the real limitation on the number of procedures and user-defined functions that a procedure file can contain depends on the amount of RAM your computer has.

OPENING MULTIPLE DATABASE FILES

Chapter 13 showed you how to open and manage multiple related database files through the queries design screen. You can also do so using dBASE IV commands. However, unlike the queries design screen, which protects data in multiple related database files through ReadOnly status, commands allow you to interact freely with these databases. This is particularly handy in complex business applications because it gives you the freedom to transfer data automatically from one database file to another. (You'll see examples of this in the chapters that follow.)

You use two primary commands to open and manage multiple database files: SELECT and USE. The SELECT command allows you to open up to ten work areas, each of which contains an open database file. These work areas are lettered A through J or numbered 1 through 10. You select a work area, then use a database file in that work area.

You can experiment with these commands directly at the dot prompt. (In actual practice, you'll use them mostly in command files.) Assuming you are logged on to the \DBASE directory where the CUSTLIST.DBF and ORDERS.DBF databases are stored, enter the commands below at the dot prompt, pressing ← after each one (you won't see immediate results, but be patient):

```
SELECT A
USE Orders
SELECT B
USE CustList
```

Now that you have multiple databases open, you must use the SELECT command rather than the USE command to access a particular database. You can use either the work area number, the work area letter, or the database name with the SELECT command to access a particular work area.

As an example, try entering

```
LIST
```

When you enter this command, you'll see the contents of the *currently selected* database: CUSTLIST. To switch to the ORDERS database (making it the currently selected database), enter the command

```
SELECT Orders
```

To verify that the ORDERS database is now the currently selected database file, again enter

```
LIST
```

This time you'll see the contents of the ORDERS database. To switch back to the CUSTLIST database, making it the currently selected database, enter the command

```
SELECT CustList
```

To verify that the CUSTLIST database is now selected, enter **LIST** again.

Once you have opened multiple database files, you must avoid using the USE command to access a particular file. Let's try a brief experiment to demonstrate the reason. If you've followed along with all these steps and are currently in work area B with the CUSTLIST database opened, enter the command

```
USE Orders
```

dBASE will beep and display the error message "File already open." dBASE signals an error because it "thinks" you want to use the ORDERS database in the current work area (B), but "knows" that the ORDERS database is already open in work area A. (To remove the error message, select Cancel from the error message submenu.)

You are now ready to define a relationship between the two open database files; things are about to become much more interesting.

DEFINING RELATIONSHIPS AMONG FILES

When two or more open databases share a common field, you can use the SET RELATION command to define relationships between them. The general syntax for the SET RELATION command is SET RELATION TO <common field name> INTO <unselected database> where <common field name> is the name of the field that links the two files and <unselected database> is the name of the database that is being linked but is not currently selected. The unselected database must be indexed on the common field, and that index must be in use.

To demonstrate, let's assume that you want to see records from the ORDERS database along with customers' names, which are stored on the related CUSTLIST database. Let's start from scratch by closing all currently open databases. To do so, enter this command at the dot prompt:

```
CLOSE DATABASES
```

Now, to open the ORDERS and CUSTLIST databases and set up a relationship based on the common CUSTNO field, enter these commands:

```
SELECT A
USE Orders
SELECT B
```

```
USE CustList ORDER CustNo
SELECT Orders
SET RELATION TO CustNo INTO CustList
```

The first two commands open the ORDERS database in work area A. The next two open the CUSTLIST database and CustNo index in work area B. Because the relationship will be set from the ORDERS database into the CUSTLIST database, the CUSTNO index must be in use with the CUSTLIST database file.

The command SELECT Orders makes ORDERS the currently selected database. The SET RELATION command tells dBASE to set up a relationship from the currently selected ORDERS database INTO the CUSTLIST database based on the common field CUSTNO.

Note that ORDERS is the currently selected database because the last SELECT command in the preceding series was SELECT Orders. Assuming you have been following along through previous chapters and your ORDERS and CUSTLIST databases already contain some data, if you now enter the command

```
LIST
```

you should see whatever data you've entered into the Orders database up to this point. But suppose you want to see the customer name (that is, the COMPANY field from the CUSTLIST database) with each order as well.

Because you've opened both databases, and defined the relationship between them, you can list data from the unselected database by specifying an *alias* (the name, or work area, of the related database file), followed by a hyphen and a greater than sign (->), and then by the name of the field. For example, to see the CUSTNO and PARTNO fields from the ORDERS database and the appropriate last name and first name from the CUSTLIST database, enter the command

```
LIST CustNo,PartNo,B->FirstName,B->LastName
```

The screen will display each record from the ORDERS database, with the appropriate name from the CUSTLIST database, as shown here:

Record #	CustNo	PartNo	B->FirstName	B->LastName
1	1001	B-222	John	Smith
2	1002	B-222	Annie	Adams

3	1001	A-111	John	Smith
4	1001	C-333	John	Smith
5	1002	A-111	Annie	Adams
6	1003	A-111	Mary	Mahoney
7	1003	B-222	Mary	Mahoney
8	1004	C-333	John	Newell
9	1005	C-333	Sandy	Beach
10	1006	C-333	Ralph	Kenney

You can define relationships among up to ten databases at one time. Just remember that you can only add records to or change data in the currently selected database. In the next chapter, you will begin developing high-powered business data processing procedures and will see some practical applications of the SELECT, USE, and SET RELATION commands.

dBASE WINDOWS

NOTE

The Applications Generator also lets you create windows, as discussed in Chapter 21.

Windows are a great technique for adding professional polish to your custom programs. A window pops up on the screen, temporarily overwriting any text behind it, to display information or options. After you select an option from the window, it disappears, revealing whatever was previously displayed in that position on the screen.

You've already seen many examples of windows in your work with dBASE IV. For example, error messages, prompt boxes, and messages that present Yes/No options are all displayed in windows. In this section, you'll learn how to create, activate, and use windows. The chapters that follow will present some practical examples.

The command for defining a window is DEFINE WINDOW, which uses the basic syntax

NOTE

Beyond the basic syntax discussed here, the DEFINE WINDOW command also provides options for creating custom borders and defining colors.

```
DEFINE WINDOW <window name> FROM <row,column> TO
   <row,column> [DOUBLE/PANEL/NONE]
```

where <window name> is a name you define, which can be up to ten characters long and may not contain spaces. The first <row,column> specifies the row and column position of the window's upper-left corner and the second <row,column> specifies the row and column position of the window's lower-right corner.

You can specify a border style with one of the last options in the command: DOUBLE (for a double-line border), PANEL (for a solid border with no lines), or NONE (no border).

Note that defining a window does not automatically display the window. To make the defined window appear on the screen, you must use the command ACTIVATE WINDOW <window name>. To remove a window from the screen, use the command DEACTI-VATE WINDOW <window name>. Defined windows are stored in RAM and so take up a little memory space. To "un-define" a window, and free up the memory it uses, use the command RELEASE WINDOW <window name>. In all three commands, <window name> refers to the name used to define the window.

To try this command, we'll create a command file named TESTWIND.PRG. At the dot prompt, enter the command MOD-IFY COMMAND TestWind. When the blank editing screen appears, type the command file exactly as shown in Figure 18.22. After typing in the file, select Save Changes and Exit from the Exit pull-down menu to return to the dot prompt.

To run the program, enter the command **DO TestWind** at the dot prompt and press ←. You will see a message at the upper-left corner of the screen. Then, very quickly, you'll see the FirstName and LastName fields from the CUSTLIST database whiz by on the

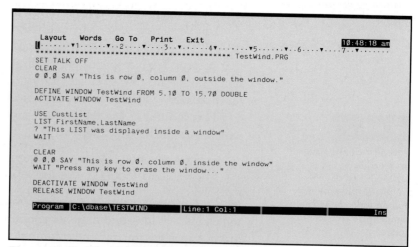

Figure 18.22: The TESTWIND.PRG command file

screen inside the window. Next, you'll see the messages "This LIST was displayed inside a window" and "Press any key to continue" displayed in the window, as shown in Figure 18.23.

After you press any key to continue, you'll see the messages "This is row zero, column 0, inside the window" and "Press any key to erase window" displayed in the window, as in Figure 18.24.

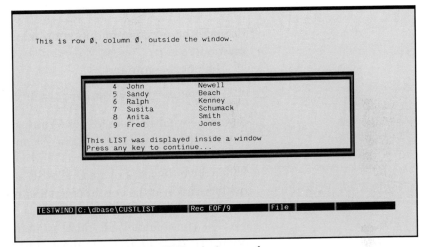

Figure 18.23: The TESTWIND window on the screen

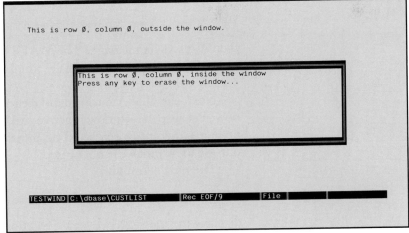

Figure 18.24: Messages displayed inside the TESTWIND window

When you press any key, the window will be erased and you will be returned to the dot prompt. Let's discuss exactly why the TESTWIND program behaves the way it does.

First, the opening commands SET TALK OFF and CLEAR turn the dBASE messages off and erase the entire screen (except for the status bar). Then the command

@ 0,0 SAY "This is row 0, column 0, outside the window."

displays the message in quotation marks at row zero, column zero, on the screen.

The next command,

DEFINE WINDOW TestWind FROM 5,10 TO 15,70 DOUBLE

defines a window named TestWind, that will extend from row 5, column 10 to row 15, column 70 on the screen. The command ACTIVATE WINDOW TestWind actually displays the window. When a window is activated, dBASE acts as though the area defined by the window is the entire screen and presents all displays within the window, as the remaining commands demonstrate.

The commands USE CustList and LIST FirstName,LastName open the CUSTLIST database and display the contents of the FirstName and LastName fields. Because the window is active, this display appears within the boundaries of the window. The command

? "This LIST was displayed inside a window"

then displays its message. The WAIT command produces the message "Press any key to continue" on the screen and waits for you to press a key.

Next, the CLEAR command clears just the contents of the window. Because the window is active, dBASE "thinks" that its boundaries are the entire screen. The message at the top of the screen, outside the window, is not erased.

The next command

@ 0,0 SAY "This is row 0, column 0, inside the window"

displays the message between quotation marks at row 0, column 0. But, once again, because dBASE "thinks" that the currently active window is the entire screen, the message actually appears at the upper-left corner of the window. The command

WAIT "Press any key to erase the window..."

displays its message on the screen, and waits for you to press any key.

After you press a key, the command DEACTIVATE WINDOW TestWind removes the window from the screen. Then the command RELEASE WINDOW TestWind removes the window from memory. Finally, the command file ends and you are returned to the dot prompt with everything back to normal.

OTHER COMMANDS

Most of the commands in this chapter have focused on programming techniques, such as user-interfacing, decision making, looping, windows, and so on. These are the basic building blocks from which you create highly sophisticated and complex dBASE IV applications.

Other commands dBASE IV offers mimic actions that you can initiate from the Control Center. You can use these commands at the dot prompt, in command files, and even while developing applications using the Applications Generator (as you'll see in Chapter 21). They allow your applications and command files to perform operations automatically that would otherwise need to be selected from options on the pull-down menus. Hence, you can develop custom programs and applications that completely bypass the Control Center. Table 18.1 lists some of these commands.

Remember, to get further information about any command, you can enter HELP <command> at the dot prompt, where <command> is a command that you want help with. In addition, the *dBASE IV Language Reference* manual that came with your dBASE IV package describes every command in detail. Rather than repeating all of that information here, the remainder of this book will demonstrate practical techniques for *using* dBASE IV commands and programming techniques for building applications.

Table 18.1: Some Useful dBASE IV Commands

Operation	Command
Activate custom form	SET FORMAT TO
Add new records	APPEND
Browse database records	BROWSE
Calculate results	CALCULATE
Copy from a database	APPEND FROM
Copy to a new database	COPY
Create a custom form	CREATE SCREEN
Create a label format	CREATE LABEL
Create a query	CREATE QUERY
Create a report format	CREATE REPORT
Edit a record	EDIT
Exit dBASE IV	QUIT
Forward search	LOCATE or LOOKUP()
Go to a record	GOTO
Index key search	SEEK or SEEK() function
Mark records for deletion	DELETE
Modify a custom form	MODIFY FORM
Modify a label format	MODIFY LABEL
Modify a query	MODIFY QUERY
Modify a report format	MODIFY REPORT
Open a database file	USE
Order records by index	SET ORDER or USE...ORDER
Print a report	REPORT FORM
Print labels	LABEL FORM
Remove marked records	PACK
Skip records	SKIP
Substitute field values	REPLACE

C H A P T E R

19

Business
Data
Processing

Fast Track

WHEN YOU BEGIN TO DEVELOP LARGER, MORE sophisticated applications, you will undoubtedly need to use a combination of all the tools that dBASE IV offers: the design screens, the Applications Generator, and programming commands and techniques. Programming is generally required to handle complex business *data processing* needs, such as managing accounts receivable, inventory, order processing, and so forth.

For example, the forms design screen lets you design custom forms for entering data into a database, as well as for making changes to existing data. The labels and reports design screens let you create formats for printing data. These screens allow you to enter data *into* the database and get information *out of* the database. This is sufficient if you use your application only for storing and retrieving information. But large, complex business applications usually need to do quite a bit of work after data is entered and before it's printed. For example, an inventory management and accounts receivable application might have to perform all of the following steps:

- Allow orders to be entered into a database.

- Check whether enough stock exists in inventory to fulfill the order.

- When an order is fulfilled, subtract the number of items shipped from the in-stock quantity to keep the inventory up to date.

- If an order cannot be fulfilled, subtract the stock that is in inventory and place the out-of-stock items on backorder.

- Prepare an invoice.

- Keep track of accounts receivable and print monthly statements.

These steps and decisions involved in fulfilling an order are all part of the data processing component of an application. Programming is usually required to achieve these steps because programming offers the precise control needed during each step in a data processing operation.

In this chapter, we'll look at some examples of business data processing programming techniques and begin building a sophisticated business management application. Be forewarned that building such a large and sophisticated application is going to take quite an investment of time on your part and a strong working knowledge of the information in all the chapters preceding this one.

Note that if you would prefer to use the sample application without investing all the time involved in creating it, you can purchase a ready-to-run copy of the application using the order form at the back of this book.

CREATING A DIRECTORY FOR THE APPLICATION

We'll store the business management application on a subdirectory named dBASE\Business. To create this subdirectory, you need to be at the DOS level. If you are currently using dBASE IV, select Quit to DOS from the Exit pull-down menu above the Control Center. Then (assuming you are using hard disk drive C), follow these steps to create the new subdirectory:

1. Type **CD** and press ◄── to log on to the root directory.

2. Type **MD \dBASE\Business** and press ◄── to create the subdirectory.

SWITCHING TO THE NEW SUBDIRECTORY

Whenever you wish to work on or use the business management application, you must first switch to the \dBASE\Business subdirectory. To do so (before you run dBASE IV), enter the command **CD \dBASE\Business** at the DOS prompt (and press ◄──, of course). If you are already in dBASE IV and the Control Center is displayed on your screen, you can switch to the \dBASE\Business directory by following these steps:

1. Select DOS Utilities from the Tools pull-down menu.

2. Select Set Default Drive:Directory from the DOS pull-down menu.

3. Specify **\dBASE\Business** as the new subdirectory (and press ◄┘).

4. Select Exit to Control Center from the Exit pull-down menu.

RUNNING dBASE IV FROM THE SUBDIRECTORY

To run dBASE IV, enter the usual command **DBASE** at the DOS prompt. (If the error message "Bad command or file name" appears, refer to Appendix B for information about how to reconfigure your AutoExec.bat file.) When the dBASE IV Control Center appears, follow these steps to create a catalog named Business.cat:

1. Select Use a Different Catalog from the Catalog pull-down menu.

2. Select <create> from the submenu that appears.

3. Type **Business** when prompted for the catalog name and press ◄┘.

In the future, whenever you run dBASE IV from the \dBASE-\Business subdirectory, the Business catalog will appear in the Control Center automatically.

BUSINESS APPLICATION DATABASE FILES

☞ NOTE

Remember: To create a database file, you select <create> from the Data panel of the Control Center.

In this chapter, we will develop some of the general data processing procedures for the sample business application. First, however, you need to create the database files for the application. After defining the structure of each database file, select Save Changes and Exit from the Exit pull-down menu.

THE CUSTOMER DATABASE FILE

The first database file that you'll create will store customer information. We'll assume for this application that most customers are companies (though the application will also allow entries for individuals who have no company affiliation). Enter the structure of the database as shown in Figure 19.1. Note that the CustNo field is indexed (marked Y in the Index column). The descriptions in Figure 19.1 are for reference only; you cannot enter these on your screen.

When you save the database structure and are prompted for a name, assign the name **Customer**.

THE MASTER DATABASE FILE

The Master database file holds information about each item in the inventory, including current in-stock (on-hand) quantities. Figure 19.2 shows the structure of the Master database, which you can create now. Note that the PartNo field is marked Y for indexing.

After creating the structure, save it and specify **Master** as the file name.

THE ITEMSREC AND ITEMHIST DATABASE FILES

As the business receives new items from its vendors to replenish its stock, it will probably want to keep a record of these newly received items and update the in-stock quantity in the Master

```
Structure for database:  C:\DBASE\BUSINESS\CUSTOMER.DBF

Num Field Name  Type        Width  Dec  Index  Description

  1  CUSTNO     Numeric       4            Y    Customer number
  2  COMPANY    Character    25            N    Company name
  3  CONTACT    Character    25            N    Contact person
  4  ADDRESS    Character    25            N    Company address
  5  CITY       Character    20            N    City
  6  STATE      Character     2            N    State
  7  ZIP        Character    10            N    Zip code
  8  PHONE      Character    13            N    Phone numbers
  9  STARTDATE  Date          8            N    Became customer
 10  TAXRATE    Numeric       5     2      N    Tax rate, if any
 11  DISCRATE   Numeric       5     2      N    Discount rate, if any
 12  YTDCHRG    Numeric       8     2      N    Year-to-date charges
 13  YTDPMT     Numeric       8     2      N    Year-to-date payments
 14  TOTCHRG    Numeric       8     2      N    Year-to-date charges
 15  TOTPMT     Numeric       8     2      N    Year-to-date payments
 16  LASTDATE   Date          8            N    Last updated (ordered)
```

Figure 19.1: Structure of the Customer database file

```
Structure for database: C:\DBASE\BUSINESS\MASTER.DBF

Num  Field Name   Type        Width  Dec  Index  Description

 1   PARTNO       Character      5           Y    Part number
 2   PARTNAME     Character     20           N    Part name
 3   CATEGORY     Character     10           N    Category
 4   INSTOCK      Numeric        4           N    In-stock (on-hand) quantity
 5   REORDER      Numeric        4           N    Reorder point
 6   PURCOST      Numeric        8     2     N    Purchase cost
 7   SELPRICE     Numeric        8     2     N    Selling price
 8   TAXABLE      Logical        1           N    Taxable?
 9   VENDOR       Character      8           N    Vendor name or code
10   VENDITEMNO   Character      8           N    Vendor's reorder number
11   LOCATION     Character     10           N    Storage location
12   LASTUPDATE   Date           8           N    Date of most recent activity
```

Figure 19.2: Structure of the Master database file

database file. The database file that keeps track of purchases (items received) is named **ItemsRec**.

The business application will initially store records of newly received items in the ItemsRec file. After it automatically updates the in-stock quantities (a procedure called *posting*), it will move the records to a separate database file named **ItemHist** (for item history). The ItemHist file has exactly the same structure as the ItemsRec file. The structure for both files is shown in Figure 19.3.

THE ORDERS AND ORDHIST DATABASE FILES

As the business sells items and accepts orders, it needs to keep track of all transactions, prepare invoices, and update the Master inventory

```
Structure for database: C:\DBASE\BUSINESS\ITEMSREC.DBF

Num  Field Name   Type        Width  Dec  Index  Description
 1   PARTNO       Character      5           Y    Part number
 2   QTY_RECVD    Numeric        3           N    Quantity received
 3   PRICE        Numeric        8     2     N    Purchase cost
 4   DATERECVD    Date           8           N    Date received
```

Figure 19.3: Structure of the ItemsRec and ItemHist database files database in-stock quantities. Initially, orders will be stored in a database named **Orders**. After an order is fulfilled, the application will move it to a file named **OrdHist** to prevent the Orders database from becoming excessively large and slowing down the whole process.

The Orders and OrdHist databases use exactly the same structures, shown in Figure 19.4. Note that the Invoice, CustNo, and PartNo fields are all indexed.

THE TRANSACT DATABASE FILE

The business application also keeps track of financial transactions to help manage accounts receivable. These are stored in a database file named **Transact**, which you should create with the structure shown in Figure 19.5. Notice that the Invoice and CustNo fields are indexed.

The application will also use a history file for old transactions, named TranHist. In addition, it will use some temporary databases to perform some aspects of the data processing. However, the application itself will create these files automatically, so you need not be concerned with them just now.

After you have created all the database files, the Data panel in the Control Center on your screen should show the names of all seven database files: Customer, ItemHist, ItemsRec, Master, Orders, OrdHist, and Transact.

```
Structure for database: C:\DBASE\BUSINESS\ORDERS.DBF


Num   Field Name   Type        Width   Dec   Index   Description
 1    INVOICE      Numeric       6             Y      Invoice number
 2    CUSTNO       Numeric       4             Y      Customer number
 3    PARTNO       Character     5             Y      Part number
 4    QTYORDERED   Numeric       3             N      Quantity ordered
 5    UNITPRICE    Numeric       8      2      N      Unit price
 6    DISCRATE     Numeric       5      2      N      Discount rate
 7    TAXRATE      Numeric       5      2      N      Tax rate
 8    SHIPPING     Numeric       8      2      N      Shipping cost
 9    ORDATE       Date          8             N      Date ordered
10    QTYSHIPPED   Numeric       3             N      Quantity shipped
11    BACKORDQTY   Numeric       3             N      Quantity backordered
12    ORDTOTAL     Numeric       8      2      N      Total order
13    CUSTPONUMB   Character    12             N      Customer P.O. number
14    INVPOSTED    Logical       1             N      Posted to inventory yet?
15    ARPOSTED     Logical       1             N      Posted to A/R yet?
```

Figure 19.4: Structure of the Orders and OrdHist database files.

```
Structure for database: C:\DBASE\BUSINESS\TRANSACT.DBF

Num Field Name  Type       Width  Dec  Index  Description
  1  INVOICE    Numeric      6           Y     Invoice number
  2  CUSTNO     Numeric      4           Y     Customer number
  3  ORDATE     Date         8           N     Order date
  4  ORDTOTAL   Numeric      9      2    N     Order total
  5  DATEPAID   Date         8           N     Date paid
  6  AMTPAID    Numeric      8      2    N     Amount paid
  7  REMARKS    Character   30           N     Remarks (reference)
  8  CUSTPOSTED Logical      1           N     Posted to customer balance?
  9  PRINTED    Logical      1           N     Printed on statement?
```

Figure 19.5: Structure of the Transact database file

THE BUSINESS
APPLICATION PROCEDURES

We will store all of the data processing components of the business application that we are building in a procedure file named BusProcs.prg. As you may recall, a procedure file is a collection of procedures and user-defined functions that you create yourself. We'll begin building the procedure file, named BusProcs.prg, now.

NUMBERING
CUSTOMERS AUTOMATICALLY

In the business application that we are developing, each customer must have a unique customer number, so that orders and invoices in the Orders and Transact files can be related to a specific customer. Rather than leaving the responsibility of ensuring that each customer has a unique number to the user of the application, we will develop a procedure that automatically assigns customer numbers, starting with number 1001.

NOTE

In this chapter, dBASE IV commands and functions are presented in uppercase letters; and field names, variable names, and file names in mixed uppercase and lowercase letters. You can, however, use any combination of uppercase and lowercase letters that you choose.

Before we actually create the procedure, let's map out the steps using a technique called *pseudocode*. Pseudocode describes the steps, in plain English, that must be performed to accomplish a goal. Then you can use the pseudocode as a guide to developing the actual procedure. Here is the pseudocode for assigning customer numbers to records in the Customer database:

```
Open the Customer database
Find the largest existing customer number
If the largest current number is zero, use 1000 instead
Add 1 to largest existing customer number to
      calculate the next available customer number

Scan for records with customer number = 0
      Replace the zero with the next customer number
      Add one to increase next customer number
Continue scanning until no more customers have customer number = 0

Save all changes
```

To convert this logic into dBASE IV code, we will use several dBASE IV commands and functions. We'll use the USE command with the ORDER option to open the Customer database, with the CustNo index determining the sort order. We will also use the MAX( ) function, which returns the largest of two values. For example, MAX(10,2) returns 10 (because 10 is larger than 2).

We will also use the REPLACE command, which replaces the contents of a field in the current database file with a new value. For example, the command REPLACE CustNo WITH 1001 puts the number 1001 in the field named CustNo in the current database record.

CREATING THE AUTOCUST PROCEDURE

We will name the procedure AutoCust and store it in the BusProcs procedure file. Here are the steps to get started:

1. Get to the dot prompt by selecting Exit to Dot Prompt from the Exit pull-down menu above the Control Center.

2. Type the command **MODIFY COMMAND BusProcs** and press ◄┘.

NOTE

You need not be concerned about how many asterisks appear at the start of a program or comment so long as there is at least one.

3. Type the AutoCust procedure *exactly* as shown in Figure 19.6, remembering to press ← at the end of each line and wherever you want a blank line to appear. (The screen will scroll, when necessary, to give you room to type everything in the figure.)

4. After typing the entire procedure, being very careful not to make any mistakes, save the procedure file by selecting Save Changes and Exit from the Exit pull-down menu.

You'll now be back at the dot prompt.

Let's discuss how the procedure works. Recall that all of the lines that begin with an asterisk (*) or double ampersands (&&) are programmer comments, which are just notes for programmers such as yourself to read and for dBASE to ignore. The first actual command, PROCEDURE AutoCust, assigns the name AutoCust to the procedure.

The command USE Customer ORDER CustNo opens the Customer database file with the CustNo index controlling the sort order. Note that you can only use the ORDER option in the USE command to activate an *existing* index, not to create a new index. Recall

```
******************************** BusProcs.PRG
*--- Procedures for order entry and editing.

*************************** Assign customer numbers.
PROCEDURE AutoCust

    *------------ Open Customer Database.
    USE Customer ORDER CustNo
    GOTO BOTTOM

    *-------- 1001 is smallest possible customer number.
    Largest = MAX(1000,CustNo)
    NextCust = Largest + 1

    *-------- Fill in customer numbers.
    USE Customer   && Deactivate index before using replace.
    SCAN FOR CustNo = 0
        REPLACE CustNo WITH NextCust
        NextCust = NextCust + 1
    ENDSCAN

    *---- Done.
    CLOSE DATABASES
RETURN
```

Figure 19.6: The AutoCust procedure

that when you initially created the Customer database, you created an index of the CustNo field by placing a Y in the Index column on the database design screen, so you can specify that order in the USE command.

As you might expect, if you open the database with the records in customer-number order, the smallest customer number will be at the top and the largest customer number will be at the bottom of the database. The command GOTO BOTTOM sends the record pointer to the last record in the Customer database, which contains the largest customer number. (If the database is empty, however, the customer number will be zero.)

The next command, Largest = MAX(1000,CustNo), stores a value in a memory variable named Largest; it stores either the number 1000 or the current customer number, whichever is larger. (That way, if the database is empty, the Largest variable contains the number 1000 rather than zero.)

The next command, NextCust = Largest + 1, calculates the next available customer number by adding 1 to the Largest memory variable and storing that result in a memory variable named NextCust. That is, the NextCust memory variable now contains the next available new customer number.

WARNING

Never use the REPLACE command to replace values in a field included in the currently active index.

The next command, USE Customer, opens the Customer database *without* the CustNo index. In a moment, the procedure is going to use the REPLACE command to start filling in new customer numbers. If the CustNo index were still active during these replacements, dBASE would re-sort the database after each individual replacement, which would lead to most customer numbers not being replaced.

The next command begins a SCAN...ENDSCAN loop. The command SCAN FOR CustNo = 0 tells dBASE to look at each record in the database and stop scanning as soon as it finds a record with the customer number equal to zero. As soon as dBASE finds the first record with the customer number equal to zero, it stops scanning and processes all commands down to the ENDSCAN command.

Within the SCAN...ENDSCAN loop, the command REPLACE CustNo WITH NextCust replaces the customer number in one record with the value stored in the NextCust memory variable. Then the command NextCust = NextCust + 1 adds 1 to the NextCust variable. The ENDSCAN command moves the record pointer to the next record in the database file and passes control back to the SCAN FOR CustNo = 0 command, which looks for the next record with zero as the customer number. The loop repeats until all records with zero customer numbers have been accessed and their customer numbers replaced with the new calculated customer numbers.

When the SCAN…ENDSCAN loop is done, processing resumes with the command CLOSE DATABASES, which closes the Customer database. This command is optional, but it's always a good idea to close a database after changing it to ensure that all changes are immediately stored on disk (portions of an open database are stored in RAM, which is susceptible to power failures and other maladies). The RETURN command marks the end of the procedure.

TESTING THE AUTOCUST PROCEDURE

To test the AutoCust procedure, you first need to add a couple of customers to the Customer database file. You do not need to return to the Control Center to do so. Instead, you can take a shortcut to the edit screen by typing the following commands at the dot prompt (press ◀━┘ after typing each command):

```
USE Customer
APPEND
```

The first command opens the Customer database and the second command, APPEND, tells dBASE that you want to add (append) new records. Type two sample customers, assigning each the customer number zero. (You must actually type the zero, even though a zero already appears on the screen, because if you press ◀━┘ without entering any data, dBASE will assume you are done entering records and return you to the dot prompt. The application we develop later will use a more elegant technique.)

For the time being, you can just fill in the CustNo and Company fields of two records, as follows:

CustNo	COMPANY
0	Adam Chandler Enterprises
0	Baker International

When you are done entering records, press Ctrl-End or select Exit from the Exit pull-down menu.

NOTE

Whenever you type a command at the dot prompt, you must press ← to send the command to dBASE.

To verify that the Customer database has two new records, enter the command

```
LIST CustNo,Company
```

at the dot prompt. You should see the two company names you just added, preceded by the customer number 0.

To test the procedure, you first need to open the procedure file by entering the following command at the dot prompt:

```
SET PROCEDURE TO BusProcs
```

dBASE will take a moment to compile the procedure and then will return you to the dot prompt. To test the AutoCust procedure, enter this command at the dot prompt:

```
DO AutoCust
```

If all went well, and you did not make any mistakes along the way, you'll be returned to the dot prompt. (If you did make a mistake, it's probably either a typographical error in the BusProcs procedure file or a misspelled field name in the Customer database file.)

To verify that the AutoCust procedure did its job, reopen the Customer database and look at the customer numbers by entering the following commands at the dot prompt:

```
USE Customer
LIST CustNo,Company
```

When we integrate this procedure into the business application later, the application user will be able to add customers to the database without entering any customer numbers. As soon as the user is finished entering new customers, the AutoCust procedure will number the customers automatically.

NUMBERING INVOICES AUTOMATICALLY

In some business applications, invoice forms are filled in on paper first, and then the information is typed into the computer from the paper form. If those paper invoices contain invoice numbers, then the invoice number can be typed directly at the screen. On the other hand, if clerks enter orders directly from phone calls or mailed order forms, then there is probably no way for the clerks to determine the next available invoice number. In this case, the application needs to number the invoices automatically.

Numbering invoices is a bit trickier than numbering customers, because several separate orders might actually belong on a single invoice. For example, suppose you receive orders from two customers, and each customer orders several items. In the Orders database, the orders might appear as follows (because initially the invoice number is not known, it is just left at zero at the time the order is entered):

Invoice	CustNo	PartNo	QtyOrdered
0	1001	A-111	10
0	1001	B-222	2
0	1002	A-111	1
0	1002	B-222	5
0	1002	C-333	20

If the last-used invoice number was 333330, then the preceding orders need to be assigned the invoice numbers shown here:

Invoice	CustNo	PartNo	QtyOrdered
333331	1001	A-111	10
333331	1001	B-222	2
333332	1002	A-111	1
333332	1002	B-222	5
333332	1002	C-333	20

As you can see, even though there are five separate orders, actually only two invoice numbers are involved. (The individual orders on an invoice are often called the invoice *detail*.)

A second problem to contend with concerns how and when you assign invoice numbers. As you'll see later, outstanding orders are stored in one database (Orders), and fulfilled orders are stored in another database (OrdHist). Depending on when the invoice numbers are assigned, the last-used invoice number will be in one database or the other.

The solutions to all these problems and the order in which they must be addressed are described in the following pseudocode (note that the smallest allowable invoice number is 100001):

```
Assume largest invoice number is 100000

Use the Orders database in invoice number order
Find the largest invoice number
If greater than 100000, then use that
    value as the largest invoice number

Use the OrdHist database in invoice-number order
Find the largest invoice number
If greater than present largest value, use it
    as the largest-used invoice number

Close the databases
Calculate the next invoice number

Use the Orders database in customer-number order
Scan for records with invoice number = 0
    Note current customer number
    Replace invoice numbers for this customer
        with calculated invoice number
    Increment invoice number by 1
    Skip back to reposition record pointer
Stop scanning when no more invoice numbers equal zero

Save all new invoice numbers
```

CREATING THE AUTOINV PROCEDURE

To add the procedure, which we'll name AutoInv, to the BusProcs procedure file, first close the procedure file. Then go to the command-file editor by entering these commands at the dot prompt:

```
CLOSE PROCEDURE
MODIFY COMMAND BusProcs
```

You will see the AutoCust procedure on the screen. You want to place the new procedure beneath the existing one, so press PgDn and the ↓ key until you get to about line 26. (After the cursor gets to the bottom of the procedure file, you can press ↩ to add new blank lines.) Then type the procedure exactly as shown in Figure 19.7. After typing the procedure, select Save Changes and Exit to return to the dot prompt.

Let's see how the procedure does its job. First, the command USE Orders ORDER Invoice opens the Orders database and selects Invoice sort order. Since this command opens the Orders database with the records in invoice-number order, the smallest invoice numbers are at the top and the largest invoice numbers are at the bottom of the database.

The command GOTO BOTTOM tells dBASE to send the record pointer to the bottom of the database file, making that record the current record. (We know that the largest invoice in the database is there, because the records are in invoice-number order.) The command Largest = MAX(100000,Invoice) stores either the invoice

NOTE

In the command USE Orders ORDER Invoice, *Orders* is the name of the database file, and *ORDER* is part of the USE command.

```
*----- Assign invoice numbers to current orders.
PROCEDURE AutoInv
    *- BusMgr application uses this procedure
    *- before printing invoices.

    *----- Find largest current invoice number.
    USE Orders ORDER Invoice
    GOTO BOTTOM
    Largest=MAX(100000,Invoice)

    USE OrdHist ORDER Invoice
    GOTO BOTTOM
    Largest=MAX(Largest,Invoice)

    CLOSE DATABASES
    NextInvNo=Largest + 1      && Next invoice number.

    *---------- Assign invoice numbers.
    USE Orders ORDER CustNo
    SCAN FOR Invoice=0
        ThisCust = CustNo
        REPLACE Invoice WITH NextInvNo ;
                WHILE CustNo = ThisCust ;
                FOR Invoice = 0
        NextInvNo = NextInvNo + 1
        SKIP -1   && Back up one record before resuming scan.
    ENDSCAN
    *----------- Done
    CLOSE DATABASES
RETURN
```

Figure 19.7: The AutoInv procedure

number from the current record or the number 100000 in a memory variable named Largest. (If the Orders database is empty, the Invoice field will contain zero.)

The next two commands, USE OrdHist ORDER Invoice and GOTO BOTTOM, move the record pointer to the bottom of the OrdHist database file, which is also sorted into invoice-number order. Then the command Largest = MAX(Largest,Invoice) stores either the current invoice number or the current largest invoice number, whichever is larger, in the memory variable named Largest.

The CLOSE DATABASES command closes the OrdHist file, because we no longer need its records in this procedure. The command NextInvNo = Largest + 1 calculates the next invoice number by adding 1 to the largest invoice number and then stores that result in the memory variable named NextInvNo.

Now that the procedure has determined the next-available invoice number, it can start assigning invoice numbers to orders in the Orders database file. Let's see how it does this, using some sample data. Suppose that the Orders database contains the following data, and the NextInvNo memory variable now contains 333331.

Invoice	CustNo	PartNo	QtyOrdered
0	1001	A-111	10
0	1001	B-222	2
0	1002	A-111	1
0	1002	B-222	5
0	1002	C-333	20

NOTE

In this case, you can use an index even though a REPLACE command is operating on the database, because the index key is CustNo, but the field being replaced is Invoice.

The command USE Orders ORDER CustNo opens the Orders database file using the CustNo index (which you created when you initially structured the database). Thus, the orders are listed in customer-number order, as in the preceding sample records.

The command SCAN FOR Invoice = 0 tells dBASE to repeat all commands between this one and the ENDSCAN command until it finds no more records with zero as the invoice number. Here is what happens inside the loop.

First, the command ThisCust = CustNo stores the current customer number in a memory variable named ThisCust. For the preceding sample records, the pointer would initially start at the first record, and therefore ThisCust would contain 1001.

The next three lines are actually one command: REPLACE Invoice WITH NextInvNo WHILE CustNo = ThisCust FOR Invoice = 0. dBASE lets you break long commands like this one into separate lines with a semicolon (;) at the end of each line break. (It's a good idea to precede the semicolon with a blank space to ensure that blank spaces appear in the command where they should.)

In English, this long REPLACE command tells dBASE to replace the invoice number with the next available invoice number WHILE (as long as) the customer number does not change; FOR (but) within these customers, do not replace records that already have an invoice number. Hence, the first time through the SCAN...ENDSCAN loop, the REPLACE command replaces records with 1001 as the customer number and stops replacing as soon as it comes to a new customer number, producing the following results (the $>>$ symbol shows where the record pointer is when the REPLACE command is finished):

	Invoice	CustNo	PartNo	QtyOrdered
	333331	1001	A-111	10
	333331	1001	B-222	2
$>>$	0	1002	A-111	1
	0	1002	B-222	5
	0	1002	C-333	20

The next command, NextInvNo = NextInvNo + 1, increments the value in the NextInvNo memory variable by 1, so now Next-InvNo contains 333332. Now if we were not very careful in our planning here, we would have a problem on our hands. The ENDSCAN command automatically moves the record pointer to the next database record before resuming the scan operation, which can cause the current record to be skipped completely.

The procedure takes care of this potential problem by moving the record pointer back a record with the command SKIP − 1, which puts the record pointer where the $>>$ symbol appears:

	Invoice	CustNo	PartNo	QtyOrdered
	333331	1001	A-111	10
$>>$	333331	1001	B-222	2
	0	1002	A-111	1
	0	1002	B-222	2
	0	1002	C-333	20

Now the ENDSCAN command moves the record pointer ahead a record, and the scan operation resumes from the position marked by >>, as shown here:

	Invoice	CustNo	PartNo	QtyOrdered
	333331	1001	A-111	10
	333331	1001	B-222	2
>>	0	1002	A-111	1
	0	1002	B-222	5
	0	1002	C-333	20

On this second pass through the loop, the command ThisCust = CustNo stores the customer number 1002 in the variable named ThisCust. Then the REPLACE command replaces records with this customer number with the new invoice number, producing these results:

	Invoice	CustNo	PartNo	QtyOrdered
	333331	1001	A-111	10
	333331	1001	B-222	2
	333332	1002	A-111	1
	333332	1002	B-222	5
	333332	1002	C-333	20
>>				

TESTING THE AUTOINV PROCEDURE

To test the AutoInv procedure, you need first to put some test data in the Orders database. To do so, enter the following commands at the dot prompt (you must actually type the zero into the Invoice field, even though a zero is already displayed):

```
USE Orders
APPEND
```

Now enter some sample orders to test the procedure. For testing purposes, you need not fill in all the fields. Instead, to mimic the examples discussed earlier in this section, you need only fill in the Invoice and CustNo fields for five records, using this data:

Invoice	CustNo
0	1001
0	1001
0	1002
0	1002
0	1002

After you've filled in some sample records, press Ctrl-End to leave the edit screen and return to the dot prompt. To test the procedure, you need to open the BusProcs procedure file and run the AutoInv procedure by entering these commands at the dot prompt:

```
SET PROCEDURE TO BusProcs
DO AutoInv
```

When the procedure is complete and the dot prompt reappears, you can check the results by entering these commands:

```
USE Orders ORDER Invoice
LIST Invoice,CustNo
```

Because you have not previously entered any orders, the invoices should be numbered starting at 100001, as follows:

Invoice	CustNo
100001	1001
100001	1001
100002	1002
100002	1002
100002	1002

Of course, the actual results will depend on what you entered as sample records, but the general logic of the results should be as follows: Each group of records with identical record numbers has the same invoice number.

The business application that we develop later will use the AutoInv procedure to automatically assign invoice numbers to all new orders. If you inadvertently added a blank record to your test data and it showed up in the results of your LIST command, don't worry about it now. The business application will automatically handle such blank records.

UPDATING THE MASTER
DATABASE FROM ITEMS RECEIVED

As the business receives purchases from its vendors, it needs to record these and update the Master database in-stock quantities accordingly. To automate the updating task, you can use the dBASE IV UPDATE command. The command requires both the database file containing the information used in the update operation and the file being updated to be open simultaneously.

The general syntax for the UPDATE command is

```
UPDATE ON <common field> FROM <unselected database> REPLACE
<field name> WITH <new value>
```

where <common field> is the name of the field that relates the two databases, <unselected database> is the database that contains data used for updating, <field name> is the name of the field in the selected database that is being updated, and <new value> defines the new value for the field being updated. You can simultaneously update several fields, as you'll see in the procedure.

The only catch in performing the update operation is that dBASE has no way of knowing what records in a database have already been used in an updating procedure. Thus, you need to devise a scheme to prevent dBASE from using records in an update more than once. The business application handles this problem by moving all *posted* (that is, already updated) transactions to a file named ItemHist. Here is the pseudocode for the procedure:

```
Open the Master database in one work area
Open the ItemsRec database in another work area

Select the Master database for updating
Update by adding qty received to in-stock qty,
     replacing the last update date with the order date,
     replacing the original cost with the current cost,

Close databases to save changes

Use the ItemHist database file
Add records from the ItemsRec file
```

Use the ItemsRec file
Delete all records
Save all changes

CREATING THE ADDITEMS PROCEDURE

The procedure for updating the Master database from items received will be named AddItems. To add this procedure to the BusProcs procedure file, follow these steps:

1. Enter the command **CLOSE PROCEDURE** to close the procedure file.

2. Enter the command **MODIFY COMMAND BusProcs** to edit the procedure file.

3. Press Ctrl-PgDn and ↓ until the cursor gets to the bottom of the procedure file.

4. If necessary, press ↵ to add a blank line or two.

5. Type the procedure exactly as shown in Figure 19.8. Note that to type the arrow, as in ItemsRec->QtyRecvd, you type a hyphen (-) followed by a greater-than sign (>).

6. After typing in the procedure, select Save Changes and Exit from the Exit pull-down menu.

Let's take a moment to see how the procedure works. The first four commands open the Master database with the PartNo index in work area A and the ItemsRec and PartNo databases in work area B.

Now let's assume that the Master database contains the following records (though, of course, it may contain many more records):

PartNo	InStock	PurCost	LastUpdate
A-111	10	500.00	01/01/91
B-222	0	50.00	01/01/91

Let's also assume that the ItemsRec database contains the following records:

PartNo	QtyRecvd	Price	DateRecvd
A-111	5	0.00	01/15/91
B-222	25	75.00	01/15/91

```
*----------------- Update Master file from items received.
PROCEDURE AddItems

    *--- Close open files, then open Master and ItemsRec.
    CLOSE DATABASES
    SELECT A
    USE Master ORDER PartNo
    SELECT B
    USE ItemsRec ORDER PartNo

    *--- Perform the update.
    SELECT Master
    UPDATE ON PartNo FROM ItemsRec REPLACE ;
        InStock WITH InStock + ItemsRec->Qty_Recvd, ;
        LastUpdate WITH ItemsRec->DateRecvd, ;
        PurCost WITH ;
        IIF(ItemsRec->Price>0,ItemsRec->Price,PurCost)

    CLOSE DATABASES
    *------------ Move updated transactions to history file.
    SET SAFETY OFF
    USE ItemHist

    *-------------- Read in completed transactions.
    APPEND FROM ItemsRec

    USE ItemsRec
    ZAP
    CLOSE DATABASES
RETURN
```

Figure 19.8: The AddItems procedure

NOTE

Note that each expression in the UPDATE command is separated by a comma. The semicolons are included to break the lengthy command into separate lines.

The command SELECT Master makes the Master database the currently selected database (the one that will be updated). Notice that in the command, field names from the unselected database, ItemsRec, are all preceded with the alias and the arrow.

The UPDATE command automatically processes every record in the unselected database (ItemsRec in this case). So for each record in ItemsRec, it adds the quantity received to the current in-stock quantity (InStock WITH InStock + ItemsRec->Qty_Recvd), replaces the LastUpdate field with the date the item was received (LastUpdate WITH ItemsRec->DateRecvd), and replaces the purchase cost with the new purchase cost (PurCost WITH IIF(ItemsRec->Price>0, ItemsRec->Price, PurCost)).

In the last expression, the IIF() function makes a decision about exactly how to perform the replacement. In some situations, the person entering data into the ItemsRec file might not know the current purchase price and would therefore leave it as zero. The IIF function says, "If the price in the ItemsRec file is greater than zero (IIF(ItemsRec->Price>0), *then* use the ItemsRec->Price value in the replacement; *otherwise*, use the PurCost field for the replacement." If the latter condition proves true, then the PurCost field is simply replaced with its own existing contents, which in essence leaves its contents unchanged.

Returning now to the sample data, after the update is complete the Master database contains the following:

PartNo	InStock	PurCost	LastUpdate
A-111	15	500.00	01/15/91
B-222	25	75.00	01/15/91

The InStock quantity for part number A-111 was 10 but is now 15, because 5 of these parts were received. The purchase cost (PurCost) is still 500.00, because no new purchase cost was entered into the ItemsRec database. The LastUpdate field, which initially contained 01/01/91, now contains 01/15/91, the date that the items were received.

No parts with part number B-222 had been in stock, but now there are 25, because 25 were received. The PurCost field now contains the new purchase price, $75.00, and the LastUpdate field now contains the date 01/15/91.

Remember that the ItemsRec database still has the same records in it, so if you were to perform the update operation again, these same quantities would once again be updated to the Master file. But that would be an error. To prevent such an error, the routine moves the records from ItemsRec to the ItemHist file. Here's how.

First, the command CLOSE DATABASES closes all open databases. Then the command SET SAFETY OFF tells dBASE not to ask for permission to overwrite files or delete records while the next steps are carried out. The command USE ItemHist opens the ItemHist database file. The command APPEND FROM ItemsRec tells dBASE to read all records from the ItemsRec file into the current ItemHist file, appending the new records to the end of the database (after any existing records).

The command USE ItemsRec then opens the ItemsRec database file, and the ZAP command deletes all records from that file. After ZAP does its job, the ItemsRec database is completely empty, but its structure still exists so that you can add new records again later.

The CLOSE DATABASES command closes all open databases, and the RETURN command marks the end of the procedure. The business application will automatically run the AddItems procedure whenever the user adds new records to the ItemsRec database file, so that updates are processed automatically, and immediately.

PROCESSING ORDERS

Order processing would be a simple task if businesses always had enough products in stock to immediately fulfill every order. Unfortunately, this is not always the case, and often items have to be backordered. However, you can develop powerful and efficient routines for updating the inventory in-stock quantities and handling backorders as orders are fulfilled.

In this section we'll develop a procedure to handle orders in the Orders database file. The logic that the procedure uses is described here in pseudocode:

```
Open the Orders database and PartNo index
Open the Master database and PartNo index

Select the Orders database for making changes
Define a relation, based on part number, in the Master database

Start at top of the Orders database
Scan for records that have not been posted
    If the qty ordered is less than or equal to in-stock qty
        Qty shipped equals qty ordered
    Otherwise
        Qty shipped equals in-stock qty
        Backorder qty equals qty ordered minus qty shipped
    Endif
    Select the Master database
    Subtract qty shipped from in-stock qty
    Select the Orders database
    Flag transaction as being posted
End scanning (all records have been processed)

Application can now print invoices
```

To add the new procedure to the BusProcs procedure file, use the same techniques that you used earlier. That is, at the dot prompt enter the command **CLOSE PROCEDURE**. Then enter the command **MODIFY COMMAND BusProcs** and position the cursor beneath the existing procedures. Then type the OrdUpdat procedure, exactly as shown in Figure 19.9. Remember to save your work after you type the entire procedure.

Now let's discuss how the order updating procedure works. First, the SELECT and USE commands open both the Orders and Master databases, each with its PartNo index in use. Then the SELECT

```
*------ Determine backorder requirements, and subtract
*------ fulfilled orders from in-stock quantities.
PROCEDURE OrdUpdat

    *-- Open Master and Orders database files.
    SELECT A
    USE Orders ORDER PartNo
    SELECT B
    USE Master ORDER PartNo

    *-- Must set up relationship if not using UPDATE command.
    SELECT Orders
    SET RELATION TO PartNo INTO Master

    *-- Update the Master in-stock quantities.
    GO TOP
    SCAN FOR .NOT. InvPosted
       *-- See if qty ordered exceeds in-stock qty.
       IF QtyOrdered <= Master->InStock
          REPLACE QtyShipped WITH QtyOrdered
       ELSE
          REPLACE QtyShipped WITH MAX(0,Master->InStock)
          REPLACE BackOrdQty WITH QtyOrdered-QtyShipped
       ENDIF
       *--- Update Master inventory database.
       SELECT Master
       REPLACE InStock WITH InStock-Orders->QtyShipped
       SELECT Orders
       REPLACE InvPosted WITH .T.
    ENDSCAN

    ********* Invoices can now be printed for posted records.
    ********* After printing invoices, must send fulfilled orders
    ********* to order history file, and convert backorders to
    ********* outstanding orders. (The application will print
    ********* invoices as soon as this procedure is done).
    CLOSE DATABASES
RETURN
```

Figure 19.9: The OrdUpdat procedure

Orders and SET RELATION TO PartNo INTO Master commands make the Orders database the current database and define a relationship, based on the common PartNo field, in the Master database file.

The GO TOP command moves the record pointer to the top (first record) in the Orders database file, and the command SCAN FOR .NOT. InvPosted sets up a loop that will process all records in the Orders database that have .F. in the InvPosted field. Within the SCAN...ENDSCAN loop, the following processes take place.

First, the command IF QtyOrdered < = Master->InStock checks whether the quantity ordered is less than or equal to the quantity in stock. If it is, the command REPLACE QtyShipped WITH QtyOrdered copies the contents of the QtyOrdered field to the QtyShipped field. If, on the other hand (ELSE), the quantity ordered is not less than or equal to the in-stock quantity, then these commands are executed:

```
REPLACE QtyShipped WITH MAX(0,Master->InStock)
REPLACE BackOrdQty WITH QtyOrdered – QtyShipped
```

The first command replaces the QtyShipped field in the Orders database with the quantity available in stock. However, if the ordering department gets ahead of the receiving department, or somebody makes an error that causes the InStock quantity to be a negative number, the QtyShipped will be a negative number, a situation we want to avoid. Thus, the procedure takes this precaution: It sets the QtyShipped value to zero or to the InStock quantity, whichever is larger (MAX(0,Master->InStock)).

The next command, REPLACE BackOrdQty WITH QtyOrdered – QtyShipped, subtracts the quantity shipped from the quantity ordered and places that value in the BackOrdQty field. The ENDIF command marks the end of the IF...ENDIF clause.

Now the Master database in-stock quantity needs to be decremented to reflect the quantity of items shipped. However, the Master database file is not currently selected, so you cannot change any of its values. This problem is easily solved by temporarily making Master the selected database file. The command SELECT Master makes the Master database file the currently selected database.

The command REPLACE InStock WITH InStock – Orders ->QtyShipped subtracts the quantity shipped from the quantity in stock. The command SELECT Orders once again makes the Orders database the currently selected database, so that its contents can be changed once again. The command REPLACE InvPosted WITH .T. places .T. in the InvPosted field, which indicates that the current order has been posted (that is, its quantity has been subtracted from the in-stock quantity). The ENDSCAN command moves the record pointer to the next record in the Orders databases and passes control back to the SCAN command. The SCAN...ENDSCAN loop and the commands within it are repeated once for each record in the Orders database that has not yet been posted.

When the SCAN...ENDSCAN loop is complete, all current orders have been checked for backordering, and the Master database in-stock quantities have been updated accordingly. Now is the perfect time for the business application to print invoices. The RETURN command marks the end of the procedure and passes control back to the (currently nonexistent) application. The application will print invoices as soon as the OrdUpdat procedure is finished.

HANDLING FULFILLED ORDERS

When orders have been fulfilled and invoices have been printed, current orders can be moved to the order-history file, OrdHist. However, backorders need to stay in the current orders database and be converted to current (outstanding) orders. The MoveOrds procedure, which we'll develop next, will handle these tasks automatically.

The basic logic for the MoveOrds procedure is shown here in pseudocode:

```
Use the order-history file
Read in all fulfilled and posted orders
Use the Orders database
Delete all fulfilled orders

For remaining orders...
    Outstanding order qty is the backorder qty
    Qty shipped is zero
    Backorder qty is zero
    Posted flag is false
    Invoice number is zero
```

To add the procedure to the BusProcs procedure file, use the usual technique. That is, at the dot prompt, enter the command **MODIFY COMMAND BusProcs** and when the procedure file appears on the screen, use the PgDn and ⏎ keys to scroll to the bottom of the procedure file. Then type the MoveOrds procedure exactly as shown in Figure 19.10. Remember to select Save Changes and Exit from the Exit pull-down menu to save your work. Let's take a moment to see how the procedure works.

First, the command USE OrdHist opens the OrdHist file, which contains records of fulfilled orders. The command APPEND FROM Orders FOR QtyShipped>0 .AND. InvPosted into the OrdHist database file reads records from the Orders database that have a quantity-shipped value greater than zero and .T. in the InvPosted field.

Next, the procedure works in the Orders database. First it opens the database, using the command USE Orders. Then it marks for deletion all orders that are not backordered and have been posted to the inventory database, using the command DELETE FOR BackOrdQty = 0 .AND. InvPosted. Then the command PACK permanently erases the records that are marked for deletion.

To convert backorders to current orders, the procedure then executes the command REPLACE ALL QtyOrdered WITH BackOrdQty, QtyShipped WITH 0, BackOrdQty WITH 0, InvPosted

```
PROCEDURE MoveOrds
     *············ Used in the BusMgr application after orders have
     *············ been fulfilled and invoices have been printed.
     USE OrdHist
     APPEND FROM Orders FOR QtyShipped > 0 .AND. InvPosted
     USE Orders
     DELETE FOR BackOrdQty = 0 .AND. InvPosted
     PACK
     REPLACE ALL QtyOrdered WITH BackOrdQty, ;
                 QtyShipped WITH 0, ;
                 BackOrdQty WITH 0, ;
                 InvPosted WITH .F., ;
                 Invoice WITH 0
RETURN
```

Figure 19.10: The MoveOrds procedure

WITH .F., Invoice WITH 0, which converts the order quantity to the backorder quantity, the quantity shipped to zero, and the backorder quantity to zero. The command also marks the record as *not* having been posted to the master inventory yet and resets the invoice number to zero.

The backorder records now are no different than any other current order records, and they will be fulfilled and invoiced automatically when stock levels permit.

CALCULATING ORDER TOTALS

Each order in the Orders database includes a quantity, (QtyShipped), unit price (UnitPrice), discount rate, (DiscRate), tax rate (TaxRate), and shipping cost (Shipping). The DiscRate and TaxRate are stored as percentage values and hence need to be divided by 100 to convert them to decimal numbers before they are used in calculations (for example, 6.5 percent divided by 100 equals 0.065).

To calculate the order total with a single expression, you need to use the calculation

$$(((\text{QtyShipped} * \text{UnitPrice}) - ((\text{DiscRate}/100) * (\text{QtyShipped} * \text{UnitPrice}))) * (1 + (\text{TaxRate}/100))) + \text{Shipping}$$

This is a complex expression, but if you test it manually, remembering that dBASE always works from the innermost parentheses outward, you'll see that it works.

For example, suppose a given order contains the following values:

QtyShipped = 2

UnitPrice = $100.00

DiscRate = 10%

TaxRate = 6.5%

Shipping = $5.00

Substituting the values into the expression results in the following formula:

$$(((2*100.00) - ((10/100)*(2*100)))*(1+(6.5/100)))+5.00$$

Performing the innermost calculations first produces

$$((200.00 - (.10*200))*(1+.065))+5.00$$

Performing the innermost remaining calculations produces

$$((200.00 - 20.00)*1.065)+5.00$$

Performing the remaining innermost expressions produces

$$(180.00*1.065)+5.00$$

This expression evaluates to

$$191.70+5.00$$

which yields the net result, 196.70.

This expression is used in the next business procedure and elsewhere in the business application.

UPDATING ACCOUNTS RECEIVABLE FROM FULFILLED ORDERS

The Transact file stores information about invoices, without the detail, for managing accounts receivable. The OrdHist database, rather than the Orders database, is used for updating the accounts receivable file because the OrdHist file contains records of fulfilled orders (those that have been invoiced).

Before dBASE copies information from the OrdHist database to the Transact database, individual orders need to be summarized into single invoices. The ARUpdate procedure handles this task with the help of the dBASE IV command TOTAL. The logic of the procedure is shown in pseudocode:

```
Use order-history file in invoice-number sort order.
Calculate total sale for each order
```

Create a summary database with invoice totals

Read the contents of the summary database
    into the AR transactions file

Use the orders-history file
Flag all records as being posted to accounts receivable

Figure 19.11 shows the ARUpdate procedure. Enter the command **MODIFY COMMAND BusProcs** at the dot prompt and then enter the procedure to the existing procedures exactly as it is shown in the figure. Be sure to select Save Changes and Exit from the Exit pull-down menu to save the procedure file after you type the new procedure.

Let's see how the procedure works. First the command USE OrdHist ORDER Invoice opens the OrdHist database with the Invoice index placing the records in sorted order from the smallest invoice number to the largest.

To examine the logic of the program, let's assume that the OrdHist database file currently contains the following records (the

```
*-------- Moves fulfilled orders to the AR transactions file.
PROCEDURE ARUpdate
     *---------- Used in BusMgr application after moving
     *---------- fulfilled orders to OrdHist file.

     *---------- First calculate order totals.
     USE OrdHist ORDER Invoice
     REPLACE OrdTotal WITH (((QtyShipped*UnitPrice)- ;
          ((Discrate/100)*(QtyShipped*UnitPrice)))* ;
          (1+(TaxRate/100)))+Shipping ;
          FOR QtyShipped > 0

     *---------- Now create temporary database of totaled orders.
     GO TOP
     SET SAFETY OFF   && Prevents dBASE from asking for permission to overwrite
     TOTAL ON Invoice FIELDS OrdTotal TO OrdTemp FOR .NOT. ARPosted
     *---------- Copy summarized totals into AR transaction file.
     USE Transact
     APPEND FROM OrdTemp
     *---------- Mark orders as being posted to the AR transaction file.
     USE OrdHist
     REPLACE ALL ARPosted WITH .T.
     CLOSE DATABASES
RETURN
```

Figure 19.11: The ARUpdate procedure

DiscRate, TaxRate, and some other fields are omitted here to save space, but you will include these values in calculations when you actually use the ARUpdate procedure):

Invoice	CustNo	PartNo	Qty Shipped	Unit Price	OrdTotal	OrDate
333333	1001	A-111	10	5.00		01/01/91
333333	1001	B-222	1	10.00		01/01/91
333333	1001	C-333	2	4.00		01/01/91
333334	1002	A-111	1	5.00		01/01/91
333334	1002	C-333	3	4.00		01/01/91

Next, the command

```
REPLACE OrdTotal WITH ((((QtyShipped*UnitPrice)-- ;
              ((DiscRate/100)*(QtyShipped*UnitPrice)))* ;
              (1 +(TaxRate/100))) + Shipping ;
              FOR QtyShipped>0
```

calculates the total of each order that has a QtyShipped value greater than zero. So now the OrdHist database looks something like this:

Invoice	CustNo	PartNo	Qty Shipped	Unit Price	OrdTotal	OrDate
333333	1001	A-111	10	5.00	50.00	01/01/91
333333	1001	B-222	1	10.00	10.00	01/01/91
333333	1001	C-333	2	4.00	8.00	01/01/91
333334	1002	A-111	1	5.00	5.00	01/01/91
333334	1002	C-333	3	4.00	12.00	01/01/91

The GO TOP command positions the record pointer at the top of the OrdHist database, and the SET SAFETY OFF command makes sure that dBASE does not ask for permission to overwrite any old copy of the OrdTemp file when the next command creates that file.

The next command, TOTAL ON Invoice FIELDS OrdTotal TO OrdTemp FOR .NOT. Posted, performs all the totaling and summarizing. The TOTAL command always creates a new database containing the totaled and summarized results. The first part of the command, TOTAL ON Invoice, tells dBASE that records are to be grouped by invoice number in the totaled results. The database being totaled must be indexed on the field used for grouping, as the Orders database is in this procedure.

The portion of the command that reads FIELDS OrdTotal tells dBASE which fields are to be totaled: OrdTotal in this example. The portion of the command that reads TO OrdTemp tells dBASE where to store summarized and totaled results. In this case, the results are stored in a database file named OrdTemp.dbf. If OrdTemp.dbf does not already exist, the TOTAL command creates it. If OrdTemp.dbf does exist, the TOTAL command attempts to overwrite it.

In this particular application, the OrdTemp.dbf database is used as a temporary database file—a holding area for summarized transactions coming out of the OrdHist database before they go into the Transact file—so it's okay for dBASE to overwrite the OrdTemp.dbf database if it already exists. dBASE would normally ask for permission before overwriting an existing file, but because the preceding command set the SAFETY feature off, dBASE will not ask for permission before overwriting the file.

The portion of the TOTAL command that reads FOR .NOT. ARPosted limits the totaling to records that have not already been posted to the Transact file. (As you'll see in a moment, posted orders are flagged with a .T. in the ARPosted field after they have been posted.)

The results of the TOTAL command are a database named OrdTemp.dbf that contains the following information, using the sample orders listed previously:

Invoice	CustNo	PartNo	Qty Shipped	Unit Price	OrdTotal	OrDate
333333	1001	A-111			68.00	01/01/91
333334	1002	C-333			17.00	01/01/91

Next, the command USE Transact opens the Transact database file, and the command APPEND FROM OrdTemp copies records from the OrdTemp.dbf database to the bottom of the Transact database. The APPEND FROM command copies only fields that have identical names in both databases. Hence, after the APPEND FROM command, Transact contains the following records (plus any other records that were already in it):

Invoice	CustNo	Ordate	OrdTotal
333333	1001	01/01/90	68.00
333334	1002	01/01/90	17.00

Next, the commands USE OrdHist and REPLACE ALL ARPosted WITH .T. place .T. in the ARPosted field of all records in the OrdHist database to indicate that the orders have been posted to the transaction file. The CLOSE DATABASES command closes open database files, and RETURN marks the end of the procedure.

DETERMINING ACCOUNT BALANCES

To determine the current account balances for each customer, the application needs to keep track of total accumulated charges and balances. The Customer database provides four fields for this: TotChrg and TotPmt, which accumulate all charges and payments, and YtdChrg and YtdPmt, which also accumulate charges and payments, but can be reset to zero at the end of the accounting year to track year-to-date charges and balances. The balance at any given time is simply the accumulated charges minus the accumulated payments.

To keep customer charges and payments current, you need a procedure that can summarize all transactions and then update the appropriate fields in the Customer database. The logic for the procedure is shown in the following pseudocode:

```
Open the Customer file with CustNo index
Open Transaction file with CustNo index

Hide posted records in the Transaction file

Select the Customer database for updating

Update Customer database by...
    adding current charges to accumulated charges
    adding current payments to accumulated payments
    replacing the last update date with today's date

Save all updates
Use the Transaction file
Mark all transactions as posted to the Customer file
```

We'll name the procedure that performs the accounts receivable posting ARPost. To add it to the BusProcs procedure, first enter the command **MODIFY COMMAND BusProcs** at the dot prompt; then position the cursor at the end of the procedure file. Type the procedure exactly as shown in Figure 19.12. Be sure to save the procedure file after typing the ARPost procedure.

Let's see how the ARPost procedure does its job. Let's assume that the Customer database includes (at least) the following two records, each of which was last updated on January 31, 1991:

CustNo	TotChrg	TotPmt	YtdChrg	YtdPmt	LastDate
1001	0.00	0.00	0.00	0.00	01/31/91
1002	100.00	10.00	100.00	10.00	01/31/91

Let's also assume that the Transact database contains the following records (note that the first record has already been posted, as indicated by .T. in the CUSTPOSTED field):

CustNo	OrdTotal	AmtPaid	CustPosted
1002	10.00		.T.
1001	500.00	0.00	.F.
1001		400.00	.F.
1002	200.00		.F.

```
*---- Update customer balances.
PROCEDURE ARPost

    SELECT A
    USE Customer ORDER CustNo
    SELECT B
    USE Transact ORDER CustNo
    *---- Exclude records that have been posted.
    SET FILTER TO .NOT. CustPosted
    GO TOP   && Always move the record pointer after SET FILTER.

    SELECT Customer
    UPDATE ON CustNo FROM Transact REPLACE ;
        TotChrg WITH TotChrg + Transact->OrdTotal, ;
        YtdChrg WITH YtdChrg + Transact->OrdTotal, ;
        TotPmt WITH TotPmt + Transact->AmtPaid, ;
        YtdPmt WITH YtdPmt + Transact->AmtPaid, ;
        LastDate WITH DATE()

    *---- Customer balances now updated, flag transactions.
    CLOSE DATABASES
    USE Transact
    REPLACE ALL CustPosted WITH .T.
    CLOSE DATABASES
RETURN
```

Figure 19.12: The ARPost procedure

(Note that both databases contain other fields as well, but these are irrelevant to the present example.)

The first four commands after the PROCEDURE command in the ARPost procedure open the Customer and Transact databases, both with the CustNo index controlling the sort order. (Later the procedure will use the UPDATE command, so both of these databases must be indexed on the field that relates the two files.)

Then the command SET FILTER TO .NOT. CustPosted tells dBASE to include only records that have .F. in the CustPosted field (that is, records that have not already been posted to the Customer database). The SET FILTER command requires you to take some action to move the record pointer immediately after the filter is set, which the ARPost procedure does through the command GO TOP. When these two commands finish their jobs, the transactions already posted are hidden, and the record pointer (indicated by > >) is at the beginning of the visible records, like this:

CustNo	OrdTotal	AmtPaid	CustPosted
> >1001	500.00	0.00	.F.
1001		400.00	.F.
1002	200.00		.F.

Next, the command SELECT Customer makes the Customer database the currently selected database, whose values will be updated. Then the long UPDATE command, broken into six separate lines with semicolons, performs the actual update operation. The databases are related using the common PartNo field, so dBASE automatically knows which charge and payment belongs to which customer.

The portion of the UPDATE command that reads TotChrg WITH TotChrg + Transact->OrdTotal adds the value in the Ord-Total field of the Transact database to the value currently in the Tot-Chrg field of the Customer database. Similar expressions are used to update the YtdChrg, TotPmt, and YtdPmt fields, with payments updated from the Transact file AmtPaid field (that is, the field named Transact->AmtPaid).

The last expression, LastDate WITH DATE( ), replaces the contents of the LastDate field in the Customer database with the current date. Assuming that the updating took place on February 28, 1991, when the UPDATE command is done the two sample records in the Customer database will contain the following new values:

CustNo	TotChrg	TotPmt	YtdChrg	YtdPmt	LastDate
1001	500.00	400.00	500.00	400.00	02/28/91
1002	300.00	10.00	300.00	10.00	02/28/91

Note that customer 1001 has now accumulated $500.00 in charges and $400.00 in payments. Customer number 1002 now has accumulated $300.00 in charges (he originally had $200.00 in charges, but another $100.00 was added during the update operation). The LastDate field in both records reflects the current date.

The CLOSE DATABASES command closes both open database files, ensuring that the updates are saved on disk. Then, to ensure that none of these transactions are posted again in the future, the procedure opens the Transact database with the USE Transact command and then uses the command REPLACE ALL CustPosted WITH .T. to replace the CustPosted field with .T. in all records. This marks the records as posted, so they will not be posted again in the future.

RESETTING YEAR-TO-DATE TOTALS

Most business applications store at least some numbers that keep track of accumulated year-to-date totals. At the end of the accounting year, these year-to-date values need to be reset to zero. A REPLACE command can handle the job easily enough, but there are some factors to take into account.

First of all, application users occasionally do not pay much attention to what is happening on their screens and therefore might unwittingly select an option to reset all year-to-date totals to zero prematurely. To prevent such accidental resetting, you can make the procedure pause and double-check whether the user really wants to reset the values.

Once the accounting year is closed, there is no need to keep all of the transactions for that entire year in the database of current transactions. Thus, the business application that we are developing will move the old transactions to a history file named TranHist. The application will create this database automatically, which is why you need not create a structure for the TranHist database.

Let's look at the pseudocode for the entire procedure, which we'll name YearEnd:

```
Ask if it is Ok to proceed

If Ok to proceed
    Replace all year-to-date totals with zero
    Copy completed transactions to the transaction history file
    Mark completed transactions for deletion
    Remove deleted transactions
End of If clause
```

As usual, to add the procedure to the end of the procedure file, first enter the command **MODIFY COMMAND BusProcs** at the dot prompt. Then use the PgDn, ↓, and ↩ keys as necessary to scroll to the end of the file. Type the YearEnd procedure exactly as shown in Figure 19.13. After typing the procedure, select Save Changes and Exit from the Exit pull-down menu to save the completed procedure file and return to the dot prompt.

```
*················· Resets year-to-date values to zero
*················· in the customer database, and moves
*················· old transactions to history file.
PROCEDURE YearEnd

    *········ Double-check for permission.
    GoAhead = .F.
    @ 4,5 SAY "Are you sure you want to reset year-to-date"
    @ 5,5 SAY "totals to zero now?  (Y/N) " GET GoAhead PICTURE "Y"
    READ

    *······ If ok to proceed, do so.
    IF GoAhead
        SET TALK ON
        SET SAFETY OFF
        USE Customer
        REPLACE ALL YtdChrg WITH 0, YtdPmt WITH 0
        USE Transact
        COPY TO TranHist FOR CustPosted .AND. Printed
        DELETE FOR CustPosted .AND. Printed
        PACK
        SET TALK OFF
    ENDIF

    CLOSE DATABASES
RETURN
```

Figure 19.13: The YearEnd procedure

Now let's examine each command in the procedure. First the command GoAhead = .F. stores *false* in a memory variable named GoAhead. Then the commands @ 4,5 SAY "Are you sure you want to reset year-to-date" and @ 5,5 SAY "totals to zero now? (Y/N) " GET GoAhead PICTURE "Y" display a two-line prompt on the screen along with the current contents of the GoAhead variable, using a template that displays .F. as N and .T. as Y, as shown here:

Are you sure you want to reset year-to-date
totals to zero now? (Y/N) [N]

The next command, READ, moves the cursor into the highlighted area where the contents of the GoAhead variable are displayed, allowing the user to change its value.

If the user does change the contents of the GoAhead variable to Y (.T.), then the IF GoAhead command is true, and dBASE executes all commands down to the ENDIF command. (If the GoAhead variable is false, then dBASE ignores all commands down to the ENDIF command.)

Within the IF...ENDIF clause, the command SET TALK ON turns on the dBASE TALK setting, which shows command progress on the screen as events take place. The command SET SAFETY OFF prevents dBASE from asking for permission later when the COPY command creates the TranHist database file. The USE Customer command opens the Customer database.

The command REPLACE ALL YtdChrg WITH 0, YtdPmt WITH 0 replaces the contents of the YtdChrg and YtdPmt fields with zero in every database record. Then the command USE Transact opens the Transact database. The command COPY TO TranHist FOR CustPosted .AND. Printed copies all records that have .T. in the CustPosted and Printed fields to a database file named TranHist. (If the TranHist file already exists because of a previous year's totals were reset to zero, the COPY command completely overwrites the existing TranHist file.)

The command DELETE FOR CustPosted .AND. Printed marks for deletion all records with .T. in the CustPosted and Printed fields, and the command PACK permanently removes those records. Then SET TALK OFF turns off the dBASE progress display, and ENDIF marks the end of the IF...ENDIF block.

Finally, the command CLOSE DATABASES closes the open database file, thereby ensuring that all changes are saved, and RETURN marks the end of the procedure.

REBUILDING INDEX FILES

As mentioned earlier, every application should include an option to rebuild index files in case these become corrupted by a power failure or some other malady. The Applications Generator includes an option for indexing a single database file, but the business application that we are developing uses many database files. Therefore, let's now write a procedure that can reindex all databases files.

The command to rebuild all the indexes associated with a particular database is REINDEX. All you need to do is issue the USE command for the database of interest and then execute the REINDEX command. For this application, we'll name the procedure to rebuild all indexes BusRendx. Figure 19.14 shows the complete procedure.

```
*----------------- Rebuild index files for all databases.
PROCEDURE BusRendx

    SET TALK ON      && Show progress
    USE Customer
    REINDEX
    USE Master
    REINDEX
    USE Orders
    REINDEX
    USE OrdHist
    REINDEX
    USE ItemsRec
    REINDEX
    USE ItemHist
    REINDEX
    USE Transact
    REINDEX
    SET TALK OFF     && Suppress progress messages.

RETURN
```

Figure 19.14: The BusRendx procedure

To add this procedure to the BusProcs procedure file, enter the command **MODIFY COMMAND BusProcs**, as usual, at the dot prompt. Then move the cursor to the end of the procedure file and type the entire procedure exactly as shown in Figure 19.14. When you are done, select Save Changes and Exit from the Exit pull-down menu to save your work and return to the dot prompt.

At this point, you have finished developing all the basic data processing procedures for the business application. But before you start actually building the application, the next chapter presents still more programming techniques that you can use to refine your business applications.

C H A P T E R

20

Intelligent
Custom Forms
for Business
Applications

THE PROCEDURES THAT YOU DEVELOPED IN THE preceding chapter will certainly help you build a powerful, integrated business management application. However, even the best business application is only as good as the data it uses. When meaningless or faulty information is entered, stored, and processed, then meaningless or faulty information appears in the various reports, such as invoices, inventory status, and so forth, printed from the database.

DATA VALIDATION

The best way to avoid erroneous or meaningless information in a business application is to try to prevent it from being stored in a database in the first place. There are two basic techniques that you can use to prevent errors: You can have your application reject obviously invalid data, and you can have the application provide feedback that allows users to quickly check their entries.

The first method of error prevention, having the application reject invalid information, prevents meaningless data from being entered into a database. For example, suppose the user enters a customer number and a part number for an order. A good application will check whether the customer number and part number entered for the order actually exist in the Customer and Master databases and if either entry is invalid, will reject the entry. The user then must reenter the order with a new value.

The second method of error prevention, having the application provide feedback, is not as foolproof as the first method, but can at least help reduce the number of errors. For example, suppose the user is entering an order for customer number 1001, but accidentally enters customer number 1010. Let's also assume that some other customer has the number 1010. The user might not catch the error unless, when the customer number is entered, the customer's name appears on the screen, as in Figure 20.1.

A quick glance at the screen tells the user the name of the customer assigned to the customer number entered. Assuming that the user knows the name of the customer for whom the order was entered, a quick glance at the screen tells the user whether the customer number is correct. As a convenience, the screen also displays that customer's standard discount and tax rates.

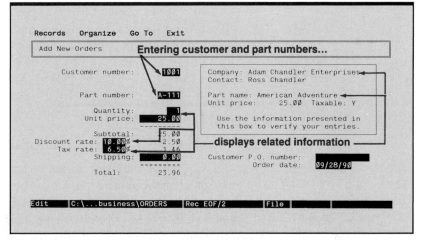

Figure 20.1: Customer information on the screen

When the user enters a part number for the order, the screen displays the name and selling price of the part. A quick glance at the screen lets the user verify the entry, once again reducing the likelihood of an error.

Developing ''intelligent'' custom forms that can trap errors and supply feedback requires some advanced programming techniques. But if you are considering developing sophisticated applications, the techniques are well worth learning, because a sophisticated *user interface* (that is, the screens for entering and editing data) is one of the hallmarks of a professional-quality application.

The basic steps involved in developing such forms are

1. Open all the necessary databases needed to enter orders and verify entries.

2. Use the forms design screen to create custom forms for entering and editing data.

3. Note the exact row and column positions of all calculated fields (including fields from related database files).

4. Save the form and create user-defined functions for validating entries and displaying calculated information.

5. Return to the forms design screen and attach the user-defined functions to specific fields using the Accept Value When edit option.

You'll see examples of how to perform each step as you develop sophisticated screens for entering and editing orders in the business application in the sections that follow.

OPENING THE DATABASES FOR ORDER ENTRY

The Orders database stores order information, including the customer number and part number for each order. To allow the application to verify customer numbers and part numbers and provide information from these databases on the screen, the Orders, Customer, and Master databases must be open simultaneously and related through the fields that link them together.

You can store the appropriate commands for opening and relating the database files in the same procedure file, BusProcs, that you developed in the preceding chapter. To do so, follow these steps:

1. At the dot prompt, enter the command **MODIFY COMMAND BusProcs**.

2. Use the PgDn, ↓, and ↵ keys to position the cursor at the end of the procedure file.

3. Type the procedure, which we'll name OrdOpen, exactly as shown in Figure 20.2.

4. After typing the entire procedure, select Save Changes and Exit from the Exit pull-down menu to save the modified procedure file.

Let's take a moment to see what the procedure does when executed. The SELECT and USE commands open the Orders, Customer, and Master databases. Notice that the Customer and Master databases are opened with indexes of the CustNo and PartNo, fields which relate them to the Orders database. The command SELECT Orders then makes the Orders database the currently selected database. Orders must be the currently selected database in this situation, because the main purpose of the form you will be developing is entering and editing orders.

The command SET RELATION TO CustNo INTO Customer, PartNo INTO Master tells dBASE to set up a relationship between Orders and Customer based on the common CustNo field, and between Orders and Master based on the common PartNo field. Figure 20.3 illustrates this relationship, assuming that all three databases contain some data.

```
*................... Opens database files and sets relations
*................... for order entry and editing.
PROCEDURE OrdOpen
   SELECT A
   USE Orders
   SELECT B
   USE Customer ORDER CustNo
   SELECT C
   USE Master ORDER PartNo

   *......... Set up relationship based on key fields.
   SELECT Orders
   SET RELATION TO CustNo INTO Customer, PartNo INTO Master
   GO TOP
RETURN
```

Figure 20.2: The OrdOpen procedure

Figure 20.3: Relationships defined among three databases

The GO TOP command simply moves the record pointer to the beginning of the Orders database, and RETURN marks the end of the procedure.

CREATING THE ORDER-ENTRY CUSTOM FORM

Now you need to create a custom form for editing orders (later you'll use this form as the basis for creating some other forms). Before you can create the form, however, you must run the OrdOpen procedure to open the appropriate databases and set up the relationships so that dBASE can verify that fields coming from related database files do indeed exist as you design the form.

To open the database files and set up the relationship, run the OrdOpen procedure by entering these commands at the dot prompt:

```
SET PROCEDURE TO BusProcs
DO OrdOpen
```

When the dot prompt reappears, rest assured that the three databases are open and related (assuming you typed the OrdOpen procedure correctly). Now go to the forms design screen to create a custom form, which we'll name EDITORD. You can bypass the Control Center and simply enter the following command at the dot prompt:

```
MODIFY SCREEN EditOrd
```

You'll see the familiar forms design screen, where you can now use the usual techniques and keys to design your customer form.

Figure 20.4 shows the completed form on the screen.

Table 20.1 lists the row and column positions of field templates on the form. To place the templates, position the cursor at the row and column indicated and select the field name from the left column of the submenu that appears.

Table 20.2 lists the row and column positions of the calculated fields on the EditOrd form. To place the calculated fields, position the cursor to the row and column indicated; then press F5 and select <create> from the right (calculated) side of the submenu. Enter the

You can enter the command DISPLAY STATUS at the dot prompt to see the names of all open database files, as well as the current status of various settings and keys.

If you need to review basic form design techniques, refer to Chapter 8.

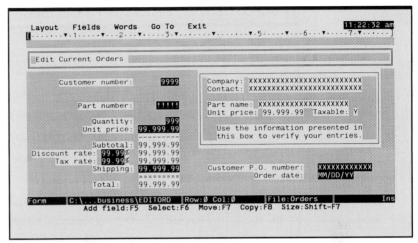

Figure 20.4: EditOrd custom form on the forms design screen

Table 20.1: Fields on the EditOrd Form

Row, column	Name
5,29	CUSTNO
8,28	PARTNO
10,30	QTYORDERED
11,24	UNITPRICE
14,16	DISCRATE
15,16	TAXRATE
16,24	SHIPPING
16,63	CUSTPONUMB
17,63	ORDATE

name and expression indicated (you can leave the description blank in each calculated field).

Use Figure 20.4 to guide you in specifying template characters as you place fields on the form. For example, as you can see in the figure, the PartNo field uses the template !!!!!.

After entering the text and field templates onto the form, you can add the boxes shown using the Box option on the Layout pull-down menu.

Table 20.2: Calculated Fields on the EditOrd Form

Row, column	Name	Expression
5,48	CustComp	Customer->Company
6,48	CustCont	Customer->Contact
8,50	PtName	Master->PartName
9,51	MPrice	Master->SelPrice
9,71	MTax	Master->Taxable
13,24	ExtPrice	QtyOrdered*UnitPrice
14,24	DiscAmt	– (DiscRate/100)*(QtyOrdered*UnitPrice)
15,24	TaxAmt	(TaxRate/100)*(QtyOrdered*UnitPrice)
18,24	TotSale	Enter as a single long expression (hint—use the F9 key to zoom): (((QtyOrdered*UnitPrice) – ((DiscRate/100)* (QtyOrdered*UnitPrice)))* (1 + (TaxRate/100))) + Shipping

NOTING
CALCULATED-FIELD LOCATIONS

If you were designing your own form rather than copying this one from the book, you would want to jot down on paper the exact location of each calculated (Calc'd) field on the form. You would also want to note the locations of regular fields that might accept new values automatically from related databases. For example, the Tax-Rate and DiscRate fields in the Orders database in the EditOrd form will be assigned values from the Customer database during data entry, so these should be included in your list.

You would also want to note the templates used for Numeric and Logical fields, as shown in Table 20.3. (It will become clear to you why this information is necessary when you develop user-defined functions in the next section.)

Table 20.3: Fields used in Recalculations on the EditOrd Form

Row, column	Expression	Template
5,48	Customer->Company	
6,48	Customer->Contact	
8,50	Master->PartName	
9,51	Master->SelPrice	99,999.99
9,71	Master->Taxable	Y
13,24	QtyOrdered*UnitPrice	99,999.99
14,24	-(DiscRate/100)* (QtyOrdered*UnitPrice)	99,999.99
15,24	(TaxRate/100)* (QtyOrdered*UnitPrice)	99,999.99
18,24	(((QtyOrdered*UnitPrice) -((DiscRate/100)* (QtyOrdered*UnitPrice))) * (1+(TaxRate/100)))+Shipping	99,999.99
11,24	UNITPRICE	99,999.99
14,16	DISCRATE	99.99
15,16	TAXRATE	99.99

When your form looks exactly like the one in Figure 20.4, select Save Changes and Exit from the Exit pull-down menu to save the form and return to the dot prompt.

At this point, you have a form that includes calculated fields for displaying information from the related Customer and Master databases and for calculating the extended price, tax amount, discount amount, and total sale. However, your job is not complete yet, because the form will not reject invalid entries during data entry. Instead, it will only show the results of the calculated field while you are editing *existing* data.

You need to add some *user-defined functions* to your BusProcs procedure to handle the data validation. As discussed in Chapter 18, a user-defined function is similar to a procedure and can be stored in a procedure file with existing procedures.

CREATING
USER-DEFINED FUNCTIONS

Before we actually develop the user-defined functions for the business application, let's take a moment to clarify exactly when these functions will be used. First, as you've seen throughout most of the preceding chapters, whenever you enter or edit database data, the screen displays a highlighted area with the cursor in it, where you can enter or change information, as shown here (where [ ] represents the highlighted area on the screen and the underline represents the cursor):

Customer number: [_]

The cursor blinks and waits for you to enter new data or change any existing data or to press some other key to move out of the field.

Regardless of which key you use to leave the field, it is at that precise moment, when the cursor leaves the field and before it moves into the next field, that your user-defined functions will be executed. These functions can perform any number of operations, including validating the entry, displaying data from related database files, and displaying calculations on the screen.

When a user-defined function is done with its task, it must return some value (as discussed in Chapter 18). Typically, in a custom screen a user-defined function returns either .T. or .F. If the function returns .T., the cursor moves to the next field on the screen as it normally would. If your function returns .F., then the cursor *does not* move to the next field on the screen. Instead, the computer beeps, the bottom line of the screen displays an error message (which you design), and the cursor stays in the current field. In other words, the entry is rejected and must be corrected.

Because you are the person who defines what is and what is not a valid entry in a user-defined function, you have enormous control over what the user can and cannot enter into the database. And because user-defined functions can perform many tasks, you also have enormous power in determining what takes place on the screen (and even in the databases) at the moment the cursor leaves a particular field on the screen.

Unfortunately, with enormous power also comes responsibility. You must be aware of one particular problem with such powerful data entry and editing screens so you can deal with it effectively. Consider the following situation.

Suppose the user is adding orders to the Orders database. Initially, the customer number, tax rate, and discount rate fields are blank, as shown here:

```
Customer number:   [ _  ]
  Part number:     [    ]
     Tax rate:     [  .  ]
Discount rate:     [  .  ]
```

As soon as the user types a customer number, your user-defined function conveniently fills in the standard discount rate and tax rate for that customer on the order form (screen), as follows:

```
Customer number:   [1001]
  Part number:     [ _  ]
     Tax rate:     [ 6.50]
Discount rate:     [10.00]
```

The user then enters the part number for the order:

```
Customer number:   [1001]
  Part number:     [A-111]
     Tax rate:     [ 6.50]
Discount rate:     [10.00]
```

Now suppose that the standard 10 percent discount rate does not apply to this particular order, so the user changes the discount rate to 0 when the cursor reaches that field, as follows:

```
Customer number:   [1001]
  Part number:     [A-111]
     Tax rate:     [ 6.50]
Discount rate:     [ 0.  ]
```

The user fills in any other fields on the screen, checks the entries, verifies that everything looks okay, and then moves on and enters several more orders. When the user is done entering orders, he or she exits the application or moves on to some other task.

Now suppose that later the user returns to the orders and decides to check them by using the edit mode and scrolling through existing orders using the PgUp and PgDn keys. It's at this moment that a real problem could arise.

As the user is scrolling through the orders, the order entered in the example reappears on the screen, as follows:

```
Customer number:   [1001]
    Part number:   [A-111]
       Tax rate:   [ 6.50]
  Discount rate:   [ 0.  ]
```

The user sees that it's okay and so presses the PgDn key to check the next record. At that precise moment, dBASE executes your user-defined function (because the cursor has left the field, as well as the entire record), and your user-defined function quickly puts the customer's standard discount rate, 10 percent, back into the discount rate field, as shown here:

```
Customer number:   [1001]
    Part number:   [A-111]
       Tax rate:   [ 6.50]
  Discount rate:   [10.00]
```

This happens so quickly—in the fraction of a second that dBASE takes to scroll from one record to the next—that chances are good that the user will not even know the change took place. But now the order is wrong, because the original discount rate of zero was the correct entry for that particular record.

How do you solve this problem? The solution is a dBASE IV built-in function named LASTKEY(). The LASTKEY() function *always* contains the ASCII code number of the most recent keypress.

You can decide for yourself which keystrokes activate your user-defined function. If the user completely filled the field highlight on the screen, then the LASTKEY() function will return a number in the range 32 to 122 (all characters from a blank to a lowercase *z*). If the user presses ← to leave the field, then LASTKEY() will contain 13. Other special keystrokes used to manage the cursor on the screen are listed here:

> **NOTE**
>
> Appendix G lists all ASCII characters and their code numbers.

Keystroke	LASTKEY( )
PgUp	18
PgDn	3
↑	5
↓	24
Tab	9
Shift-Tab	− 400
Esc	27
Ctrl-End	23

For the user-defined functions in this chapter, we'll assume that if the user presses any letter or number (a key in the range 32 to 122) or presses ◄─┘ (number 13), the user-defined function will be executed. If the user presses any other key (such as PgUp, PgDn, Tab, or an arrow key), the function will assume the user is just scrolling and will not modify existing entries. To make this decision, we'll use an IF clause that starts with the command IF LASTKEY( ) = 13 .OR. (LASTKEY( ) > = 32 .AND. LASTKEY( ) < = 122) in our user-defined function, as you'll see in a moment.

VALIDATING CUSTOMER NUMBERS

The first user-defined function that you will develop will perform the tasks shown here in pseudocode:

```
In case user leaves customer number blank to exit
    Skip validation
    Return "Ok"
In case a valid customer number was entered
    Display the company name
    Display the contact
    If user not just scrolling
        Replace order discount rate with customer discount rate
        Allow discount rate to be changed for this order
        If item is taxable
            Replace order tax rate with customer tax rate
        Else
            Replace order tax rate with zero
        End "taxable" IF clause
```

Allow tax rate to be changed for this order
Recalculate screen
Return Ok

In case invalid customer number ordered
Reject entry and display "No such customer!"
Return "not Ok"

To add the user-defined function to the BusProcs procedure file, use the same basic technique you used to add new procedures. That is, first enter the command **CLOSE PROCEDURE** at the dot prompt. Then enter the command **MODIFY COMMAND BusProcs**, and position the cursor beneath the existing procedures. Then enter the complete user-defined function, as shown in Figure 20.5. Be sure to save the BusProcs procedure after adding the IsCust function by selecting the Save Changes and Exit option from the Exit pull-down menu.

```
*............................. Validate customer number.
FUNCTION IsCust
PARAMETERS MCustNo
   DO CASE

      *- If user is exiting, do nothing.
      CASE McustNo = 0
         Ok=.T.

      *.......... Customer number was entered.
      CASE SEEK(MCustNo,"Customer")
         a 5,48 SAY Customer->Company
         a 6,48 SAY Customer->Contact
         *--- Recalculate (depnding on last keypress).
         IF LASTKEY()=13 .OR. (LASTKEY()>=32.AND.LASTKEY()<=122)
            REPLACE Orders->DiscRate WITH Customer->DiscRate
            a 14,16 GET DiscRate PICTURE "99.99"
            IF Master->Taxable
               REPLACE Orders->TaxRate WITH Customer->TaxRate
            ELSE
               REPLACE Orders->TaxRate WITH 0
            ENDIF &&taxable
            a 15,16 GET TaxRate PICTURE "99.99"
            Ok=Recalc(QtyOrdered)
         ENDIF  && last keypress
         Ok=.T.
      OTHERWISE
         a 5,48 SAY "No such customer!        "
         a 6,48 SAY SPACE(25)
         Ok=.F.
   ENDCASE
RETURN (Ok)
```

Figure 20.5: The IsCust user-defined function

Now let's examine this user-defined function and its commands. The first command, FUNCTION IsCust, defines the name of the user-defined function as IsCust. The command PARAMETERS MCustNo assigns the temporary name MCustNo to the value passed to the function. (As you'll see later, this function is called from the custom screen using the syntax IsCust(CustNo), where CustNo is the customer number that the user entered and is also the value passed to the user-defined function.)

The command DO CASE (discussed in Chapter 18) sets up a clause in which the first true condition will be the only one executed between the DO CASE and ENDCASE commands. The first CASE statement, CASE MCustNo = 0, checks whether the user just pressed ◄┘ without entering a customer number, which implies that he or she has finished entering orders. If this is the case, then the command Ok = .T. stores .T. in the memory variable named Ok, and dBASE ignores all other CASE conditions. (The Ok memory variable plays an important role in this user-defined function, as you'll see.)

If the user did indeed enter a new customer number for the current order, then the next CASE statement, CASE SEEK(MCustNo, "Customer"), is evaluated. The SEEK() function very quickly searches for its first argument in the current index of the database specified in its second argument. Let us see how this operation works.

The OrdOpen procedure, which you created earlier in this chapter, opens the Customer database with the CustNo index controlling the sort order. The memory variable MCustNo currently contains the customer number that the user entered on the screen. Therefore, the expression SEEK(MCustNo, "Customer") searches the CustNo index of the Customer database for a customer number that matches the one the user entered on the screen.

If the SEEK() function does *not* find a matching customer number, it returns .F., and dBASE then ignores all commands up to the OTHERWISE command in the DO CASE clause. If, on the other hand, the SEEK() function *does* find a matching customer number, it returns .T., in which case dBASE executes all commands between the CASE SEEK(MCustNo, "Customer") and OTHERWISE commands and ignores the commands between OTHERWISE and ENDCASE.

Assuming that the SEEK() function did indeed find a matching customer number in the Customer database, dBASE executes the

NOTE

dBASE IV includes both a command called SEEK and a built-in function named SEEK(). Both the command and the function search the currently active index file only.

NOTE

Even though it takes quite a while to *explain* some of the operations performed in these user-defined functions, dBASE IV actually executes them in a fraction of a second.

following commands. First, the @ 5,48 SAY Customer ->Company command displays on the form the company name from the related record on the Customer database. That is, if the user entered **1001** as the customer for the current order and customer number 1001 identifies Adam Chandler Enterprises in the Customer database, then Adam Chandler Enterprises is the company name displayed on the screen. If you are wondering why the company name needs to be displayed specifically at row 5, column 48, refer back to Figure 20.4 or Table 20.2; you'll see that this is precisely where the company name is displayed on the custom form you developed earlier.

The next command processed if the customer number was valid is @ 6,48 SAY Customer->Contact, which displays the Contact field from the Customer database directly beneath the company name.

The command IF LASTKEY() = 13 .OR. (LASTKEY() > =32 .AND. LASTKEY() < =122) checks whether the user last typed a letter or character or pressed ←┘. If the user did so, dBASE processes all commands between this command and the ENDIF && last keypress command. If the user presses any other key (such as PgUp, PgDn, or some other scrolling key), the IF statement evaluates to false, and dBASE ignores all commands between this command and the ENDIF && last keypress command.

The next command, REPLACE Orders->DiscRate WITH Customer->DiscRate copies the customer's standard discount rate into the current record on the Orders database. But this value may need to be changed for a particular order, so the next command, @ 14,16 GET DiscRate PICTURE "99.99", places the field, with its new contents, back on the screen so that it can be changed if necessary. (If the user changes the discount rate, it is changed for the current order only in the Orders database, *not* in the Customer database.)

Note that the command @ 14,16 GET DiscRate PICTURE "99.99" exactly matches the row and column position, field name, and template (99.99) specified back in Table 20.2. This command displays the new discount rate at exactly the same position, using exactly the same template, that the EditOrd custom screen does.

Next, an IF...ENDIF clause, nested within the IF...ENDIF clause that determined the last key that the user pressed, determines how to present the tax rate. If the user is editing an existing record, then the part number is already on the screen and in the database record. The first command, IF Master->Taxable, determines whether the related item from the Master database is taxable. If the item is taxable, then TaxRate in the current record of the orders database is replaced with the customer's standard tax rate. The command REPLACE Orders->TaxRate WITH Customer->TaxRate effects the replacement.

If the item ordered is *not* taxable (ELSE), then the command REPLACE Orders->TaxRate WITH 0 puts a zero in the TaxRate field of the order currently being entered or edited. The ENDIF &&taxable command marks the end of the IF...ENDIF decision clause for determining the tax rate for the current order.

In case the default tax rate assigned to the order needs to be changed for the current order, the command @ 15,16 GET TaxRate PICTURE ''99.99'' displays the customer's tax rate on the screen and makes it available for editing. Again, the command uses exactly the same row and column positions and template that was specified in the EditOrd custom form.

The command Ok = Recalc(QtyOrdered) activates another user-defined function, named *Recalc*, which we'll develop later. The Recalc function will recalculate all the subtotals and totals on the screen and then return .T. dBASE stores this .T. in the memory variable named Ok. Later, this .T. will be returned to the custom form, indicating that a valid part number was entered and the user can proceed with the order.

The next command, ENDIF &&last keypress, marks the end of the IF...ENDIF clause that was used to determine the last key that the user pressed. The next command, Ok = .T., stores the value .T. in the memory variable named Ok, which this user-defined function will return to the field that called it (as you'll see later).

The commands beneath the OTHERWISE command are executed only if neither of the preceding CASE conditions is true (that is, the user is not exiting, and the user did not enter a valid customer number). If the OTHERWISE condition is executed, then the IsCust user-defined function displays the message ''No such customer!'' at exactly the position where a valid customer name would appear (row 5, column 48). The next command, @ 6,48 SAY SPACE(25), displays 25 blank spaces where the customer contact name would appear, thereby overwriting any previous contact name at that screen position.

Next, the command Ok = .F. stores .F. in the memory variable named Ok, because if the entire OTHERWISE clause is executed, then the customer number that the user entered is not valid (that is, it does not exist in the Customer database). When this .F. is returned to the custom form, the cursor will not move to the next field on the form, but instead will wait for a new, valid customer number to be entered (as you'll see later). The ENDCASE command marks the end of the DO CASE...ENDCASE decision clause.

The last command in the IsCust user-defined function, RETURN (Ok), returns the value currently stored in the memory variable named Ok to the custom form that initially called the procedure. You'll see how to attach the IsCust user-defined function to the customer field in the EditOrd custom screen soon.

For now, suffice it to say that if the customer number that the user entered was valid, or if the user was just scrolling or exiting, then the Ok value returned will allow the user to proceed. However, if the Ok value returned is .F. (that is, the customer number for the current order is invalid), then the user will need to enter a different, valid customer number before moving to the next field in the custom screen.

VALIDATING PART NUMBERS

The user-defined function for validating part numbers, named IsPart, validates part numbers as they are entered or edited in the current Orders database. The IsPart procedure uses the same basic logic and the same programming techniques as the IsCust user-defined function. The main difference is that the IsPart function validates part numbers rather than customer numbers as they are entered or changed on the screen, and it displays related data from the Master, rather than the Customer, database file.

Also, the IsPart user-defined function does not need to check whether the user is just exiting, because dBASE exits a custom screen only if the first field on the custom form (CustNo in this example) is left blank. So the IsPart function uses a simple IF...ENDIF clause to determine whether the part number that the user entered was valid (IF SEEK(MPartNo,"Master"), or not (ELSE).

The basic logic of the IsPart user-defined function is shown here in pseudocode:

```
*- - - - - - - - - - - - - - - - - - - - - - - - - - - - - Validate part number
FUNCTION IsPart
PARAMETERS MPartNo
If a valid part number was entered
    Display part name
    Display selling price
    Display taxable status
    If the user is not just scrolling
        Replace the order unit price with the selling price
            REPLACE Orders->UnitPrice WITH Master->SelPrice
            Allow suggested selling price to be changed for this order
            If the item is taxable
                Replace order tax rate with customer's tax rate
            Else
                Replace order tax rate with zero
            End IF (for taxable status)
            Allow order tax rate to be changed
            Recalculate screen
    Endif (for last keypress)
    Entry is Ok
Else
    Display error message "No such part number!"
    Reject entry
End If (part number validation)
```

To add the IsPart user-defined function to the BusProcs procedure file, follow these steps:

1. At the dot prompt, enter the command **MODIFY COMMAND BusProcs** to edit the BusProcs procedure file.

2. Position the cursor at the end of the file (beneath the IsCust user-defined function).

3. Enter the IsPart user-defined function exactly as shown in Figure 20.6.

4. After typing the new user-defined function, select Save Changes and Exit from the Exit pull-down menu to save the modified BusProcs procedure file.

```
*- - - - - - - - - - - - - - - - - - - - - - - - - - - - - - - - - Validate part number
FUNCTION IsPart
PARAMETERS MPartNo
   IF SEEK(MPartNo,"MASTER")
      @ 8,50 SAY Master->PartName
      @ 9,51 SAY Master->SelPrice PICTURE "99,999.99"
      @ 9,71 SAY Master->Taxable PICTURE "Y"

      IF LASTKEY()=13 .OR. (LASTKEY()>=32.AND.LASTKEY()<=122)
         REPLACE Orders->UnitPrice WITH Master->SelPrice
         @ 11,24 GET UnitPrice PICTURE "99,999.99"
         *- - - - If item not taxable, replace tax rate with 0
         IF Master->Taxable
            REPLACE Orders->TaxRate WITH Customer->TaxRate
         ELSE
            REPLACE Orders->TaxRate WITH 0
         ENDIF
         @ 15,16 GET TaxRate PICTURE "99.99"
         Ok = Recalc(QtyOrdered)
      ENDIF &&lastkey
      Ok=.T.

   *- - - Invalid part number.
   ELSE
         @ 8,50 SAY "No such part number!    "
         Ok=.F.
   ENDIF && seek() true or false.

RETURN (Ok)
```

Figure 20.6: The IsPart user-defined function

RECALCULATING TOTALS

As mentioned previously, dBASE will automatically recalculate subtotals and totals as you scroll through existing records in the database, because of the various calculated fields that you placed on the form. But these fields will not recalculate while the user is entering new data. Therefore, you need a user-defined function to force recalculation to take place whenever you want it to.

The name of the recalculation user-defined function is Recalc( ). To add this function to the BusProcs procedure, enter the command **MODIFY COMMAND BusProcs** at the dot prompt and then position the cursor at the bottom of the procedure file. Type the procedure as shown in Figure 20.7. Be sure to save the procedure file after adding the new function.

If you compare the contents of the Recalc function to the row and column positions of calculated fields listed previously in Table 20.2,

```
*------------------- Recalculate totals for screen display.
FUNCTION Recalc
PARAMETERS MQty
   @ 13,24 SAY QtyOrdered*UnitPrice PICTURE "99,999.99"
   @ 14,24 SAY -(DiscRate/100)*(QtyOrdered*Unitprice) PICTURE "99,999.99"
   @ 15,24 SAY (TaxRate/100)*((1-Discrate/100)*(QtyOrdered*UnitPrice)) ;
     PICTURE "99,999.99"
   @ 18,24 SAY ((QtyOrdered*UnitPrice)- ;
     ((DiscRate/100)*(QtyOrdered*UnitPrice)))* ;
     (1+(TaxRate/100)) + Shipping;
     PICTURE "99,999.99"
   Ok=.T.
RETURN (Ok)
```

Figure 20.7: The Recalc user-defined function

you'll see that it basically performs the same calculations as the calculated fields in the form. But again, because we can control when the Recalc function does its job, we gain control over when recalculations occur on the screen.

All user-defined functions must return some value, so the Recalc function always returns .T. (in a variable named Ok). Unlike the previous user-defined functions, which return .F. when invalid data is entered into a field, the Recalc function never rejects data. Its job is simply to recalculate, not to validate.

You may recall that both the IsCust and IsPart user-defined functions included the command Ok = Recalc(QtyOrdered). This command forces the Recalc function to recalculate all the subtotals and totals on the screen and then stores .T. in the variable named Ok.

ATTACHING
USER-DEFINED FUNCTIONS TO FIELDS

Now that you have created all of your user-defined functions for order entry, you need to go back to your custom screen and determine when each user-defined function is executed. As you do so, dBASE will check to make sure each user-defined function is available, so the procedure file must be open. Assuming that the dot prompt is showing on your screen, open the BusProcs procedure file now by entering the command

SET PROCEDURE TO BusProcs

To work with the EditOrd screen, the Orders, Customer, and Master databases must be open simultaneously as well. To open all three files, enter the command

DO OrdOpen

to execute the OrdOpen procedure.

To get back to the forms design screen with the EditOrd form displayed, enter the command

MODIFY SCREEN EditOrd

ATTACHING THE ISCUST FUNCTION

To attach a particular user-defined function to a particular field on the form, you need to move the cursor to the appropriate field template, press the Field (F5) key, and use the appropriate syntax for the user-defined function as the Accept Value When edit option. Let's work through the exact steps involved in attaching the IsCust user-defined function to the Customer field template.

1. Position the cursor on the CustNo field template (row 5, column 29).

2. Press Field (F5).

3. Select Edit Options.

4. Select Accept Value When.

5. Type the expression **IsCust(CustNo)** and press ←⏎.

6. Select Unaccepted Message, type the message **Please re-enter a valid customer number**, and press ←⏎.

When you are done, your screen should look like Figure 20.8 (dBASE adds the curly braces automatically; you do not type them).

Let's take a moment to review what this step has done. As soon as the user adds or changes a customer number, the Accept Value

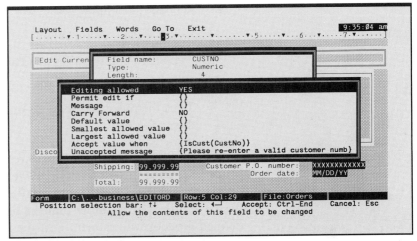

Figure 20.8: IsCust function attached to the CustNo field

When option executes the custom IsCust function, passing it the customer number (CustNo) that the user entered. The IsCust user-defined function will do the jobs you specified and return either .T. (if the entry is valid) or .F. (if the entry is invalid).

If the IsCust function returns .T., the Accept Value When option accepts the entry and moves the cursor to the next field on the form. If the IsCust function returns .F., then the Accept Value When option rejects the entry, displays the Unaccepted Message, and waits for a new entry. The cursor remains in the CustNo field on the form until the user enters a valid customer number (that is, the IsCust function returns .T.).

After defining the Accept Value When and Unaccepted Message fields, press Ctrl-End twice to return to the form.

ATTACHING THE ISPART FUNCTION

Next, to validate part numbers attach the IsPart user-defined function to the PartNo field template on the form. Use the same basic steps that you used before:

1. Move the cursor to the PartNo field template (row 8, column 28).

2. Press Field (F5).

3. Select Edit Options.

4. Select Accept Value When.

5. Type the expression **IsPart(PartNo)** and press ◄─┘.

6. Select Unaccepted Message.

7. Type the message **Please re-enter a valid part number** and then press ◄─┘.

Figure 20.9 shows how your screen should look when you've properly entered the expressions. Note that the Accept Value When option for this field activates the IsPart user-defined function and passes to it the part number that the user entered. The IsPart user-defined function will return .T. if the part number is valid. Otherwise, it will return .F., and the form will not accept the entry. Press Ctrl-End twice to return to the forms design screen.

ATTACHING THE RECALC FUNCTION

Whenever the user changes the quantity, unit price, discount rate, tax rate, or shipping information on the order-entry screen, the subtotals and total need to be recalculated. Therefore, you need to attach the Recalc user-defined function to each of these fields. The expression you use to activate the Recalc function is Recalc(QtyOrdered).

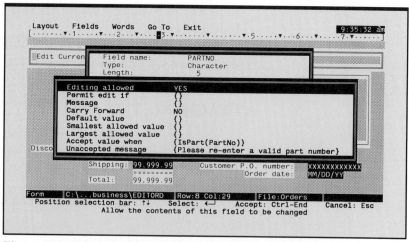

Figure 20.9: IsPart function attached to the PartNo field

Here are the steps to follow to attach the Recalc function to the QtyOrdered field:

1. Move the cursor to the QtyOrdered field template (row 10, column 30).

2. Press Field (F5).

3. Select Edit Options.

4. Select Accept Value When.

5. Type **Recalc(QtyOrdered)** and press ⏎.

6. Press Ctrl-End twice to return to the forms design screen.

You did not define an Unaccepted Message in the preceding steps because the Recalc function always returns .T. Again, its job is not to validate data, but rather to recalculate. Nonetheless, as soon as the cursor leaves the QtyOrdered field on the form, the Accept Value When option will force the Recalc function to do its job.

Now repeat steps 2 through 6 for each of the field templates listed here (in place of step 1, first position the cursor on the field template at the row and column positions indicated):

Field template	Position
UnitPrice	Row 11, column 24
DiscRate	Row 14, column 16
TaxRate	Row 15, column 16
Shipping	Row 16, column 24

SETTING A DEFAULT DATE

Before you save the current form, you might first want to make the default order date equal to the current date. To do so, follow these steps:

1. Position the cursor on the Ordate field template (row 17, column 63).

2. Press Field (F5).

3. Select Edit Options.

4. Select Default Value.

5. Type the expression **DATE( )** and press ←.

6. Press Ctrl-End twice.

SAVING THE FORM FOR ORDER EDITING

You actually need two forms for managing orders: one for editing orders and one for adding orders. The form for editing orders is done, so follow these steps to save the forms yet stay on the forms design screen:

1. Select Save This Form from the Layout pull-down menu.

2. Press ← to accept the suggested name EditOrd.

SAVING THE FORM FOR ORDER ENTRY

The form for entering new orders is basically the same as the editing form, but there is no need to display the calculated field templates that appear on the form. (These would be accurate only while scrolling through existing records.) Thus, you can delete these for the order entry form.

First move the cursor to the title Edit Current Orders and change it to Add New Orders. Then delete each of the calculated field templates by moving the cursor to the field template and pressing the Del key. Be careful to delete *only* the following calculated fields:

Field name	Position
ExtPrice	Row 13, column 24
DiscAmt	Row 14, column 24
TaxAmt	Row 15, column 24
TotSale	Row 18, column 24
CustName	Row 5, column 48
CustCont	Row 6, column 48
PtName	Row 8, column 50
Price	Row 9, column 51
Taxable	Row 9, column 71

When you are done, your screen should look like Figure 20.10.

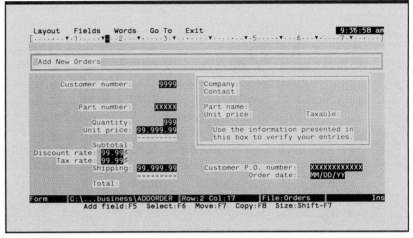

Figure 20.10: Form for entering new orders

To save this form with the file name AddOrder, follow these steps:

1. Select Save This Form from the Layout pull-down menu.

2. Press Backspace 11 times to erase EditOrd.scr and then type the new form name **ADDORDER**.

3. Press ↵.

Now select Abandon Changes and Exit from the Exit pull-down menu. You'll be returned to the dot prompt.

TESTING THE FORMS

Both the Customer and Master databases need to have some information in them before you can enter orders into the Orders database. Let's check the status of the databases now and, if necessary, add some data. At the dot prompt enter the command **CLOSE DATABASES** to close all currently open databases. Enter the command **USE Customer** to open the Customer database and then enter the command **EDIT**. If you get an error message indicating that the end-of-file was encountered immediately, the file is empty; enter the command **APPEND** instead to add new records.

Add some sample records (or edit existing ones) so that the database contains at least the two records shown here (you can press F2 to

In this section, you'll use dot-prompt commands to test your forms, but after you build the business application, you'll be able to access the forms through simpler menu selection.

switch to the browse screen if you prefer):

CustNo:	1001
Company:	Adam Chandler Enterprises
Contact:	Ross Chandler
Address:	1221 West Gaines
City:	Pine Valley
State:	NY
Zip:	12345
Phone:	(123)555-0123
StartDate:	12/01/91
TaxRate:	6.50
DiscRate	10.00
YtdChrg:	0.00
YtdPmt:	0.00
TotChrg:	0.00
TotPmt:	0.00
LastDate:	/ /

CustNo:	1002
Company:	Baker International
Contact:	Linda Grey
Address:	456 Ocean St.
City:	San Diego
State:	CA
Zip:	92067
Phone:	(619)555-0912
StartDate:	12/01/91
TaxRate:	0.00
DiscRate	0.00
YtdChrg:	0.00
YtdPmt:	0.00
TotChrg:	0.00
TotPmt:	0.00
LastDate:	/ /

Press Ctrl-End after adding or editing records to save them and return to the dot prompt. Note that the first customer, 1001, has a discount rate of 10 percent, and a tax rate of 6.5 percent. The second customer has zero as both these rates.

Now add or edit some Master database file records. First enter the command **USE Master** to open the Master database. Then enter the command **EDIT** (or **APPEND**, if you get an error message). Enter at least two records with the following characteristics:

PartNo:	A-111
PartName:	American Adventure
Category:	BOOK
InStock:	10
Reorder:	20
PurCost:	10.00
SelPrice:	25.00
Taxable:	T
Vendor:	HBJ
VendItemNo:	HBJ-101
Location:	WH-A10
LastUpdate:	/ /

PartNo:	B-222
PartName:	Data Base Master
Category:	MAGAZINE
InStock:	30
Reorder:	5
PurCost:	3.50
SelPrice:	5.00
Taxable:	F
Vendor:	ZD
VendItemNo:	Z-444-01
Location:	WH-001
LastUpdate:	/ /

Press Ctrl-End after adding at least these two records. Note that the first item, A-111, is taxable, and the second is not. Press Ctrl-End when you are done to return to the dot prompt.

Now you are ready to start testing. First make sure the BusProcs procedure file is open by entering the command **SET PROCE-DURE TO BusProcs**. Then open the required databases by entering the command **DO OrdOpen**.

The dot prompt command for activating a custom form is **SET FORMAT**. To activate the AddOrder form, enter the command **SET FORMAT TO AddOrder** (initially, only the dot prompt will appear). Then, to start adding new records, enter the command **APPEND**. You should see the AddOrder custom form on the screen, ready to accept data, as in Figure 20.11.

First try entering an invalid customer number such as 4444. You should see the message ''No such customer!'' in the single-line box

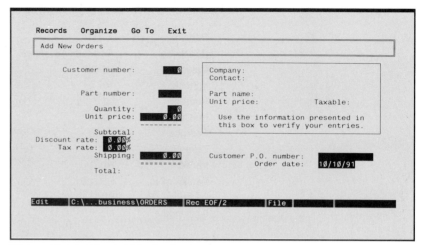

```
   Records   Organize   Go To   Exit
  ┌─────────────────────────────────────────────────────────────────┐
  │ Add New Orders                                                    │
  └─────────────────────────────────────────────────────────────────┘


         Customer number:      ▐    0   ┌──────────────────────────────┐
                                        │ Company:                     │
                                        │ Contact:                     │
            Part number:      ▐      ▌  │                              │
                                        │ Part name:                   │
               Quantity:      ▐     0   │ Unit price:        Taxable:  │
             Unit price:      ▐  0.00   │                              │
                                 ─────  │   Use the information presented in │
                Subtotal:               │   this box to verify your entries. │
     Discount rate: ▐0.00%               └──────────────────────────────┘
         Tax rate: ▐0.00%
              Shipping:      ▐   0.00    Customer P.O. number:
                                 ═════      Order date: ▐10/10/91▌
                  Total:
```

```
 Edit  │C:\...business\ORDERS │Rec EOF/2      │File    │          │
```

Figure 20.11: The AddOrder form, ready to accept data

and the message "Please re-enter a valid customer number (press
SPACE)." Press the space bar and then enter a valid customer number, such as **1001**.

The screen should immediately display the customer information, as shown in Figure 20.12. (The tax rate is initially set to zero,
however, because you have not yet entered a part number.)

Now try entering an invalid part number, such as W-333. You
should see an error message indicating that no such part number
exists and asking you to press the space bar. Enter a valid part number, such as **A-111**, and you should see the name, unit price, and taxable status (Y or N) of the part on the screen.

Next enter a quantity, such as **10**. Immediately, the screen calculates the subtotal, discount, tax, and total, as shown in Figure 20.13.
At this point, you can change any of the other fields (if necessary) to
finish entering the order, or just press PgDn to enter the next order.

Feel free to experiment with the form for as long as you wish.
After you enter at least two sample orders, you can leave the customer number as zero on a new, blank record or press Ctrl-End to
save your work and return to the dot prompt.

To review or change the orders you've entered, use the EditOrd
screen and the EDIT command. At the dot prompt, enter

```
SET FORMAT TO EditOrd
EDIT 1
```

When the editing screen appears, you can use the PgUp and PgDn keys to scroll through the records. Again, feel free to experiment. Press Ctrl-End when you are done experimenting.

In the next chapter, we'll develop some additional custom forms and report formats for the business application and use the Applications Generator to tie everything together into a single, integrated application. For future reference, Figure 20.14 shows the entire completed BusProcs procedure file.

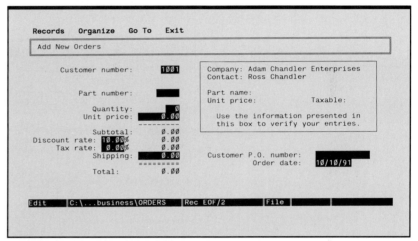

Figure 20.12: Valid customer number entered on the screen

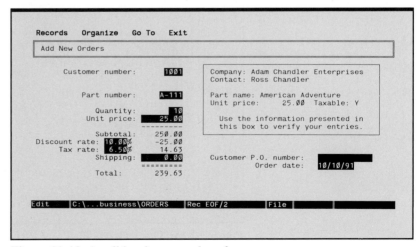

Figure 20.13: A valid order entered on the screen

```
****************************************** BusProcs.PRG
*---- Procedures for order entry and editing.

**************************** Assign customer numbers.
PROCEDURE AutoCust

   *---------- Open Customer database.
   USE Customer ORDER CustNo
   GOTO BOTTOM

   *---------- 1001 is lowest possible customer number.
   Largest = MAX(1000,CustNo)
   NextCust = Largest + 1

   *---------- Fill in customer numbers.
   USE Customer   && Deactivate index before using REPLACE.
   SCAN FOR CustNo = 0
     REPLACE CustNo WITH NextCust
     NextCust = NextCust + 1
   ENDSCAN

   *--- Done
   CLOSE DATABASES
RETURN

*---------- Assign invoice numbers to current orders.
PROCEDURE AutoInv

   * BusMgr application uses this procedure
   * before printing the invoices.

   *---- Find largest current invoice number
   USE Orders ORDER Invoice
   GOTO BOTTOM
   Largest = MAX(100000,Invoice)

   USE OrdHist ORDER Invoice
   GOTO Bottom
   Largest=MAX(Largest,Invoice)

   CLOSE DATABASES
   NextInvNo = Largest + 1   && Next invoice number.

   *------ Assign invoice numbers.
   USE Orders ORDER CustNo
   SCAN FOR Invoice = 0
     ThisCust = CustNo
     REPLACE Invoice WITH NextInvNo ;
         WHILE CustNo = ThisCust ;
         FOR Invoice = 0
     NextInvNo = NextInvNo + 1
     SKIP -1
   ENDSCAN
   *--- Done
```

Figure 20.14: The complete BusProcs.PRG procedure file

```
       CLOSE DATABASES
    RETURN

    *----------------- Update Master file from items received.
    PROCEDURE AddItems

       *--- Close open files, then open Master and ItemsRec.
       CLOSE DATABASES
       SELECT A
       USE Master ORDER PartNo
       SELECT B
       USE ItemsRec ORDER PartNo

       *-------- Perform the update.
       SELECT Master
       UPDATE ON PartNo FROM ItemsRec REPLACE ;
          InStock WITH InStock + ItemsRec->Qty_Recvd, ;
          LastUpdate WITH ItemsRec->DateRecvd, ;
          PurCost WITH ;
          IIF(ItemsRec->Price > 0,ItemsRec->Price,PurCost)

       CLOSE DATABASES

       *------------- Move updated transactions to history file.
       SET SAFETY OFF   && So dBASE does not ask for permission.
       USE ItemHist     && History file for ItemsRec database.

       *------------- Read in completed transactions.
       APPEND FROM ItemsRec

       *---------- Remove completed transactions from ItemsRec file.
       USE ItemsRec
       ZAP
       CLOSE DATABASES
    RETURN

    *------ Determine backorder requirements, and subtract
    *------ orders from in-stock quantities.
    PROCEDURE OrdUpdat

       *-- Open Master and Orders database files.
       SELECT A
       USE Orders ORDER PartNo
       SELECT B
       USE Master ORDER PartNo

       *-- Must set up relationship if not using UPDATE command.
       SELECT Orders
       SET RELATION TO PartNo INTO Master

       *-- Update the Master in-stock quantities.
       GO TOP
       SCAN FOR .NOT. InvPosted
          *-- See whether or not qty ordered exceeds in stock qty.
       IF QtyOrdered <= Master->InStock
```

Figure 20.14: The complete BusProcs.PRG procedure file (continued)

```
              REPLACE QtyShipped WITH QtyOrdered
          ELSE
              REPLACE QtyShipped WITH MAX(0,Master->InStock)
              REPLACE BackOrdQty WITH QtyOrdered-QtyShipped
          ENDIF
          *---------- Update Master inventory database.
          SELECT Master
          REPLACE InStock WITH InStock-Orders->QtyShipped
          SELECT Orders
          REPLACE InvPosted WITH .T.
          ENDSCAN

          ********* Invoices can now be printed for posted records.
          ********* After printing invoices, must send fulfilled orders
          ********* to order history file, and convert backorders to
          ********* outstanding orders.  (The application will print
          ********* invoices as soon as this procedure is done).
          CLOSE DATABASES
RETURN


PROCEDURE MoveOrds
    *---- Used in the BusMgr application after orders have
    *---- been fulfilled and invoices have been printed.
    USE OrdHist
    APPEND FROM Orders FOR QtyShipped > 0 .AND. InvPosted
    USE Orders
    DELETE FOR BackOrdQty = 0 .AND. InvPosted
    PACK
    REPLACE ALL QtyOrdered WITH BackOrdQty, ;
            QtyShipped WITH 0, ;
            BackOrdQty WITH 0, ;
            InvPosted WITH .F., ;
            Invoice WITH 0
RETURN

*--------- Moves fulfilled orders to the AR transaction file.
PROCEDURE ARUpdate
    *--- Used in BusMgr application after moving
    *--- fulfilled orders to OrdHist file.

    *--- First calculate order totals.
    USE OrdHist ORDER Invoice
    REPLACE OrdTotal WITH (((QtyShipped*UnitPrice)- ;
        ((DiscRate/100)*(QtyShipped*UnitPrice)))* ;
        (1+(TaxRate/100)))+Shipping ;
        FOR QtyShipped > 0

    *--- Now create temporary database of totaled orders.
    GO TOP
    SET SAFETY OFF
    TOTAL ON Invoice FIELDS OrdTotal TO OrdTemp FOR .NOT. ARPosted
    *---- Copy summarized totals into the AR transaction file.
    USE Transact
    APPEND FROM OrdTemp
    *--- Mark orders as being posted to the AR transaction file.
```

Figure 20.14: The complete BusProcs.PRG procedure file (continued)

```
      USE OrdHist
      REPLACE ALL ARPosted WITH .T.
      CLOSE DATABASES
RETURN

*--- Update customer balances
PROCEDURE ARPost

   SELECT A
   USE Customer ORDER CustNo
   SELECT B
   USE Transact ORDER CustNo
   *-- Exclude records that have been posted.
   SET FILTER TO .NOT. CustPosted
   GO TOP   && Always move the record pointer after a SET FILTER.

   SELECT Customer
   UPDATE ON CustNo FROM Transact REPLACE ;
      TotChrg WITH TotChrg + Transact->OrdTotal, ;
      YtdChrg WITH YtdChrg + Transact->OrdTotal, ;
      TotPmt WITH TotPmt + Transact->AmtPaid, ;
      YtdPmt WITH YtdPmt + Transact->AmtPaid, ;
      LastDate WITH DATE()

   *----- Customer balances now updated, flag transactions.
   CLOSE DATABASES
   USE Transact
   REPLACE ALL CustPosted WITH .T.
   CLOSE DATABASES
RETURN

*---- Resets year-to-date values to zero
*---- in the customer database, and moves
*---- old transactions to history file.
PROCEDURE YearEnd

   *--- Double-check for permission.
   GoAhead = .F.
   @ 4,5 SAY " Are you sure you want to reset year-to-date"
   @ 5,5 SAY "totals to zero now? (Y/N) " GET GoAhead PICTURE "Y"
   READ

   *-- If Ok to proceed, do so.
   IF GoAhead
      SET TALK ON
      SET SAFETY OFF
      USE Customer
      REPLACE ALL YtdChrg WITH 0, YtdPmt WITH 0
      USE Transact
      COPY TO TranHist FOR CustPosted .AND. Printed
      DELETE FOR CustPosted .AND. Printed
      PACK
      SET TALK OFF
   ENDIF
```

Figure 20.14: The complete BusProcs.PRG procedure file (continued)

```
     CLOSE DATABASES
RETURN


*---- Rebuild index files for all databases.
PROCEDURE BusRendx

     SET TALK ON     && Show progress
     USE Customer
     REINDEX
     USE Master
     REINDEX
     USE Orders
     REINDEX
     USE OrdHist
     REINDEX
     USE ItemsRec
     REINDEX
     USE ItemHist
     REINDEX
     USE Transact
     REINDEX
     SET TALK OFF && Suppress progress messages.
RETURN


*----------------- Opens database files and sets relations
*----------------- for order entry and editing.
PROCEDURE OrdOpen
   SELECT A
   USE Orders
   SELECT B
   USE Customer ORDER CustNo
   SELECT C
   USE Master ORDER PartNo

   *--- Set up relationship based on key fields.
   SELECT Orders
   SET RELATION TO CustNo INTO Customer, PartNo INTO Master
   GO TOP
RETURN


*--------- Validate customer number.
FUNCTION IsCust
PARAMETERS MCustNo
   DO CASE
      *-- Is user is exiting, do nothing.
      CASE MCustNo = 0
         Ok=.T.

      *-- Customer number was entered.
      CASE SEEK(MCustNo,"Customer")
           @ 5,48 SAY Customer->Company
           @ 6,48 SAY Customer->Contact
           *-- Recalculate (depending on last keypress)
           IF LASTKEY()=13 .OR. (LASTKEY()>=32.AND.LASTKEY()<=122)
```

Figure 20.14: The complete BusProcs.PRG procedure file (continued)

```
               REPLACE Orders->DiscRate WITH Customer->DiscRate
               @ 14,16 GET DiscRate PICTURE "99.99"
               IF Master->Taxable
                   REPLACE Orders->TaxRate WITH Customer->TaxRate
               ELSE
                   REPLACE Orders->TaxRate WITH 0
               ENDIF  && taxable
               @ 15,16 GET TaxRate PICTURE "99.99"
               Ok=Recalc(QtyOrdered)
               ENDIF && last keypress
               Ok=.T.
           OTHERWISE
               @ 5,48 SAY "No such customer!"
               @ 6,48 SAY SPACE(25)
               Ok=.F.
       ENDCASE
RETURN (Ok)

*------------------------ Validate part number.
FUNCTION IsPart
PARAMETERS MPartNo
    IF SEEK(MPartNo,"Master")
       @ 8,50 SAY Master->PartName
       @ 9,51 SAY Master->SelPrice PICTURE "99,999.99"
       @ 9,71 SAY Master->Taxable PICTURE "Y"

       IF LASTKEY()=13 .OR. (LASTKEY()>=32.AND.LASTKEY()<=122)
           REPLACE Orders->UnitPrice WITH Master->SelPrice
           @ 11,24 GET UnitPrice PICTURE "99,999.99"
           *--- If item not taxable, replace tax rate with zero.
           IF Master->Taxable
               REPLACE Orders->TaxRate WITH Customer->TaxRate
           ELSE
               REPLACE Orders->TaxRate WITH 0
           ENDIF
           @ 15,16 GET TaxRate PICTURE "99.99"
           Ok = Recalc(QtyOrdered)
       ENDIF &&lastkey
       Ok=.T.

    *--- Invalid entry.
    ELSE
       @ 8,50 SAY "No such part number!    "
       Ok=.F.
    ENDIF  && seek() true or false

RETURN (Ok)

*---------------- Recalculate totals for screen display.
FUNCTION Recalc
PARAMETERS MQty
    @ 13,24 SAY QtyOrdered*UnitPrice PICTURE "99,999.99"
    @ 14,24 SAY -(DiscRate/100)*(QtyOrdered*UnitPrice) PICTURE "99,999.99"
    @ 15,24 SAY (TaxRate/100)*((1-DiscRate/100)*(QtyOrdered*UnitPrice)) ;
```

Figure 20.14: The complete BusProcs.PRG procedure file (continued)

```
       PICTURE "99,999.99"
   a 18,24 SAY ((QtyOrdered*UnitPrice)- ;
           ((DiscRate/100)*(QtyOrdered*UnitPrice)))* ;
           (1+(TaxRate/100)) + Shipping;
           PICTURE "99,999.99"
   Ok=.T.
RETURN (Ok)
```

Figure 20.14: The complete BusProcs.PRG procedure file (continued)

C H A P T E R

21

The Business
Management
Application

IN CHAPTERS 19 AND 20, WE BUILT THE DATABASE structures, procedure file, and two custom forms for the business application. In this chapter, we'll complete the application by designing the remaining screens and report formats and then use the Applications Generator to pull all the pieces together into an integrated system with pull-down menus.

DESIGNING THE CUSTOM FORMS

In Chapter 20, you created the AddOrder and EditOrd screens for entering and editing orders in the Orders database. Now you need to develop forms for entering and editing data in the Customer, Master, ItemsRec, and Transact files. This section will present examples of various forms, though you can design the forms in any way you wish.

You can create each form using the forms design screen from the Control Center. If the dot prompt is displayed on your screen right now, enter the command **ASSIST** to return to the Control Center. You should see the names of the various files you created in Chapter 19 listed in the panels. (Don't forget that you must be on the \dBASE\Business subdirectory and the Business.cat catalog must be displayed on the screen when you use the business application.)

DESIGNING THE FORMS
FOR THE CUSTOMER DATABASE

If you need reminders about techniques or special keys that you use to create and edit custom forms, refer to Chapter 8.

To create forms for the Customer database, open the Customer database and select <create> from the Forms pull-down menu. Figure 21.1 shows a suggested format for the form. Table 21.1 lists the exact locations of field templates on the form. Special display attributes assigned to the fields, such as picture functions or default values, are listed to the right of the field name. The template that each field uses on the form is visible in the figure.

Figure 21.1: The EditCust custom form on the forms design screen

Remember: To add a field template or change a field template, picture functions, or edit options, use the F5 key.

Note that Balance is a calculated field. Remember: To place a calculated field on the screen, you position the cursor at the field's location, press F5, and select <create> from the Calculated column. Then type a name for the calculated field (**Balance** in this example) and the expression (**TotChrg – TotPmt** in this example).

After you create the form, select the Save This Form option from the Layout pull-down menu and save the form using the name **Edit-Cust**. Then remove the Customer number: prompt and the CustNo field template and change the form title as shown in Figure 21.2. After making the changes, again select Save This Form from the Layout menu, and then save the modified form with the name **Add-Cust**. After saving the forms, you can select Abandon Changes and Exit to return to the Control Center.

DESIGNING THE FORMS FOR THE MASTER INVENTORY

The forms for the Master database are named AddParts and EditPart. To create these forms, first open the Master database and then use the PartNo index by pressing Data (F2) and selecting the

Table 21.1: Fields and Options on the EditCust Form

Row, Column	Field Name	Options
5, 21	CUSTNO	Edit option: Editing Allowed: NO
6, 21	COMPANY	
7, 21	CONTACT	
8, 21	ADDRESS	
9, 21	CITY	
9, 43	STATE	
9, 47	ZIP	
10, 21	PHONE	
11, 21	STARTDATE	Edit option: Default Value: DATE( )
11, 51	DISCRATE	
12, 51	TAXRATE	
14, 27	YTDCHRG	
14, 60	TOTCHRG	
15, 27	YTDPMT	
15, 60	TOTPMT	
17, 60	(Calculated field) Name: BALANCE Expression: TOTCHRG – TOTPMT	

Order Records by Index option from the Organize pull-down menu. Then press Ctrl-End to return to the Control Center.

Next, select <create> from the Forms panel. Design the form to your own liking or use the suggested format shown in Figure 21.3. The row and column locations, picture functions, and edit options associated with each field are listed in Table 21.2.

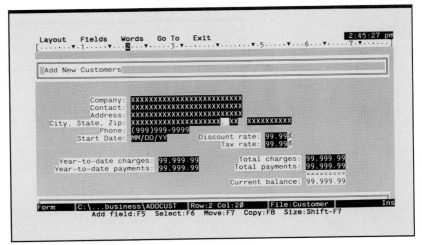

Figure 21.2: The AddCust custom form

Figure 21.3: Suggested format for the AddParts custom form

Note that the Accept Value When expression, .NOT. SEEK (PartNo, "Master"), rejects the entry when the part number entered already exists in the database (the SEEK function searches the index, and hence this feature works only if the PartNo index is in use during data entry). After creating the AddParts custom form, select Save

Table 21.2: Fields and Options on the AddParts Form

Row, Column	Field Name	Options
5, 16	PARTNO	Picture Function: ! Edit option: Accept Value When .NOT. SEEK(PARTNO, "MASTER") Unaccepted Message: Each part must have a unique part number!
7, 16	PARTNAME	
7, 48	CATEGORY	
11, 5	INSTOCK	
11, 18	REORDER	
11, 30	PURCOST	
11, 45	SELPRICE	
11, 61	TAXABLE	
14, 11	VENDOR	
14, 37	VENDITEMNO	
14, 67	LOCATION	

This Form from the Layout pull-down menu and save the form with the file name AddParts.

To create the form for editing the part information, leave the AddParts custom form on the screen and remove the Accept Value When and Unaccepted Message edit options from the PartNo field. Then change the Editing Allowed option for the PartNo field from Yes to No. Modify the form to look like Figure 21.4. Save the modified version of the form with the file name EditPart. Then you can select Abandon Changes and Exit from the Exit pull-down menu to return to the Control Center.

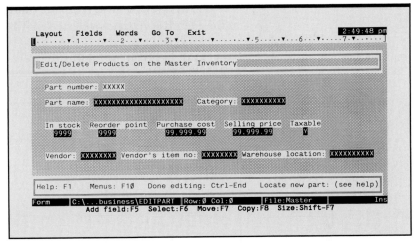

Figure 21.4: Suggested format for the EditPart custom form

DESIGNING THE FORM
FOR THE ITEMSREC DATABASE

The ItemsRec database file holds information about newly received purchases (items that the business received to replenish its stock). To create the form, first open the ItemsRec database file and then select <create> from the Forms panel. Figure 21.5 shows a suggested format for the custom form.

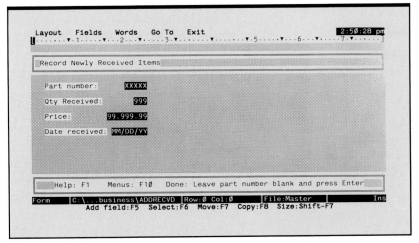

Figure 21.5: AddRecvd custom form for recording purchases

The locations of field templates and the display attribute assigned to the DateRecvd field are listed in Table 21.3.

Table 21.3: Fields on the AddRecvd Custom Form

Row, Column	Field Name	Options
5, 21	PARTNO	
7, 23	QTY_RECVD	
9, 17	PRICE	
11, 18	DATERECVD	Edit option: Default Value: DATE( )

After creating the form, select Save Changes and Exit from the Exit pull-down menu and assign the name AddRecvd when prompted.

DESIGNING THE FORMS FOR THE TRANSACTION DATABASE

Most of the information on the Transact (transactions) database comes from the Orders database automatically. However, you do need a couple of forms to view and change existing data, as well as to record customers' payments. To create these forms, first open the Transact database, then select <create> from the Forms panel.

VIEWING AND EDITING TRANSACTIONS   Figure 21.6 shows a suggested screen format for editing transactions. Field template positions and display attributes are listed in Table 21.4. Note that most fields use the Permit Edit If edit option with the expression .NOT. (Printed .OR. CustPosted). This edit option prevents the user from editing transactions that have already been billed and updated and are reflected in the Customer balances. (As you'll see later, to change transactions that have already been printed and posted, the user can enter adjustment transactions, which provide an audit trail.) Name the form EDTRANS when saving it.

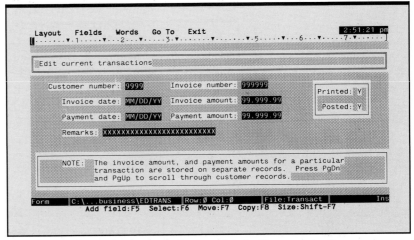

Figure 21.6: The EdTrans custom form for the Transact database

ENTERING PAYMENTS   The form for entering payments displays only a few fields from the Transact database. The form requires no special display attributes, except that you might want to use DATE( ) as the Default Value edit option so that the current date is filled in automatically. Figure 21.7 shows a suggested format for the custom form on the forms design screen. Create the form in the usual manner and save it using the file name AddPmts.

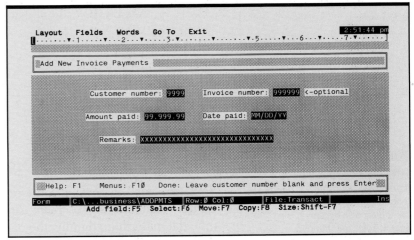

Figure 21.7: The AddPmts custom form on the forms design screen

Table 21.4: Fields on the EdTrans Custom Form

Row, Column	Field Name	Options
5, 21	CUSTNO	Edit option: Permit Edit If: .NOT. (Printed .OR. CustPosted)
5, 47	INVOICE	Edit option: Permit Edit If: .NOT. (Printed .OR. CustPosted)
6, 73	PRINTED	Edit option: Editing Allowed: No
7, 21	ORDATE	Edit option: Permit Edit If: .NOT. (Printed .OR. CustPosted)
7, 47	ORDTOTAL	Edit option: Permit Edit If: .NOT. (Printed .OR. CustPosted)
8, 73	CUSTPOSTED	Edit option: Editing Allowed: No
9, 21	DATEPAID	Edit option: Permit Edit If: .NOT. (Printed .OR. CustPosted)
9, 47	AMTPAID	Edit option: Permit Edit If: .NOT. (Printed .OR. CustPosted)
11, 16	REMARKS	

DESIGNING THE REPORT FORMATS

If you need additional reminders about how to use the reports design screen, refer to Chapters 7 and 9.

Next, you need to develop some report formats for the business application. Remember: To create a report format, you must first open the database that contains the data that the report is to print. Then select <create> from the Reports panel in the Control Center.

DESIGNING THE CUSTOMER LIST REPORT

The Customer List report displays names and addresses, charges, payments, and the current balance for each customer. Figure 21.8 shows a suggested format for the report on the reports design screen. Figure 21.9 shows two records from the Customer database printed with the suggested format.

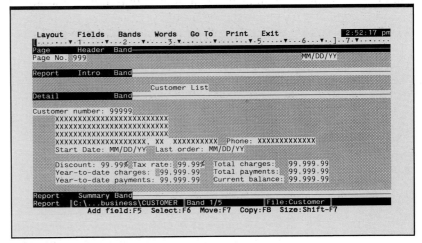

Figure 21.8: Suggested format for the Customer report

Note that in the suggested format, the current balance is a calculated field named Balance that uses the expression TotChrg – TotPmt. All other fields are taken directly from the database. The large field templates beneath the customer number are the Company, Contact, Address, City, State, and Zip fields, in that order from top to bottom.

After you create the report format, save it using the file name **Customer**. When you return to the Control Center, you'll be ready to develop the report formats for the Master inventory database.

DESIGNING THE MASTER INVENTORY REPORTS

The business application uses two report formats for displaying data from the Master inventory: One shows the entire current inventory, and the other lists items that need to be reordered.

The dates shown in sample reports are for the example only.

```
Page No.   1                                                    01/30/92

                              Customer List

Customer number:  1001
      Adam Chandler Enterprises
      Ross Chandler
      1221 West Gaines
      Pine Valley, NY  12345                 Phone: (123)555-0123
      Start Date: 12/01/91  Last order: 01/23/92

      Discount: 10.00% Tax rate:   6.50%  Total charges:        0.00
      Year-to-date charges:         0.00  Total payments:       0.00
      Year-to-date payments:        0.00  Current balance:      0.00


Customer number:  1002
      Baker International
      Linda Grey
      3456 Ocean St.
      San Diego, CA  92067                   Phone: (619)555-0912
      Start Date: 12/01/91  Last order: 01/23/92

      Discount:  0.00% Tax rate:   0.00%  Total charges:        0.00
      Year-to-date charges:         0.00  Total payments:       0.00
      Year-to-date payments:        0.00  Current balance:      0.00
```

Figure 21.9: Customer records printed using the Customer format

MASTER INVENTORY REPORT   The Master Inventory report displays the current status of all items in stock. Figure 21.10 shows a suggested format for the report. Figure 21.11 shows some sample records from the Master database printed with the suggested format. To create the Master Inventory report, first make sure that the Master database file is open and then select <create> from the Reports panel.

Note that in the suggested format, the templates displayed as XXXXXX : XXXXXXXXXXXXXXXXXXXXX are the field templates for the PartNo and PartName fields, respectively, separated by a colon. The field template beneath the Cost heading is for the PurCost field, and the field template beneath the Price heading is for the SelPrice field. After creating the report format, save it with the file name MastRept.

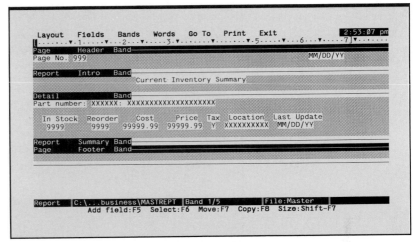

Figure 21.10: Suggested format for the Master Inventory report

```
Page No.   1                                          02/28/91

                         Current Inventory Summary

Part number: A-111: American Adventure

   In Stock   Reorder     Cost     Price  Tax  Location  Last Update
      10        20        10.00     25.00  Y   WH-A10    01/01/91

Part number: B-222: Data Base Master

   In Stock   Reorder     Cost     Price  Tax  Location  Last Update
      30         5         3.50      5.00  N   WH-001    01/05/91
```

Figure 21.11: Sample records printed using the MastRept format

REORDER REPORT   To create the Reorder report, once again be sure that the Master database file is open and then select <create> from the Reports panel. Figure 21.12 shows a suggested format for the report. Figure 21.13 shows some sample data printed using the format. After you create the report format, save it using the file name ReordRpt.

Figure 21.12: Suggested format for the ReordRpt report

Figure 21.13: Sample record printed using the ReordRpt format

PRINTING INVOICES AND AN INVOICE SUMMARY

To print invoices and an invoice summary (or invoice register, as it is often called), you need data from three separate databases: the Customer database, for customers' names and addresses; the Orders database, for current orders; and the Master database, for part names. Recall that in Chapter 20 you created a procedure named

OrdOpen to open and relate these three database files. So rather than go through all the steps again, you can just run the OrdOpen procedure following these steps:

1. From the Control Center, select Exit to Dot Prompt from the Exit pull-down menu.

2. At the dot prompt, open the procedure file by entering the command **SET PROCEDURE TO BusProcs**.

3. When the dot prompt reappears, enter the command **DO OrdOpen**. When the dot prompt reappears again, you can be sure that the three databases are open and related.

DESIGNING THE INVOICE FORMAT

Now that the three required database files are open, you can create the invoice report format, which we'll name Invoices. You can go directly to the reports design screen, bypassing the Control Center, by entering the command **MODIFY REPORT Invoices.**

Figure 21.14 shows a suggested format for the report. Figure 21.15 shows a sample invoice for one customer.

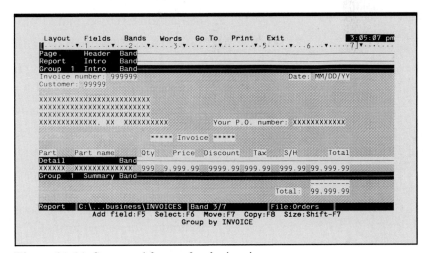

Figure 21.14: Suggested format for the invoices

```
Invoice number: 100003                                    Date: 02/28/91
Customer:  1001

Adam Chandler Enterprises
Ross Chandler
1221 West Gaines
Pine Valley, NY  12345                  Your P.O. number: 123-45-6789

                       ***** Invoice *****

Part      Part name      Qty    Price  Discount   Tax    S/H      Total
A-111     American Adve    2     25.00    -5.00    2.93   0.00     47.93
B-222     Data Base Mas    1      3.50     0.35    0.00   0.00      3.15
                                                              ---------
                                                     Total:       51.08
```

Figure 21.15: Sample printed invoice

The Invoices report format uses many of the techniques discussed in Chapter 13 for printing invoices. To get started (assuming that you are already at the reports design screen), follow these steps:

1. Move the cursor into the Report Intro band border (so that "Band 2/5" appears in the status bar).

2. Select Add a Group Band from the Bands pull-down menu.

3. Select Field Value from the submenu.

4. Select Invoice as the grouping field, (because you want each invoice to print all orders for a specific invoice number).

5. Move the the Page Header band border (band 1/7) and press ⏎ to close the band.

6. Move to the Report Intro band border (band 2/7) and press ⏎ to close that band.

7. Use the same basic techniques to close the Report Summary band (band 6/7) and Page Footer band (band 7/7) near the bottom of the report format.

8. Move the cursor to the Group 1 Intro band border (band 3/7), select Begin Band on New Page from the Bands pull-down menu, and press the space bar until the setting reads

"Yes." This ensures that each invoice is printed on a separate page.

Remember: To add a blank line to a report band, move the cursor inside the band and press Ctrl-N.

Next, you need to place field templates in the Group 1 Summary Band. The date in the upper-right corner of the band (line 0, column 62) is the Date from the Predefined column that appears when you press F5. The following table lists the row and column positions of fields from the Orders database. To place these on the report format, position the cursor at the row and column position shown, press F5, and select the field name from the Orders column of the submenu that appears.

Line, Column	Name
0, 16	Invoice
1, 10	CustNo
6, 57	CustPONumb

The rest of the fields in the Group 1 Summary band are calculated fields. To place these, position the cursor at the line and column position shown, press F5, and select <create> from the Calculated column. Leave the Name entry blank, and enter the Expression shown here:

TIP

When using a calculated field to display data from separate databases, it's best not to assign a name to that calculated field.

Line, Column	Expression
3, 0	Customer->Company
4, 0	Customer->Contact
5, 0	Customer->Address
6, 0	Customer->City
6, 15	Customer->State
6, 19	Customer->Zip

Next you can enter the field templates in the Detail band. Note that fitting all of the information into the Detail band of the invoice is a tight squeeze. Therefore, you need to reduce most of the field templates to the smallest acceptable size. Here, the part-name template is reduced to only 13 spaces wide. If your printer is capable of compressed print, you could widen the margins and thereby make more room for the part name. You could also use the Vertical Stretch picture function to word-wrap the part name onto two separate lines if you prefer.

Detail band fields, taken directly from the Orders database, are listed here:

Line, Column	Name
0, 0	PartNo
0, 23	QtyShipped
0, 28	UnitPrice
0, 54	Shipping

The following table lists the position, name, and expression for each calculated field in the Detail band (note that some expressions are broken into several lines here to fit into the book, but you must enter each expression as a single line):

Line, Column	Name	Expression
0, 8		Master->PartName
0, 38	DISCAMT	$-$(DiscRate/100) *(QtyShipped*UnitPrice)
0, 46	TAXAMT	(TaxRate/100) *((QtyShipped*UnitPrice) $-$((DiscRate/100) *(QtyShipped*UnitPrice)))
0, 61	TOTSALE	(((QtyShipped*UnitPrice) $-$((DiscRate/100) *(QtyShipped*UnitPrice))) *(1 +(TaxRate/100))) +Shipping

The total for each invoice appears in the Group 1 Summary band at line 1, column 61. To place this field, position the cursor, press F5, and assign the name SumTotSal. Select SUM as the Operation and

TotSale as the field to summarize on and set Reset Every to Invoice (so the total is reset to zero before each invoice is printed).

When you have finished designing the report, select Save This Report from the Layout pull-down menu and press ⏎ to accept Invoices as the file name.

DESIGNING THE INVOICE SUMMARY FORMAT

The invoice summary report allows the application user to preview printed invoices before they are printed to check for errors. It uses a format similar to the invoices report, but more compressed. Figure 21.16 shows a suggested format on the reports design screen, and Figure 21.17 shows some sample data printed using the format.

To modify the Invoices report format to create the invoice summary report format, move the cursor to the Group 1 Intro band border (band 3/7), select Begin Band on New Page from the Bands menu, and change the setting to No. Then select Modify Group from the Bands pull-down menu, select Field Value, and specify CustNo as the field to group on.

Invoice numbers are not assigned until invoices are printed, so you can also delete the Invoice Number field template in row 0 of the Group 1 Intro band. Also, because the invoice summary report is

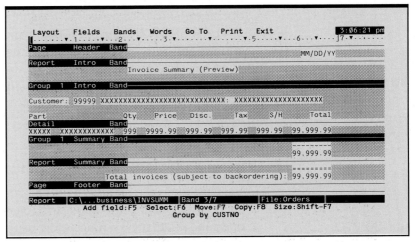

Figure 21.16: Suggested format for the InvSumm report

```
                                                            01/30/91
                       Invoice  Summary  (Preview)


 Customer:   1001 Adam Chandler Enterprises: Ross Chandler

 Part                    Qty    Price   Disc.    Tax    S/H     Total
 A-111    American Adve   2     25.00   -5.00   2.93   0.00     47.93
 B-222    Data Base Mas   1      3.50    0.35   0.00   0.00      3.15
                                                              ---------
                                                      Total:    51.08

 Customer:   1002 Baker International: Linda Grey

 Part                    Qty    Price   Disc.    Tax    S/H     Total
 B-222    Data Base Mas   1      3.50    0.00   0.00   0.00      3.50
                                                              ---------
                                                      Total:     3.50


                                                              =========
                  Total invoices (subject to backordering):    54.58
```

Figure 21.17: Sample data printed using the InvSumm format

printed prior to the actual fulfillment (and possible backordering) of orders, you need to delete the QtyShipped field template from the Detail band (near line 0, column 23) and replace it with a field template for the QtyOrdered field.

The grand total of invoices, displayed in the Report Summary band, is a summary field named GrandTot that uses SUM as its operation and TotSale as the field to summarize on and is Reset Every REPORT. You may also want to remove the customer's address and add the report title, as shown in the suggested format.

After creating the report format, select Save This Report from the Layout pull-down menu and assign the file name InvSumm to the report format. Then you can select Abandon Changes and Exit to return to the dot prompt.

PRINTING CUSTOMER STATEMENTS

Customer statements are printed once a month to display current charges, payments, and balances. To create this report, you need to open and relate the Transact and Customer databases. From the dot prompt, enter this series of commands:

```
CLOSE DATABASES

SELECT A
USE Transact ORDER Custno

SELECT B
USE Customer ORDER CustNo

SELECT A
SET RELATION TO CustNo INTO Customer
```

Then, to get to the reports design screen to create the report format, named Statmnts, enter this command:

```
MODIFY REPORT Statmnts
```

Figure 21.18 shows a suggested format for the Statmnts report on the reports design screen. Figure 21.19 shows a sample printed statement. The Group band is based on the field value CustNo. After adding the Group band, select Begin Band on New Page from the Bands pull-down menu and change the setting to Yes to print each statement on a separate page.

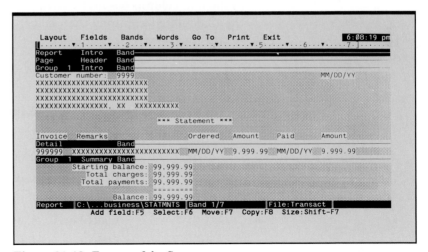

Figure 21.18: Format of the Statmnts report

```
Customer number:  1001                                            02/28/91
Adam Chandler Enterprises
Ross Chandler
1221 West Gaines
Pine Valley, NY  12345


                        *** Statement ***


Invoice  Remarks                  Ordered    Amount    Paid      Amount
100003                            01/30/91   27.11
100005                            02/08/91  100.00
100003   Check # 552                 /  /                02/05/91  27.11

         Starting balance:       0.00
            Total charges:     127.11
           Total payments:      27.11
                              =========
                 Balance:     $100.00
```

Figure 21.19: Sample data printed using the Statmnts report format

The Group 1 Intro Band contains Regular, Predefined, and Calculated fields. The location, type, and expression of each is listed below. For example, to place the first field template, move the cursor into the Group 1 Intro band, press F5, then select CUSTNO from the first column of the menu that appears, and press Ctrl-End to leave the submenu. When adding calculated fields, move the cursor to the line/column position shown, press F5, select <create> from the Calculated column, then select Expression and type in the expression shown (for example, CUSTOMER->Company). Then press ⏎ and Ctrl-End. As with the Invoices report, you don't want to use names with these calculated fields:

Line,Column	Type	Expression
0,18	Regular	CUSTNO
0,64	Predefined	DATE
1,0	Calculated	Customer->Company
2,0	Calculated	Customer->Contact
3,0	Calculated	Customer->Address
4,0	Calculated	Customer->City
4,18	Calculated	Customer->State
4,22	Calculated	Customer->Zip

The Detail band contains templates for fields from the Transact database. From left to right, the fields are Invoice, Remarks, Ordate, Ordtotal, Datepaid, and Amtpaid.

The Group 1 Summary band contains two calculated fields and two summary fields. The first calculated field, called StartBal, appears at line 0, column 26 and uses the expression Customer->TotChrg – Customer->TotPmt. At line 1, column 26, the summary field named CurrChrg sums the OrdTotal field and is Reset Every CustNo. At line 2, column 26, a summary field named CurrPmts sums the AmtPaid field, and it, too, is Reset Every CustNo. Line 4, column 26 contains a calculated field that is named CurrBal and uses the expression STARTBAL + CURRCHRG – CURRPMTS.

After creating the report format, select Save Changes and Exit from the Exit pull-down menu to return to the dot prompt. When you get back to the dot prompt, enter the following command to close the database files and return to the Control Center:

```
CLOSE DATABASES
ASSIST
```

BUILDING THE APPLICATION

We have now created all the objects needed for the business management application, including the database structures, custom procedures and functions, screens, and report formats. Now we need to pull these together into an integrated application with easy-to-use pull-down menus. Of course, we'll use the dBASE IV Applications Generator for this phase of the operation.

Figure 21.20 shows the menu tree for the business management application, including the names of the various menus. You'll use the Applications Generator to design the menus and assign an action to each menu item.

DEFINING THE APPLICATION

To begin, select <create> from the Applications panel of the Control Center. From the submenu that appears, select Applications Generator. Then, when you get to the Application Definition dialog box, fill it in as shown in Figure 21.21.

NOTE

If you need to take a break during the design of the application, mark the place in the book where you left off and select Save Changes and Exit from the Exit pull-down menu.

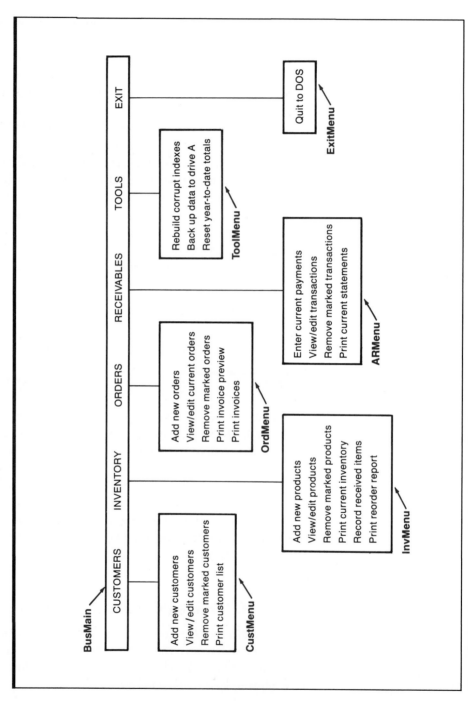

Figure 21.20: Menu tree for the business application

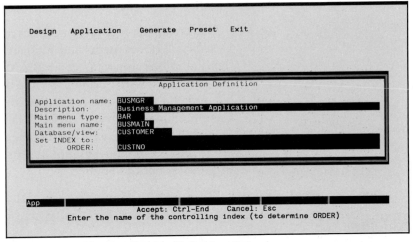

Figure 21.21: The Application Definition dialog box

We've defined the main menu type as (horizontal) BAR, and given it the name BUSMAIN. Later, we'll actually create a menu with that name. The applications generator also requires that a database be opened right away, even if the application will manage many databases. In this example, it's not particularly important which database is opened when the application is first run, so we've somewhat arbitrarily selected CUSTOMER as the database and the CUSTNO tag as the index that controls the sort order. (The Set INDEX To option is required only if you want the application to use dBASE III PLUS .NDX files.)

The business application uses many database files. But dBASE requires that a default database and index be defined with the application definition. Thus, this application specifies the Customer database with the CustNo index, though you could specify any database and order that the application uses.

CREATING THE SIGN-ON BANNER

After defining the application, press Ctrl-End to get to the Applications Generator design screen. You can modify the sign-on banner to match that shown in Figure 21.22. If you want the application to display the sign-on banner, remember to select Display Sign-on Banner from the Application pull-down menu and change its setting to Yes.

CREATING THE MAIN MENU

To create the main menu, select Horizontal Bar Menu from the Design pull-down menu and <create> from the submenu. When the dialog box appears, enter **BusMain** as the menu name. You can then press Ctrl-End to leave the other options blank. When the blank menu bar appears at the top of the screen, enter the options **Customers**, **Inventory**, **Orders**, **Receivables**, **Tools**, and **Exit**, each separated by three spaces. (Remember to press the F5 key before and after typing each item.) Figure 21.23 shows the horizontal bar menu with the six options entered.

CREATING THE PULL-DOWN MENUS

The business application uses six pull-down menus, which you can begin designing now. Note that for this application, each pull-down menu will use the IN EFFECT AT RUN TIME option as the default database. This setting is used because the application uses many different databases. Any particular option might use one or several database files. So rather than assigning a particular database to each individual pull-down menu, the application tells dBASE just to use whatever database is open at the moment.

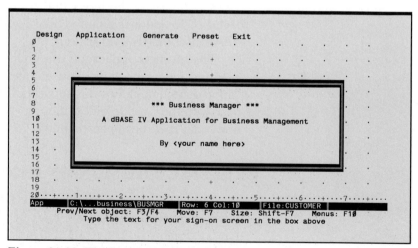

Figure 21.22: The BusMgr sign-on banner

Each of the six pull-down menus that you will create will require you to follow these eight general steps (but don't do them now):

1. Select Pop-Up Menu from the Design pull-down menu.

2. Select <create> from the submenu that appears.

3. Enter the menu name, an optional description, and an optional message line prompt in the dialog box that appears and then press Ctrl-End (specific information for each menu will be provided).

4. Press Size (Shift-F7) to enlarge the menu frame as necessary and press ⏎ when done sizing.

5. Type the menu options, using Size as necessary to adjust the menu frame (specific information will be provided).

6. After creating the menu, select Override Assigned Database or View from the Menu pull-down menu (*not* from the Item pull-down menu) and press the space bar until the IN EFFECT AT RUN TIME option is displayed. Then press Ctrl-End.

7. Press the Move (F7) key, select Entire Frame, and move the

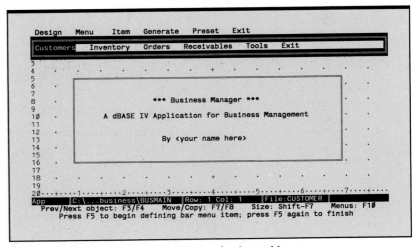

Figure 21.23: The business application horizontal bar menu

completed menu to beneath the main menu option it is associated with (the exact location will be provided).

8. Select Put Away Current Menu from the Menu pull-down menu and Save Changes from the submenu that appears.

In the descriptions that follow, use the preceding general steps to create each pull-down menu, but fill in the specific information provided for each menu. The descriptions list just this particular information, with the step number to which the information applies indicated in parentheses.

CUSTMENU PULL-DOWN MENU   The CustMenu pull-down menu provides options for managing the Customer database. Here is the specific information for the menu:

(Step 3)   Name: CUSTMENU
           Message line prompt: Manage the Customer
           database

(Step 5)   Specific menu options:
           Add new customers
           View/edit customers
           Remove marked customers
           Print customer list

(Step 6)   Menu database file/view: IN EFFECT AT RUN
           TIME

(Step 7)   Upper-left corner of menu frame aligned beneath
           the first *s* in Customers on the main menu

INVMENU PULL-DOWN MENU   The menu for managing the Master inventory database is named InvMenu. Repeat the general steps for creating a pull-down menu, using the specific information listed here:

(Step 3)   Name: INVMENU
           Message line prompt: Manage the Master
           inventory database

(Step 5) Specific menu options:
Add new products
View/edit products
Remove marked products
Print current inventory
Record received items
Print reorder report

(Step 6) Menu database file/view: IN EFFECT AT RUN TIME

(Step 7) Upper-left corner of menu frame aligned beneath the *v* in Inventory on the main menu

ORDMENU PULL-DOWN MENU The menu for managing orders is named OrdMenu. Follow the preceding general steps, using the specific information presented here, to create the menu:

(Step 3) Name: ORDMENU
Message line prompt: Manage current orders and invoices

(Step 5) Specific menu options:
Add new orders
View/edit current orders
Remove marked orders
Print invoice preview
Print invoices

(Step 6) Menu database file/view: IN EFFECT AT RUN TIME

(Step 7) Upper-left corner of menu frame aligned beneath the *d* in Orders on the main menu

ARMENU PULL-DOWN MENU The ARMenu pull-down menu provides options for managing accounts receivable. Use the preceding general steps to create the menu, filling in the specific information listed here:

(Step 3) Name: ARMENU
Message line prompt: Manage accounts receivable and customer statements

(Step 5)   Specific menu options:
            Enter current payments
            View/edit transactions
            Remove marked transactions
            Print current statements
            -
            Print all current invoices before
            printing customer statements

(Step 6)   Menu database file/view: IN EFFECT AT RUN
            TIME

(Step 7)   Upper-left corner of menu frame aligned beneath
            the *c* in Receivables on the main menu

TOOLMENU PULL-DOWN MENU   The ToolMenu pull-down
menu provides general tools for the business application. To create
the menu, follow the general steps listed previously, filling in the specific information provided here:

(Step 3)   Name: TOOLMENU
            Message line prompt: General purpose file
            management tools

(Step 5)   Specific menu options:
            Rebuild corrupted indexes
            Backup data to drive A
            Reset year-to-date totals

(Step 6)   Menu database file/view: IN EFFECT AT RUN
            TIME

(Step 7)   Upper-left corner of menu frame aligned beneath
            the second *o* in Tools on the main menu

EXITMENU PULL-DOWN MENU   The ExitMenu pull-down
menu provides a single option to exit the application. Follow the eight
general steps, filling in the specific information provided here:

(Step 3)   Name: EXITMENU
            Message line prompt: Exit the application and
            return to DOS

(Step 5)   Specific menu options:
Quit to DOS

(Step 6)   Menu database file/view: IN EFFECT AT RUN
TIME

(Step 7)   Upper-left corner of menu frame aligned beneath
the *i* in Exit on the main menu

OPENING THE PROCEDURE FILE

At this point, you've designed all of the menus for your application. Remember too that earlier you developed many custom procedures for the application, and you want to make sure the application can use them. Therefore, you need the application to execute a SET PROCEDURE TO BusProcs as one of its first steps. To do so, embed the command above (before) the application main menu. Here are the steps to follow:

1. Press the F4 key until the frame on the BUSMAIN horizontal bar menu (the one that contains the options Customer, Inventory, Receivables, and so forth) is highlighted.

2. Select Embed Code from the Menu pull-down menu (*not* the Item pull-down menu—I'll explain the difference in a moment).

3. Select BEFORE.

4. Type the following two lines (pressing ◄┘ after typing each line) as shown in Figure 21.24:

    ```
    *--- Open the procedure file.
    SET PROCEDURE TO BUSPROCS
    ```

5. Press Ctrl-End three times to save your changes and return to the application design screen.

If you need to take a break, now would be a good time to do so. Select Clear Work Surface from the Menu pull-down menu and select Save Changes when prompted. Then select Save All Changes and Exit from the Exit pull-down menu to return to the Control Center. When

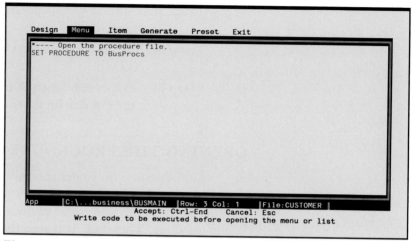

Figure 21.24: Command to open the BusProcs procedure file

time permits, you can resume your work by switching to the C:\
dBASE\Business subdirectory and running dBASE IV. Then proceed
with the next section.

ASSIGNING ACTIONS TO MENU OPTIONS

The next step in building the business application is to assign
actions to each menu option and batch-process operation. To begin,
we will assign actions to the main menu options.

ASSIGNING ACTIONS TO THE MAIN MENU

If you have taken a break and exited dBASE IV, you'll need to
get back to the applications design screen. To do so, highlight
BusMgr in the Applications panel of the Control Center and press
←┘. Then select Modify Application. To bring the application's horizontal bar menu back onto the applications design screen, select Horizontal Bar Menu from the Design pull-down menu and BUSMAIN
from the submenu that appears.

If you did not take a break, make sure that the horizontal bar menu is the current object by pressing the F4 key until the horizontal bar menu frame is highlighted.

Before assigning actions, make sure the first menu option, Customers, is highlighted (if necessary, move the cursor to that option using the ← and → keys). Then press F10 and select Change Action from the Item pull-down menu. For each menu option, follow these five general steps, using the specific information provided later:

1. Select Open a Menu.

2. Specify POP-UP as the menu type and press ↵.

3. Press Shift-F1 to view menu names and select the appropriate name for the current option (as specified later).

4. Press Ctrl-End.

5. Press PgDn to move to the next menu option (its name is centered in the status bar near the bottom of the screen).

The following list shows the name of each menu assigned to each action in the application main menu. Select the name shown when you perform step 3:

Option	Opens this menu
Customers	CUSTMENU
Inventory	INVMENU
Orders	ORDMENU
Receivables	ARMENU
Tools	TOOLMENU
Exit	EXITMENU

ATTACHING THE PULL-DOWN MENUS

After you have assigned the Open a Menu action to each of the six main menu options, select Attach Pull-Down Menus from the Menu pull-down menu and then select the Yes option.

ASSIGNING ACTIONS TO PULL-DOWN MENUS

In the sections that follow, you will assign actions to each option in each pull-down menu. In addition, most options will use *embedded code* to perform custom operations, and some will use windows to display progress. Let's take a moment to discuss these topics in general before you start working on the pull-down menu actions, so that you can better understand why they are used and how to use them.

USING EMBEDDED CODE

Use the usual dBASE IV editing techniques to enter and change text while writing embedded code.

From this point on, in this particular application, you should never select Embed Code from the Menu pull-down menu. Always select Embed Code from the Item pull-down menu. To remind you of this, the following sections will tell you when to embed code using the phrase "*Item* Embed Code Before or After" to remind you that you want to select Embed Code from the Item pull-down menu.

Both the Menu and the Item pull-down menus on the application design screen provide an option called Embed Code. When you select this option, you'll be provided with two options: Before and After. The Before option lets you enter up to 19 lines of dBASE commands to be executed before the action assigned to a menu option is executed. The After option lets you enter up to 19 lines of dBASE code to be executed after the menu action takes place.

Embedded code lets you call your custom procedures when they are required for a specific task. You can also use embedded code to open and close databases and to define relationships among databases as necessary while the application is running. This feature gives you a great deal of control over exactly when various operations take place and also lets you manage the many multiple databases in the application with great efficiency.

There is one area of potential confusion in using embedded code that you must watch out for very carefully when developing an application: Even though both the Menu and the Item pull-down menus provide the Embed Code option, there is a big difference between the two. When you select Embed Code from the *Menu* pull-down menu, any commands that you enter will be executed before or after the *menu* is displayed when the user runs the application. When you select Embed Code from the *Items* pull-down menu, any commands that you embed will be executed before or after the current menu *option* performs its action.

USING LOGICAL WINDOWS

Some operations will use windows, discussed in Chapter 18, to show command progress as the business application is performing a lengthy task. The Applications Generator allows you to set up logical windows via a dialog box, as shown in Figure 21.25.

All of the logical windows in this application will use **Double** as the border. You need not be concerned with colors or custom borders in this application. When windows are used, you'll be given the name to assign to the window as well as the upper-left and lower-right row and column coordinates for each window.

GENERAL STEPS FOR ASSIGNING ACTIONS

To assign actions to pull-down menus, you first need to make the pull-down menu the current object. Then you need to perform the five general steps listed here for each option on your pull-down menu (you'll be provided with specific information for each step in the sections that follow):

1. Press F10 and move to the Item pull-down menu.

2. Select Change Action and assign the appropriate action for the item (specific information will be provided later).

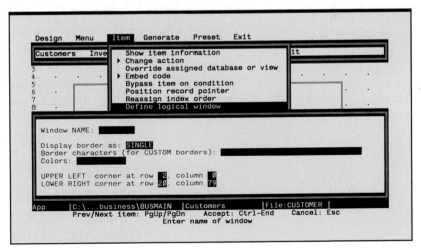

Figure 21.25: The Define Logical Window dialog box

3. If the option requires embedded code, select Embed Code and Before or After (as indicated by the specific information provided later). Press Ctrl-End twice to save the code and leave the Before or After submenu.

4. If the option requires a logical window, select Define Logical Window and enter the window name and coordinates (as specified later). Press Ctrl-End to return to the Item pull-down menu.

5. Press PgDn to move to the next menu item (it appears in the status bar).

Follow these steps for each option in each pull-down menu (note that some options do not require embedded code or logical windows, and you can skip these steps for those options).

ASSIGNING CUSTMENU ACTIONS

To begin assigning actions to the CustMenu pull-down menu, first make it the current object by selecting Pop-Up Menu from the Design pull-down menu and CUSTMENU from the submenu that appears. Then use the five general steps to assign actions and embedded code to each menu option as specified.

ADD NEW CUSTOMERS   The Add New Customers option lets the user add new customers to the Customer database and then automatically numbers them. To ensure that the Customer database is open when the user selects this option, you need to specify Embed Code Before to open the Customer database. To have the application automatically number customers, you need to specify Embed Code After to have the application execute the AutoCust procedure.

Using the five general steps, assign the actions and enter the embedded code specified here (Figure 21.26 shows how the ''before'' embedded code should look on your screen after you enter it.)

(Step 2)   Action: Edit form (add, delete, edit)
Format file: ADDCUST
Mode: APPEND

(Step 3)   *Item* Embed Code Before:

```
*--- Open Customer database to add new customers.
USE Customer
```

Item Embed Code After:

```
*--- After adding new customers, number them.
DO AutoCust
```

VIEW/EDIT CUSTOMERS   The View/Edit Customers menu option uses the Customer database with the CustNo index to allow the user to search for, view, and if necessary, modify customer information using the EditCust form that you created earlier. The specific embedded code and actions are listed here:

(Step 2)   Action: Edit form (add, delete, edit)
Format file: EDITCUST
Mode: EDIT
Options: Allow Record Add?: NO

(Step 3)   *Item* Embed Code Before:

```
*--- View/edit customers with CustNo index in control.
USE Customer ORDER CustNo
```

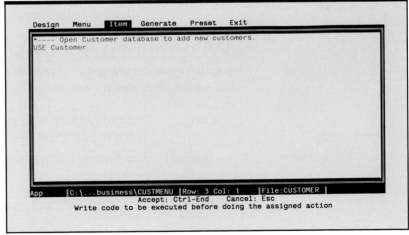

Figure 21.26: Sample embedded code typed on the screen

Item Embed Code After:

```
*--- Save changes and close database.
CLOSE DATABASES
```

REMOVE MARKED CUSTOMERS The Remove Marked Customers menu option packs the Customer database and displays its progress through a window named PakWindo. Here are the specifics for this menu option:

(Step 2) Action: Perform file operation
          Discard marked records

(Step 3) *Item* Embed Code Before:

```
*--- Pack Customer database.
USE Customer
```

Item Embed Code After:

```
*--- Save changes and close database.
CLOSE DATABASES
```

(Step 4) Define Logical Window:
          Name: PAKWINDO
          Border: DOUBLE
          Upper-left corner: 10, 10
          Lower-right corner: 20, 60

PRINT CUSTOMER LIST The Print Customer List prints all customer information using the Customer report format that you developed earlier. Specifics for this option are as follows:

(Step 2) Action: Display or print report
          Form name: Customer

(Step 3) *Item* Embed Code Before:

```
*--- Print customer list.
USE Customer ORDER CustNo
```

Item Embed Code After:

```
*--- Close database
CLOSE DATABASES
```

After you have assigned actions to all of the options on the Customer pull-down menu, select Put Away Current Menu from the Menu pull-down menu and Save Changes from the options that appear.

ASSIGNING INVMENU ACTIONS

To assign actions to the InvMenu options, first make InvMenu the current object by selecting Pop-Up Menu from the Design pull-down menu and InvMenu from the submenu. Then assign actions, define windows, and embed codes using the five general steps listed previously and the specific information provided.

ADD NEW PRODUCTS   The Add New products option lets the user add new products to the master inventory file. Specific actions and embedded code for this menu option are listed here:

(Step 2)   Action: Edit form (add, delete, edit)
Format file: ADDPARTS
Mode: APPEND

(Step 3)   *Item* Embed Code Before:

```
*--- Use Master database to add new items to the inventory.
USE Master ORDER PartNo
```

Item Embed Code After:

```
*--- Save changes and close.
CLOSE DATABASES
```

VIEW/EDIT PRODUCTS   The View/Edit Products option lets the user search for and, optionally, change or delete products in the inventory. The specific actions and embedded code for this menu option are as follows:

> (Step 2) Action: Edit form (add delete, edit)
> Format file: EDITPART
> Mode: EDIT
> Allow Record Add?: No
>
> (Step 3) *Item* Embed Code Before:

```
*--- Use Master database with PartNo index.
USE Master ORDER Partno
```

> *Item* Embed Code After:

```
*--- Save changes and close file.
CLOSE DATABASES
```

REMOVE MARKED PRODUCTS The Remove Marked Products option packs the database, thereby removing any records that were marked for deletion during editing. Specific actions, windows, and embedded code for this option are listed here:

> (Step 2) Action: Perform file operation
> Discard marked records
>
> (Step 3) *Item* Embed Code Before:

```
*--- Use Master database for packing.
USE Master
```

> *Item* Embed Code After:

```
*--- Save changes and close database.
CLOSE DATABASES
```

> (Step 4) Define Logical Window:
> Name: WINDOW2
> Border: DOUBLE
> Upper-left corner: 10, 10
> Lower-right corner: 20, 60

PRINT CURRENT INVENTORY The Print Current Inventory option prints the current inventory. Specific actions and embedded code for this option are listed here:

(Step 2) Action: Display or print: report
Form Name: MASTREPT

(Step 3) *Item* Embed Code Before:

```
*--- Use Master database to print current inventory.
USE Master ORDER PartNo
```

Item Embed Code After:

```
*--- Close the database.
CLOSE DATABASES
```

RECORD RECEIVED ITEMS The Record Received Items option lets the user record received purchases in the ItemsRec database. This option uses the AddItems procedure that you developed earlier to update the Master database in-stock quantities and move the updated records to a history file named ItemHist.

Note that the "after" embedded code for this option defines, activates, and closes a window to display progress during the update operation. We use embedded code, rather than the Define Logical Window option, in this instance, because we want the application to display the window only during the updating process, not while the user is entering records.

The specific actions, embedded code and windows for this menu option are listed here:

(Step 2) Action: Edit form (add delete, edit)
Format file: ADDRECVD
Mode: APPEND

(Step 3) *Item* Embed Code Before:

```
*--- Use ItemsRec for recording received purchases.
USE ItemsRec
```

Item Embed Code After:

```
DEFINE WINDOW UpdatWin FROM 10,5 TO 20,65 DOUBLE
ACTIVATE WINDOW UpdatWin
```

```
SET TALK ON   && Show progress on screen.

*--- In case records were marked for deletion
*--- during entry, pack the database.
USE ItemsRec
PACK
*--- Now update the MASTER inventory.
DO AddItems


SET TALK OFF

*--- Get rid of window.
DEACTIVATE WINDOW UpdatWin
RELEASE WINDOW UpdatWin
```

PRINT REORDER REPORT   The Print Reorder Report option displays items in the inventory whose in-stock quantities are at or below the level specified in the reorder report. This option uses the ReordRpt report format with the filter condition FOR INSTOCK < = REORDER to display the appropriate records. Here are the specific embedded code and actions for this option:

(Step 2)   Action: Display or print: report
            Form name: REORDREPT
            For: InStock < = Reorder

(Step 3)   *Item* Embed Code Before:

```
*--- Print reorder report in part number order.
USE Master ORDER PartNo
```

Item Embed Code After:

```
*--- Close database.
CLOSE DATABASES
```

Now that you have assigned actions to each option on the InvMenu pull-down menu, select Put Away Current Menu from the Menu pull-down menu, and Save Changes from the submenu that appears.

ASSIGNING ORDMENU ACTIONS

The OrdMenu lets the user enter new orders, preview and change current orders, and print the invoices. Options on this menu use many of the custom procedures that you developed earlier to manage information.

To start assigning actions and embedded code to the options on this menu, first make this menu the current object by selecting Pop-Up Menu from the Design pull-down menu and then OrdMenu from the submenu that appears.

ADD NEW ORDERS   The Add New Orders option needs to open all the databases required to enter orders through the AddOrder custom screen. It uses the OrdOpen procedure that you developed earlier to accomplish this task. The specific embedded code and actions assigned to this option are listed here:

(Step 2)   Action: Edit form (add, delete, edit)
Format file: ADDORDER
Mode: APPEND

(Step 3)   *Item* Embed Code Before:

```
*--- Open databases for entering orders.
DO OrdOpen
```

Item Embed Code After:

```
*--- Closes the databases
CLOSE DATABASES
```

VIEW/EDIT CURRENT ORDERS   The option View/Edit Current Orders allows the user to scroll through current orders (that is, those that have not been fulfilled) and make changes or corrections if necessary. The specific actions and embedded code for this option are listed here:

(Step 2)   Action: Edit form (add, delete, edit)
Format file: EDITORD

Mode: EDIT
Allow Record Add?: No

(Step 3)   *Item* Embed Code Before:

```
*--- Open related database files.
DO OrdOpen
SELECT Orders
SET ORDER TO CustNo
GO TOP
```

Item Embed Code After:

```
*--- Close databases after action is complete.
CLOSE DATABASES
```

REMOVE MARKED ORDERS   The Remove Marked Orders option packs the Orders database to remove any records that may have been marked for deletion during editing. This option uses a window named PakWindo to display progress. The specific actions and embedded code for this menu option are listed here:

(Step 2)   Action: Perform file operation
           Discard marked records

(Step 3)   *Item* Embed Code Before:

```
*--- Pack the Orders database only.
USE Orders
```

Item Embed Code After:

```
*--- Close after action complete.
CLOSE DATABASES
```

(Step 4)   Define Logical Window:
               Name: PAKWINDO
               Border: DOUBLE
               Upper-left corner: 10, 10
               Lower-right corner: 20, 60

PRINT INVOICE PREVIEW The Print Invoice Preview option displays current orders using the format InvSumm report format that you created earlier. The specific embedded code and actions for this menu option are listed here:

      (Step 2)   Action: Display or print: report
                         Form name: INVSUMM

      (Step 3)   *Item* Embed Code Before:

```
*--- Open related database files.
DO OrdOpen

*--- Specify sort order.
SELECT Orders
SET ORDER TO Invoice
```

                       Item Embed Code After:

```
*--- Close databases.
CLOSE DATABASES
```

PRINT INVOICES The Print Invoices option performs several operations. First, it checks all current orders for backordering and adjusts the Orders database accordingly (it uses the OrdUpdat procedure you developed earlier to perform this job). Then it uses the AutoInv procedure to automatically assign invoice numbers to outstanding orders.

The menu option then prints the invoices. After printing the invoices, it moves fulfilled orders to the OrdHist database using the MoveOrds procedure that you developed earlier. This option also adds outstanding orders to the accounts receivable transaction file, Transact, using the ARUpdate procedure that you developed earlier.

Specific embedded code and actions assigned to this menu option are listed here:

      (Step 2)   Action: Display or Print: report
                         Form Name: INVOICES
                         For: QtyShipped $>$ 0

(Step 3)   *Item* Embed Code Before:

```
*--- Update master inventory before printing invoices.
CLOSE DATABASES
DO OrdUpdat


*--- Automatically assign invoice numbers.
DO AutoInv


*--- Open databases for printing invoices.
DO OrdOpen


*--- Specify sort order.
SELECT Orders
SET ORDER TO Invoice
```

Item Embed Code After:

```
*--- Move invoiced transactions to history file.
DO MoveOrds


*--- Summarize orders and move to transaction file.
DO ARUpdate


*(ARUpdate procedure closes databases when done).
```

Now that you have assigned actions to all the options on the Ord-Menu menu, you can select Put Away Current Menu from the Menu pull-down menu and Save Changes from the submenu that appears.

ASSIGNING ARMENU ACTIONS

The ARMenu pull-down menu provides options for managing the accounts receivable database, Transact. To begin assigning actions to this menu, first make it the current object by selecting Pop-Up menu from the Design pull-down menu and ARMenu from the submenu that appears.

ENTER CURRENT PAYMENTS   The Enter Current Payments option lets the user record invoice payments as they are received. The actions and embedded code for this option are listed here:

(Step 2)   Action: Edit form (add, delete, edit)
           Format file: ADDPMTS
           Mode: APPEND

(Step 3)   *Item* Embed Code Before:

```
*--- Store payments in transaction file.
USE Transact
```

Item Embed Code After:

```
*--- Save changes and close.
CLOSE DATABASES
```

VIEW/EDIT TRANSACTIONS   The View/Edit Transactions option lets the user view all transactions, but allows him or her to edit only those that have not been printed and posted. (Adjustment transactions, discussed later, allow corrections to printed and posted transactions.) The specific actions and embedded code required for this menu option are listed here:

(Step 2)   Action: Edit form (add, delete, edit)
           Format file: EDTRANS
           Mode: EDIT

(Step 3)   *Item* Embed Code Before:

```
*--- Open transaction database in customer order for editing.
USE Transact ORDER CustNo
```

Item Embed Code After:

```
*--- Save changes and close database.
CLOSE DATABASES
```

REMOVE MARKED TRANSACTIONS   The Remove Marked Transactions option erases any records that may have been marked for deletion while the user was editing. The specific action, embedded code, and window requirements for this option are listed here:

(Step 2)   Action: Perform file operation: Discard marked records

(Step 3)   *Item* Embed Code Before:

```
*--- Open the transaction database.
USE Transact
```

Item Embed Code After:

```
*--- Save changes and close database file.
CLOSE DATABASES
```

(Step 4)   Define Logical Window:
                Name: PAKWINDO
                Border: DOUBLE
                Upper-left corner: 10, 10
                Lower-right corner: 20, 60

PRINT CURRENT STATEMENTS   The Print Current Statements option prints the customer statements, updates the balances in the Customer database, and marks all records as printed and posted. This option uses the Statmnts report format to print the statements. The specific actions and embedded code for this option are listed here:

(Step 2)   Action: Display or print: report
                Format File: STATMNTS
                For: .NOT. Printed

(Step 3)   *Item* Embed Code Before:

```
*--- Open files needed to print statements.
SELECT A
USE Transact ORDER CustNo
SELECT B
USE Customer ORDER CustNo

*--- Set up relationship.
SELECT A
SET RELATION TO CustNo INTO Customer
```

* * * * * * * * (Application will now print statements)

Item Embed Code After:

*--- After printing statements, flag transactions.
SELECT Transact
REPLACE ALL Printed WITH .T.
CLOSE DATABASES

*--- Next, update Customer database charges and payments.
DO ARPost

*---(ARPost procedure closes databases when done)

At this point, you can select Put Away Current Menu from the Menu pull-down menu and Save Changes from the submenu that appears.

ASSIGNING TOOLMENU OPTIONS

The ToolMenu menu provides general-purpose options for managing the business application database files. To assign actions to this menu, first make it the current object by selecting Pop-Up Menu from the Design pull-down menu and ToolMenu from the submenu that appears.

REBUILD CORRUPTED INDEXES　The Rebuild Corrupted Indexes option rebuilds all indexes using the BusRendx procedure that you developed earlier. This option does not require embedded code. Specific requirements for this option are listed here:

(Step 2)　　Action: Run program
　　　　　Do dBASE program: BUSRENDX

(Step 4)　　Define Logical Window:
　　　　　　Name: RNDXWIND
　　　　　　Border: DOUBLE
　　　　　　Upper-left corner: 10, 5
　　　　　　Lower-right corner: 20, 75

BACK UP DATA TO DRIVE A The Back up Data to Drive A option copies all database (.dbf) files from the current directory to a floppy disk in drive A. This option requires only that you assign an action to it, as listed here:

(Step 2)   Action: Run program
Run DOS program
Program: COPY
Parameters: *.DBF A:

RESET YEAR-TO-DATE TOTALS The Reset Year-to-Date Totals option resets all customer year-to-date charges and payments to zero and moves old transactions to the TranHist history file. It uses the YearEnd procedure that you developed earlier to accomplish this task. The specific window settings and action required for this option are listed here:

(Step 2)   Action: Run program
Do dBASE Program
Program: YEAREND

(Step 4)   Define Logical Window:
Name: YEARWIND
Border: DOUBLE
Upper-left corner: 10, 5
Lower-right corner: 20, 70

At this point, you have finished assigning actions to the ToolMenu menu options. Select Put Away Current Menu from the Menu pull-down menu and select Save Changes from the submenu.

ASSIGNING EXITMENU OPTIONS

To assign an action to the ExitMenu pull-down menu, first make it the current object by selecting Pop-Up Menu from the Design pull-down menu and then ExitMenu from the submenu that appears.

QUIT TO DOS   The action for the Quit to Dos menu option is described here:

(Step 2)   Action: Quit
             Quit to DOS

After assigning the action, select Put Away Current Menu from the Menu pull-down menu and Save Changes from the submenu.

GENERATING THE APPLICATION

When you have finished assigning actions to each option in every menu and batch process for the application, you can have the Applications Generator write all of the code for the completed application. Here are the steps:

1. Select Clear Work Surface from the Application (or Menu) pull-down menu.

2. If prompted, select Save Changes.

3. Select Select Template from the Generate pull-down menu.

4. If necessary, change the template name to Menu.gen.

5. Press ◄┘.

6. Select Display during Generation and change the setting to Yes.

7. Select Begin Generating.

8. When generation is complete, press any key to continue, as prompted on the screen.

9. Select Save All Changes and Exit from the Exit pull-down menu to return to the Control Center.

At this point, you have (finally) completed the entire business management application. You should be at the Control Center, and the BusMgr application name should appear in the Applications panel.

USING THE COMPLETED APPLICATION

The remainder of this chapter discusses general techniques for using the completed application. If you plan to use the application in an actual business setting, be sure to use it in parallel with any existing manual or automated system for a while to make sure that it is adequate for your needs.

STARTING THE APPLICATION

To start the application directly from the DOS prompt (before starting dBASE IV), follow these steps:

1. Enter the command **CD\dBASE\Business** at the DOS prompt to switch to the application directory.
2. At the DOS prompt, enter the command **dBASE BusMgr**.
3. Press ← when prompted to leave the copyright screen.

If dBASE IV is already up and running on your computer, you can run the business application by following these steps:

1. Select DOS Utilities from the Tools pull-down menu.
2. Select Set Default Drive\Directory from the DOS pull-down menu.
3. Specify **C:\dBASE\Business** as the default drive and directory.
4. Select Exit to Control Center from the Exit pull-down menu.
5. If the Business catalog does not appear on your screen, select Use a Different Catalog from the Catalog pull-down menu.
6. Select BUSINESS.CAT from the submenu that appears.
7. Highlight BUSMGR in the Applications panel, press ←, select Run Application, and select Yes if prompted.

In a moment, you will see the application sign-on banner appear on the screen along with the message "Press ← to continue." Do so to access the pull-down menus.

MANAGING CUSTOMER RECORDS

The pull-down menu under the Customer option allows you to manage customer data. Note that you must enter customer information into the Customer database before you can place orders for the customer.

ADDING NEW CUSTOMER RECORDS   You can add new customers to the customer database at any time by selecting Add New Customers from the Customer pull-down menu. You will not be prompted to enter a customer number, as the application numbers customers automatically. When you are done entering new customers, leave the Company field blank on a new record and press ←.

VIEWING AND EDITING CUSTOMER RECORDS   To view or edit customer data, select View/Edit Customer data from the Customers pull-down menu. To locate a particular customer by number, follow these steps:

1. Press F10 and select Index Key Search from the Go To pull-down menu.

2. Enter the customer number you want to find and press ←.

To locate a customer by company, contact, or some other field, use the Forward Search option from the Go To pull-down menu, as discussed in Chapter 6.

Charges and payments for all customers are maintained automatically by the application, so you will rarely, if ever, want to modify these fields. Note, however, that these values are updated only after customer statements are printed, and so the values you see on the screen are accurate only to the last printing. (Do not change these values to make them more current, because when the system updates them automatically in the future, it will not be aware that you have already made changes.)

To delete a customer, press Ctrl-U while the customer record appears on the screen (the word "Del" appears in the lower-right corner of the screen when a customer is marked for deletion). When you are done editing, press Ctrl-End to save your changes and return to the application menus.

REMOVING MARKED CUSTOMER RECORDS   If you marked any records for deletion while editing customer records, you can permanently remove these records by selecting Remove Marked Customers from the Customers pull-down menu. The application displays some messages in a window indicating that the deletion is in progress and then returns you to the application menus.

PRINTING CUSTOMER DATA   To print a list of all customers, select Print Customer List from the Customers pull-down menu. Note that the charges and payments in the report are current only to the date of the last printing of customer statements. For this reason, it might be a good idea to print the customer list immediately after printing customer statements.

MANAGING THE INVENTORY

The Inventory pull-down menu lets you manage the current inventory. Note that you must store information about a product in the master inventory database before you can process orders for that product.

ADDING NEW PRODUCTS   Whenever you add a new product to your product line, you need to assign a unique part number to that product and then add a record for that product to the master inventory database. Use the Add New Products option from the Inventory pull-down menu to do so. If you enter a part number that already exists, the screen will reject it, and you will need to enter a new part number (or press Esc to exit and then try again later).

When you have finished entering new products, leave the PartNo field blank and press ⏎ or Esc. (Alternatively, you can select Exit from the Exit pull-down menu.)

VIEWING OR EDITING PRODUCT INFORMATION To view or change product information, select View/Edit Products from the Inventory pull-down menu. To search for a particular product by part number, follow these steps:

1. Press F10 and select Index Key Search from the Go To pull-down menu.

2. Enter the part number to search for (using uppercase letters if part numbers include letters) and press ⏎.

Note that in-stock quantities are updated immediately after invoices are printed, and therefore are accurate only to that date. Do not change the in-stock quantity to reflect the actual in-stock quantity, unless you are sure that invoices have been printed recently and in-stock quantities in the Master database are therefore truly up to date.

To delete a product from the master inventory database, display the product name on the edit screen and press Ctrl-U. Then press Ctrl-End or select Exit from the Exit pull-down menu.

REMOVING MARKED PRODUCT RECORDS If you marked any records for deletion while editing the database, select Remove Marked Products to permanently remove those marked records from the database.

PRINTING THE CURRENT INVENTORY To print a list of the current inventory, select Print Current Inventory from the Inventory pull-down menu. Once again note that in-stock quantities are updated after invoices are printed and therefore are most accurate immediately after you print a batch of invoices.

RECORDING PURCHASES As you place orders and receive new items to replenish your stock, you can record these purchases by selecting Record Received Items from the Inventory pull-down menu. For each shipment received, include the part number and quantity received. If possible, record the purchase price as well (if you leave this value at zero, it remains unchanged on the Master database.)

After recording all shipments received, leave the Part Number field blank on a new record and press ←⏎. The master inventory in-stock quantities will be updated immediately to reflect these newly received shipments.

PRINTING THE REORDER REPORT   To print a list of items that need to be reordered, select Print Reorder Report from the Inventory pull-down menu. After the report is printed, you'll be returned to the application menus.

MANAGING ORDERS

The Orders pull-down menu provides options for entering and editing orders and for printing invoices.

ENTERING NEW ORDERS   To enter new orders, select Add New Orders from the Orders pull-down menu. You can fill in as many orders as necessary. Note that an invalid customer number or part number will be rejected. Also note that the customer's standard discount rate and tax rate (if the item being ordered is taxable) is automatically displayed on the screen and used in calculations, but either of these two standard values can be changed directly on the current screen.

If the customer used a purchase order to place an order, you can record that number in the Customer P.O. Number field, and it will be printed on the invoice.

When you are done entering orders, press ←⏎ while a blank record appears on the screen and a zero still appears in the Customer Number field.

PREVIEWING INVOICES   Before printing invoices, you can print an invoice summary by selecting Print Invoice Preview from the Orders pull-down menu. Check the printout for errors. If you find any errors, you can still change them at this point, using the option discussed next.

VIEWING AND EDITING CURRENT ORDERS   Current orders are those that have not yet been invoiced. You can change any current orders by selecting View/Edit Current Orders from the Orders pull-down menu. To search for a particular order by customer number, select Index Key Search from the Go To pull-down menu, enter the customer number, and press ◄─┘. Use the PgDn and PgUp keys to scroll through multiple orders for that customer.

To delete a particular order, bring that order onto the edit screen and press Ctrl-U. The Del indicator will appear in the status bar.

After viewing and, optionally, changing current orders, press Ctrl-End or select Exit from the Exit pull-down menu to return to the application menus.

REMOVING MARKED ORDERS   If during editing, you marked some orders for deletion, you can select the Remove Marked Orders option from the Orders pull-down menu to permanently erase the marked orders.

PRINTING INVOICES   When you are ready to print the invoices and fulfill the orders, select Print Invoices from the Orders pull-down menu. The application will quickly check whether backordering is required and will make adjustments accordingly. In addition, the option will calculate the invoice numbers. (This process may take a while, so don't be alarmed if invoices don't start printing immediately.)

The option then will print invoices that bill only for the quantity shipped, not the quantity backordered. Later, when in-stock quantities permit, backorders will automatically be fulfilled and invoiced.

After invoices have been printed, you may not make changes through the View/Edit Current Orders option. However, you can make corrections by entering adjustment transactions, as discussed later in this chapter.

MANAGING RECEIVABLES

Most of the data used to manage accounts receivable comes directly from fulfilled orders. However, you do need to keep track of payments and print monthly customer statements. The options to do so are on the Receivables pull-down menu.

RECORDING CURRENT PAYMENTS   As customers send in payments, record these by selecting Enter Current Payments from the Receivables pull-down menu. You must enter a customer number for each payment, though entering an invoice number is optional. Use the Remarks field to reference the payments (for example, enter "Check no. 555" or "Credit for Returned Items").

After recording all current payments, leave the customer number on a new blank record as zero and press ←⏎.

EDITING TRANSACTIONS   Any time during the month, you can view all financial transactions. However, you can edit only transactions that have not yet been posted to the customer's balances or printed on a customer statement (you'll need to use adjustment transactions to make such changes).

To locate transactions for a particular customer, select Index Key Search from the Go To pull-down menu, enter the customer number, and press ←⏎. Use the PgDn and PgUp keys to scroll through that customer's transactions. To delete a transaction, bring the transaction to the screen and press Ctrl-U. When you are done editing current transactions, press Ctrl-End or select Exit from the Exit pull-down menu.

REMOVING MARKED TRANSACTIONS   If you mark any records for deletion while editing the transactions database, you can select Remove Marked Transactions from the Receivables pull-down menu to permanently erase those records.

PRINTING CUSTOMER STATEMENTS   You can print customer statements at any time during the month, but note that individual payments and invoices are printed only once (not on every statement). For that reason, you may want to print customer statements only once, perhaps at the end of the month. Printing customer statements automatically updates all current charges, payments, and balances in the Customer database.

USING THE GENERAL-PURPOSE TOOLS

The Tools pull-down menu provides general-purpose tools for managing the overall application.

REBUILDING CORRUPTED INDEXES A sudden power outage or other mishap might cause database indexes to become corrupted. Then the application will tend to fail regularly and display an error message specifying a problem with an index. If this problem occurs, select Rebuild Corrupted Indexes from the Tools menu. The option will rebuild all indexes and return you to the application menu, where you can resume your work.

BACKING UP DATA From time to time, you should make copies of all the application database files. To do so, put a formatted disk in drive A (either a blank one or one you use only for making backup copies), and then select Backup Data to Drive A from the Tools pull-down menu. When copying is done, you'll be returned to the application menus.

RESETTING YEAR-TO-DATE TOTALS At the end of each accounting year, you can reset customer year-to-date charges and payments to zero by selecting Reset Year-To-Date Totals from the Tools pull-down menu. To verify that you did not select this option in error, a window will appear asking for verification. If you are sure you want to reset year-to-date totals, type **Y**. Otherwise, press ↵ to select the default answer, no.

ENTERING ADJUSTMENT TRANSACTIONS

When an error or some other problem occurs that disrupts the normal flow of information through the business application, you can respond in any of several ways. Let's look at an example.

Suppose that customer number 1001 pays for an invoice, and the payment goes through and is posted to the customer's current payments. Later you discover that the check bounced. You cannot alter the original payment record, because it has already been posted. You *could* simply edit the customer's balance in the customer database (for example, subtract $100 from the customer's total payments), but doing so leaves no audit trail.

A better method would be to enter an *adjustment transaction*, which corrects the balances and leaves a record of when and why the change occurred. In the example of the bounced check for customer number

CH. 21

1001, you could use the Enter Current Payments option from the Receivables pull-down menu to add a new payment to the transaction database that specifies a negative payment amount equal to the check (plus your charges, if any). Figure 21.27 shows an example.

Note that the entry specifies – 110.00 as the payment amount (assuming that the check that bounced was for $100.00, and you've charged $10.00 as a returned check fee). The remark for the entry explains the negative payment value.

Later, when you print customer statements, the adjustment will appear on the customer's bill, and the negative value will indeed be subtracted from the customer's total payments. The customer's balance will still be correct, and the adjustment will be recorded in the transaction database for future reference.

Let's look at another example. Suppose a customer returns two of part number B-222 because he hadn't actually ordered these items (someone made a mistake while entering orders). To put the items back into the in-stock inventory quantities, you select Record Received Items and enter the two received items as though they were received from a vendor. Automatically, the application will add the two returned products to the in-stock quantity, and you will have a record of the transaction on the ItemHist database.

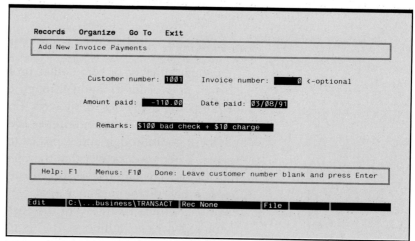

Figure 21.27: An adjustment transaction for a bounced check

Then select the Enter Current Payments option from the Receivables pull-down menu and enter a payment equal to whatever the customer was charged for the two items. In the remarks field, enter a description such as "Credit for returned items." The transaction is logged as a payment, therefore keeping the customer's balance correct. In addition, the customer's statement will reflect the adjustment, so he can be sure that he received credit for the mistake.

Note that you cannot make adjustments through the Add New Orders option on the Orders pull-down menu, because a negative quantity will not be calculated correctly (because of all the computation involved in backordering). However, you should be able to make any adjustments through the Record Received Items option in the Inventory pull-down menu and the Enter Current Payments option on the Receivables pull-down menu.

LEAVING THE APPLICATION

You can leave the application and return to dBASE IV by pressing Esc rather than selecting Quit to DOS.

When you have finished a session with the business manager application and want to stop using dBASE, select Quit to DOS from the Exit pull-down menu. All your work will be saved, and you will be returned to DOS, at which time you can turn off your computer or run another program.

WHERE DO YOU GO FROM HERE?

At this point you've seen examples of practically every feature that the dBASE IV Control Center and its various design screens have to offer, had a lot of hands-on experience in creating database objects, and have also learned a little bit about the dBASE IV programming language.

Where you go from here depends largely on what you want to do with dBASE IV. If you are still feeling a bit overwhelmed by all these capabilities, you might want to stay in the Control Center and design screens, and practice creating databases, queries, forms, and report and label formats on your own, and perhaps even some applications.

If you want to focus on creating applications, you'd be better off "graduating" to a more advanced book that focuses on the dBASE IV programming language and/or applications development. I might recommend my own dBASE IV Programmer's Reference Guide, also published by SYBEX, which picks up where this book leaves off and covers the entire programming language in great detail.

APPENDIX A

A DOS Primer

IF YOU'VE NEVER USED A COMPUTER BEFORE, YOU'D be wise to invest a little time in learning a few things about your computer's *operating system*. Even though you are probably ready to start putting dBASE IV to work now, the time you spend learning about your computer's operating system will be well spent. The more you know about the operating system, the more easily you will get along with your computer, and with dBASE IV as well.

The operating system acts as a sort of a middleman between the *hardware* of the computer and the *software* that you are using. The fact that you are reading this book indicates that your hardware is probably an IBM or compatible microcomputer. The operating system that you are using is probably DOS, or perhaps OS/2. DOS is an acronym for disk operating system. OS/2, which stands for operating system 2, is a newer version of DOS. The specific software package (or program) that you will be using in this book is dBASE IV.

Note that even though there are some differences between DOS and OS/2, both use identical commands for performing the types of operations used in this book. Therefore, this book refers to the operating system simply as DOS.

DISKS AND DISK DRIVES

Information that you store in the computer, whether it be a sales report, customer list, graph, or letter, is *written* in a *file*. Programs, such as dBASE IV, are also stored in files. Each file is stored on a disk, similar to the way that a song is stored on a compact disk or cassette tape. Your tape or disk player lets you hear your cassette tapes and compact disks; your computer lets you *read* the contents of a file on your computer disk.

Most computers can use at least two types of disks for storing files. One type is removable and is called a *floppy disk* or *diskette*. The other type of disk is a *hard* or *fixed disk*. A hard disk cannot be removed.

FLOPPY DISKS

Removable disks come in two sizes: $5\frac{1}{4}$-inch minifloppy disks and $3\frac{1}{2}$-inch microfloppy disks. Your computer might accept one size or both. Figure A.1 shows the 5¼-inch and 3½-inch diskettes.

To access the files stored on a disk, you first have to put the disk into the *disk drive* of your computer. Always insert the disk with the label facing upward and toward you. Most 5¼-inch disk drives have a latch or door that you must close after inserting the disk. To remove the disk, open the drive door or latch. The disk will pop out slightly. Gently pull the disk out of the drive to remove it.

The 3½-inch disk drives do not have a door or latch. Instead, you push the disk in until it clicks and pops into the drive. To remove a 3½-inch disk, you press the eject button, which is usually slightly below and to the right of the slot where you insert the disk. The disk will pop out slightly. Gently pull the disk the rest of the way out of the slot.

The write-protect notch on a 5¼-inch disk lets you protect the files stored on the disk. When the notch is uncovered, you have full access to the files on that disk. That is, you can read and copy information from the disk, change files on the disk, copy new files to the disk, and erase files from the disk.

If you cover the notch with one of the tabs that comes with a box of disks, you can only read or copy files from the disk; you cannot add, erase, or change any of the files that are already stored on the disk.

Figure A.1: A 5¼-inch and a 3½-inch disk

The 3½-inch disks use a sliding tab to protect files. (Some have two sliding tabs, others have only one.) When the sliding tab is closed, you have full access to the files on the disk. You can read, copy, change, erase, and add new files to the disk. When the sliding tab is open, you can only read or copy files from the disk; you cannot add new files or erase or change existing ones.

HARD DISKS

Your computer is probably equipped with at least one hard disk (or fixed disk) drive as well as a floppy disk drive. You can't see the hard disk because it's inside the main unit of the computer. The hard disk has certain advantages over a floppy disk. For instance, a single hard disk can hold much more information than a floppy disk; it can hold perhaps as much as 100 disks. A hard disk is also much faster than a floppy disk, which makes all your work on the computer faster.

The reason the computer has both hard and floppy disk drives is that you need some way to transport files from one computer to another. The removable floppy disks provide that capability. For example, when you buy dBASE IV, it comes to you on floppy disks. Before using the program, you *install* it, which includes copying dBASE IV from the disks on which it was delivered to the hard disk in your computer.

Floppy disks are also useful for making backup copies of important information. For example, if you store all your accounting data on a hard disk, you might also want to make an extra copy and store it on a floppy disk. You can store that extra copy in a safe place. If someone accidentally erases the accounting data from your hard disk, you can then recopy it from the backup disk onto your hard disk.

You might also want to copy information from your hard disk to a floppy disk for use on another computer. For example, you might want to give a copy of the accounting data to someone else for use elsewhere. Or if you have computers both at home and in your office, you might want to copy data from the hard disk on one computer for use on the other.

DISK DRIVE NAMES

DOS identifies each disk drive on your computer with a single letter. Typically, if your computer has one floppy disk drive and one hard disk, the floppy disk drive is named A and the hard disk is named C. If you have two floppy disk drives and one hard disk, the floppy drives are named A and B, with A usually being the one on the top or at the left. The hard disk is still named C.

Your computer might have additional hard disks named D, E, F, and so on. For example, if you share a computer with other users in a network, you might work on a hard disk named E or F. The network administrator (that is, the person in charge of the computer) can tell you the letter assigned to the drive that you are using.

DIRECTORIES AND FILES

A single hard disk can store many thousands of files. To help keep all of these files organized, you can create separate work areas, called *directories* (or *subdirectories*). Each directory holds its own set of files, just like each department in a company has its own set of files.

DIRECTORY NAMES

Each directory on a disk has a name, which you assign. The name can be up to eight characters long, but it cannot contain any blank spaces or punctuation. You can use numbers and the underline character (_) in a directory name. Table A.1 lists examples of valid and invalid directory names.

DOS often precedes a directory name with a backslash (\) to distinguish it from a file name. For example, the DBASE directory might be identified as \DBASE. To pinpoint the *exact* location of a particular directory, DOS often precedes the directory name with the drive name, followed by a colon (:) and a backslash. For example, C:\DBASE identifies a directory named DBASE on disk drive C.

Table A.1: Valid and Invalid Directory Names

Directory name	Status
DBASE	Valid
ACCOUNTS	Valid
JAN1991	Valid
GL	Valid
ACCT_REC	Valid
FIRST QTR	Invalid (contains a blank space)
RECEIVABLES	Invalid (too long)
ACCT:REC	Invalid (colon is a punctuation mark)

SUBDIRECTORIES

You can also create subdirectories on your disk. The name of a subdirectory can also be up to eight characters long. A subdirectory name is always preceded by the names of higher-level directories and a backslash. For example, suppose you create a directory named SALES to store information for the sales department of your company. Also suppose you want to keep the accounting data and personnel data for the sales department on separate subdirectories. To do so, you could create one subdirectory named SALES\ACCTNG and another subdirectory named SALES\PERSONNL. Note that the directory and subdirectory names are separated by a backslash.

DIRECTORY TREES

You can envision the directory structure (or directory *tree,* as it's sometimes called), on a disk as a hierarchy. The *root* directory (which every computer has) is the highest level directory. The root directory is always named simply \. There can be any number of directories and subdirectories beneath the root directory. Figure A.2 shows a sample directory tree (the directory on your computer is probably much different).

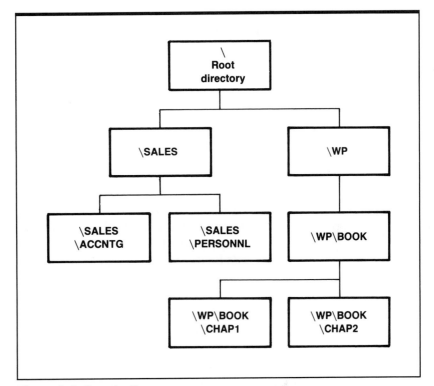

Figure A.2: Sample directory structure

The terms *parent* and *child* are often used to describe the hierarchical relationships between directories and subdirectories. For example, in Figure A.2 the SALES (or \SALES) directory is the *parent* to both \SALES\ACCTNG and \SALES\PERSONNL. The \SALES\ACCTNG subdirectory is a *child* to the \SALES directory, as is \SALES\PERSONNL.

Be aware that the terms *directory* and *subdirectory* are used interchangeably in most computer literature. For example, it is not unusual to see a phrase such as "switch to the \SALES\ACCTNG directory" or even "the \SALES subdirectory."

The reason for this loose terminology stems from the fact that, from the computer's standpoint, directories and subdirectories are pretty much the same thing: each is just a place on the disk where files are stored. Subdirectory names, such as \SALES\ACCTNG, are for human convenience. That is, when you see the subdirectory name \SALES\ACCTNG, you can quickly recall that the sales department's accounting information is stored in that work area. But the computer just sees a work area named \SALES\ACCTNG (and has no idea that the information stored there has anything to do with your sales department or with accounting).

FILE NAMES

Each directory (and subdirectory) on a disk may contain many files, such as a file containing a customer list; another file containing a parts list; and other files containing letters, graphs, and programs such as dBASE IV. Each file has a name that, like a directory name, can be up to eight letters long and cannot contain spaces. Numbers and the underline character (_) are allowed.

A file name can also have an *extension* (or last name). The extension can be up to three letters long and is always preceded by a period. Usually, the file name identifies the contents of a file and the extension identifies the type of information in the file. (When using dBASE IV, you usually provide the file name, and dBASE automatically adds the extension.)

Table A.2 lists examples of valid and invalid file names. Table A.3 lists examples of file name extensions and indicates the type of data stored in the files. (Appendix B lists all file name extensions that dBASE IV automatically assigns to different types of files.)

The exact location of specific information filed on a disk is often displayed by DOS (and dBASE IV) as a combination of the disk drive, directory (and subdirectory) names, and the file name preceded by a backslash. For example, the complete name C:\DBASE-\MYDATA.DBF identifies a database file named MYDATA.DBF stored on the \DBASE directory on disk drive C. The complete name C:\SALES\PERSONNL\NAMELIST.TXT identifies a text file named NAMELIST.TXT on the \SALES\PERSONNL subdirectory on disk drive C.

Now suppose that, while using dBASE IV, you create a database containing customer names and addresses. You assign the name CUSTLIST to this database and store it on a directory named

Table A.2: Valid and Invalid File Names

File name	Status
MYREPORT.TXT	Valid
ACCTREC.DAT	Valid
QRT1.91	Valid
1991TAX.FRM	Valid
JAN_1991.DBF	Valid
MAIL LIST.DAT	Invalid (contains a space)
1991SUMMARY.REP	Invalid (file name too long)
MAILIST.DATA	Invalid (extension too long)

Table A.3: Examples of File Name Extensions

Extension	Type of information
.TXT	Text (such as a letter, report, or document)
.BAK	Backup copy of another file
.DBF	dBASE database file
.COM	Program
.EXE	Another extension used for programs

\DBASE on drive C. Because dBASE automatically adds the extension .DBF, the customer names and addresses will actually be stored in a file named CUSTLIST.DBF. To completely identify the location and name of the customer list, DOS (and dBASE) use C:\DBASE\CUSTLIST.DBF. Figure A.3 illustrates how the CUSTLIST database is stored on a disk.

Another term that you may encounter while using DOS or dBASE IV is *path*. The path refers to the disk drive, directory, and subdirectory name (if any) that describes the location of a file. Figure A.4 shows an example of a path, using a file named FORMLET.TXT stored on the \WP\LETTERS subdirectory of drive C.

Other
directories and
subdirectories

Custlist.DBF

Smith	John	ABC Co
Adams	Annie	
Mahoney	Mary	
Newell	John	LoTech
Beach	Sandy	Americ
Kenney	Ralph	
Schumack	Susita	SMS So

Disk
drive C:

\DBASE
directory

C:\DBASE\CUSTLIST.DBF
**is complete location and name
of the CUSTLIST database**

Figure A.3: CUSTLIST.DBF database stored on a disk

THE DOS PROMPT

If your computer automatically displays a menu or ''DOS Shell'' at startup, you'll need to find an option for exiting or for accessing the DOS Command Prompt to get to the DOS prompt.

When you first turn on your computer, DOS automatically *boots* the system and takes control. Your screen shows the *DOS prompt,* which consists of the name of the current disk drive, followed by the > sign. The DOS prompt will probably be C > on your computer (if you boot from a hard disk) or A > (if you boot from a floppy disk).

When the DOS prompt is showing, the computer is ready to accept certain *DOS commands.* The following sections discuss some basic DOS commands that can help you use your computer more effectively. For a more complete discussion of DOS commands, refer to the manual that came with your copy of DOS (or OS/2).

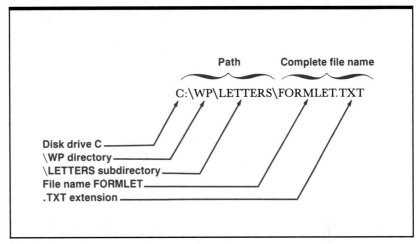

Figure A.4: A file name, preceded by its path

SETTING THE DATE AND TIME

Your computer stores the current date (sometimes called the *system date*) in its memory, and dBASE IV can access that date. To see if the date is correct, type the command **DATE** next to the DOS prompt. (If you make a mistake, you can back up by pressing the Backspace key.) After typing the DATE command, press ← (called the Enter or Return key on some keyboards).

Your screen will display a prompt such as this one:

Current date is Sat 12/31/1990
Enter new date (mm-dd-yy)

If the date shown on your screen is not correct, type a new date in *mm-dd-yy* format (for example, 11/15/91 for November 15, 1991). Press ← after typing the new date, and you'll be returned to the DOS prompt.

To check and correct the system time, type the command **TIME** and press ←. The screen will display the current time and a prompt for entering the correct time, as follows:

Current time is 12:26:15.92
Enter new time:

If the current time shown is not correct, type the new time using a 24-hour clock format. (You need not enter seconds or hundredths of seconds.) For example, if the current time is 8:30 A.M., type **8:30** and press ◄─┘. If the current time is 2:15 P.M., type **14:15** and press ◄─┘. You'll then be returned to the DOS prompt.

SWITCHING TO A DISK DRIVE

To switch to a particular disk drive, type the letter of that drive followed by a colon and press the ◄─┘ key. (You can only switch to a floppy disk drive if there is a disk in the drive and the drive door, if any, is closed.) For example, if you are currently on disk drive A and want to switch to hard disk drive C, you would enter the command **C:** and then press ◄─┘. (This command works, of course, only if your computer has a hard disk named C.)

SWITCHING TO A DIRECTORY

NOTE

Be sure to use the back-slash (\) rather than the forward slash (/) when specifying directory names.

To switch to a directory or subdirectory, use the DOS CHDIR (for Change Directory) command or the abbreviation CD. For example, after you have installed dBASE on your computer, you can switch to the \DBASE directory by typing the command **CD \DBASE** and pressing ◄─┘. To switch to a subdirectory, enter both the parent and child directory names. For example, if your computer has a directory named \DBASE\SAMPLES, you switch to that subdirectory by typing the command **CD \DBASE\SAMPLES** and pressing ◄─┘.

VIEWING THE
CURRENT DIRECTORY NAME

If you switch to a new directory and its name does not appear next to the DOS prompt, you can see the directory name by typing

NOTE

Whatever directory you happen to be on at the moment is the *current* directory.

the command **PROMPT PG** and pressing ◄━┘. The current disk drive and directory will appear at the DOS prompt. For example, if you are currently on the \DBASE directory on drive C, the DOS prompt will be followed by C:\DBASE>. This technique is very handy for keeping track of which directory you are currently on.

VIEWING FILE NAMES

NOTE

All DOS commands require you to press ◄━┘ after typing the command. Hence, the phrase "enter the command" means "type the command and then press ◄━┘."

To view the names of files stored on the current directory, you can enter the DIR command at the DOS prompt. If the directory contains many files, you can enter the command **DIR /W** to display the file names in a wide (columnar) format, or you can enter the command **DIR /P** to have DOS pause after it presents each screenful of file names. (Press any key after each pause to view the next screenful.)

When DIR displays file names, it does not show a period between the file name and the extension. Instead, it displays the name and extension in separate columns. If you do not use the /W option for a wide display, DIR also shows the size of each file and the date and time that the file was created or was last changed. DIR also shows the names of directories that are children to the current directory. These have <DIR>, rather than a file size, in the third column of the list.

Here is a sample DIR display (your computer will show something completely different):

Directory of C:\

ASSIGN	COM	1536	2-11-90	12:00p
DBASE	<DIR>		3-31-90	8:00a
DISKCOPY	COM	39456	2-11-90	12:00p
FIND	EXE	27424	2-11-90	12:00p
PRINT	COM	28492	2-11-90	12:00p

The first row shows that there is a file named ASSIGN.COM on the current directory and that this file occupies 1536 *bytes* of disk space. (A byte is the same as a character; for example, the word *CAT* contains three bytes.) ASSIGN.COM was created (or last changed) at 12:00 P.M. on 2/11/90 in this example.

The second row shows that a directory named \DBASE exists on the disk. That directory was created on 3-31-90 at 8:00 A.M.

VIEWING THE DIRECTORY TREE

To view the names of all directories and subdirectories on the current disk drive, switch to the root directory and enter the TREE command. For example, to see the names of directories on disk drive C, you would enter these commands (press ◄─┘ after typing each command):

```
C:      ◄─┘
CD\     ◄─┘
TREE    ◄─┘
```

The C: command brings you to drive C. The CD\ command brings you to the root directory, which is always named \. The TREE command runs a DOS program named TREE, which displays the directory tree. Note that if the TREE.COM program is not accessible from the root directory, DOS displays only the message "Bad command or file name." Don't worry about this; you can still use the other commands discussed in this chapter.

If a particular directory has child directories beneath it, these are listed separately. For example, suppose your TREE display includes

Path: \DBASE

Sub-directories: SQLHOME
                 DBTUTOR
                 SAMPLES

This display informs you that the hard disk includes a directory named \DBASE, with subdirectories \DBASE\SQLHOME, \DBASE\DBTUTOR, and \DBASE\SAMPLES.

To switch to the \DBASE directory, you would enter the command **CD \DBASE**. To switch to the \DBASE\SAMPLES subdirectory, you would enter the command **CD \DBASE\SAMPLES**.

Then you could enter the DIR command to see the names of files on the directory (or subdirectory).

CREATING DIRECTORIES

To create a new directory (or subdirectory) on your hard disk, you use the DOS MKDIR command (or the abbreviation MD). Include the full directory name and a preceding backslash. For example, to create a directory named \DBASE, you enter **MD \DBASE** at the DOS prompt. (You need not create any new directories right now.) To switch to that new directory, you would then enter the command **CD \DBASE** ↵.

RUNNING PROGRAMS
FROM THE DOS PROMPT

All programs are stored in files that have the extension .COM, .EXE, or .BAT. To run a program, you usually need to switch to the appropriate directory and type the program name (without the extension).

For example, after you install dBASE IV (according to the instructions in Appendix B), the dBASE IV program and its associated files will be stored in a directory named \DBASE. The main dBASE IV program is named DBASE.EXE. Therefore, to run dBASE IV, you will first need to switch to the \DBASE directory on drive C and then to enter the command DBASE at the DOS prompt. The exact commands you enter at the DOS prompt are

```
C:              ↵
CD\DBASE        ↵
DBASE           ↵
```

If you attempt to run a program that is not on the current disk drive and directory, DOS will respond with the message "Bad command or File Name" (or something equivalent, depending on the version of DOS that you are using).

There is an exception to the rule of having to be on a particular directory before running a program. The next section discusses this exception.

FILE SEARCH PATHS

Normally, when you ask DOS to run a program (such as dBASE IV), you must be on the directory that the program or file is stored in. However, DOS offers a command, PATH, that tells the computer to search other directories if it cannot find a particular program on the current directory.

When you install dBASE IV on your computer (as discussed in Appendix B), it will ask if you want to be able to start dBASE IV from any directory. If you answer Yes to this question, the installation automatically creates the appropriate PATH so that you can run dBASE IV from any directory.

You can check the current PATH at any time by entering the command **PATH** at the DOS prompt. After you have installed dBASE IV, you should see C:\DBASE as one of the paths displayed on the screen. For example, you might see PATH = C:\DBASE. If other files are included in the path, you'll see these as well, each separated by a semicolon. For example, if the root directory, a directory named \WP, and the \DBASE directory are included in the search path, you'll see PATH = C:\;C:\WP;C:\DBASE.

If for some reason, you find that you cannot start dBASE from directories other than the \DBASE directory, you can alter the DOS path using the DBSETUP program discussed in Appendix B.

APPENDIX

B

Installing
dBASE IV

BEFORE YOU CAN USE dBASE IV ON YOUR COMPUTER, it needs to be installed. You need only go through the installation process once. This appendix discusses general techniques for installing dBASE IV on a single-user computer. If you wish to install dBASE IV on a network, refer to the network installation instructions that came with your dBASE IV package.

HARDWARE REQUIREMENTS

The minimum hardware requirements for running dBASE IV are:

- An IBM PC, AT, PC/XT, or PS/2 model 30, 50, 60, or 80; a Compaq Deskpro 386; or any 100 percent compatible microcomputer.

- IBM DOS or MS-DOS version 2.0 or higher for the DOS version of dBASE IV, or OS/2 for the OS/2 version.

- At least 640K total RAM, with 450K available when starting dBASE IV.

- A hard disk with about 4 megabytes (Mb) of available disk space.

LOCATING YOUR SERIAL NUMBER

If this is the first time you are installing this copy of dBASE IV, you should jot down your Ashton-Tate serial number. If you are upgrading from version 1.0 of dBASE to version 1.1, your serial number is printed on the label of the version 1.0 System Disk. It also appears on the copyright screen when you start version 1.0 of dBASE using the DBASE (as opposed to dBASE /T) command.

If you are not upgrading from a previous version of dBASE IV, the serial number is printed on your dBASE IV version 1.1 System Disk #1.

PREVIOUS VERSIONS OF dBASE

If you have an earlier version of dBASE, such as dBASE IV version 1.0 or dBASE III PLUS, on your computer, you might want to "uninstall" those, or move them to another directory. You can use the install program that came with that earlier version of program to uninstall it.

If you want to keep an earlier version of dBASE on your hard disk, make sure that you do not install dBASE IV on the same directory as that earlier version. Either move the earlier version to another directory, or use a new directory name when installing dBASE IV.

DISK CACHING

Disk caching (pronounced "cashing") is a technique version 1.1 of dBASE IV uses to speed processing. It stores heavily used data in extended (EMS) or expanded (LIM) memory to reduce the slower hard disk activity. To use the disk caching option, you need to know whether or not your computer has extended or expanded memory, and if so, which one. Here are some guidelines to help you determine this:

- If you have an 8088 or 8086 computer (such as an IBM PC or XT), you don't have extended memory. You may, however, have expanded memory if you've purchased and installed an expanded memory board.

- If you have an AT-type (80286) computer, chances are you have extended memory.

- An 80386 computer generally has extended memory, which can easily be converted to expanded memory using the device driver in the CONFIG.SYS file.

- If you have DOS version 4, you can enter the command **MEM** (and press ◄─┘) to see what memory is available. You might also have some other utility that can provide this information.

If you are not sure which type of memory is available on your computer, take a guess. If you make a mistake, you'll find out later and can fix it then (as discussed in the section "Reinstalling Disk Caching" later in this chapter).

INSTALLING dBASE IV

In this appendix, we'll cover the basic single-user installation of dBASE IV. Installing dBASE IV on a network is trickier and varies with the type of network in use. Please refer to the documentation that came with your dBASE IV package if you will be installing it on a network.

To begin the actual single-user installation, follow these steps:

1. Start your computer in the usual manner and get to the DOS command prompt.

2. Insert the dBASE IV Install Disk #0 in disk drive A, and close the drive door (if any).

3. Type **A:** and press ◄── to switch to drive A.

4. Type **INSTALL** and press ◄──.

5. After a few moments, you'll see a dBASE IV screen followed by a Copyright screen. When instructed at the bottom of the screen, press ◄── to proceed with the installation.

6. Select QUICK when you see the dBASE IV Installation screen by using the ← or → key to highlight that option and pressing ◄──.

> **NOTE**
>
> If the arrow keys don't work on your keyboard, press NumLock, then try again.

7. On the next screen, dBASE suggests C:\DBASE as the installation drive and directory. Press ◄── to accept this suggestion, or change it using the arrow keys, then press ◄──.

8. If dBASE already exists in the directory specified in the previous step, you'll see a message indicating this. Select Proceed to overwrite the previous version, or select Change Drive:Directory to repeat step 7 and assign a different drive and directory. (If you proceed, it may take a few minutes for the program to uninstall the previous version.)

9. When prompted, remove the Install disk from drive A, and put in the dBASE IV System Disk #1. Then press ◄──.

10. If this is the first time this copy of dBASE IV is being installed, you'll see a screen for registering your copy of dBASE IV. As prompted on the screen, type either your name, your company

name, or both. Also, type in your serial number. When done, press ← and follow the instructions on the screen.

11. Next you'll be asked if you want to install caching for extended/expanded memory. Answer Yes if your computer has extended or expanded memory, then choose either Extended or LIM(expanded) from the next menu to appear.

12. Follow the instructions on the screen: replace the disk in drive A and press ← so the dBASE IV files can be copied to your hard disk.

13. When copying is complete, you'll see a screen asking for permission to modify your AUTOEXEC.BAT file in order to place the dBASE IV directory in the PATH statement. Press ← to proceed, or Esc to modify AUTOEXEC.BAT yourself later, if you prefer.

14. Next you'll see a screen asking for permission to modify your CONFIG.SYS file so that FILES is set to at least 15, and BUFFERS is set to at least 40, the minimum settings for dBASE IV. Press ← to proceed, or Esc if you prefer to check and modify the CONFIG.SYS file later on your own.

15. Next you'll see a message indicating that installation is complete. Press ← to end the installation.

At this point, the basic installation is complete, and you should be at the drive and directory where dBASE IV was installed (typically C:\DBASE).

INSTALLING THE DEVELOPER'S EDITION FILES

If you have the dBASE IV Developer's Edition as opposed to the standard edition, you might want to install the RunTime and Template Language files that come with that version of the program (though these are topics that are beyond the scope of this introductory-level book). The RunTime file needs about 1.4Mb, and the Template Language Toolkit requires about 0.5Mb of storage.

If you have sufficient hard disk space and want to copy those files now, follow these steps:

1. Go to the directory that dBASE is stored on (typically C:\DBASE).

2. Place the Runtime Disk 1, or Utilities and Template Language disk (depending on which you're copying) in drive A or B.

3. Type **INSTALL** and press ←┘.

4. Press ←┘ when prompted to continue.

5. Select MENU-DRIVEN (by typing the letter M).

6. Select Transfer Other Files.

7. Select RunTime (if you want to install the RunTime files), or select dBASE Template Language if you want to install those files.

8. Indicate the drive you used in step 2 (either A or B) when prompted, and press ←┘.

9. Press any key, then follow the instructions that appear on the screen.

From this point on you should be able to just follow the prompts on the screen. When asked about installing disk caching for RunTime, you can select Yes and whichever type of memory your computer has.

When you've finished copying all the Developer's Edition RunTime and/or Template Language files, select Exit to DOS from the Exit pull-down menu to return to the DOS command prompt.

INSTALLING PRINTERS

TIP

You can use DBSETUP at any time to install a new printer for use with dBASE IV.

To install one or more printers with dBASE IV, follow these steps:

1. Assuming you are at the DOS command prompt on the dBASE IV (C:\DBASE) directory, type **DBSETUP** and press ←┘.

2. Press ⏎ again to leave the opening screen.

3. Select Modify Existing CONFIG.DB by pressing ⏎ when that option is highlighted.

4. If the drive and directory shown is where you've stored dBASE IV, press ⏎. Otherwise, enter the correct drive and directory, then press ⏎.

5. Select Drivers from the Printer pull-down menu (by pressing ⏎).

6. For each of up to four printers, press Shift-F1 while the cursor is in the Printer Name column. Use the ↑, ↓, PgUp, and PgDn keys to move the highlighter to the name of the company that made your printer, then press ⏎.

7. Use the same keys to highlight the printer model on the next menu to appear, and press ⏎ to select it.

8. When the cursor is in the Device column, press Shift-F1 to see a list of printer ports, then highlight the appropriate port for that printer and press ⏎.

You can use the LJII printer drivers for the HP LaserJet IIP and LaserJet III printers.

9. You can repeat steps 6–8 for up to four printers, or four "versions" of the same printer (for example, the Hewlett-Packard LaserJet IID offers 6.5 lpi (lines per inch), 6 lpi, 2-side, and land (landscape or "sideways" printing) options), which allows you to easily switch among these various features of the same printer while using dBASE IV.

10. Press Ctrl-End after selecting your printers.

11. When prompted, specify the drive\directory for storing the printer drivers, or just press ⏎ if the suggested drive\directory is correct. The program will extract the appropriate printer drivers for the DRIVERS.EXE file located on the dBASE IV directory.

12. Next, select Default Printer by highlighting that option and pressing ⏎.

13. Choose the printer driver you want to use for general-purpose printing. (If you forgot the name of the driver, press Esc, then select Drivers again to review the driver names. Then press Ctrl-End and repeat step 12.)

If your printer offers a variety of built-in fonts, and you know the codes for starting and ending those fonts, you can install those fonts now. Or, you can install them later after you've had a chance to check your printer manual. Either way, you can refer to the section "Installing Printer Fonts" later in this appendix for information.

OPTIMIZING THE DISPLAY

Some CGA monitors produce "snow" (interference) when used with dBASE IV. You can check for snow now (while you're still in DBSETUP) by following these steps:

1. Press → until the Display pull-down menu appears.

2. Select Optimize Color Display by typing **O** or highlighting the option and pressing ←┘.

3. Press ←┘ to select Proceed.

4. Type **Y** if you see interference (snow), otherwise type **N**.

5. Press any key to return to the menu.

This completes the basic installation of dBASE IV. To save all changes and exit, follow these steps:

1. Press → until the Exit pull-down menu is displayed.

2. Press ←┘ to select Save and Exit.

3. Press ←┘ again to accept the suggested drive\directory name (which should be the same as the drive\directory that dBASE IV is stored on).

4. Select Ok when asked for permission to overwrite.

5. Select Exit to Dos from the Exit menu on the next screen to appear.

Now you've installed dBASE, one or more printers, your monitor, and perhaps disk caching. The next section describes how to test the installation.

STARTING dBASE IV

To check your installation, follow these steps to start dBASE IV:

1. If you changed the AUTOEXEC.BAT or CONFIG.SYS files during installation (or are not sure whether you did or not), reboot by removing any floppy disks from their drives and simultaneously pressing the Ctrl, Alt, and Del keys momentarily.

2. When the DOS command prompt appears, go to the directory that you installed dBASE on. For example, if you stored dBASE on C:\DBASE, type **C:** and press ←, then type **CD\DBASE** and press ←.

3. Type **DBASE** and press ←.

If you opted to install disk caching, and did so properly, you should see a brief message indicating that the Hyperdisk disk caching software is being loaded. If instead you see a message indicating the Hyperdisk was *not* installed, refer to the following section titled "Reinstalling Disk Caching."

Then you should see the dBASE IV copyright screen and the message to press ←. Do so to get to the dBASE IV Control Center (which is discussed in Chapter 2).

To exit dBASE, press Alt-E (hold down the Alt key and type the letter E), then type the letter Q to select Quit to DOS. You will be reminded of these steps when you actually start putting dBASE to work in Chapter 2.

 TIP

To start dBASE without the full trademark screen, enter the command **DBASE /T** rather than **DBASE** at the DOS prompt.

REINSTALLING DISK CACHING

If you attempted to install disk caching, but received a message indicating that Hyperdisk was not installed when you ran dBASE, then one of the following things is wrong:

- You selected the wrong type of memory (extended rather than expanded, or vice versa).

- Your computer has neither expanded nor extended memory.

- An incompatible TSR (terminate stay resident) program is already in memory.

- An incompatible memory manager is already in place and will not relinquish control to the dBASE disk cache.

If either of the first two is the problem, the solution is fairly simple. Follow these steps:

1. Make sure you are still at the drive\directory where dBASE is stored.

2. Type **CACHEDB** <**type**> where <type> is either EXT (for extended memory), LIM (for expanded memory), or OFF (for no disk caching). For example, the command **CACHEDB EXT** sets up disk caching to use extended memory.

3. Press ◄─┘.

4. Run dBASE again to see if the current memory type is acceptable.

If neither the EXT nor LIM options work, then either your computer does not have extended or expanded memory, or some other memory manager is in control.

If the problem concerns other TSR programs that are already loaded, add the command **DEVICE = C:\DBASE\DBCINIT** to your AUTOEXEC.BAT file. Place this command above any other commands in the AUTOEXEC.BAT file that load TSR programs, so that DBCINIT is loaded first.

If the problem is an incompatible memory manager, such as HIMEM.SYS (used with Windows 3.0), you simply have to choose between one or the other. For example, while Windows 3.0 is running, HIMEM.SYS is in control of memory, and if you run dBASE IV from within Windows, you'll see a message indicating that disk caching cannot be loaded because of incompatibility with HIMEM's XMS extended memory. (dBASE will still run, but without the cache.)

However, if you exit Windows before running dBASE (and have installed DBCACHE for extended memory), dBASE IV caching will be installed when you run dBASE IV.

NOTE

If you are unfamiliar with DOS, TSR programs, and other topics discussed here, skip to the section titled "Customizing dBASE IV with DBSETUP" later in this section until you learn more about DOS.

Also, if a disk cache is already in operation on the computer when you start dBASE IV, the dBASE cache may still be installed, creating a sort of "cache within a cache." This could actually impede performance, so you may want to disable the dBASE caching in that case.

DOS 4.01, SHARE, AND FASTOPEN

If you are running dBASE IV with DOS 4.01 and a hard disk partition larger than 30Mb or are using the SHARE command in an earlier version of DOS, or if you use the DOS FASTOPEN disk cache, you must add the command **FCBS = 16,16** to your CONFIG.SYS file.

FINE TUNING dBASE IV PERFORMANCE

When you use dBASE, it creates many temporary files that are later erased when you exit dBASE normally. Two DOS environmental variables, TMP and DBTMP, define where dBASE IV temporary files will be created. TMP is a general area that programs other than dBASE IV will use, while DBTMP is used by dBASE IV only.

dBASE IV will check the DOS environment for a directory defined by DBTMP first to determine where to store temporary files. If DBTMP is not defined in the environment, dBASE will then check for a directory defined by the TMP variable in the environment, and use that directory for storing temporary files. If neither DBTMP nor TMP are defined in the environment, dBASE will store temporary files on the same directory that dBASE IV (dBASE.EXE) is stored on.

NOTE

DBCACHE uses whatever extended or expanded memory is available, but anything over 1.6Mb does not increase performance significantly.

One way to speed up the execution of dBASE IV (a little bit) is to use a RAM disk to store the temporary files, but only if you have over 2Mb of extended or expanded memory, and only if you are well enough versed in DOS already to know how to set up a RAM disk in extended or expanded memory. (This is a DOS topic, and space does not allows us to teach advanced DOS topics right here and now.) Leave at least 1.6Mb of memory free for DBCACHE.

The RAM disk must be created before you can use it for storing temporary files. Typically, you create a RAM disk by using the VDISK or RAMDISK device driver (which are part of DOS, not dBASE) in your DOS CONFIG.SYS file.

For example, suppose your system has 4Mb of extended memory. Depending on your version of DOS, you could include a command like the one below to use 1Mb of that memory as a RAM disk:

```
DEVICE = C:\DOS\VDISK.SYS 1024 /E
```

Assuming that your computer already has drives named C:, D:, and E:, the RAM disk will be drive F:.

Your AUTOEXEC.BAT file could then contain the command

```
SET TMP = F:\
```

or

```
SET DBTMP = F:\
```

dBASE would then use the fast RAM disk (drive F:) to store temporary files.

CUSTOMIZING dBASE IV WITH DBSETUP

This section describes additional features of the DBSETUP program which you can use to refine and customize dBASE IV to your liking.

RUNNING DBSETUP

To run the DBSETUP program, follow these steps:

1. Assuming you are at the DOS command prompt on the dBASE IV (C:\DBASE) directory, type **DBSETUP** and press ←┘.

2. Press ←┘ again to leave the opening screen.

3. Select Modify Existing CONFIG.DB by pressing ←┘ when that option is highlighted.

4. If the drive and directory shown is where you've stored dBASE IV, press ←┘. Otherwise, enter the correct drive and directory, then press ←┘.

This brings you to the DBSETUP main menu. The sections that follow assume that you are starting your selections from this point. As usual, you can select any menu option by moving the highlighter to it with the arrow keys and pressing ⏎.

CHANGING THE SCREEN COLORS

If you find that the screen colors used by dBASE IV are not adequate for your needs, and want to change them for all future sessions with dBASE, select the Display option on the DBSETUP main menu. There, you can experiment with different color combinations using the color palette. (See Chapter 14 for information on using the color palette.)

INSTALLING FONTS

dBASE IV can access only built-in (resident) fonts, not downloadable soft fonts stored on disk.

You can use up to five additional fonts (beyond the default font) for printing with dBASE IV, provided your printer offers additional fonts. (That is, dBASE IV can't *create* a font; it can only *use* a font that's built into your printer.) You can check your printer manual to see what, if any, additional fonts are available to you.

To get access to additional fonts, you need to install them for use with dBASE IV via the DBSETUP program. If you are using a Postscript printer, please skip to the section titled "PostScript Printing" below for information on using PostScript fonts. Otherwise, continue reading in this section.

The first step to using printer fonts is to determine the codes used to activate and deactivate that font. These codes are usually available in your printer manual or, in some cases, by printing a Font List directly from the printer.

You may also need to know which is the normal default font for your printer, and the code for activating that font, so you can use that as the ending code to terminate another font. (Courier 10pt is the default font on most laser printers.)

When choosing your fonts, keep in mind that there is no need to select the Italic, Bold, and other styles of a single typeface, as these can be activated in the reports design screen within dBASE. Also, you have three choices of sizes within dBASE, Condensed, Pica,

Elite (16.67, 10, and 12 lpi), so you need not select more than one of these sizes for a particular typeface.

When you locate the codes for using fonts in your printer manual, keep in mind the following points:

- dBASE requires that you represent the Escape character as {Esc}, though your printer manual might represent this character as <Esc>, Escape, \027, CHR(27), CHR$(27), or some other character.

- Ctrl-*key* characters must be represented as {Ctrl-A}, {Ctrl-B}, and so forth, in dBASE, where {Ctrl-A} is ASCII character 1, {Ctrl-B} is ASCII character 2, and so forth, up to {Ctrl-Z}, which is ASCII character 26.

- A null character (ASCII character 0) is represented as {Null} in dBASE.

You need not define the printer's default font as one of your "extra" fonts, as dBASE always has access to the default font.

Your printer manual may represent the Escape key as <Esc> or <027> or \027, but you want to use {Esc} to represent the Esc key with dBASE.

As an example of setting up fonts for use with dBASE IV, suppose you have a Hewlett-Packard Laserjet III Printer. In going through the printer documentation, you find that you can get a listing of all the available fonts and their start codes by taking the printer off line and pressing the Print Fonts key. (Don't forget to put the printer back on line after printing the fonts.)

You also discover that the default font is Courier 10 pitch, and the startup code for that font is:

{Esc}(8U{Esc}(s0p10.00h12.0v0s0b3T

so you know that is the ending code for each optional font you choose.

Suppose you decide to create the following fonts, and determine the startup codes as below:

Font	Start Code
Huge Univers-24pt	{Esc}(8U{Esc}(s1p24.00v0s0b4148T
Large CG Times-16pt	{Esc}(8U{Esc}(s1p16.00v0s0b4101T
Large Unvers-16pt	{Esc}(8U{Esc}(s1p16.00v0s0b4148T
CG Times-12pt	{Esc}(8U{Esc}(s1p12.00v0s0b4101T
Line Printer-8.5pt	{Esc}(8U{Esc}(s0p16.67h8.5v0s0b0T

The end code for each font would be the code used for specifying the default Courier 10 pitch font.

The steps to installing the fonts for use with dBASE IV are as follows:

1. If you are not already at the DBSETUP main menu, follow the instructions under "Running DBSETUP" earlier in this section to get to that menu.

2. Select Fonts from the Printer pull-down menu.

3. Press PgDn (Page Down) until the description of the printer that you want to install fonts for is displayed at the top of the window (next to Printer Number).

4. Type in a name (of your choosing) to describe the font, then press ←⏎.

5. Type in the exact start code for activating the font, then press ←⏎.

6. Type in the code for ending the font, or for activating the default font.

7. Repeat steps 4 through 6 for up to five fonts.

8. Press Ctrl-End when done.

Keep in mind that this series of steps assigns fonts for only one printer driver. If you have more than one driver for a printer, for example, both Portrait and Landscape drivers for a Laserjet, you'll need to set up fonts for each driver separately. When you've finished installing fonts for your printers, either proceed with the next section or proceed to Saving CONFIG.DB Settings later in this section.

INTERNATIONALIZING dBASE IV

dBASE IV initially comes configured to display dates and currencies in American formats. You can change the formats of currencies and dates using the DBSETUP program.

CHANGING THE DATE FORMAT   By default, dBASE displays dates in the format MM/DD/YY. To use a different date format in all future sessions of dBASE IV, select the Modify Existing

CONFIG.DB option from the CONFIG.DB pull-down menu in DBSETUP. Press ◄┘ to accept the suggested drive and directory and then move the highlight to the General option on the menu bar. Then move the highlight to the Date option and press the space bar to scroll through the various options. Table B.1 displays the date format that each option uses.

Table B.1: International Date Formats for dBASE IV

Option	Format	Example
American	MM/DD/YY	12/31/90
Ansi	YY.MM.DD	90.12.31
British	DD/MM/YY	31/12/90
French	DD/MM/YY	31/12/90
German	DD.MM.YY	31.12.90
Italian	DD-MM-YY	31-12-90
Japanese	YY/MM/DD	90/12/31
USA	MM-DD-YY	12-31-90
MDY	MM/DD/YY	12/31/90
DMY	DD/MM/YY	31/12/90
YMD	YY/MM/DD	90/12/31

You can convert any date format so that it accepts and displays the year as a four-digit number (for example, 1991) rather than a two-digit number (for example, 91). To do so, highlight the Century option on the General pull-down menu and press the space bar to change the setting to On.

CHANGING THE CURRENCY FORMAT   By default, dBASE IV prints currency amounts that use currency templates or picture functions with a leading dollar sign (for example, $123.45). You can modify the display of these currency amounts by changing the currency symbol, the position of the currency symbol, and the character used as the decimal place. Select the Modify Existing CONFIG.DB option from the CONFIG.DB pull-down menu in DBSETUP, press ⏎ to accept the drive and directory, and then move the highlight to the General pull-down menu.

To change the currency symbol, highlight Currency and press ⏎; then select Symbol. The symbol that you enter can be up to ten characters long. However, to prevent the symbol from being repeated in displays (that is, to display $123.45 rather than $$$$123.45), you should make the first character a blank space (by pressing the space bar).

To use currency symbols that are not available from the keyboard, hold down the Alt key and type the three-digit ASCII code for the symbol on the numeric keypad. (You must use the numeric keypad, not the numbers at the top of the keyboard.) The symbol appears on the screen after you type all three digits and then release the Alt key. Table B.2 shows currency symbols and their ASCII codes.

Table B.2: International Currency Symbols

Code	Symbol	Meaning
155	¢	Cent
156	£	Pound
157	¥	Yen
158	Pt	Peseta
159	ƒ	Franc

To display the currency sign to the right of a number rather than to the left, select Justification from the Currency pull-down menu and press the space bar to change the setting from Left to Right.

To use a character other than a period as the decimal point, select Point from the General pull-down menu. When prompted, type the character to use (for example, a comma) and press ⏎. To use a character other than a comma to separate thousands, select Separator from the General pull-down menu. Then type the character you wish to use as the separator.

Note that regardless of the format you define while in CON-FIG.DB, you still must enter numeric values in the usual manner later when storing data, (for example, **12345.67**) in the database. However, when you design a custom form or report format to print the data, the number will be formatted according to the template or picture function you define at that time.

For example, suppose you define *f* as the currency symbol, Right as the currency justification, the comma (,) as the point, and the period (.) as the separator. If you design a report or custom form and use the Financial Format picture function and the template 999,999.99 to display the field, the number 12345.67 will be displayed as 12.345,67*f*.

CHANGING THE CLOCK FORMAT   The Control Center always displays a clock in the upper-right corner of the screen. You can use DBSETUP to remove the clock, change its position, or change its format. From the DBSETUP main menu, select CONFIG.DB. Press ← to accept the suggested drive and directory and then move the highlight to the General pull-down menu.

To turn the clock off, first select Clock. On the submenu that appears, highlight the Clock option and press ← to change the setting to Off. To change the position of the clock, leave the Clock setting and select Screen Row and Screen Column, specifying a location for each setting. The upper-left corner of the screen is row 0, column 0.

To change the clock display from a 12-hour clock (for example, 1:00 P.M.) to a 24-hour-clock (for example, 1300), highlight the Hours option on the General pull-down menu, and press the space bar to change the setting to 24.

SAVING CONFIG.DB SETTINGS

After customizing any options from the CONFIG.DB pull-down menu, select Save Changes and Exit from the Exit pull-down menu. When prompted for the drive and directory of the CONFIG.DB file, press ← to reuse the original drive and directory. To exit the DBSET-UP program, select Exit to DOS from the Exit pull-down menu.

POSTSCRIPT PRINTING

Chapter 7 discusses creating and printing reports, in general, with dBASE IV. This section talks about features that are unique to printing on PostScript printers, and overlaps with the material in Chapter 7.

PostScript is a *page description language* used by certain types of laser printers such as the Apple LaserWriter. If you have a PostScript printer (even if it is not an Apple LaserWriter), you should install the Apple LaserWriter as one of your printers, and use it as the driver when printing on your PostScript printer.

INSTALLING POSTSCRIPT FONTS

You can use three typefaces from your PostScript printer, Courier, Times, and Helvetica. To install these three fonts for use with dBASE IV, follow the steps for installing fonts as described in the section "Installing Fonts" earlier in this appendix. When you get to step 7, be sure to press PgUp or PgDn until the Apple LaserWriter is the selected printer.

In steps 4–6, set up the screen using *exactly* the font names, begin codes, and end codes shown below:

Font name	Begin code	End code
1FONT	1FONT{32}	1FONT{32}
2FONT	2FONT{32}	1FONT{32}
3FONT	3FONT{32}	1FONT{32}

Then resume with the remaining steps in that section to save your changes.

Later, when selecting fonts at the reports design screen (Chapter 7), remember that 1FONT is Courier, 2FONT is Helvetica, and 3FONT is Times Roman. If you are printing a columnar report, you should use only the Courier (a monospaced font) for the Detail band to ensure that the printed data aligns properly in each column.

SENDING SPECIAL CODES TO POSTSCRIPT PRINTERS

This section describes techniques for activating special features of a PostScript printer for a particular report. That is, while defining a report design (as described in Chapter 7), you can initiate the codes described here on the Print pull-down menu so they affect the current report only. If you want to change the default value for any of these features, so that all future reports use that feature, see the section "Changing PostScript Defaults" later in this appendix.

LANDSCAPE PRINTING WITH POSTSCRIPT   If you want a particular report to be printed in landscape mode (sideways on the page) on your PostScript printer, follow these steps while designing your report at the reports design screen:

1. Press Alt-P to pull down the Print menu.
2. Select Control of Printer.
3. Select Starting Control Codes.
4. Type **LAND** then press the space bar.
5. Press ←⏎.
6. Select Ending Control Codes.
7. Type PORT and press the space bar.
8. Press → to leave the menu.
9. Select Page Dimensions.
10. Select Length of Page.
11. Type **45** and press ←⏎.
12. Press → to leave the menu.

NOTE

Use all uppercase, or all lowercase letters when typing commands such as LAND and PORT for your PostScript printer.

Save your report format and the new print form settings in the usual manner. It's important to press the space bar after typing LAND and PORT so that the options appear as

```
{LAND  }
{PORT  }
```

rather than

```
{LAND}
{PORT}
```

on the menu, otherwise the codes will be ignored.

CHOOSING LEGAL PAPER SIZE WITH A POSTSCRIPT PRINTER   If your PostScript printer supports legal size (8.5 × 14 inch) paper, you can select the legal paper size as the page length for the report you are currently designing by following these steps:

1. At the reports design screen for the report, press Alt-P to access the Print pull-down menu.

2. Select Control of Printer.

3. Select Starting Control Codes.

4. Type **LEGAL** and press the space bar.

5. Press ←⏎.

6. Select Ending Control Codes.

7. Type **LETTER** and press the space bar.

8. Press ←⏎.

9. Press → to leave the submenu.

10. Select Page Dimensions.

11. Select Length of Page.

12. Type **78** and press ←⏎.

13. Press → to leave the submenu.

Save your report format and print form settings in the usual manner.

COMBINING POSTSCRIPT COMMANDS   If you want to print in Landscape mode on legal size paper, you can combine the LAND and LEGAL command in the Starting Control Codes option of the Print menu. Be sure to press the space bar after each command so that the Starting Control Codes appear as

  {LAND LEGAL   }

in the menu, and the Ending Control Codes appear as

  {PORT LETTER   }

on the menu.

SETTING THE LINES PER INCH WITH POSTSCRIPT PRINTERS   If you are printing in Portrait rather than Landscape mode on your PostScript printer, you can adjust the number of lines per inch to be printed by following these steps:

1. At the reports design screen for the report, press Alt-P to access the Print pull-down menu.

2. Select Control of Printer.

3. Select Starting Control Codes.

4. Type **60LPP** and press the space bar if you want 60 lines per page, or type **66LPP** and press the space bar if you want 66 lines per page.

5. Press ←⏎.

6. Press → to leave the submenu.

7. Select Page Dimensions.

8. Select Length of Page.

9. Type either **60** or **66** to match your selection in step 4, then press ←⏎.

10. Press → to leave the submenu.

Save your report format and print form settings in the usual manner.

CHANGING POSTSCRIPT PRINTER DEFAULTS

dBASE uses an ASCII text file named PostScri.dld to send information to your PostScript printer. This file contains the PostScript printer defaults, and also accepts changes to those defaults, such as LAND, LEGAL, fonts changes, and so forth, that an individual report may use.

The PostScri.dld file is actually a "PostScript program" which you can modify. But be forewarned—you must be well versed in editing ASCII text files and aware that if your text editor adds a Ctrl-Z file to the end of the PostScript.dld file (as most do), chances are all future reports will "time out" before they're printed (that is, printing appears to be going along normally, the printer light blinks as though its going to print, but the printed report never appears).

If you encounter this particular problem after editing your PostScript.dld file, you can remove the Ctrl-Z from the end of the file using the DOS COPY command. For example, if you suspect that your current PostScript.dld file has a Ctrl-Z at the end of it, the following DOS commands will remove that Ctrl-Z:

```
COPY PostScri.dld PostScri.tmp     ←┘
COPY PostScri.tmp /A
PostScript.dld /B                  ←┘
```

To play it doubly safe, you should first make a copy of your original, unmodified PostScri.dld file, perhaps with the name Postscri.org (for "PostScript Original") and never make changes to that particular file. That way, if you make a mistake and your modified PostScri.dld file does not work, you can just copy the Postscri.org file to the PostScri.dld file (using the DOS COPY command) to "undo" any changes. (You can also pull a copy of the original PostScri.dld file from the dBASE DRIVERS.EXE file by entering the command **DRIVERS PostScri.dld** at the DOS command prompt on the dBASE IV directory.)

I'd also recommend that you get a book about the PostScript language as well (such as SYBEX's *Understanding PostScript Programming* by David A. Holzgang) if you plan on utilizing your PostScript printer to its utmost capacity.

CHANGING THE DEFAULT ORIENTATION AND PAGE LENGTH   The PostScri.dld file assumes that you will be using letter (8.5 × 11 inch) paper. If you want to use legal (8.5 × 14 inch) paper, change the line

```
/paper 1 def  %(1 = letter,2 = legal)
```

to

```
/paper 2 def  %(1 = letter,2 = legal)
```

in the PostScri.dld file.

dBASE also assumes that you will normally print in portrait (normal) mode rather than in landscape (sideways) mode. If you prefer to change the default orientation for your PostScript printer to Landscape, change the command

```
/orient 1 def  %(1 = portrait,2 = landscape)
```

to

```
/orient 2 def  %(1 = portrait,2 = landscape)
```

The line

```
/nLPP 60 def  %lines per page (60,66, or 78
                for portrait; 45 for landscape)
```

in the PostScri.dld file specifies the default number of lines to print per page. You should adjust this setting to match your default page size, as below:

```
/nLPP 60 def      (letter portrait, 6 lines per inch)
/nLPP 66 def      (letter portrait, 6.48 lines per inch)
/nLPP 78 def      (legal portrait)
/nLPP 45 def      (landscape)
```

If you do change the number of lines per page, you should make the corresponding change to the Length of Page option on the Print pull-down menu, and save that change in Reports.prf, as described in Chapter 7.

CHANGING THE DEFAULT POSTSCRIPT OFFSET   If text is not properly aligned on your printed PostScript pages, you can modify the printer offsets in the PostScri.dld file. There are four pairs of offsets, each measured in points, as shown below:

A *point* is approximately $1/72$ inch.

```
% printer-dependent portrait offsets
/tpxoff 18 def % x (letter)
/tpyoff 28 def % y (letter)
/gpxoff 22 def % x (legal)
/gpyoff 26 def % y (legal)
% printer-dependent landscape offsets
/tlxoff 10 def % x (letter)
```

```
/tlyoff 44 def % y (letter)
/glxoff 14 def % x (legal)
/glyoff 80 def % y (legal)
```

Notice that one pair of offsets, tpxoff and tpyoff, is for letter-size paper, portrait mode. The other three pairs are for portrait legal, letter landscape, and legal landscape modes. These are entirely independent of one another.

Each pair has an x value and a y value. To move the printing to the right on a page, increase the x-offset number. To move text to the left on the page, decrease the x-offset value.

To move printing up (higher) on the page, increase the y-offset value. To move printing down in the page, decrease the y-offset value.

For example, suppose that you want to increase the left margin on your printed letter portrait paper by ½ inch (36 points). In the PostScri.dld file, you would want to change

```
% printer-dependent portrait offsets
/tpxoff 18 def % x (letter)
```

to

```
% printer-dependent portrait offsets
/tpxoff 54 def % x (letter)
```

CHANGING THE DEFAULT POINT SIZES When designing reports, dBASE gives you three point sizes to choose from for each report band (as discussed in Chapter 7):

Pica	12pt
Elite	10pt
Compressed	8pt

You may prefer to use Pica and Compressed for printing your data (in the Detail band) and a larger font for report titles and such. For example, you might want to change the definition of Elite to 20 points for printing very large titles.

The point definitions are in the section of the PostScri.dld file shown below:

```
% point sizes to use
/PicaPoint 12 def                    % Pica
/ElitePoint 10 def                   % Elite
/CompressedPoint 8 def               % compressed
```

To convert Elite to a 20-point size, simply change its definition as below:

```
/ElitePoint 20 def                   % Elite
```

When designing your reports later (in the dBASE IV reports design screen), remember that any band that you assign the ELITE text pitch to will actually be printed in the large 20-point size.

When designing reports, you have the option of selecting the default font, which is Pica on PostScript printers. If you want to change the default size to Elite or Compressed, change the line that reads

```
/CurPoint    PicaPoint def  % initial pointsize
```

to either

```
/CurPoint    ElitePoint def % initial pointsize
```

to make Elite the default, or

```
/CurPoint    CompressedPoint def % initial pointsize
```

to use compressed print as the default.

CHANGING THE DEFAULT POSTSCRIPT FONTS   There are three fonts offered in dBASE for use with PostScript printers: 1FONT (Courier), 2FONT (Helvetica), and 3FONT (Times Roman). These are defined in the PostScri.dld file in Figure B.1.

You can assign a different font to either 1FONT, 2FONT, or 3FONT, provided that you know the correct name of the font (as defined in your printer manual). For example, if your printer has a resident Palatino font, and you want to use that instead of

```
/CurFSet 1 def % default font set
/FSet (
        /CurFSet exch def
        % Font Set 1 (default)
        /n    /Courier def                     % normal
        /b    /Courier-Bold def                % bold
        /i    /Courier-Oblique def              % italic
        /bi   /Courier-BoldOblique def % bold+italic
        CurFSet 2 eq
            (
            /n     /Helvetica def
            /b     /Helvetica-Bold def
            /i     /Helvetica-Oblique def
            /bi    /Helvetica-BoldOblique def
            ) if
        CurFSet 3 eq
            (
            /n     /Times-Roman def
            /b     /Times-Bold def
            /i     /Times-Italic def
            /bi    /Times-BoldItalic def
            ) if
        /FontNorm n def
        /FontBold b def
        /FontItal i def
        /FontBoldItal bi def
        Norm
    ) def
%  --------- End User-adjustable parameters -------
```

Figure B.1: Three fonts defined in PostScri.dld

Times-Roman as the 3FONT, you would change the CurFSet 3 portion of the file to

```
CurFSet 3 eq
{
    /n  /Palatino def
    /b  /Palatino-Bold def
    /i  /Palatino-Italic def
    /bi /Palatino-BoldItalic def
} if
```

ADDING A POSTSCRIPT FONT You can also add up to two new fonts to your PostScri.dld file, for a total of five fonts. You need to know the proper name of the additional fonts (as defined in your printer manual), and make additions to the PostScri.dld file in three places. Name the additional fonts 4FONT and 5FONT.

As an example, the section of the modified PostScri.dld file below shows the addition of ITC Bookman as a fourth font beneath the existing 3FONT in the PostScri.dld file:

```
CurFSet 3 eq
{
  /n
/Times-Roman
def        /b  /Times-Bold def
  /i
/Times-Italic
def        /bi /Times-BoldItalic def
} if
CurFSet 4 eq
{
  /n
/Bookman-Light
def        /b  /Bookman-Demi def
  /i
/Bookman-LightItalic
def        /bi /Bookman-DemiItalic def
} if
/FontNorm n def
```

Next, the 4FONT and synonyms need to be defined a little lower in the PostScri.dld file in this section:

```
/1Font   {1 FSet} def
/2Font   {2 FSet} def
/3Font   {3 FSet} def
/4Font   {4 FSet} def
```

and in this section:

```
/1FONT {1Font} def /1font {1Font} def
/2FONT {2Font} def /2font {2Font} def
/3FONT {3Font} def /3font {3Font} def
/4FONT {4Font} def /4font {4Font} def
```

Any new fonts that you add to the PostScri.dld file must also be installed for use with dBASE, using DBSETUP as described under "Installing PostScript Fonts" previously in this appendix. Otherwise, the font will not even appear as an option on the reports design screen when you design reports later (see Chapter 7).

C

Summary of Changes in dBASE

FOR EXPERIENCED dBASE III AND dBASE III PLUS users, dBASE IV offers many new and exciting features. This appendix highlights some of the more impressive new features and, where applicable, provides references to further information in this book. The later portion of this chapter describes changes between version 1.0 and version 1.1 of dBASE IV.

THE CONTROL CENTER

The dBASE III PLUS Assistant menu has been replaced by the much more functional and easier-to-use Control Center. The Control Center provides access to all design screens and data and displays the names of all files in a catalog. Unlike earlier versions of dBASE, the Control Center provides access to nearly all dBASE IV features (see Chapter 2).

In addition, the Control Center offers the DOS utilities screen for managing files and directories. This screen allows you to perform most DOS operations in an interactive fashion without leaving dBASE or entering DOS commands (see Chapter 14).

IMPROVED HELP SYSTEM

Context-sensitive help is available at all times. In addition, the built-in help system provides a table of contents, with various levels of specificity, to simplify the search for related information (see Chapter 2).

For a quick reminder of the syntax and options for a particular dBASE IV command or function, enter the command **HELP <command/function>** at the dot prompt, where <command/function> is the name of the command or function for which you need help (see Chapter 17).

INCREASED LIMIT VALUES

The allowable values for several dBASE III PLUS limitations have been increased in dBASE IV. A single database record can contain up to 255 fields, with a maximum combined length of 4,000 characters. Up to 99 files can be opened simultaneously, 10 of which can be database files.

NEW DATA TYPE

dBASE IV also includes the new data type, Float, for storing floating-point decimal numbers (see Chapters 3 and 9).

IMPROVED DATE HANDLING

You no longer need to use CTOD( ) and DTOC( ) to manage dates. To define the Date data type, just enclose the date in curly braces, as in {01/01/91} (see Chapter 6).

To index a database to display dates sorted on a date field, you can use the DTOS( ) function in an index expression. DTOS( ) converts a date to a character string in YYYYMMDD format (that is, it converts 12/31/90 to 19901231), which ensures proper sort order (see Chapter 12).

IMPROVED MEMO FIELDS

Memo fields, which were quite unwieldy in earlier versions of dBASE, are much improved (see Chapter 10).

- Memo fields can now be displayed in windows on custom forms.
- Deleting and packing database records now deletes and packs memo fields as well, thereby preventing the memo field file from growing too large.
- Queries can now search memo fields.

IMPROVED INDEX MANAGEMENT

dBASE III PLUS stored all indexes in separate database files and made the user responsible for keeping them current. dBASE IV stores all indexes in a single production index file that has the same name as the database file but the extension .MDX. As soon as you open a database file, the production index file is automatically opened and all indexes are instantly adjusted to changes in the database as they happen (see Chapter 5).

The COPY INDEXES command lets you convert existing dBASE III PLUS .NDX index files to dBASE IV production (.MDX) indexes (see Appendix D).

dBASE IV also supports both ascending and descending index sort orders (see Chapter 5).

IMPROVED BROWSE AND EDIT MODES

You can now switch between the browse and edit screens simply by pressing the Data key (F2). In addition, both screens provide pull-down menus for immediate access to operations such as adding new records, deleting records, searching for a record, and undoing recent changes (see Chapter 4).

Any special features used in a custom form, including templates and picture functions, multiple-choice options, and data validation, can be carried over to a browse screen, giving you equal control over data entry and editing in a custom form and on the browse screen (see Chapter 16).

QUERY BY EXAMPLE

The dBASE III PLUS query form has been replaced by a much-improved queries design screen, which provides an interactive query-by-example technique for searching and isolating database records. You can also perform SOUNDEX searches, which locate records that sound like a particular spelling. For example, a search for SOUNDEX("Kinny") will locate Kinny, Kinney, Kenney, and Kenny (see Chapter 6).

The queries design screen also lets you perform calculations such as those for totals, subtotals, averages, and statistical operations on the fly (see Chapter 9).

Queries can also perform global replacement operations, such as increasing prices by 10 percent in any or all records (see Chapter 11).

IMPROVED REPORTS AND LABELS

The dBASE III PLUS Report Generator has been replaced by a much improved reports design screen. New features of the reports design screen include

- A WYSIWYG (What-you-see-is-what-you-get) work surface with *bands* defining page headers and footers, as well as report and group (subtotal) introductory and summary bands.

- Unlimited levels of subtotaling.

- Easy access to printer features such as boldfacing, underlining, and special fonts and pitches.

- Word-wrap and search-and-replace editing for easy creation and editing of form letters.

- A form layout, which makes stacking fields in printed reports easy.

- Seven summary operators for calculations: Average, Count, Max, Min, Sum, Std (standard deviation), and Var (variance).

- Improved techniques for moving and copying field templates.

The labels design screen is also greatly improved and offers many of the same features that the reports design screen does (see Chapters 7 and 10).

IMPROVED FORMS

The dBASE III PLUS Screen Painter has been replaced by a much-improved forms design screen. New features of the forms design screen include

- Automatic layout of all database fields to speed form design.
- Coloring of individual fields and boxed areas on the form.
- Easier access to custom graphics characters.
- Calculated fields.
- Multiple-choice fields that allow a user to scroll through options.
- Edit options that support conditional editing (permit edit if…), data validation, on-screen calculations, custom navigation line messages for each field, and carry-forward for individual fields.

(See Chapter 8.)

MULTIPLE CHILD FILES PER PARENT

A single database file can now be related to multiple related "child" files simultaneously (see Chapters 13 and 19).

KEYSTROKE MACROS

You can store and play back any series of keystrokes in dBASE IV (see Chapter 14).

FINANCIAL FUNCTIONS

dBASE IV includes three new financial functions: FV() (future value), PV() (present value), and PAYMENT() (payment on a loan) (see Appendix E).

AUTOMATIC COMPILATION

To maximize processing speed, dBASE IV automatically compiles all programs into a format that is more quickly executed by the computer. All objects that you create, including report formats, label formats, custom screens, queries, and calculations, are converted to dBASE IV source code, which you can modify or embed in your own custom programs. All of the objects are also compiled automatically for maximum execution speed (see Chapter 17).

APPLICATIONS GENERATOR

dBASE IV provides a much improved, more functional Applications Generator, which you can use to build applications of any complexity using pull-down menus, pop-up menus, and windows. Many applications can be developed without any programming whatsoever.

Experienced programmers and application developers need not write all the tedious code for managing menus, windows, or complex custom forms. Instead, the developer can focus on developing a few procedures and user-defined functions to handle the complex data processing components of an application and call the procedures from the application design (see Chapters 19 through 21).

SEEK() and LOOKUP()

The SEEK and LOCATE commands now have counterparts as functions, which return .T. if a value is found and .F. if a value is not found. These functions are particularly handy in custom forms that require looking up data in a separate database for validation (see Chapters 20 and 21).

SCAN...ENDSCAN LOOPS

The SCAN...ENDSCAN loop provides a compact and efficient alternative to the DO WHILE .NOT. EOF() loop. For example, the

DO WHILE loop

```
USE AnyFile
GO TOP
DO WHILE .NOT. EOF()
   IF PartNo = "A-111"
      REPLACE UnitPrice WITH 1.10*UnitPrice
      ? PartNo,UnitPrice
   ENDIF
   SKIP
ENDDO
```

can be converted to the simpler loop

```
USE AnyFile
SCAN FOR PartNo = "A-111"
   REPLACE UnitPrice WITH 1.10*UnitPrice
   ? PartNo,UnitPrice
ENDSCAN
```

(See Chapter 19.)

USER-DEFINED FUNCTIONS

You can now create your own dBASE IV functions and use them in commands, report columns, custom forms, and any other place where you normally use the standard built-in functions. You can also attach a user-defined function to a field in a custom form to add sophisticated validation and on-screen calculation capabilities (see Chapters 18 and 20).

dBASE WINDOWS

dBASE IV supports windowing, which you can use to enhance the appearance of applications (see Chapters 18 and 21).

ARRAYS

Like most programming languages, dBASE IV offers arrays. An array is a collection of *subscripted memory variables,* each with the same name but a different subscript. For example, an array with the name PartName might consist of the array *elements* PartName[1], PartName[2], and PartName[3] (pronounced part name sub-one, part name sub-two, and part name sub-three).

An array can have either one dimension or two. A one-dimensional array has a single subscript, as in the preceding PartName example. A two-dimensional array has two subscripts, such as Score[1,1]. You can envision a two-dimensional array as a table with rows and columns. The first subscript represents the row number, and the second subscript represents the column. For example, you can envision the arrangement of elements in an array named Score that has three rows and four columns as follows:

```
Score[1,1]   Score[1,2]   Score[1,3]   Score[1,4]
Score[2,1]   Score[2,2]   Score[2,3]   Score[2,4]
Score[3,1]   Score[3,2]   Score[3,3]   Score[3,4]
```

To create an array, you use the syntax

```
DECLARE <array name> [<rows> [<,columns>]]
```

where <array name> is any valid memory variable name, <rows> is the number of rows (elements) in the array, and <columns> is an option number of columns. The outermost brackets ([]) are required.

The DECLARE command simply allocates memory for the array. To enter data into the array, you need to assign values just as you do for any other memory variable. You can also use the COPY TO ARRAY command to copy data from a database into an array, or APPEND FROM ARRAY to copy data from an array into a database.

Figure C.1 shows a simple array that stores abbreviations of day names to a one-dimensional array named Day. Note that the DECLARE command creates an array named Day that consists of seven elements (DECLARE Day[7]). The commands that follow the DECLARE commands assign a day abbreviation to each array element.

```
***************************** TArray.PRG
*············ Test a one-dimensional array.
SET TALK OFF
CLEAR

*·········· Set up an array of day abbreviations.
DECLARE Day[7]
Day[1] = "Sun."
Day[2] = "Mon."
Day[3] = "Tue."
Day[4] = "Wed."
Day[5] = "Thur."
Day[6] = "Fri."
Day[7] = "Sat."

*········ Ask for a date.
AnyDate = (  /  /  )
@ 10,10 SAY "Enter any date " GET AnyDate
READ

*········ Store day of week (number) in a memory variable.
DayOfWeek = DOW(AnyDate)

*········ Use memory variable as subscript to display day abbreviation.
?
? Day[DayOfWeek]
?
```

Figure C.1: Sample command file with a one-dimensional array

If you run the program and enter a date when prompted, the command DayOfWeek = DOW(AnyDate) stores the day of the week as a number between 1 and 7 in a memory variable named DayOfWeek. The command ? Day[DayOfWeek] prints the abbreviation for the day of the week. That is, if DayOfWeek is 7, then the command becomes ? Day[7]. Looking at the array, you can see that Day[7] is "Sat."

Note that, by default, the memory variables in an array are private to the command file (or procedure) that they are created in (as are other memory variables). If you want the elements in an array to be available to all command files and procedures in an application, use the command PUBLIC ARRAY rather than DECLARE. For example, the command PUBLIC ARRAY Score[3,4] creates an array of memory variables named Score, which are public rather than private.

dBASE IV DEVELOPER'S EDITION

The dBASE IV Developer's Edition provides additional tools, including a template language, a run-time package, and network management, for advanced applications developers. For more information, refer to a more advanced book that focuses on the Developer's Edition.

SUMMARY OF CHANGES FROM VERSION 1.0 TO VERSION 1.1 OF dBASE IV

Version 1.1 of dBASE IV addresses and resolves most of the bugs in version 1.0, producing a more reliable and robust product. Many changes and improvements were made in the programming language and SQL components of dBASE, topics you can read about in a more advanced dBASE book. New and improved features that are relevant to the Control Center and other topics discussed in this book are summarized in the sections that follow.

REDUCED MEMORY REQUIREMENT

dBASE IV Release 1.1 requires 450K available memory, as opposed to 516K required by Version 1.0. You still need 640K total RAM; however, only 450K of it needs to be available to run dBASE IV.

ACCESS TO INDEXES THROUGH THE BROWSE AND EDIT SCREENS

You no longer need to work your way all the way back to the database design screen to create or activate an index—the Organize pull-down menu is available at both the Browse and Edit screens (see Chapter 5).

NARROWED QUERY COLUMNS

Fields widths on the Queries design screen default to the width of the field name, allowing you to see more columns at a glance. As you add data to a column, it automatically widens to accommodate your entry if necessary (see Chapter 6).

POSTSCRIPT SUPPORT

dBASE IV version 1.1 offers some support of PostScript printers, including letter and legal paper sizes, landscape and portrait mode, and up to five typefaces and three font sizes (see Appendix B).

PRINTING LABELS ON LASER PRINTERS

dBASE IV version 1.1 offers better control over the margins when printing labels, which in turn provides more control over printing labels on laser printers.

IMPROVED CALCULATED FIELDS CALCULATIONS

Calculated and summary fields in reports and forms seem to be improved in version 1.1 of dBASE IV, but still a little tricky at times. An understanding of the order of precedence of calculations, however, can help resolve miscalculations (see Chapter 9).

APPLICATIONS GENERATOR IMPROVEMENTS

Some of the commands used to display menus have changed in version 1.1, and the template for generating applications (MENU-.GEN) has apparently been altered as well. Therefore, you should re-generate any applications created under version 1.0 of dBASE IV before using them with version 1.1.

Starting an application with a batch process still tends to produce somewhat confusing results. Therefore, the version of the BusMgr (Business Management) application in this book (Chapter 21) uses the Embed Code feature, rather than a batch process, to load the BusProcs procedure file, with much more reliable results.

"QUERIED" INDEXES

Queries are no longer the only way to limit access to certain records in the database. Now you can create indexes that access only records that meet some criterion. This technique is probably more useful to dBASE programmers than Control Center users, but nonetheless is available from the Organize pull-down menu (see Chapter 12).

DISK CACHING AND PERFORMANCE TUNING

Version 1.1 has its own disk caching program that can use extended or expanded memory to greatly increase speed. You can also use a RAM disk to store temporary files, which can further increase speed (see Appendix B).

**Interfacing
with Other
Programs**

dBASE IV OFFERS SEVERAL OPTIONS FOR DIRECTLY importing and exporting data in a variety of formats. These are discussed at the beginning of this appendix and illustrated in an example of importing and exporting data from a Lotus 1-2-3 spreadsheet.

In some cases, you may want to transfer data to software products that dBASE IV does not support. In those situations, you will need to use one of the following alternative methods to complete the transfer.

If the foreign software product has the ability to transfer dBASE IV, dBASE III, or dBASE III PLUS database files, use the foreign software's transfer capabilities (dBASE IV can read dBASE III and dBASE III PLUS database files directly). If the foreign software product does not support dBASE file transfers, but does allow exporting of ASCII text files, then use the ASCII text files as intermediary files to complete the transfer.

The examples presented later in this appendix demonstrate numerous general techniques for importing and exporting dBASE IV data.

BUILT-IN IMPORT AND EXPORT OPTIONS

To export data from a dBASE IV database to a format used by another program, select the Export option from the Tools pull-down menu. You will see a submenu of exporting formats, each of which is summarized in the sections that follow.

RAPIDFILE

This option copies data to the format used by RapidFile and assigns the extension .RPD to that file.

dBASE II

This option copies data to dBASE II format and assigns the extension .DB2 to the file. Do not change the name of the .DB2 file to the .DBF extension until you've moved it to another directory, disk drive, or computer. If you change the name of the .DB2 file to .DBF while it is still on the same directory as the dBASE IV database, you may overwrite your original dBASE IV database.

FRAMEWORK II

This option copies data in a dBASE IV database to a file with the extension .FW2, which can be used in Framework II.

LOTUS 1-2-3

This option copies a dBASE IV database to a file with the extension .WKS, which can be used by Lotus 1-2-3 (as well as Symphony and Quattro). Different versions of 1-2-3 and Symphony require different extensions (for example, version 2 of 1-2-3 uses the .WK1 extension). If necessary, use 1-2-3 or Symphony to change a .WKS file to a .WK1 file.

VISICALC

This option copies a dBASE IV database to a VisiCalc .DIF file.

PFS:FILE

This option copies a dBASE IV database to a format that can be read by PFS:FILE. The name of the copied file will have no extension.

SYLK-MULTIPLAN

This option copies a dBASE IV database to a Multiplan SYLK file. The file name for the copied file will not include an extension.

TEXT FIXED-LENGTH FIELDS

This option copies a dBASE IV database to a text file that lists fields in equal-width columns (called SDF format in earlier versions of dBASE). The copied file with have the extension .TXT.

BLANK DELIMITED

This option copies a dBASE IV database to a text file that includes a single blank space between each field. The copied file will have the extension .TXT.

CHARACTER DELIMITED (")

This option copies a dBASE IV database to a delimited text file with a general format that most software packages can import. When you select this option, you can specify a delimiter other than the default quotation marks. (Quotation marks are the most common delimiter, however.)

EXAMPLE 1: IMPORTING DATA FROM LOTUS 1-2-3

Database files store data in even rows and columns, whereas spreadsheets allow data to be stored in any format. If you want to import data from a spreadsheet to a dBASE IV database, you should import only that portion of the spreadsheet that stores data in even rows and columns, as the example that follows demonstrates.

Suppose you have a Lotus 1-2-3 spreadsheet in which you've stored data for invoices, and you wish to switch to dBASE IV to manage the database. For this example, let's assume that the invoices are stored in a Lotus 1-2-3 spreadsheet file named INVOICES.WK1, which is stored on a directory named C:\123. Let's go through the steps required to import the spreadsheet data to a dBASE IV database named INVOICES.DBF on the C:\DBASE directory.

ISOLATING DATA TO IMPORT

The first phase of the importation process is to isolate the data to be imported to a dBASE IV database. Assuming that both Lotus 1-2-3 and the file to import are on the C:\123 directory, and that you are currently at the DOS prompt (not in dBASE), you would follow these steps:

1. At the DOS prompt, enter the command CD\123 to switch to the 123 directory.

2. Enter the command 123 to start Lotus 1-2-3.

3. Type **/FR** (File Retrieve) and select the name of the file that you want to copy to dBASE IV (INVOICES in this example).

4. Move the cell pointer to the upper-left corner of the range to export the file to dBASE IV.

5. Type **/FXV** (File Xtract Values) to begin extracting data.

6. Enter a drive, directory, and file name for the exported file. To simplify matters, be sure to specify the drive and directory on which you want the imported database file to be stored. For example, in this case you want to store the imported data on the C:\DBASE directory, so press Esc twice to erase the suggested drive and directory and then enter as the file name **C:\DBASE\TRANSFER**. (Version 2 of 1-2-3 will automatically add the .WK1 extension. If you are using some version other than 2, include the .WK1 extension; that is, enter **C:\DBASE\TRANSFER.WK1**.)

7. Highlight the data to copy to dBASE IV, excluding column titles, underscores, totals, or any other spreadsheet embellishments. Figure D.1 shows an example. Press ⏎ after specifying the range to export, and you'll be prompted for a file name.

8. Type **/QY** (Quit Yes) to leave 1-2-3 and return to DOS.

IMPORTING THE SPREADSHEET DATA

To import the spreadsheet data to dBASE IV, you first need to get dBASE up and running, then use the Import option from the Tools pull-down menu. Here are the steps:

1. Enter the command **CD\DBASE** to switch to the dBASE directory.

```
F16: (D1) [W11] +D16+30                                              POINT
Enter extract range: A4..F16
         A         B            C       D          E         F
1  Customer Invoices
2
3  Invoice   Customer        InvAmt InvDate       PdAmt DatePaid
4    10001 Smith Electric   $392.39 06-Oct-90   $392.39 05-Nov-90
5    10002 Toy World        $177.90 06-Oct-90   $177.90 05-Nov-90
6    10003 CompuGames        $84.26 06-Oct-90    $84.26 05-Nov-90
7    10004 Rainbird         $250.73 06-Oct-90   $250.73 05-Nov-90
8    10005 SMS Software     $460.22 06-Oct-90
9    10006 DEK Video        $911.44 06-Oct-90   $911.44 05-Nov-90
10   10007 Compugames       $276.69 06-Oct-90   $276.69 05-Nov-90
11   10008 Rainbird         $600.26 07-Oct-90   $600.26 06-Nov-90
12   10009 SMS Software     $962.91 07-Oct-90   $962.91 06-Nov-90
13   10010 DEK Video        $291.88 07-Oct-90
14   10011 Toy World        $972.70 07-Oct-90   $972.70 06-Nov-90
15   10012 CompuGames       $344.25 07-Oct-90   $344.25 06-Nov-90
16   10013 Rainbird         $477.22 07-Oct-90   $477.22 06-Nov-90
17   -----------            -----------         -----------
18 Totals                  $6,202.85            $5,450.75
19
20
```

Figure D.1: Export range highlighted

2. Enter the command **DBASE** to run dBASE IV.

3. Press F10 and select Import from the Tools pull-down menu above the Control Center.

4. Select Lotus 1-2-3.

5. Select the name of the extracted spreadsheet file (TRANS-FER.WK1 in this example).

6. If a database file named TRANSFER.DBF already exists, dBASE will ask for permission to overwrite it. Select Overwrite to proceed (and lose any data currently in TRANS-FER.DBF). You'll be returned to the Control Center, with the name of the new database, TRANSFER, above the line in the data panel.

7. With the highlight on TRANSFER in the data panel, press F2 to see the database's contents (use the F2 and PgUp keys to switch back and forth between browse and edit and to scroll through records).

Figure D.2 shows how the file appears on the browse screen after importation. dBASE has assigned the simple field names A, B, C, D, and so on to the fields (you will probably want to change these names).

```
  Records    Organize    Fields    Go To    Exit

 A              B                    C            D            E            F

    10001.00  Smith Electric       392.39    10/06/90       392.39    11/05/90
    10002.00  Toy World            177.90    10/06/90       177.90    11/05/90
    10003.00  CompuGames            84.26    10/06/90        84.26    11/05/90
    10004.00  Rainbird             250.73    10/06/90       250.73    11/05/90
    10005.00  SMS Software         460.22    10/06/90
    10006.00  DEK Video            911.44    10/06/90       911.44    11/05/90
    10007.00  Compugames           276.69    10/06/90       276.69    11/05/90
    10008.00  Rainbird             600.26    10/07/90       600.26    11/06/90
    10009.00  SMS Software         962.91    10/07/90       962.91    11/06/90
    10010.00  DEK Video            291.88    10/07/90
    10011.00  Toy World            972.70    10/07/90       972.70    11/06/90
    10012.00  CompuGames           344.25    10/07/90       344.25    11/06/90
    10013.00  Rainbird             477.22    10/07/90       477.22    11/06/90




 Browse   C:\dbase\TRANSFER            Rec 1/13          File
```

Figure D.2: Sample data imported from Lotus 1-2-3

REFINING THE DATA TYPES

Next you'll want to see what data types dBASE has assigned to the imported fields. Follow these steps:

1. If the browse or edit screen is displayed, press Esc to return to the Control Center.

2. With the highlight still on TRANSFER, press Design (Shift-F2) to switch to the database design screen.

3. Press Esc to remove the Organize pull-down menu.

Figure D.3 shows the structure of the imported file. Note that dBASE automatically assigned two decimal places to Numeric fields and specified the Character fields as Date fields.

You can change the data types of any fields and also mark fields for indexing. However, during this phase you should not perform any other operations, such as renaming, adding, or deleting fields. (dBASE may become confused when copying backup data back into the database and probably will lose some of your data.)

Figure D.4 shows a suggested structure for the imported database. After making appropriate changes, select Save Changes and Exit from the Exit pull-down menus and Yes from the prompt box that appears.

Figure D.3: Initial structure of the imported file

Figure D.4: More accurate data types for the imported database

When you get back to the Control Center, you can press F2 and PgUp to view the data and verify that the changes are correct. Then press Esc to return to the Control Center.

RENAMING FIELDS

You probably want to use field names that are more descriptive than the single-letter names that dBASE assigned. To do so, follow these steps:

1. With the highlight on TRANSFER in the Control Center, press Design (Shift-F2) to get to the database design screen.

2. Press Esc to leave the Organize pull-down menu.

3. Enter new field names, but do not make any other changes to the database structure. (Figure D.5 shows some suggested field names for this example.)

4. Select Save Changes and Exit from the Exit pull-down menu.

5. Answer Yes to the prompts that appear until you get back to the Control Center.

6. To view the database and verify your changes, press Data (F2) and PgUp.

The database will appear on the edit or browse screen with the new field names. To return to the Control Center after viewing your data, press Esc. At this point, the entire importation is complete, and you can use the imported data just as you would any dBASE IV database file. If you wish to change the name of the imported database, use the Rename option in the Operations pull-down menu on the DOS utilities screen (see Chapter 14).

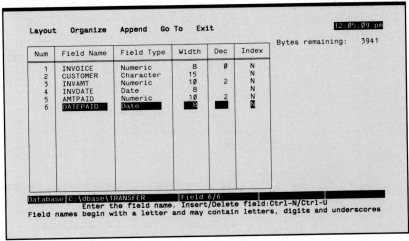

Figure D.5: New field names assigned to the imported database

EXAMPLE 2:
EXPORTING DATA TO LOTUS 1-2-3

Suppose you have a dBASE IV database file named ORDERS-.DBF on the C:\DBASE directory, and you want to use Lotus 1-2-3 to print a graph of total orders for each part number stored in the database. Assume that the ORDERS.DBF has the structure shown in Figure D.6. Figure D.7 shows a small portion of the sample database (additional records are scrolled off the bottom of the screen).

Before you actually export the database to Lotus 1-2-3 in this example, you need to generate total sales for each part number, because that is the information that you want to graph. To do so, you follow these steps:

1. Open the ORDERS database by highlighting its name in the data panel, pressing ◄┘, and selecting Use File.

2. Select <create> from the Queries panel.

3. Press F10 and select Include Indexes from the Fields pulldown menu.

4. Set up a query to total the Qty field for each part number, as in Figure D.8.

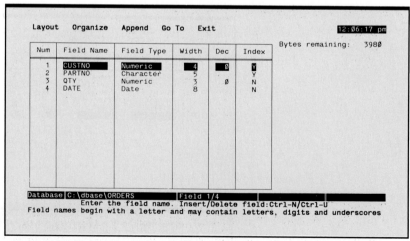

Figure D.6: Structure of the sample ORDERS database

5. Press F2 to test the query and view the results; then select Transfer to Query Design from the Exit pull-down menu.

6. Create a database file from the results of the query by selecting Write View as Database File from the Layout pull-down menu.

7. When prompted, enter a file name for the new database file (such as **ORDTOTS** in this example). You can leave the description blank by pressing ←↵.

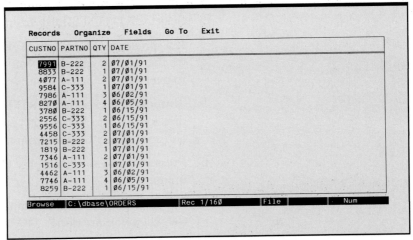

Figure D.7: Some sample data in the ORDERS database

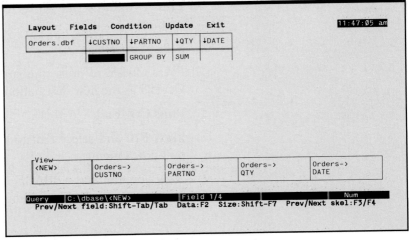

Figure D.8: Query to total orders by part number

8. Press F10 and select Abandon Changes and Exit from the Exit pull-down menu and Yes when prompted for verification.

When you get back to the Control Center, you are ready to export the totaled data in ORDTOTS.DBF to Lotus 1-2-3. To do so, you follow these steps:

1. Press F10 and select Export from the Tools pull-down menu.

2. Select Lotus 1-2-3.

3. Select ORDTOTS.DBF from the submenu that appears.

4. If a spreadsheet file named ORDTOTS.WKS already exists on the current database, you'll be prompted for permission to overwrite it. Select Overwrite.

5. To move the exported ORDTOTS.WKS file to the C:\123 directory (where Lotus 1-2-3 is presumably stored), press F10 and select DOS Utilities from the Tools pull-down menu.

6. Press F10 and select Display Only from the Files pull-down menu.

7. Select Display Only and change the setting to **.WKS**. Press ⏎ when you are done.

8. Use the PgDn and arrow keys to locate and highlight ORD-TOTS.WKS in the files list.

9. Press F10 and select Move from the Operations pull-down menu.

10. Select Single File.

11. Press Ctrl-Y to erase the suggested destination and type **C:\123** as the new destination.

12. Press Ctrl-End.

13. Press F10 and select Exit to Control Center from the Exit pull-down menu.

14. Now you can leave dBASE IV by selecting Quit to DOS from the Exit pull-down menu.

Now you want to load the exported data into Lotus 1-2-3 and build the graph. First you need to switch to the appropriate directory (C:\123 in this example), run 1-2-3, and retrieve the file. Here are the steps:

1. Enter the command **CD\123** at the DOS prompt.

2. Enter the command **123** at the DOS prompt to run 1-2-3.

3. When the blank spreadsheet appears, type **/FR** (File Retrieve) and select the name of the exported dBASE IV file (ORDTOTS.WKS in this example).

4. You'll see the exported totals on the spreadsheet. As necessary, use the /WCS (Worksheet, Column, Set-Width) options to alter column widths in the spreadsheet.

5. Type **/GTB** (Graph Type Bar) to select a graph type.

6. Select X and highlight X-axis titles (part numbers in the range B2..B7 in this example) as shown in Figure D.9.

7. Select A and specify the values to plot on the graph (C2..C7 in this example).

8. Select View.

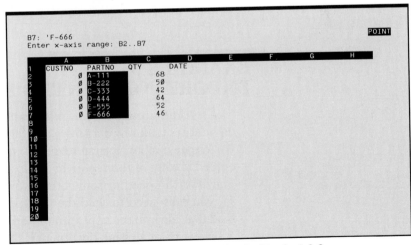

Figure D.9: Part names selected as the X-axis titles in 1-2-3

The graph will appear on the screen. You can use other 1-2-3 graph options to add titles or other features, as in the example shown in Figure D.10. After viewing the graph, press any key to return to the spreadsheet. You can treat the imported data as you would any other spreadsheet data. Remember: If you wish to save any changes to the spreadsheet, use the 1-2-3 **/FS** (File Save) options. To leave 1-2-3, type **/QY** (Quit Yes).

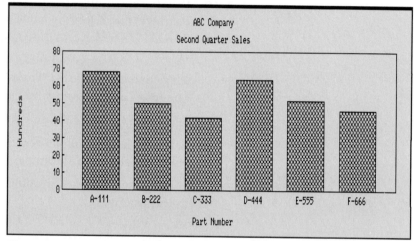

Figure D.10: Sample graph printed from the ORDERS database file

EXAMPLE 3:
EXPORTING PRINTED REPORTS

In some situations, you may want to export printed, formatted data rather than raw data from a database file. For example, suppose you create a report format to display totals and subtotals and wish to embed a copy of the report in a document you created with Word-Star, WordPerfect, or some other word processing program. To do so, you only need to send the printed report to a disk file and then read that file into the appropriate word processing document (or into a new word processing document).

CREATING THE TEXT FILE

In this section, we'll discuss the general steps for creating a text file from a report or label format. We'll use the CUSTLIST.DBF database and the LIST report format in the LEARN catalog as examples.

1. Open the database (CUSTLIST in this example) by highlighting its name in the Data panel of the Control Center, pressing ◄─┘, and selecting Use File.

2. To export only certain records or to sort the database, create a query or use an existing query to display the appropriate records (as discussed in Chapter 6). Press F2 to verify the query and then return to the Control Center.

3. Highlight the name of the report format in the Reports panel (LIST in this example), press ◄─┘, and select Print Report.

4. Select Destination and press the space bar to change the setting to DOS File.

5. Select Name of File and note the suggested file name (LIST.PRT in this example) or change the drive, directory, or suggested file name.

6. To view the report on the screen as it is stored on disk, select Echo to Screen and press ◄─┘ to change the setting to Yes.

7. Press Ctrl-End.

8. Select Begin Printing.

9. When you get back to the Control Center, select Quit to DOS from the Exit pull-down menu to leave dBASE IV.

You can use the DOS TYPE command to verify that the file exists. In this example, you would enter the command **TYPE LIST.PRT** (and press ◄─┘) at the DOS prompt. You should see the entire formatted report.

READING THE REPORT INTO WORDSTAR

If you use WordStar as your word processor, you can follow these general steps to read the printed report into a word processing document:

1. Enter the DOS command **CD** to switch to the directory that contains WordStar or the WordStar document into which you want to insert the report.

2. Run WordStar in the usual manner (that is, type **WS** at the dot prompt and press ◄─┘).

3. Type **D** to select Document and then enter the name of a new or existing document file.

4. If you are inserting the report into an existing document, move the cursor to exactly the place that you want the incoming report to be inserted.

5. Press Ctrl-KR and, when prompted, type the full path and file name of the file to insert (**C:\DBASE\LIST.PRT** in this example). Press ◄─┘.

You will see the formatted report appear in your document. Use the PgUp and PgDn keys to scroll and make changes if necessary. Save the document after inserting the report using the usual Ctrl-KD, Ctrl-KS, or Ctrl-KX keystrokes.

READING THE REPORT INTO WORDPERFECT

To read the formatted report into a WordPerfect document, follow these general steps:

1. Enter the DOS **CD** command to switch to the directory that contains WordPerfect or the document into which you want to insert the formatted report.

2. If you want to read the formatted report into a new document, run WordPerfect by entering the command **WP** at the DOS prompt. If you want to read the report into an existing WordPerfect document, start WordPerfect by entering the command **WP <filename>**, where <filename> is the name of the existing WordPerfect document.

3. If you are inserting the formatted report into an existing document, move the cursor to the location where you want the inserted report to appear.

4. Press Ctrl-F5.

5. Select option 1, and then option 2.

6. Enter the full path and file name of the formatted report (**C:\DBASE\LIST.PRT** in this example) and press ⏎.

You'll see the formatted report embedded in the document. Use the usual scrolling keys to verify that the entire file was inserted and to make any changes, if necessary. Save the document using the usual F7 key.

EXAMPLE 4: EXPORTING TO WORDSTAR MAILMERGE FILES

Suppose you wish to use dBASE IV to manage names and addresses and to use WordStar to print form letters. To do so, you need to export records from the DBASE IV database to an ASCII text file that delimits (separates) each field with a comma. Then you need to use the WordStar MailMerge dot commands in a form letter to read in the exported data.

Let's look at an example, where we will export data from the CUSTLIST database to a WordStar MailMerge file named CUST-LIST.MRG on a directory named C:\WS4. Here are the steps to get started:

1. Press F10 and select Export from the Tools pull-down menu.

2. Highlight Character Delimited, and press ⏎ to accept the quotation mark (ASCII character number 34) as the delimiter.

3. Select CUSTLIST.DBF.

4. When the exportation is done, select Quit to DOS from the Exit pull-down menu.

At the DOS prompt, you can verify that the exportation was successful by entering the command **TYPE CustList.TXT**. You should see the CUSTLIST database records, with Character data surrounded by quotation marks and commas between each field. A sample record is shown here:

```
1001,"Smith","John","ABC Co.","123 A St.","San Diego",
"CA","92067","(619)555-1234",19901115,Y
```

Now suppose you want to store a copy of this exported file on a directory named WS4 (where WordStar is stored) and to change its name to CUSTLIST.MRG. To do so, enter this command at the DOS prompt:

```
COPY CustList.TXT C:\WS4\CustList.MRG
```

After you press ⏎ and the copy operation is complete, you can switch to the C:\WS4 directory by entering the command **CD\WS4**. Now you need to create a form letter, following these steps:

1. At the DOS prompt, enter the usual command for running WordStar (usually **WS**).

2. Select D and enter a name for the form letter (for example, **FORMLET.TXT**).

3. Press Ctrl-O and then S1 to set line spacing to 1.

Figure D.11 shows a sample form letter that is capable of printing letters using exported data in the CUSTLIST.MRG file. Note that the .DF dot command specifies the name of the file containing the data to merge. The .RV command assigns a variable name to each field in the merge file. Note that you must include a variable name for each field in the merge file, whether or not you plan to actually use it in the letter, and you must use the same left-to-right order as the fields in the merge file.

To place data from the merge file onto the printed letter, use the variable name assigned in the .RV command surrounded by ampersands. If you think that a particular field may be blank in some records (such as COMPANY in the CUSTLIST database), add /o to the right of the variable name, as in the example &Company/o&.

```
      C:FORMLET.TXT           PØ1 L16 C23 Insert Align
    L----!----!----!----!----!----!----!----!----!--------R
    .MT 8                                                             1
    .DF CustList.MRG                                                  :
    .RV CustNo,Last,First,Company,Address,City,State,Zip,Phone,Start,Paid :
    .OP                                                               :
    .LS1                                                              <

    June 11, 1991                                                    <
                                                                     <
    &First& &Last&                                                   <
    &Company/o&                                                      <
    &Address&                                                        <
    &City&, &State&   &Zip&                                          <
                                                                     <
    Dear &First&:                                                    <

    This is a sample WordStar form letter.  The name and address
    above were exported from a dBASE IV database to a delimited text
    file, which in turn was used as a mailmerge file to print these
    letters.                                                         <
                                                                     <
    (etc... etc... etc...)                                           <
                                                                     <
    .PA                                                              .
```

Figure D.11: Sample WordStar form letter

Doing so ensures that WordStar will close the gap left by this empty variable, rather than printing a blank line.

After creating the form letter, save it using the usual Ctrl-KD command. Then select M (for Merge Print) and specify the name of the form letter file (FORMLET.TXT in this example). Press Esc to bypass other options and begin printing.

IMPORTING ASCII TEXT FILES

If neither dBASE IV nor a foreign software product provide built-in options for interfacing, you'll usually need to use an ASCII text file as an intermediary file for the transfer operation. Most software products, even those with very limited interfacing capability, have some means of storing data in ASCII text files.

If you can use that foreign software product to produce the ASCII text file, then chances are that you can import that text file into a dBASE IV database. There are several general steps involved, listed in the next sections. (The general steps are illustrated in an example that follows.)

STEP 1: CREATE THE ASCII TEXT FILE

Suppose that you are using a product, which we'll name FlashBase, to store data and you want to transfer copies of that data to a dBASE IV database. You need to look in the FlashBase manual for information about creating ASCII text files, either through a file exporting option or by storing printed reports or data on disk files. Use whatever means are available to create the file and note the disk drive, directory, and complete file name of the exported ASCII text file.

STEP 2: NOTE THE STRUCTURE OF THE ASCII TEXT FILE

The next step is to look at the ASCII text file and ascertain its structure. To do so, starting from the DOS prompt, switch to the directory where the file is stored and use the DOS TYPE command to look at the contents of the file. For example, if the ASCII text file is stored in C:\FBASE\EXPORTED.DAT, you enter the following commands at the DOS prompt to view the contents of the file:

```
CD\FBASE
TYPE Exported.DAT
```

Most likely, the file will be in one of three formats: delimited, blank delimited, or fixed field length (also called structured data format, or SDF). Delimited ASCII files generally place a comma between each field and surround character strings with quotation marks or some other character. Blank-delimited files separate each field with a single blank space, and individual fields contain no blank spaces. Fixed field-length storage places each field in evenly spaced columns. Figure D.12 shows examples of these three formats.

Note that in the example in the figure, the delimited file uses double quotation marks as delimiters. If, while viewing the file, you notice that some other character is used to delimit character strings, make a note of this character to remind yourself later. For example, the following text file uses apostrophes (') to delimit character strings:

```
1001,'Smith','John','ABC Co.','123 A St.','San Diego'
1002,'Adams','Annie','','3456 Ocean St.','Santa Monica'
```

Delimited (with ") format:

```
1001,"Smith","John",19901115,T
1002,"Adams","Annie",19910101,F
```

Blank-delimited format:

```
1001 Smith John 19901115 T
1002 Adams Annie 19910101 F
```

Fixed field-length (SDF) format:

```
1001Smith           John                19901115T
1002Adams           Annie               19910101F
```

Figure D.12: Examples of ASCII file formats

Note that you may find that the file uses none of the formats discussed in this section, in which case you might need to write a program to perform the conversion. WordPerfect secondary (mailmerge) files are an example of files that use a very unusual format which cannot be easily imported into or exported from dBASE IV database files.

STEP 3: PLAN A dBASE IV DATABASE STRUCTURE

While viewing the contents of the ASCII text file on your screen, you need to plan a structure for the dBASE IV database. Assign a name, data type, width, and number of decimal places (for numbers) to each field. Be sure to list file names in the same order that they are listed, from left to right, in the text file.

If the fields in the file are separated by commas or single blank spaces, then you can assign any width that you wish to each field. If, however, the file has the SDF structure, the width you assign to your dBASE IV database must exactly match the widths of the fields in the ASCII text file.

STEP 4: COPY AND RENAME THE TEXT FILE

Next, you copy the file to the C:\DBASE directory and change the extension to .TXT. (If you have a DOS redirect or move utility, you can move the file instead.) For example, to copy the C:\FBASE\ EXPORTED.DAT file to C:\DBASE\EXPORTED.TXT, you enter this command below at the DOS prompt:

COPY C:\DBASE\Exported.DAT C:\DBASE\Exported.TXT

STEP 5: CREATE THE DATABASE STRUCTURE

Now you can switch to the DBASE directory and run dBASE, by entering the commands

CD\DBASE
DBASE

When the Control Center appears, select <create> from the Data panel and design a database with the field names and data types that you noted earlier. Save the database structure using the Save This Database File Structure option from the Database Design screen Layout pull-down menu. Then select Copy Records from Non-dBASE File from the Append pull-down menu in the database design screen and the appropriate option from the submenu that appears (Figure D.13 shows that submenu).

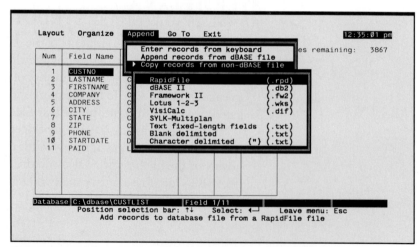

Figure D.13: Menu for importing data into a database file

The next section demonstrates some of these steps, showing you how to import data from a WordStar mailmerge file into a dBASE database.

EXAMPLE 5: IMPORTING WORDSTAR MAILMERGE DATA

Suppose you have already created a fairly large list of names and addresses for WordStar MailMerge operations, simply by typing them using WordStar. Now that you have dBASE IV, you want to import those names and addresses to a database file and use dBASE to manage them. You can easily import this list to a dBASE IV database. (Because WordStar MailMerge files are already in ASCII delimited format, you need not take any action to export them to a different format.)

For example, suppose you have stored the names and addresses in a file named C:\WS4\NAMES.MRG. Here is how you import them to a dBASE IV database:

1. From the DOS prompt, enter the command **CD\WS4** to switch to the WS4 directory.

2. To view the contents of the file, enter the command **TYPE NAMES.MRG** at the DOS prompt.

3. Suppose now that the screen displays the contents of the NAMES.MRG file, as shown in Figure D.14. Jot down notes about the file and define field names and data types, as follows (because commas separate fields in this example, you can assign any widths that you wish to each field):

   Format: Delimited (with ")
LastName	Character	15
FirstName	Character	15
Company	Character	20
Address	Character	30
City	Character	20
State	Character	2
Zip	Character	10

```
C:\WS4>TYPE Names.MRG
"Smith","John","ABC Co.","123 A St.","San Diego","CA",92067
"Adams","Annie","","3456 Ocean St.","Santa Monica","CA",92001
"Mahoney","Mary","","211 Seahawk St.","Seattle","WA",88977
"Newell","John","LoTech Co.","734 Rainbow Dr.","Butte","MT",54321
"Beach","Sandy","American Widget","11 Elm St.","Portland","OR",76543
"Kenney","Ralph","","1101 Rainbow Ct.","Los Angeles","CA",96607
"Schumack","Susita","SMS Software","47 Broad St.","Philadelphia","PA",45543
"Smith","Anita","Zeerocks, Inc.","2001 Engine Dr.","Hideaway","CA",92220
"Jones","Fred","American Sneaker","P.O. Box 3381","Newark","NJ",01234


C:\WS4>
```

Figure D.14: Contents of a WordStar MailMerge file

4. Copy the text file to the \DBASE directory and change its extension to .TXT by entering the command **COPY C:\WS4\NAMES.MRG C:\DBASE\NAMES.TXT** at the DOS prompt.

5. Log on to the dBASE directory by entering the command **CD\DBASE** at the DOS prompt.

6. Run dBASE in the usual manner (enter the command **DBASE** at the DOS prompt).

7. Select <create> from the Data panel in the Control Center.

8. Design the database according to your earlier notes, as in Figure D.15.

9. Select Save This Database File Structure from the Layout pull-down menu and assign a valid file name (such as **NAMES**).

10. Select Copy Records from non-dBASE File from the Append pull-down menu.

11. Select Character Delimited from the submenu.

12. Because the text file uses quotation marks as delimiters, and the submenu that appears suggests this character, just press ←┘.

Figure D.15: Structure of the database to receive MailMerge records

13. Select the name of the text file (NAMES.TXT in this example) from the submenu that appears.

14. Select Save Changes and Exit from the Exit pull-down menu.

The importation is now complete. You can press F2 to switch to the edit and browse screens and use the PgUp, PgDn, and arrow keys to scroll through the database and verify that all appropriate records were imported.

EXAMPLE 6:
EXPORTING TO WORDPERFECT
SECONDARY MERGE FILES

In some cases you need to use a little ingenuity to get your files transferred. WordPerfect secondary merge files (used for printing form letters and such) are a good example, because dBASE does not have an option for exporting directly to such files.

However, if you were to check the menu on the WordPerfect Convert program (the one that comes with WordPerfect 5.1), you'd see that it has an option to import DIF (Data Interchange Format) files into Secondary Merge Files. dBASE IV, in turn, can export to DIF. Hence, you need to export from dBASE to DIF, then import from DIF to Word-Perfect. Here are the steps using CUSTLIST.DBF as the sample database being exported to WordPerfect 5.1. These steps assume that dBASE IV is stored on C:\DBASE and WordPerfect 5.1 is stored on C:\WP51 (you would need to change the drive\directory names accordingly if your copies are stored elsewhere):

1. Run dBASE IV in the usual manner so that the Control Center appears.

2. If the catalog containing the database file you want to export does not appear, use the Use a Different Catalog option on the Catalog pull-down menu to go to the appropriate catalog.

3. Select Export from the Tools pull-down menu.

4. Select VisiCalc (.dif) from the Export submenu.

5. Select the name of the file you want to export from the submenu of database names (the exported file will have the same first name, but the extension .DIF rather than .DBF).

6. Select Quit to Dos from the Exit pull-down menu to leave dBASE IV.

7. Switch to the WordPerfect directory (**CD \WP51** ← if you are using WordPerfect 5.1, and if it's stored on C:\WP51).

8. Enter the CONVERT command followed by the location and name of the exported DIF file, a blank space, and the location and name of the new WordPerfect secondary merge file you'll be creating. For example, if you were exporting CUSTLIST.DBF, you would type

    CONVERT C:\DBASE\CUSTLIST.DIF CUSTLIST.SCD

    and press ←.

9. Select A Spreadsheet DIF to WordPerfect Secondary Merge.

That completes the exportation. You can now run WordPerfect and retrieve the exported file (CUSTLIST.SCD in this example) using the Retrieve (Shift-F10) key or List Files (F5). There will, however, be a couple of problems you need to repair.

First, the new secondary merge file will have the dBASE IV field names as the first record. These can help you determine the number of each imported field because as you scroll up and down in this file, the number of each field appears in the lower-left corner of the screen. However, you probably don't want to print these field names either. So, at your leisure you can delete them by highlighting everything from the top of the file to the first {END RECORD} (or ^E) merge command and pressing Delete (Del).

The second problem is that any dates that were exported will be in the generic format yyyymmdd (such as 19901231 for 12/31/90). To display dates in the more familiar mm/dd/yy (12/31/90) format, you would need to use a merge expression with the {MID} macro command to isolate each component of the date and display it in the format you want. Assuming that the date is stored in field 9, the exact expression is

```
{MID}{FIELD}9~ ~4~2~/{MID}
     {FIELD}9~ ~6~2~/{MID}{FIELD}9~ ~2~2~
```

To create each {MID} expression on your WordPerfect primary merge file, you need to follow these general steps (assuming your WordPerfect primary file is on your WordPerfect Edit screen ready for editing):

1. Place the cursor to where you want the imported date to appear in your primary merge file.

2. Press Merge Codes (Shift-F9) and select More.

3. Select {MID}expr ~ offset ~ count ~ .

4. Press ← when prompted to enter an expression.

5. When prompted for an Offset, type **4** and press ←.

6. When prompted for a count, type **2** and press ←.

7. Press ← enough times to move the cursor to beneath the first tilde (~), to the right of the }.

8. Press Merge Codes (Shift-F9).

9. Select More.

10. Select {FIELD}field ˜ .

11. Type the number of the field to display and press ← (**9** in this example because the imported date is in Field 9).

12. Press Home → to move to the end of the expression.

13. Type **/** (because you want the expression to type a / here).

At this point you will have typed **{MID}{FIELD}9 ˜ ˜ 4 ˜ 2 ˜ /** (assuming the date is in Field 9), which tells WordPerfect to print the month followed by a slash—the 4 refers to the fourth character in the string where the first character is number 0, and the 2 refers to the length. Hence, if the imported date is 19901231, then **{MID}-{FIELD}9 ˜ ˜ 4 ˜ 2 ˜** / will display 12/ after the merge.

You need to repeat the general steps above to complete the entire expression, displaying the portion {MID}{FIELD}9 ˜ ˜ 6 ˜ 2 ˜ (the day of the month) the second time, followed by a slash, and then displaying the portion {MID}{FIELD}9 ˜ ˜ 2 ˜ 2 ˜ on the third time through (the two characters representing the year).

Figure D.16 shows a sample WordPerfect 5.1 primary merge file that can print letters using data that was exported to dBASE IV, both

```
{FIELD}2˜ {FIELD}1˜
{FIELD}3?˜
{FIELD}4?˜
{FIELD}5˜, {FIELD}6˜  {FIELD}7˜

Dear {FIELD}2˜:

Thanks for joining our club. We have your starting date on file as
{MID}{FIELD}9˜˜4˜2˜/{MID}{FIELD}9˜˜6˜2˜/{MID}{FIELD}9˜˜2˜2˜ and will start sendi
following month.

C:\WP51\WPFILES\CUSTLIST.PRM                        Doc 1 Pg 1 Ln 1" Pos 1"
▲        ▲         ▲         ▲         ▲         ▲         }     ▲    ▲
[Mrg:FIELD]2˜ [Mrg:FIELD]1˜[HRt]
[Mrg:FIELD]3?˜[HRt]
[Mrg:FIELD]4?˜[HRt]
[Mrg:FIELD]5˜, [Mrg:FIELD]6˜  [Mrg:FIELD]7˜[HRt]
[HRt]
Dear [Mrg:FIELD]2˜:[HRt]
[HRt]
Thanks for joining our club. We have your starting date on file as[SRt]
[Mrg:MID][Mrg:FIELD]9˜˜4˜2˜/[Mrg:MID][Mrg:FIELD]9˜˜6˜2˜/[Mrg:MID][Mrg:FIELD]9˜˜2
˜2˜ and will start sending your newsletter the[SRt]

Press Reveal Codes to restore screen
```

Figure D.16: Sample WordPerfect 5.1 primary merge file

See your WordPerfect manual or a WordPerfect book for additional information on merging with WordPerfect.

on the normal Edit screen and on the Reveal Codes screen. All of the merge codes shown in curly braces ({}) were placed using the Merge Codes key (Shift-F9). Once you've completed your primary merge file, you can use the Merge key (Ctrl-F9) to merge the primary and secondary files in the usual manner.

EXAMPLE 7: IMPORTING FROM WORDPERFECT SECONDARY MERGE FILES

Importing data from a WordPerfect secondary merge file into a dBASE database also takes a little ingenuity, primarily because the Import option on the Tools pull-down menu has nothing that's compatible with WordPerfect's Convert program. However, you can add records from a DIF file to an existing database file. That is, you first need to create a dBASE database with the appropriate structure. For each field in the WordPerfect secondary merge file, there must be a corresponding field in the dBASE database.

If you will be importing any dates from the WordPerfect file (typed or entered with the WordPerfect Date Text key in 12/31/90 format), define the dBASE fields that will store those as the Character data type with a length of 8. You might want to use a temporary name for this field. For example, if the third field in the WordPerfect secondary file contains a date, then you might want the third field in your dBASE database structure to be named IMPDATE, have a Character data type, and a length of 8.

Similarly, even though WordPerfect does not support the Logical data type per se, you might have used some sort of Yes/No or Y/N field in your secondary merge file. If that is the case, make the dBASE field that will be receiving that field the Character data type as well, with a length of 1.

After creating that dBASE database, which in this example we'll assume is named FROMWP.DBF, you need to go to the directory where the WordPerfect secondary file is stored, and use the Word-Perfect Convert program to make a copy of that file converted to DIF format. For example, if the WordPerfect secondary merge file is named MEMBERS.SCD, you could enter this command to initiate the exportation:

CONVERT C:\WP51\MEMBERS.SCD
C:\DBASE\MEMBERS.DIF

When the Convert menu appears, select option **1** WordPerfect to Another Format. Then select **8** WordPerfect Secondary Merge File to Spreadsheet DIF. The DIF version of the file will be stored on the C:\DBASE drive and directory in this example.

Next, go back to the dBASE directory and run dBASE. At the Control Center, highlight the name of the database file that you want to import records to (from WP in this example). Press Design (Shift-F2), then press Alt-A and select Copy Records from Non-dBASE File. Highlight the name of the DIF file (MEMBER.DIF in this example) and press ◄┘.

When the importation is complete you can return to the Control Center by pressing Control-End.

If the imported data contained any dates, you may want to convert them to the dBASE Date data type now. For example, if you imported dates into a Character field named IMPDATE, you might want to go back to the database design screen and add a new field to the database named STARTDATE (or whichever database you want to import to), giving the Date data type. Save the database structure and get to the dot prompt. At the dot prompt, enter the command:

REPLACE ALL STARTDATE WITH CTOD(IMPDATE)

The STARTDATE field will then have "real" dBASE dates. You can then return to the dBASE database design screen, remove the IMPDATE field, and (immediately) save the new database structure.

If you imported Logical data into a Character field, named IMPLOGIC for example, in your database, you can use a similar technique to convert that to a Logic field. After the importation, add a new field to the database with whatever name you want (we'll use PAIDYET in this example), and make it the Logical data type. Save the new structure, and get to the dot prompt.

Assuming the IMPLOGIC field contains either Y (for true) or N (for false), you could use the following command to convert those values to Logical values in the PAIDYET field:

REPL ALL PAIDYET WITH IIF(IMPLOGIC = "Y",.T.,.F.)

When the replacement is finished, you can go back to the database design screen and remove the IMPLOGIC field. Then save the database structure immediately.

I have found one flaw with this technique: the first record from the WordPerfect secondary merge file is not appended from the DIF file, because this is where field names are usually stored. To ensure that all of your WordPerfect secondary merge records are exported, place a blank record at the top of that file before exporting to DIF format.

CONVERTING FROM dBASE III PLUS TO dBASE IV

If you want to use your dBASE III PLUS databases, reports, and so forth with dBASE IV, you should go through the following steps to bring all the files up to date:

1. Copy all the dBASE III PLUS database (.DBF and .DBT), index (.NDX), screen (.SCR), report (.FRM), label (.LBL), and program (.PRG) files to a separate directory where they can be converted to dBASE IV format. You can use the DOS COPY command, or the dBASE IV DOS Utilities options covered in Chapter 14.

2. Start dBASE IV from the new directory, and create a catalog for the old dBASE III PLUS files (see Chapter 14).

3. After creating the catalog, add the various files from dBASE III PLUS to it (Chapter 14).

4. Open a database in the Data panel.

5. Update each Form, Report, and Label format for that database by first highlighting its name in the Control Center and pressing Design (Shift-F2). This will bring that object to the appropriate design screen for that object.

6. Make any changes you want to the object then save the object by pressing Ctrl-End or by selecting Save Changes and Exit from the Exit pull-down menu.

7. Repeat steps 5 and 6 for each Form, Report, and Label format in each database so that a dBASE IV version of the file is generated.

You can also update any dBASE III PLUS view (.VUE) files by bringing a copy to the Queries panel of the Control Center and pressing Design (Shift-F2) to modify the view. However, not all dBASE III PLUS views are easily translated to dBASE IV, so you may have to re-create a portion of each view before saving them as dBASE IV query (view) files.

CONVERTING INDEX FILES

You will probably want to combine any dBASE III PLUS index (.NDX) files into dBASE IV multiple index (.MDX) files, since this is by far a more convenient way to manage indexes. You can use the COPY INDEX command (from the dBASE dot prompt) to do this.

To see how you would convert dBASE III PLUS index files to dBASE IV indexes, suppose you have a dBASE III PLUS database named PRODUCTS.DBF that uses two index files named PROD-NO.NDX and PRODDATE.NDX. First, run dBASE IV in the usual manner and then, from the Control Center, press Esc and select Yes to get to the dot prompt. At the dot prompt, open the database file and both indexes by entering the command

USE Products INDEX ProdNo,ProdDate

To copy both indexes to a production index file named PRODUCTS.MDX, enter the command

COPY INDEX ProdNo,ProdDate

(The default production index name, Products.MDX in this example, is assumed by the COPY INDEX command.) When the dot prompt reappears, the conversion is complete.

To avoid confusion between the new and old indexes, you can delete the dBASE III PLUS .NDX files now by entering the following series of commands at the dot prompt:

```
CLOSE ALL
ERASE ProdNo.NDX
ERASE ProdDate.NDX
```

To open the Products database and both indexes, you simply need to enter the command

```
USE Products
```

When the dot prompt reappears, enter the command

```
DISPLAY STATUS
```

You'll notice that the status report displays the following (with the directory, file name, and index names for your converted files substituted):

```
Currently selected database:
Select area: 1, Database in Use: C:\DBASE\PRODUCTS.DBF
Production    MDX file:    C:\DBASE\PRODUCTS.MDX
              Index TAG:   PRODNO    Key: partno
              Index TAG:   PRODDATE  Key: Date
```

At the moment, the database file and both indexes are open. However, no particular index is controlling the sort order, nor can any of the indexes currently be searched with a SEEK or FIND command. But if you add, change, or delete data, both indexes will be updated automatically.

Note that each index within a production index file includes a *tag*. A tag is simply the name of the individual index within the larger production index file.

To select one of the indexes for ordering records or searching with a SEEK or FIND command, use the SET ORDER command:

```
SET ORDER TO ProdNo
```

The ProdNo index will control the sort order and can be searched. Other indexes within the production index file are still updated automatically whenever data is added, changed, or deleted.

Note that if you now attempt to use the dBASE III PLUS command SET INDEX TO ProdNo, dBASE IV will still attempt to find an index file named ProdNo.NDX. However, you've erased that index file, so dBASE displays the error message "File not found."

To open the database with one of the indexes controlling the sort order, use the syntax USE <database> ORDER <index tag>. For example, the command

USE Products ORDER ProdDate

opens the Products database with the ProdDate index controlling the sort order. (Of course, all other indexes in the production index file are open and will be updated to include any new, changed, or deleted data.)

Note that if you attempted to use the dBASE III PLUS command USE Products INDEX ProdDate, dBASE IV would attempt to find the ProdDate.NDX index file, which you've erased. The error message "File not found" would appear.

The dBASE IV INDEX ON command will still create an .NDX index file unless you specify the TAG option in place of the TO option. For example, the following command creates an index named PartName, which is stored in the production index file with other indexes:

INDEX ON PartName TAG PartName

The following dBASE IV command creates a dBASE III .NDX index file, which is stored outside the production index file:

INDEX ON PartName TO PartName

COMPILER WARNINGS

dBASE IV will automatically compile a dBASE III PLUS program the first time it is executed and whenever it is modified in the future. If the dBASE III PLUS program includes remarks to the right of ENDDO, ENDIF, ENDCASE, or other commands that terminate program clauses, dBASE will present a warning, such as the one shown here, when compiling the line:

```
ENDDO (while not eof)                              .
Warning on line XXX: Extra characters ignored at end of command
```

The warning will not prevent the program from compiling or running properly. However, if you want to prevent future compilations from displaying the warning message, precede all such comments with double ampersands, as follows:

ENDDO &&(while not eof)

COPYING CATALOGS AND APPLICATIONS ACROSS PCs

In this section we'll talk about interacting with multiple (licensed) copies of dBASE IV on several PCs in terms of copying and moving catalogs and applications between these PCs. In this situation there is no need to actually translate data, since you are just going from dBASE IV on one machine to dBASE IV on another machine. However, there are some potential confusions about how to go about copying entire applications and catalogs, which we'll discuss here.

COPYING APPLICATIONS

As mentioned in the chapters on creating applications, it's always a good idea to create each new application on its own, unique directory. If you do so, it's simple to copy an application from one computer to another. When describing how to do this, we'll refer to the computer that currently has the application stored on it as the *source* computer, and the computer that you want to copy the application to as the *target* computer.

NOTE

See the MKDIR, CHDIR, and COPY commands in your DOS manual for additional information on directories and copying files. The more comfortable you are with these commands, the better.

Basically you need to create a directory on the target computer (using the DOS MKDIR or MD command) with the same name as the directory used to store the application on the source computer.

Then, you simply need to copy every file from the application's directory on the source computer to the directory with the same name on the target directory. You can use the DOS COPY command (COPY *.*) or the dBASE IV DOS Utilities screen to do so. If you are using floppy disks as an intermediary (that is, copying from the source to a floppy, then from the floppy to the target), you may need to use more than one disk, or erase files from the floppy after they've been copied to the target directory to make room for more files.

As an alternative to using floppies, you can use a linking program such as LapLink or Brooklyn Bridge (available at most computer or software stores) to simply send the file through a wire (if the computers are close enough to each other). Optionally, you can use a modem if the two computers are far apart. Whichever technique you use to copy the application, just make sure to copy every file from the application's directory on the source computer to the corresponding directory on the target computer.

After copying the files to the target computer, run dBASE IV from the application's directory on the target computer (which, of course, assumes that the dBASE IV directory is already in the PATH statement on the target computer). If the application's catalog does not appear in the Control Center when you first start dBASE on the target computer, select Use a Different Catalog from the Catalog pull-down menu, then select the catalog name (if it appears) from the submenu, or select <create> from that submenu, type in the catalog's name, and press ◄—┘. You should then see the entire application's catalog with all its file names appear on your screen.

COPYING CATALOGS

I've often been asked how one goes about copying a catalog (meaning the catalog itself, and all the files within it) from one computer to another. Intuitively, it seems as though this should be a simple process—simply copy the catalog.

However, intuition is not correct in this case, mainly because a catalog is only a collection of file *names,* not a collection of the actual files. As a matter of fact, a catalog is actually a dBASE database file with a predefined structure and the extension .CAT. You can see this for yourself by experimenting at the dot prompt. For example, if you've created all (or some) of the files in the LEARN catalog used throughout the first few chapters of this book, you can follow the steps below to view the contents of the LEARN.CAT file:

1. Start dBASE IV from its usual directory (typically C:\DBASE) in the normal manner.

2. At the Control Center, press Esc and then type Y to get to the dot prompt.

3. Type the command **SET CATALOG TO** and press ◄─┘ to close any open catalogs.

4. Type **USE LEARN.CAT** and press ◄─┘ (you can substitute any catalog name on the current directory for LEARN.CAT).

5. Type **BROWSE** and press ◄─┘.

If you browse through this database with the Tab, Shift-Tab, ↑ and ↓ keys, you'll see the names of files, their types, descriptions, and so forth stored within this database.

If you were to copy this catalog (that is, the .CAT file) to another computer, disk, or directory, the only thing you would be copying is this list of names. The actual files that the catalog refers to would *not* be copied, hence the catalog is useless in whatever location you've moved it to.

Before we proceed, let me mention that to leave this browse screen and get back to the Control Center, you first need to close all files. Here are the steps to return to the Control Center from this browse screen:

1. Press Esc to leave the browse screen.

2. Type **CLOSE ALL** and press ◄─┘ to close all open files.

3. Type **ASSIST** and press ◄─┘ to return to the Control Center.

A second problem with catalogs concerns the fact that they are actually incomplete. For example, every database (.DBF) file may also have a multiple index (.MDX) file and memo field (.DBT) file associated with it, but these files are not included in the catalog. Similarly, an application (.APP) file also may have several other files associated with it, such as a bar (.BAR) menu, pop-up (.POP) menus, program (.PRG) files, and so forth. These additional files are also excluded from the catalog. Why? Because dBASE is designed to search for these additional files automatically and "behind the scenes."

Unfortunately, neither the DOS COPY command, nor the Copy option on the dBASE DOS Utilities menu is quite so smart. Which leaves us with the conclusion that, while catalogs are useful for keeping families of files together within the Control Center, they are of virtually no use outside of dBASE, and therefore there is no easy way to copy a catalog and its contents from one drive\directory to another unless that catalog is stored in its own directory (in which case you can simply copy all the files on the directory as described under copying applications above). You must copy each file in the catalog individually (more on this in a moment).

With some dBASE IV programming, you *could* write a command file that will copy every file that's listed in a .CAT file to another drive or directory, and even catch all the .MDX, .DBT, and other files in the process. But there would be no easy way to write a program that could also copy all the unlisted files that belong in the Applications panel of that catalog. Therefore, my best recommendation at the moment to those of you who will need to copy catalogs and their associated files to other computers is to be sure to create each catalog on its own directory, and to create only one catalog on each directory.

If it's too late for that, and you need to copy a catalog that's on a directory with other catalogs, you can copy each file individually by following these general steps:

- At the dBASE IV Control Center, select Use a Different Catalog from the Catalog pull-down menu, then select the name of the catalog that you want to copy, so that catalog appears on your screen.

- Jot down a list of all the names of objects that you want to copy from the various panels of the Control Center.

- Jot down the name of the catalog itself.

- Exit dBASE IV to get to the DOS command prompt.

- Use the DOS COPY command to copy the catalog (using .CAT as the extension), and use a * to represent the extension on other object names.

For example, suppose you want to copy a catalog named RESEARCH that contains a database file named MYDATA and a report named MYREPORT to a disk in drive A. At the DOS command prompt, the following commands would do the trick:

```
COPY RESEARCH.CAT A:
COPY MYDATA.* A:
COPY MYREPORT.* A:
```

To copy the catalog and its files from that floppy to another PC, go to the directory on the other PC (where you want to store the catalog and its objects) and use the DOS command COPY A:*.* to copy all the files from disk drive A to the current directory.

Finally, run dBASE IV and select Use a Different Catalog from the Catalog pull-down menu when the Control Center appears. If the name of the catalog you just copied appears in the list, select that name. If that name does not appear in the list, select <create>, type in the name of the catalog you just copied, and press ◄─┘.

USING dBASE IV WITH WINDOWS 3.0

You can run dBASE IV directly from Windows 3.0, and if you have a 386 machine, you can run other programs while dBASE is running (perhaps play a little Reversi while dBASE is printing your invoices). Of course, dBASE IV is not a true Windows application, so there are a couple of potential problems to be aware of when starting dBASE IV from Windows:

- The DBCACHE program is incompatible with Windows' XMS memory manager. You'll still be able to run dBASE, but you may see an error message indicating that HyperDisk has not been installed. dBASE will still work fine, but may be a little slower without its own cache.

- dBASE IV is not a mouse-driven product. If you try to use the mouse with dBASE IV (under Windows) the keyboard will hang (the keys just beep when you press them), because Windows thinks you are trying to cut and paste. You can "unhang" the keyboard by single-clicking the right mouse button.

Depending on when you've installed Windows and dBASE IV, the *Ashton Tate dBase* icon might already appear in your Non-Windows Applications window, in which case you need only double-click that icon to run dBASE IV. Most likely, dBASE IV will take over the entire screen until you exit. However, if you have a 386 machine, you can run dBASE IV in its own window, as discussed later in this section.

CREATING THE DBASE IV ICON

These sections assume you already know the basics of using Windows 3.0. Refer to your Windows 3.0 manual for more detailed information.

If there is no icon for dBASE in your Non-Windows Applications window, and you would like to add one, follow these steps:

1. Run Windows in the usual manner so that the Program Manager window appears.

2. Open the Main window if it is not already open.

3. Double-click the Windows Setup icon.

4. Pull down the Options menu.

5. Select Set Up Applications.

6. Click on the ↓ next to *Setup will search* and click on the drive that dBASE IV is stored on.

7. Click on Ok.

8. When the search is complete, click on *Ashton Tate dBase*. If more than one appears, you can click on one and look to the bottom of the screen to see which directory each refers to. When you've identified which refers to dBASE Version 1.1, select that one only, clicking on any others to "unselect" them.

9. Click on *Add*→.

10. Click on Ok.

11. Close the Windows Setup window.

12. Open the Non-Windows Applications window by double-clicking its icon.

At this point you should see an icon and be able to run dBASE IV simply by double-clicking its icon in the Non-Windows Applications window. When you exit dBASE, you'll actually be returned to Windows.

If you are not completely satisfied with Windows' "automatic" installation of dBASE IV in the application, and want to make changes, keep reading. We'll start by discussing how to change the icon itself.

CHANGING THE DBASE ICON AND PIF

As you may know, Windows uses a Program Information File (PIF) to help start non-Windows applications from within Windows. There are actually several dBASE PIFs shipped with Windows (DBASE.PIF, DBASE0.PIF, DBASE1.PIF, and so forth) because you might want to create a separate PIF for each dBASE application. For example, you could start an inventory management system with one Windows icon, and a dBASE Customer list management application with a different icon. (We'll discuss multiple PIFs in a little more detail later.)

But the first step in getting dBASE IV 1.1 to run properly under Windows is to identify which PIF the automatic setup procedure selected for you. This is simple to do.

1. In the Non-Windows Applications window, click once on the icon you want to use to run dBASE IV.

2. Open the File pull-down menu on the Program Manager frame.

3. Select Properties.

4. You might want to change the description from *Ashton Tate dBase* to *dBASE IV Ver 1.1,* or something similar, so that the icon is more specific. To do so, just press Backspace, then type in your new title.

5. If you want to select a different icon, click on Change Icon, then click on View Next until the icon you want is displayed. Then click on Ok.

6. Jot down or memorize the name of the file in the Command Line box; it will most likely be one of the dBASE PIF files such as DBASE0.PIF.

7. Click on Ok to save any changes.

If you merely wanted to change the icon or its title, you're done. If you'd like to make additional changes or refinements to the PIF file, keep reading. Otherwise, you can follow these steps to modify the PIF file used to run dBASE IV:

1. Double-click the Accessories icon in the Program Manager window.

2. Double-click the PIF Editor icon in the Accessories window.

3. Pull down the File menu and select Open.

4. Click on the PIF file name from step 6 in the earlier steps, then select Ok.

Figure D.17 shows an example of setting up a PIF file on a 386 computer under 386 enhanced mode. In this example, dBASE IV Version 1.1 is assumed to be stored on the \DBASE directory of drive C:. If it is not, be sure to specify the current drive and directory in the

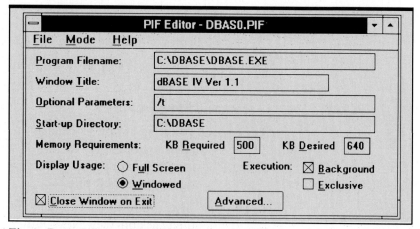

Figure D.17: Windows 3.0 PIF settings on a 386

Program Filename and *Start-up Directory* boxes. Keep in mind that these are only suggested settings; you may want to make adjustments to maximize performance on your own computer.

Note that the Windowed option, rather than the Full Screen option, is selected to allow other applications to run while dBASE IV is running (available only on 386- and 486-based computers). Figure D.18 shows some suggested Advanced settings for dBASE IV, again on a 386-based computer. (The Advanced options are not available on 286- or lower-based computers.) On a 386, you get to this screen by clicking on the Advanced button shown in Figure D.17. After making your Advanced selections, you can click on Ok to return to the previous window.

Figure D.18: Windows 3.0 Advanced PIF settings on a 386

When installing on a 286-based machine, you'll have only one screen of PIF options. You can use the same settings shown in Figures D.17 and D.18 wherever your screen presents a similar option.

Remember, these settings are only suggestions and you may want to try other settings to get maximum performance on your computer.

SAVING YOUR CHANGES Whether you've adjusted your PIF settings for a 286 or 386 computer, you can now follow these steps to save those changes:

1. Pull down the File menu on the PIF Editor window.

2. Select Exit.

3. If you made changes, click on Yes when asked about saving those changes (unless you prefer to abandon them).

4. Close the Accessories window.

To test your new PIF file, double-click on your dBASE IV Version 1.1 icon in the Non-Windows Applications window once again.

If you set up dBASE IV for a windowed environment, and want to try running another program while dBASE IV is running, you can just click on the contents of the other window(s), or press Ctrl-Esc, or use the Switch To option on the pull-down menu to go to another window, as described in your Windows 3.0 documentation.

MULTIPLE PIF FILES You can create multiple PIF files with Windows 3.0—one for each dBASE IV application you create. For example, in the latter chapters of this book, you'll create an application named BUSMGR (Business Manager) on the \DBASE\BUSI-NESS subdirectory.

To start this application with its own icon, you could create a new icon in the Non-Windows Applications window, and give it a unique name, such as *Business Manager*. The PIF file could have the following settings (again assuming that dBASE IV Version 1.1 is stored on C:\DBASE):

```
Program Filename:     C:\DBASE\DBASE.EXE
Window Title:  dBASE IV Business Manager
Optional Parameters:     /t BusMgr
Start-up Directory:     C:\DBASE\BUSINESS
```

For more information about Windows 3.0 PIF files, see your Windows 3.0 documentation.

DBASE CACHING AND WINDOWS

If you start dBASE IV from within Windows, the XMS memory management system will be active, and therefore the DBCACHE system will not be installed. However, if you've set CACHEDB to EXT or LIM (depending on your system) at the DOS command prompt, and exit Windows before starting dBASE IV, dBASE caching may be installed automatically when you start dBASE IV from the DOS command prompt.

If you want to see whether or not caching is in use during a dBASE session, and how much memory is dedicated to it, go to the dBASE dot prompt, type **!DBCACHE**, and press ◄┘. You'll get the complete lowdown on the current status of dBASE caching on your screen, or the message *HyperDisk is not installed* if dBASE caching is not installed at the moment.

dBASE IV
Functions

THIS APPENDIX CATEGORIZES AND SUMMARIZES ALL dBASE IV functions. Functions can be used in any dBASE IV expression and with any command. Each function must use the appropriate syntax and operate on the appropriate data type.

For the syntax, data type, and further information about a particular function, type the command **HELP <function name>**, where <function name> is the function for which you want help. For example, typing **HELP PAYMENT( )** displays helpful information about the PAYMENT function.

Chapter 12 presents practical examples of using functions to sort, group, and manipulate data. For additional information, refer to the language reference manual that came with your dBASE IV package or to a dBASE IV programmer's reference guide.

DATE FUNCTIONS

The date functions operate upon the Data data type and return numeric, date, or character results.

CDOW( )	Returns the day for the week as a character string (for example, Monday).
CMONTH( )	Returns the month as a character string (for example, April).
DATE( )	Returns the current system date.
DAY( )	Returns the day of the month as a number.
DMY( )	Returns a date converted to date, month, year format (for example, 31 December 91).
DOW( )	Returns the day of the week as a number.
DTOS( )	Converts a date to a character string in the format "19911231".
MDY( )	Returns a date converted to month, date, year format (for example, December 31, 90).
MONTH( )	Returns the month as a number (1 to 12).
TIME( )	Returns the current system time.
YEAR( )	Returns the year of a date.

STRING FUNCTIONS

The string functions allow you to manipulate data stored as the Character data type. The term *string* refers to any Character data. For example, "XYZ" is a string of 3 characters, and "Hello there" is a string of 11 characters (spaces always count as characters).

Many functions manipulate *substrings*. A substring is any string embedded in a larger string. For example, the letters "ABC" are a substring of the sentence "Now I know my ABC's..." because ABC appears in the larger sentence.

&	Indicates macro substitution.
ASC( )	Returns the numeric ASCII code for a character.
AT( )	Returns the position of a substring within a string.
CHR( )	Returns the ASCII character for a number.
DIFFERENCE( )	Returns the difference between two SOUNDEX codes.
LEFT( )	Returns a substring of the leftmost characters.
LEN( )	Returns the length of a character string.
LOWER( )	Returns the lowercase equivalent of string.
LTRIM( )	Trims leading blanks.
REPLICATE( )	Repeats a character string.
RIGHT( )	Returns a substring of the rightmost characters.
RTRIM( )	Removes trailing blanks.
SOUNDEX( )	Returns the SOUNDEX code of a character string.
SPACE( )	Generates blank spaces.
STUFF( )	Replaces or inserts a substring in a character string.

SUBSTR( )	Returns a substring from a larger character string.
TAG( )	Returns the tag name of an index.
TRANSFORM( )	Displays data in a predefined format.
TRIM( )	Removes leading and trailing blanks.
UPPER( )	Returns the uppercase equivalent of a string.

MEMO FIELD FUNCTIONS

The Memo field functions return information about Memo fields.

| MEMLINES( ) | Returns the number of lines required to print a Memo field. |
| MLINE( ) | Returns a specified line from a Memo field. |

NUMERIC FUNCTIONS

The numeric functions return the results of calculations on Numeric and Float data types.

ABS( )	Returns the absolute (positive) value.
CEILING( )	Returns the smallest integer that is greater than or equal to the specified number.
EXP( )	Returns the exponential (value of e^x).
FLOOR( )	Returns the largest integer that is less than or equal to the specified number.
INT( )	Returns the integer value with any decimal value truncated.
LOG( )	Returns the natural logarithm.
LOG10( )	Returns the common log to the base 10.
MAX( )	Returns the larger of two numbers.

MIN( )	Returns the smaller of two numbers.
MOD( )	Returns the modulus (remainder) of dividing two numbers.
PI( )	Returns π (approximately 3.14159265).
RAND( )	Returns a random number between 0 and 1.
ROUND( )	Rounds a number to the specified decimal place.
SIGN( )	Returns 1 for a positive number, -1 for a negative number, and 0 for zero.
SQRT( )	Returns the square root of the specified number.

FINANCIAL FUNCTIONS

The financial functions perform common financial calculations. When using the financial functions PAYMENT( ), FV( ), and PV( ), you must make sure that all parameters refer to the same time period. For example, if you want to determine the *monthly* payment on a loan given the *annual* percentage rate and a term expressed in *years*, then you must divide the annual interest rate by 12 to obtain the monthly rate and multiply the term of the loan by 12 to determine the number of months.

For example, suppose you want to calculate the *monthly* payment on a loan given an *annual* interest rate of 6.75 percent and a term of 30 *years*. First you need to convert the percentage rate, 6.75 percent, to the decimal value 0.0675 by dividing by 100. Then you need to divide the resulting annual decimal rate by 12 to obtain the monthly percentage rate. Finally, you need to convert the *years* for the loan to months by multiplying by 12.

You can perform all of the appropriate conversions directly in the expression used to calculate the payment. If the loan principal is stored in a field or variable named PRINCIPAL, the annual interest is stored in a field or variable named APR, and the term is stored in a field or variable named YEARS, then the expression to calculate the monthly payment is PAYMENT(Principal,APR/1200,YEARS*12).

FV( )	Returns the future value of equal, regular deposits into an investment.
NPV( )	Returns the net present value of a series of future cash flows (used only with the CALCULATE command).
PAYMENT( )	Returns the periodic payment on a loan.
PV( )	Returns the present value of equal, regular deposits into an investment.

TRIGONOMETRIC FUNCTIONS

The trigonometric functions assume that their arguments are expressed in radians. You can use the DTOR( ) function to convert degrees to radians. For example, COS(DTOR(45)) returns the cosine, in radians, of a 45-degree angle. The RTOD( ) function converts radians to degrees. The expression RTOD(COS(DTOR(45))) returns the cosine, in degrees, of a 45-degree angle.

ACOS( )	Returns the arccosine, in radians, of a cosine expressed in radians.
ASIN( )	Returns the arcsine, in radians, of a sine expressed in radians.
ATAN( )	Returns the arctangent, in radians, of any tangent.
ATN2( )	Returns the two-quadrant arctangent of a sine.
COS( )	Returns the cosine, expressed in radians, of an angle expressed in radians.
DTOR( )	Converts degrees to radians.
RTOD( )	Converts radians to degrees.
SIN( )	Returns the sine, in radians, of an angle expressed in radians.
TAN( )	Returns the trigonometric tangent of an angle expressed in radians.

DATA TYPE CONVERSION FUNCTIONS

The functions described in this section all convert values from one data type to another.

CTOD( )	Converts Character data to Date data.
DTOC( )	Converts Date data to Character data in MM/DD/YY format.
DTOS( )	Converts Date data to Character data in YYYYMMDD format.
FIXED( )	Converts Float data to Numeric data.
FLOAT( )	Converts Numeric data to Float data.
STR( )	Converts Numeric data to Character data.
VAL( )	Converts Character data to Numeric data.

KEYPRESS FUNCTIONS

The keypress functions return information regarding the most recent keypress.

INKEY( )	Returns the numeric code of keypress without interrupting program execution.
LASTKEY( )	Returns the ASCII numeric value of the most recent keypress.
READKEY( )	Returns the ASCII code used to exit a full-screen editing session.

MENU FUNCTIONS

The menu functions return information about horizontal bar, pop-up, and pull-down menus used in applications.

BAR( )	Returns the number of the last-selected option from a pop-up or pull-down menu.
MENU( )	Returns the name of the currently active menu.
PAD( )	Returns the name of the currently selected horizontal bar menu option.
POPUP( )	Returns the name of the currently active pop-up menu.
PROMPT( )	Returns the prompt of the most recently selected menu option.

IDENTIFICATION AND TESTING FUNCTIONS

The identification and testing functions return information about the current environment.

ALIAS( )	Returns the alias assigned to a work area.
BOF( )	Returns .T. when the record pointer is at the beginning of a database file.
CERROR( )	Returns the number associated with the last error during compilation.
COL( )	Returns the current column position of the cursor on the screen.
COMPLETED( )	Returns .T. if a transaction has been completed.
DBF( )	Returns the name of the database file currently in use.
DELETED( )	Returns .T. if the current record is marked for deletion.
DISKSPACE( )	Returns the amount of available disk space in bytes.

EOF( )	Returns .T. when the record pointer is past the last record in a database file.
ERROR( )	Returns the number generated by an ON ERROR command.
FIELD( )	Returns the name of a field in database file.
FILE( )	Returns .T. if the specified file exists.
FKLABEL( )	Returns the name of a function key.
FKMAX( )	Returns the number of function keys on the keyboard.
FOUND( )	Returns .T. if the record being searched for was found.
GETENV( )	Returns information about the operating system environment.
IIF( )	Immediate IF, embedded inside command lines or report columns; selects one of two alternatives.
ISALPHA( )	Returns .T. if the first character is a letter.
ISCOLOR( )	Returns .T. if a color monitor is in use.
ISLOWER( )	Returns .T. if the first character is a lowercase letter.
ISMARKED( )	Returns .T. if a database is in a state of change.
ISUPPER( )	Returns .T. if the first character is an uppercase letter.
KEY( )	Returns the index expression associated with an index file or tag.
LIKE( )	Compares a value to a wildcard string and returns .T. if they match.
LINENO( )	Returns the line number of the next command to be executed in a command file.
LUPDATE( )	Returns the date of most recent change to a database file.

MDX( )	Returns the name of the currently open production index file.
MEMORY( )	Returns the amount of available RAM in kilobytes.
MESSAGE( )	Returns the error message that triggered an ON ERROR condition.
NDX( )	Returns the name of the active index (.NDX) file.
ORDER( )	Returns the name of the index currently controlling the sort order.
OS( )	Returns the name of the operating system in use.
PCOL( )	Returns the current printer column position.
PRINTSTATUS( )	Returns .T. if the printer is ready to accept data.
PROGRAM( )	Returns the name of the program or procedure in which an error occurred.
PROW( )	Returns the current printer row position.
RECCOUNT( )	Returns the number of records in a database file.
RECNO( )	Returns the number (position) of the current record.
RECSIZE( )	Returns the size of each record in database file.
ROLLBACK( )	Returns .T. if the most recent transaction rollback was successful.
ROW( )	Returns the current row position of the cursor on the screen.
RUN( )	Sends a command to DOS and returns a 0.
SELECT( )	Returns the number of the highest unused work area (between 1 and 0).

SET( )	Returns the current status of a SET command.
TYPE( )	Returns the data type of current field or variable.
VARREAD( )	Returns the name of the highlighted field or memory variable being edited.
VERSION( )	Returns the version number of the dBASE program in use.
WINDOW( )	Returns the name of the currently active window.

FUNCTIONS THAT MIMIC COMMANDS

The following functions operate similarly to the CALL, SEEK, and LOCATE commands:

CALL( )	Executes a loaded binary program.
LOOKUP( )	Searches any field for a value and returns .T. if the value is located.
SEEK( )	Searches an index for a value and returns .T. if the value is located.

NETWORK FUNCTIONS

The network functions can be used when developing applications that run on a network. (Note that the Applications Generator always develops applications that are ready for use on either a single-user system or a network.)

| ACCESS( ) | Returns the level of access for the last logged-in user. |
| CHANGE( ) | Returns .T. if a value has been changed by a network user. |

FLOCK( )	Locks a database file.
LKSYS( )	Returns the time, date, and user name of a locked file.
LOCK( )	Locks a database record.
NETWORK( )	Returns .T. if dBASE is currently installed on a network.
RLOCK( )	Same as LOCK.
USER( )	Returns the log-in name of a network user.

F

dBASE IV
Commands

THIS APPENDIX CATEGORIZES AND SUMMARIZES ALL dBASE IV commands. Remember that you need be concerned with these commands only if you want to go beyond the capabilities of the Control Center and Applications Generator to develop highly sophisticated custom programs and applications.

You can use any of the commands in a command file or as Applications Generator embedded codes. You can also enter most commands directly at the dot prompt (exceptions are programming clause commands such as DO WHILE...ENDDO, DO CASE...ENDCASE, IF...ENDIF, SCAN...ENDSCAN, and TEXT...ENDTEXT).

Each command must be entered on a single line and must use proper syntax. For the exact syntax of a command, refer to the dBASE IV language reference manual that came with your dBASE IV package or type the command **HELP** followed by the command at the dot prompt. For example, to get help regarding the BROWSE command, you type **HELP BROWSE** at the dot prompt and press ◄─┘.

Chapter 17 provides additional information about entering commands, creating command files, and interpreting syntax charts, and the sample application in Chapter 21 demonstrates Applications Generator embedded codes. However, an in-depth discussion of all programming commands and techniques is beyond the scope of this book.

COMMANDS TO
CREATE AND USE DATABASE FILES

CLOSE DATABASES	Closes all open database files, saving their contents to disk.
CREATE	Enters the database design screen to create a new database file.
SELECT	Specifies a work area, from A to J or 1 to 10, in which to open a database file. Also used to switch among currently open database files.

SET RELATION Defines the relationship between two or more open database files based on a common field, which must be indexed in the nonselected database file.

USE Opens a database file for use.

COMMANDS TO
ENTER AND EDIT DATABASE DATA

APPEND Adds new records to the bottom of the current database through the edit or browse screen. If a custom form has been activated through the SET FORMAT command, that form is used instead of the edit screen.

APPEND BLANK Adds a new blank record to the end of a database file.

APPEND FROM Copies records from a separate or foreign database file or an array to the currently open database file.

BEGIN
TRANSACTION Records changes to a database file, permitting ROLLBACK to undo those changes.

BROWSE Enters the browse screen for entering or editing database data.

CHANGE Same as EDIT.

DELETE Marks records for deletion.

EDIT Allows data in the currently open database to be edited, using either the default edit screen or a custom form opened with the SET FORMAT command.

END TRANSACTION	Marks the bottom of a BEGIN TRANSACTION block and commits any changes to the database.
INSERT	Inserts a new record into a database.
PACK	Permanently removes from a database records that have been marked for deletion with the DELETE, CHANGE, EDIT, or BROWSE command.
RECALL	Reclaims records that have been marked for deletion.
REPLACE	Replaces the data in a database field with a new value.
ROLLBACK	Undoes all changes to a database file since the last BEGIN TRANSACTION command.
ZAP	Erases all records from a database file, but leaves the structure intact.

COMMANDS TO SORT AND INDEX

COPY TAG	Converts production indexes to individual index (.NDX) files.
DELETE TAG	Removes an index from a production (.MDX) index file.
INDEX	Creates an index if TAG is specified or an index file with the .NDX extension if TO is specified.
REINDEX	Rebuilds all indexes in the current production index file.
SET ORDER	Selects an index from the production index file to determine the sort order and the field that can be used for SEEK and FIND searches.

SORT	Creates a new, sorted database file from the currently open database file.
USE...ORDER	Through the ORDER option, specifies a controlling index for the database being opened.

COMMANDS TO LOCATE A RECORD

CONTINUE	Used in conjunction with the LOCATE command to find the next record matching the search criterion.
FIND	Locates a value in the controlling index (.NDX) file.
GO or GOTO	Moves the record to a specific record according to its record number or position (that is, TOP or BOTTOM, or a specified record number).
LOCATE	Positions the record pointer at the first record in the database that matches a search criterion.
SEEK	Locates a value in the current index (the one controlling the sort order).
SKIP	Moves the record pointer forward or backward relative to its current position.

COMMANDS TO DISPLAY DATA

@...SAY	Specifies a row and column position on the screen or printer and displays data.
@...TO	Draws a line or box.
?	Prints information starting on a new line or prints a blank line when used alone.

??	Prints information at the current cursor or printer position.
???	Sends special characters to the printer without changing the printing position.
DISPLAY	Displays the contents of a database record or of several records.
LABEL FORM	Prints mailing labels in the format specified by the CREATE LABEL command.
LIST	Displays database records.
REPORT FORM	Prints a report with the format specified by the CREATE REPORT command.

COMMANDS TO CALCULATE DATA

AVERAGE	Calculates and displays the average of a numeric field in a database.
CALCULATE	Calculates the sum, average, count, highest value, lowest value, net present value, standard deviation, or variance using numeric fields.
COUNT	Counts the number of records in a database that meet some criterion.
REPLACE	Replaces the contents of specified database records with a new value.
SUM	Calculates and displays the sum of a numeric field in a database.
TOTAL	Creates a summary of an existing file containing totals of specified numeric fields.
UPDATE	Changes the values of fields in one database based upon the fields in a separate, related database.

COMMANDS TO
COPY AND MOVE DATABASE DATA

APPEND FROM	Adds records from a separate or foreign database file to the end of the currently open database file.
COPY	Copies the currently open database to another database or to a foreign file format.
COPY STRUCTURE	Copies a database structure to a new database file.
JOIN	Combines the fields from two related databases into a new database.

COMMANDS TO
MANAGE MEMO FIELDS

APPEND MEMO	Copies external data to a Memo field.
COPY MEMO	Copies a Memo field to another file.
SET WINDOW OF MEMO	Uses a defined window for editing a Memo field during browse and edit operations.

COMMANDS TO
CREATE NEW OBJECTS

CREATE	Enters the database design screen to create a new database file.
CREATE APPLICATION	Enters the Applications Generator to create a new application.

CREATE LABEL	Calls up the labels design screen to create a new label format for the currently open database.
CREATE QUERY	Calls up the queries design screen to create a new query for the currently open database.
CREATE REPORT	Calls up the reports design screen to create a new report format for the currently open database.
CREATE SCREEN	Calls up the forms design screen to create a new custom form for the currently open database.
CREATE VIEW	For compatibilty purposes, creates a dBASE III PLUS view file from the currently selected database files and relationships.
MODIFY COMMAND	Creates or modifies a command file (or program) with the file extension .PRG.

COMMANDS TO MODIFY EXISTING OBJECTS

MODIFY APPLICATION	Enters the Applications Generator to modify an existing application.
MODIFY COMMAND	Enters the editor to create or modify a command file or procedure file.
MODIFY LABEL	Enters the labels design screen to modify a label format.
MODIFY QUERY	Enters the query design screen to modify an existing query.
MODIFY REPORT	Enters the reports design screen to modify an existing report format.

MODIFY SCREEN	Enters the forms design screen to modify an existing custom form.
MODIFY STRUCTURE	Enters the database design screen to modify the current database file.

COMMANDS TO MANAGE DISK FILES

COPY FILE	Copies any file to another file name, drive, or directory.
DELETE FILE	Erases a disk file.
ERASE	Erases a file from the directory (same as DELETE FILE).
RENAME	Changes the name of any file.
SET ALTERNATE	Activates the screen-capture file defined by the SET ALTERNATE TO command.
SET ALTERNATE TO	Creates a file to capture all screen activity.

COMMANDS TO MANAGE KEYSTROKE MACROS

KEYBOARD	Stores keystrokes in the buffer as though they had been typed.
PLAY MACRO	Executes a keystroke macro.
RESTORE MACROS	Copies recorded keystroke macros from a disk file into memory.
SAVE MACROS	Saves recorded keystroke macros to a disk file.

COMMANDS TO
IMPORT OR EXPORT DATA

APPEND FROM	Appends data from foreign software to the currently open database file.
COPY	Copies data from the currently open database file to a foreign file format.
COPY INDEXES	Copies dBASE III PLUS .NDX index files to dBASE IV production (.MDX) index files.
EXPORT	Exports dBASE data to a new foreign file.
IMPORT	Imports data from a foreign file format to a new dBASE IV database file.

COMMANDS TO GET ASSISTANCE

ASSIST	Switches from the interactive dot-prompt mode to the Control Center.
DIR	Displays the names of files in a directory.
DISPLAY STATUS	Displays information about the database files currently in use and other dBASE environmental parameters.
DISPLAY STRUCTURE	Displays the structure of the currently open database file.
HELP	Provides on-line assistance for specific dBASE commands as well as other information.
TYPE	Displays the contents of an ASCII text file.

COMMANDS TO CREATE
AND CONTROL COMMAND FILES

CANCEL	Terminates command-file processing and returns control to the dot prompt.
CASE	Begins an option within a DO CASE clause (must be placed between DO CASE and ENDCASE commands).
COMPILE	Converts a command (.PRG) file to an executable object-code (.DBO) file.
DO	Executes a command file or procedure.
DO CASE	Begins a block of several mutually exclusive routines (must be terminated with an ENDCASE command).
DO WHILE	Begins a loop in a command file (must be terminated with an ENDDO command).
ELSE	Used within an IF clause as the alternate path when the IF expression is false (must be enclosed between IF and ENDIF commands).
ENDCASE	Marks the end of a DO CASE clause.
ENDDO	Marks the end of a DO WHILE loop.
ENDIF	Marks the end of an IF clause.
ENDSCAN	Marks the end of a SCAN...ENDSCAN loop.
ENDTEXT	Marks the end of a TEXT block.
EXIT	Passes control outside of a loop.
IF	Makes a decision based on a single expression (must be terminated with an ENDIF command).
LOOP	Passes control to the beginning of a DO WHILE loop.
ON ERROR	Executes a specified command when an error occurs.

ON ESCAPE	Executes a specified command when the Esc key is pressed (SET ESCAPE parameter must be on).
ON KEY	Executes a specified command when the user presses any key.
OTHERWISE	Used as an alternative path in a DO CASE clause when no CASE statement evaluates to true (must be enclosed between DO CASE and ENDCASE commands).
QUIT	Terminates command file processing, closes all open files, and leaves dBASE IV.
RETURN TO MASTER	Returns control to the first calling program in a series of DO commands.
SCAN	Marks the beginning of a loop to process database records.
TEXT	Begins a block of text in the command file to be displayed on the screen or printer.

COMMANDS FOR PROCEDURES AND USER-DEFINED FUNCTIONS

CLOSE PROCEDURE	Closes a procedure file.
DO...WITH	Calls a command file or procedure and passes parameters to it.
FUNCTION	Marks the beginning and defines the name of a user-defined function.
PARAMETERS	Specifies internal names for values passed to a procedure, user-defined function, or command file.
PROCEDURE	Marks the beginning of and assigns a name to a procedure.

RETURN   Marks the end of a procedure or
              user-defined function, passes control back
              to a calling command file or procedure,
              and resumes processing at the next line.

SET   Opens a procedure file.
PROCEDURE

COMMANDS TO
ADD COMMENTS TO COMMAND FILES

*   Specifies a programmer comment when used as the
         first character in a line.

&&   Specifies a programmer comment to the right of a
         command line in a program.

NOTE   Marks a programmer comment in a command file
         (same as *).

COMMANDS TO MANAGE
MEMORY VARIABLES AND ARRAYS

APPEND FROM   Copies data from an array to a database
ARRAY   file.

CLEAR ALL   Closes all open database files and
              removes all windows, menus, and
              memory variables from memory.

CLEAR   Erases all current memory variables.
MEMORY

DECLARE   Defines the name and dimensions of an
              array.

DISPLAY   Displays the names, data types, and
MEMORY   contents of all currently active memory
              variables and arrays.

PRIVATE	Specifies that a memory variable is local to a given command file or procedure.
PUBLIC	Makes a memory variable global to all levels of command files and procedures.
RELEASE	Erases memory variables.
RESTORE	Brings memory variables that have been stored on disk in a .MEM file back into memory.
REPLACE FROM ARRAY	Updates one or more records with the contents of an array.
SAVE	Saves memory variables and arrays in a memory (.MEM) file on disk.
STORE	Creates a memory variable and assigns a value to it.

COMMANDS FOR INTERFACING WITH USERS

@...SAY...GET	Displays a message and the current contents of a field or memory variable for editing.
ACCEPT	Stores user input in a Character memory variable.
INPUT	Waits for user entry and stores input in a Numeric memory variable.
READ	Allows data to be entered via the @...SAY...GET command.
WAIT	Waits for the user to press a single key and optionally stores that keypress in a Character memory variable.

COMMANDS TO CONTROL
THE SCREEN AND WINDOWS

@...FILL	Colors an isolated portion of the screen.
ACTIVATE SCREEN	Sends all output to the entire screen, covering but not removing active windows.
ACTIVATE WINDOW	Activates and displays an existing window.
CLEAR	Clears any windows, menus, custom forms, or pending GETs on the screen.
DEACTIVATE WINDOW	Removes a window from the screen, but leaves its definition intact for future use.
DEFINE BOX	Defines the border and location of a box.
DEFINE WINDOW	Defines the name, border type, and screen position of a window.
MOVE WINDOW	Moves a window to a new screen location.
READ	Allows data to be entered through a custom form if one has been activated by SET FORMAT.
RELEASE WINDOW	Removes a defined window from memory.
RESTORE SCREEN	Redisplays a saved screen.
SAVE SCREEN	Saves the current screen image in memory, which can be redisplayed with RESTORE SCREEN.
SAVE WINDOW	Saves a window definition to a disk file.
SET COLOR	Determines colors used on screen displays.

SET FORMAT TO	Determines the format file to be used with APPEND, EDIT, and READ commands.
SET WINDOW OF MEMO	Uses a defined window for editing a Memo field during browse and edit operations.

COMMANDS TO MANAGE MENUS

ACTIVATE MENU	Activates an existing horizontal bar menu.
ACTIVATE POPUP	Activates an existing pop-up menu.
DEACTIVATE MENU	Deactivates a bar menu and erases it from the screen.
DEACTIVATE POPUP	Deactivates a pop-up menu and removes it from the screen.
DEFINE BAR	Defines an option in a pop-up menu.
DEFINE MENU	Defines a horizontal bar menu.
DEFINE PAD	Defines an option in a horizontal bar menu.
DEFINE POPUP	Defines a pop-up menu.
ON SELECTION	Assigns an action to a horizontal bar menu option (PAD) or pop-up menu option (POPUP), to be executed when the option is selected.
RELEASE MENUS	Removes defined horizontal bar menus from memory.
RELEASE POPUP	Removes defined pop-up menus from memory.
SHOW MENU	Displays a horizontal bar menu without activating it.

SHOW POPUP   Displays a pop-up menu without
                    activating it.

COMMANDS
TO CONTROL THE PRINTER

EJECT   Ejects the page in the printer.

EJECT PAGE   Similar to the EJECT command, but can
                    be sent to any device, such as a disk file
                    or the screen.

ENDPRINTJOB   Marks the end of a print operation.

PRINTJOB   Marks the beginning of a print
                    operation.

SET DEVICE   When DEVICE is set to PRINT,
                    @...SAY, output is directed to the
                    printer rather than to the screen.

SET PRINTER   Sets printing on or off for commands that
                    display data.

COMMANDS TO INTERFACE
WITH EXTERNAL PROGRAMS

CALL   Runs an assembly language (binary) subroutine
                    that has already been loaded into memory.

LOAD   Copies an assembly language subroutine into
                    memory.

RELEASE   Removes a loaded assembly language
MODULE   subroutine from memory.

RUN   Runs an external DOS program and
                    automatically returns control to the dot prompt.

!   Same as RUN.

COMMANDS TO AID DEBUGGING

DEBUG	Activates the dBASE IV debugger.
DISPLAY HISTORY	Displays commands stored in the history file.
LIST HISTORY	Same as DISPLAY HISTORY, but does not pause each after each screenful of information.
RESUME	Resumes command-file processing after temporary suspension.
SET DEBUG	Sends the results of the SET ECHO command to the printer rather than the screen.
SET ECHO	Displays command lines from command files on the screen before executing them.
SET HISTORY	Specifies the number of lines to be recorded in the history file.
SET STEP	Pauses execution after every line in a command file.
SUSPEND	Temporarily suspends processing of a command file and returns control to the dot prompt.

COMMANDS TO CONTROL THE dBASE ENVIRONMENT

SET	Displays a menu for interactively changing dBASE environmental settings.
SET AUTOSAVE	Determines whether database changes are saved immediately.
SET BELL	Determines whether the bell sounds during data entry and editing.

SET BELL TO	Determines the pitch and duration of the bell tone.
SET BLOCKSIZE	Defines the block size for storing memory variables.
SET BORDER	Defines the border for menus and windows.
SET CARRY	Determines whether data from the previous record is carried over to the next record during data entry.
SET CARRY TO	Determines which fields are carried to new records when SET CARRY is on.
SET CATALOG	Determines whether new files are added to an active catalog.
SET CATALOG TO	Creates, opens, or closes a catalog file.
SET CENTURY	Determines whether the century appears in dates.
SET CLOCK	Determines whether the clock appears on the screen.
SET CLOCK TO	Determines the position of the clock on the screen.
SET COLOR	Automatically set at startup, depending on whether a monochrome or color monitor is in use.
SET COLOR TO	Determines colors (or shading) for the screen.
SET CONFIRM	Determines whether a carriage return is required after a data entry field is filled in.
SET CONSOLE	Turns the screen on or off.
SET CURRENCY	Determines whether currency symbols are displayed to the left or right of numbers.

SET CURRENCY TO	Defines the currency sign.
SET CURSOR	Lets you hide (OFF) or display (ON) the cursor.
SET DATE	Sets a format for displaying dates.
SET DBTRAP	Protects against errors caused during complex event processing.
SET DECIMALS	Determines the number of decimal places displayed in the results of mathematical calculations.
SET DEFAULT	Specifies the disk drive used to store and retrieve files.
SET DELETED	When set to On, does not display records that are marked for deletion.
SET DELIMITERS	Determines whether delimiters appear around fields on screen displays.
SET DELIMITERS TO	Specifies the characters to use as delimiters around fields on screen displays.
SET DESIGN	Determines whether design screens can be accessed from the dot prompt or Control Center.
SET DEVELOPMENT	Turns automatic compilation and recompilation on or off.
SET DIRECTORY	Lets you define the current drive and directory from within dBASE IV.
SET DISPLAY	Sets the screen display mode to monochrome, color, EGA, or VGA.
SET DOHISTORY	Retained in dBASE IV for compatibility with dBASE III PLUS, but performs no action (the DEBUG command is used for debugging).
SET ECHO	Determines whether lines from command files are displayed on the screen before execution.

SET ESCAPE	Determines whether pressing the Esc key interrupts command file processing.
SET EXACT	Determines whether exact matches are required in character-string searches.
SET FIELDS	Activates or deactivates the most recent SET FIELDS command.
SET FIELDS TO	Determines which fields from a database or from multiple related databases are displayed and edited.
SET FILTER	Hides database records that do not match a specified search criterion.
SET FIXED	Determines whether a fixed number of decimal places are displayed (use in conjunction with SET DECIMALS).
SET FULLPATH	When on, mimics dBASE III PLUS by including the pathname in file names returned by functions such as DBF( ).
SET FUNCTION	Assigns tasks to function keys.
SET HEADING	Determines whether field names appear at the beginning of the output from LIST and DISPLAY commands.
SET HELP	Determines whether the "Do you want some help?" message appears on the screen after an error occurs.
SET HISTORY	Determines whether commands are recorded in the history file.
SET HISTORY TO	Determines the number of lines to be recorded in the history file.
SET HOURS	Determines whether the clock display uses 12-hour or 24-hour format.
SET INDEX	Opens index (.NDX) files for the database currently in use.

SET INSTRUCT	Determines whether Control Center prompt boxes appear on the screen.
SET INTENSITY	Determines whether enhanced display with reverse video is used for full-screen operations.
SET MARGIN	Adjusts the left margin setting on the printer.
SET MARK	Changes the separator used in dates.
SET MEMOWIDTH	Determines the display width of Memo fields.
SET MENU	Retained in dBASE IV to maintain compatibility with dBASE III PLUS, but performs no function (replaced by SET INSTRUCT).
SET MESSAGE	Displays a message centered at the bottom of the screen (if SET STATUS is on).
SET NEAR	Determines whether or not FIND, SEEK, and SEEK( ) go to the nearest record when an exact match can't be found.
SET ODOMETER	Determines the frequency of updating on the odometer displayed with COPY and other commands (when SET TALK is on).
SET ORDER	Determines which index in a production index file is used for the sort order and for SEEK searches.
SET PATH	Specifies a path of directories to search for files.
SET PAUSE	When on, the SQL SELECT command pauses for a key press like the DISPLAY ALL command.
SET POINT	Determines the character used as the decimal point in numeric values.

SET PRECISION	Determines the decimal accuracy used in fixed-point arithmetic.
SET PRINTER	Determines whether or not output is directed to the printer.
SET PRINTER TO	Directs printing to a specified device or file.
SET SAFETY	Determines whether the overwrite warnings appear on the screen.
SET SCOREBOARD	Determines whether dBASE messages appear in the status bar (or in row zero on the screen if SET STATUS is off).
SET SEPARATOR	Determines the character used to separate thousands in numeric displays.
SET SKIP	Determines the order in which multiple related database files are changed during update operations.
SET SPACE	When on, prints a blank space between fields displayed with **?** and **??** commands.
SET SQL	When on, dBASE IV accepts SQL commands.
SET STATUS	Determines whether the status bar appears near the bottom of the screen.
SET STEP	Determines whether dBASE pauses before processing each line in a command file.
SET TALK	Determines whether the results of commands and calculations are displayed on the screen.
SET TITLE	Determines whether the SET CATALOG command prompts for file names as new files are added to the catalog.

SET TRAP	When on, the dBASE IV debugger is activated whenever an error occurs during program execution.
SET TYPEAHEAD	Specifies the number of keystrokes stored in the typeahead buffer.
SET UNIQUE	Determines whether only unique records are included in an index.
SET VIEW	Opens multiple database files and sets up their relationships based upon a previous CREATE QUERY or MODIFY QUERY command.

COMMANDS FOR NETWORKING

CONVERT	Adds a field to a database for multiuser lock detection.
DISPLAY/LIST USERS	Displays the names of all currently logged dBASE network users.
LIST/DISPLAY STATUS	Displays information about the current status of dBASE IV in the network.
LOGOUT	Logs a user out of the network, allowing a new user to log in.
PROTECT	Activates the dBASE IV file security system.
RETRY	Returns to a calling program and executes the same line.
SET ENCRYPTION	Determines whether protected files are encrypted when copied.
SET EXCLUSIVE	Sets a file open attribute to either exclusive or shared mode.
SET LOCK	Determines whether automatic record locking is activated.
SET PRINTER	Selects a printer on the network.

SET REFRESH	Determines the interval for checking multiuser database changes and updating user screens.
SET REPROCESS	Sets the number of times dBASE tries to access a network file or data lock before quitting.
UNLOCK	Removes record and file locks.

APPENDIX

G

ASCII
Chart

ASCII CHART

ASCII Value	Character	ASCII Value	Character
000	(null)	037	%
001	☺	038	&
002	●	039	'
003	♥	040	(
004	♦	041	)
005	♣	042	*
006	♠	043	+
007	(beep)	044	,
008	▫	045	-
009	(tab)	046	.
010	(line feed)	047	/
011	(home)	048	0
012	(form feed)	049	1
013	(carriage return)	050	2
014	♫	051	3
015	☼	052	4
016	►	053	5
017	◄	054	6
018	↕	055	7
019	‼	056	8
020	¶	057	9
021	§	058	:
022	▬	059	;
023	↨	060	<
024	↑	061	=
025	↓	062	>
026	→	063	?
027	←	064	@
028	(cursor right)	065	A
029	(cursor left)	066	B
030	(cursor up)	067	C
031	(cursor down)	068	D
032	(space)	069	E
033	!	070	F
034	"	071	G
035	#	072	H
036	$	073	I

ASCII Value	Character	ASCII Value	Character
074	J	113	q
075	K	114	r
076	L	115	s
077	M	116	t
078	N	117	u
079	O	118	v
080	P	119	w
081	Q	120	x
082	R	121	y
083	S	122	z
084	T	123	{
085	U	124	¦
086	V	125	}
087	W	126	~
088	X	127	⌂
089	Y	128	Ç
090	Z	129	ü
091	[	130	é
092	\	131	â
093	]	132	ä
094	∧	133	à
095	—	134	å
096	`	135	ç
097	a	136	ê
098	b	137	ë
099	c	138	è
100	d	139	ï
101	e	140	î
102	f	141	ì
103	g	142	Ä
104	h	143	Å
105	i	144	É
106	j	145	æ
107	k	146	Æ
108	l	147	ô
109	m	148	ö
110	n	149	ò
111	o	150	û
112	p	151	ù

ASCII Value	Character	ASCII Value	Character
152	ÿ	191	┐
153	Ö	192	└
154	Ü	193	┴
155	¢	194	┬
156	£	195	├
157	¥	196	─
158	Pt	197	┼
159	ƒ	198	╞
160	á	199	╟
161	í	200	╚
162	ó	201	╔
163	ú	202	╩
164	ñ	203	╦
165	Ñ	204	╠
166	ª	205	═
167	º	206	╬
168	¿	207	╧
169	⌐	208	╨
170	¬	209	╤
171	½	210	╥
172	¼	211	╙
173	¡	212	╘
174	«	213	╒
175	»	214	╓
176	░	215	╫
177	▒	216	╪
178	▓	217	┘
179	│	218	┌
180	┤	219	█
181	╡	220	▄
182	╢	221	▌
183	╖	222	▐
184	╕	223	▀
185	╣	224	α
186	║	225	β
187	╗	226	Γ
188	╝	227	π
189	╜	228	Σ
190	╛	229	σ

ASCII Value	Character	ASCII Value	Character
230	μ	243	$\leq$
231	$\top$	244	$\lceil$
232	Φ	245	J
233	Θ	246	$\div$
234	Ω	247	$\approx$
235	δ	248	$^{\circ}$
236	∞	249	$\bullet$
237	$\varnothing$	250	$\cdot$
238	ϵ	251	$\sqrt{}$
239	$\cap$	252	^{n}
240	$\equiv$	253	^{2}
241	$\pm$	254	■
242	$\geq$	255	(blank 'FF')

INDEX

An *n* next to a page number indicates margin note.

G

R

S

Selections from The SYBEX Library

DATABASES

The ABC's of dBASE III PLUS
Robert Cowart
264pp. Ref. 379-1
The most efficient way to get beginners up and running with dBASE. Every 'how' and 'why' of database management is demonstrated through tutorials and practical dBASE III PLUS applications.

The ABC's of dBASE IV
Robert Cowart
338pp. Ref. 531-X
This superb tutorial introduces beginners to the concept of databases and practical dBASE IV applications featuring the new menu-driven interface, the new report writer, and Query by Example.

The ABC's of Paradox
Charles Siegel
300pp. Ref. 573-5
Easy to understand and use, this introduction is written so that the computer novice can create, edit, and manage complex Paradox databases. This primer is filled with examples of the Paradox 3.0 menu structure.

Advanced Techniques in dBASE III PLUS
Alan Simpson
454pp. Ref. 369-4
A full course in database design and structured programming, with routines for inventory control, accounts receivable, system management, and integrated databases.

dBASE Instant Reference
SYBEX Prompter Series
Alan Simpson
471pp. Ref. 484-4; 4 ¾" × 8"
Comprehensive information at a glance: a brief explanation of syntax and usage for every dBASE command, with step-by-step instructions and exact keystroke sequences. Commands are grouped by function in twenty precise categories.

dBASE III PLUS Programmer's Reference Guide
SYBEX Ready Reference Series
Alan Simpson
1056pp. Ref. 508-5
Programmers will save untold hours and effort using this comprehensive, well-organized dBASE encyclopedia. Complete technical details on commands and functions, plus scores of often-needed algorithms.

dBASE IV Programmer's Instant Reference
SYBEX Prompter Series
Alan Simpson
544pp. Ref. 538-7, 4 ¾" × 8"
This comprehensive reference to every dBASE command and function has everything for the dBASE programmer in a compact, pocket-sized book. Fast and easy access to adding data, sorting, performing calculations, managing multiple databases, memory variables and arrays, windows and menus, networking, and much more. Version 1.1.

dBASE IV User's Desktop Companion SYBEX Ready Reference Series
Alan Simpson
950pp. Ref. 523-9

This easy-to-use reference provides an exhaustive resource guide to taking full advantage of the powerful non-programming features of the dBASE IV Control Center. This book discusses query by example, custom reports and data entry screens, macros, the application generator, and the dBASE command and programming language.

dBASE IV User's Instant Reference SYBEX Prompter Series
Alan Simpson
349pp. Ref. 605-7, 4 ¾" × 8"

This handy pocket-sized reference book gives every new dBASE IV user fast and easy access to any dBASE command. Arranged alphabetically and by function, each entry includes a description, exact syntax, an example, and special tips from Alan Simpson.

Mastering dBASE III PLUS: A Structured Approach
Carl Townsend
342pp. Ref. 372-4

In-depth treatment of structured programming for custom dBASE solutions. An ideal study and reference guide for applications developers, new and experienced users with an interest in efficient programming.

Mastering dBASE IV Programming
Carl Townsend
496pp. Ref. 540-9

This task-oriented book introduces structured dBASE IV programming and commands by setting up a general ledger system, an invoice system, and a quotation management system. The author carefully explores the unique character of dBASE IV based on his in-depth understanding of the program.

Mastering FoxPro
Charles Seigel
639pp. Ref. 671-5

This guide to the powerful FoxPro DBMS offers a tutorial on database basics, then enables the reader to master new skills and features as needed -- with many examples from business. An in-depth tutorial guides users through the development of a complete mailing list system.

Mastering Paradox (Fourth Edition)
Alan Simpson
636pp. Ref. 612-X

Best selling author Alan Simpson simplifies all aspects of Paradox for the beginning to intermediate user. The book starts with database basics, covers multiple tables, graphics, custom applications with PAL, and the Personal Programmer. For Version 3.0.

Mastering Q & A (Second Edition)
Greg Harvey
540pp. Ref. 452-6

This hands-on tutorial explores the Q & A Write, File, and Report modules, and the Intelligent Assistant. English-language command processor, macro creation, interfacing with other software, and more, using practical business examples.

Power User's Guide to R:BASE
Alan Simpson
Cheryl Currid
Craig Gillett
446pp. Ref. 354-6

Supercharge your R:BASE applications with this straightforward tutorial that covers system design, structured programming, managing multiple data tables, and more. Sample applications include ready-to-run mailing, inventory and accounts receivable systems. Through Version 2.11.

Quick Guide to dBASE: The Visual Approach
David Kolodney
382pp. Ref. 596-4

This illustrated tutorial provides the beginner with a working knowledge of all the basic functions of dBASE IV. Images of each successive dBASE screen tell how to create and modify a database, add, edit, sort and select records, and print custom labels and reports.

Understanding dBASE III
Alan Simpson
300pp. Ref. 267-1
dBASE commands and concepts are illustrated throughout with practical, business oriented examples—for mailing list handling, accounts receivable, and inventory design. Contains scores of tips and techniques for maximizing efficiency and meeting special needs.

Understanding dBASE III PLUS
Alan Simpson
415pp. Ref. 349-X
A solid sourcebook of training and ongoing support. Everything from creating a first database to command file programming is presented in working examples, with tips and techniques you won't find anywhere else.

Understanding Oracle
James T. Perry
Joseph G. Lateer
634pp. Ref. 534-4
A comprehensive guide to the Oracle database management system for administrators, users, and applications developers. Covers everything in Version 5 from database basics to multi-user systems, performance, and development tools including SQL*Forms, SQL*Report, and SQL*Calc. Includes Fast Track speed notes.

Understanding Professional File
Gerry Litton
463pp. Re. 669-3
Build practical data management skills in an orderly fashion with this complete step-by-step tutorial -- from creating a simple database, to building customized business applications.

Understanding R:BASE
Alan Simpson
Karen Watterson
609pp. Ref. 503-4
This is the definitive R:BASE tutorial, for use with either OS/2 or DOS. Hands-on lessons cover every aspect of the software, from creating and using a database, to custom systems. Includes Fast Track speed notes.

Understanding SQL
Martin Gruber
400pp. Ref. 644-8
This comprehensive tutorial in Structured Query Language (SQL) is suitable for beginners, and for SQL users wishing to increase their skills. From basic principles to complex SQL applications, the text builds fluency and confidence using concise hands-on lessons and easy-to-follow examples.

Up & Running with Q&A
Ranier Bartel
140pp. Ref. 645-6
Obtain practical results with Q&A in the shortest possible time. Learn to design and program forms, use macros, format text, use utilities, and more. Or use the book to help you decide whether to purchase the program.

OPERATING SYSTEMS

The ABC's of DOS 4
Alan R. Miller
275pp. Ref. 583-2
This step-by-step introduction to using DOS 4 is written especially for beginners. Filled with simple examples, *The ABC's of DOS 4* covers the basics of hardware, software, disks, the system editor EDLIN, DOS commands, and more.

ABC's of MS-DOS
(Second Edition)
Alan R. Miller
233pp. Ref. 493-3
This handy guide to MS-DOS is all many PC users need to manage their computer files, organize floppy and hard disks, use EDLIN, and keep their computers organized. Additional information is given about utilities like Sidekick, and there is a DOS command and program summary. The second edition is fully updated for Version 3.3.

DOS Assembly Language
Programming
Alan R. Miller
365pp. 487-9
This book covers PC-DOS through 3.3, and gives clear explanations of how to assemble, link, and debug 8086, 8088, 80286, and 80386 programs. The example assembly language routines are valuable for students and programmers alike.

DOS Instant Reference
SYBEX Prompter Series
Greg Harvey
Kay Yarborough Nelson
220pp. Ref. 477-1, 4 ¾" × 8"
A complete fingertip reference for fast, easy on-line help:command summaries, syntax, usage and error messages. Organized by function—system commands, file commands, disk management, directories, batch files, I/O, networking, programming, and more. Through Version 3.3.

DOS User's Desktop Companion
SYBEX Ready Reference Series
Judd Robbins
969pp. Ref. 505-0
This comprehensive reference covers DOS commands, batch files, memory enhancements, printing, communications and more information on optimizing each user's DOS environment. Written with step-by-step instructions and plenty of examples, this volume covers all versions through 3.3.

Encyclopedia DOS
Judd Robbins
1030pp. Ref. 699-5
A comprehensive reference and user's guide to all versions of DOS through 4.0. Offers complete information on every DOS command, with all possible switches and parameters -- plus examples of effective usage. An invaluable tool.

Essential OS/2
(Second Edition)
Judd Robbins
445pp. Ref. 609-X
Written by an OS/2 expert, this is the guide to the powerful new resources of the OS/2 operating system standard edition 1.1 with presentation manager. Robbins introduces the standard edition, and details multitasking under OS/2, and the range of commands for installing, starting up, configuring, and running applications. For Version 1.1 Standard Edition.

Essential PC-DOS
(Second Edition)
Myril Clement Shaw
Susan Soltis Shaw
332pp. Ref. 413-5
An authoritative guide to PC-DOS, including version 3.2. Designed to make experts out of beginners, it explores everything from disk management to batch file programming. Includes an 85-page command summary. Through Version 3.2.

Graphics Programming
Under Windows
Brian Myers
Chris Doner
646pp. Ref. 448-8
Straightforward discussion, abundant examples, and a concise reference guide to graphics commands make this book a must for Windows programmers. Topics range from how Windows works to programming for business, animation, CAD, and desktop publishing. For Version 2.

Hard Disk Instant Reference
SYBEX Prompter Series
Judd Robbins

256pp. Ref. 587-5, 4 ¾" × 8"

Compact yet comprehensive, this pocket-sized reference presents the essential information on DOS commands used in managing directories and files, and in optimizing disk configuration. Includes a survey of third-party utility capabilities. Through DOS 4.0.

The IBM PC-DOS Handbook
(Third Edition)
Richard Allen King

359pp. Ref. 512-3

A guide to the inner workings of PC-DOS 3.2, for intermediate to advanced users and programmers of the IBM PC series. Topics include disk, screen and port control, batch files, networks, compatibility, and more. Through Version 3.3.

Inside DOS: A Programmer's Guide
Michael J. Young

490pp. Ref. 710-X

A collection of practical techniques (with source code listings) designed to help you take advantage of the rich resources intrinsic to MS-DOS machines. Designed for the experienced programmer with a basic understanding of C and 8086 assembly language, and DOS fundamentals.

Mastering DOS
(Second Edition)
Judd Robbins

722pp. Ref. 555-7

"The most useful DOS book." This seven-part, in-depth tutorial addresses the needs of users at all levels. Topics range from running applications, to managing files and directories, configuring the system, batch file programming, and techniques for system developers. Through Version 4.

MS-DOS Advanced Programming
Michael J. Young

490pp. Ref. 578-6

Practical techniques for maximizing performance in MS-DOS software by making best use of system resources. Topics include functions, interrupts, devices, multitasking, memory residency and more, with examples in C and assembler. Through Version 3.3.

MS-DOS Handbook
(Third Edition)
Richard Allen King

362pp. Ref. 492-5

This classic has been fully expanded and revised to include the latest features of MS-DOS Version 3.3. Two reference books in one, this title has separate sections for programmer and user. Multi-DOS partitons, 3 ½-inch disk format, batch file call and return feature, and comprehensive coverage of MS-DOS commands are included. Through Version 3.3.

MS-DOS Power User's Guide, Volume I
(Second Edition)
Jonathan Kamin

482pp. Ref. 473-9

A fully revised, expanded edition of our best-selling guide to high-performance DOS techniques and utilities—with details on Version 3.3. Configuration, I/O, directory structures, hard disks, RAM disks, batch file programming, the ANSI.SYS device driver, more. Through Version 3.3.

Programmer's Guide to Windows
(Second Edition)
David Durant
Geta Carlson
Paul Yao

704pp. Ref. 496-8

The first edition of this programmer's guide was hailed as a classic. This new edition covers Windows 2 and Windows/386 in depth. Special emphasis is given to over fifty new routines to the Windows interface, and to preparation for OS/2 Presentation Manager compatibility.

Understanding DOS 3.3
Judd Robbins

678pp. Ref. 648-0

This best selling, in-depth tutorial addresses the needs of users at all levels with many examples and hands-on exercises. Robbins discusses the fundamentals of DOS, then covers manipulating files and directories, using the DOS editor, printing, communicating, and finishes with a full section on batch files.

Understanding Hard Disk Management on the PC
Jonathan Kamin

500pp. Ref. 561-1

This title is a key productivity tool for all hard disk users who want efficient, error-free file management and organization. Includes details on the best ways to conserve hard disk space when using several memory-guzzling programs. Through DOS 4.

Up & Running with Your Hard Disk
Klaus M Rubsam

140pp. Ref. 666-9

A far-sighted, compact introduction to hard disk installation and basic DOS use. Perfect for PC users who want the practical essentials in the shortest possible time. In 20 basic steps, learn to choose your hard disk, work with accessories, back up data, use DOS utilities to save time, and more.

Up & Running with Windows 286/386
Gabriele Wentges

132pp. Ref. 691-X

This handy 20-step overview gives PC users all the essentials of using Windows -- whether for evaluating the software, or getting a fast start. Each self-contained lesson takes just 15 minutes to one hour to complete.

Programmers Guide to the OS/2 Presentation Manager
Michael J. Young

683pp. Ref. 569-7

This is the definitive tutorial guide to writing programs for the OS/2 Presentation Manager. Young starts with basic architecture, and explores every important feature including scroll bars, keyboard and mouse interface, menus and accelerators, dialogue boxes, clipboards, multitasking, and much more.

UTILITIES

Mastering the Norton Utilities
Peter Dyson

373pp. Ref. 575-1

In-depth descriptions of each Norton utility make this book invaluable for beginning and experienced users alike. Each utility is described clearly with examples and the text is organized so that readers can put Norton to work right away. Version 4.5.

Mastering PC Tools Deluxe
Peter Dyson

400pp. Ref. 654-5

A complete hands-on guide to the timesaving—and "lifesaving"—utility programs in Version 5.5 of PC Tools Deluxe. Contains concise tutorials and in-depth discussion of every aspect of using PC Tools—from high speed backups, to data recovery, to using Desktop applications.

Mastering SideKick Plus
Gene Weisskopf

394pp. Ref. 558-1

Employ all of Sidekick's powerful and expanded features with this hands-on guide to the popular utility. Features include comprehensive and detailed coverage of time management, note taking, outlining, auto dialing, DOS file management, math, and copy-and-paste functions.

Up & Running with Norton Utilities
Rainer Bartel
140pp. Ref. 659-6

Get up and running in the shortest possible time in just 20 lessons or "steps." Learn to restore disks and files, use UnErase, edit your floppy disks, retrieve lost data and more. Or use the book to evaluate the software before you purchase. Through Version 4.2.

Up & Running with PC Tools Deluxe 6
Thomas Holste
180pp. Ref.678-2

Learn to use this software program in just 20 basic steps. Readers get a quick, inexpensive introduction to using the Tools for disaster recovery, disk and file management, and more.

COMMUNICATIONS

Mastering Crosstalk XVI (Second Edition)
Peter W. Gofton
225pp. Ref. 642-1

Introducing the communications program Crosstalk XVI for the IBM PC. As well as providing extensive examples of command and script files for programming Crosstalk, this book includes a detailed description of how to use the program's more advanced features, such as windows, talking to mini or mainframe, customizing the keyboard and answering calls and background mode.

Mastering PROCOMM PLUS
Bob Campbell
400pp. Ref. 657-X

Learn all about communications and information retrieval as you master and use PROCOMM PLUS. Topics include choosing and using a modem; automatic dialing; using on-line services (featuring CompuServe) and more. Through Version 1.1b; also covers PROCOMM, the "shareware" version.

Mastering Serial Communications
Peter W. Gofton
289pp. Ref. 180-2

The software side of communications, with details on the IBM PC's serial programming, the XMODEM and Kermit protocols, non-ASCII data transfer, interrupt-level programming and more. Sample programs in C, assembly language and BASIC.

NETWORKS

The ABC's of Local Area Networks
Michael Dortch
212pp. Ref. 664-2

This jargon-free introduction to LANs is fur current and prospective users who see general information, comparative options, a look at the future, and tips for effective LANs use today. With comparisons of Token-Ring, PC Network, Novell, and others.

The ABC's of Novell Netware
Jeff Woodward
282pp. Ref. 614-6

For users who are new to PC's or networks, this entry-level tutorial outlines each basic element and operation of Novell. The ABC's introduces computer hardware and software, DOS, network organization and security, and printing and communicating over the netware system.

Mastering Novell Netware
Cheryl C. Currid
Craig A. Gillett
500pp. Ref. 630-8

This book is a thorough guide for System Administrators to installing and operating a microcomputer network using Novell Netware. Mastering covers actually setting up a network from start to finish, design, administration, maintenance, and troubleshooting.

Networking with TOPS
Steven William Rimmer
350pp. Ref. 565-4

A hands on guide to the most popular user friendly network available. This book will walk a user through setting up the hardware and software of a variety of TOPS configurations, from simple two station networks through whole offices. It explains the realities of sharing files between PC compatibles and Macintoshes, of sharing printers and other peripherals and, most important, of the real world performance one can expect when the network is running.

SPREADSHEETS AND INTEGRATED SOFTWARE

1-2-3 for Scientists and Engineers
William J. Orvis
341pp. Ref. 407-0

Fast, elegant solutions to common problems in science and engineering, using Lotus 1-2-3. Tables and plotting, curve fitting, statistics, derivatives, integrals and differentials, solving systems of equations, and more.

The ABC's of 1-2-3 (Second Edition)
Chris Gilbert
Laurie Williams
245pp. Ref. 355-4

Online Today recommends it as "an easy and comfortable way to get started with the program." An essential tutorial for novices, it will remain on your desk as a valuable source of ongoing reference and support. For Release 2.

The ABC's of 1-2-3 Release 2.2
Chris Gilbert
Laurie Williams
340pp. Ref. 623-5

New Lotus 1-2-3 users delight in this book's step-by-step approach to building trouble-free spreadsheets, displaying graphs, and efficiently building databases. The authors cover the ins and outs of the latest version including easier calculations, file linking, and better graphic presentation.

The ABC's of 1-2-3 Release 3
Judd Robbins
290pp. Ref. 519-0

The ideal book for beginners who are new to Lotus or new to Release 3. This step-by-step approach to the 1-2-3 spreadsheet software gets the reader up and running with spreadsheet, database, graphics, and macro functions.

The ABC's of Excel on the IBM PC
Douglas Hergert
326pp. Ref. 567-0

This book is a brisk and friendly introduction to the most important features of Microsoft Excel for PC's. This beginner's book discusses worksheets, charts, database operations, and macros, all with hands-on examples. Written for all versions through Version 2.

The ABC's of Quattro
Alan Simpson
Douglas J. Wolf
286pp. Ref. 560-3

Especially for users new to spreadsheets, this is an introduction to the basic concepts and a guide to instant productivity through editing and using spreadsheet formulas and functions. Includes how to print out graphs and data for presentation. For Quattro 1.1.

The Complete Lotus 1-2-3 Release 2.2 Handbook
Greg Harvey
750pp. Ref. 625-1

This comprehensive handbook discusses every 1-2-3 operating with clear instructions and practical tips. This volume especially emphasizes the new improved graphics, high-speed recalculation techniques, and spreadsheet linking available with Release 2.2.

The Complete Lotus 1-2-3 Release 3 Handbook
Greg Harvey
700pp. Ref. 600-6

Everything you ever wanted to know about 1-2-3 is in this definitive handbook. As a Release 3 guide, it features the design and use of 3D worksheets, and improved graphics, along with using Lotus under DOS or OS/2. Problems, exercises, and helpful insights are included.

Lotus 1-2-3 Desktop Companion SYBEX Ready Reference Series
Greg Harvey
976pp. Ref. 501-8

A full-time consultant, right on your desk. Hundreds of self-contained entries cover every 1-2-3 feature, organized by topic, indexed and cross-referenced, and supplemented by tips, macros and working examples. For Release 2.

Lotus 1-2-3 Instant Reference Release 2.2 SYBEX Prompter Series
Greg Harvey
Kay Yarborough Nelson
254pp. Ref. 635-9, 4 ¾" × 8"

The reader gets quick and easy access to any operation in 1-2-3 Version 2.2 in this handy pocket-sized encyclopedia. Organized by menu function, each command and function has a summary description, the exact key sequence, and a discussion of the options.

Lotus 1-2-3 Tips and Tricks (2nd edition)
Gene Weisskopf
425pp. Ref. 668-5

This outstanding collection of tips, shortcuts and cautions for longtime Lotus users is in an expanded new edition covering Release 2.2. Topics include macros, range names, spreadsheet design, hardware and operating system tips, data

analysis, printing, data interchange, applications development, and more.

Mastering 1-2-3 (Second Edition)
Carolyn Jorgensen
702pp. Ref. 528-X

Get the most from 1-2-3 Release 2.01 with this step-by-step guide emphasizing advanced features and practical uses. Topics include data sharing, macros, spreadsheet security, expanded memory, and graphics enhancements.

Mastering 1-2-3 Release 3
Carolyn Jorgensen
682pp. Ref. 517-4

For new Release 3 and experienced Release 2 users, "Mastering" starts with a basic spreadsheet, then introduces spreadsheet and database commands, functions, and macros, and then tells how to analyze 3D spreadsheets and make high-impact reports and graphs. Lotus add-ons are discussed and Fast Tracks are included.

Mastering Enable
Keith D. Bishop
517pp. Ref. 440-2

A comprehensive, practical, hands-on guide to Enable 2.0—integrated word processing, spreadsheet, database management, graphics, and communications—from basic concepts to custom menus, macros and the Enable Procedural Language.

Mastering Enable/OA
Christopher Van Buren
Robert Bixby
540pp. Ref 637-5

This is a structured, hands-on guide to integrated business computing, for users who want to achieve productivity in the shortest possible time. Separate in-depth sections cover word processing, spreadsheets, databases, telecommunications, task integration and macros.

Alan Simpson's
Understanding dBASE IV
Optional Companion Disks

If you want to use the sample databases, reports, custom forms, and the membership and business management applications presented in this book without keying them in yourself, you can send for a set of companion disks containing all the files. You can use these files to speed your learning (less typing!), or as modifiable applications that you can refine to better suit your own needs. You must already have access to dBASE IV to use these files.

To obtain the companion disks, please complete the order form below and return it with a check, money order, or purchase order for $30.00 U.S. Currency (plus sales tax for California residents) to the address shown on the coupon. Or, we can bill you later. Sorry, we cannot accept credit cards.

If you prefer, you can return the coupon without making a purchase to receive periodic newsletters and updates about Alan Simpson's latest books and products.

SMS Software
P.O. Box 2802
La Jolla, CA 92038-2802
(619)756-1354

□ Please send the companion disk for *Understanding dBASE IV*

□ No disk thanks, but please send free newsletters from Alan Simpson

Name_____

Company_____

Address_____

City, State, Zip _____

Country_____ P.O. Number (if applicable)_____

Check one:
       □ Payment enclosed ($30.00 + sales tax for CA residents) made payable to SMS Software
       □ Bill me later
       □ No charge (mailing list only)

Check one disk size:
       □ 5 1/4-inch disk   □ 3 1/2-inch disk

Understanding dBASE IV Version 1.1

TO JOIN THE SYBEX MAILING LIST OR ORDER BOOKS
PLEASE COMPLETE THIS FORM

NAME _____ COMPANY _____

STREET _____ STATE _____ ZIP _____

☐ PLEASE MAIL ME MORE INFORMATION ABOUT **SYBEX** TITLES

ORDER FORM (There is no obligation to order)

PLEASE SEND ME THE FOLLOWING:

TITLE	QTY	PRICE
_____	____	____
_____	____	____
_____	____	____
_____	____	____

TOTAL BOOK ORDER _____ $_____

CUSTOMER SIGNATURE _____

SHIPPING AND HANDLING PLEASE ADD $2.00 PER BOOK VIA UPS _____

FOR OVERSEAS SURFACE ADD $5.25 PER BOOK PLUS $4.40 REGISTRATION FEE _____

FOR OVERSEAS AIRMAIL ADD $18.25 PER BOOK PLUS $4.40 REGISTRATION FEE _____

CALIFORNIA RESIDENTS PLEASE ADD APPLICABLE SALES TAX _____

TOTAL AMOUNT PAYABLE _____

☐ CHECK ENCLOSED   ☐ VISA
☐ MASTERCARD   ☐ AMERICAN EXPRESS

ACCOUNT NUMBER _____

EXPIR. DATE _____ DAYTIME PHONE _____

CHECK AREA OF COMPUTER INTEREST:

☐ BUSINESS SOFTWARE

☐ TECHNICAL PROGRAMMING

☐ OTHER: _____

THE FACTOR THAT WAS MOST IMPORTANT IN YOUR SELECTION:

☐ THE SYBEX NAME

☐ QUALITY

☐ PRICE

☐ EXTRA FEATURES

☐ COMPREHENSIVENESS

☐ CLEAR WRITING

☐ OTHER _____

OTHER COMPUTER TITLES YOU WOULD LIKE TO SEE IN PRINT:

_____

_____

OCCUPATION

☐ PROGRAMMER   ☐ TEACHER

☐ SENIOR EXECUTIVE   ☐ HOMEMAKER

☐ COMPUTER CONSULTANT ☐ RETIRED

☐ SUPERVISOR   ☐ STUDENT

☐ MIDDLE MANAGEMENT   ☐ OTHER:

☐ ENGINEER/TECHNICAL _____

☐ CLERICAL/SERVICE

☐ BUSINESS OWNER/SELF EMPLOYED

CHECK YOUR LEVEL OF COMPUTER USE

☐ NEW TO COMPUTERS

☐ INFREQUENT COMPUTER USER

☐ FREQUENT USER OF ONE SOFTWARE

   PACKAGE:

   NAME _____

☐ FREQUENT USER OF MANY SOFTWARE

   PACKAGES

☐ PROFESSIONAL PROGRAMMER

OTHER COMMENTS:

_____

_____

_____

_____

_____

_____

PLEASE FOLD, SEAL, AND MAIL TO SYBEX

SYBEX, INC.
2021 CHALLENGER DR. #100
ALAMEDA, CALIFORNIA USA
               94501

SEAL

The Labels, Reports, and Forms Design Screens

You use the labels, reports, and forms design screens to design custom formats for displaying data. All three use the same keys to perform tasks. The forms design screen shown here presents a custom format for displaying data from the CUSTLIST database.

(CHAPTERS 7 AND 8)

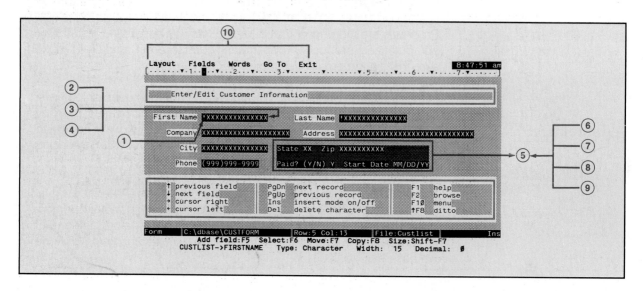

If you want to:	Here's how:	See page:
① Position cursor	Use arrow keys, Home, End, PgUp, PgDn	167
② Add or modify field template	Position cursor and press Field (F5)	186,214
③ Delete field template	Position cursor and press Del	186
④ Size field template	Position cursor and press Size (Shift-F7)	217
⑤ Select field or area for operation	Position cursor and press Select (F6)	168
⑥ Move selected field or area	Press Move (F7) after making selection	187
⑦ Copy selected field or area	Press Copy (F8) after making selection	187
⑧ Delete selected field or area	Press Del after making selection	168
⑨ Unselect selected area	Press Escape	168
⑩ Access pull-down menus	Press Menu (F10)	23